SOUTH AFRICA

5th Edition

**Where to Stay and Eat
for All Budgets**

**Must-See Sights
and Local Secrets**

Ratings You Can Trust

Fodor's Travel Publications   New York, Toronto, London, Sydney, Auckland
www.fodors.com

FODOR'S SOUTH AFRICA

Editors: Alexis Kelly, Shannon Kelly

Editorial Contributors: Jade Archer, Claire Melissa Baranowski, Brian Berkman, Sanja Cloete-Jones, Tracy Gielink, Debra A. Klein, Lee Middleton, Karena du Plessis, Kate Turkington, Tara Turkington

Production Editor: Jennifer DePrima
Maps & Illustrations: David Lindroth and Mark Stroud, *cartographers;* Bob Blake, Rebecca Baer, *map editors;* William Wu, *information graphics*
Design: Fabrizio La Rocca, *creative director;* Guido Caroti, Siobhan O'Hare, *art directors;* Tina Malaney, Chie Ushio, Ann McBride, Jessica Walsh, *designers;* Melanie Marin, *senior picture editor*
Cover Photo: (Kokerboom trees): Russell Burden/Index Stock Imagery
Production Manager: Angela L. McLean

COPYRIGHT

Copyright © 2010 by Fodor's Travel, a division of Random House, Inc.

Fodor's is a registered trademark of Random House, Inc.

All rights reserved. Published in the United States by Fodor's Travel, a division of Random House, Inc., and simultaneously in Canada by Random House of Canada, Limited, Toronto. Distributed by Random House, Inc., New York.

No maps, illustrations, or other portions of this book may be reproduced in any form without written permission from the publisher.

5th Edition

ISBN 978-1-4000-0879-7

ISSN 1091-4757

SPECIAL SALES

This book is available at special discounts for bulk purchases for sales promotions or premiums. Special editions, including personalized covers, excerpts of existing books, and corporate imprints, can be created in large quantities for special needs. For more information, write to Special Markets/Premium Sales, 1745 Broadway, MD 6-2, New York, New York 10019, or e-mail specialmarkets@randomhouse.com.

AN IMPORTANT TIP & AN INVITATION

Although all prices, opening times, and other details in this book are based on information supplied to us at press time, changes occur all the time in the travel world, and Fodor's cannot accept responsibility for facts that become outdated or for inadvertent errors or omissions. So **always confirm information when it matters,** especially if you're making a detour to visit a specific place. Your experiences—positive and negative—matter to us. If we have missed or misstated something, **please write to us.** We follow up on all suggestions. Contact the South Africa editor at editors@fodors.com or c/o Fodor's at 1745 Broadway, New York, NY 10019.

PRINTED IN THE UNITED STATES OF AMERICA

10 9 8 7 6 5 4 3 2 1

Be a Fodor's Correspondent

Your opinion matters. It matters to us. It matters to your fellow Fodor's travelers, too. And we'd like to hear it. In fact, we need to hear it.

When you share your experiences and opinions, you become an active member of the Fodor's community. That means we'll not only use your feedback to make our books better, but we'll publish your names and comments whenever possible. Throughout our guides, look for "Word of Mouth," excerpts of your unvarnished feedback.

Here's how you can help improve Fodor's for all of us.

Tell us when we're right. We rely on local writers to give you an insider's perspective. But our writers and staff editors—who are the best in the business—depend on you. Your positive feedback is a vote to renew our recommendations for the next edition.

Tell us when we're wrong. We're proud that we update most of our guides every year. But we're not perfect. Things change. Hotels cut services. Museums change hours. Charming cafés lose charm. If our writer didn't quite capture the essence of a place, tell us how you'd do it differently. If any of our descriptions are inaccurate or inadequate, we'll incorporate your changes in the next edition and will correct factual errors at fodors.com immediately.

Tell us what to include. You probably have had fantastic travel experiences that aren't yet in Fodor's. Why not share them with a community of like-minded travelers? Maybe you chanced upon a beach or bistro or B&B that you don't want to keep to yourself. Tell us why we should include it. And share your discoveries and experiences with everyone directly at fodors.com. Your input may lead us to add a new listing or highlight a place we cover with a "Highly Recommended" star or with our highest rating, "Fodor's Choice."

Give us your opinion instantly at our feedback center at www.fodors.com/feedback. You may also e-mail editors@fodors.com with the subject line "South Africa Editor." Or send your nominations, comments, and complaints by mail to South Africa Editor, Fodor's, 1745 Broadway, New York, NY 10019.

You and travelers like you are the heart of the Fodor's community. Make our community richer by sharing your experiences. Be a Fodor's correspondent.

Happy traveling!

Tim Jarrell, Publisher

CONTENTS

Fodor's Features

MAPS

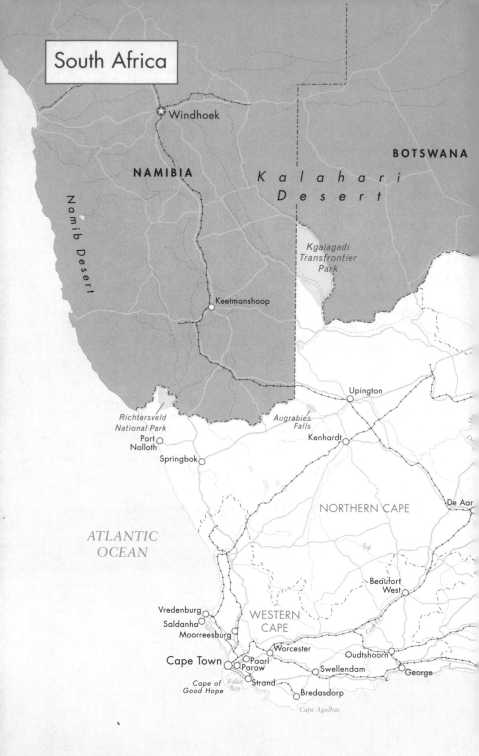

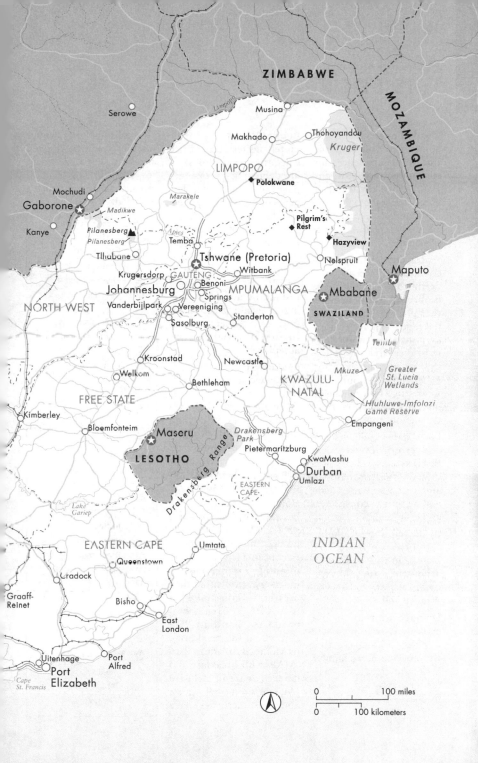

ABOUT THIS BOOK

Our Ratings

Sometimes you find terrific travel experiences and sometimes they just find you. But usually it's up to you to select the right combination of experiences. That's where our ratings come in.

As travelers we've all discovered a place so wonderful that its worthiness is obvious. And sometimes that place is so experiential that superlatives don't do it justice: you just have to be there to know. These sights, properties, and experiences get our highest rating, **Fodor's Choice,** indicated by orange stars throughout this book.

Black stars highlight sights and properties we deem **Highly Recommended,** places that our writers, editors, and readers praise again and again for consistency and excellence.

By default, there's another category: any place we include in this book is by definition worth your time, unless we say otherwise. And we will.

Disagree with any of our choices? Care to nominate a place or suggest that we rate one more highly? Visit our feedback center at www.fodors.com/feedback.

Budget Well

Hotel and restaurant price categories from ¢ to $$$$ are defined in the opening pages of each chapter. For attractions, we always give standard adult admission fees; reductions are usually available for children, students, and senior citizens. Want to pay with plastic? **AE, DC, MC, V** following restaurant and hotel listings indicate if American Express, Diners Club, MasterCard, and Visa are accepted.

Restaurants

Unless we state otherwise, restaurants are open for lunch and dinner daily. We mention dress only when there's a specific requirement and reservations only when they're essential or not accepted—it's always best to book ahead.

Hotels

Hotels have private bath, phone, TV, and air-conditioning and operate on the European Plan (a.k.a. EP, meaning without meals), unless we specify that they use the Continental Plan (CP, with a Continental breakfast), Breakfast Plan (BP, with a full breakfast), or Modified American Plan (MAP, with breakfast and dinner), or are all-inclusive (AI, including all meals and most activities). We

always list facilities but not whether you'll be charged an extra fee to use them, so when pricing accommodations, find out what's included.

Many Listings

★ Fodor's Choice
★ Highly recommended
⊠ Physical address
✦ Directions or Map coordinates
🕮 Mailing address
☎ Telephone
🖷 Fax
⊕ On the Web
✑ E-mail
🎟 Admission fee
☉ Open/closed times
Ⓜ Metro stations
🖃 Credit cards

Hotels & Restaurants

🏨 Hotel
🛏 Number of rooms
⚴ Facilities
🍴 Meal plans
✗ Restaurant
⚱ Reservations
🏛 Dress code
⚐ Smoking
🍸 BYOB

Outdoors

⛳ Golf
⛺ Camping

Other

☕ Family-friendly
⇨ See also
⊠ Branch address
☞ Take note

Experience
South Africa

WORD OF MOUTH

"One night our ranger asked if we wanted to go with him to investigate some lions roaring not far from the lodge. We had heard roars before, but never so up close and never in the pitch of darkness. I'll never forget this experience."

—debwarr

"We have always been quite lucky with sightings. We've concluded that it's because we drive slowly and take our time. We take the recommended driving times and double them and then we're pretty much on schedule. Either that or we are just incredibly lucky!"

—canadian_robin

WHAT'S WHERE

1 Cape Town and the Peninsula. Backed by Table Mountain, this onetime refueling station between Europe and the East anchors a stunning coastline: mountains cascading into the sea, miles of beaches, and inland wineries dating to the 17th century.

2 The Winelands and Beaches: The Western Cape. Stellenbosch, Paarl, and Franschhoek make popular day trips from Cape Town. The Overberg is a region of tranquil farms and popular beach resorts. Whale-watching site Hermanus is near Cape Agulhas, the southernmost tip of Africa.

3 The Garden Route and the Little Karoo. The aptly named Garden Route is 208 km (130 mi) of forested mountains, waterways, and beaches. The Little Karoo, separated from the coast by the Outeniqua Mountains, is famous for ostrich farms and the underground Cango Caves.

4 The Eastern Cape. One of South Africa's most populated and diverse provinces, the Cape is home to seaside family getaways, hundreds of bird species, and the nation's premiere elephant sanctuary at Addo.

5 Durban and KwaZulu-Natal. Inland from Durban, a bustling port city with a tropical feel, are the battlefields where Boers, Britons, and Zulu struggled for control of the country and the beautiful Drakensberg, a sanctuary for hikers. Wildlife-viewing in the far-north reserves rivals that at Kruger.

6 Johannesburg. Constitution Hill and the Museum of Apartheid reside in this historic gold town, orbited by the capital of Pretoria and the Soweto township. See some of the world's oldest human fossils at the nearby Cradle of Humankind.

7 Victoria Falls. The Zambezi River joins Botswana's Chobe River here to form the vast plunge between Zambia and Zimbabwe. Two towns share the flow of visitors: Livingstone, in Zambia, and Victoria Falls, in Zimbabwe.

8 South Africa's Safaris. Kruger National Park and adjacent northeastern reserves are the safari hot spots, but in South Africa you can also combine beaches and safaris in KwaZulu-Natal or opt for vast desert wilderness at Kgalagadi, on the Botswana border.

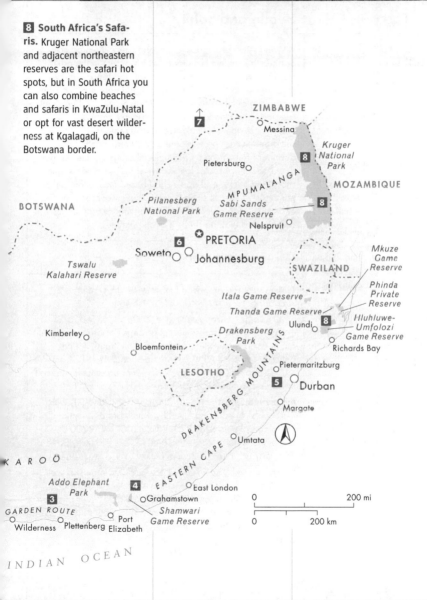

ZIMBABWE

7

Messina

Kruger National Park

Pietersburg

MOZAMBIQUE

MPUMALANGA

BOTSWANA

Pilanesberg National Park

Sabi Sands Game Reserve

Nelspruit

6 ✪ PRETORIA

Soweto Johannesburg

SWAZILAND

Mkuze Game Reserve

Tswalu Kalahari Reserve

Phinda Private Reserve

Itala Game Reserve

Thanda Game Reserve

Ulundi

Hluhluwe-Umfolozi Game Reserve

Kimberley

Drakensberg Park

Bloemfontein

Richards Bay

LESOTHO

Pietermaritzburg

5 Durban

DRAKENSBERG MOUNTAINS

Margate

KAROO

Umtata

Addo Elephant Park

4

EASTERN CAPE

East London

3

Grahamstown

GARDEN ROUTE

Shamwari Game Reserve

Wilderness

Plettenberg

Port Elizabeth

0   200 mi

0   200 km

INDIAN OCEAN

SOUTH AFRICA PLANNER

Fast Facts

Size 1,221,037 square km (471,442 square mi)

Number of National Parks 21

Number of Private Game and Nature Reserves Dozens in each state

Population Approximately 47.9 million

Big Five Lions, leopards, rhinos, elephants, and Cape buffalo

Language 11 official languages: Afrikaans, English, Ndebele, North and South Sotho, Swati, Tsonga, Tswana, Venda, Xhosa, and Zulu. English is widely spoken.

Time SAST (South African Standard Time), seven hours ahead of North American Eastern Standard Time.

Health and Safety

HIV and AIDS are endemic. Beyond these, the most serious health problem is malaria, which occurs in the prime game-viewing areas of Mpumalanga and Limpopo provinces (home to Kruger, Sabi Sands) and northern KwaZulu-Natal (site of Hluhluwe-Imfolozi, Mkuze, and Ithala game reserves, and Phinda and Thanda private reserves). Travelers heading to malaria-endemic regions should consult a health-care professional at least one month before departure for advice on antimalarial drugs. As the sun goes down, wear light-color long-sleeve shirts, long pants, and shoes and socks, and apply DEET-based mosquito repellent generously. Always sleep in a mosquito-proof room or tent and keep a fan going. If you're pregnant or trying to conceive, avoid malaria areas if at all possible.

Important Details

Embassies The **American Embassy** (✉ *877 Pretorius St., Arcadia* ☎ *021/431–4000*) is in Tshwane.

Emergencies Europ Assistance (☎ *0860/635–635* ⊕ *www.europassistance.co.za*) arranges emergency evacuation. For a general emergency, dial the **South Africa Police Service** (*SAPS* ☎ *10111 from landline, 112 from mobile phone* ⊕ *www.saps.gov.za*). For an ambulance, call the **special ambulance number** (☎ *10177*) or SAPS.

Money Matters. The unit of currency is the rand (R), with 100 cents (¢) equaling R1. Bills, which are differentiated by color, come in R10, R20, R50, R100, and R200 denominations. Coins are minted in R5, R2, R1, 50¢, 20¢, 10¢, 5¢, 2¢, and 1¢ denominations.

Passports and Visas. A valid passport (for infants as well as adults) with two blank facing visa pages is needed to enter South Africa for visits of up to 90 days. Your passport must be valid for at least six months after your return date, or you will be denied entry. There is no visa fee for Americans.

Getting Here and Around

As the air hub for all of southern Africa, Johannesburg is linked to the rest of the world by major carriers, including U.S.-based airlines and their overseas partners. There are regularly scheduled domestic flights throughout the country, as well as an intricate network of landing strips served by various charter airlines flying to and from safari camps. Charter companies run both scheduled routes and on-demand services, catering to travelers who wish to make their own itineraries.

Luxury train services run between Pretoria and Cape Town; less expensive trains ply the same routes. Regional trains, such as those serving metro Johannesburg and Pretoria, are not considered safe for tourists (or locals). Budget minded travelers can, instead, use a backpacker bus service that makes regular stops along the popular tourist path from Cape Town to Johannesburg and dips into Swaziland on some routes.

Self-drive holidays are common between Johannesburg and Kruger National Park, as well from Cape Town through the Winelands and along the Garden Route.

Prearranged airport car services with drivers can take you door to door. Taxis are available at airports, but as a safety precaution it is best to have your accommodation send one for you rather than just hiring one yourself.

Hop-on, hop-off tourist buses ply the routes of Cape Town's major tourist attractions.

WHAT IT COSTS IN SOUTH AFRICAN RAND

	¢	$	$$	$$$	$$$$
Restaurants	under R50	R50–R75	R76–R100	R101–R125	over R125
Lodging	under R500	R500–R1,000	R1,001–R2,000	R2,001–R3,000	over R3,000
Full-service Safari Lodging	under R2,000	R2,000–R5,000	R5,001–R8,000	R8,001–R12,000	over R12,000

Restaurant prices are per person for a main course at dinner, a main course equivalent, or a prix-fixe meal. Hotel and lodging prices are for a standard double room in high season, including 14% tax.

When to Go

Johannesburg has one of the world's best climates. Summers are sunny and hot (never humid), with short afternoon thunderstorms. Winter days are bright and sunny, but nights can be frosty. Although November through January is Cape Town's most popular time, with glorious sunshine and long, light evenings, the best weather is between February and March. Cape winters (May through August) are unpredictable with cold, windy, rainy days interspersed with glorious sun. The coastal areas of KwaZulu-Natal are warm year-round, but summers are steamy and hot. The ocean water is warmest in February, but it seldom dips below 17°C (65°F).

The best time to go on safari is in winter, May through September. The vegetation is sparse so it's easier to spot game, and water is scarce so game congregates around photo-friendly water holes. However, although it's very hot in summer (October through April), the bush looks its best; there will be lots of young animals, and the summer bird migrants will have returned. That said, keep in mind that hotel prices rise dramatically and accommodations are at a premium November through March. At most private game lodges you'll see game year-round.

For weather forecasts for the whole country, check out **South Africa Weather Service** (www.weathersa.co.za) .

TOP ATTRACTIONS

Kruger National Park

Whether you drive yourself and stay at campsites, as many South Africans do, or fly in to a neighboring reserve for an all-inclusive guided luxury safari experience, Kruger Park delivers the Africa wildlife tableaux of your dreams. See a zebra at a watering hole, a giraffe so close you can touch it, or lion cubs scampering across fields back home to their mothers at dusk.

Cape Town

This part of the country is popular with visitors because it combines history, scenery, seascapes, and culture in spectacular natural surroundings. Spend the day touring the best museums, shopping for crafts at the V&A Waterfront, or browsing the shops around the bustling Greenmarket Square. Watch buskers or sip wine in a contemporary setting, or venture into the Bo Kaap district for an authentic Cape Malay meal.

Robben Island

This is an essential stop to comprehend the scope of the anti-apartheid movement. After a scenic boat ride out of Cape Town's harbor and onto the seas, you'll ride in a bus past scrub and bunnies— the penal colony's current residents—before seeing the actual cell where Nelson Mandela served most of his sentence. Former inmates conduct the tours.

Table Mountain

High above Cape Town, looking out over the city, it's just tourists, rock hyraxes, and stunning views. Those with limited time, or limited interest in hiking, can take the cable car to the top. Hardier visitors can hike up and walk down, but be sure to go in groups and bring along a coat for the always changeable weather. Check the forecast in the morning; high winds mean the cable car can't go up.

Cradle of Humankind

Technically everyone's Motherland, this site of fossils, footprints, and evolutionary evidence dates back millions of years and is said to be the place from which our prehistoric ancestors ventured out to the rest of the world. Explore mankind's family tree at the on-site interactive museum, just an hour outside Johannesburg.

Soweto Township

Take an organized tour of the largest township outside Johannesburg and learn how the community has continued to thrive despite hardships. Dine in a restaurant near Nelson Mandela's and Desmond Tutu's homes and add a stop in the Apartheid Museum downtown. This is truly the heart of South African life.

Southernmost Point in Africa

Geography buffs will want to stand at Cape Agulhas, the southernmost point on the African continent and the place where the Indian and Atlantic Ocean currents collide. Shipwrecks dot the coastline, as do migrant waterfowl, while thousands of wildflowers pepper the landscape between May and September.

Winelands

Spend lazy afternoons watching the sun pull shadows across peaks that look like they belong on wine labels, and nights sampling savory African, French, or Indian fare. Or slip away to a spa ringed by vineyards growing some of the world's tastiest whites and varietals. Classic Cape Dutch buildings provide the backdrop for historical walking tours in South Africa's oldest university town, Stellenbosch; afterwards relax at a plush inn.

TOP EXPERIENCES

Splurge for a Night
Choose a decadent luxury safari camp or a five-star hotel in Cape Town or Johannesburg—South Africa's sky-high standards of hospitality gleam at the country's top accommodations, which truly set a gold standard in terms of service. View the added expense as an investment in your travel future; from here on out you'll have the highest benchmark against which to measure all future trips.

Get to Know Some Locals
Guesthouses, many of which are of far higher standards than most other countries' B&Bs, abound throughout the country. Enjoy an opportunity to chat with the local owners and South African guests at breakfast to get a better perspective on the country and the progress it's made. On safari, ask your guide or tracker about his or her insights. Engage your long-haul driver in conversation. South Africans are warm and friendly and happy to discuss their country. You'll enrich your memories of your time if you can uncover this often hidden attraction of South Africa—the warm and friendly people throughout the country.

Get Closer to Wildlife
You can spend hours looking for cheetah to photograph on a game drive and come up empty, but The Cheetah Outreach Park at the Spier Estate in Stellenbosch lets you fulfill your desire to touch one, too. You can also get an educational view of the cats at the De Wildt Cheetah and Wildlife Trust Center between Johannesburg and Pretoria and have close encounters with monkeys, ostriches, and elephants, among others, at various places around the country.

Eat Out . . . Way Out
Drums beat, hyenas trill, and flames flicker as you enter the dirt-floored *boma*, a traditional African space open to the night skies, for an essential safari treat—a bush dinner. Sign up ahead of time for one of the organized Kruger Park evenings, where only a mere wall of thatch separates you from the lions and elephants you feared hours earlier in broad daylight. If you're staying at a luxury reserve, most will happily serve you and your partner a romantic dinner for two under the stars.

Explore Apartheid
Learn more about the legacy of apartheid at Cape Town's Robben Island, the prison colony where Nelson Mandela and others served out their sentences. Visit the District Six Museum to learn about apartheid's effects on one local Cape Town community. In Johannesburg's Apartheid Museum, hold a replica "pass card"—the document all black South Africans were required to carry during apartheid. Also worth visiting are the Mandela Family Museum, the Hector Pieterson Memorial and Museum, and the Regina Mundi Church in Soweto.

See the Sea
Swim with the penguins at Boulders Beach on the Cape Peninsula or cage dive alongside great white sharks along the southern coast off Gansbaai, in the Overberg. Landlubbers can whale-watch from July to November from the cliff-top walkways of Hermanus or get a closer view from a boat in Plettenberg Bay. Bottlenose dolphins live in these waters all year.

Rise Above It

Whether by charter-plane transfer or hot-air balloon ride, do your best to experience the country's topography from up high. Even a trip up Table Mountain for sky-high views will allow you to see the different worlds that exist side by side, from shanty towns to luxury estates to spectacular mountain ranges all in one swoop.

Do Good

You may not have a week to volunteer in a township, but you might be able to help out struggling communities with a purchase of arts and crafts made by women who live there. Ask questions and read labels in gift shops and while taking tours. Your dollar might be able to do more than purchase your keepsake; it may help someone less fortunate. For those with more time on their hands, several groups run day- or weeklong volunteer opportunities to townships, hospitals, schools, or animal conservation centers.

Get Cultured

The Limpopo district's Sekhukhune attractions include the villages of Ndebele people, known for colorful beadwork, large geometric murals, and fanciful dress. Visit a Zulu village to immerse yourself in that distinct tradition that also includes costumes covered in beadwork and an annual ritual Reed dance. Stay overnight in the Dumazulu Traditional Village and Lodge for the complete experience, including dance and traditional foods.

SOUTH AFRICA'S HISTORY

The First Known Inhabitants

Two-million-year-old hominid fossils of the earliest known prehuman ancestors were found in South Africa, at the Sterkfontein Caves, about an hour's drive from Johannesburg. This area is now known as the Cradle of Humankind.

The descendants of these prehistoric Africans, the San, were Stone Age hunter-gatherers. From AD 200 to 400, people speaking various Bantu languages moved into the area that is now South Africa's Eastern Cape and KwaZulu-Natal, bringing with them Iron Age culture. Between AD 500 and the 1300s, the Khoikhoi, nomadic cattle herders, moved south and interacted, as well as clashed, with the San, as did a later group of farmers from the north. As the population increased, powerful kingdoms developed.

European Colonization

The Portuguese were the first to land in the Cape—in 1487—when pioneering a sea route to India, but it was the Dutch who decided to set up a refreshment station in 1652, so that their ships could stock up on food and water en route to the East Indies. Station commander Jan van Riebeeck later established a permanent settlement and imported a large number of slaves, mostly from the East Indies. The Cape Colony started to expand outward and the Khoikhoi, who were living in the Cape, lost most of their livestock, grazing areas, and population; those who remained became marginalized servants. The Afrikaans language developed—a mix of mainly Dutch, as well as some words and sounds from the languages of other European settlers, slaves, and San and Khoikhoi servants.

Over the next 100 years, the Dutch pushed farther inland, sometimes clashing with indigenous inhabitants. Official control see-sawed between the Dutch and the British until the region was formally recognized by the 1815 Congress of Vienna as a British colony.

The Great Trek

The British government subsequently annexed the Cape Colony and outlawed slavery in 1834. The Boers, or Afrikaners, fled inland, setting up new communities and drawing up constitutions explicitly prohibiting racial equality in church and state.

Also known as the Voortrekkers (or pioneers), the Boers traveled into lands occupied by Bantu-speaking peoples, including the Zulu kingdom. Ruled by Shaka, the Zulus evolved during the 1820s into the most powerful black African kingdom in southern Africa and occupied most of what is now KwaZulu-Natal.

Between 1837 and 1838, Afrikaner farmer and businessman Piet Retief attempted to negotiate a land agreement with the Zulu king, Dingane. Instead, the Zulus killed Retief and more than 500 Voortrekkers.

In retaliation, a Boer raiding party defeated the Zulus at the Battle of Blood River in 1838 and set up the independent Republic of Natalia, now roughly the province of KwaZulu-Natal. Also around that time, two Boer republics were established: the South African Republic (now Mpumalanga, North West and Limpopo provinces) and the Orange Free State (now Free State).

Prosperity and Conflict

The discovery of diamonds in Kimberley in 1867 and then gold in 1886 outside Johannesburg changed South Africa's fortunes forever. The economic center moved from the British-controlled Cape to the Boer republics and transformed

an agricultural society to an urbanized, industrial one.

Mining companies required a great deal of labor, supplied by black, male migrant workers, who were forced to live in single-sex hostels or compounds. Workers had to carry passes, and their movements were tightly controlled. The British had financial interest in the mines and wanted to control the entire country and thus its mineral wealth. To this end, they took over Natalia and invaded Zulu territory, successfully bringing it under imperial control. They next turned their attention to the two Boer republics.

To preempt an invasion by the British, the Boers declared war in 1899. The Anglo-Boer war (now called the South African War) lasted until 1902. A "scorched earth" policy by the British meant farms were burned and women and children were put into concentration camps. The Boers eventually surrendered, but bitterness toward the British remained. By 1910 the former British colonies were united as the Union of South Africa, and Afrikaners were appointed to government positions in an attempt to reconcile English and Afrikaans speakers.

Apartheid

In 1913, the first Union government established the Natives Land Act, which divided the country into black and white areas. Blacks were given less than 10% of land, thus forcing many to become migrant workers on white-owned farms and mines. Black political leaders established the South African Native National Congress (SANNC) in 1912, a forerunner to the African National Congress (ANC), to protest against such measures.

During World War I, South Africa, as part of the British Empire, was at war with Germany, and invaded German South West Africa (later Namibia). White Afrikaners tried to exploit this opportunity to win back their country but failed. Between the World Wars, the country was ruled by an Afrikaner-dominated government. The ANC continued to peacefully protest its plight, with little success.

Once World War II began, the Union voted to support the British by a small majority; many Afrikaners openly supported Nazi Germany. The National Party won the 1948 election on the platform of pro-apartheid policies, the cornerstone of which, the 1950 Population Registration Act, classified all South Africans according to race and established separate schools, universities, residential areas, and public facilities.

Opposition to Apartheid

The government in turn introduced severe penalties for opposition to apartheid and banned the ANC and Pan Africanist Congress (PAC)—a faction of the ANC, which went underground or into exile.

ANC leaders, Nelson Mandela among them, were arrested two years later, and, after a lengthy detention and trial, sentenced to life imprisonment on Robben Island in 1964. This further weakened the black protest.

By the mid-1970s the anti-apartheid struggle was revived, aided by condemnation from other countries, including South Africa's neighbors, who were no longer sympathetic to the white regime. In 1976 several thousand black African schoolchildren marched through the township of Soweto to protest Afrikaans becoming the language of instruction. During what became known as the Soweto Uprising, police opened fire on crowds, killing between 200 and 500 people and injuring thousands. After this, the government was increasingly forced to rely on the police force and army to crush resistance and impose order; it never fully regained control.

By the 1980s, international condemnation of, and reaction to, apartheid had reached a fever pitch: celebrities boycotted appearances in South Africa, sports teams were shunned abroad, and U.S. college students held rallies demanding their universities divest their assets from the country. Despite this, the government continued to arrest South African journalists, student leaders, and other opponents, detaining them without trial. Prominent apartheid opponents were killed in neighboring countries. However, sanctions, boycotts, strikes, and campaigns by the liberation organizations were damaging the economy, and business began to be badly affected.

The Dawn of Democracy

F.W. de Klerk became president of South Africa in December 1989 and in his first speech to Parliament two months after his election, he made the unexpected and astonishing announcement: Mandela and other political prisoners were to be released and the ANC and PAC were to be unbanned. Talks began between government and the liberation movements, although racial tensions remained. In 1994, South Africa had its first democratic election, which the ANC won by a large majority. It was a time of great joy and exultation for many. Mandela became president, and South Africa rejoined the rest of the world on the political stage, resuming full participation in the UN and the Commonwealth, and sending its first racially integrated team to the Olympics.

A government-appointed panel called the Truth and Reconciliation Commission (TRC), headed by Desmond Tutu, an Anglican archbishop, began public hearings across the country to probe human-rights violations during the apartheid years. People could talk about their experiences, and the full extent of apartheid atrocities came to light; many considered this to be an important healing process.

Mandela was succeeded in 1999 by Thabo Mbeki, who continued to guide the transformation process from a white-dominated, apartheid government to a democratic one.

The Present

In 2008, Jacob Zuma became leader of the ANC and succeeded Mbeki as president in the 2009 elections. South Africans hope for continued progress toward a better future under Zuma and that his populist utterances will translate into action that will improve the lives of people, the majority of whom still live in poverty. Despite South Africa's modern economy, prosperous gold and diamond mines, and the export of raw materials, the country continues to face numerous problems, including an unskilled labor force, failing infrastructure, violent crime, chronic unemployment, and the highest rate of HIV infection in the world.

SOUTH AFRICA TODAY

The Rainbow Nation

The "Rainbow Nation" of South Africa is one in which people intermingle racially far more than they did in the past. You can expect to find a once-segregated population living side by side as equals: as guests in game lodges, dining together in air-conditioned malls, and in the workplace.

However, vast economic disparities and racial tensions still exist. The physical legacy of apartheid remains, and large shantytown communities inhabited by black South Africans can be found on the outskirts of urban areas and suburban communities; for many of the country's poor, things have not changed substantially in the past 15 years. Much of the tourism industry is managed by whites, and you'll find that it's not easy to meet South African blacks on an equal footing.

When it comes to religion, more than 80% of South Africans are Christians, with African Independent churches making up the majority of affiliations; the Zion African Church has the largest following, and you might see its members wearing hexagram pendants. About 3% of the population follow other religions, including Hinduism, Islam, and Judaism. About 13% of the population claim to have no affiliation.

Sports and the World Cup

As far as South Africa is concerned, the 2010 FIFA World Cup is more than a global competition. It's seen as the first real test of the relatively new nation's ability to deliver a smoothly orchestrated high-profile event. With stadiums to build, roads to repair, and lodgings to create, the world will be watching to see if the country takes its logical place as Africa's leader on the world stage.

South Africans are ardent fans of football (soccer), supporting Bafana Bafana, the national team. They also go crazy for rugby and cricket. The national rugby team, the Springboks, is known worldwide for its prowess and has legions of international fans. The Proteas, the national cricket team, also has a large fan base.

The natural beauty and mild climate of South Africa combine to offer an incredible range of outdoor activities for sports enthusiasts. Besides golf, tennis, surfing, diving, kayaking, hiking, and sailing, there is a great range of adventure activities on offer, many of them adrenaline fueled. Kloofing (which basically entails jumping into a canyon) is popular in the Western Cape, and you can also paraglide, take a hot-air balloon, abseil, bungee jump, or even ski.

Music, Dance, and Drama

Cape Town, Durban, and Johannesburg all have lively arts scenes. And while permanent venues are found in most of the major cities, annual festivals, such as the Grahamstown Arts Festival in July, are great places to experience innovative performing and visual arts trends in the country.

On the music front, Johnny Clegg has a huge following in France, and Ladysmith Black Mambazo received international recognition after performing on Paul Simon's *Graceland* album. The best-selling genre of music in South Africa, however, is African gospel, and jazz is popular with older crowds. Popular sounds among urban black youth are *kwaito* and local hip-hop; American R&B and rap also have massive followings. White South Africans prefer international pop, and indeed, with such a small white population, local bands find

it hard to get an audience, although the Afro-fusion band Freshlyground and the dance music duo Goldfish are receiving recognition internationally.

Dance companies post-apartheid have begun to use movement as a form of expression to explore the country's legacy. The dance form called Afrofusion, named by Moving Into Dance Company's Sylvia Glasser, combines classic and traditional movements. Companies such as Glasser's and Cape Town's Jazzart Dance Theatre, the oldest in the country, experiment with styles and expression. Local theaters feature international productions as well as the work of homegrown authors such as Athol Fugard.

Literature

Most South African literature is published in English and Afrikaans. One reason is that in previous decades indigenous languages were not recognized and African experiences not valued. Contemporary African writers find themselves writing in English or Afrikaans, too, to assure

themselves of a larger audience than if they write solely in their regional language. Increasingly, however, works are being translated, often for a foreign market as well. Experiences, culture, and language vary so widely throughout the country that there isn't really a unified concept of South African literature.

The first fictional works written in South Africa tended to deal with colonial attitudes and adventures; the hero was often an Englishman, and indigenous people, when they featured, were either savages or servants.

Much of apartheid-era writing tends towards realism and such themes as the white minority's sense of psychological and physical alienation, the black struggle living under the apartheid regime—themes that are still being addressed today as South Africa forges a new identity. Well-known novelists include Nobel Prize for literature winners Nadine Gordimer and J.M. Coetzee (who also won the Booker prize twice).

IF YOU LIKE

Drop-Dead Luxury

Not into roughing it? No problem. Our favorite luxe properties will tempt you to defect from the real world and live like kings and queens.

Lion Sands, Sabi Sands Reserve. Family-owned and operated for more than 80 years, the camp's location across from Kruger National Park guarantees awesome animal sightings from just about every vantage point, including your plush king-sized bed. Your every need will be catered to from the moment you arrive.

MalaMala, Sabi Sands Reserve. One of the oldest and most distinguished of all southern African bush lodges, this is the haunt of royalty, celebs, and the jet set.

One and Only Cape Town. Large rooms, a large swimming pool, name-brand restaurants, and a view of Table Mountain are all part of the newest, swankiest hotel on the scene.

Rovos Rail. Some travelers just can't bear to stay put when on a journey. For them, Rovos Rail's plush cars are the best way to stay pampered while on the move.

Thanda Main Lodge, KwaZulu-Natal. This exquisite lodge has beehive-shape dwellings that blend elements of royal Zulu with an eclectic pan-African feel. Shaka never had it this good.

The Twelve Apostles Hotel and Spa, Cape Town. Sinfully comfy rooms with ocean views in front and those looming Cape Town palisades make this luxury retreat a favorite of those wanting to get a good view of nature.

The Westcliff, Johannesburg. If you can't stay the night, at least come for tea at Johannesburg's cushy grand hotel, cascading down a hillside, interspersed with gardens.

Rubbing Shoulders With Locals

South Africa's rich cultural offerings run from the rhythms of Soweto to the jazz riffs of Cape Town's clubs. Crafts, drama, and dance combine to form the rich cultural mosaic of South Africa, where native beats mingle with European traditions. Step out like a local, or visit some locals and soak it in.

Jazz Tours, Cape Town. Join like-eared aficionados for a tour that will show you the roots of jazz and expose you to some local ear candy.

Jazzart Dance Theatre, Cape Town. The country's oldest modern dance company has a range of programs and teaches in disadvantaged communities.

Kirtsenbosch National Botanical Gardens, Cape Town. The 1,304 acres feature indigenous southern African plants that captivate even the locals. Come for lawn picnics in the shadow of Table Mountain and stay to listen to the Winter Concert Series.

Market Theatre, Johannesburg. One of the country's renowned venues showcasing new works, with a rich legacy. During the era of apartheid it was one of South Africa's only venues where all races could watch together.

Sisal Cooperative, Madikwe. Learn how locals turn sisal fiber to acid-free paper used for colorful gift tags and cards in this workshop adjacent to a mill.

Thusanang Training and Development Project, Klerksdorp. For decades, single mothers have worked together here, creating crafts for resale.

Staying in Fair-Trade Properties

Never sacrificing luxury, these spots look after the environment, the local communities, and the wildlife, so you can feel good while you're having fun.

Cape Grace. Synonymous with understated luxury and smack on Cape Town's V&A Waterfront, this hotel's commitment to the welfare of its staff and to improving the community with job training programs earned it certification by South Africa's Fair Trade in Tourism program.

Chiwa Camp, Zambia. A family-owned and -managed property, the camp supports the surrounding Lower Zambezi area through conservation, wildlife education, and community involvement and works to reintroduce wild cheetahs and the ground hornbill to the area.

Grootbus Private Nature Reserve. On 2,500 acres overlooking Walker Bay in the Western Cape, Grootbus is home to the largest private fynbos garden in the world. You can tour tropical rain forests, watch for whales, and dine on locally grown produce. The reserve's foundation contributes to community education and employment.

Hog Hollow Country Lodge. Once an overgrown wasteland, lodge owners worked tirelessly to return the land to its original, indigenous state. The lodge employs and trains local people from surrounding communities.

Shiluvari Lakeside Lodge. If you're out to bag souvenir beads, textiles, or pottery, make this tranquil lakeside retreat—home to many well-known artists—your base. The community created a source of revenue and relaxation in a serene corner of the country.

Vuyatela, Djuma. Near the Sabi Sands Reserve, the game-viewing at Djuma is among the best there is. The owner-run camp was built with local labor and no machinery to lessen the impact on the environment. The camp's owners also built a day-care center for the local community.

The Beach

South Africa's coastline stretches from tiny towns to desolate windswept acres, and most beach lovers can find exactly what they're after, be it a private cove or an endless stretch of sand.

Boulders Beach, Simon's Town. The sparkling coves ringed by dramatic boulders are also home to a colony of African penguins. Share your spot in the sand with these curious creatures, but a warning: they can be quite loud.

Camps Bay. A broad Atlantic beach backed by looming Table Mountain and a street full of umbrella-shaded cafés. The perfect place to watch a sunset or take a stroll.

Diaz Beach, Cape Point. Many consider this secluded spot, reachable only on foot via a short trail, the Cape's most beautiful beach. Unfortunately the currents are pretty strong, and swimming is not advised.

Rocktail Bay Lodge. If you're in the mood for pristine beaches, surf fishing, snorkeling, or sunbathing, then coming to this lodge nestled in the Maputaland Coastal Reserve will be the perfect beach getaway after your safari.

St. James. Just south of Kalk Bay's shops, St. James's colorful changing cabanas are photo icons. The gentle surf and tidal pool on False Bay are perfect for kids.

Zimbali Lodge. With direct access to the beach, this lodge near Durban is set in

one of the last remaining coastal forests in the KwaZulu-Natal province. Play golf, go horseback riding, or swim in the pool on the beach.

Getting Out of the Vehicle

Game drives are thrilling and often action-packed, but sometimes, particularly if you are a second-time visitor to Africa and have ticked off your Big Five, you'd like to get up close and personal with the African bush and its inhabitants. Here are some of the best ways to really get down to nature.

Elephant Safaris. If you prefer your wildlife a bit more tame, visit the Addo Elephant Sanctuary, where you'll meet some trained African elephants available for short rides, walks, petting, and feeding.

Rhino Tracking. Seeing a rhino on foot is quite a different experience from viewing one from a jeep. Depending on your level of interest, you can organize a walking safari within a special area of Kruger for several hours or several days. Along the way, the guide will point out interesting grasses, smaller animals.

Stargazing Safaris. Ask if your lodge has a guide trained in astronomy for a night safari of the Southern Hemisphere's sky.

Turtle Watching. From St. Lucia to Kosi Bay, join a safari to look for loggerhead and leatherback turtles laying their eggs.

Walking Safaris. For some, feeling the grass on their legs and hearing the rustle under their feet is the best way to experience the land. Amble with trained guides for several hours to gain a new perspective on creatures large and small—you may spot the "little five" up close in many locations throughout the country.

Kid-Friendly Destinations

More and more families want their kids to share in their safari experience, and more lodges are catering to kids with programs designed especially for them. Always find out in advance which camps welcome kids, as many still don't allow children under 12. And try for one of the malaria-free reserves to avoid the added worry of antimalarial medication.

Berg-en-Dal. Kids can explore in safety at this attractive, fenced camp, which has a great pool and curio shop. Get them to walk around the camp's perimeter and spot game.

Jaci's Lodges, Madikwe. Whereas many other safari camps hide their family offerings so as not to frighten off other clients, Jaci's celebrates children with Jungle Drives for the littlest adventurers and Family Drives for Mom and Dad, too. Even the food is kid-friendly, with spaghetti and hot dogs on the menu.

Pafuri Camp, Kruger. This lovely camp in Kruger's far north has a superb children's program and special family accommodations that give everybody privacy. Kids love Crooks Corner, where baddies-on-the-run used to hide.

Shamwari Riverdene Lodge. Malaria-free Shamwari constructs family-specific itineraries on-site and even gives kids a gift pack to welcome them. Kid-friendly side trips include a big cat rescue center and wildlife hospital.

Thakadu Tented Camp, Madikwe. Four of the 12 tented suites at this camp in malaria-free Madikwe are designed for families. It's a smaller reserve, but that means less time in the vehicle for antsy kids—and Madikwe does have more than enough game to keep adults happy.

GREAT ITINERARIES

South Africa in 7 Days

With only one week, you can still enjoy the best of South Africa, including Johannesburg and Cape Town highlights, as well as a safari.

Days 1–3: R and R at Kruger Fly-in Safari. To make the most of your time, arrange for a direct flight from O.R. Tambo Airport to a safari lodge at one of Kruger's fly-in reserves. International flights arrive in the morning, making it easy logistically to board the daily midmorning South African Airlink flight to the airfield at Mala-Mala, a reserve bordering Kruger and Sabi Sands. Recoup from your long-haul flight by lazing at a luxury lodge or being driven around to gaze at scenery. Meals are all arranged for you and bedtime is early.

Experience your first full safari day on Day 2. You'll awake before sunrise for a quick caffeine jolt before setting out on a game drive (usually with a stop for morning tea) and then return to the lodge for lunch and a rest during the midday heat. Depending on where you stay, you may be able to arrange for a massage or spa treatment during this time. After a hearty and proper afternoon tea of sweet and savory options, you're off in the vehicle again. Sundowners as the sun sets is an experience you'll never forget. After the evening drive, it's back to the lodge for cleanup, drinks, and dinner and maybe some stargazing.

You'll have time for a morning game drive before you depart the camp on Day 3. Head back to Johannesburg via car so you can stop at the sites along the Mpumalanga Panoramic Route through Blyde Canyon's breathtaking scenery, arriving in Johannesburg late in the day. Shoppers might select a small B&B or guesthouse in the thick of things (e.g., the Melville

or Parktown neighborhoods); those looking for retail therapy should opt for tony Sandton. To experience life outside the cloistered environment and walk down a street or sit at a café, Melville is ideal.

Days 4–7: Johannesburg to Cape Town. Prearrange a township tour to Soweto to learn about the roots of apartheid and the way entrepreneurs are changing lives within the community. Include a stop at the Apartheid Museum for a full taste of the country's history. Catch a late-afternoon or early-evening flight to Cape Town and overnight along the V&A Waterfront at the Cape Grace. That will give you time to step outside your accommodations to grab dinner waterside, with Table Mountain looming behind you.

Get the first boat to Robben Island on your fifth day, to see where Nelson Mandela spent decades and inhale that bracing fresh sea air. When you return, grab a taxi to the base of Table Mountain and ride

up the cable car for magnificent views. If you're a shopper, spend the afternoon browsing in Greenmarket Square and then grab a snack in one of Long Street's cafés. If you're more of an explorer, rent a car to visit Kirstenbosch National Botanic Gardens to see magnificent protea plants and views (in summer there are concerts on the lawns). You may even have time to dip into some nearby wine-tasting rooms before heading to Camps Bay for sunset cocktails and a light dinner, followed by a stroll along the beach.

Head to the university town of Stellenbosch, less than an hour from Cape Town, on Day 6. Check out the historic downtown's Cape Dutch architecture before settling into a typical South African B&B. Book some spa time at Lanzerac Manor and enjoy lunch there gazing out at spectacular scenery. Stop for some wine tastings at Fairview or Boechendal Wine Farm along the road leading back to town, then book dinner at Moyo at the Spier estate to taste a variety of wines and dig into an elaborate and entertaining meal of typical South African game in the whimsical outdoor café. Come early to visit the cheetahs.

Get an early start on your last morning to take the long way to Cape Town, turning left when you hit the water to visit Strand and Gordon's Bay. Reverse course to return to Cape Town, taking in more beach communities like Kalk. See the penguins at Boulders and visit the Cape Peninsula National Park and Cape Point before finishing up at Cape Town airport for a flight home that evening.

South Africa in 10 Days

With 10 days you can spend the majority of your time on safari and finish up with highlights of the Cape.

Days 1–3: A Private Fly-in Reserve. Begin your vacation in true luxury by opting to fly in to a private game reserve. Madikwe on the border with Botswana may not have the vast open savannah of your African dreams, but with the Big Five, watering holes, plenty of options for accommodations, and wild dogs, you won't feel shortchanged.

Spend the morning of Day 2 visiting a community program just outside the reserve's gates. Enjoy the still air and hot breeze of the middle of the day from a private balcony or a luxury lodge's plunge pool. Night drives may bring out the elusive leopard or lions feasting on a kill. The small size of the reserve will enable you to return to see your favorite animals more than once in the course of a stay.

Go on a morning safari on Day 3 before heading to Kruger with an overnight in Pretoria or drive straight through. The road will give you views of real-life African villages, massive mining operations, as well as the distant Waterberg and Pilanesberg ranges. If you drive straight through, be sure to get through Kruger's gates before sundown so you can get settled at your lodge.

Days 4–7: Kruger National Park. If you decided to stop in Pretoria, rise early on Day 4, so you can meander through the scenic Blyde River Canyon with views of the distant Drakensberg Range. Consider visiting the Three Rondavels and God's Window, a lookout where you can see clear to Mozambique some days. Stop for lunch in quaint Pilgrim's Rest, a former mining town. Remember to get through Kruger's gates before sundown (check times) so you can join in evening activities at your first accommodation, possibly one of the basic rest camps. Or if you want to splurge on more luxury, try Ivory Lodge at the Lion Sands Private Reserve or Singita Lebombo Lodge.

If you arrived at Kruger the night before, you can choose to sleep in, have a spa treatment, participate in a walking safari, or visit a local community, in addition to taking a game drive.

If Day 5 is your first full day in Kruger, consider joining an organized guided trip to get your bearings, before trying to spot game on your own. If you do drive yourself, take your time and go slowly to spot game. No matter when you arrived, join a ranger-led walk for a different perspective and expertise in the afternoon. Book a dinner at a boma under the stars or a stargazing safari for a memorable only-in-Africa experience.

Days 6 and 7 should be spent exploring the park in detail, viewing your favorite animals for as long as you wish.

Days 8–10: Cape Town. Return to Johannesburg in time for a midday flight to Cape Town. This will put you in town with enough time for a quick peek at the Greenmarket Square shopping area or the legendary tea at the Mount Nelson Hotel. If you choose sightseeing, book dinner at the V&A Waterfront or one of the swank new eateries at the One&Only hotel. Shop late in the arts-and-crafts collective, which benefits area artists. For a low-key option, stay at Camps Bay and dine along the water at the foot of the Twelve Apostles mountain range.

Rent a car for Day 9 and head out early to hit highlights outside town, including beaches and the National Park at Cape Point. Watch out for aggressive baboons! Stop for fish-and-chips in Simon's Town or a tranquil waterside rest at one of the beach communities, such as Kalk Bay, on the way. Finish your long day with a relaxing evening out at the charming Theatre on the Bay at Camps Bay—you can even dine there.

Day 10: City Highlights. Plan to visit Table Mountain and Robben Island. Lace up your hiking shoes and try walking downhill for spectacular views and some leg stretching before your lengthy flight home.

South Africa in Two Weeks

Start this itinerary from the bottom up. Fly into Cape Town and fly out of Johannesburg, with a quick overnight jaunt up to Victoria Falls.

Days 1–3: Cape Town and Environs. With two weeks in South Africa you can enjoy Cape Town's attractions at a leisurely pace. Take the time to explore the city's diverse collection of museums surrounding the Company's Gardens Park. Window-shop along Long Street, and later explore the African crafts galleries along the V&A Waterfront. To save money and feel a bit like you're in a home away from

home, rent one of the many apartment units available in and around the city. The Cape Cadogan Apartments are ideally located off Kloof Street in refurbished homes.

Day 2 can include a small loop that takes in Kirstenbosch National Botanic Gardens, with plenty of time for a leisurely picnic, and a visit to Table Mountain. It also leaves time for hiking at both or just enjoying the view. You can drive into Constantia and visit a winery and enjoy vineyard scenery. Take a taxi to dinner in the Bo Kaap district or dine along the waterfront.

Use Day 3 to make a full loop of the Cape Peninsula, heading out of town through Hout Bay with stops in Kalk Bay, and time to walk through the boardwalk with the penguins at Boulders Beach. You can even hike Cape Peninsula National Park. On the way back visit an ostrich farm to learn about this unique South African industry.

Days 4–5: The Winelands. Heading out from Cape Town you'll have plenty of time to linger over wine-and-cheese tastings in Stellenbosch, dine on gourmet French food in Franschhoek, and stroll alongside Paarl's mix of Cape Dutch, Edwardian, Victorian, and art deco architecture lining the main street. Take an afternoon to bike the back roads or indulge in a spa treatment. With so many excellent guesthouses to chose from, part of the fun is deciding which fantasy accommodation suits you best—from tranquil lakeside cottages set in the midst of the vines to a historic B&B right off Stellenbosch's main street.

Begin Day 5 with a hot-air balloon ride over the valley or a refreshing round of golf. Loll in a nature reserve and spend the afternoon at leisure meandering among the wineries. Tonight, go to a dinner under the stars at Moyo's outpost at Spier Winery.

Days 6–8: The Garden Route. Continue with a drive to the Garden Route with an overnight in the tranquil valley town of George. Along the way, make stops in Knysna, Plettenberg Bay, and Tsitsikamma National Park, exploring whatever captures your fancy. You may want to bungee jump off Africa's highest bridge or just amble along a trail in the national park. Make time for a visit to Cape Agulhas, South Africa's southernmost point, or stop in Hermanus for some whale-watching.

Take your time on Day 7 as you make your way to the outskirts of Port Elizabeth, driving the coast and stopping in at old fishing villages on the way. If you're brave, this is the place to arrange for a shark cage dive off the coast in Shark Alley. Overnight in town or on Day 8 finish up your tour with some R and R and light game-viewing at Samara Game Reserve outside Port Elizabeth. Or if you're a fan of pachyderms, pack in a night at Addo National Elephant Sanctuary. For something different, the beautiful and unique Samara Game Reserve is off the beaten track—about a two-hour drive from Port Elizabeth. You can relax by the pool or go on a walk, without pressure to do every game drive.

Days 9–12: Private Reserve Safari. By now you'll have had your fill of driving, so board a flight from Port Elizabeth and let someone else take over the wheel. Head to Phinda Private Game reserve in the Eastern Cape, where you can participate in a range of activities, from walking safaris to rhino tracking to canoeing and specialized leopard research safaris.

1

On Day 10 you'll have your first full day on safari and a chance to relax and get accustomed to the rhythms of the camp. You can ask your guide to show you particular animals or to suggest a recent sighting of interest. Unless you elect to participate in a special activity, the safari camp will structure your days. All you will need to do is eat, take pictures, listen to the knowledgeable guides, and relax.

For a different perspective, take today's safari by water. Choose to explore in a sturdy guided canoe ride during the day or riverboat in the evening when the crocs laze on the banks eyeing you. An alternative is a visit to nearby Greater St. Lucia Wetland Park, a World Heritage area, to look at a different type of ecosystem.

On your final safari day, take the opportunity to check out your favorites or participate in an intensive research safari on leopards. Make your last night special and arrange for a private dinner under the stars.

Days 13–14: Victoria Falls. Plan on Day 13 being a travel day, as you'll have just enough time to fly into Johannesburg and right back out to Victoria Falls on the Zambia side. You may have time and energy once you've checked into the Royal Livingstone to take a taxi into Livingstone to explore the town's colonial remnants and stop in at Kubu Crafts for curios and tea. Unlike many of Africa's big cities, the pace of life in Livingstone is relaxed. Go slow, stroll, soak up the atmosphere, then taxi back to the hotel when you are through. Walk "over" the border on the bridge in front of the falls and "into" Zimbabwe, and then enjoy sunset cocktails under the big tree with mischievous monkeys, a small herd of zebra, and maybe a black mamba snake as company.

On your last morning, visit the falls early for more souvenirs at the large crafts market near the bridge. Your flight from Livingstone will land in O.R. Tambo Airport with time to shop at the outstanding duty-free facilities before your evening flight back home.

FLAVORS OF SOUTH AFRICA

South Africa's rich cultural legacy comes alive on the plate, in the array of flavors and tastes influenced by the mélange of people who have lived here, as well as in the global cuisine. Restaurants score well in international awards and subscribe to the highest food safety standards. Confusingly, an entrée in South Africa is considered an appetizer rather than a main course.

BBQ Traditions

South Africans love to *braai* (rhymes with rye)—i.e., barbecue—at any opportunity. In black townships, literally hundreds of people meet and socialize around an outdoor fire at recreational sites, after purchasing meat from nearby butchers and drinks from a corner shebeen (neighborhood tavern). But it's in the homes of South Africans that the braai comes to life.

Boerewors (pronounced *boo-*rah-vors)— beef and pork sausage with heady doses of coriander seed, lamb chops, and chicken pieces—is a braai staple. *Sosaties* (so-*sah*-teez), skewers of meat with fruit or vegetables, are also popular. Potatoes and sweet potatoes, known as *patats* (pah-*tutzz*), are often wrapped in foil and cooked among the coals. *Broodjies* (brew-kiss) are sandwiches (typically onion and tomato) cooked on the fire to the perfect consistency: crisp on the outside, moist on the inside. A *potjie* (phoi-kee) is a three-legged cast-iron pot as well as the name of the dish typically prepared in it: meat on the bone is layered with vegetables (potatoes, onions, garlic, dried beans) and cooked over low coals for at least three hours (think paella).

During the grape harvest (March–April) a soft, sweet bread is made from the grape must. Called *mosbolletjies* (*mohss*-ball-eh-keys), it's irresistible if purchased fresh from the oven.

Indigenous South African Dishes

Pap (pronounced pup; also known as *samp*) is made from maize meal and cooked to varying consistencies—*krummel* (*krah*-muhl) is dry and crumbly, whereas *stywe* (*stay*-ver) is like a stiff porridge. A staple across the continent, it's served alongside stewed vegetables or meats. The texture is like couscous, and the flavor is mild enough to take on the taste of whatever is served with it, such as chicken or a vegetable stew of sugar beans, onions, and potatoes. Other vegetables abundant in South African recipes include gem squash, butternut squash, pumpkin, green beans, tomatoes, and cabbage. You may also come across the following confusing terms: rocket (arugula), peppadew (a cross between a pepper and cherry tomato), or *waterblommetjiebredie* (literally flower stew, made from the buds of a Western Cape flower).

For dessert expect *malva* (muhl-vah) pudding, its sweet and sour notes created by pouring an apricot-jam-and-vinegar sauce over sponge cake. *Melktert* (melk-tet) is a thick custard typically dusted with cinnamon or nutmeg. *Koeksisters* (cook-sis-ter) is braided sweet dough boiled in cinnamon-spiced syrup. Finger-shaped coconut doughnuts usually available only at Cape Malay restaurants or at carnivals are also called koeksisters.

Immigrant Influences

Despite the name, the cuisine of Cape Town's Malay community is not Malaysian, but instead mixes the flavors, spices, and preparations of Indonesia, China, Africa, and Europe. *Bobotie*, a curried, minced beef with raisins, topped with a savory custard mixture, most closely

resembles English shepherd's pie—with a kick. *Bredie* is another way of saying stew and is often made with tomatoes. You'll find *samoosas* (samosas—pronounced sah-*moo*-sah here)—curry-mince or vegetable-filled, deep-fried three-cornered nibbles—at every corner café. *Rootis* (rotis—pronounced *root*-ee), a soft, griddled tortilla, when filled with curry mince is called a *salomi* (pronounced sah-*low*-me). Sure to cause indigestion, the Gatsby is a long roll packed with lettuce, tomatoes, french fries, and melted cheese; a proteinlike sausage or steak is added and then topped with anything from mayonnaise to *peri-peri* (fiery tomato-and-chili sauce that originated in Mozambique). You will find them at roadside cafés in half or full portions. "Bunny chow," made famous in Durban by indentured Asian laborers who couldn't sit down to eat, is a half or quarter white-bread loaf that's hollowed out, filled with curry, and capped by the leftover bread. Top your snacks with *chakalaka* (a spicy vegetable relish) or peri-peri, which is perfect with grilled seafood.

Beyond Beef

Similar to beef jerky, *biltong* is a popular snack that's found just about everywhere from roadside stands to high-end markets. Types range from beef and ostrich to game (kudu is a favorite) and can be flavored with spices. Dried sausage and crisp, thin biltong pieces known as snap sticks perfectly accompany a beer.

Frikkadels, mini lamb *rissoles* (small croquettes), are occasionally wrapped in cabbage leaves and flavored with nutmeg, reminiscent of Eastern European stuffed cabbage dishes or the little Greek meatballs called *keftedes.*

Many restaurants serve game such as ostrich and springbok but also wildebeest, impala, and kudu. Karoo lamb is the most delicious lamb you will find, on account of the herby Santolina bush the animals eat in the arid Karoo region. The meat has an almost perfumed quality to it.

Succulent Seafood

In a country surrounded on three sides by water, it's no surprise that a major source of protein comes from the sea. Once used as bait, rock lobster (also known as crayfish) is now highly sought after and closely resembles New England lobster. Costly perlemoen or abalone, which is almost on the brink of extinction, is tough and best described as similar to calamari steak. Local fish include kingklip (a firm white fish), hake (a flaky, white fish called haddock once smoked), and snoek (pronounced snook), an oily fish with many long bones. Line-caught fish includes Cape salmon (also known as *geelbek*), which isn't salmon at all but is sure to be on the menu. You may come across *kabeljou* (*cabal*-yoh), also known as kob, a firm fish similar in appearance to salmon. The best prawns and langoustines usually come from Mozambique. Tuna is often seared; it's divine with a pepper crust. Unexpectedly, the best seafood is in landlocked Johannesburg, as merchants send their best quality to the biggest market.

Eating on Safari

Since most, if not all, of the ingredients must be flown in or grown locally in small quantities, you might expect meals to be limited. However, you'll usually have a choice of entrée options (two to three), and you'll be amazed at the delicious and innovative creations that come out of the kitchen. You'll also have plenty of

opportunity to try new varieties of fish or game and South African wines. Breads and pastries are generally fresh baked, and any dietary concerns are catered to as best as possible. Don't be surprised if you gain a few pounds. It's not unheard of to eat six or seven times a day. Dining is truly a pastime on safari.

Taste at Your Own Risk

Odd-sounding treats are often presented on a township tour. Two of the most common are *smileys* (sheep's heads cooked in the fire) and *walkie-talkies*, which appropriately enough, are made from chicken heads and feet. You may also be offered Mopane worms, a tofulike, protein-rich staple that tends to take on the taste of other ingredients; it's typically cooked with tomatoes and onions. More Afrikaner than African, *skilpadjies* (skul-*pai*-keys) is calf liver covered by caul fat, and *poffaddertjies* (*pohf*-aader) is liver and kidneys stuffed into a sheep's intestine and cooked on the braai.

Wetting Your Whistle

South Africa's world-renowned wines are shockingly inexpensive. Tastings at wineries average R20 to try five wines and you'll be hard-pressed to find a bottle of wine on the menu for more than R250.

Pinotage, a cross between pinot noir and Cinsaut varieties, is truly a South African original and will always be on a wine list. Grassy or mineral-y sauvignon blanc is a very good food wine. Local chardonnays, especially the costlier ones that have benefited from oaking, are renowned. Red wine vineyards are younger in South Africa and produce different flavors than expected for cabernet sauvignon, Shiraz, and pinot noir. Chenin blanc, one of the best value wines available, often appears as "steen."

Much as in wine-growing regions from California to Australia and New Zealand, the dining emphasis is on the freshest greens, light flavors, and experimental dishes that complement the relaxed atmosphere. Many vineyards have cafés attached so you can eat a light meal between tastings if you plan ahead.

South Africans consume more beer than any other nation on the continent; this area was settled by the Dutch, Germans, and English, after all. South African Breweries (SAB) controls most of the beer market, and its most popular brew is Castle Lager. You'll also find Windhoek lager, a Namibian beer, on offer. If you like hard cider, keep an eye out for Hunters Gold and Savanna Dry.

South Africans have created nectars like muscadels (muscatels) filled with intense fruits, to creamy liqueurs best served over ice under a full moon. Amarula, South Africa's unique creamy fruit liqueur with the elephant on the label, is popular. Some say it's similar to Bailey's Irish Cream. South Africa's brandy regularly beats cognacs in blind tastings.

Teetotalers might prefer to quaff *rooibos* (pronounced *roy*-boss), the unique South African red bush tea. Ginger beer, a carbonated soft drink, is another tasty option, while the local answer to root beer is Irn-Bru (an orange-colored soft drink). Fruit-based drinks such as Appletiser (carbonated) or LiquiFruit (noncarbonated) are very good. As a fruit-producing region, top quality fruit is always available at supermarkets. The *naartjie* (*nah*-chee) is an easy-peeling small citrus, while melons like *spanspek* (*spun*-speck) and paw-paw (papaya) are available elsewhere and are usually served at breakfast.

WORLD CUP 411

Held since 1958, the FIFA (Federation Internationale de Football Association) World Cup is truly a worldwide event; more than 40 billion fans in 200 countries tuned in for the monthlong 2006 World Cup, in Germany. The 2010 World Cup (June 11–July 11), anticipates an even larger audience, and South Africa, the host nation, has been hard at work preparing for its moment to shine. Airports have received makeovers, neighborhoods have been revamped, and cities are putting the finishing touches on the 10 venues that will host the 64 matches. Some stadiums were built from scratch, while others were modernized and expanded.

More than a year before the event some venues and matches were already sellouts. Large public viewing areas called **fan parks** outside many of the stadiums are planned for those without tickets.

THE MASCOT AND LOGO

The official logo, called a "symbol of hope" by some officials, was inspired by Khoi San rock paintings and pictures a soccer player over the shape of Africa in the colors of the South African flag.

The name of the mascot, Zakumi, a playful, green-haired leopard with a soccer ball, is an amalgamation of *ZA*, the abbreviation for South Africa, and *kumi*, which means "ten" in several African languages.

WHO'S PLAYING?

Thirty-two teams compete in the World Cup, with allocations made geographically. Europe will enter 13 teams; the Americas, 8; Africa, 6, including the one automatically allotted to the host nation. Asia will have 4 teams, and a fifth slot will go to the winner of a playoff with the Oceania region. Qualifying matches started in 2007.

WHERE ARE THE GAMES?

Matches will be spread across the country, in 10 stadiums in nine cities.

Soccer City
Near Soweto, where nearly 40% of Johannesburg's residents live, Soccer City is the tournament's main venue. The old stadium on this site hosted several historic events, including Nelson Mandela's first mass rally after his release. The overhauled stadium, a new landmark for Johannesburg, was designed to resemble an African bowl, or calabash (gourd), in daytime and a traditional African cooking pot when lit at night.

Hosting: Opening and closing matches; first- and second-round and quarterfinal play

Location: Johannesburg

Capacity: 94,000

Ellis Park
A 15-minute walk to the Johannesburg city center, Ellis Park was originally constructed as a rugby venue and was the site of the 1995 Rugby World Cup final when South Africa bested New Zealand. The arena has been refitted with new upper tiers at either goal post.

Hosting: First- and second-round and quarterfinal play.

Location: Johannesburg

Capacity: 61,000

Cape Town Stadium
Planted between Cape Town's V&A Waterfront and Signal Hill in Green Point, the country's costliest new stadium has a retractable dome, just in case the "Cape

doctor" comes to call (that's the nickname for the unpredictable Cape weather, which can be chilly and wet in June and July).

Hosting: Semifinal play

Location: Cape Town

Capacity: 70,000

Moses Mabhida Stadium

Upgrades to this stadium near Durban's Golden Mile include new roofed upper tiers, which make it a three-tier stadium. Dramatic arches cross the stadium's rooftop and a slatted facade protect against the elements but still allow views to the outside. The stadium is part of the Kings Park Sporting Precinct, developed to aid in Durban's 2020 Olympics bid.

Hosting: First- and second-round and semifinal play

Location: Durban

Capacity: 70,000

Nelson Mandela Bay Stadium

Soccer teams will trade kicks and passes in this modern stadium, built specifically for the games.

Hosting: First- and second-round and semifinal play

Location: Port Elizabeth

Capacity: 50,000

Loftus Versfeld Stadium

In the vicinity of Embassy Row in South Africa's executive capital, this stadium is home to Sundowns, a South African soccer club.

Hosting: First- and second-round play

Location: Tshwane (Pretoria)

Capacity: 50,000

Royal Bafokeng Stadium

Only minor renovations will bring the relatively new stadium—named for the local Bafokeng people—up to FIFA standards.

The stadium's location, just 90 minutes outside Johannesburg, means that you can gamble in Sun City between matches.

Hosting: First- and second-round play

Location: Rustenburg, North West Province

Capacity: 42,000

Peter Mokaba Stadium

In the capital of Limpopo Province (previously Pietersburg), the stadium is named after controversial anti-apartheid activist Peter Mokaba, a native of the area. The arena was built fresh alongside the previously existing field.

Hosting: First-round play

Location: Polokwane, Limpopo Province

Capacity: 46,000

Mbombela Stadium

This brand-new, aptly named stadium—*Mbombela* means many people together in a small place—was purposely built close to the city center, local airport, and game parks.

Hosting: First-round play

Location: Nelspruit, Mpumalanga Province

Capacity: 46,000

Free State Stadium

The arena is getting some new additions including a second tier on the main grandstand, a new electronic scoreboard, and a new sound system—perfect for hearing the announcer over the din of the crowd.

Hosting: First- and second-round play

Location: Bloemfontein, Free State Province

Capacity: 48,000

ADVENTURE SPORTS

If coming face to mane with a lion isn't spine tingling enough for you, try some of these only-in-South Africa thrills instead. From coast to coast, above and below the sea, and even in the air, the country's adventure offerings are sure to raise the hairs on the back of your neck.

Hang Ten. The South African coast is one of the world's top surf destinations, and dudes and dudettes come from all over to check out the sometimes-empty scene. But along with killer waves, surfers have to worry about, well, being killed. These are shark-infested waters. If you're experienced, check out Dungeons in Cape Town, Jeffreys Bay in the Eastern Cape, and the area dubbed Point Break Heaven south of Durban in KwaZulu-Natal.

Swim with Sharks. If you actually *want* to see sharks close up, a few hours' drive from Cape Town and 5 mi out at sea is the great white shark highway called Shark Alley, where daredevils can test their mettle by diving into the water, separated from the ocean's most feared predators by just a few spindly bars of a shark cage. Can't scuba dive? Lost your nerve? You can also watch from the boat deck.

Dive with Crocs. If you prefer your deadly predator encounters to be land-based, arrange to come face to snout with Nile crocodiles. The people at Cango Wildlife Ranch will happily dunk you into clear water in Oudtshoorn with a mask and a snorkel, inside a cage. You don't really even need to know how to swim. They'll snap your picture so you can prove you did it when you make it back home.

Surf Without Water. The Western Cape has some of the gnarliest sand this side of the shore break. If you want to hang ten without getting wet, grab a plank of wood, or sign up with a company that outfits you with the needed equipment and then point yourself downhill on a seemingly endless sandy dune. They call it sandboarding, and adrenaline junkies surf the grains at Lost City, Atlantis, or Betty's Bay to get a blast of hot grit.

Cave by Candlelight. A mining country like South Africa has plenty of caves to explore all over. Experienced spelunkers can find caves in Mpumalanga and the North West provinces. Many small towns have caves, and some of the more popular places—such as the Cango Caves—are tourist attractions. Outside of these, be sure you go with someone local if you've never been.

Jump off a Bridge. South Africa has the world's highest bungee jump on the border between the Eastern Cape and Western Cape, along the N2 Garden Route. Bloukrans Bridge is a span full of superlatives: largest single span arched bridge in the world, highest bridge in South Africa and third highest in the world. If jumping off it is unappealing, you can ride the "flying fox" out to the arch. Or if that sounds like too much excitement, just walk it.

Jump out of a Plane. Skydiving is popular in South Africa, with clubs all over the country—the largest is in Pretoria. Novice jumpers can learn the ropes in Johannesburg or do tandem jumps in Cape Town, creating a Table Mountain photo opportunity to rival the scariest lion shot.

Cape Town and Peninsula

WORD OF MOUTH

"On day trips we did the Baboon Walk, which was fantastic, and a pelagic-waters cruise. It was cool to see Cape Point from below and beyond. And wonderful fish and chips at Kalky's!"

—Numbat83

"We were bowled over by the attentive service at the Cape Grace. Our room was large and, to our surprise, we could actually see Table Mountain! The light on it changes during the course of the day and it's so dramatic. I found myself completely mesmerized by this mountain."

—Tripgirl

Updated by
Lee Middleton
and Brian
Berkman

If you visit only one place in South Africa, make it Cape Town. Whether you're partaking of the Capetonian inclination for alfresco fine dining (the so-called "Mother City" is home to many of the country's best restaurants) or sipping wine atop Table Mountain, you sense—correctly—that this is South Africa's most urbane, civilized city.

Here elegant Cape Dutch buildings abut ornate Victorian architecture and imposing British monuments. In the Bo-Kaap neighborhood, the call to prayer echoes through cobbled streets lined with houses painted in bright pastels, while the sweet tang of Malay curry wafts through the air. Flower sellers, newspapers hawkers, and numerous markets keep street life pulsing, and every lamppost advertises another festival, concert, or cultural happening.

But as impressive as Cape Town's urban offerings are, what you'll ultimately recall about this city is the sheer grandeur of its setting—the mesmerizing beauty of Table Mountain rising above the city, the stunning drama of the mountains cascading into the sea, and the gorgeous hues of the two oceans. Francis Drake wasn't exaggerating when he said this was "the fairest Cape we saw in the whole circumference of the earth," and he would have little cause to change his opinion today.

A visit to Cape Town is often synonymous with a visit to the peninsula beneath the city, and for good reason. With pristine white-sand beaches, hundreds of mountain trails, and numerous activities from surfing to paragliding to mountain biking, the accessibility, variety, and pure beauty of the great outdoors will keep nature lovers and outdoor adventurers occupied for hours, if not days. You could spend a week exploring just the city and peninsula.

Often likened to San Francisco, Cape Town has two things that the City by the Bay doesn't—Table Mountain and Africa. The mountain, or tabletop, is vital to Cape Town's identity. It dominates the city in a way that's difficult to comprehend until you visit. In the afternoon, when creeping fingers of clouds spill over Table Mountain and reach toward the city, the whole town seems to shiver and hold its breath. Meanwhile, for all of its bon-vivant European vibe, Cape Town also reflects the diversity, vitality, and spirit of the many African peoples who call this city home.

ORIENTATION AND PLANNING

GETTING ORIENTED

Cape Town lies at the northern end of the Cape Peninsula, a 75-km (47-mi) tail of mountains that ends at the Cape of Good Hope. Drive 15 minutes out of town, and you may lose yourself in a stunning landscape

TOP REASONS TO GO

City Sophistication. Cape Town is a cosmopolitan city with a rich heritage that's proudly on display. It might be more laid-back than Johannesburg, but it has shaken off its sleepy, parochial air and now bristles with world-class shops and restaurants and cutting-edge art and design.

Lofty Aspirations. Fantastic Table Mountain towers over Cape Town and dominates the whole peninsula. Exploring the mountain is a must; you can either take the cable car to the top or hike up various routes.

Nature's Playground. Capetonians are proud of their city's stylish good looks and make the most of the mountain and beaches. In summer you'll find professionals shrugging off their suits as they head for the beach after work, surfboards, picnics, and sundowners in tow. In winter they bundle up against the cold and go walking, mountain biking, or running in the city's countless green spaces.

To Market, to Market. Cape Town's markets are the best in the country— informal, creative, funky, and with a good selection of both tacky and splendid African curios.

Historical Heritage. Cape Town is saturated with an extremely rich and fascinating history. At Robben Island you can stand in Mandela's old cell and learn about political and social banishment during apartheid, while the District Six Museum tells the poignant tale of the destruction of one of the country's most vibrant inner-city neighborhoods.

of 18th-century Cape Dutch manors, historic wineries, and white-sand beaches backed by sheer mountains.

Everyone uses Table Mountain for orientation. Cape Town's aptly named heart, the City Bowl fills the basin between the lower northern slopes of the mountain to the rim of the harbor. Though it's called interchangeably the "City Centre" or "Cape Town Central," the City Bowl actually encompasses Cape Town Central as well as adjacent neighborhoods located in the bowl, such as Gardens and Bo-Kaap. But don't get hung up on names: Cape Town is compact, with neighborhoods quickly morphing one into the next, and even locals disagree as to where the boundaries fall.

As you face Table Mountain from within the City Bowl, the distinctive triangular-shape mountain on the left is Devil's Peak; on the right are Lion's Head and Signal Hill, which takes its name from a gun fired there every day at noon. Lion's Head looks southwest (out to sea) past Table Mountain. Over Signal Hill and Lion's Head (and therefore outside the bowl) lies the fashionable Atlantic Seaboard, also known as Millionaire's Row, which includes cosmopolitan Green Point and Sea Point through to the exclusive suburbs of Clifton and Camps Bay. Cape Town's Southern Suburbs—Rondebosch, Newlands, Claremont, and the posh Constantia—are on the southern side of Table Mountain.

The vibrant V&A Waterfront lies at the northern end of the City Bowl across the freeways that separate the docks from downtown; nearby Waterkant is a fashionable and largely gay neighborhood between Green

Point and the Bo-Kaap. Beyond the predominantly white suburbs surrounding Cape Town's city center, the infamous townships of the Cape Flats stretch over what were once dunes and wetlands. Though separated from the city by highways, the continually expanding townships of Khayelitsha, Nyanga, Langa, and Gugulethu are integral to Cape Town's life, housing the majority of the city's nonwhite workers and influxes of immigrants.

> **A WORD OF EXPLANATION**
>
> Street signs in Cape Town alternate between English and Afrikaans. For example, *Wale* is English and *Waal* is Afrikaans, but they mean the same thing. In Afrikaans you don't put a space between the name and the street. So an address could be Orange Street or Oranjestraat. Kaapstad is Afrikaans for Cape Town.

Table Mountain National Park. Running north-south through the Cape Peninsula from Cape Town, Table Mountain National Park's 85 square mi include Table Mountain itself, most of the high-lying land in the mountain chain that runs down the center of the peninsula from Table Mountain south, the Cape of Good Hope nature reserve at the peninsula's end, and beautiful valleys, rugged cliffs, sandy flats, and some of the world's most stunning beaches. The park is bordered by the Atlantic Ocean to the west and False Bay to the east.

Cape Town Central. The small area roughly bounded by Hans Strijdom to the north, Buitenkant to the east, Buitengracht to the west, and the Company's Garden to the south is Cape Town's central business district and the only part of the city where you're likely to find anything approaching a skyscraper. The head offices of banks and big businesses, Parliament, the central railway and bus stations, some great architecture, and a good number of the city's tourist attractions are found here.

Bo-Kaap. Gracing the lower slopes of Signal Hill, wedged between the hill, De Waterkant, and Cape Town Central, this small City Bowl neighborhood is the historic home of the city's Muslim population, and remains strongly Muslim to this day. Its main thoroughfare is Wale Street.

Gardens. The affluent Gardens neighborhood begins at the southern end of the Company's Garden, stretching south toward the base of Table Mountain and Lion's Head. Most shops and restaurants are centered on Kloof Street.

V&A Waterfront. Once a seedy harbor, the V&A (Victoria & Alfred) Waterfront, often simply referred to as the Waterfront, is now one of South Africa's premier tourist destinations. Each year millions flock to this commercial area between the bay and Table Mountain to shop, eat at one of the many outdoor restaurants and bars, or just people-watch. The working harbor and buskers performing in public squares add character to the shopping malls, expensive hotels, and plush apartments lining the water's edge.

Southern Suburbs. Southeast of the City Bowl and at the base of Table Mountain's "backside" are the mainly residential neighborhoods known collectively as the Southern Suburbs, where the fantastic Kirstenbosch Botanic Gardens is located, along with a few other worthwhile attractions.

The Peninsula and Beaches. The Cape Peninsula, much of which is included in Table Mountain National Park, extends for around 40 km (25 mi) from the city through to Cape Point. The peninsula's eastern border is False Bay, whose Indian Ocean waters are (relatively) warmer and calmer than those of the peninsula's wilder, emptier, and arguably more beautiful Atlantic side. A coastal road and railway line connects east-coast towns.

PLANNING

WHEN TO GO
Whatever activities you hope to accomplish in Cape Town, head up Table Mountain as soon as the wind isn't blowing. Cape Town wind is notorious, and the mountain can be shut for days on end when there are gales. Summer (October–March) is the windiest time of the year, and during December winds can reach 60 km (37 mi) an hour. If you're planning to visit Robben Island during peak season, it's also wise to book well in advance. One of the best months to visit is April, when the heat and wind have abated and the Cape is bathed in warm autumnal hues. The rains in winter can put off visitors, but this time of the year holds its own charm: the countryside is a brilliant green, and come early spring (September) you have the whales and wildflowers to look forward to.

GETTING HERE AND AROUND
AIR TRAVEL
Cape Town International Airport lies about 12 mi from the city center. The domestic and international terminals both have booths run by Cape Town Tourism, which are open from 7:30 until the last flight comes in. It should take about 20 minutes to get from the airport to the city; during rush hour it can easily be double that.

There is no scheduled public transport to or from the airport, but private operators abound. Metered taxis and shuttle services (usually minivans) are based inside the domestic baggage hall and outside the international and domestic terminals and can also be phoned for airport drop-offs. Rates vary depending on the operator, number of passengers, destination, and time of arrival.

One person going into the city center alone pays about R280 in a metered taxi; a group of up to four will usually pay the same rate. △ Reports of overcharging are common, so check the fare first. Touch Down Taxis is the only officially authorized airport taxi. Look for the ACSA symbol on the vehicles. Shawn Casey Taxi Service charges a fixed rate of R220 for the vehicle (up to four passengers) but must be booked ahead. For single travelers, a prearranged shared shuttle with Legend Tours and Transfers or Magic Bus is the most economical, costing about R150–R180 per person; however, it will likely be slower because of numerous drop-offs. A surcharge of up to R50 is sometimes levied from

Cape History at a Glance

It's said that Cape Town owes its very existence to Table Mountain. The freshwater streams running off its slopes were what first prompted early explorers to anchor here. In 1652 Jan van Riebeeck and 90 Dutch settlers established a refreshment station for ships of the Dutch East India Company (VOC) on the long voyage east. The settlement represented the first European toehold in South Africa, and Cape Town is still called the Mother City.

Those first Dutch settlers soon ventured into the interior to establish their own farms, and 140 years later the settlement supported a population of 20,000 whites and 25,000 slaves brought from distant lands like Java, Madagascar, and Guinea. Its strategic position on the cusp of Africa, however, meant that the colony never enjoyed any real stability. The British occupied the Cape twice, first in 1795 and then more permanently in 1806, bringing with them additional slaves from Ceylon, India, and the Philippines. Destroyed or assimilated in this colonial expansion were the indigenous Khoekhoen (previously called Khoikhoi and Hottentots), who once herded cattle and foraged along the coast.

Diamond and gold discoveries in central and northern South Africa in the late 1800s pulled focus away from Cape Town, and Pretoria, near Johannesburg, was designated the capital in 1860. In 1910, Cape Town was named the legislative capital, and it remains so today. The diamond and gold boom fueled rapid development in Cape Town and throughout the country.

The wounds of the 20th century belong to apartheid (⇨ *South Africa's History, in Chapter 1)*. While apartheid ended in the 1990s, its legacy still festers, and although the city is made up of many nationalities that mingle happily, it remains divided along racial, economic, and physical lines. As you drive into town along the N2 from the airport, you can't miss the shacks built on shifting dunes as far as the eye can see—a sobering contrast to the first-world luxury of the city center.

Much of South Africa's rich and fascinating history is reflected in Cape Town. Most of the sites worth seeing are packed into a small area, which means you can see a lot in just a few hours. Mandela's tiny jail cell at Robben Island has been preserved, and you can learn about his banishment there as well as about the ecological significance of the island. The District Six Museum tells the heartbreaking story of the apartheid-era demolition of one of Cape Town's most vibrant neighborhoods, and the Bo-Kaap Museum tells the story of the city's Muslim community, who settled here after the abolition of slavery. For a taste of the city's long naval history, visit Simon's Town. The Castle of Good Hope, former seat of the British and Dutch governments and still the city's military headquarters, is the oldest colonial building still standing in South Africa.

10 PM until early morning, and some shuttles charge more for arrivals than for departures to cover waiting time. For the ultimate luxury ride you can hire a six-seat Lincoln stretch limo from Cape Limousine Services. Rates are R1,400 for the first two hours and R200 per hour thereafter (add extra for gas if you travel outside the Cape Town area).

All major car-rental companies have counters at Cape Town International, and driving to the City Bowl or V&A Waterfront is straightforward in daylight. If your flight arrives after dark, consider prearranging transportation through your hotel.

⇨ *For airline contact information, see Air Travel, in the Travel Smart South Africa chapter.*

Airport Cape Town International Airport (☎ 021/937–1200, 086/727–7888 *flight information* ⊕ www.airports.co.za).

Airport Transfers Cape Limousine Services (☎ 021/785–3100). City Hopper (☎ 021/386–0077). Legend Tours and Transfers (☎ 021/704–9140 ⊕ www.legendtours.co.za). Magic Bus Airport Transfers (☎ 021/505–6300 ⊕ www.magicbus.co.za). Marine Taxis (☎ 021/434–0434). Shawn Casey Taxi (☎ 082/954–1867). Touch Down Taxis (☎ 021/919–4659).

BUS TRAVEL

Overall, Intercape Mainliner is the best option for Western Cape destinations. Other operators include Greyhound, Translux/City-to-City (for less serviced destinations like Umtata), and Baz Bus. Common routes from Cape Town include Johannesburg and Tshwane, Springbok, Windhoek, George, Port Elizabeth, and Durban. All the main bus companies operate from the bus terminal alongside the central train station on Adderley Street, and most have their offices there.

Within Cape Town, Golden Arrow runs an extensive network of routes from the main Golden Acre terminal on the Grand Parade (Castle Street side). These city buses are by far the cheapest form of transportation (much to the frustration of the minibus taxi operators). You'll get to most destinations for R5–R10, and you can save by buying 10-ride clip cards. The bus runs from the central train station to the Waterfront (R4.10) and to Kirstenbosch (R6.90), and there's also service departing from the Cape Town Tourism Information Office in the city center.

■TIP→ The service has a timetable, but buses often run late and you'll need a certain level of knowledge regarding its operation. Bus shelters and lamppost markers indicate stops. Route maps are not available in leaflet form, but they are displayed at all major depots. Alternatively, phone the Golden Arrow hotline, or ask people at a bus stop for info on which ones go your way.

For short trips locals generally use minibus taxis, which waste no time getting you to your destination and, for the modest fare of R5–R20, provide you with some local atmosphere. You can hop on and off the *combis* (minivans) quite easily; small gatherings on the roadside usually indicate a stop. However, don't expect to leave the starting point until the taxi is full, which can slow you down outside of peak hours or away from busy routes. The main minibus stop in the city center is above the train station on Adderley Street, but you can flag combis down just about anywhere. Most taxis are sound, but watch out for those held together with tape and wire (literally). There are no route maps for minibus taxis; ask the drivers where they're going. If you don't have the exact change, you may have to wait until the guy taking the fares gets your change. Overcharging is not common, but it's best to discreetly ask other passengers what the fare should be. Taxis are crowded, so watch out for pickpockets.

Contacts Baz Bus (☎ *021/439–2323* ⊕ *www.bazbus.com*). **Golden Arrow** (☎ *080/065–6463* ⊕ *www.gabs.co.za*). **Greyhound** (☎ *083/915–9000* ⊕ *www. greyhound.co.za*). **Intercape Mainliner** (☎ *021/380–4400* or *0861/287–287* ⊕ *www.intercape.co.za*). **Translux/City-to-City** (☎ *0861/589–282* ⊕ *www. translux.co.za*).

CAR TRAVEL

A car is by far the best way to get around Cape Town, particularly in the evening, when public transportation closes down. Cape Town's roads are excellent, but they are unusual in a few respects and can be a bit confusing. Signage is inconsistent, switching between Afrikaans and English, between different names for the same road (especially highways), and between different destinations on the same route. Sometimes the signs simply vanish. ⚠ **Cape Town is also littered with signs indicating** CAPE TOWN **instead of** CITY CENTRE, **as well as** KAPSTAAD, **which is Afrikaans for Cape Town.** Good one-page maps are essential and freely available from car-rental agencies and tourism information desks. Among the hazards are pedestrians running across highways, speeding vehicles, and minibus taxis. Roadblocks for document and DWI checks are also becoming more frequent.

Parking attendants organized by municipal authorities and private business networks provide a valuable service. Most wear brightly colored vests; pay them R2–R3 for a short daytime stop and R5–R10 in the evening. Parking in the city center can be a hassle. Longer-stay parking spaces are scarce, and most hotels charge extra for them (even then you won't be guaranteed a space). There are numerous pay-and-display (i.e., put a ticket in your windshield) and pay-on-exit parking lots around the city. For central attractions like Greenmarket Square, the Company's Garden, the South African National Gallery, and the Castle of Good Hope, park around the Grand Parade in Darling Street. The Sanlam Golden Acre Parking Garage on Adderley Street offers covered parking, as does the Parkade on Strand Street.

The main arteries leading out of the city are the N1, which bypasses the city's Northern Suburbs en route to Paarl and, ultimately, Johannesburg; and the N2, which heads out past Khayelitsha and through Somerset West to the Overberg and the Garden Route before continuing on through the Eastern Cape to Durban. Branching off the N1, the N7 goes to Namibia. The M3 splits off from the N2 near Observatory, leading to the False Bay side of the Peninsula via Claremont and Constantia; it's the main route to the False Bay towns like Muizenberg. Rush hour affects all major arteries into the city from 7 to 9, and out of the city from 4 to 6:30.

MOTORCYCLE TRAVEL

Renting a scooter or motorbike (motorcycle license and deposit required) is a great option within the city. Eurojet Scooters has scooters for around R150 a day. Motorcycles can be rented from Moto Berlin at R1,000–R1,650 per day for a 650-cc to 1,200-cc machine. Cheaper rates apply for weekly rentals. LDV Biking in Gardens rents scooters and motorcycles, starting at R120 a day for scooters, and R210 for motorcycles.

Contacts **Eurojet Scooters** (✆ *021/424–4131* ⊕ *www.eurojet.co.za*). **LDV Biking** (✆ *021/423–5000* ⊕ *www.ldvbiking.co.za*). **Moto Berlin** (✆ *021/439–0662 or 083/377–8833* ⊕ *www.motoberlin.com*).

RIKKI TRAVEL

Rikkis are London taxi-style cars that provide a cheap (but slow) alternative to metered taxis. Service is door-to-door, but unlike a metered cab, a rikki may stop at several other doors to pick up additional passengers en route. Rikkis operate 24 hours a day in the City Bowl, and go everywhere in the city for R20–R25. They also have service to and around Hout Bay and Simon's Town. Hours in Hout Bay are 6:30 AM–2:30 AM weekdays, and 24 hours a day on weekends. Rikkis also can be booked for farther destinations, like Kirstenbosch (R120, up to four people). The Simon's Town rikkis can also take you anywhere, but the most popular trip is to Cape Point. A two-hour trip for two is about R760.

Contacts **Rikkis** (✆ *0861/745–547, 072/387–4366 in Simon's Town* ⊕ *www.rikkis.co.za*).

TAXI TRAVEL

Taxis are expensive compared with other forms of transportation but offer a quick way to get around the city center. Don't expect to see the throngs of cabs you find in London or New York, as most people in Cape Town use public transportation or their own cars. You'll be lucky to hail one on the street. Taxis rarely use roof lights to indicate availability, but if you flag down an occupied cab the driver may radio another car for you. Your best bet is to summon a cab by phone or head to one of the major taxi stands, such as at Greenmarket Square or either end of Adderley Street (near the Slave Lodge and outside the train station). For lower rates at night, try prebooking the Backpacker Bus, a shuttle service on Adderley Street. Sea Point Taxis charges R11 per kilometer and R60 an hour for waiting time. Expect to pay R50–R70 for a trip from the city center to the Waterfront. In addition to the companies listed here, ask your hotel or guesthouse which company it recommends. Lodging establishments often have a relationship with particular companies and/or drivers, and this way you will be assured of safe, reliable service.

Contacts **Backpacker Bus** (✆ *021/439–7600* ⊕ *www.backpackerbus.co.za*). **Excite Taxis** (✆ *021/448–4444*). **Marine Taxis** (✆ *021/434–0434*). **Sea Point Taxis** (✆ *021/434–4444*). **Unicab** (✆ *021/486–1600*).

TRAIN TRAVEL

Cape Town's train station is on Adderley Street, in the heart of the city, surrounded by lively rows of street vendors and a taxi stand. The station building and facilities are unattractive but functional, servicing local, interprovincial, and luxury lines.

Metrorail, Cape Town's commuter line, offers regular service to the Northern Suburbs, including Parow and Bellville; the Cape Flats townships Langa, Nyanga, Mitchell's Plain, and Khayelitsha; the Southern and False Bay suburbs of Observatory, Claremont, Wynberg, Muizenberg, St. James, Kalk Bay, Fish Hoek, and Simon's Town; and the Winelands towns of Paarl, Stellenbosch, and Franschoek *(⇨ Chapter 3)*. The trip to Simon's Town takes 60–70 minutes and costs about R24 for a first-class round-trip ticket, R15 for third class. The train to Khayelitsha costs R17 round-trip first class, about half that for third-class. The last train leaves about 8 PM on weekdays (though it's not advisable to take trains after dark), and weekend service is reduced. Timetables change often. If you travel on Metrorail during off-peak periods, avoid isolated cars and compartments, and be alert to your surroundings when the train stops. Muggers work trains intensively, slipping on and off with ease. Train security is erratic at best. You're safer standing in a cramped third-class car than sitting comfortably in splendid isolation in an empty first-class one, but watch your pockets.

National carrier Shosholoza Meyl runs the Trans-Karoo daily between Cape Town and Johannesburg; the trip takes about 26 hours and costs between R310–R570 on tourist class and R160–R180 on economy class, depending what time of year you travel. Tourist class cars have sleeping compartments. A weekly train to Durban, the Trans-Oranjia, departs on Wednesdays, takes two days, and costs R660 tourist class. You need to make tourist-class reservations by phone (bookings open three months before date of travel) and then pay at the station in advance (not just before departure). Credit cards cannot be taken over the phone. For a third-class ticket you can pay just before you go. The reservations office at the train station is open 8–4 weekdays and 8–10 AM weekends. Despite its name, Shongololo Express runs multiday journey-tours, with its Good Hope train traveling from Cape Town through the Karoo and the Garden Route to Johannesburg over 16 days.

Looking to travel in high style? Check out the luxurious and leisurely Blue Train, which travels between Cape Town and Tshwane once a week, and Rovos Rail's Pride of Africa, which runs from Cape Town to Tshwane every Monday *(⇨ Train Travel, in Travel Smart South Africa chapter)*. Shosholoza Meyl also runs a Premier Classe train that is a major step up from its tourist class, but far more affordable than the above luxury trains.

Contacts Metrorail (☎ 080/065–6463 ⊕ *www.metrorail.co.za*). **Shongololo Express** (☎ 011/483–0657 or 011/483–0658 ⊕ *www.shongololo.com*). **Shosholoza Meyl** (☎ 086/000–8888 ⊕ *www.spoornet.co.za/ShosholozaMeyl*).

HEALTH AND SAFETY

There's no reason for paranoia in Cape Town, but there are a few things to look out for. Aside from busy nightlife zones like Long Street, avoid the City Bowl at night and on Saturday afternoons and Sundays, when it's very quiet. Street kids and roving teens are blamed for much of the petty crime, but sophisticated crime syndicates are often involved, and many of Cape Town's fraudsters are smartly dressed. Cell phones can be snatched from car seats through open windows and even out of people's hands while in use. Watch your pockets at busy transportation interchanges and on trains. Pick a crowded car; if you suddenly find yourself alone, move to another one. Public transportation collapses after dark. Unless you're at the Waterfront or are in a large group, use metered taxis. Better still, rent a car, but don't leave valuables visible and don't park in isolated areas. Despite thousands of safe visits every year, Table Mountain, which couldn't look less threatening, has been the location of several knife-point robberies in daylight. The point is, never be completely off guard.

Poor signage is an issue in Cape Town, especially in the black townships, where most streets still have numbers rather than names and many streets are not signed at all. Carry a good map, and visit township attractions only as part of an organized tour with a reputable operator. Women and couples are strongly advised not to walk in isolated places after dark. If you want to walk somewhere in the evening, make sure you do so in a large group, stay vigilant at all times, and keep flashy jewelry and expensive cameras hidden, or better yet, at the hotel.

As in other major cities, drug use is a problem in Cape Town. IV-drug use carries a high risk of HIV transmission, as does the sex trade (which also carries the risk of other sexually transmitted diseases). AIDS is a huge problem in South Africa, so exercise appropriate caution. The drug of choice for children on the street is glue, and increasingly "tic" or methamphetamine. You will undoubtedly come across many people begging in Cape Town, including kids. Please do not give cash directly to children, as this often supports either a glue habit or adults lurking in the background. If you are concerned and wish to contribute, consider supporting people who sell *The Big Issue* magazine (associated with a worthy organization of the same name) or giving food instead of money.

EMERGENCIES

There are several numbers you can call for general emergencies, including Vodacom mobile networks. Metrorail has its own security/emergency number. If you get lost on Table Mountain, call Metro Medical Emergency Services, and for all sea emergencies, call the National Sea Rescue Institute (NSRI).

Emergency services at public hospitals are overworked, understaffed, and underfunded. Visitors are advised to use private hospitals, which are open 24/7 and have ambulances linked to their private hospital group (although these services can transport patients to any health facility). Most public hospitals have facilities for private patients at lower rates than the fully private hospitals. Make sure you have medical insurance that's good in South Africa before you leave home.

Emergency Services **Ambulance** (☎ *10177*). **Metro Medical Emergency Services** (☎ *021/937–0300*). **Metrorail** (☎ *0800/210–081*). **National Sea Rescue Institute** (☎ *021/449–3500*). **Police** (☎ *10111*). **Police, fire, and ambulance services** (☎ *107 from landline*). **Vodacom emergency services** (☎ *112 from mobile phone*).

Hospitals **Christiaan Barnard Hospital** (✉ *181 Longmarket St., Cape Town Central* ☎ *021/480–6111*). **Constantiaberg Medi-clinic** (✉ *Burnham Rd., Plumstead* ☎ *021/799–2911*).

TAKE IT ALL IN

3 Days: With three days you can manage to see many of the city's major sights—including Company's Garden, Castle of Good Hope, District Six Museum, and the Bo-Kaap—on your own or with a tour. Weather permitting, try to also work in a Robben Island tour, which will take around 3½ hours, and lunch at one of the outdoor restaurants at the V&A Waterfront, where you can eat while watching working tugboats maneuver past sleek million-dollar yachts. The cable-car ride to the summit of Table Mountain is a must; go in the morning, and in the afternoon, drive out to Camps Bay, where you can kick off your shoes to stroll along the beach. To round out the evening, find a sophisticated sea-facing bar for a sundowner before going on to dinner. On another evening, discover the rhythm of Africa by heading to the Green Dolphin at the V&A Waterfront, where you can listen to terrific jazz. Or for a real taste of contemporary African music, go to Long Street's Mama Africa or Zulu Bar to hear pulsing marimba music or great local DJs.

5 or More Days: With at least five days, you can enjoy all the sights listed above as well as a trip to the Winelands in Constantia, Stellenbosch, Franschhoek, and Paarl. From the harbor you can take a cruise to Seal Island or, for a more adventurous activity, admire the sunset from the back of a horse at Noordhoek. Wend your way along the False Bay coast to Boulders Beach, in Table Mountain National Park, where you'll find African penguins in profusion. From here, follow the road to the Cape of Good Hope and Cape Point. You can take the steep walk to the point or ride the funicular. It looks as if this is where the Indian and Atlantic oceans meet—sometimes there is even a line of foam stretching out to sea—but of course it's not. (That happens at Cape Agulhas, on the Cape's southern coast.) For a late lunch make your way back to the pretty fishing village of Kalk Bay, where the streets are lined with antiques shops and there are plenty of excellent restaurants to relax in. However you spend your time, on your last night back in Cape Town have a drink at the Bascule bar at the Cape Grace (at the V&A Waterfront) and watch the gulls wheel overhead against Table Mountain. Chances are, you won't want to leave.

DISCOUNTS

If you're keen to explore South Africa's many wilderness areas, including Table Mountain National Park, consider buying a SANParks Wild Card, but be sure to read all the fine print. There are several types of passes covering different clusters of parks for individuals, couples, and families.

Contacts **SANParks Wild Card** (⊕ *www.wildcard.co.za*).

OUT ON THE TOWN

Cape etc. is a great bimonthly roundup of Cape Town's entertainment. For weekly updates try "Friday," the entertainment supplement of the *Mail & Guardian,* or the "Top of the Times" in Friday's *Cape Times.* Both are informed, opinionated, and up-to-date. The *Argus* newspaper's "Tonight" section gives you a complete daily listing of what's on, plus contact numbers. Tickets for almost every cultural and sporting event in the country (including movies) can be purchased through Computicket. Cape Town is a very gay-friendly city. For information on the gay scene, contact Africa Outing. Geared toward gay and lesbian travelers, Gay Net Cape Town provides information on events and venues in Cape Town.

Contacts Computicket (☎ *083/915–8000* ⊕ *www.computicket.co.za*). **Gay Net Cape Town** (⊕ *www.gaynetcapetown.co.za*).

AT THE BEACH

Cape Town's beaches on both the Atlantic and False Bay sides are legendary. The beaches at Milnerton, Blouberg, and Long Beach (in Noordhoek) stretch endlessly, and you can walk for miles without seeing a fast-food outlet or drink stand. You'll see seagulls, dolphins, penguins, and whales (in season). Forget about swimming in the Atlantic, though; even a quick dip will freeze your toes. The "in" crowd flocks to Clifton, a must for sunbathers. If you must swim, head to the warmer waters from Muizenberg to Simon's Town, where the warm Benguela current sweeps along the False Bay side of the peninsula. The beaches are dotted with tidal pools, which are safe for kids and make swimming more comfortable. Windsurfers congregate at Blouberg, where several competitions are held. At Boulders or Seaforth you can sunbathe and snorkel in the coves and pools, sheltered by huge granite rocks, often with penguins. Cape Town's surfing community appreciates Muizenberg, Kommetjie, Fish Hoek, and Blouberg. For kite surfing, Strandfontein and Sunrise beaches are the places to try (or to watch). Don't be tempted to kite surf for the first time when the wind is pumping, however—it's far too dangerous.

MONEY MATTERS

Most shops, restaurants, hotels, and B&Bs in Cape Town take credit cards, but you need cash to buy gas. ■TIP→ Don't even think about changing money at your hotel. The rates at most hotels are outrageous, and the city has plenty of banks and *bureaux de change* (exchange counters) offering better rates; most are open during business hours (weekdays and Saturday mornings). Rennies Bank's Waterfront branch is open until 9 PM daily. At the airport, Foreign Exchange exchanges currency weekdays 7 AM–11 PM and weekends 8 AM–11 PM.

Exchange Services American Express (⊠ *Ground fl., Sahara House, Thibault Sq., Cape Town Central* ☎ *021/425–7991* ⊠ *Shop 11A, Alfred Mall, Waterfront* ☎ *021/419–3917* ⊕ *www.amex.co.za*). **Rennies Bank** (⊠ *2 St. George's Mall, Cape Town Central* ☎ *021/418–1206* ⊠ *Lower Level, Victoria Wharf, Waterfront* ☎ *021/418–3744*).

TOURS

Numerous companies offer guided tours of the city center, the peninsula, the Winelands, and any place else in the Cape (or beyond) that you might wish to visit. They differ in type of transportation used, focus, and size. The following list provides an idea of what is generally available, as well as pointing out some of the more unique offerings. For comprehensive information on touring companies, head to one of the Cape Town Tourism offices; alternately, ask for recommendations at your hotel.

BOAT TOURS

The Waterfront Boat Company offers trips on a range of boats, from yachts to large motor cruisers. A 1½-hour sunset cruise from the V&A Waterfront costs about R200 and includes a glass of bubbly. Tigger 2 also runs boats from the Waterfront to Clifton 4th beach or Table Bay. Drumbeat Charters runs a variety of trips in the Hout Bay area, ranging from sunset cruises to full-day crayfishing expeditions. A trip from Hout Bay to Seal Island with Drumbeat Charters costs R60 for adults, R25 for kids. ■ TIP→ The only boat trip to actually land on Robben Island is the museum's ferry.

Tour Operators **Drumbeat Charters** (☎ 021/791–4441 ⊕ www.drumbeatcharters.co.za). **Tigger 2 Charters** (☎ 021/790–5256 ⊕ www.tigger2.co.za). **Waterfront Boat Company** (☎ 021/418–0134 ⊕ www.waterfrontboats.co.za).

BUS AND CAR TOURS

Large- and small-group bus tours are operated by African Eagle Day Tours and Hylton Ross, among others. Expect to pay R350–R500 for a half-day trip and about R500–R800 for a full-day tour (the smaller and more personalized the tour, the higher the price). There's a huge selection of tours to choose from. A day trip might include such highlights as the Cape Point nature reserve and Boulders Beach, or winetasting in Stellenbosch; a half-day trip could involve a visit to a local township. Many of the companies will also tailor private trips to suit your needs.

The hop-on/hop-off red City Sightseeing bus is a pleasant way to familiarize yourself with Cape Town; a day ticket costs R120, and there are two routes to choose from. The Red Route runs through the city, and you can get on and off at major museums, the V&A Waterfront, Table Mountain Cableway, Two Oceans Aquarium, and other attractions. The Blue Route takes you farther afield—to Kirstenbosch National Botanic Gardens, Hout Bay, and Camps Bay, to name a few destinations. Tickets are available at the Waterfront outside the Aquarium or on the bus.

Cape Point Route custom-designs tours that focus on the peninsula, including the eco-adventure family tour and the extreme-sports corporate tour (R595–R1,250 for full-day tours).

The Cape Safari tour with iKapa Tours & Travel departs at 6:30 AM, and takes you to Aquila Private Game Reserve (R1,880) or Inverdoorn Game Reserve (R1,550). It includes a three-hour game drive, all meals, and champagne. Both reserves are about a 2½-hour drive from the city.

Grassroute Tours offers a range of half-day township experiences (R360) that demonstrate just how fragmented South African society is. Stops include the Bo-Kaap, District Six, and the Cape Flats. The full-day version of this tour includes Robben Island (R530). Evening township tours (R450) include drinks at a shebeen and a traditional dinner with a local family; overnight township tours (R670) combine the day and evening tours with a stay with a host family.

For something more historical, Western Cape Action Tours provides insight into Cape Town's experience of apartheid and resistance. Lead by a group of MK veterans (former cadres of the ANC's armed wing), these unique tours (R300–R550) visit locations important during the armed struggle.

Coffeebeans Routes storyteller tours pay evening visits to the homes of Cape Town storytellers for a yarn (R495). Their famous Jazz Safari (R650) takes small groups to meet key musicians of Cape Town's jazz scene in their homes for dinner, followed by a visit to non-touristy jazz clubs in the Cape Flats.

Friends of Dorothy leads small group tours for gay travelers. And for those looking for something really different, Cape Sidecar Adventures offers full-day trips around the peninsula in a World War II sidecar: your guide drives and you sit in the sidecar (R895).

Though many of the above operators specialize in niche tours, they usually also cover mainstream trips like Cape Point and the Winelands.

Tour Operators African Eagle Day Tours (☎ 021/464–4260 ⊕ www.africa-adventure.org/a/africaneagle). **Cape Point Route** (☎ 021/782–9356 ⊕ www.capepointroute.co.za). **Cape Sidecar Adventures** (☎ 021/434–9855 ⊕ www.sidecars.co.za). **Coffeebeans Routes** (☎ 021/424–3572 ⊕ www.coffeebeansroutes.com). **Friends of Dorothy** (☎ 021/465–1871 ⊕ www.friendsofdorothytours.co.za). **Grassroute Tours** (☎ 021/464–4269 ⊕ www.grassroutetours.co.za). **Hylton Ross Tours** (☎ 021/511–1784 ⊕ www.hyltonross.co.za). **iKapa Tours & Travel** (☎ 021/510–8666 ⊕ www.ikapa.co.za). **Western Cape Action Tours** (☎ 021/448–5760 ⊕ www.dacpm.org.za).

HELICOPTER TOURS

Fly from the V&A Waterfront for a tour of the city and surrounding area on a three- to six-seat chopper. Most operators charge between R2,000–R4,200 for a 20-minute trip, and R6,300 to R12,600 for an hour in the air. Custom tours can also be arranged, and the price varies according to how many people are flying.

Tour Operators Civair Helicopters (☎ 021/419–5182 ⊕ www.civair.co.za). **NAC/Makana Aviation** (☎ 021/425–3868 ⊕ www.nacmakana.com).

WALKING TOURS

Cape Town on Foot offers fun city walking tours that last about 2½ hours. The tours cover major historical attractions, architecture, and highlights of modern-day Cape Town. Its Bo-Kaap tour includes the Bo-Kaap Museum. Expect to pay around R150–R200 for 2½ hours.

For a more Bo-Kaap–centric experience, Shireen Misbach-Habib of Tana Baru Tours leads walking tours (R250) through the neighborhood where she was born and lives. Shireen's tours conclude with tea and Malay cakes in her home.

Footsteps to Freedom offers two really good walking tours—one of the city and its historical sites and the other of the V&A Waterfront. The guides are friendly and well informed and offer a rare insight into the city; they can also help with tours of the Bo-Kaap and townships. Ilios Travel offers a walking tour of Langa Township (R385), including a tour of the Bo-Kaap and the District 6 Museum. The guides explain the social structures and lifestyles of Cape Town's oldest African precinct, as well as the cultural history of the area.

Pamphlets for a self-guided walking tour of city-center attractions can be picked up at Cape Town Tourism.

Tour Operators Cape Town on Foot (☎ 021/462–4252 ⊕ www.wanderlust. co.za). **Footsteps to Freedom** (☎ 021/426–4260 or 083/452–1112 ⊕ www. footstepstofreedom.co.za). **Ilios Travel** (☎ 021/697–4056 ⊕ www.ilios.co.za). **Tana Baru Tours** (021/424–0719 or 073/237–3800).

VISITOR INFORMATION

Cape Town Tourism is the city's official tourist body, providing information on tours, hotels, restaurants, rental cars, and shops. It has a coffee shop and Internet café. The staff make hotel, tour, and travel reservations. From October to March, the office in town is open weekdays 8–6, Saturday 8:30–2, and Sunday 9–1; from April to September, it's open weekdays 8–5:30, Saturday 8:30–1, and Sunday 9–1.The branch at the Waterfront is now run by Cape Town Routes Unlimited (CTRU) but offers the same services and is open daily 9–7.

Contacts Cape Town Routes Unlimited (⊠ Shop 107, Clock Tower Centre, South Arm Rd., Waterfront ☎ 021/405–4500 ⊕ www.tourismcapetown.co.za). **Cape Town Tourism** (⊠ The Pinnacle Building, Burg and Castle Sts., Cape Town Central ☎ 021/487–6800 ⊕ www.tourismcapetown.co.za).

EXPLORING CAPE TOWN

Cape Town has grown as a city in a way that few others in the world have. Take a good look at the street names. Strand and Waterkant streets (meaning "beach" and "waterside," respectively) are now far from the sea. However, when they were named they were right on the beach. An enormous program of dumping rubble into the ocean extended the city by a good few square miles (thanks to the Dutch obsession with reclaiming land from the sea). Almost all the city on the seaward side of Strand and Waterkant is part of the reclaimed area of the city known as the Foreshore. If you look at old paintings of the city, you will see that originally waves lapped at the very walls of the castle, now more than half a mile from the ocean.

TABLE MOUNTAIN NATIONAL PARK

Nowhere else in the world does an area of such spectacular beauty and rich biodiversity exist almost entirely within a metropolitan area. Large swaths of the Cape Peninsula are devoted to this spectacular

85-square-mi park, which is home to countless hiking trails and gorgeous beaches, as well as two world-renowned landmarks: the eponymous Table Mountain and the legendary Cape of Good Hope. The park requires entrance payments only at three points—Cape of Good Hope, Boulders, and Silvermine. The rest of the park is open and free for all to enjoy.

TIMING AND PRECAUTIONS

It would be easy for nature lovers to spend days in the park. Most visitors spend a minimum of three hours to go up Table Mountain (by cable car), and another half day to visit Cape Point. For the fit, hiking up Table Mountain (and taking the cable car down) is a far more rewarding experience but requires good weather and at least half a day. To experience the wild beauty of Cape Point, a full day is recommended to visit the point (by funicular), walk to the Cape of Good Hope, and explore the gorgeous empty beaches around Olifantsbos or Platboom. Within Cape Point, the main safety issue is baboons: they are dangerous and should not be messed with. Do not feed them. Much of the park is bordered by city neighborhoods, and muggings can occur in isolated areas. Don't walk alone, and don't carry valuables if you can avoid it. Finally, when hiking on the mountain, be aware that dramatic weather changes can occur, and regardless of conditions when you set out, always carry extra layers of clothing, water, a hat, and sunscreen.

TOP ATTRACTIONS

The sights below are marked on the Cape Town and Cape Town Peninsula maps.

③④ Cape Point and the Cape of Good Hope. Once a nature reserve on its own, this section of Table Mountain National Park covers more than 19,000 acres. Much of the park consists of rolling hills covered with fynbos and laced with miles of walking trails, for which maps are available at the park entrance. It also has beautiful deserted beaches (you can swim at some of these beaches, but note that there are no amenities or lifeguards). Eland, baboon, ostrich, and bontebok (a colorful antelope nearly hunted to extinction in the early 20th century) are among the animals that roam the park. A paved road runs 12½ km (8 mi) to the tip of the peninsula, and a turnoff leads to the Cape of Good Hope, a rocky cape that is the southwesternmost point of the continent. A plaque marks the spot—otherwise you would never know you're standing on a site of such significance.

Fodor's Choice
★

The opposite is true of Cape Point, a dramatic knife's edge of rock that slices into the Atlantic. Looking out to sea from the viewing platform, you feel you're at the tip of Africa, even though that honor officially belongs to Cape Agulhas, about 160 km (100 mi) to the southeast. From Cape Point the views of False Bay and the Hottentots Holland Mountains are astonishing. The walk up to the viewing platform and the old lighthouse is very steep; a funicular (R40 round-trip, R36 one way) makes the run every three or four minutes. Take a jacket or sweater—the wind can be fierce. It took six years, from 1913 to 1919, to build the old lighthouse, 816 feet above the high-water mark. On a clear day the old lighthouse was a great navigational mark, but when the mists rolled in it was useless, so a new and much lower lighthouse (286 feet) was built at Dias Lookout Point. The newer, revolving lighthouse, the most powerful on the South African coast, emits a group of three flashes every 30 seconds. It has prevented a number of ships from ending up on Bellows or Albatross Rock below. You can't go into the lighthouses, but the views from their bases are spectacular.

Stark reminders of the ships that didn't make it are dotted around the Cape. You'll see their rusty remains on some of the beaches. One of the more famous wrecks is the *Thomas T. Tucker,* one of hundreds of Liberty Ships produced by the United States to enable the Allies to move vast amounts of supplies during World War II. It wasn't the German U-boats patrolling the coastline that did the ship in. Rather the fog closed in, and on her maiden voyage in 1942, she ended up on Olifantsbos Point. Fortunately, all on board were saved, but the wreck soon broke up in the rough seas that pound the coast.

The park has some excellent land-based whale-watching spots. About June to November, whales return to these waters to calve. You're most likely to see the Southern Right whale in False Bay, but the occasional humpback and Bryde's whale also show up. When the water is calm you may even be lucky enough to see a school of dolphins looping past. The Rooikrans parking lot is good for whale-watching, but there are any number of lookout points. It's just a matter of driving around until you see the characteristic spray or a shiny black fluke.

The mast you see on the western slopes of Cape Point near the lighthouse belongs to the Global Atmosphere Watch Station (GAW). The South African Weather Bureau, together with the Fraunhofer Institute in Garmisch, Germany, maintains a research laboratory here to monitor long-term changes in the chemistry of the earth's atmosphere, which may impact climate. This is one of 20 GAWs throughout the world, chosen because the air at Cape Point is considered particularly pure most of the time.

The large sit-down Two Oceans Restaurant has spectacular views, and recent changes in management have vastly improved the food. Also here are a kiosk selling snacks and three gift shops. During peak season (December–January), visit Cape Point as early in the day as you can; otherwise you'll be swamped by horrendous numbers of tour buses and their occupants. A fun alternative is an overnight hike with comfortable basic accommodations and incredible views, booked through South African National Parks. ⚠ **Be wary of baboons in the parking lot; they have been known to steal food and can be dangerous if provoked. Do not feed them.** Unfortunately the indigenous chacma baboons are increasingly under threat, and the Peninsula's population is currently estimated at only 350–400 individuals. Many baboons have been shot for raiding homes and stealing food. Baboon-feeding tourists only exacerbate this serious situation. ✉ *Off the M65 (Plateau Rd.)* ☎ *021/780–9526 or 021/780–9204* ⊕ *www.sanparks.org* 💳 *R60* ⊗ *Apr.–Sept., daily 7–5; Oct.–Mar., daily 6–6; last exit 1 hr after closing.*

★ **Hoerikwaggo Trail.** A great way to get acquainted with Table Mountain and all its moods is to hike part of the Hoerikwaggo Trail, which opened in 2006. The trail follows the spine of the mountains that run the length of the peninsula, linking four tented camps from the Table Mountain lower cable station all the way to the Cape Point lighthouse. The camps are located at Orangekloof, Silvermine, Slangkop, and Smitswinkel Bay. Hikes are guided and portered, but you'll have to bring your own food, which will be portered. Built on wooden platforms, the tented camps have beds, hot showers, kitchens, and *braais* (barbecues). You can opt for a single night at any of the tented camps (R420 per person, per night); the adventurous can take on the whole trail (four nights). Alternately, there's the three-day "table mountain" trail aimed at international tourists, which starts at the Waterfront and ends at Kirstenbosch. It's guided and fully catered and accommodation (in cottages) is top-notch. Expect to pay around R1,900 (no Wild Card discounts). ☎ *021/422–2816* ⊕ *www.sanparks.org.*

㉕ **Table Mountain.** Along with Victoria Falls on the border of Zimbabwe

Fodor's Choice and Zambia, this is one of southern Africa's most beautiful and impres-

★ sive natural wonders. The views from its summit are awe-inspiring. The mountain rises more than 3,500 feet above the city, and its distinctive flat top is visible to sailors 65 km (40 mi) out to sea. In summer, when the southeaster blows, moist air from False Bay funnels over the tabletop, condensing in the colder, higher air to form a cloud "tablecloth." Legend attributes this low-lying cloud to a pipe-smoking contest between the devil and Jan van Hunks, a pirate who settled on Devil's Peak. The devil lost, and the cloud serves to remind him of his defeat.

Climbing the mountain will take two to three hours, depending on your fitness level. There is no water along the route; you *must* take at least two liters (a half gallon) of water per person. Table Mountain can be dangerous if you're not familiar with the terrain. Many paths that look like good routes down the mountain end at treacherous cliffs. Platteklip Gorge trail is the most straightforward and popular route up. ■**TIP→ Do not underestimate this mountain.** It may be in the middle of a city, but it is not a genteel town park. Wear sturdy shoes or hiking boots, always take warm clothes, such as a windbreaker, and a mobile phone; and let someone know of your plans. The mountain is safe if you stick to known paths. However, when there's heavy cloud cover it's easy to become disoriented even on marked paths. Look for the Table Mountain map by Peter Slingsby at most major outdoor stores or the shop at the Lower Cable Station. If you're on the mountain and the weather changes dramatically (heavy rain, mist) and you can't tell where you are, just sit tight and call Metro Medical Emergency Services (⇨ *Emergencies, above*) to let them know you're in trouble. You will be rescued as soon as the weather permits. Walking around in the mist is very dangerous. Also be aware that in light of occasional muggings here, it's unwise to walk alone on the mountain. It's recommended that you travel in a group or, better yet, with a guide.

Atop the mountain, well-marked trails offering 10- to 40-minute jaunts crisscross the western Table near the Upper Cable Station. Many other trails lead to the other side of Platteklip Gorge and into the mountain's catchment area, where you'll find reservoirs, hidden streams, and incredible views. Feeling adventurous? Try a rappel from the top—it's

The Wilds of Table Mountain

Despite being virtually surrounded by the city, Table Mountain is a remarkably unspoiled wilderness. Most of the Cape Peninsula's 2,200 species of flora—about as many plant species as there are in all of North America and Europe combined—are found on the mountain. This includes magnificent examples of Cape Town's wild indigenous flowers known as *fynbos*, Afrikaans for "fine bush," a reference to the tiny leaves characteristic of these heathlike plants. The best time to see the mountain in bloom is between September and March, although you're sure to find flowers throughout the year.

Long gone are the days when Cape lions, zebras, and hyenas roamed the mountain, but you can still glimpse *grysboks* (small antelopes), baboons, and rabbitlike *dassies* (rhymes with "fussy"). Although these creatures, also called rock hyraxes, look like oversize guinea pigs, this is where the similarities end; the dassie's closest relative is the elephant. They congregate in large numbers near the Upper Cable Station, where they've learned to beg for food. Over the years a diet of junk food has seriously compromised their health. ■TIP→Do not feed the dassies, no matter how endearing they look.

only about 350 feet, but you're hanging out over 3,300 feet of air (⇨ *Rappelling, in Sports and the Outdoors*). A shop at the top of the mountain, appropriately called the Shop at the Top, sells gifts and curios. ☎ *021/424–8181* ⊕ *www.sanparks.org.*

NEED A BREAK? During the warm summer months, Capetonians are fond of taking picnic baskets up the mountain. The best time to picnic is after 5, as some say sipping a glass of chilled Cape wine while watching the sun set from Table Mountain is one of life's great joys. The large self-service restaurant called, quite simply, **The Restaurant** (☎ *021/424–8181*) serves good hot breakfasts, light meals, sandwiches, and local wine, and has a salad bar. **The Cocktail Bar** (☎ *021/424–8181*) dishes up a spectacular view along with cocktails and bar snacks from 2 until the last cable car. As you might expect, the place has a good wine list, with local labels predominating.

㉕ **Table Mountain Aerial Cableway.** This is a slick operation. Two large,
Fodor's Choice wheelchair-friendly revolving cars that provide spectacular views take
★ three to five minutes to reach the summit. Operating times vary from month to month according to season, daylight hours, and weather. To avoid disappointment, phone ahead for exact times. You can't prebook for the cable car, but the longest you'll have to wait is about a half hour, and then only in peak season (December 15–January 15). Several tour operators include a trip up the mountain in their schedules.

The Lower Cable Station lies on the slope of Table Mountain near its western end. It's a long way from the city on foot, and you're better off traveling by car, taxi, or *rikki* (a shared taxi). To get there from the City Bowl, take Buitengracht Street toward the mountain. Buitengracht turns into Kloof Nek Road, which continues all the way to a traffic circle where you turn left on Tafelberg Road. Follow signs to the Table Mountain Aerial Cableway. Taxis from the city center to the Lower Cable Station (one way) cost about R60; rikkis cost R30 per person. ⊠ *Tafelberg Rd.* ☎ *021/424–8181* ⊕ *www.tablemountain.net* ⊠ *R145 round-trip, R74 one way* ⊘ *Hrs vary so it's best to check when you arrive, but usually daily 8:30–7:30.*

WORTH NOTING

㉓ Lion's Head and Signal Hill. The prominent peak to the right of Table Mountain is Lion's Head, a favorite hiking spot for locals. The hike takes about 1½ hours (each way), with 360-degree views of the city unfolding as you spiral up the "lion" as well as from the top. The trail is gorgeous, well marked, and on a nice day, enjoys a good flow of hikers. Though easier than hiking up Table Mountain, the last quarter will still earn you that beer or *malva* pudding (a baked sponge cake sauced with orange juice, apricot jam, and vinegar). As always, don't hike alone, and keep alert, especially as sunset approaches. For those less inclined to sweat, Signal Hill is the smaller flat-topped hill extending from the northern lower slopes of Lion's Head, also sometimes called the "Lion's Rump." Once the location for signal flags communicating weather warnings to ships visiting the bay, Signal Hill is also the home of the Noon Gun, still operated by the South African Navy and South African Astronomical Observatory. Both Lion's Head and Signal Hill are accessed by Signal Hill Road, which ends at the Signal Hill parking lot. The lot has spectacular views of Sea Point and Table Bay. Be careful around here, however, especially if it's deserted. There have been incidents of violent crime.

㉔ Tafelberg Road. This is a very popular walking road for locals, especially when the weather is fine and windless, as it's perfectly flat with fabulous views over the City Bowl and Table Bay. The road crosses the northern side of Table Mountain before ending at Devil's Peak, providing access to the lower cable station, as well as trailheads for Platteklip Gorge (easiest ascent of Table Mountain) and Devil's Peak. After the Devil's Peak trailhead, the road is restricted to foot traffic and bicycles. As always, take the usual precautions about walking in groups and staying alert.

CAPE TOWN CENTRAL

In Cape Town's city center, glistening glass-and-steel office blocks soar over street vendors selling everything from seasonal fruit and flowers to clothes and cigarettes. Sandwiched in between these modern high-rises are historic buildings dating to the 1600s. There's also an impressive collection of art-deco buildings undergoing restoration. Don't try to navigate the center of Cape Town by car. It's small enough to walk, and this way you'll be able to explore the many galleries, coffee shops, and markets that appear on every corner.

TIMING AND PRECAUTIONS

If you are pressed for time, you can explore the city in a day, getting the lay of the land and a feel for the people of Cape Town while visiting or skipping sights as your interests dictate. However, if you'd like to linger in various museums and galleries, you could easily fill two or three days. Start at about 9, when most workers have finished their commute, and then stop for a long, leisurely lunch, finishing the tour in the late afternoon. If you have to head out of town on either the N1 or N2, be sure to depart before 4, when rush-hour congestion takes over.

Except for the top end of Long Street and around Heritage Square where there are lots of bars and cafés, the city center dies at night, and you are advised not to wander the streets after dark. The last commuters leave around 6 (note that the city center can also be deserted on weekends). The biggest threat is being mugged for your cell phone, jewelry, or money. Fortunately many of the old city buildings are being converted into upscale apartments, thus rejuvenating the city center.

TOP ATTRACTIONS

The sights below are marked on the Cape Town map.

❹ ★ Castle of Good Hope. Despite its name, the castle isn't the fairy-tale fantasy type but rather a squat fortress that hunkers down as if to avoid shellfire. Built between 1665 and 1676 by the Dutch East India Company (VOC) to replace an earthen fort constructed in 1652 by Jan van Riebeeck, the Dutch commander who settled Cape Town, it's the oldest building in the country. Its pentagonal plan, with a diamond-shape bastion at each corner, is typical of the Old Netherlands defense system adopted in the early 17th century. The design was intended to allow covering fire for every portion of the castle. As added protection, the whole fortification was surrounded by a moat, and back in the day, the sea nearly washed up against its walls. The castle served as both the VOC headquarters and the official governor's residence, and still houses the regional headquarters of the National Defence Force. Despite the bellicose origins of the castle, no shot has ever been fired from its ramparts, except ceremonially.

You can wander around on your own or join one of the highly informative guided tours at no extra cost. Also worth seeing is the excellent William Fehr Collection. Housed in the governor's residence, it consists of antiques, artifacts, and paintings of early Cape Town and South Africa. ⊠ *1 Buitenkant St., Cape Town Central* ☎ *021/787-1240* ⊕ *www.castleofgoodhope.co.za* ⊡ *R25* ⊙ *Daily 9–3:30; tours at 11, noon, and 2.*

❽ ★ Company's Garden. These are all that remain of a 43-acre garden laid out by Jan van Riebeeck in April 1652 to supply fresh vegetables to ships on their way to the Dutch East Indies. By 1700 free burghers were cultivating plenty of crops on their own land, and in time the VOC vegetable patch was transformed into a botanic garden. It remains a delightful haven in the city center, graced by fountains, exotic trees, rose gardens, and a pleasant outdoor café. At the bottom of the gardens, close to Government Avenue, look for an **old well** that used to provide water for the town's residents and the garden. The old water pump, engraved with the maker's name and the date 1842, has been overtaken by an oak tree and now juts out of the tree's trunk some 6 feet above the ground. A huge **statue of Cecil Rhodes,** the Cape's prime minister in the late 19th century, looms over the path that runs through the center of the gardens. He points to the north, and an inscription reads, YOUR HINTER-LAND IS THERE, a reference to Rhodes's dream of extending the British Empire from the Cape to Cairo. Continue past the pond and toward the South African Museum, outside of which the **Delville Wood Monument** honors South Africans who died in the fight for Delville Wood during the great three-day Somme offensive of 1916. A self-guided walking brochure with detailed historical information about the garden is sold (R10) at the office just outside the restaurant. ✉ *Between Government Ave. and Queen Victoria St., Cape Town Central* ☎ *021/400–2521* 📠 *Free* ☉ *Summer, daily 7–7; winter, daily 7–6.*

⑤ District Six Museum. Housed in the Buitenkant Methodist Church, this
★ museum preserves the memory of one of Cape Town's most vibrant multicultural neighborhoods and of the district's destruction in one of the cruelest acts of the apartheid-era Nationalist government. District Six was proclaimed a white area in 1966, and existing residents were evicted from their homes, which were razed to make way for a white suburb. The people were forced to resettle in bleak outlying areas on the Cape Flats, and by the 1970s all the buildings here, except churches and mosques, had been demolished. Huge controversy accompanied the proposed redevelopment of the area, and only a small housing component, Zonnebloem, and the campus of the Cape Technicon have been built, leaving much of the ground still bare—a grim reminder of the past. There are plans to bring former residents back into the area and reestablish the suburb; however, the old swinging District Six can never be re-created. The museum consists of street signs, photographs, life stories of the people who lived there, and a huge map, where former residents can identify the sites of their homes and record their names. This map is being used to help sort out land claims. You can arrange in advance for a two-hour walking tour of the district for a nominal amount. Two blocks from the District Six Museum is **Fields of Play** (✉ *15 Buitenkant St., Cape Town Central8000* ☎ *021/466–7100*), the museum's new annex. Through photographs, interviews, and objects, this museum exposes the history and role of soccer in Cape Town's different communities, and is a fascinating look at how the game linked and divided these communities. ✉ *25 Buitenkant St., Cape Town Central* ☎ *021/466–7208* ⊕ *www.districtsix.co.za* 📠 *R15* ☉ *Mon. 9–2, Tues.–Sat. 9–4, Sun. by appointment.*

**NEED A
BREAK?**

Perhaps the only really good restaurant in the immediate area, **Dias Tavern** (✉ *15 Caledon St., District 6, Cape Town Central* ☎ *021/465–7547*) serves fantastic and filling Portuguese fare, including *trinchado* (spicy braised beef), calamari, grilled meats of all varieties, and pastas. This casual tavern setting has nonpanoramic but nice views of Table Mountain and is a favorite of office workers in the area.

⑰ Gold of Africa Museum. This museum in the historic Martin Melck House
★ chronicles the history and artistry of African gold and houses arguably one of the best collections in the world. The exquisite exhibition upstairs, cleverly displayed in a darkened room, may leave you gasping—artisans from Mali, Senegal, Ghana, and the Ivory Coast certainly

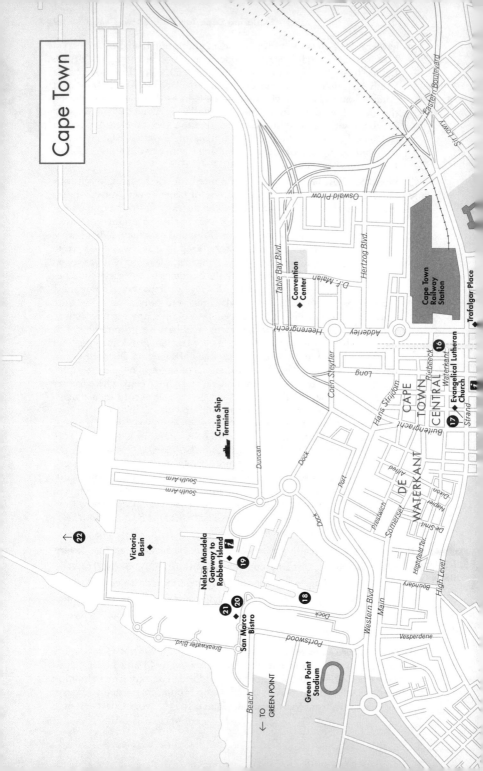

Cape Town

Convention Center

Cruise Ship Terminal

Cape Town Railway Station

Trafalgar Place

16 ◆ Evangelical Lutheran Church

17

CAPE TOWN CENTRAL

DE WATERKANT

Victoria Basin

22

Nelson Mandela Gateway to Robben Island

19

20

21

San Marco Bistro

18

Green Point Stadium

← TO GREEN POINT

Beach

Streets: Eastern Boulevard, Sir Lowry, Oswald Pirow, Table Bay Blvd., Hertzog Blvd., D.F. Malan, Heerengracht, Adderley, Coen Steytler, Long, Hans Strijdom, Riebeeck, Waterkant, Strand, Buitengracht, Duncan, Dock, Port, Alfred, Dixon, Napier, Prestwich, Somerset, De Smit, Highfield Rd., Western Blvd., Main, Boundary, High Level, Vesperdene, Breakwater Blvd., Portswood, South Arm

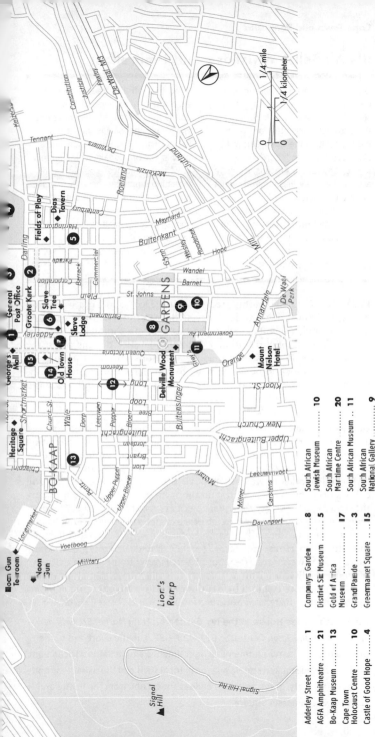

It's All Bells, Whistles—and Umbrellas!

One of the greatest celebrations in Cape Town is the annual Cape Coon New Year Carnival, also known as the Cape Town Minstrel Carnival or, more simply, as the Coon Carnival. (Although the term "coon" does rankle some South Africans, it's more accepted in Cape lingo than it would be in the United States or Great Britain, and hence remains the popular name of the festival.) The origins of this January festival date to the early colonial period, when this was the one day of the year that slaves were given time off. The tradition continued even after the emancipation of slaves and is the most visible reminder of a way of life that saw its finest flowering in District Six. Today thousands of wild celebrants take to the streets in vibrant costumes—complete with matching umbrellas—to sing *moppies* (pronounced a somewhat guttural *more peas*, they're vaudeville-style songs), accompanied by banjos, drums, and whistles. The celebration lasts one or two days.

knew how to transform this precious metal. Downstairs is a workshop where you can watch jewelers busy at their craft. When you've taken in all the opulence you can, visit the excellent gift shop where you can buy replicas of some traditional Ghanaian jewelry designs or escape to the lovely café in a secluded courtyard. Book ahead for a Pangolin Night Tour (R40; two-person minimum), which includes a guided flash-lighted tour of the collection and a glass of wine with gold flakes. ⊠ 96 *Strand St., Cape Town Central* ☎ *021/405–1540* ⊕ *www.goldofafrica. com* ⊠ *R25* ⊙ *Mon.–Sat. 10–5.*

⑮ ★ Greenmarket Square. For more than a century this cobbled square served as a forum for public announcements, including the 1834 declaration abolishing slavery, which was read from the balcony of the Old Town House, overlooking the square. In the 19th century the square became a vegetable market as well as a popular watering hole, and you can still enjoy a drink at an open-air restaurant or hotel veranda while watching the crowds go by. Today the square has a great outdoor market *(⇨ Shopping)*, and is flanked by some of the best examples of art-deco architecture in South Africa. A beautiful example of urban Cape Dutch architecture, the **Old Town House** (☎ *021/481–3933* ⊕ *www.iziko.org.za/michaelis* ⊠ *Free* ⊙ *Weekdays 10–5, Sat. 10–4*) is now home to the extensive **Michaelis Collection.** This 17th-century collection of Dutch paintings includes evocative etchings by Rembrandt, as well as changing exhibits. ⊠ *Longmarket, Burg, and Shortmarket Sts., Cape Town Central.*

NEED A BREAK?

The **Scotch Coffee House at the Ivy Garden** (⊠ *Long Market St., Greenmarket Sq., Cape Town Central* ☎ *021/423–0322*), in the courtyard of the Old Town House, serves homemade light lunches with a South African bent (try the braised smoked snoek, a favorite local fish) and the usual teas and coffees. This leafy, green setting is a pleasant escape from the hustle and bustle of Greenmarket Square.

2

WORTH NOTING

❶ Adderley Street. Originally named Heerengracht after a canal that once ran the length of the avenue, this street has always been Cape Town's principal thoroughfare. It was once the favored address of the city's leading families, and its

oak-shaded sidewalks served as a promenade for those who wanted to see and be seen. By the mid-19th century the oaks had all been chopped down and the canal covered, as Adderley became the main commercial street. By 1908 it had become so busy that the city planners paved it with wooden blocks in an attempt to dampen the noise of countless wagons, carts, and hooves. In recent years Adderley Street has lost most of its charm. Although there are a couple of beautiful old buildings dating to the early 1900s, they are mostly crowded out by uninspiring office buildings, and the sidewalks are packed with street hawkers selling everything from fruits and vegetables to cell-phone covers and tea towels. City management is trying to halt the urban decay, however, and there's plenty of evidence of regeneration. A lot of old office buildings are now being converted to upscale apartments, and beautiful old art-deco buildings are getting the spit and polish they so desperately need. ⊠ *Cape Town Central.*

❻ Church Square. Church Square bore witness to much of Cape Town's dark history. On the square's northern end is the former **Slave Lodge** (⊠ *49 Wale St., Cape Town Central* ☎ *021/460–8242* ⊕ *www.iziko.org. za/slavelodge* ⊠ *R15* ☉ *Weekdays 10–4:30, Sat. 10–1*). Built in 1679 by the Dutch East India Company to house slaves, convicts, and lunatics, it also housed the supreme court from 1815 to 1914. The lodge now holds a museum with a sobering account of slavery in the Cape, as well as excellent and evocative temporary exhibits that tend to examine apartheid and racism.

An inconspicuous concrete plaque along Spin Street's median is all that's left of the **Slave Tree,** an enormous Canadian pine under which slaves were reportedly auctioned off. A section of the tree is on display at the District Six Museum.

Across from the slave tree on the square's eastern end is the entrance to the Gothic-style **Groote Kerk** (⊠ *Parliament St., Cape Town Central* ☎ *021/422–0569* ⊠ *Free* ☉ *Weekdays 10–2; services Sun. at 10 and 7*). One of South Africa's most famous churches, the Groote Kerk (Great Church) was built in 1841 on the site of an earlier Dutch Reformed church dating from 1704. The adjoining clock tower is all that remains of that earlier building. Among the building's interesting features are the enclosed pews, each with its own door—prominent families would buy these so they wouldn't have to pray with the masses. The enormous pulpit is the joint work of famous sculptor Anton Anreith and carpenter Jan Jacob Graaff. The lions supporting it are carved from local stinkwood; the upper portion is Burmese teak. The organ, with nearly 6,000 pipes, is the largest in the Southern Hemisphere. Approximately 200 people are buried beneath the Batavian soapstone floor, including eight governors. There are free guided tours on request.

⑭ **Church Street Arcade.** The center of Cape Town's art and antiques business, this section of Church Street is a pedestrian mall filled with art galleries, antiques dealers, and small cafés. A daily antiques and flea market is held here. ⊠ *Church St. between Burg and Long Sts., Cape Town Central.*

❷ **City Hall.** Though this attractive Edwardian building constructed in 1905 is in need of sprucing up, it's still a commanding presence overlooking the Grand Parade. What was the seat of local administration is now home to the Cape Town Philharmonic Orchestra (the acoustics in the main hall are phenomenal) and a traffic department. Some of the building's stone was imported from Bath, England, and the clock is a scaled-down replica of Big Ben. From a balcony overlooking Darling Street, Nelson Mandela gave his historic speech upon his release from prison in 1990. ⊠ *Darling St., Cape Town Central* 🔁 *Free.*

❸ **Grand Parade.** Once a military parade ground, this is now just a bleak parking lot with a statue of Edward VII serving as a parking attendant and seagull resting post. But it was here that more than 100,000 of Nelson Mandela's supporters gathered on February 11, 1990, when, after 27 years in prison, he addressed an adoring crowd from the balcony at City Hall. The Grand Parade will be temporarily transformed into a fan park for the 2010 World Cup. ⊠ *Darling, Lower Plein, and Buitenkant Sts., Cape Town Central.*

⑫ **Long Street.** The section of Long between Orange and Wale streets is lined with magnificently restored Georgian and Victorian buildings. Wrought-iron balconies and fancy curlicues on these colorful houses evoke the French Quarter in New Orleans. In the 1960s, Long Street played host to bars, prostitutes, and sleazy hotels, but today antiques dealers, secondhand bookstores, pawnshops, the Pan-African Market, and funky clothing outlets make this the best browsing street in the city. Lodgings here range from backpackers' digs to the more exclusive Grand Daddy. At the mountain end is Long Street Baths, an indoor swimming pool and old Turkish *hammam* (steam bath). ⊠ *Cape Town Central.*

> ### WHO'S THAT?
>
> The imposing statue with his back turned toward the Slave Lodge is of Jan Smuts, a statesman, soldier, naturalist, and philosopher. In the mid-20th century he was also the leader of the United Party, which believed in a unified South Africa. Had he not been defeated by the National Party in 1948, South African history would have taken a very different turn.

NEED A BREAK?

Amid the dozens of great joints around Long and Loop streets, **Zorina's** (⊠ *172 Loop St., Cape Town Central* ☎ *021/424–9301*) is a hole-in-the-wall that's famous for great Cape Malay curries and samosas. On the other end of the spectrum, if you can't stand the idea of another heavy meal, head to funky **Portobello Café** (⊠ *111 Long St., Cape Town Central* ☎ *021/426–1418*), which serves fantastic vegetarian cuisine, smoothies, and fresh fruit juices that even meat-eaters will love.

7 St. George's Cathedral. This cathedral was once the religious seat of one of the most recognizable faces—and voices—in the fight against apartheid, Archbishop Desmond Tutu. In his position as the first black archbishop of Cape Town (he was elected in 1986), he vociferously denounced apartheid and relentlessly pressed for a democratic government. It was from these steps that he led a demonstration of more than 30,000 people and coined the phrase the Rainbow People to describe South Africans in all their glorious diversity. The Anglican cathedral was designed by Sir Herbert Baker in the Gothic Revival style; construction began in 1901, using sandstone from Table Mountain. The structure contains the largest stained-glass window in the country, some beautiful examples of late-Victorian stained glass, and a 1,000-year-old Coptic cross. If you want to hear the magnificent organ, go to the choral evensong at 7 on Sunday evening. ⊠ *5 Wale St., Cape Town Central* ☎ *021/424–7360* ✆ *Free* ☉ *Daily 8–5; services weekdays at 7:15* AM *and 1:15* PM, *Sat. at 8* AM, *Sun. at 7* AM, *8* AM, *10* AM, *7* PM.

16 St. George's Mall. This promenade stretches from the city center almost all the way to the Foreshore. Shops and cafés line the mall, and street vendors hawk everything from T-shirts to African arts and crafts. Street performers and dancers gather daily to entertain crowds of locals and visitors, who rub shoulders on their way to and from work or while sightseeing. ⊠ *Between Long and Adderley Sts., from Wale St. to Prestwich St., Cape Town Central.*

11 South African Museum. This museum has some excellent examples of rock art that will give you insight into the ancient Khoisan culture. The museum also has an interesting section on the fossil remains of prehistoric reptiles and other animals, and the Whale Well, where musical recitals are often held under suspended life-size casts of enormous marine mammals. Shark World thrills children with exhibits on the sharks that ply the oceans. The adjoining planetarium stages a variety of shows throughout the week, some of which are specifically designed for children as young as five. ⊠ *25 Queen Victoria St., Cape Town Central* ☎ *021/481–3800* ⊕ *www.iziko.org.za/sam* ✆ *Museum R15, planetarium R20* ☉ *Museum daily 10–5; planetarium shows weekdays at 2, plus Tues. at 8* PM, *and weekends at noon, 1, and 2:30.*

BO-KAAP

You'll know you're in the Bo-Kaap (Afrikaans for "on top of the Cape") when you catch the heady smell wafting from Atlas Trading Co., which is often packed with housewives stocking up on fresh spices, or when you hear the call of the muezzin from one of the many mosques in the area. You might even have to sidestep lights, cameras, and film stars, since the district is an oft-used setting for movies and magazine shoots—the brightly colored houses make a stunning backdrop. Bo-Kaap is the historic home of the city's Muslim population, brought from the East as slaves in the late 17th and early 18th centuries. So it's no surprise that it's also home to the Auwal Mosque, the oldest mosque in South Africa, built in 1798. Today the area remains strongly Muslim, and it's fascinating to wander the narrow, cobbled lanes past mosques and the largest collection of pre-1840 architecture in South Africa. The Bo-Kaap is also known as the Malay quarter, even though its inhabitants originated from all over, including the Indonesian archipelago, India, Turkey, and Madagascar.

TIMING AND PRECAUTIONS
To experience all that the area has to offer and because there have been a few muggings in the Bo-Kaap, we recommend that you take a guided tour (⇨ *Walking Tours, in Planning, at the beginning of the chapter)* or stick to Wale, Dorp, and Shortmarket streets.

TOP ATTRACTIONS
The sights below are marked on the Cape Town map.

⑬ Bo-Kaap Museum. Built in the 18th century, this museum was originally the home of Abu Bakr Effendi, a well-known Turkish scholar and prominent leader in the Muslim community. He was brought here in the mid-19th century to help quell feuding between Muslim factions and is believed to have written one of the first books in Afrikaans. The house has been furnished to re-create the lifestyle of a typical Malay family in the 19th century. (Since the exhibits aren't labeled, you might do better to visit the museum as part of a guided tour of the Malay quarter.) Look for works by artist Gregoire Boonzaire, who is famous for capturing both the chaos and charm of neighborhoods such as the Bo-Kaap and District Six. ⊠ *71 Wale St., Bo-Kaap* ☏ *021/481–3939* ⊕ *www.iziko. org.za/bokaap* ⊠ *R10* ☉ *Mon.–Sat. 10–5.*

NEED A BREAK?

Noon Gun Tearoom and Restaurant (⊠ *273 Longmarket St., Bo-Kaap* ☏ *021/424–0529*) on the slopes of Signal Hill is a good place to stop for a breather and some traditional, home-cooked Malay food. Your entertaining hostess, Zaine Misbach, cooks up a mean curry and *biryani* (a spicy rice-based dish). And her samosas are to die for. The menu is limited, but Zaine's repertoire is anything but; she's chatty and engaging and also offers cooking lessons.

GARDENS

An affluent city neighborhood, Gardens is populated largely by young professionals. Gardens has numerous restaurants, cafés, hotels, and shops, as well as many beautiful homes. Main thoroughfares like Kloof Street are packed with funky boutiques and are pleasant to stroll and explore.

TIMING AND PRECAUTIONS
Unlike Cape Town Central, Gardens' commercial zone remains relatively lively into the evening. From where Kloof Street begins (at the end of Long Street) until it intersects with Camp Street, restaurants, cafés, and Cape Town's art-house cinema make the area lively and safe for walking until about 9 PM. In other areas take the usual precautions.

TOP ATTRACTIONS

The sights below are marked on the Cape Town map.

⑩ ★ **Cape Town Holocaust Centre.** The center is both a memorial to the 6 million Jews and other victims who were killed during the Holocaust and an education center whose aim is to create a caring and just society in which human rights and diversity are valued. The permanent exhibit is excellent and very moving. A multimedia display, comprising photo panels, text, film footage, and music, creates a chilling reminder of the dangers of prejudice, racism, and discrimination. The center is next to the South African Jewish Museum. ⊠ *88 Hatfield St., Gardens* ☎ *021/462–5553* ⊕ *www.ctholocaust.co.za* ⊠ *Free* ☉ *Sun.–Thurs. 10–5, Fri. 10–2.*

⑩ ★ **South African Jewish Museum.** Housed in the Old Synagogue—South Africa's first synagogue, built in 1863—this museum lies adjacent to the Cape Town Holocaust Centre and spans 150 years of South African Jewry. The themes of Memories (immigrant experiences), Reality (integration into South Africa), and Dreams (visions) exhibits are conveyed with high-tech multimedia and interactive displays, models, and artifacts. The complex also includes the Great Synagogue (built in 1905), an active place of worship, a computerized Discovery Center that can help you trace your family roots, a temporary gallery for changing exhibits, an auditorium, and a museum restaurant and shop. ⊠ *88 Hatfield St., Gardens* ☎ *021/465–1546* ⊕ *www.sajewishmuseum.co.za* ⊠ *R50* ☉ *Sun.–Thurs. 10–5, Fri. 10–2.*

NEED A BREAK? | Government Avenue ends opposite the impressive gateway to the Mount Nelson Hotel (⊠ **76 Orange St., Gardens** ☎ **021/483-1000** ⊕ **www.mount-nelson.co.za**), complete with two pith-helmeted gatekeepers. The Nellie, as it's known, was erected in 1899 to welcome the Prince of Wales on his visit to the Cape and today remains one of Cape Town's most fashionable and genteel social venues. Don't miss the legendary high tea. Served from 2:30 to 5:30, the pastry selection can tempt even the most jaded palate, and the savory treats make for a scrumptious meal.

⑨ ★ **South African National Gallery.** This museum houses a good collection of 19th- and 20th-century European art, but its most interesting exhibits are the South African works, many of which reflect the country's traumatic history. The gallery owns an enormous body of work, so exhibitions change regularly, but there's always something provocative—whether it's documentary photographs or a multimedia exhibit chronicling South Africa's struggles with HIV/AIDS. The new director, Riason Naidoo, plans to maintain the edgy and sometimes controversial exhibitions that his predecessor Marilyn Martin was known for, as well as establish the museum as a leader of contemporary and traditional African art. Free guided tours on Tuesday and Thursday take about an hour. ⊠ *Government Ave., Gardens* ☎ *021/467–4660* ⊕ *www.iziko.org.za/sang* ⊠ *R15* ☉ *Tues.–Sun. 10–5; tours Tues. and Thurs. at 11, noon, and 1.*

V&A WATERFRONT

The V&A (Victoria & Alfred) Waterfront is the culmination of a long-term project undertaken to breathe new life into the historical dockland of the city. Although some Capetonians deem the Waterfront too "mallish," it remains one of Cape Town's most popular and vibrant attractions, and construction is ongoing. Expensive apartments are being built at the marina, and hundreds of shops, movie theaters, restaurants, and bars share quarters in restored warehouses and dock buildings, all connected by pedestrian plazas and promenades. A major plus is that it's clean, safe, and car-free.

TIMING AND PRECAUTIONS

You could see the area's major sights in half a day, but that won't give you much time for shopping, coffee stops, or lunch, or for all that the aquarium has to offer. A more leisurely approach would be to set aside a whole day, at the end of which you could find a waterside restaurant or bar to enjoy a cold glass of wine or a cocktail.

With its crowds of people, security cameras, and guards, this is one of the safest places to shop and hang out in the city. That said, you should still keep an eye on your belongings and be aware of pickpockets.

TOP ATTRACTIONS

The sights below are marked on the Cape Town map.

㉒ **Robben Island.** Made famous by its most illustrious inhabitant, Nelson
Fodor's Choice Mandela, this island, whose name is Dutch for "seals," has a long and
★ sad history. At various times a prison, leper colony, mental institution, and military base, it is finally filling a positive, enlightening, and empowering role in its latest incarnation as a museum. Robert Sobukwe and Walter Sisulu were also imprisoned here for their role in opposing apartheid. For many years the African National Congress secretary-general, Sisulu died in 2003 in his early nineties and was given a hero's burial. Sobukwe, founding president of the Pan Africanist Congress, proved to be such a thorn in the government's side that he was imprisoned in the 1960s under the special Sobukwe Clause, which had to be renewed every year to keep him in jail. John Voster, then the country's minister, said of Sobukwe, "He is a man with magnetic personality, great organizing ability, and a divine sense of mission," and it was these very qualities that made him such a threat. He was treated slightly better than other prisoners but was kept completely isolated from them—an especially terrible punishment for a man with such a strong sense of community. In addition to these more recent prisoners, other fascinating (and reluctant) people have inhabited this at once formidable and beautiful place. One of the first prisoners was Autshumato, known to the early Dutch settlers as Harry the Hottentot. He was one of the main interpreters for Jan van Riebeeck in the mid-17th century and was imprisoned for opposing British colonial rule, as was his niece Krotoa. In 1820 the British thought they could solve some of the problems they were having on the Eastern Cape frontier by banishing Xhosa leader Makhanda to the island. Both Autshumato and Makhanda (also spelled Makana) escaped by rowboat, but Makhanda didn't make it.

Declared a World Heritage site on December 1, 1997, Robben Island has become a symbol of the triumph of the human spirit. In 1997 around 90,000 made the pilgrimage; in 2006 more than 300,000 crossed the water to see where some of the greatest South Africans spent much of their lives. Visiting the island is a sobering experience, which begins at the modern Nelson Mandela Gateway to Robben Island, an impressive embarkation center that doubles as a conference center. Interactive exhibits display historic photos of prison life. Next make the journey across the water, remembering to watch Table Mountain recede in the distance and imagine what it must have been like to have just received a 20-year jail sentence. Boats leave on the hour (every other hour in winter), and the crossing takes 30 minutes.

Tours are organized by the Robben Island Museum. (Other operators advertise Robben Island tours but just take visitors on a boat trip *around* the island.) As a result of the reconciliation process, most tour guides are former political prisoners. During the 2½-hour tour you walk through the prison and see the cells where Mandela and other leaders were imprisoned. You also tour the lime quarry, where Mandela spent so many years pounding rocks; in summer the reflection off the rock is blinding, and Mandela's eyesight—but thankfully not his insight—was irreparably damaged by the glare. The tour also takes you past Robert Sobukwe's place of confinement and the leper church. In recent years, many of the prison buildings and the houses where the wardens used to live were renovated, and are now home to former prisoners who act as current tour guides. Due to increased demand for tickets during peak season (December–January), make bookings at least three weeks in advance. Take sunglasses and a hat in summer. ■TIP➔ You are advised to tip your guide only if you feel that the tour has been informative. *Waterfront* ☎ *021/413–4220 or 021/413–4221 for information, 021/413–4209 or 021/413–4211 for reservations, 021/413–4219 for ticket sales* ⊕ *www.robben-island.org.za* ☜ *R180* ☉ *Summer, boats depart from the Nelson Mandela Gateway daily 9–3; winter, daily 9–1; last boat generally leaves the island at 6 in summer and 4 in winter (opening times and boat departures can vary, so phone ahead to check).*

⓲ ☺ **Two Oceans Aquarium.** This aquarium is considered one of the finest in the world. Stunning displays reveal the marine life of the warm Indian Ocean and the icy Atlantic. It's a hands-on place, with a touch pool for children and opportunities for certified divers to explore the vast, five-story kelp forest or the predator tank, where you share the water with a couple of large ragged-tooth sharks (*Carcharias taurus*) and get a legal adrenaline rush (R485, R380 with own gear). If you don't fancy getting wet, you can still watch the feeding in the predator tank every day at 3. But there's more to the aquarium than just snapping jaws. Look for the endangered African penguins, also known as jackass penguins because of the awkward braying noise they make; pulsating moon jellies and spider crabs; and a new frog exhibit. ⊠ *Dock Rd., Waterfront* ☎ *021/418–3823* ⊕ *www.aquarium.co.za* ☜ *R85* ☉ *Daily 9:30–6.*

Fodor's Choice
★

WORTH NOTING

㉑ AGFA Amphitheatre. This popular outdoor space mounts performances ranging from concerts by the Cape Town Philharmonic Orchestra to gigs by jazz and rock bands. (Check with the Waterfront's Cape Town Tourism office for a schedule of events.) The amphitheater stands on the site where, in 1860, a teenage Prince Alfred inaugurated the construction of a breakwater to protect ships in the harbor from devastating northwesterly winds. ⊠ *Near Market Sq., Waterfront* ☎ *021/408–7600 for schedule* ⊕ *www.waterfront.co.za.*

⑲ Chavonne's Cannon Battery Museum. An archeological sight housing the remains of Cape Town's oldest cannon battery, this museum, which opened in 2008, reconstructs the outer battlements and underground rooms that formed one of the major defense outposts on the Cape. Detailed miniature replicas of the cannons and the different types of projectiles are fascinating, as are interpretative materials about the Cape's natural heritage at the time that the battery was in use. ⊠ *Clock Tower Precinct, opposite Mandela Gateway, Waterfront* ☎ *021/416–6230* ⊕ *www.chavonnesmuseum.co.za* ⊠ *R25* ⊙ *Wed.–Sun. 9–4.*

NEED A BREAK?

San Marco Bistro (⊠ *Shop 128 Victoria Wharf, Waterfront* ☎ *021/418–5434*) offers a wide variety of options from sandwiches and salads to hearty pasta, meat, and seafood entrées. This reasonably priced spot is a good place to refuel while shopping and has one the best alfresco locations on the waterfront. For what many would argue is Cape Town's best sushi head to **Willoughby's** (⊠ *Shop 6132 Victoria Wharf, Waterfront* ☎ *021/418–6115*). Unfortunately, there are no views.

---

⑳ South African Maritime Centre. Inside the Union-Castle House, this museum explains the Cape's long history with the sea. Recently renovated, the center documents the history of the Union-Castle shipping line. Before World War II many English-speaking South Africans looked upon England as home, even if they had never been there. The emotional link between the two countries was symbolized most strongly by the mail steamers, carrying both mail and passengers that sailed weekly between South Africa and England. Models of ships are accompanied by memorabilia such as a collection of postcards sold from the ships between 1910 and 1960. A fascinating re-creation of Cape Town harbor as it appeared in 1885, which was built by convicts, is on permanent display, as is a chilling exhibit about the SS *Mendi*, a cargo vessel turned troopship that was carrying the South African Native Labour Contingent to help with the war effort in France. She was accidentally rammed by a British cargo ship, resulting in the deaths of 607 black troops. ⊠ *Union-Castle Building, Dock Rd., Quay 4, Waterfront* ☎ *021/405–2880* ⊕ *www.iziko.org.za/maritime* ⊠ *Free* ⊙ *Daily 10–5.*

SOUTHERN SUBURBS

Lying largely in the shadow and protection of Table Mountain, the Southern Suburbs are known for their leafy, affluent charm. Home to the University of Cape Town (UCT), this area also boasts attractions like the Kirstenbosch Botanic Gardens, UCT's Baxter Theatre (⇨ *Nightlife and the Arts)*, and the Irma Stern Museum. If you don't have time for the Winelands but still want to experience the Cape's stellar wines, Constantia's excellent estates are a lovely compromise.

TIMING AND PRECAUTIONS
These mainly residential suburbs tend to shut down at night. An exception is the bohemian student neighborhood around Observatory, which, though full of interesting little cafés and nightlife spots, is also notorious for muggings and car theft.

TOP ATTRACTIONS
The sights below are marked on the Cape Peninsula map.

㉙ ★ Groot Constantia. The town of Constantia takes its name from the wine estate established here in 1685 by Simon van der Stel, one of the first Dutch governors of the Cape. After his death in 1712 the land was subdivided, with the heart of the estate preserved at Groot Constantia. The enormous complex enjoys the status of a national monument and is by far the most commercial and touristy of the wineries. Van der Stel's magnificent homestead, the oldest in the Cape, lies at the center of Groot Constantia. It's built in traditional Cape Dutch style, with thick, whitewashed walls, a thatch roof, small-paned windows, and ornate gables. The house is a museum furnished with exquisite period pieces. The old wine cellar sits behind the manor house. Built in 1791, it is most famous for its own ornate gable, which contains a sculpture designed by Anton Anreith. The sculpture, depicting fertility, is regarded as one of the most important in the country.

In the 19th century the sweet wines of Groot Constantia were highly regarded in Europe, but today Groot Constantia is known for its splendid red wines. The best is the excellent Bordeaux-style Gouverneurs Reserve, made mostly from cabernet sauvignon grapes with smaller amounts of merlot and cabernet franc. The pinotage is consistently good, too, reaching its velvety prime in about five years. The estate operates two restaurants: the elegant Jonkershuis and Simon's, which serve sophisticated meals in a spectacular setting. You can also bring your own picnic—or buy a picnic for two from Jonkershuis (R250 for two)—and relax on the lawns behind the wine cellar. ⊠ *Off Constantia Rd., Constantia* ☎ *021/794-5128 winery, 021/795-5140 museum, 021/794-6255 Jonkershuis, 021/794-1143 Simon's* ▱ *Museum R10, tastings R20, cellar tour with tastings R25* ☉ *Museum daily 10–5. Winery May–Sept., daily 9–5; Oct.–Apr., daily 9–6. Tours 7 times per day starting at 10.*

㉗ ★ Irma Stern Museum. This small but wonderful museum is dedicated to the works and art collection of Irma Stern (1894–1966), one of South Africa's greatest painters. The museum is administered by the University of Cape Town and occupies the Firs, the artist's home for 38 years. She is best known for African studies, particularly her paintings of indigenous people inspired by trips to the Congo and Zanzibar. Her collection of African artifacts, including priceless Congolese stools and carvings, is superb. ⊠ *Cecil Rd., Rosebank* ☎ *021/685-5686* ⊕ *www.irmastern.co.za* ▱ *R10* ☉ *Tues.–Sat. 10–5.*

㉘ Kirstenbosch National Botanic Gardens. Spectacular in each season, these world-famous gardens showcase stunning South African flora in a magnificent setting, extending up the eastern slopes of Table Mountain and overlooking the sprawling city and the distant Hottentots Holland Mountains. No wonder the gardens are photographed from every angle. They aren't just enjoyed by out-of-town visitors; on weekends Capetonians flock here with their families to lie on the lawns and read their newspapers while the kids run riot. Walking trails meander through the gardens, and grassy banks are ideal for a picnic or afternoon nap. The plantings are limited to species indigenous to southern Africa, including fynbos—hardy, thin-leaved plants that proliferate in the Cape. Among these are proteas, including silver trees and king proteas, ericas, and *restios* (reeds). Magnificent sculptures from Zimbabwe are displayed around the gardens, too.

Garden highlights include a large cycad garden, the Bird Bath (a beautiful stone pool built around a crystal-clear spring), and the fragrance garden, which is wheelchair-friendly and has a tapping rail and Braille interpretive boards. Those who have difficulty walking can take a comprehensive tour lasting one hour (R35, hourly 9–3) in seven-person (excluding the driver) golf carts. Another wheelchair trail leads from the main paths into the wilder section of the park, getting close to the feel of the mountain walks. Concerts featuring the best of South African entertainment—from classical music to township jazz to rock and roll—are held on summer Sundays starting an hour before sunset. But get there early, as the space fills quickly with picnicking music lovers. A visitor center by the conservatory houses a restaurant, bookstore, and coffee shop. Unfortunately, muggings have become increasingly more common in the gardens' isolated areas, and women are advised not to walk alone in the upper reaches of the park far from general activity. ⊠ *Rhodes Ave., Newlands* ☎ *021/799–8783* ⊕ *www.nbi.ac.za* 🖃 *R35* ۩ *Apr.–Aug., daily 8–6; Sept.–Mar., daily 8–7.*

WORTH NOTING

㉚ Buitenverwachting. Once part of Dutch governor Simon van der Stel's original Constantia farm, Buitenverwachting (which means "beyond expectation" and is roughly pronounced "Bait-in-fur-WAGH-ting") has an absolutely gorgeous setting. An oak-lined avenue leads past the Cape Dutch homestead to the modern cellar. Acres of vines spread up hillsides flanked by more towering oaks and the rocky crags of Constantiaberg Mountain. Buitenverwachting's wine is just as good as the view. The biggest seller is the slightly dry Buiten Blanc, an easy-drinking blend of a few varietals. The best red is Christine, a blend of mostly cabernet sauvignon and merlot. The winery's eponymous restaurant is one of the country's best. ⊠ *Off Klein Constantia Rd., Constantia* ☎ *021/794–5190* 🖃 *Tastings free* ۩ *Weekdays 9–5, Sat. 9–1.*

> **NEED A BREAK?** **Buitenverwachting** (⊠ *Off Klein Constantia Rd., Constantia* ☎ *021/794–1012*) serves great picnic lunches during the summer months (November–April) under the oaks on the estate's lawns. It's an idyllic setting and a most civilized way to cap a morning of wine tasting. Each picnic basket is packed with a selection of breads, chicken and other meat, pâtés, and cheeses.

You can buy a bottle of estate wine as an accompaniment. The picnic costs R110 per person, and reservations are essential.

 Rhodes Memorial. Rhodes served as prime minister of the Cape from 1890 to 1896. He made his fortune in the Kimberley diamond rush, but his greatest dream was to forge a Cape–Cairo railway, a tangible symbol of British dominion in Africa. The classical-style granite memorial sits high on the slopes of Devil's Peak, on part of Rhodes's old estate, Groote Schuur. A mounted rider symbolizing energy faces north toward the continent for which Rhodes felt such passion. A bust of Rhodes dominates the temple—ironically, he's leaning on one hand as if he's about to nod off. ⊠ *Off Rhodes Dr., Rondebosch* ⊡ *Free.*

NEED A BREAK? The **Rhodes Memorial Restaurant** (⊠ *Off Rhodes Dr., Rondebosch* ☎ *021/689–9151*), tucked under towering pines behind the memorial, is a pleasant spot that serves breakfast, tea, and a light lunch.

THE PENINSULA

The Peninsula is a treat for any Cape Town visitor, and a round-trip drive that takes in both the False Bay coastline and the Atlantic Ocean is a memorable experience. Among the highlights of the False Bay coast are the quaint fishing village of Kalk Bay and Boulders Beach, with its African penguin colony. Cape Point and the Cape of Good Hope nature reserve are at the tip of the peninsula, and few fail to fall in love with the area's windswept beauty. The wilder and more rugged Atlantic coastline is one of the most stunning in the world. Highlights include a drive along the "Misty Cliffs" between Scarborough and Witsands, and horseback riding down Noordhoek beach. Beautiful Chapman's Peak Drive, if open, is a must, and Hout Bay's Mariners Wharf and weekend market are thoroughly charming. You might even consider spending a night or two in one of the many B&Bs that dot the coast, or even inside the Cape Point Nature Reserve at one of the cottages on Olifantsbos Beach.

TIMING AND PRECAUTIONS

Distances on the peninsula are not that great, so it's certainly possible to drive the loop in a day, visiting a few sights of interest to you. It's equally possible, and far more rewarding, to spend three days here, either moving slowly around the peninsula and staying in a different guesthouse each night or returning to a central spot in the Southern Suburbs at the end of each day. Just remember, however, that during peak season (generally mid-November–mid-January) and holidays, traffic can keep you gridlocked for many frustrating hours. Although touring the peninsula poses no obvious danger, you are advised not to park or walk alone in isolated areas. And watch out for baboons at Cape Point. If you're carrying food, they invite themselves to lunch and can be highly aggressive.

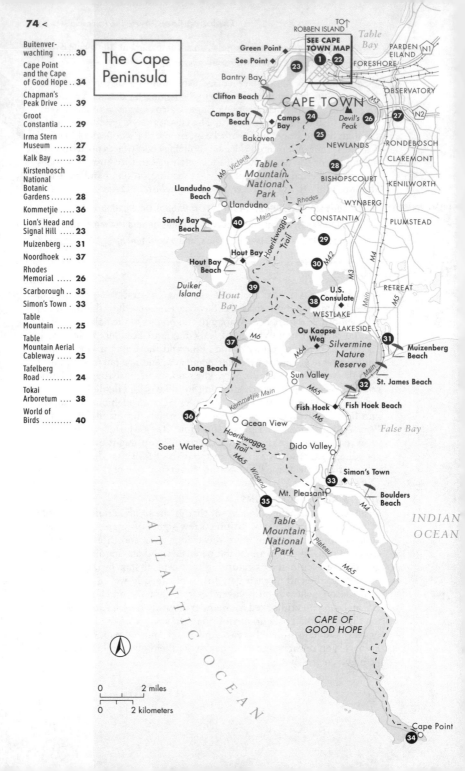

The Cape Peninsula

Robben Island

Table Bay

SEE CAPE TOWN MAP **1** – **22**

PARDEN EILAND

N1

FORESHORE

Green Point ◆

See Point ◆ **23**

OBSERVATORY

Bantry Bay

CAPE TOWN

M3

Clifton Beach

Camps Bay Beach

◆ Camps Bay **24**

Devil's Peak **26** **27** N2

Bakoven **25**

RONDEBOSCH

NEWLANDS

CLAREMONT

Victoria

M6

Table Mountain National Park

28

BISHOPSCOURT

KENILWORTH

Llandudno Beach

Rhodes

WYNBERG

○ Llandudno

Main

CONSTANTIA

PLUMSTEAD

Sandy Bay Beach **40**

29

Hout Bay

Hout Bay Beach

30 M42

M4

M3

39

Duiker Island

Hout Bay

U.S. Consulate

38 ◆

WESTLAKE

LAKESIDE

RETREAT

Ou Kaapse Weg ◆

31

Muizenberg Beach

37 M6

M64

Silvermine Nature Reserve

Main

M5

Long Beach

Sun Valley

32 St. James Beach

M65

Kommetjie Main

Fish Hoek ◆ Fish Hoek Beach

M6

36

○ Ocean View

Hoerikwaggo Trail

Dido Valley

False Bay

Soet Water

M65

Wildand

Simon's Town

33 ◆

35

Mt. Pleasant

Boulders Beach

M4

INDIAN OCEAN

Table Mountain National Park

Plateau

M65

CAPE OF GOOD HOPE

A T L A N T I C   O C E A N

0 ——— 2 miles

0 ——— 2 kilometers

Cape Point ○

34

TOP ATTRACTIONS

The sights below are marked on the Cape Peninsula map.

Fodor's Choice ★ **Boulders Beach.** This series of small coves lies among giant boulders on the southern outskirts of Simon's Town. Part of Table Mountain National Park, the beach is best known for its resident colony of African penguins. You must stay out of the fenced-off breeding beach, but don't be surprised if a wandering bird comes waddling up to you to take a look. Penguin-viewing platforms, accessible from either the Boulders Beach or Seaforth side, provide close-up looks at these comical birds. When you've had enough penguin peering, you can stroll back to Boulders Beach for some excellent swimming in the quiet coves. This beach is great for children because it is so protected, and the sea is warm(ish) and calm. It can get crowded in summer, though, so go early. Without traffic, it takes about 45 minutes to get here from town, less from the Southern Suburbs. ⌂ *Follow signs from Bellvue Rd., Simon's Town* ☎ *021/786–2329* ⊕ *www.sanparks.org* ⌂*R30* ⊙ *Daily, Dec. and Jan. 7 AM–7:30 PM, Feb., Mar., Oct., and Nov. 8–6:30.*

(NOT SO) HAPPY FEET

As comical as the African penguin may seem, their predicament is sobering: they are regarded as an endangered species. Newspaper reports in early 2007 suggested that the African penguin (*Spheniscus demersus*) population had taken a hammering as a result of declining anchovy and sardine stocks. Up to 50,000 of the birds—who call Boulders Beach and Stony Point near Betty's Bay (⇨ *Chapter 3)* in the Overberg home—were lost in just two years and the current population hovers around 2,700. Penguins mate for life and have been known to return to the same nesting site for up to 15 years.

NEED A BREAK?

Don't be fooled by its low-key, casual atmosphere, **Boulders Beach Lodge and Restaurant** (⌂ *Boulders Beach parking lot* ☎ *021/786-1758)* serves seriously good food, worth a visit even without the penguins. Sitting on the huge veranda with stunning views over False Bay, expect to enjoy spectacular and reasonably priced Pacific Rim–inspired cuisine using the freshest seafood, as well as great burgers, salads, and killer breakfasts.

③⑨ ★ **Chapman's Peak Drive.** Rock slides and unstable cliff faces mean this fantastically scenic drive can often be closed for maintenance, as it was for the greater part of 2008–2009. Work began on the drive in 1910, when it was considered an impossibility. Charl Marais, a mining surveyor, wasn't deterred by the task and set about surveying a route by sending a worker ahead of him to chop out footholds and create rudimentary platforms for his theodolite. There are stories of him hanging on to the side of the cliff by ropes and nearly losing his life on a number of occasions. His tenacity paid off, and with the help of 700 convicts, a road was chipped and blasted out of the rock. Chapman's Peak Drive officially opened in 1922 with views rivaling those of California's Pacific Route 1 to Big Sur. When open, you can access the drive from both Noordhoek and Hout Bay. ☎ *021/791–8222.*

㉜ Kalk Bay. This small, fascinating harbor, which shelters a weathered fishing fleet, takes its name from the seashells that were once baked in large kilns near the shore to produce lime (*kalk*). Tiny cottages crowd the narrow cobbled streets, clinging to the mountain, and funky clothing shops, galleries, antiques shops, and cozy bistros can fill a whole day of rambling. Here gnarled fisherfolk rub shoulders with artists, writers, surfers, yuppies, New Age trendies, and genteel ladies with blue hair rinses. During whale seasons the gentle giants rub up against the harbor wall, and if you time your visit right you can almost touch them. You can also walk up any of the steep stairways to Boyes Drive and from there up the mountain, or relax and down a few beers in the sun at the Brass Bell while local surfers strut their stuff on Kalk Bay Reef. Other possibilities on your to-do list might include dropping your own line off the pier (fishing supplies are available from the small supermarket on the Main Road) or watching the harbor seals that loll around waiting for fishy discards when the boats come in. The lives of the fisherfolk are changing rapidly due to declining fish stocks, and many are now shorebound without an income, due in part to the controversial requirement for fishing permits.

NEED A BREAK?

Kalky's (✉ *Kalk Bay Harbour, Kalk Bay* ☎ *021/788–6396*), right on the harbor, is a great place to get generous portions of fish-and-chips. The seagulls will fight for any of your leftover scraps, as will Robby, the resident seal. The **Olympia Café** (✉ *134 Main Rd., Kalk Bay* ☎ *021/788–6396*), a Mediterranean café, is one of the best places to eat in Cape Town and is usually packed to capacity, especially on weekends. At the affiliated bakery just around the corner, you can buy take-away cappuccinos, melt-in-your-mouth croissants, and pasties filled with springbok and sometimes even rabbit. Pop in, elbow your way through the locals who won't start their day without something from "The Deli" (as it's fondly known), and take whatever you've bought to the harbor wall (just a two-minute walk away), where you can eat and watch the seals gambol in front of you.

㉝ Simon's Town. Picturesque Simon's Town has many lovely old buildings and possibly the peninsula's best swimming beaches at Seaforth and Boulders. The town has had a long association with the Royal Navy. British troops landed here in 1795 before defeating the Dutch at the Battle of Muizenberg, and the town served as a base for the Royal Navy from 1814 to 1957, when it was handed over to the South African navy. Today you are bound to see plenty of men and women decked out in crisp white uniforms.

Jubilee Square, a dockside plaza that serves as the de facto town center, is just off the main road (St. George's Road). Next to the dock wall stands a **statue of Just Nuisance,** a Great Dane adopted as a mascot by the Royal Navy during World War II. Just Nuisance apparently liked his pint of beer and would accompany sailors on the train into Cape Town. He had the endearing habit of leading drunken sailors—and only sailors—that he found in the city back to the station in time to catch the last train. The navy went so far as to induct him into the service as

2

an able seaman attached to the HMS *Afrikander*. He died at the age of seven in April 1944 and was given a military funeral. Just below Jubilee Square is the popular Simon's Town Waterfront, with numerous shops and restaurants. Day cruises, deep-sea fishing trips, and kayaking trips leave from the harbor.

If you're looking for something to entertain children, the area has quite a few child-friendly options. The somewhat rustic **Simon's Town Museum** (☎ *021/786–3046* ⛶ *Free* ☉ *Weekdays 9–4, Sat. 10–1, Sun. 11–3*) features historical exhibits of the town, including numerous photographs and memorabilia from former non-white residents who were removed to the townships of the Cape Flats in the 1960s. The **Naval Museum** (☎ *021/787–4635* ☉ *Daily 9:30–3:30*) is filled with model ships, old navigational equipment, old South African Navy divers' equipment, a few real, life-sized boats, and, oddly enough, a helicopter. You can also climb to the top of the building's clock tower. The **Toy Museum** (☎ *021/786–1395* ☉ *Daily 9–5*) is great for kids, brimming with hundreds of models of all things locomotive: from cars to trains to tanks, these miniature vehicles date from the 1920s to the present. A fairly large collection of dolls is also on exhibit. A small selection of (modern) toy cars and dolls is for sale. At **Scratch Patch and Mineral World** (☎ *021/786–2020* ☉ *Weekdays 8:30–4:45, weekends 9–5:30*), a gemstone factory about 1 km north of town, you can buy and fill a bag (R14–R85, depending on size) with gemstones that you pick from a garden filled ankle-deep with semiprecious stones.

NEED A BREAK?

The Sweetest Thing (✉ *82 St. George's St., Simon's Town* ☎ *021/786–4200*) has amazing homemade cakes, pastries, cookies, as well as light lunch options like savory pies and quiches.

WORTH NOTING

③⑥ ♻ **Kommetjie.** A pleasant, somewhat isolated village, Kommetjie has a scenic 45-minute walk down Long Beach that leads to the wreck of the *Kakapo*, a steamship that ran aground on her maiden voyage in 1900. This is a surfer's paradise, with some really big waves and a few gentler breaks. Because of a series of attacks on Long Beach, you are advised to walk here only in a group. If you don't have security in numbers, walk instead to the **Slangkoppunt lighthouse** (☎ *021/783–1717* ☉ *Daily 10–3*). At 111 feet, it's the tallest cast-iron tower on South Africa's coast and is located almost exactly midway between Robben Island and Cape Point. The lighthouse has a 5-million-candlepower light and a range of 30 nautical mi, with four flashes every 30 seconds. Lighthouse keeper Peter Dennett is known for giving great tours.

③⑦ **Noordhoek.** This popular beach community has stunning white sands that stretch all the way to Kommetjie along the aptly named Long Beach. The small bordering Noordhoek Farm Village has become a retreat for the arts-and-crafts community, with a couple of galleries and boutiques showcasing local work. Long Beach is very popular with surfers and runners, and you can walk all the way to Kommetjie. But don't walk alone or when the beach is deserted, as attacks are not uncommon. Horseback riding along the beach and through the fynbos-covered dunes is a memorable and highly worthwhile excursion.

NEED A
BREAK?

Nestled behind Chapman's Peak and minutes away from Noordhoek Beach, Café Roux (⊠ *Chapman's Peak Dr., Noordhoek Farm Village, Noordhoek* ☎ *021/789–2538*) is an unpretentious outdoor café with great homemade food and fabulous South African wines at competitive prices. The Toad in the Village (☎ *021/789–2973*), which is next to Café Roux, is a country pub and restaurant with a beer garden, deck in the trees, good kids' menu, and live music in the evenings.

③⑤ Scarborough. This tiny vacation community has one of the best beaches on the peninsula, and is populated by a disproportionate number of conservation biologists. Look no further than the setting to explain that one. From Scarborough to Kommetjie, the M65 hugs the shoreline, snaking between the mountains and the crashing surf. This part of the shore is considered unsafe for swimming, but experienced surfers, boogie boarders, and windsurfers revel in the wind and waves, and the scenery is heart-stopping.

③⑧ Tokai Arboretum. This gorgeous and tranquil national forest is planted with hundreds of tree species from all over the world, including Californian redwoods and a variety of oaks. A favorite spot for picnickers and cyclists, the Arboretum also has a simple tea garden that serves hearty home-style meals and delicious cakes. On the way in to the Arboretum is a crumbling Cape Dutch manor. Built in 1795 with a façade designed by famed architect Louis Michel Thibault, the homestead, which is not open to the public, is reputedly haunted. ⊠ *Tokai Rd., Tokai* ۞ *Daily, sunrise to sunset.*

④⓪ World of Birds. Here you can walk through aviaries housing 450 species of indigenous and exotic birds, including eagles, vultures, penguins, and flamingos. No cages separate you from most of the birds, so you can get some pretty good photographs; however, the big raptors are kept behind fences. ⊠ *Valley Rd., Hout Bay* ☎ *021/790–2730* ⊕ *www. worldofbirds.org.za* ☜ *R59* ۞ *Daily 9–5.*

BEACHES

With panoramic views of mountains tumbling to the ocean, the stunning sandy beaches of the Cape Peninsula are a major draw for Capetonians and visitors alike. Beautiful as the beaches may be, don't expect to spend hours splashing in the surf: the water around Cape Town is very, very cold (although you get used to it). Beaches on the Atlantic are washed by the Benguela Current flowing up from the Antarctic, and in midsummer the water hovers around 10°C–15°C (50°F–60°F). The water on the False Bay side is usually 5°C (9°F) warmer, so if it's warmer waters you seek, head to False Bay beaches such as Muizenberg, Fish Hoek, and Boulders. Cape beaches are renowned for their clean, snow-white, powdery sand. Beachcombers will find every kind of beach to suit them, from intimate coves to sheltered bays and wild, wide beaches stretching forever. If you are looking for more tropical water temperatures, head for the warm Indian Ocean waters of KwaZulu-Natal or the Garden Route.

The major factor that affects any day at a Cape beach is wind. In summer howling southeasters, known collectively as the Cape Doctor, are all too common and can ruin a trip to the beach; during these gales you're better off at Clifton or Llandudno, on the Atlantic side; the sheltered but very small St. James Beach, on the False Bay side; and maybe even the southern corner of False Bay's Fish Hoek Beach or one of the pools along Jager's Walk. Boulders (⇨ *Cape Peninsula Top Attractions, above*) and Seaforth are also often sheltered from southeasters.

Every False Bay community has its own beach, but most are not reviewed here. In comparison with Atlantic beaches, most of them are rather small and often crowded, sandwiched between the sea and the commuter rail line, with Fish Hoek a major exception. South of Simon's Town the beaches tend to be wilder and less developed, except for the very popular Seaforth and Millers Point beaches.

TIMING AND PRECAUTIONS

The closest beaches to town are Clifton and Camps Bay, which are just minutes away during non-rush-hour traffic. But in summer, when you can't move for traffic, getting anywhere—and especially to the beaches—can take a frustratingly long time. If you want an adventure and are eager to avoid the holiday traffic, jump on the train that runs by the False Bay beaches of Muizenberg, Fish Hoek, and Boulders. From the center of town it will take you about 40 minutes to get to Fish Hoek, and the views from the train across the bay from Muizenberg onward are absolutely spectacular.

At many beaches there may be powerful waves, a strong undertow, and dangerous riptides. The lifeguard situation is haphazard and varies according to funding and the availability of the lifeguards; the service combines voluntary and professional guards. Lifeguards work the main beaches, but only on weekends and during school breaks. Other beaches are unpatrolled. Although it's nice to stroll along a lonely beach, remember it's risky to wander off on your own in a deserted area. ⚠ **Toilet facilities at beaches are limited.**

Southeasters can also bring blue bottles—Portuguese men of war. As these jellyfishlike creatures can sting, you should avoid swimming at these times. (If you see them washed up on the shore, that's a good sign to stay out of the water.)

The beaches below are marked on the Cape Peninsula map.

ATLANTIC COAST

Blouberg Beach. Make the 25-km (16-mi) trip north from the city to the other side of Table Bay and you'll be rewarded with an exceptional (and the most famous) view of Cape Town and Table Mountain. Blouberg is divided into two parts: Big Bay, which hosts surfing and windsurfing contests, and Little Bay, better suited to sunbathers and families. It's frequently windy here, which is fine if you want to fly a kite but a nuisance otherwise. (The Kite Shop in Victoria Wharf at the V&A Waterfront has many colorful, high-tech numbers for sale.) Kite surfing has become extremely popular, and adrenaline junkies blow off work to come here and ride the waves. For safety, swim in front of the lifeguard club. The lawns of the Blue Peter Hotel are a favorite sunset cocktail spot, especially with tired kite- and windsurfers. ⊠ *N1 north to R27 to Milnerton and Bloubergstrand, Blouberg.*

Camps Bay Beach. The spectacular western edge of Table Mountain, known as the Twelve Apostles, provides the backdrop for this long, sandy beach that slopes gently to the very cold water from a grassy verge. Playing Frisbee or volleyball is very popular on this beach. The surf is powerful, but sunbathers can cool off in a tidal pool or under cool outdoor showers. The popular bars and restaurants of Camps Bay lie only yards away across Victoria Road. One drawback is the wind, which can blow hard here. It's also a popular vacation resort for Cape Town's models, movie stars, and the rich and famous; some people find it pretentious. ⊠ *Victoria Rd., Camps Bay* Ⓜ *Hout Bay bus from OK Bazaars on Adderley St.*

★ **Clifton Beach.** A fantastic beach area that's almost always wind-free, this is where the in crowd comes to see and be seen. Some of the Cape's most desirable houses cling to the slopes above the beach, and elegant yachts often anchor in the calm water beyond the breakers. Granite outcroppings divide the beach into four segments, unimaginatively known as First, Second, Third, and Fourth beaches. Fourth Beach is popular with families, whereas the others support a strong social and singles' scene. Swimming is reasonably safe here, although the undertow is strong and the water, again, freezing. Lifeguards are on duty on weekends and in peak season. During holidays Clifton can be a madhouse, and your chances of finding parking at these times are nil. If you plan to visit the beaches in midsummer, consider renting a scooter or motorcycle instead of a car, taking a shuttle from your hotel, or going early in the morning, when the beautiful people are still sleeping off their champagne from the night before. Clifton is also a favorite for sundowners and picnics, but take care with containers, as officially alcohol on this beach is prohibited. ⊠ *Off Victoria Rd., Clifton* Ⓜ *Hout Bay bus from OK Bazaars on Adderley St.*

Hout Bay Beach. Cradled in a lovely bay of the same name and guarded by a 1,000-foot peak known as the Sentinel, Hout Bay is the center of Cape Town's crayfishing industry, and the town operates several fish-processing plants. It also has knockout views of the mountains, gentle surf, and easy access to the restaurants and bars of Mariner's Wharf. Unfortunately, however, because this is a working harbor, the beach can be polluted, and the water often has an oily film on the surface. You are advised not to swim here.

If you're getting hungry, head to Mariner's Wharf, which is Hout Bay's salty answer to the Waterfront in Cape Town. You can buy fresh fish at a seafood market and take it outside to be grilled. You should also try *snoek,* a barracuda-like fish that is traditionally eaten smoked. Cruise boats *(⇨ Boat Tours, in Planning, at the beginning of the chapter)* depart from Hout Bay's harbor to view the Cape fur seal colony on Duiker Island. ⊠ *Off the M6, Hout Bay* Ⓜ *Hout Bay bus from OK Bazaars on Adderley St.*

★ **Llandudno Beach.** Die-hard fans return to this beach again and again, and who can blame them? Its setting, among giant boulders at the base of a mountain, is glorious, and sunsets here attract their own aficionados. The surf can be very powerful on the northern side of the beach (where you'll find all the surfers, of course), but the southern side is fine for a quick dip—and in this water that's all you'll want.

SPOTTING SHARKS

Shark spotters are employed at several of Cape Town's beaches to warn bathers when sharks are out and about. Great white sharks are usually found close to the shore in the summer months (September–March), and spotters record around 170 sightings per year.

Lifeguards are on duty on weekends and in season. If you come by bus, brace yourself for a long walk down (and back up) the mountain from the bus stop on the M6. Parking is a nightmare, but most hotels run shuttles in summer. ⊠ *Llandudno exit off M6, Llandudno* Ⓜ *Hout Bay bus from OK Bazaars on Adderley St.*

Long Beach. A vast expanse of white sand stretching 6½ km (4 mi) from the base of Chapman's Peak to Kommetjie, this is one of the wildest and least populated beaches, backed by a lagoon and private nature reserve. Because of the wind and the space, it attracts horseback riders and walkers rather than sunbathers, and the surfing is excellent. There are no lifeguards and there is no bus service, and, as at some other beaches, there are real safety concerns. Despite patrollers on horseback and an all-terrain vehicle, crime is an issue here, and women in particular should be careful. You'd do well not to visit this beach unless it is well populated. ⊠ *Off M6, Noordhoek.*

FALSE BAY COAST
⇨ *For Boulders Beach, see Cape Peninsula Top Attractions, above.*

☾ **Fish Hoek Beach.** With the southern corner protected from the southeaster by Elsies Peak, this sandy beach attracts retirees and families with young kids, who appreciate the calm, clear water—it may be the safest bathing beach in the Cape, although sharks are sighted fairly regularly in the bay between September and March (though that doesn't stop people from swimming, surfing, and boogie boarding here); shark spotters are employed to keep an eye out. The middle and northern end of the beach are also popular with catamaran sailors and windsurfers, who often stage regattas offshore. Jager's Walk, from the south side of Fish Hoek Beach to Sunny Cove, is a pleasant, scenic, wheelchair-friendly pathway that meanders through the rocks, providing access to some sheltered natural rock pools that are just great for swimming. The snorkeling is good, and it's a great beach for boogie boarding. It's also one of the best places to see whales during calving season—approximately August to November—though there have been whale sightings as early as June and as late as January. Outside of peak traffic, it takes about 40 minutes to get from Cape Town to Fish Hoek, but over Christmas and New Year's the roads get very congested, so leave early to miss the crowds. ⊠ *Beach Rd., Fish Hoek.*

ↂ **Muizenberg Beach.** Once the fashionable resort of South African high society, this long, sandy beach has, unfortunately, lost much of its glamour and now appeals to families and beginner surfers. Surf shops offering lessons and rental boards and wet suits line the beachfront. A tacky pavilion houses a swimming pool, waterslides, toilets, changing rooms, and snack shops. The beach is lined with colorful bathing boxes of the type once popular at British resorts. Lifeguards are on duty, and the sea is shallow and reasonably safe. Many of the beautiful art-deco beachfront buildings that were fast becoming slums have been renovated into upscale apartments. New restaurants like the popular Knead (and great Sinnful ice-cream shop next door) have opened, and property prices are soaring. If you're keen on stretching your legs, you can walk along the beach or take the picturesque concrete path known as the Catwalk, which connects Muizenberg to St. James. ✉ *Off the M4, Muizenberg.*

WHERE TO EAT

Updated by
Brian Berkman

Cape Town is the culinary capital of South Africa. Nowhere else in the country is the populace so discerning about food, and nowhere else is there such a wide selection of restaurants. Western culinary history here dates back more than 350 years—Cape Town was founded specifically to grow food—and that heritage is reflected in the city's cuisine. A number of restaurants operate in historic town houses and 18th-century wine estates, and many include heritage dishes on their menus.

Today dining in the city and its suburbs can offer a truly global culinary experience, since Cape chefs are now showing the same enthusiasm for global trends as their counterparts worldwide. French and Italian food has long been available here, but in the last decade, with the introduction of Thai and Pan-Asian flavors, locals have embraced the chili. Kurdish, Pakistani, Persian, Ethiopian, Lebanese, and regional Chinese cuisines are now easily available, and other Asian fare is commonplace. Sushi is ubiquitous. If there is a cuisine trend it is toward organic produce and healthful dishes made with foams rather than creams.

WINE

Wine lists at many restaurants reflect the enormous expansion and resurgence of the Cape wine industry, with some establishments compiling exciting selections of lesser-known gems. More and more restaurants employ a sommelier to offer guidance on wine, but diners, even in modest establishments, can expect staff to be well versed about both wine lists and menus. Wines are expensive in restaurants (often three times what you'd pay in a wineshop), and connoisseurs are often irritated at corkage charges (around R25). Only a handful of restaurants will refuse to open a bottle you bring, often the same ones that refuse to provide tap water despite its being perfectly potable.

TIMING AND WHAT TO WEAR

During summer months restaurants in trendier areas are geared up for late-night dining but will accept dinner orders from about 6. In winter locals tend to dine earlier, but there are venues that stay open late, particularly at the Waterfront and the strip along the main road between

BEST BETS FOR CAPE TOWN DINING

With many restaurants to choose from, how will you decide where to eat? Fodor's writers and editors have selected their favorite restaurants by price, cuisine, and experience in the lists below. Fodor's Choice properties represent the "best of the best" in every price category. You can also search by neighborhood—just peruse our reviews on the following pages.

Fodor's Choice★

Aubergine, $$$$, p. 87
bizerca, $$, p. 85
La Colombe, $$$$, p. 98
Myoga, $$$, p. 99
Nobu, $$$, p. 89

By Price

¢

Birds Boutique Café, p. 84
Cafe Orca, p. 94
Giovanni's Deliworld, p. 88
Ocean Basket, p. 87
Raith Gourmet, p. 88

$

Café Roux , p. 100
Olympia Café, p. 101
Mano's, p. 89

$$

bizerca, p. 85
Carne SA, p. 85
Food Barn & Deli, p. 100

95 Keerom, p. 86
Salt, p. 96

$$$

Catharina's, p. 97
Constantia Uitsig, p. 97
Ginja, p. 85
Maze, p. 89
Myoga, p. 99
Nobu, p. 89

$$$$

Aubergine, p. 87
Buitenverwachting, p. 96
Haiku, p. 85
Jardine, p. 86
La Colombe, p. 98

By Cuisine

SOUTH AFRICAN

Africa Cafe, $$, p. 84
Azure, $$$$, p. 93
Cape Malay, $$$$, p. 97
Jonkershuis, $, p. 98
Signal, $$$, p. 93

SEAFOOD

Belthazar, $$$, p. 88
Cafe Orca, ¢, p. 94
Harbour House, $$$, p. 101
Panama Jack's, $$, p. 92
Pigalle, $$$$, p. 92

By Experience

BUSINESS

Aubergine, $$$$, p. 87
Constantia Uitsig, $$$, p. 97
La Colombe, $$$$, p. 98
95 Keerom, $$, p. 86
Savoy Cabbage, $$$, p. 86

QUIET

Aubergine, $$$$, p. 87
Buitenverwachting, p. 96
Constantia Uitsig, $$$, p. 97
Savoy Cabbage, $$$, p. 86

GREAT SEA VIEW

Azure, $$$$, p. 93
Black Marlin, $$, p. 99
Harbour House, $$$, p. 101
Salt, $$, p. 96

CHILD-FRIENDLY

Cafe Orca, ¢, p. 94
Café Roux, $, p. 100
Food Barn & Deli, $$, p. 100
Jonkershuis, $, p. 98
Ocean Basket, ¢, p. 87

MOST ROMANTIC

Atlantic, $$, p. 88
Azure, $$$$, p. 93
Cape Colony, $$, p. 87
La Colombe, $$$$, p. 98
Pigalle, $$$$, p. 92

QUICK LUNCH

Birds Boutique Café, ¢, p. 84
Empire Cafe, ¢, p. 100
Giovanni's Deliworld, ¢, p. 88
Mano's, $, p. 89
Raith Gourmet, ¢, p. 88

BEST BREAKFAST

Atlantic, $$, p. 88
Azure, $$$$, p. 93
Catharina's, $$$, p. 97
Maze, $$$, p. 89
River Café, $, p. 99

the city and Green Point. Other areas that are meccas for food lovers include Kloof Street (dubbed Restaurant Mile) in the City Bowl and the beachfront road in Camps Bay along the Atlantic seaboard. Many restaurants are crowded in high season, so it's best to book in advance whenever possible. With the exception of the fancier hotel restaurants—where a jacket is suggested—the dress code in Cape Town is casual (but no shorts).

⇨ For more information on South Africa food, see Flavors of South Africa, in Chapter 1.

WHAT IT COSTS IN SOUTH AFRICAN RAND					
	¢	$	$$	$$$	$$$$
Restaurants	under R75	R75–R100	R101–R125	R126–R140	over R140

Prices are per person for a main course at dinner, a main course equivalent, or a prix-fixe meal.

The restaurants below are marked on the Where to Eat and Stay in Cape Town map.

CAPE TOWN CENTRAL

$$

AFRICAN

✕ **Africa Cafe.** Tourist oriented it may be, but it would nevertheless be a pity to miss out on this vibrant restaurant in a historic 18th-century former home, with its African decor and city views. Fresh-fruit cocktails accompany a communal feast, with dishes originating from Ethiopia to Zambia, from Kenya to Angola. There are no starters or entrées, but rather a tasty series of patties, puffs, and pastries accompanied by addictive dips, along with dishes like Bostwanan *seswaa masala,* a game-meat curry traditionally served at weddings and funerals, and an East African *mchicha wa nazi* (spinach cooked in a coconut milk sauce). Vegetarian dishes are plentiful, including the Soweto *chakalaka* (a fiery cooked-vegetable relish). Poppy seed cake with vanilla ice cream is the prix-fixe dessert. The cost of this colorful prix-fixe abundance is R125 per person. Wines from Cape estates are available, or you can ask for *umqomboti* beer, brewed from sorghum or millet. ⊠ *Heritage Square, 108 Shortmarket St., Cape Town Central* ☎ *021/422–0221* ⊕ *www. africacafe.co.za* ⊟ *AE, DC, MC, V* ⊙ *Closed Sun. No lunch.*

¢

CAFÉ

✕ **Birds Boutique Café.** There's something so charming about this café that most diners are willing to overlook the discomfort of sitting on plastic milk crates or sharing a roughly hewn trestle table with other patrons. Bird-song records play, bird images abound, and the German owners roost over patrons like tall cranes. However inexplicable, it's so delightful that people tend to stay far longer than they intend. Teas are served sprouting fresh herbs and twigs, and for the most part salads and quiches incorporate organic produce. The chicken pie shaped like an egg is legendary, and the butternut-squash-and-feta quiche is delicious, as is the wide selection of salads. Chocolate scones, like everything at Birds, are made daily and written up on the chalkboard menu or scrawled on poster paper. A large selection of sugar-free and wheat-free items impresses diabetics. ☒ *127 Bree St., Cape Town Central* ☎ *021/426–2534* ▤ *AE, DC, MC, V* ☻ *Closed weekends. No dinner.*

$$ ✗ **bizerca.** Here, it's all about the food, and diners will encounter superb cuisine in a monochromatic bistro setting. The raw Norwegian salmon salad is enlivened by ginger and soy flavors before being dressed in a sauce of finely minced shallots in butter with reduced meat stock. The braised pig trotter with a seared scallop and truffle oil is a triumph. Served off the bone and encased in a crispy caul-fat envelope, it delivers taste and texture. Culinary magic transforms chicken into a dish that invokes the best childhood memories of when chicken tasted wholesome and delicious. The dish is served with corn, coriander polenta, asparagus, and tomato salsa. A red-pepper sauce is the final flavor accent. Atmosphere at lunch is better than dinner. ☒ *Jetty St., Foreshore* ☎ *021/418–0001* ⊕ *www.bizerca.com* ⌕ *Reservations essential* ▤ *MC, V* ☻ *Closed Sun. No lunch Sat.*

FRENCH

Fodor'sChoice

★

$$ ✗ **Carne SA.** Sister to the acclaimed 95 Keerom and directly across the way, this is carnivore heaven. Beef and lamb come directly from the owner's farm in the Karoo, which is certified organic. Interiors are blond-wood tables and Philippe Starck ghost chairs—a clean plate for the meat. Start with the ravioli of slow-cooked lamb shoulder in brown butter or kudu (venison) tartar. Adventurous palates should try the offal—the sweetbreads and kidneys are very good—as an intermediary course. Don't neglect grilled steak or lamb chops. The T-bone is a classic meal-for-two, but lighter cuts like the hanger steak, drawn from near the kidneys, are hard to find elsewhere. Mashed potato, matchstick fries, or green beans with garlic are perfect side dishes. For dessert there's a cheese trolley to pick from if the crema cotta (baked cream) or legendary chocolate soufflé don't entice. ☒ *70 Keerom St., Cape Town Central* ☎ *021/424–3460* ⊕ *www.carne-sa.com* ⌕ *Reservations essential* ▤ *AE, DC, MC, V* ☻ *Closed Sun. No lunch.*

ITALIAN

$$$ ✗ **Ginja.** Ginja's position in the culinary firmament is well deserved, but it does mean advance booking and dining at one of two sittings staggered from 7 PM during high season. Order the Around the World in a Spoon starter from the eclectic menu: six delicious mouthfuls, from eggplant with Parmesan to avocado sushi with ginger. Springbok Wellington with caramelized red cabbage and green beans is a delicious main course. End with chocolate-cherry parfait or lemon meringue with a twist. Service is slick, and the narrow entrance corridor, red walls, and black-and-white images of forks hint at the drama to unfold. Watch your step as you enter. ☒ *70 New Church St., Gardens* ☎ *083/578–7502* ⌕ *Reservations essential* ▤ *AE, DC, MC, V* ☻ *Closed Sun. No lunch.*

ECLECTIC

★

$$$$ ✗ **Haiku.** This is still the best Pan-Asian restaurant in town, and it's worth putting up with the waiting lists, multiple seatings, and a complex menu of dim sum, sushi, and wok-fried items. A tip: allow your server to order for you, though we do suggest starting with steamed scallop *siu mai* (a traditional Chinese dumpling) with salmon roe for tongue fireworks. The Peking duck with paper-thin pancakes is delicious. Grills include mint lamb chops served with dry red chilies and garlic. On the sushi menu, the salmon roses—thin sashimi curls filled with mayonnaise and topped with pink caviar—are outstanding. Four kitchens mean

ASIAN

★

2

that dishes arrive when ready. Although this provides the freshest dining experience, it may mean fellow diners watch while you eat, or vice versa. The owners of Haiku also own Bukhara, the excellent Indian restaurant above it. There's a minimum per person of R170. ⊠ *33 Burg St., Cape Town Central* ☎ *021/424–7000* ⊕ *www.haikurestaurant.com* ⚶ *Reservations essential* ☰ *AE, DC, MC, V* ☺ *No lunch Sun.*

$$$$ ✕ **Jardine.** Highly acclaimed for its tasting menu and signature Cape lob-
ECLECTIC   ster risotto, you can also expect slow-cooked pork belly with star anise
★   or rib-eye with braised ox cheek bourguignon and dauphinoise potato on the ever-changing menu. The tasting menu contains experimental dishes like cauliflower foam over crispy duck. While some complain about the noise that reflects off many hard surfaces, others consider it the best place to eat in the city. The best croissant and coffee is at its adjoining Jardine Bakery on Bloem Street. ⊠ *185 Bree St., Cape Town Central* ☎ *021/424–5640* ⊕ *www.jardineonbree.co.za* ⚶ *Reservations essential* ☰ *AE, DC, MC, V* ☺ *Closed Sun. No lunch.*

$$ ✕ **95 Keerom.** Chef-owner Giorgio Nava is so passionate about using
ITALIAN   only the finest ingredients that he catches his own fish and farms his own
★   beef. Diners will be hard-pressed to find better Milanese cuisine. The paper-thin beef carpaccio "95" is drizzled with homemade mayonnaise and topped with fresh arugula and Parmesan shavings. When Nava manages to catch tuna, he serves it seared with cherry tomatoes, capers, and olives. The butternut-squash-filled ravioli with brown sage butter is sublime, and the soft-centered chocolate soufflé is the benchmark for every other. With its bentwood chairs, the upstairs interior is Eames-inspired; downstairs, the exposed stone reveals the building's ancient history, which began in 1682. ⊠ *95 Keerom St., Cape Town Central* ☎ *021/422–0765* ⊕ *www.95keerom.com* ⚶ *Reservations essential* ☰ *AE, DC, MC, V* ☺ *Closed Sun. Lunch Thurs. and Fri. only.*

$$$ ✕ **Savoy Cabbage.** Heritage Square, with its near-crumbling brick walls
ECLECTIC   and original timber ceilings, is one of the oldest inner-city spaces, dating from the late 18th century. Today it houses a fine hotel and many good eateries, including the Savoy Cabbage, which attracts business deal-makers during the day and serious foodies by night. The place is famous for its themed events, where winemakers or opera-house stars make an evening of it, and mini-festivals such as chef Peter Pankhurst's paean to offal for an entire week in winter. Expect high-level service from the mostly career waiters. The menu changes daily, but the focus is on organic ingredients whenever possible, especially game. Beef fillet is served on a potato cake with onions cooked in red wine sauce. The fish of the day might be prepared with beetroot mash and braised leek and parsley sauce. Brine-cured warthog is paired with sour fig sauce, and other game is often served with port sauce and spaetzle. ⊠ *101 Hout St., Cape Town Central* ☎ *021/424–2626* ⊕ *www.savoycabbage.co.za* ☰ *AE, DC, MC, V* ☺ *Closed Sun. No lunch Sat.*

GARDENS

$$$$
ECLECTIC
Fodor'sChoice
★

✕**Aubergine.** Aubergine's timber-and-glass interior matches chef-owner Harald Bresselschmidt's classic-with-a-twist cuisine. A beaded Strelitzia flower in the entrance hall is a clue to what will come: South African produce, prepared with strong classical methods that echo the Austrian chef's roots, surprises and requires a closer look. This is serious cuisine. You may notice yourself sitting more upright than usual—not because of stuffiness or any pretentious formality, but out of respect for the food. There is a superb wine selection, and servers double as sommeliers. The fish on the menu is line-caught—never frozen. Yellowtail (a fleshy local catch) is poached in saffron and served with a beetroot sorbet and fennel salad. Heartier options include pork and pancetta pralines with cumin cabbage and blue-cheese wontons. The highly recommended surprise du chef selection of mini-desserts might include melon soup with wine gelée and rhubarb sorbet, chocolate fondant with cherry ragout, crème brûlée, magnificent apricot linzer tartlet, and passion-fruit ice-parfait with deep-fried chocolate. Although showered with every award possible, the Cinq à Sept (served between 5 and 7 in the evening) is unexpectedly affordable with a median price of R80. ⊠ *39 Barnet St., Gardens* ☎ *021/465–4909* ⊕ *www.aubergine.co.za* ⚓ *Reservations essential* ☐ *AE, DC, MC, V* ⊗ *Closed Sun. No lunch Mon., Tues., and Sat.*

$$
ECLECTIC

✕**Cape Colony Restaurant.** There's a new chef at the helm of this elegant restaurant, one of the most glamorous rooms in the city. The tall bay windows, a high domed ceiling, and a giant trompe-l'oeil mural of Table Mountain creates a fitting setting for the city's most unashamedly colonial hotel. This is a good place to come for a stylish night out, enhanced by a band. Although the menu changes regularly, expect geranium (fynbos) and lemon–cured salmon with prawn and avocado salad, or *naartjie* (local citrus) and *rooibos-* (bush tea–) smoked duck breast with *vetkoek* (deep-fried savory pastry), *moskonfyt* (sugar-preserved melon often flavored with ginger), and duck rillette (shredded confit). Game is in the form of springbok, where the loin is honey glazed and cooked with beetroot. The dish is served with a shank pie, butternut-squash puree and a chakalaka-stuffed onion. ⊠ *Mount Nelson Hotel, 76 Orange St., Gardens* ☎ *021/483 1000* ⚓ *Reservations essential* ☐ *AE, DC, MC, V.*

¢
SEAFOOD
☾

✕**Ocean Basket.** On Restaurant Mile along the city fringe, this informal spot has few competitors in the field of bargain-price, ocean-fresh, well-cooked seafood. You can sit facing the street or find a table in the courtyard, complete with a fountain, at the back. Calamari—stewed, grilled, pickled, or in a salad—features prominently among the starters, which include a mezes selection. The catch of the day is listed on the many blackboards lining the mustard-yellow walls, but delicately flavored hake-and-chips is the budget draw card. Standard entrées range from excellent Cajun-style grilled calamari to a huge seafood platter for two. Prices for the seafood platters and crayfish run higher than for other dishes. Tartar, chili, and garlic sauces come on the side, and Greek salads are authentic. Desserts are average. ⊠ *75 Kloof St., Gardens* ☎ *021/422–0322* ☐ *AE, DC, MC, V.*

¢   ✕ **Raith Gourmet.** So much German is spoken by patrons here it's easy
GERMAN   to forget you're in Cape Town. People come to this pristine deli for
the largest selection of raw sausages and authentic German breads and
also for the great value ready-made lunches. Expect pea or potato-and-
leek soups as standards and single-plate items like farmer's omelets or
smoked pork chops. It's easy to get carried away and ratchet up the bill
while selecting cheeses and imported meats, so beware. Ask the helpful servers to slice your bread, cut a selection of cheese and meats, and
package some salads for an impromptu picnic in the Company Gardens
nearby. Another option is to grab a coffee and ready-made salami-and-
mozzarella roll. Don't miss the barrel sauerkraut or selection of pickled
gherkins. ⊠ *Shop 38, Gardens Centre, Mill St., Gardens* ☎ *021/465–
2729* ⊕ *www.raithgourmet.com* ☰ *AE, DC, MC, V* ☉ *No dinner.*

V&A WATERFRONT

$$ ✕ **Atlantic.** The elegant flagship restaurant at the luxurious Table Bay
ECLECTIC   Hotel holds a prime position at the city's waterfront. On balmy eve-
nings diners seated on the terrace have stunning views of working docks
against a mountain backdrop. A tower starter of citrus-marinated
salmon with blood orange and ruby grapefruit is as exquisite to look
at as it is to eat, while duck breast is set on red-onion marmalade with
butternut-squash gnocchi and béarnaise sauce, braised red cabbage,
and pumpkin chips. Vegetarians will enjoy soups, salads, and pasta
dishes. For the wheat averse, there is a flourless Black Forest gateau
with Kirsch panna cotta and chocolate ice cream. A kumquat compote
cuts the richness. The extensive wine list covers the best of the Cape,
supplemented by a selection of New World labels. The Sunday jazz
lunch is recommended. The Table Bay hotel offers the best breakfast
in town, which is served in the Atlantic restaurant. If you're looking
for a place to celebrate a special occasion, then the formal but friendly
service will make an event of any meal. ⊠ *Table Bay Hotel, Quay 6,
Waterfront* ☎ *021/406–5688* ☰ *AE, DC, MC, V* ☉ *Closed Sun. and
Mon. No lunch.*

$$$ ✕ **Belthazar.** Boasting one of the largest selections of wines by the glass
STEAK   (about 100) in the land, Belthazar is also recommended for its consis-
tently good steak and seafood. Steaks are cut and matured by an in-
house butcher, and a team of sommeliers will recommend the best wine
match for your meal. The springbok fillet served with a chocolate-chili
sauce is a good choice. The Chicago-cut beef is a little more than a
pound of on-the-bone deliciousness. The deep-fried onion blossom is a
visual treat but the creamed spinach or spiced beetroot is a better choice
for a side. Combo steak, prawn, and calamari platters are good options
too. Outside seating under umbrellas (heated in winter) provides views
over the harbor, though it's more comfortable inside. The service is
excellent. ⊠ *Shop 138, V&A Wharf, Waterfront* ☎ *021/421–3753 or
021/421–3756* ⚹ *Reservations essential* ☰ *AE, DC, MC, V.*

¢   ✕ **Giovanni's Deliworld.** Floor-to-ceiling shelves are stacked with every-
CAFÉ   thing delicious from French champagne to stock cubes. Fridges have
fresh pasta dishes and greens, but the deli section and espresso bar is
where most will congregate. At possibly the oldest deli in the area,

locals jostle for a seat with models and film-industry folk who come for the coffee and vibe. While a little chaotic at peak times and not especially comfortable to eat at the raised counters, it shouldn't be missed. There might be Italian meatballs with spaghetti or Thai plum chicken on offer. There's always a wide selection of hams and cold cuts as well as global cheeses. Get anything from pumpkin-seed rolls to fresh-cut flowers and the daily newspaper. And it's just a block away from the soccer stadium. ⊠ *103 Main Rd., Green Point* ☎ *021/434–6893* ▭ *AE, DC, MC, V* ⊘ *No dinner.*

$ ✕**Mano's.** A chic city diner serving good, unpretentious, and reasonably
CAFÉ   priced crowd-pleasers, Mano's is the perfect spot for a relaxed evening with friends. Start with grilled calamari or share one of the huge salads. The bacon, avocado, and blue cheese salad is about as decadent as a salad gets. A healthier option is the fresh flavors of the Greek peasant salad—chopped cucumber, feta, tomatoes, and olives. The prawn curry is subtle and delicately spiced, and the fillet in a creamy béarnaise is perfectly cooked. A good and well-priced wine list, and great cocktails from the swanky bar, are no doubt also responsible for the lively buzz coming from big groups and couples alike. Efficient, competent service will keep you coming back for more. ⊠ *39 Main Rd., Green Point* ☎ *021/434–1090* ⊕ *www.mano.co.za* ▭ *AE, DC, MC, V* ⊘ *Closed Sun.*

$$$ ✕**Maze.** Gordon Ramsay's first restaurant in Africa is a combination of
BRITISH   Ramsay's other restaurants Gordon Ramsay Maze and Gordon Ramsay
★   Maze Grill. Guests enter through a glass wall with more than 5,000 wine bottles into a vast three-story space of contemporary chandeliers. Start with carpaccio of veal and tuna or share items tapas-style. The white-onion risotto is very good. The menu is varied with crowd-pleasers such as a sensational Caesar salad with the option of butter-poached chicken breast or Cape lobster (crayfish) tail. Meat—local, Namibian and Australian Wagyu beef (among the most costly and tender in the world)—is cooked over coal before being broiled. Sides are extra but the thin-cut chips with garlic and sherry-cooked mushrooms are both must-haves. Order the Assiette of Maze desserts to share, bite-size portions of nearly the entire dessert menu. ⊠ *One&Only Cape Town, Dock Rd., Waterfront* ☎ *021/431–5222* ⊕ *www.oneandonlyresorts. com* ⚄ *Reservations essential* ▭ *AE, DC, MC, V.*

$$$ ✕**Nobu.** Exceptional new-style Japanese cuisine with a South American
JAPANESE   twist has recently come to Cape Town. Guests dine in a vast hall-like
Fodor's Choice   restaurant with ceilings more than three stories high. With no views to
★   speak of, food is always the main event. If budget allows, the Omakase seven-course tasting menu is the way to go for a culinary and visual surprise that takes into account personal dietary restrictions. It is equally delicious to order à la carte. Costly Alaskan black cod and Australian Wagyu (similar to beer-fed Kobe beef) aside, the menu is largely affordable. The sake-roasted kingklip (firm local white fish) with Sansho salsa is excellent. If you're lucky you'll be served by staff from one of the other more established Nobu venues, which will only add to the remarkable dining experience. There is a stellar selection of sake and, of course, excellent local wines. ⊠ *One&Only Cape Town, Dock Rd.,*

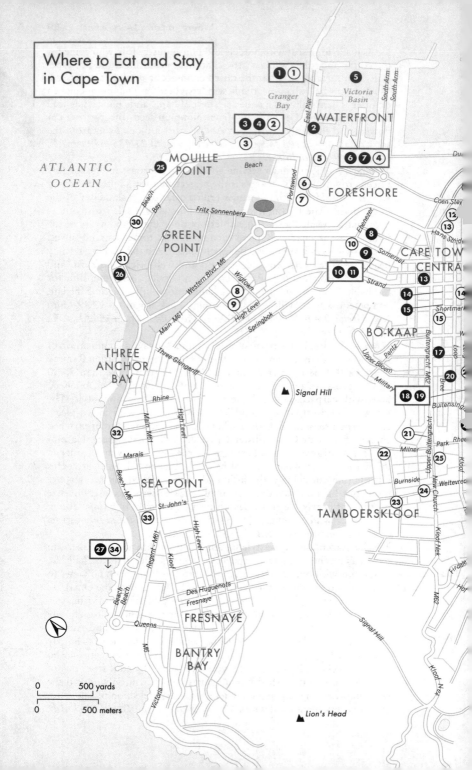

Where to Eat and Stay in Cape Town

ATLANTIC OCEAN

Granger Bay

Victoria Basin

WATERFRONT

MOUILLE POINT

Beach

FORESHORE

GREEN POINT

Fritz Sonnenberg

CAPE TOWN CENTRAL

BO-KAAP

THREE ANCHOR BAY

Signal Hill

SEA POINT

TAMBOERSKLOOF

FRESNAYE

BANTRY BAY

Lion's Head

0   500 yards
0   500 meters

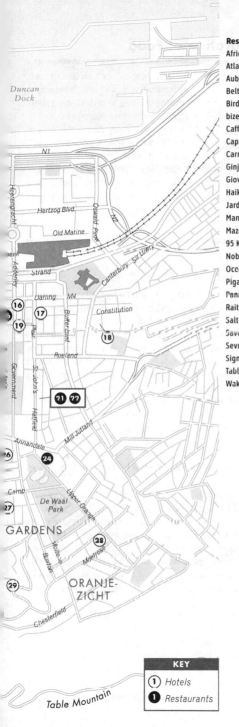

① Hotels
● Restaurants

Restaurants ▼		Hotels ▼	
Africa Cafe	15	Adderley Hotel	19
Atlantic	1	Best Western Cape Suites Hotel	18
Aubergine	22	Cape Grace	4
Belthazar	5	Cape Heritage Hotel	15
Birds Boutique Café	17	Cape Milner Hotel	22
bizerca	12	Cape Town Backpack	21
Caffe Neo	26	Cape Victoria Guest House	8
Cape Colony Restaurant	21	The Commodore Hotel	7
Carne SA	19	Daddy Long Legs Boutique Hotel	20
Ginja	13	Dock House	6
Giovanni's Deliworld	9	Dolphin Inn	30
Haiku	16	Ellerman House	34
Jardine	20	Kensington Place	29
Mano's	10	La Splendida Luxury Suites	31
Maze	4	La Villa Belle Ombre	23
95 Keerom	18	The Grand Daddy	14
Nobu	3	Mandela Rhodes Place	16
Ocean Basket	23	More Cape Cadogan	24
Pigalle	11	Mount Nelson Hotel	26
Panama Jack's	6	One&Only Cape Town	2
Raith Gourmet	24	Peninsula All Suites Hotel	33
Salt	27	Protea Fire & Ice	25
Savoy Cabbage	14	Protea Hotel North Wharf	13
Sevruga	2	Protea Hotel Victoria Junction	10
Signal Restaurant	7	Radisson Blu Hotel	3
Table Thirteen	8	Romney Park Hotel & Spa	9
Wakame	25	Southern Sun Cullinan Cape Town Waterfront	12
		Table Bay Hotel	1
		Townhouse Hotel	17
		Victoria & Alfred Hotel	5
		Villa Belmonte	28
		Welgelegen Guest House	27
		Westin Grand Arabella Quays Hotel Cape Town	11
		Winchester Mansions Hotel	32

2

CLOSE UP

A Cape Town Celebration of Food

The **Gourmet Festival** (☎ 021/797–4500 ⊕ www.gourmetsa.com) is an exclamation mark on the Cape culinary calendar. The festival usually begins in mid-May with the announcement of the Swiss Air wine awards, followed by the Table of Unity—a fund-raising dinner on the slopes of Table Mountain. The last weekend in May, thousands visit the Good Food and Wine Show at the International Convention Centre for three days of foodie exhibitions and presentations by international celebrity (TV) chefs, cooking courses, wine tastings, coffee salons, and more. Food-related events throughout the city during this period in May include special-priced menus at restaurants to coax hibernating locals out as the chill of winter sets in. The festival culminates with a gala banquet prepared by a team of the visiting and local chefs.

Waterfront ☎ *021/431–5111* ⊕ *www.oneandonlyresorts.com* ⚘ *Reservations essential* ▤ *AE, DC, MC, V* ☉ *No lunch.*

$$
SEAFOOD
✕ **Panama Jack's.** In this raw-timber structure in the heart of the docks, about 3 mi north of other V&A venues, the music is loud, the tables are crowded, and the decor is nonexistent, but nowhere in town will you find bigger crayfish. Your choice, made from large open tanks, is weighed before being grilled or steamed. Expect to pay upwards of R515 per kilogram for this delicacy and a whopping R1,100 a kilogram for the scarce and endangered wild abalone, which is being poached nearly to extinction. Large prawns range in price from R250 for 10 to about R77 each for Mozambique langoustines. There is plenty of less expensive seafood as well, and daily specials such as baby squid and local line-caught fish are competitively priced. It can be difficult to find this place at night, so you may want to come for lunch, which is far more affordable, if it's your first visit. ⊠ *Quay 500, Waterfront* ☎ *021/447–3992* ⊕ *www.panamajacks.net* ▤ *AE, DC, MC, V* ☉ *No lunch Sat.*

$$$$
SEAFOOD
✕ **Pigalle.** Entering this plush venue graced with art-nouveau fixtures, huge chandeliers, and a wall of Andy Warhol Elvis reproductions transports one to an otherworldly realm. Spectacular shellfish and Portuguese spicing are the draws here. Though the lobster thermidor with black cherries is fabulous, the simple perfection of grilled langoustines basted with lemon-garlic or peri-peri (chili sauce) can't be beat. The scallops with spring-onion risotto are heavenly, and steaks are good too. Though open for lunch, do yourself a favor and come for dinner when a jazz band croons Sinatra-esque tunes, turning up the tempo for twirling couples as the evening progresses. Exceptional waiters complete this uniquely enjoyable experience. ⊠ *57A Somerset Rd., Green Point* ☎ *021/421–4848* ⊕ *www.pigallerestaurants.co.za* ⚘ *Reservations essential* ▤ *AE, DC, MC, V* ☉ *Closed Sun.*

$$$$
SEAFOOD
✕ **Sevruga.** In a prime quayside location on Cape Town's busy Waterfront, swank Sevruga (sister restaurant to popular Beluga) offers upscale dining with a menu that has something for everyone. The tome-like

menu bursts with an almost overwhelming array of culinary options and an impressive wine list. The sushi is fresh and inventive, and other seafood options are fresh, local catches typically grilled with mashed potato, tomato salsa, and lemon crème fraiche. Not up for fruits of the sea? A huge variety of signature dishes like truffle beef fillet or the slow-roasted lamb with white beans and potato dumplings is offered. With its modern-elegant atmosphere and key location, Sevruga is a popular choice. ⊠ *Shop 4, Quay 5, Victoria Wharf Waterfront* ☎ *021/421–5134* ⊕ *www.sevruga.co.za* ▤ *AE, D, DC, MC, V.*

2

$$$ ✕ **Signal Restaurant.** Housed in Cape Town's gorgeous Cape Grace Hotel, newly opened Signal Restaurant caters to all guests with its accommodating hours and a menu featuring both international and "Cape" cuisine. Reflecting the area's multiculturalism, Signal's kitchen blends Malay and Indian-influenced Cape cuisine with numerous French, Asian, and English options. Classics like the mouthwatering slow-cooked Karoo lamb shoulder and divine passion-fruit gratin flout conventional wisdom regarding cuisine at large hotels. Aged yellow-wood furniture, crisp white linens, and handcrafted chandeliers create a warm and understated elegance. Breakfast in the light-filled conservatory is worthwhile, even if you're not sleeping over. In keeping with Cape Grace standards, service is impeccable. ⊠ *Cape Grace Hotel, West Quay Rd., Waterfront* ☎ *021/410–7080* ⊕ *www.capegrace.com* ▤ *AE, DC, MC, V.*

ECLECTIC

¢ ✕ **Table Thirteen.** Marble-topped wrought-iron bistro tables, comfy wood chairs, multiple chandeliers, and other objects are all for sale as part of adjacent interiors shop T&CO. For this reason, and its proximity to the headquarters of a magazine publisher, regulars are mainly media and design folk who treat it as a meeting place and canteen. Food is fresh. The smell of freshly baked goods makes it very difficult to resist the large display of cakes and cookies. For more filling meals there's a small menu of salads, but it's the daily deli offering of three or four warm dishes that deserves the most attention. Specials are entirely seasonal and you can expect hearty fish chowder or Moroccan chicken tagine, along with a selection of wholesome sides like caramelized fennel, pomegranate, and feta salad or red onion, thyme, and pine-nut couscous. ⊠ *Unit 78, Victoria Junction, Ebenezer Rd., Green Point* ☎ *021/418–0739* ▤ *AE, DC, MC, V* ☺ *No dinner.*

CAFÉ

ATLANTIC COAST

The restaurants below are marked on the Where to Eat and Stay in Cape Town *and the* Where to Eat and Stay in the Cape Peninsula *maps.*

$$$$ ✕ **Azure.** Blue leather armchairs and crisp white napery confirm the Twelve Apostles Hotel's nautical bent and Azure's smart interior. The menu—with its focus on seafood, game, and the indigenous fynbos plants—works well with views of the Atlantic Ocean as far as the eye can see and Table Mountain. Presented in a martini glass on a bed of greens, the crayfish-and-prawn cocktail is one of the restaurant's signature dishes. The chicken noodle soup, another signature dish, with perogan (mince pie) is delicious. The giant-tiger-prawn tempura, served with chili-

ECLECTIC

tomato salsa and pickled cucumber, is an extravagant feast. Slow-roasted duck comes with roasted potatoes and panfried vegetables, glazed baby apples, and a caramelized citrus reduction. The Cape Malay Curry with chicken and prawns is a good example of regional cuisine that's been given new life. Oversized napkins provide unexpected luxury for messy eaters. ■ TIP➜ Ask for a window table. ✉ *Twelve Apostles Hotel and Spa, Victoria Rd., Camps Bay* ☎ *021/437–9029* ✇ *www.12apostleshotel.com* ⚐ *Reservations essential* ▭ *AE, DC, MC, V.*

¢ ✕ **Cafe Orca.** It may be laid-back and shabby, but this tiny eatery in a for-

SEAFOOD   mer fishing village enjoys views overlooking a stretch of pristine beach. There are salads, burgers, and toasted sandwiches on the menu, but the seafood combos and baskets—which combine fish with calamari, shrimp, mussels, or chicken—are the most popular items. At R229, the seafood platter for two is probably the best bargain of its kind. Don't be tempted to order a garlic-and-cheese roll; you need to save space for what's to come. Service is friendly but can be slow. ✉ *88 Beach Rd., Melkbosstrand* ☎ *021/553–4120* ⚐ *Reservations essential* ▭ *AE, DC, MC, V* ✆ *No dinner Sun. and Tues.*

¢ ✕ **Caffe Neo.** You'll pay more for a sandwich than you should have to

MEDITERRANEAN   here, but the place and people are pretty and the free Wi-Fi is the great appeal. Excellent lighthouse and sea views from the balcony seating is also a great draw, but many people, especially those with computers, favor the long communal table. The shaved turkey sandwich is accept-able, but you'll do better with coffee and a selection of Greek biscuits or a grilled haloumi (a mild and salty Greek cheese) salad. Most over-look the poor service and consider the hipster vibe reason enough to visit. This is a good spot for breakfast. ✉ *129 Beach Rd., Mouille Point* ☎ *021/433–0849* ▭ *AE, DC, MC, V* ✆ *No dinner.*

$$$ ✕ **Paranga.** Attracting models and folks hoping to spot celebrities along

CAFÉ   Camps Bay's beach strip, Paranga is a high-attitude, stylish vantage point and an acceptable place to eat. The terrace is shaded by a Bedouin-style tarpaulin. It's mostly popular with locals for a leisurely weekend breakfast, as the place can get very warm by lunchtime. A wide selec-tion of salads will appeal to most palates. Start with the goat-cheese cake served inside crispy deep-fried *kataifi* (Greek-style shredded phyllo dough) with a spicy chili jam. Kingklip is served with a pineapple salsa, while burgers get fusion treatment with garlic aioli and tomato salsa. The balsamic marinated fillet is deliciously tender. The lounge-style music selection is a focal point, and, as at Ibiza's famed seafront Café del Mar, it's available to purchase. Check menu prices carefully, as some are out of kilter. Reservations are essential for summertime dinners. ✉ *Shop No. 1, The Promenade, Victoria Rd., Camps Bay* ☎ *021/438–0404* ✇ *www.paranga.co.za* ▭ *AE, DC, MC, V.*

$$$$ ✕ **The Round House Restaurant.** Rather than a lion or zebra, the trophy

FRENCH   at this 18th-century Table Mountain–side hunting lodge is fine dining. Start with skate and foie gras terrine with pickled octopus on roasted brioche or gnocchi with braised rabbit before exploring the roasted catch of the day served with baby roasted potatoes, bacon, capers, and a lemon *buerre noisette* sauce. Although the Somerset Room offers sea views, it can be very noisy. The private room for up to eight guests

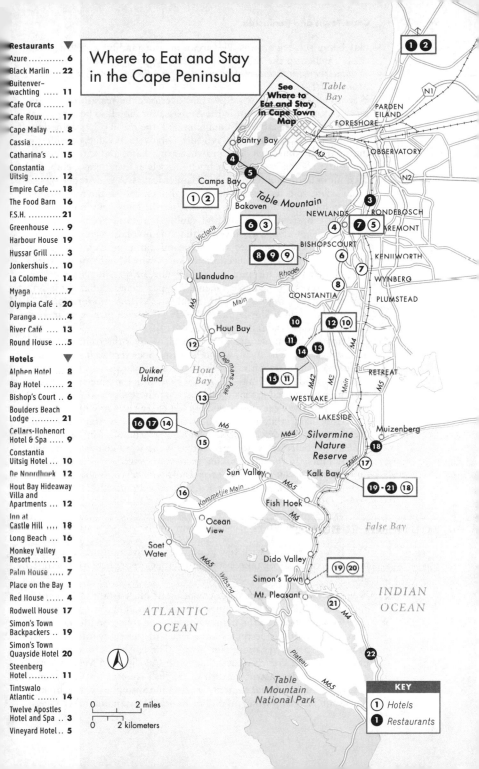

Where to Eat and Stay in the Cape Peninsula

See Where to Eat and Stay in Cape Town Map

KEY

① Hotels
❶ Restaurants

0   2 miles

0   2 kilometers

may better suit big groups. Beware of the outstanding wine list: it can easily ratchet up the bill. ⊠ *The Glen Camps Bay* ☎ *021/438–4347* ⊕ *www.theroundhouserestaurant.com* ⊟ *AE, DC, MC, V* ⊘ *Closed Mon. and Tues.*

$$ ✕ **Salt.** Floor-to-ceiling windows that overlook the sea afford marvel-
ECLECTIC   ous views at this restaurant in the Ambassador Hotel, so be sure to ask for a window-side table. Although limited, the menu offers something for most palates, and the food is a surprisingly good value, considering the smart surroundings. The prawn, Parma ham, and saffron risotto is a hearty starter, as are the steamed mussels in lemongrass, chili, and coconut milk topped with fresh coriander leaves. A wide range of sea-sonal salads suits as a quick lunch; for dinner, choose the more robust venison loin with blue-cheese polenta, mushrooms, and mulled wine. The lentil, butternut squash, and cauliflower curry accompanied by pilaf rice bejeweled with slivered almonds invokes vegetarian India. The plate of cookies, especially the peanut butter and chocolate chip ones, or the mini-dessert selection (to share), which might include sticky toffee bread and butter pudding, a lime tart, or homemade ice cream, are must-haves on the dessert menu. A tapas menu is offered for sun-downers. This is a great spot for breakfast. ⊠ *Ambassador Hotel, 34 Victoria Rd., Bantry Bay* ☎ *021/439–7258* ⊕ *www.saltrestaurant.co.za* ⊜ *Reservations essential* ⊟ *AE, DC, MC, V.*

$$ ✕ **Wakame.** The simple interior allows views over the Atlantic to take
ASIAN   precedence here. The sushi, which Wakame does very well, is sufficient reason to visit. Start with the crispy, fried, salted calamari with hoisin sauce, coriander, and lime. Then move on to the sesame-crusted tuna with ponzu-flavored greens (ponzu is a Japanese citrus-vinegar sauce) with deep-fried sweet potato or Thai red-curry chicken with lime fried rice. Chocolate fondant with a butterscotch sauce or star anise–and–coconut crème brûlée are dessert highlights. Smoking is permitted on the narrow balcony, which means that if the wind changes direction, nearby diners in the nonsmoking section may suffer the smell. Wafu, on the upper level, is excellent for drinks and serves a good dim sum menu. ⊠ *Surry Pl. and Beach Rd., Mouille Point* ☎ *021/433–2377* ⊟ *AE, DC, MC, V.*

SOUTHERN SUBURBS

This is a pricey area with few good, inexpensive options. You'll also need to rent a car or take a taxi just about everywhere you want to go.

$$$$ ✕ **Buitenverwachting.** On a historic wine estate in Constantia, this superb
ECLECTIC   and gracious restaurant occupies a modern building on one side of a
★   grassy court ringed by the manor house, wine cellar, and former slave quarters. Window-side tables have views of the vineyards in serried rows along the lower mountain slopes. The cuisine is innovative but based on strong French basics. Start with Crayfish and Melons for an experimental, deconstructed dish of crayfish ice cream to experience flavors out of their usual context, or select the Springbok with Christine (the estate's flagship wine) jus and *madumbi* (African potato) croquette

for a more traditional main dish. If in season, it might be accompanied by celery root puree and Hanepoot grape chutney. The raspberry soufflé with a parfait is as much a treat for the eyes as it is for the palate. The adjoining Café Petit serves lighter and more affordable options. ⊠ *Klein Constantia Rd., Constantia* ☎ *021/794–3522* ⊕ *www.buitenverwachting.co.za* ⚠ *Reservations essential* ⊟ *AE, DC, MC, V* ☉ *Closed Sun. Closed Mon. May–Oct.*

$$$$
SOUTH AFRICAN

✕ **The Cape Malay.** In an 18th-century manor house, the finest traditional Cape cuisine is served in three courses with your choice of starter and dessert. The carrot-and-cumin soup is recommended over the garden salad or smoked snoek (an oily local fish), while four main-course dishes are shared with the table. Fish *bobotie* (with a savory custard topping) is good, but the lamb-and-butternut-squash *bredie* (stew) is the winner. A *dhall* (dal) curry is the only vegetarian option, while the chicken curry with cumin, fennel seeds, and yogurt delivers a spicy bite. Accompaniments include a roti (a griddled flour tortilla), *sambal* (a spicy chutney-like sauce), and *atchars* (a spicy relish often made with mangos). Basmati rice is also served. All three desserts—malva pudding, lemon meringue, and *boeber* (a traditional dish of warm milk and *lokshen* pudding with almonds, cinnamon, and rosewater)—are excellent to share. Coffee or tea and *koeksisters* (plaited dough that is deep-fried and doused in syrup) is another delicious way to end the meal. ⊠ *Cellars-Hohenort, 93 Brommersvlei St., Constantia* ☎ *021/794–2137* ⊕ *www.cellars-hohenort.com* ⊟ *AE, DC, MC, V* ☉ *Closed Tues. and Wed. in winter.*

$$$
ECLECTIC
★

✕ **Catharina's.** The old winery on this historic estate has had a major renovation replacing one wall with windows that take in extravagant mountain and vineyard views. At lunchtime you can sit on the oak-shaded terrace overlooking manicured lawns and whitewashed homestead. A global menu with Cape influences includes asparagus-and-field-mushroom risotto served with slow-roasted Rosa tomatoes, goat feta, and watercress before being anointed with white-truffle oil. Beef fillet is served with an oxtail cake, porcini flan, *pomme Maxim* (a fried circle of scalloped potatoes), and foie gras butter finished with a beef jus. The tasting menu is recommended for serious foodies, and the Sunday lunch buffet with jazz quartet is the best the city has to offer. ⊠ *Steenberg Hotel, Steenberg and Tokai Rds., Tokai* ☎ *021/713 2222* ⊕ *www.steenberghotel.com* ⊟ *AE, DC, MC, V.*

$$$
ITALIAN
★

✕ **Constantia Uitsig.** Reserve a table on the enclosed veranda or outside on the patio for tremendous views of the mountains at this restored farmstead house. The menu is a harmonious blend of northern Italian and Provençal cuisines. Many diners start with homemade pasta or fish carpaccio (served with nori and a rice cube). They may then move on to such main courses as line fish served on mashed sweet potato with baby spinach and a verjuice (gentle grape astringent) vinaigrette or the classic *trippa alla Fiorentina* (tripe braised in tomato, carrot, and celery sauce). Veal sweetbreads are cooked with artichokes, prosciutto, and baby peas. The *marquise au chocolat* is calorific splendor: dark-chocolate mousse in a spiderweb pool of crème anglaise. ⊠ *Constantia*

Uitsig Farm, Spaanschemat River Rd., Constantia ☎ *021/794–4480* ⚐ *Reservations essential* ▤ *AE, DC, MC, V.*

$$$$ ✗ **The Greenhouse.** Aptly named, this conservatory-like dining room
ECLECTIC built around a 350-year-old oak overlooks the beautiful gardens of the Cellars-Hohenort Hotel. A bistro menu with owner Liz McGrath's own Steak and Kidney Pie and crispy fish-and-chips recipe is competitively priced for lunch. The dinner menu offers more elegant options such as truffled celery root soup with a shallot tarte tatin and celery root rémoulade or *tian* of soft-shell crab with aubergine and avocado as starters. Panfried sole served with scallop paupiettes, steamed potatoes, tomato fondue, baby fennel, and ginger velouté is a great entrée option. Roasted quail and veal sweatbreads are joined by mushroom mille-feuille, ham and leeks, pumpkin, and a sherry quail jus. Mrs M's Dark and White Chocolate Plate is taken from the owner's published cookbook, *The Collection Cookbook* (2003). Ask for beverage manager Miguel Chan's assistance with ordering the wine, as he has succeeded in securing every vintage of nearby Klein Constantia's famous Vin de Constance. ✉ *Cellars-Hohenort Hotel, 15 Hohenort Ave., Constantia* ☎ *021/794–2137* ⚐ *Reservations essential* ▤ *AE, DC, MC, V.*

$$$ ✗ **Hussar Grill.** Now a franchise of three with other branches in Green
STEAKHOUSE Point and Camps Bay, this opened in 1964 and has served steaks and lip-smacking ribs since. Although recently accused of passing off pork as warthog ribs, the service is always good and food reasonably priced. Close to the Baxter Theatre and a favorite for preshow dinners, interiors are packed with wine crates and historic photographs. The gin-and-tomato soup or chicken livers with garlic, brandy, and cream are good. Aside from the usual, this is one of the few local places that serves a Cobb salad. The R50 beef burger with sauce is a good choice. ✉ *10 Main Rd., Rondebosch* ☎ *021/689–9516* ⊕ *www.hussargrill.com* ▤ *AE, DC, MC, V* ⊘ *No lunch weekends.*

$ ✗ **Jonkershuis.** This 19th-century building adjoins the gracious manor
SOUTH AFRICAN house at Groot Constantia, the Cape's oldest wine estate. The Malay platter provides a hearty taste of the Cape's culinary heritage with *bobotie* (spiced minced beef studded with dried fruit and topped with a savory baked custard), lamb curry with *sambals* (condiments), tomato-based chicken *bredie*, samosas, fish cakes, cinnamon-spiced butternut squash, rice, and *papadum* (crispy flatbread). Smoked snoek (fragrant Cape oily fish) pâté is a good way to start your meal. A wide selection of contemporary dishes includes grilled squid and chorizo salad served with rocket (arugula), roasted tomatoes, and a warm orange-and-lime vinaigrette. The South African dessert *melktert,* or milk tart—similar to baked custard—is both traditional and delicious. ✉ *Groot Constantia, Main Rd., Constantia* ☎ *021/794–6255* ⚐ *Reservations essential* ▤ *AE, DC, MC, V* ⊘ *No dinner Sun.*

$$$$ ✗ **La Colombe.** Constantia Uitsig is home to three good restaurants, but
FRENCH it's La Colombe, with chef Luke Dale-Roberts's excellent Provence-
Fodor's Choice inspired food with an Asian sensibility, that attracts the most atten-
★ tion and garners every award. The seven-course Elements tasting menu, inspired by the restaurant's direct environment, is an exquisite culinary experience served on custom-designed plates made by a community arts

project. The regular chalkboard menu items are equally excellent but not as edgy. Expect pressed terrine of confit rabbit, chorizo, foie gras, and fig jelly served with port-poached fig and mascarpone mousse, or springbok loin cooked in port with truffles, panfried foie gras, and bush tea–preserved quince. Although costly, this is a not-to-be-missed culinary experience. ✉ *Constantia Uitsig Farm, Spaanschemat River Rd., Constantia* ☎ *021/794–2390* ⚞ *Reservations essential* ☰ *AE, DC, MC, V.*

$$$$
FRENCH
Fodor's Choice
★

✕**Myoga.** This relaxed fusion-glam eatery in the posh Vineyard Hotel & Spa outside Cape Town has all the makings of an über-hip, foodie hot spot, minus the hipsters. The well-heeled regulars come for chef Mike Basset's fusion flair, evidenced in dishes like lamb three ways on one plate: slow-cooked belly with green apple, noisette with chorizo, and sticky glazed ribs with wilted greens and chips. Like many dishes here, each plate has four or five elements. Wakame salmon is teriyaki-glazed with lemon peel emulsion before being served with avocado-and-cauliflower mousse and scallop-and-wasabi gremolata; salmon tartare on a potato blini completes the dish. High-backed sofas and black chandeliers lend a touch of Alice in Wonderland to the art-deco-meets-Japanese-nightclub-cool aesthetic. Portions are tasting-menu size, so plan to order three. Don't neglect the fabulous wine list, which features many of the country's best. ✉ *Vineyard Hotel & Spa, 60 Colinton Rd., Newlands* ☎ *021/657 1515* ⊕ *www.myoga.co.za* ⚞ *Reservations essential* ☰ *AE, DC, MC, V* ☾ *Closed Sun.*

$
CAFÉ

✕**River Café.** For informal feasting on country fare in idyllic surroundings, this pretty spot with a lavender-fringed terrace is hard to beat. The place really shines at breakfast time with classics like eggs Florentine and Benedict, along with the usual fry-ups; on peak-season weekends cars line up waiting for the doors to the café to open. Local favorites include smoked-salmon bagels, lamb burgers, and beef fillet, which are always available on a frequently changing seasonal menu. Norwegian salmon on chive mashed potatoes with asparagus and a béarnaise sauce is another good option. Sticky pudding with star-anise caramel and vanilla ice cream is a nice way to round off the meal. ✉ *Constantia Uitsig Farm, Spaanschemat River Rd., Constantia* ☎ *021/794–3010* ⊕ *www.constantiauitsig.co.za* ☰ *AE, DC, MC, V* ☾ *No dinner.*

FALSE BAY

$$
SEAFOOD

✕**Black Marlin.** Black Marlin's position overlooking the Indian Ocean is unrivaled, and its popularity is well deserved (it's largely supported by tour bus business). Ask for a table outside amid the bougainvillea. Seafood is the hero here, and it's fairly affordable. Calamari rings paired with chili-mango jam are tasty, but if you're looking for local fare, select the Cape Malay fish cakes or black mussels in a cream-and-white-wine sauce. The bayside platter, with fish, calamari rings, and mussels, is a good value, but be sure to leave room for angel's dark delight: a devilish dessert of baked dark-chocolate mousse served with orange sorbet. ✉ *Main Rd., Millers Point, Simon's Town* ☎ *021/786–1621* ⊕ *www.blackmarlin.co.za* ⚞ *Reservations essential* ☰ *AE, DC, MC, V* ☾ *No dinner Sun.*

$ **✗ Café Roux.** Easy eating in a family-friendly atmosphere doesn't get
CAFÉ much better than at this spot. Sit outside or in and take in the environment—alternative shops and barefoot, nature-loving folk. The twice-
baked cheese and courgette (baby marrow) soufflé although small is very
rich, as is the roasted butternut squash with sun-dried tomato–and-spin-
ach penne in a cream-and-Gorgonzola sauce. Unexpectedly, the burger
with aged cheddar is a lighter option. The chicken, mushroom, and leek
pie comes in a phyllo pastry. Breakfast treats include a French-toast
stack with fried banana and a berry coulis. Bacon is an optional extra.
Kids have their own menu and a dedicated play area with a minder.
⊠ *Noordhoek Farm Village, Village La., Noordhoek* ☎ *021/789–2538*
⊕ *www.caferoux.co.za* ☰ *AE, DC, MC, V* ☻ *No dinner.*

¢ **✗ Empire Cafe.** A picture window overlooks the surfers' beach, and folks
CAFÉ will visit barefooted with sand still between their toes. The food is unexpectedly good, even if the service isn't. The lamb rump steak is fabulous:
it's served on sautéed spinach with chickpeas, rooibos-tea-soaked raisins
(rooibos is a Cederberg mountain plant), garlic butter, and eggplant,
with dribbled garlic aioli. Also popular is the burger with a surprisingly
good mushroom sauce. Although the butternut-squash-and-feta salad
is good, it comes with crisp butternut-squash chips that are more easily
enjoyed by hand than with the cutlery provided. The café's confection-
ery skill is renowned, and people visit just to buy breads and pastries.
As desserts go, the malva pudding delivers the perfect balance of sweet
and sticky with vinegar undertones. The coffee is delicious. Some will
find the laid-back vibe irritating, while others will find it's exactly what
they were looking for. ⊠ *11 York Rd., Muizenberg* ☎ *021/788–1250*
⌕ *Reservations essential* ☰ *AE, DC, MC, V* ☻ *No dinner Sun.–Tues.*

$$ **✗ The Food Barn & Deli.** When Franck Dangereux left La Colombe, the
FRENCH culinary world held its breath. Fortunately, everyone can breathe a sigh
★ of relief. Whether enjoying "fine dining" in the à la carte venue or just
relaxing with coffee and cake in the Deli, diners will not be disappointed.
Braised veal sweetbreads are served over mashed potatoes with confit
tomato and rocket, finished with a niçoise-thyme jus, while roasted
rack of lamb gets an herb crust before being served with Dangereux's
favorite ingredient, lentils, which are mixed with hummus in a spring
roll; the dish is finished with a cumin-scented and fresh coriander jus.
Deli items include the Moroccan chicken tram, a toasted *trammezzini*
with mozzarella cheese, free-range chicken, *harissa* (a North African
hot red paste) mayonnaise, candied onions, and coriander. It's delicious.
⊠ *Noordhoek Farm Village, Village Lane, Noordhoek* ☎ *021/789–1390*
⊕ *www.thefoodbarn.co.za* ☰ *AE, DC, MC, V* ☻ *Call for hours.*

$ **✗ FSH.** This restaurant supports the SASSI (South African Sustainable
SEAFOOD Seafood Initiative) fish program, so diners can be assured that fish
served is fresh and not endangered. Aside from the sushi menu and
starters such as Malay-style pickled fish with apple-and-leaf salad or
prawn-and-avocado ceviche, diners select raw fish from a fridge that
is then cut and weighed to order before being grilled or fried. Wine
lovers will enjoy the "tasting card" system—patrons put money on a
card that's used at automatic wine dispensers. Again, it's DIY, but here
patrons select from 24 wines in sample sizes or full glasses. Expect good

family dining in a relaxed environment with inside and outdoor seating. ✉ *The Quays, Majestic Village, Main Rd., Kalk Bay* ☎ *021/788–1869* 🚫 *AE, DC, MC, V.*

$$$ ✗ **Harbour House.** Don't be put off by the unremarkable entrance here;
SEAFOOD once you're upstairs and seated at a window table you'll be entranced by views across the bay, where fishing boats chug back and forth and whales spout for much of the year. Bring a keen appetite. Starter salads are substantial, and you can follow them with just-landed, olive oil–brushed fish, or Mediterranean calamari with garlic, chili, black olives, and giant capers. The smoked-salmon-sushi sandwich (layers of fish, sushi rice, and nori) is as delicious as the deep-fried calamari rings dusted with curry powder and served with garlic mayo. Rib-eye steaks come with spinach and cream-cheese ravioli. There's also a tempting dessert list. ■**TIP→ If you're looking for something a bit more casual, try Polana just downstairs for a similar seafood menu but at lower prices.** ✉ *Kalk Bay Harbour, Main Rd., Kalk Bay* ☎ *021/788–4133* ⊕ *www.harbourhouse.co.za* 🚫 *AE, DC, MC, V.*

$ ✗ **Olympia Café.** This tiny Kalk Bay landmark, furnished with mismatched
CAFÉ tables and a counter along the window, has long been a well-kept secret among locals and regular visitors. The quality of the mostly Mediterranean fare is consistently high, and the servers are consistently sassy. A delectable vegetarian dish of eggplant rolls—filled with butternut squash, ricotta, and sweet potato and sauced with piquant tomato—is always popular. A choice of pasta may include fresh tuna when available or tomato with fresh basil and chili. During peak times people will queue to get in, so get there early. The croissants and crusty loaves from the café's bakery around the corner are available to purchase to take home. ✉ *134 Main Rd., Kalk Bay* ☎ *021/788–6396* ⚓ *Reservations not accepted* 🚫 *AE, DC, MC, V.*

NORTHERN SUBURBS

$$ ✗ **Cassia.** With a large deck overlooking the farm's reservoir, this barn-
ECLECTIC style restaurant is the go-to place in the Durbanville Hill's wine valley. Service is slick and cuisine simple. Watch the chefs in the glass kitchen or gaze out at views over the vineyards. Decoration is minimal, so the food speaks. Seared salmon is served with a paprika–beurre blanc sauce, while baked kingklip is served atop *charmoula* chickpeas (seasoned with a Moroccan spice mix) with *tzatziki* (Greek yogurt-cucumber sauce). When available, the slow-braised springbok shanks served with mashed potatoes and *waterblommetjies* (a local water lily) are lip-smackingly delicious. ✉ *Tygervalley Rd., Durbanville Hills* ☎ *021/976–0640* 🚫 *AE, DC, MC, V* ⊗ *Closed Mon. No dinner Sun.*

WHERE TO STAY

Updated by
Brian Berkman

Finding lodging in Cape Town can be a nightmare during peak travel season (December–January), as many of the more reasonable accommodations are booked up. It's worth traveling between April and August, if you can, to take advantage of the "secret season" discounts that are sometimes half the high-season rate. If you arrive in Cape Town without a reservation, head for the Tourism Office, which has a helpful accommodations desk.

Hotels in the city center are a good option if you're here on business or are here for only a short stay. During the day the historic city center is a vibrant place. At night, though, it's shut up tight (though this is changing slowly as more office buildings are converted into apartment complexes); night owls may prefer a hotel amid the nonstop action of Long Street or the Waterfront. Hotels and bed-and-breakfasts in the Southern Suburbs, especially Constantia, offer unrivaled beauty and tranquility and make an ideal base if you're exploring the peninsula. You'll need a car, though, and should plan on 25–45 minutes to get into town. Atlantic Coast hotels provide the closest thing in Cape Town to a beach-vacation atmosphere despite the cold ocean waters.

Keep in mind that international flights from the United States and Europe arrive in the morning and return flights depart in the evening. Because most hotels have an 11 AM checkout, you may have to wait for a room if you've just arrived; if you're leaving, you will be hauled kicking and screaming out of your room hours before your flight. Most hotels will try to accommodate you, but they often have no choice in peak season. Some of the larger hotels have residents-only lounges where you can spend the hours awaiting your flight. Note that many small luxury accommodations either do not permit children or have minimum-age restrictions. It's a good idea to inquire in advance if this will be an issue. Cape Town has led the global trend of not smoking in public places. All hotels will have no-smoking rooms, and some have no-smoking floors or are entirely smoke-free.

B&BS AND GUESTHOUSES

When South Africans travel they often stay in guesthouses or B&Bs, which are numerous in Cape Town. Don't be put off by the names—choosing a B&B or guesthouse doesn't mean you'll have to eat breakfast with the family or help wash up afterwards! Instead, there are some very classy and professionally run establishments that offer everything a hotel does but on a smaller, more personal scale.

The most reliable source of good B&B establishments is **South African Accommodation** (☎ 021/794–0030 ⊕ *www.bookabed.co.za*). The **Portfolio of Places** (☎ 021/689–4020 ⊕ *www.portfoliocollection.com*) brochure includes guesthouses, B&Bs, villas, and more. If you don't like tiptoeing around someone's house or you want to save money, consider renting a fully furnished apartment, especially if you're staying two or more weeks. **CAPSOL Property & Tourism Solutions** (☎ 021/422–3521 ⊕ *www.capsol.co.za*) has around 1,500 high-quality, furnished, fully stocked villas and apart-

BEST BETS FOR CAPE TOWN LODGING

Fodor's offers a selective listing of quality lodging experiences in every price range, from the city's best budget beds to its most sophisticated luxury hotels. Here, we've compiled our top recommendations by price and experience. The very best properties—in other words, those that provide a particularly remarkable experience in their price range—are designated in the listings with the Fodor's Choice logo.

2

Fodor'sChoice★

Cape Grace, $$$$, p. 111
Dock House, $$$$, p. 112
Ellerman House, $$$$, p. 115
Mount Nelson Hotel, $$$$, p. 109
Steenberg Hotel, $$$, p. 122
Twelve Apostles, $$$$, p. 119

By Price

¢

Daddy Long Legs, p. 105
Dolphin Inn, p. 115
Grand Daddy, p. 105
Townhouse, p. 106

$

Constantia Uitsig Hotel, p. 121
Monkey Valley Resort, p. 117

Palm House, p. 121
Protea Hotel Victoria Junction, p. 113
Vineyard Hotel & Spa, p. 122

$$

Cape Heritage Hotel, p. 104
Westin Grand Arabella Quays Hotel Cape Town, p. 106
Winchester Mansions Hotel, p. 119

$$$

Cellars-Hohenort Hotel & Spa, p. 120
Rodwell House, p. 124
Radisson Blu, p. 113
Steenberg Hotel, p. 122

$$$$

Cape Grace, p. 111
Ellerman House, p. 115
Long Beach, p. 117

Mount Nelson Hotel, p. 109
Twelve Apostles, p. 119

By Experience

BEST HOTEL BARS

Alphen, $, p. 119
Mount Nelson Hotel, $$$$, p. 109
One&Only Cape Town, $$$$, p. 112
Table Bay Hotel, $$$$, p. 114
Westin Grand Arabella Quays Hotel Cape Town, $$, p. 106

BEST SPA

Cape Grace, $$$$, p. 111
Ellerman House, $$$$, p. 115
Constantia Uitsig Hotel, $, p. 121
Mount Nelson Hotel, $$$$, p. 109

One&Only Cape Town, $$$$, p. 112
Vineyard Hotel & Spa, $, p. 122

BEST FOR ROMANCE

Cape Heritage Hotel, $$, p. 104
Cellars-Hohenort Hotel & Spa, $$$, p. 120
Constantia Uitsig Hotel, $, p. 121
Ellerman House, $$$$, p. 115
Long Beach, $$$$, p. 117

BEST LOBBY

One&Only Cape Town, $$$$, p. 112
Radisson Blu, $$$, p. 113
Table Bay Hotel, $$$$, p. 114
Westin Grand Arabella Quays Hotel Cape Town, $$, p. 106

ments on its books. **Cape Stay** (☎ *021/674–3104* ⊕ *www.capestay.co.za*) has a wide selection of accommodations to suit different needs.

Village & Life (✉ *1 Loader St., Cape Town Central* ☎ *021/437–9700* ⊕ *www.villageandlife.com*) manages **De Waterkant Village,** Cape Town's first and only guest street. The more than 40 beautifully restored, self-catering (with cooking facilities) houses are unusual, trendy, classy, and quite charming. Houses come with daily housekeeping services and have between one and four bedrooms. If you don't feel like cooking, you could stay in the Charles Café and Rooms, a guesthouse in the heart of the village. The high-season double-occupancy rate is around R1,650 per night.

Cape Town is regarded as one of the top backpacker destinations in the world, with plenty of hostels to choose from. Contact **Backpacking South Africa** (*BTSA* ⊕ *www.btsa.co.za*) for information.

WHAT IT COSTS IN SOUTH AFRICAN RAND					
	¢	$	$$	$$$	$$$$
Hotels	under R1,000	R1,000–R2,000	R2,001–R3,000	R3,001–R4,000	over R4,000

Prices are for a standard double room in high season, including 14% tax.

CAPE TOWN CENTRAL

The hotels below are marked on the Where to Stay and Eat in Cape Town map.

$ ⊡ **Adderley Hotel.** If you're looking for an inner-city accommodation that's well priced and far away from the late-night noise of Long Street but close enough to enjoy the nightlife, the Adderley is for you. Each suite has separate dining and work areas, as well as a fully stocked kitchen. The beds are outfitted in comfy white linens, while only part of the bathroom is fully enclosed with basin and tub in the bedroom section and shower and toilet behind frosted glass. For those who aren't interested in self-catering, the well-priced restaurant, Bowl, on the first floor serves breakfast and good light fare such as salads and sandwiches by day, and heartier dishes like confit duck on Chinese noodles and a Thai chicken green curry for dinner. During the day you're in the center of the action, but at night it's very quiet. **Pros:** near van Riebeeck's 1655 Fort (called The Castle by locals), St. George's Anglican Cathedral, which, aside from its beauty, has been the site of many political protests, and the Company Botanical Gardens established by van Riebeeck. **Cons:** although patrolled and covered by CCTV cameras, the inner city can be scary. ✉ *31 Adderley St., Central Cape Town* ☎ *021/469–1900* ⊕ *www.relaishotels.com/adderley* ↩ *27 suites* ⚅ *In-room: safe, kitchen, refrigerator, Internet, Wi-Fi (some). In-hotel: restaurant, room service, bar, pool, laundry service, Internet terminal, Wi-Fi, parking (paid)* ▭ *AE, D, DC, MC, V* ⦿ *BP.*

$$ ⊡ **Cape Heritage Hotel.** Built as a private home in 1771, this friendly,
★   attractive, well-run hotel is part of the Heritage Square development

2

and as such has direct access to a host of restaurants and a couple of shops. Teak-beamed ceilings and foot-wide yellowwood floorboards echo the building's gracious past, and the spacious rooms are individually decorated. Some have four-poster beds, others exposed brickwork, but each has its own special charm. Rooms overlooking the pleasant courtyard—complete with tables sheltered by what is claimed to be the oldest grapevine in South Africa—may be a little noisy, but the revelry stops at midnight sharp, when the bar quits serving. Parking is across the street in a section of a public lot with good security. **Pros:** good eateries in adjoining Heritage Square; private hospital across the way; free Wi-Fi in rooms and public areas. **Cons:** bordered by busy roads; homeless people hang around parking area. ⊠ *90 Bree St., Cape Town Central* ☎ *021/424–4646* ⊕ *www.capeheritage.co.za* ⊃ *17 rooms* ⚭ *In-room: safe, DVD, Wi-Fi. In-hotel: 6 restaurants, room service, bar, laundry service, Internet terminal, Wi-Fi, parking (paid)* ⊟ *AE, DC, MC, V* ⏻ *BP.*

¢ ⊞ **Daddy Long Legs Boutique Hotel.** Independent travelers with artistic
★ streaks love this place. It was built to represent the creative community of Cape Town, and well-known local artists—including poet-author Finuala Dowling and architect Andre Vorster—were given a budget and invited to decorate a room to their tastes. The results are fantastic. In the Photo Booth room, a huge portrait behind the bed is made up of 3,240 black-and-white photos of Capetonians, while a funky room by the fusion band Freshlyground has a bright red throw, portraits of the band members, and music. But it's not all about show—the amenities are all in place as well. The linen is crisp and clean, the staff is friendly, and the only real drawback is finding parking on Long Street (it's fine after hours but a crush during the day). **Pros:** loads of dash without cash; the hotel has had lots of positive global media coverage, and your chums will be impressed that you stayed here. **Cons:** small rooms; Long Street is noisy until late into the night. ⊠ *134 Long St., Cape Town Central* ☎ *021/422–3074* ⊕ *www.daddylonglegs.co.za* ⊃ *13 rooms* ⚭ *In-room: no phone, no TV (some), Wi-Fi. In-hotel: bar, laundry service, Wi-Fi* ⊟ *AE, DC, MC, V.*

¢ ⊞ **The Grand Daddy.** The Metropole closed amid scandal, and new owners opened the Grand Daddy in its place. This is a stylish inner-city, glamorous spot that's also good value for travelers. The decor—clever without being overbearing—is done by local designers with images such as ostrich silhouette wallpaper and protea-flower prints on lamp shades. For a new experience, stay in one of the uniquely themed rooftop Airstream trailers, which are available at the same price as the rooms. The same team owns Daddy Long Legs, and guests can expect the same quirky and outlandish interiors completed by artists and musicians. The Afro Funk trailer has broad, curved, brown stripes and fabrics with Nelson Mandela's image, while in Dorothy everything (even the kettle) is blue and covered in white polka dots—except for the ruby slippers to bring you home safely from Oz. If you're staying for more than a night, book one night in an Airstream and the others in the hotel. Ask for a corner room, which has three large windows. The in-house café is run by renowned chef Bruce Robertson and serves weigh-and-pay breakfast and lunch buffets, while dinner items include good burgers and a curry or two. The Daddy Cool bar on the first floor is high bling with gold-chain curtains; a gold-and-black, Versace fabric–covered couch; and rapper-style chunky jewelry as decor. **Pros:** great value for money; in the heart of Long Street. **Cons:** noise from the street and bar/club until late; neighbors include student bars and African crafts shops. ⊠ *38 Long St., Cape Town Central* ☎ *021/424–7247* ⊕ *www.granddaddy.co.za* ➵ *23 rooms, 3 suites ₺ In-room: safe, Wi-Fi. In-hotel: restaurant, room service, bar, laundry service, Internet terminal, Wi-Fi, parking (paid).*

\$ ⊡ **Mandela Rhodes Place.** Occupying an entire city block, this mixed-use complex of apartments, offices, a winery, retail space, and a hotel spearheaded the inner-city's rejuvenation. The hotel is comprised of five buildings, the Tower being the most contemporary and spacious with two-bedroom apartments. The apartments in the Fairbairn have an art-deco bent; those in the Kendall benefit from wood flooring and inlaid stone work while the Winery overlooks the only inner-city winery. This location is excellent for exploring the city and environs on foot during the day, but it can feel daunting to freely walk about at night. Luckily, there are good restaurants on-site. Synergy is operated by the hotel and serves elegant Mediterranean cuisine like saddle of lamb with butternut squash, capers, and mint. Doppio Zero is an Italian family-dining franchise on the lower level, and, directly across the street, Haiku serves superb Pan Asian, and Bukhara equally good North Indian cuisine. For views of Table Mountain and the Harbor, book as high in the Tower as possible. Rooms in the Winery tend to be noisier, as the reception area is directly beneath. **Pros:** money-savers like self-catering and laundry facilities make this a good value, especially for families. **Cons:** decent supply of hot water can be insufficient at peak times; slow and costly Wi-Fi. ⊠ *Wale and St. George's Sts., Cape Town Central* ☎ *021/481–4000* ⊕ *www.mandelarhodesplace.co.za* ➵ *110 rooms ₺ In-room: safe, kitchen, refrigerator, DVD (some), Internet, Wi-Fi. In-hotel: 2 restaurants, room service, bar, pool, gym, spa, laundry facilities, laundry service, Internet terminal, Wi-Fi, parking (paid)* ⊟ *AE, DC, MC, V.*

¢ ⊡ **Townhouse Hotel.** Its proximity to government buildings and its easy-going atmosphere (not to mention extremely competitive rates) make the Townhouse a popular choice, especially for the business traveler. It was upgraded in 2009 to a sexier scheme of browns with great lighting and succeeds in providing a restful retreat from the hubbub of the city. Request a room with a view of the mountain. Some rates include breakfast. **Pros:** near Long St., St. George's Cathedral, and the Castle; helpful staff. **Cons:** not a great area to walk around in at night; parking is costly (about R40 per day) and slightly challenging as it's in a nearby building accessed by one-way roads. ⊠ *60 Corporation St., Box 5053, Cape Town Central* ☎ *021/465–7050* ⊕ *www.townhouse.co.za* ➵ *104 rooms ₺ In-room: safe, Wi-Fi. In-hotel: restaurant, room service, bars, pool, gym, laundry service, Internet terminal, Wi-Fi, parking (free)* ⊟ *AE, DC, MC, V.*

\$\$ ⊡ **Westin Grand Arabella Quays Hotel Cape Town.** The super-sophisticated e-butler service in the foyer is enough to get excited about—and that's

2

before you've even set foot in the rooms. Since the hotel is linked to the Cape Town International Convention Centre, rooms are geared toward working guests, but that doesn't mean they're spartan. The decor is modern minimalist with touches of African creativity, perhaps in pillowcases or a quirky wall color. Workstations are cleverly partitioned away from the sleeping area, so even if you have to burn the midnight oil, you can do it in comfort and style. Everything glides and whirls at the touch of a button, and service is seamless. Take special note of the artwork in the lobby and foyer area. This hotel group collects and supports local art. Don't miss the spa at the top of the hotel or a water-taxi ride from the hotel to the Waterfront. **Pros:** stellar views over the harbor and Signal Hill on one side and city and Table Mountain on the other from the top-floor restaurant; gym, infinity pool, and great spa; Louis B's cigar bar. **Cons:** busy corporate hotel; not much within easy walking distance. ⊠ *Convention Sq., Lower Long St., Cape Town Central* ⌖ *Box 50095, Waterfront 8002* ☎ *021/412–9999* ⊕ *www.starwood. com* ⌖ *451 rooms, 32 suites* ⌖ *In-room: safe, Wi-Fi. In-hotel: 2 restaurants, room service, bars, gym, spa, laundry service, Internet terminal, Wi-Fi, parking (free)* ⊟ *AE, DC, MC, V* ⊠ *BP.*

GARDENS

$$ ⚹ **Best Western Cape Suites Hotel.** This village-style hotel, with low buildings and adjoining individual units, is 10 minutes from the center of Cape Town, close to District Six, and a brisk 20-minute walk from the Waterfront, although walking is not recommended. Some guests find the complex security (high walls, electric fence, cameras) a bit off-putting, but others like the peace of mind it gives them. Rooms are spacious and pleasantly furnished in a cheerful and contemporary style, and all come with a fully equipped kitchen. Some rooms have mountain views; others look into the city. Although it's on a corner site, the hotel is well insulated, so traffic noise is not a major problem; inner rooms tend to be quieter. If you have a car, you can park it virtually outside your room. A free shuttle takes you to popular sights within about 13 km (8 mi) of the hotel. Some stays include a full breakfast. **Pros:** easy highway access; proximity to Wembley Square mall. **Cons:** vibrant nearby student life including pubs and music venues. ⊠ *Constitution and de Villiers Sts., Zonnebloem* ⌖ *Box 51085, Waterfront 8002* ☎ *021/461– 0727* ⊕ *www.capesuites.co.za* ⌖ *123 suites* ⌖ *In-room: safe, kitchen, refrigerator. In-hotel: 2 restaurants, bars, pool, laundry facilities, laundry service, Internet terminal, Wi-Fi, parking (free), some pets allowed* ⊟ *AE, DC, MC, V.*

$ ⚹ **Cape Milner Hotel.** Tamboerskloof is an ideal location from which to explore the city and farther afield. The look at this attractive hotel is clean and contemporary, with rooms decorated in earth tones. Public areas are high-energy, with hip music and TV with news or fashion channels on, but still chic. Each room has a tea/coffeemaker, and there's a gym for those who need to work off some of their holiday excesses. The hotel shuttle service to the Waterfront and nearby beaches is a real plus. The terrace has wonderful views of Table Mountain. It's largely supported by film and commercials crews, which may annoy some when folks lugging lighting rigs pass the bar, but others will enjoy the healthy, mostly shirts-off crew. **Pros:** great location minutes from city; good dining options within walking distance; near Table Mountain. **Cons:** one-way roads make it tricky to access; overlooks a road that's busy at peak times. ⊠ *2 Milner Rd., Tamboerskloof* ☎ *021/426–1101* ⊕ *www. capemilner.com* ➱ *56 rooms, 2 suites* ⏣ *In-room: safe, Wi-Fi. In-hotel: restaurant, room service, bar, pool, gym, laundry service, Internet terminal, Wi-Fi, parking (free)* ⊟ *AE, DC, MC, V* ❏❏ *BP.*

¢ 🖭 **Cape Town Backpack.** Billed as a "luxury backpack" you'll stay here because the rooms are clean and cheap, but you'll return because of the community vibe created by the hands-on owners. Perhaps you'll make new friends at the Tuesday evening communal braai (barbecue) where meat and snoek (oily local fish) and sides are served at very reasonable prices (R90), or you'll appreciate its Fair Trade credentials and participate in its knitting project—there are knitting needles and wool in the common areas to make blankets for needy community members. There are 100 beds available, spread across four adjoining Cape Victorian houses, a large pool, and shared kitchen if you'd rather do your own cooking. The location is the great prize here, with Table Mountain in full view from outdoor areas. You're within easy walking distance of many great eateries and, if you're up to it, the steep walk up the hill to the Mountain cable-station. Although there's no on-site parking, there is a door guard who keeps his eye on the nearby public parking at night. **Pros:** good value for money; on-site travel center to book excursions; café with good coffee and reasonably priced meals such as filled tortilla wraps for R30. **Cons:** you're staying in a hostel; guests staying in dorm rooms may be noisy after a night's partying. ⊠ *74 New Church St., Cape Town Central* ☎ *021/423–4530* ⊕ *www.backpack.co.za* ➱ *100 beds* ⏣ *In-room: no phone, safe (some), no TV, Wi-Fi. In-hotel: restaurant, pool, laundry facilities, laundry service, Internet terminal, Wi-Fi* ⊟ *AE, DC, MC, V.*

$$$ 🖭 **Kensington Place.** The lovely garden entrance leads you into this contemporary space that smells amazing. The staff is helpful and accommodating and will arrange everything from dinner reservations to daily excursions. Each spacious suite comes equipped with an iPod docking station and beach-ready bag—a nice touch if you've left these essentials at home. The king-size beds are outfitted in gorgeous white linens, and your gas fireplace adds to the already comforting atmosphere. If the weather's nice and the view clear, opt for breakfast on your terrace. Molton Brown bath products add a luxe touch to a very sleek bathroom; be careful—the tub is a bit difficult to get in and out of. **Pros:** great views of Cape Town and Table Mountain from some balconies; heated floors in the bathroom; laptops in every room with free Wi-Fi. **Cons:** not within walking distance of town; breakfast is the only meal served; lots of stairs and no elevator could be a problem for some. ⊠ *32 Kensington Crescent, Higgovale* ☎ *021/424–4744* ⊕ *www. kensingtonplace.co.za* ➱ *8 rooms* ⏣ *In-room: safe, refrigerator (some), DVD (some), Wi-Fi. In-hotel: room service, bar, laundry service, Wi-Fi, parking (free), no kids under 12* ⊟ *AE, DC, MC, V* ❏❏ *BP.*

¢ ⊡ **La Villa Belle Ombre.** This B&B is in a converted Cape Victorian mansion that was built in 1870 on the edge of the city and within walking distance of Table Mountain. All five rooms have en suite bathrooms with either a bath or a shower and some rooms have wood-burning fireplaces. Public spaces are warm and comfortable with a communal TV in the lounge. Views from the wooden sash windows either look out to the pretty garden, where there's a table under the bougainvillea, or over the pepper or orange tree. Rooms are basic but clean. Although Room 5 is the smallest, it's on the sunny side of the house and has African furniture and a queen-size bed. You'll see the mountain as soon as you step outside. **Pros:** excellent value for money; good breakfast included in the rates; very reasonable airport transfers. **Cons:** insufficient closet space in some bedrooms. ⊠ *16 Belle Ombre Rd., Tamboerskloof* ☎ *021/424–2727* ⊕ *www.villabelleombre.com* ↵ *5 rooms* ⟡ *In-room: no TV, Wi-Fi. In-hotel: laundry service, Internet terminal, Wi-Fi, parking (free)* ⊟ *AE, D, DC, MC, V* ⟦◎⟧ *BP.*

$$ ⊡ **More Cape Cadogan.** Declared a national monument in 1984, this
★ lovely space is housed in a Georgian and Victorian building that dates back to the beginning of the 19th century. Public areas, such as a library, lounge with wood-burning fireplace, and patio area, are great places to relax and collect oneself before heading out or on returning from the day's travels. The staff are pleasant and accommodating and will help you arrange just about anything you need. The rooms are decorated with contemporary and antique furnishings, and the bathrooms feature the fabulous locally made Charlotte Rhys products—you'll want to pick some up while you're in town. Those interested in self-catering will find the More Quarters, a series of apartments in four historic homes just feet from the hotel, the ideal lodging option. **Pros:** minutes from the busy and popular Long and Kloof streets; beautiful, historic accommodations; apartments available for those who want to self-cater. **Cons:** traffic noise (hooting minibus taxis at nearby intersection). ⊠ *5 Upper Union St., Tamboerskloof* ☎ *021/480–8080* ⊕ *www.capecadogan.co.za* ↵ *8 rooms, 4 suites, 1 villa* ⟡ *In-room: safe, refrigerator, Internet. In-hotel: restaurant, room service, pool, laundry service, Internet terminal, Wi-Fi, parking (free)* ⊟ *AE, DC, MC, V* ⟦◎⟧ *BP.*

$$$$ ⊡ **Mount Nelson Hotel.** This distinctive pink landmark is the grande dame
Fodor's Choice of Cape Town. Since it opened its doors in 1899 to accommodate pas-
★ sengers just off the Union-Castle steamships, it has been the focal point of Cape social life. It retains a traditional charm and gentility that other luxury hotels often lack: a lavish afternoon tea is served in the lounge to piano accompaniment, the Planet Champagne Bar is very glam, and the staff almost outnumber the guests. Rooms are decorated with fine antiques and fresh flowers and have an air of aristocracy about them. The hotel stands at the top of Government Avenue, but, surrounded as it is by 9 acres of manicured gardens, it might as well be in the country. Once a week the head gardener leads a guided tour through the magnificent gardens, and tea is served afterward. Very civilized! For peak season, December–March, it's advisable to book a year in advance. **Pros:** the most glamorous hotel in town; guests include movie stars and diplomats; everyone in Cape Town knows it. **Cons:** breakfast and lunch

restaurant overlooks guests at the pool; Friday nights in the Planet Bar are legendary, and the main building is abuzz until late. ⊠ *76 Orange St., Gardens* ☎ *021/483–1000* ⊕ *www.mountnelson.co.za* ⟲ *145 rooms, 56 suites* ₺ *In-room: safe, DVD, Wi-Fi. In-hotel: 2 restaurants, room service, bar, tennis courts, pools, gym, spa, laundry service, Internet terminal, Wi-Fi, parking (free)* ⊟ *AE, DC, MC, V* ⦿ *BP.*

$ ⛯ **Protea Fire & Ice.** Initially built as an Extreme Hotel—interior elements like elevators dressed like a shark cage under water or a Table Mountain cable car mid-journey, and a "climbing wall" still exist—the hotel is more user-friendly now for the average visitor (or anyone over 21) while still remaining edgy. Rooms are very small but otherwise you are getting four- and even five-star facilities for three-star rates. Everything you'll want in a room is here including Bose iPod docking stations. Thoughtful additions include free local newspapers in the public areas and free popcorn at the bar. **Pros:** location at the edge of the city means good dining and other activities available on foot; brilliant views of Table Mountain especially from rooms above the fifth floor. **Cons:** some will be irritated by the zany decoration, like public toilets with full-size Adam and Eve images with a hand-towel instead of fig leaf. ⊠ *New Church and Victoria Sts., Tamboerskloof* ☎ *021/488–2555* ⊕ *www.proteahotels.com* ⟲ *200 rooms* ₺ *In-room: safe, DVD (some), Internet, Wi-Fi. In-hotel: restaurant, room service, bar, pool, gym, laundry service, Internet terminal, Wi-Fi, parking (paid)* ⊟ *AE, DC, MC, V.*

$$ ⛯ **Villa Belmonte.** In a quiet residential neighborhood on the slopes above the city, this small guesthouse offers privacy and luxury in an attractive Dutch Revival residence. The owners have sought to create the feeling of an Italian villa through the use of marbling, molded ceilings, and natural wood floors. Wide verandas afford superb views of the city, Table Mountain, and Devil's Peak. Rooms have colorful draperies, luxurious finishes, wicker furniture, and small-pane windows. It's a 20-minute walk to the city center. **Pros:** amazing mountain, city views; award-winning wine collection. **Cons:** not many restaurant choices within walking distance; decor could use an update. ⊠ *33 Belmont Ave., Oranjezicht* ☎ *021/462–1576* ⊕ *www.villabelmontehotel.co.za* ⟲ *14 rooms* ₺ *In-room: safe, Internet. In-hotel: restaurant, room service, bar, pool, laundry service, Internet terminal, parking (free), no kids under 8* ⊟ *AE, DC, MC, V* ⦿ *BP.*

$$ ⛯ **Welgelegen Guest House.** In Afrikaans, *welgelegen* means "well situated," and this classy guesthouse in two beautifully restored Victorian mansions is just that: it's nestled under Table Mountain and just minutes away from city attractions. Each room is individually and stylishly decorated. The look is a mixture of African chic and romantic whimsy, and the pretty courtyard is a good place to relax after a busy day. If you want more independence, you can opt for a two-bedroom, self-catering cottage down the road. **Pros:** great staff make guests feel like part of the family; recycling program, which is not common in Cape Town; support community-based projects. **Cons:** sometimes old sash windows rattle in the wind; not all rooms are updated; no elevator. ⊠ *6 Stephen St., Gardens* ☎ *021/426–2373 or 021/426–2374* ⊕ *www. welgelegen.co.za* ⟲ *13 rooms, 1 cottage* ₺ *In-room: Wi-Fi. In-hotel:*

room service, pool, laundry service, Internet terminal, Wi-Fi, parking (free) = AE, DC, MC, V ⎮◎⎮ BP.

V&A WATERFRONT

$$$$ 🖭 **Cape Grace.** The recent refurbishment of Cape Town's beloved Cape
Fodor's Choice   Grace has transformed this storied hotel's look from period French
★   to a mélange of indigenous and foreign influences that have come to
epitomize the region. Hand-painted fabrics embellished with proteas, antiques like old cane fishing rods and Dutch china, and nautical murals add to the new eclectic decor. Though some may miss its former French elegance, this award winner remains a bastion of perfect service. Cape Grace continues to charm with its library where guests can take afternoon tea, enjoy views of the harbor, or cozy up by a fire. The Spirit of the Cape is the hotel's luxury motor yacht, which is available for harbor cruises, fishing trips, or overnights. **Pros:** mountain and harbor views from all rooms; spa; complimentary shuttle within city center; child-friendly; excellent waterfront location. **Cons:** lacks the intimacy of a boutique hotel. ⊠ *West Quay Rd., Box 51387, Waterfront* ☎ *021/410–7100* ⊕ *www.capegrace.com* ⇆ *121 rooms* ⚭ *In-room: DVD, Internet, Wi-Fi. In-hotel: restaurant, room service, bar, pool, gym, spa, children's programs (all ages), laundry service, Internet terminal, Wi-Fi, parking (free)* = *AE, DC, MC, V* ⎮◎⎮ *BP.*

$ 🖭 **Cape Victoria Guest House.** Only a five-minute drive and a brisk 20-minute walk from the waterfront, this charming guesthouse is a luxurious refuge from the bustle of the city. Each room is individually decorated, and there are quirky touches throughout—from an enormous Victorian bath to an African inspired room for those wishing they were on safari. The owner, Lily Kaplan, is a gem who knows Cape Town inside out, so she can give you all the hot tips when you arrive. The breakfasts are legendary; you will be fortified for the rest of the day, especially if you have a strong cup of coffee together with a slice of the freshly baked almond tart or Lily's special banana bread packed with fruit and nuts. The plunge pool on the terrace overlooking the city rooftops is a great place to unwind with a glass of wine at the end of a busy day. **Pros:** Lily is reason alone to stay here to benefit from her clued-in knowledge of the latest and greatest, combined with her loving grandmotherly attitude; good daytime eating options within walking distance. **Cons:** noise from guests in the other rooms can be heard as rooms aren't soundproofed; wooden floors and staircase in the hotel and rooms creak; tricky one-way roads make it difficult to access by car. ⊠ *13 Torbay Rd., Green Point* ☎ *021/439–7721* ⊕ *www.capevictoria. co.za* ⇆ *10 rooms* ⚭ *In-room: Internet. In-hotel: pool, laundry service, parking (free), no kids under 12* = *AE, DC, MC, V* ⎮◎⎮ *BP.*

$$$ 🖭 **The Commodore Hotel.** A nautical theme embraces The Commodore with shiny brass, rope barriers, and bent-wood archways overhead to suggest life on a tall ship. Rooms are comfortable but feel corporate in the plain way in which they're decorated. Once-splendid views of Table Mountain are now marred by the new One&Only property across the way. Guests will appreciate being a few steps away from the action. You can also stay at the Portswood, the adjacent four-star property.

Pros: situated in historic buildings. **Cons:** costly on-site parking of more than R80 a day. ✉ *Portwood Rd., Waterfront* ☎ *021/415–1000* ⊕ *www. legacyhotels.co.za* ⇨ *232 rooms* ♿ *In-room: safe, DVD (some), Internet, Wi-Fi. In-hotel: restaurant, room service, bar, pool, gym, laundry service, Internet terminal, Wi-Fi, parking (paid)* ⊟ *AE, DC, MC, V* ⦿⦿ *BP.*

$$$$
Fodor's Choice
★

⊡ **Dock House.** Victorian splendor meets modern glam at this stunning boutique hotel perched over Cape Town's trendy and ever-popular Waterfront. The Dock House, with only a handful of rooms and butler-style service, oozes pampered privacy. Antique silver artifacts, crystal chandeliers, edgy artwork, and bathrooms are sure to impress. The staff, dressed in white linen tunics, provides immaculate yet understated service. The property's prime location means visitors can freely (and safely) explore the Waterfront's plethora of dining, shopping, and other attractions. But, with a private chef dishing up divine room-service meals, a pool and bar overlooking the harbor, and a full range of treatments and gym facilities at the OneWellness spa annex, it's entirely possible you'll never want to leave. **Pros:** the hotel's elegant interior has been featured in decor magazines; close to activities, dining, and shopping; excellent room service; complimentary minibar. **Cons:** guests have to leave the building to reach the gym and spa; staircases and wooden floors in the bedrooms creak; rooms aren't soundproofed. ✉ *Portswood Close, Portswood Ridge, Waterfront* ☎ *021/421–9334* ⊕ *www. dockhouse.co.za* ⇨ *5 rooms, 1 suite* ♿ *In-room: safe, Internet, Wi-Fi. In-hotel: Wi-Fi, room service, bar, gym, spa, laundry service, parking (free)* ⊟ *AE, DC, MC, V* ⦿⦿ *BP.*

$$$$
★

⊡ **One&Only Cape Town.** Sol Kerzner helped put South Africa on the international tourism map with his Southern Sun Group and Sun City. After moving operations abroad to launch Atlantis in the Bahamas and Dubai and One&Only resorts, he has returned to South Africa with the One&Only Cape Town. The hotel opened in April 2009 amid international fanfare and celebrity guests, including Mariah Carey and Robert De Niro (a partner in the on-site Nobu Restaurant) and British TV chef Gordon Ramsey, who's behind Maze restaurant. There are audible gasps when people enter for the first time and see Table Mountain framed in splendid four-story-high glass windows of the sunken lounge and bar. Access to the Island suites and Spa is through the lounge and downstairs. All rooms are larger than in most other hotels and furnished to a very high contemporary standard. Deluxe rooms have two full bathrooms with freestanding tubs and dual dressing areas. The Island's free-form pools are oxygenated, promising clean water and enhanced youthfulness. **Pros:** two exceptional restaurants in Nobu and Maze (⇨ *Where to Eat)*; exclusive high-end fashion labels available at boutique; excellent spa with Bastian Gonzales nail studios; impressive KidsOnly facility. **Cons:** Marina Rise guests must walk through the lounge in their swimming trunks to reach the pool; as a big hotel it can feel a little impersonal. ✉ *Dock Rd., Waterfront* ☎ *021/431–5888* ⊕ *www.oneandonlyresorts.com* ⇨ *91 rooms, 40 suites* ♿ *In-room: safe, DVD, Internet, Wi-Fi. In-hotel: 3 restaurants, room service, bar, pool, gym, spa, children's programs (ages 4–17), laundry service, Internet terminal, Wi-Fi, parking (free)* ⊟ *AE, DC, MC, V* ⦿⦿ *BP.*

2

$ ⚇**Protea Hotel North Wharf.** A favorite with businesspeople and families who like apartment-style living, each room is outfitted with a full kitchen and laundry facilities. Decor is upscale but unfussy, and the views of the mountain or city from fully opening sliding doors are amazing. The hotel is adjacent to the Cullinan hotel so it feels safer, despite its city location. There are good daytime dining options within walking distance. **Pros:** there's loads of creative energy in the building as a major architectural firm occupies the top floor; secure parking access; affordable rooms close to the Waterfront. **Cons:** on the edge of the city and a little dodgy at night; basement gym is claustrophobic. ⊠ *1 Lower Bree St., Foreshore* ☎ *021/443–4600* ⊕ *www.proteahotels.com* ⤵ *67 rooms* �& *In-room: kitchen, refrigerator DVD (some), Internet, Wi-Fi. In-hotel: restaurant, room service, bar, pool, gym, laundry facilities, laundry service, Internet terminal, Wi-Fi, parking (paid)* ⊟ *AE, DC, MC, V.*

$ ⚇**Protea Hotel Victoria Junction.** With funky art-deco decor, this hotel, adjacent to the Waterfront and De Waterkant, is popular with those looking for something different. Spacious, high-ceilinged loft rooms have large double beds on an upper level; you have to be fairly nimble to climb in. Standard rooms have ordinary knee-level beds but are still quite chic. The Set restaurant serves buffet breakfasts and is good for business lunches as it's quiet. The menu offers a great range of salads and something to satisfy most palettes. The bar always jumps at happy hour, especially with film and TV crews. **Pros:** suites have coffee machines; good dining options within walking distance. **Cons:** hotel pool is a distance away and narrow; evenings are noisy because of the nearby nightclubs in edgy Somerset Road. ⊠ *Somerset and Ebenezer Rds., Box 51234, Green Point* ☎ *021/418–1234* ⊕ *www.proteahotels. com* ⤵ *172 rooms* �& *In-room: safe, kitchen (some), refrigerator (some), DVD, Internet. In-hotel: restaurant, bar, pool, laundry service, Internet terminal, Wi-Fi, parking (free)* ⊟ *AE, DC, MC, V* ⏏❙*BP.*

$$$ ⚇**Radisson Blu Hotel.** Location, location, location. When it comes to the perfect position, this hotel is one of Cape Town's front-runners, perched right on the edge of the Atlantic Ocean. You may be a five-minute walk from the V&A Waterfront, but it's easy to imagine that you're on a yacht out at sea. The hotel overlooks a private marina, which explains why you'll find some wealthy yacht owners swanning about. The rooms are spacious and pleasantly decorated in nautical blues and creams and are in the process of being updated; be sure to ask for a recently upgraded sea-facing room. Make time to enjoy the infinity pool and a meal and drink at Tobago's Restaurant and Terrace, where Cape Town's cool set gathers for drinks after work. **Pros:** sound of the water crashing against the breakwater; proximity to stadium and golf course; airport shuttle available. **Cons:** first-generation rooms don't warrant the cost. ⊠ *Beach Rd., Granger Bay, Waterfront* ☎ *021/441–3000* ⊕ *www. radissonblu.com* ⤵ *182 rooms* �& *In-room: safe, DVD, Wi-Fi. In-hotel: restaurant, room service, bar, tennis court, pool, gym, spa, laundry service, Wi-Fi, parking (paid)* ⊟ *AE, D, MC, V* ⏏❙*BP.*

$ ⚇**Romney Park Hotel & Spa.** This converted apartment block incorporates adjoining houses to provide luxury sea-facing suites, all with generous balconies and fully fitted kitchens. Elegantly decorated in an

African-colonial style, what this property lacks in gardens and outdoor space it makes up for in generously apportioned suites. Breakfasts are available, but with self-catering facilities in suites, you might prefer to fix your own and enjoy it while watching the sea from your balcony. Or head down to Somerset Road on foot for a host of deli-dining options. The adjoining spa is well known for good, reasonably priced treatments. **Pros:** free Wi-Fi; underfloor heating. **Cons:** on-site parking spaces are limited; no gym. ⊠ *Corner of Hill and Romney Rds., Green Point* ☎ *021/439–4555* ⊕ *www.romneypark.co.za* ⮒ *57 rooms* ⅍ *In-room: safe, kitchen, refrigerator, DVD (some), Internet, Wi-Fi. In-hotel: restaurant, room service, bar, pool, spa, laundry service, Internet terminal, Wi-Fi, parking (paid)* ⊟ *AE, DC, MC, V.*

$$$ ☷ **Southern Sun Cullinan Cape Town Waterfront.** This sparkling white hotel is just opposite the entrance to the Waterfront but still requires a significant walk across a busy road to the V&A malls. It has a spacious marble-tile lobby, huge picture windows draped in rose and gold that lead out to the pool, and an enormous double-curving gilt staircase that completes the picture. Rooms are quite restrained, with muted green carpets and floral notes, and bathrooms are well laid out, with separate showers in white tile and gray marble. But the views of Table Mountain and the harbor steal the show. There's an efficient shuttle service that runs 8 AM–11 PM, so you'll be able to get around easily. **Pros:** high-power shower; within walking distance of the V&A (but across a very busy, multilane road). **Cons:** unheated pool; some complain that "Don't Disturb" signs are ignored; doesn't handle peak-season business well. ⊠ *1 Cullinan St., Waterfront* ☎ *021/418–6920* ⊕ *www.southernsun. com* ⮒ *410 rooms* ⅍ *In-room: safe, Internet, Wi-Fi. In-hotel: restaurant, room service, bar, pool, gym, Internet terminal, Wi-Fi, parking (free)* ⊟ *AE, DC, MC, V* ⑩ *BP.*

$$$$ ☷ **Table Bay Hotel.** This glitzy hotel has a prime spot at the tip of the
★ V&A Waterfront. The decor is sunny, with huge picture windows looking onto the mountain, marble mosaic and parquet floors, and lots of plants, including the hotel's trademark floral arrangements. In the lounge you can browse through a selection of international newspapers as you sit by the fire, relaxing to live piano music. Rooms, although traditionally decorated with hints of dark wood, are bright and have marble-and-tile bathrooms with roomy showers. There's also a business center full of modern conveniences, including helpful administrators who can make your life easier. The hotel has direct access to the large Waterfront mall. **Pros:** direct access to Victoria Wharf mall; attentive service despite being a large hotel. **Cons:** shallow pool; magnetic key cards often fail. ⊠ *Quay 6, Waterfront* ☎ *021/406–5000* ⊕ *www. suninternational.com* ⮒ *311 rooms, 18 suites* ⅍ *In-room: safe, DVD (some), Internet. In-hotel: 2 restaurants, room service, bar, pool, gym, spa, laundry service, Internet terminal, Wi-Fi, parking (free)* ⊟ *AE, DC, MC, V* ⑩ *BP.*

$$$ ☷ **Victoria & Alfred Hotel.** This upscale hotel in a converted warehouse is
★ smack in the middle of the Waterfront and surrounded by shops, bars, and restaurants. Rooms are huge and luxurious, with crisp linens and elegant throws. Views from the costlier mountain-facing rooms are

spectacular, encompassing not only Table Mountain but the city and docks as well. The terrace is a great place to relax. **Pros:** best value at the Waterfront; excellent breakfasts include healthy and diabetic options; great service from restaurant and hotel staff. **Cons:** there's a drawbridge nearby that seafarers have to alert with a whistle; buskers in the piazza are loud; pool and gym an effort to find. ⊠ *On the Waterfront Pierhead, Waterfront* ☎ *021/419–6677* ⊕ *www.vahotel.co.za* ➴ *94 rooms* ⚭ *In-room: safe, Internet, Wi-Fi. In-hotel: restaurant, room service, bar, gym, laundry service, Internet terminal, Wi-Fi, parking (free)* ▭ *AE, DC, MC, V* �f⊙f *BP.*

ATLANTIC COAST

The hotels below are marked on the Where to Eat and Stay in Cape Town and the Where to Eat and Stay in the Cape Peninsula maps.

$$ **Bay Hotel.** This beach hotel in Camps Bay is the most relaxed and unpretentious of the luxury lodgings in and around Cape Town. It's across the road from a white-sand beach and is backed by the towering cliffs of the Twelve Apostles. From the raised pool deck you can look out over sea and sand and onto one of the coolest strips in South Africa, where all the beautiful people congregate. The decor is contemporary, clean, and bright, and the rooms incorporate a sophisticated range of neutral shades. Service is excellent, and although you're only 10 minutes from the hurly-burly of the city, it feels like a lifetime away. Be prepared to pay upwards of R4,560 for a premier room if you want a sea view. **Pros:** popular beach across the way; at the epicenter of high-season social life; airport shuttle available. **Cons:** road between hotel and beach is often busy and sometimes gridlocked; unpleasant when the Southeaster wind blows hard. ⊠ *69 Victoria Rd., Box 32021, Camps Bay* ☎ *021/438–4444* ⊕ *www.thebay.co.za* ➴ *78 rooms* ⚭ *In-room: safe, DVD, Internet. In-hotel: 2 restaurants, room service, bars, pools, tennis court, gym, spa, beachfront, laundry service, Internet terminal, Wi-Fi, parking (free), no kids under 12* ▭ *AE, DC, MC, V* f⊙f *FAP.*

¢ **Dolphin Inn.** An excellent value-for-money location on Mouille Point's sought-after strip of expensive condominiums that overlook the sea. Close to the Waterfront and the new soccer stadium, accommodations are basic without any of the luxury charms (robes, slippers, etc.) but are neat and comfortable. There is a self-catering apartment on the first floor. The lounge overlooks the sea with comfy leather couches. Owners are friendly and helpful. **Pros:** great location and price make up for basic amenities. **Cons:** basic amenities might leave you wanting more; sea-facing rooms are noisy as they are next to the hotel entrance and directly on the road, which is very busy at times; expect to hear every other guest arriving and departing; restaurant only serves breakfast. ⊠ *75 Beach Rd., Mouille Point* ☎ *021/434–3175* ⊕ *www.dolphin-inn.co.za* ➴ *8 rooms* ⚭ *In-room: safe (some), kitchen (some). In-hotel: restaurant, beachfront, laundry service, Internet terminal* ▭ *AE, DC, MC, V.*

$$$$
Fodor'sChoice
★ **Ellerman House.** Without a doubt, this is one of the finest (and most exclusive) hotels in South Africa. Built in 1912 for shipping magnate Sir John Ellerman, the hotel sits high on a hill in Bantry Bay and has

stupendous views of the sea. Broad, terraced lawns fronted by elegant balustrades step down the hillside to a sparkling pool. The drawing and living rooms, decorated in Regency style, are elegant yet not forbiddingly formal. Guest rooms have enormous picture windows, high ceilings, and exquisite bathrooms. The hotel accommodates only a handful of guests, and a highly trained staff caters to their every whim. In the kitchen chefs prepare whatever guests request—whether it's on the menu or not. All drinks except wine and champagne are included in the rates. If you're traveling with a group, or want absolute privacy, the adjacent Ellerman Villa is the way to go. Although costly (upwards of R40,000 a night), the villa can sleep up to 10 people. It is fitted out with all the newest media and lighting gizmos, as well as spalike bathrooms that are hard to leave. The views and service are the same as at the main house, but high-profile guests in search of absolute privacy book here. An additional R10,000 a day and the spa and its therapists are yours too. **Pros:** important local art collection adorns the walls; free airport transfers; hand-finished laundry packed in tissue paper; free, fully stocked guest pantry. **Cons:** Kloof Road is busy, and paparazzi could be waiting as your limo exits; often booked a year in advance. ⊠ *180 Kloof Rd., Box 515, Sea Point* ☎ *021/430–3200* ⊕ *www.ellerman.co.za* ⌨ *11 rooms* ♨ *In-room: safe, DVD, Wi-Fi. In-hotel: restaurant, room service, bar, pool, gym, spa, laundry service, Internet terminal, Wi-Fi, parking (free), no kids under 14* ⊟ *AE, DC, MC, V* ⊗ *Closed June 15–July 15* � BP.

$$ 🌃 **Hout Bay Hideaway Villa and Apartments.** You know you're in an exceptional place when you can lie in an outdoor bath surrounded by indigenous trees and an astonishing view of the mountains. Hout Bay Hideaway is a luxury retreat. All rooms are individually and beautifully decorated with original antiques and artwork. To complete the stylish picture, you can rent one of the beautifully restored Jaguars so that you can tool around Cape Town in style. **Pros:** wood-burning fires and underfloor heating; airport shuttle available. **Cons:** smokers aren't welcome. ⊠ *37 Skaife St., Hout Bay* ☎ *021/790–8040* ⊕ *www.houtbay-hideaway.com* ⌨ *5 suites* ♨ *In-room: no phone, safe, kitchen, refrigerator, DVD, Internet, Wi-Fi. In-hotel: room service, pool, Wi-Fi, parking (free)* ⊟ *MC, V* � CP.

$ 🌃 **Hout Bay Manor.** A recent renovation of this 1871 classic Cape Dutch mansion has given it some funky, contemporary African style. Situated in Hout Bay—a fishing village turned trendy refuge from the city— the Manor's location encourages exploration of the area's many shops and restaurants, not to mention the multitude of stunning attractions. The Manor's fine-dining restaurant, Pure, will blow your mind with its dreamlike lighting and fabulous culinary creations. The lovely garden gets fresh sea breezes. **Pros:** friendly service; child-friendly offerings (crayons, jars of candy); fine linens; free airport shuttle. **Cons:** no gym. ⊠ *Baviaanskloof, Hout Bay* ☎ *021/790–0116 or 021/790–0118* ⊕ *www.houtbaymanor.co.za* ⌨ *20 rooms, 1 suite* ♨ *In-room: refrigerator, Wi-Fi. In-hotel: 2 restaurants, room service, bar, pool, spa, laundry service, Wi-Fi, parking (free)* ⊟ *AE, D, DC, MC, V.*

2

$ ⬚ **La Splendida Luxury Suites.** Designed to look like an art-deco hotel in Miami's South Beach, this trendy all-suites lodging has a great location—the V&A Waterfront is a 15-minute walk. Ask for a sea- or mountain-facing room, either of which will have great views. Natural fabrics decorate the well-proportioned rooms, and the overall feeling is light and airy. The hotel restaurant specializes in contemporary Italian food: great pizzas and pastas and fresh salads. You have a choice of executive or penthouse suites (slightly larger and a bit more expensive), but whichever you choose, you'll be very comfortable. **Pros:** sea-facing rooms overlook grassed area and seaside promenade; reasonably priced rooms; near soccer stadium. **Cons:** major upgrade scheduled for late 2010, so things might be loud, chaotic, and messy; security is a bit lax as restaurant patrons can access hotel elevators. ⊠ *121 Beach Rd., Mouille Point* ☎ *021/439–5119* ⊕ *www.lasplendida.co.za* ⇆ *24 suites* ♿ *In-room: safe, Wi-Fi. In-hotel: restaurant, room service, bar, laundry service, Internet terminal, Wi-Fi, parking (paid)* ▤ *AE, DC, MC, V.*

$$$$ ⬚ **Long Beach.** Superbly spacious rooms are decorated in a beach-house
★ theme with shower and soaking tub exposed on a platform behind the bed. Toilet is enclosed for total privacy. All rooms have balconies with sea views; you are, after all, on the beach. Public areas are very comfortable, and the small staff make a point of introducing themselves and other guests (never more than 12 of you). When you're not basking on the sundeck (good for whale-watching during the season, approximately June–November), you can explore the Kommetjie beach. Playful touches include colorful towels and beach hats in a basket at the ready. Romantic turndown service with candles and petals is also a nice touch. **Pros:** complimentary minibar and nuts and dried-fruit snacks in the room; free Wi-Fi in entire hotel; staff make you feel like they are there to serve only you. **Cons:** need a car to get around; poor mobile phone reception in lower-level rooms. ⊠ *1 Kirsten Ave., Kommetjie* ☎ *021/794–6561* ⊕ *www.thelastword.co.za* ⇆ *6 rooms* ♿ *In-room: safe, DVD, Wi-Fi. In-hotel: room service, bar, pool, beachfront, laundry service, Internet terminal, Wi-Fi, parking (free)* ▤ *AE, DC, MC, V* ⬚ *BP.*

$ ⬚ **Monkey Valley Resort.** This secluded resort is one of the best places
☾ on the peninsula for families and is very popular for small conferences.
★ Built on stilts, the self-catering thatch log cottages lie in an indigenous milk wood forest overlooking a nature reserve and the white sands of Noordhoek Beach. Cottages have two or three bedrooms, fully equipped kitchens, and large balconies. The wood interiors are attractive and rustic, brightened by floral fabrics, cottage-style furniture, and wood-burning fireplaces. Rooms are similarly decorated, and some have pretty Victorian bathrooms. There's a large grocery store 5 km (3 mi) away. Owner Judy Sole runs an outstanding establishment and is a character in her own right. Children's programs for all ages can be arranged on request. **Pros:** expansive views of sea and mountains; close to nature; great low-season specials; airport shuttle available. **Cons:** no a/c in the rooms; thatched roof invites insects; other than beach, not much available on foot. ⊠ *Mountain Rd., Box 114, Noordhoek* ☎ *021/789–1391* ⊕ *www.monkeyvalleyresort.com* ⇆ *32 rooms, 16 cottages* ♿ *In-room:*

kitchen (some), refrigerator (some). In-hotel: restaurant, room service, bar, pool, laundry service, Internet terminal, parking (free) ☰ *AE, DC, MC, V* ⦿❘ *BP.*

$ ⊡ **Peninsula All Suites Hotel.** In an 11-story building just across the road from the ocean and a 4-mi paved promenade, these accommodations are ideal for families or groups of friends. You can choose from a variety of rooms that sleep from four to eight people and have incredible views of the sea. The larger suites are the most attractive, full of light and air, thanks to picture windows, sliding doors, wide balconies, and white-tile floors. Small "studio suites" are more like conventional hotel rooms. Each unit has a fully equipped kitchen with a microwave oven. The hotel is a time-share property, so booking during the busy December holiday could be a problem. There are children's programs mid-December to mid-January. **Pros:** airport shuttle available; although the hotel has a pool, there's a saltwater Olympic-sized public pool very close by; good supermarket and deli a block away; good dining options within walking distance; free shuttle to Waterfront and beaches. **Cons:** outside noise can be a bit obtrusive; limited on-site parking. ⊠ *313 Beach Rd., Sea Point* ⦿ *Box 768, Sea Point 8060* ☎ *021/430–7777* ⊕ *www.peninsula.co.za* ⇨ *100 suites* ⚭ *In-room: safe, kitchen, refrigerator, Wi-Fi. In-hotel: restaurant, room service, bar, pools, gym, beachfront, children's programs (ages infant–12), laundry service, Internet terminal, Wi-Fi, parking (free)* ☰ *AE, DC, MC, V* ⦿❘ *BP.*

$ ⊡ **Place on the Bay.** Now also incorporating the Fairways hotel, these luxury self-catering apartments are on the beachfront in Camps Bay, within easy walking distance of a host of restaurants and bars. Apartments are tasteful, modern affairs that make extensive use of glass. Many units have good sea views from their balconies. If you really want to have it all, take the magnificent penthouse, which occupies the entire top floor and comes with its own plunge pool. All units have daily housekeeping service. **Pros:** great location; management responds seriously to concerns and complaints; medi-spa on-site. **Cons:** limited parking; traffic noise from Victoria Road. ⊠ *Fairways and Victoria Rds., Camps Bay* ☎ *021/437–8500* ⊕ *www.placeonthebay.co.za* ⇨ *27 apartments* ⚭ *In-room: safe, kitchen, refrigerator, Wi-Fi. In-hotel: restaurant, room service, pool, beachfront, laundry service, Wi-Fi, parking (free)* ☰ *AE, DC, MC, V.*

$$$$ ⊡ **Tintswalo Atlantic.** Visitors attracted to the Cape Peninsula for its natural grandeur will think they've died and gone to heaven at this discreetly luxurious boutique hotel. Directly off Chapman's Peak Drive (a contender for world's most scenic road) and built around a wonderland of native fynbos plants and milk wood trees, Tintswalo Atlantic is the only beachfront development in Table Mountain National Park. Themed after different islands, 11 roomy suites all have breathtaking views of Hout Bay from verandas and bathtubs, wood-burning stoves, and heavenly bedding—all against the sound of breaking waves. Only 20 minutes from Cape Town, guests can enjoy the city but may also opt to watch the whales playing in the bay. Exquisite four-course meals, an impressive wine cellar, and excellent service complete the pampering at this exclusive and truly unique hideaway. **Pros:** whale-watching; stupendous

breakfast. **Cons:** no gym; must drive to all activities and sights. ⊠ *Km 2, Chapman's Peak Dr., Chapman's Peak, Hout Bay* ☎ *011/464–1070* ⊕ *www.tintswalo.com* 🔊 *10 island suites, 1 Atlantic Presidential Suite* & *In-room: DVD, Wi-Fi. In-hotel: restaurant, room service, bar, pool, spa, beachfront, water sports, laundry service, Internet terminal, Wi-Fi, no kids under 13 (except Dec. 15–Jan. 15)* 🖹 *AE, DC, MC, V* ⏁ *BP.*

$$$$ 🖬 **Twelve Apostles Hotel and Spa.** Fancy taking a helicopter to the airport
Fodor'sChoice or lazing in a bubble bath while looking out floor-to-ceiling windows at
★ sea and mountains? If this sounds like you, then opt for this luxurious hotel and spa. The only building between Camps Bay and Llandudno and bordering the Table Mountain National Park, it was built amid controversy just before the park's status was proclaimed. The hotel has spectacular views and an enormous indigenous garden that disappears up the mountain. Each room is unique, decorated in either cool blues and whites to reflect the colors of the ocean or warmer tones to conjure up the lifestyle of Africa's explorers. A shuttle runs to the Waterfront every hour during the day. Children's programs are available in December. On-site restaurant Azure is excellent for its Cape fynbos (botanical) menu and Portuguese-inspired seafood dishes. Breakfasts at Azure are also notable (free-flowing sparkling wine and live oysters included in the breakfast buffet). **Pros:** guests are well looked after by an attentive staff; Table Mountain is your back garden; good DVD selection; views, views, views. **Cons:** overlooks a road that gets busy; nearest off-site restaurant is at least 10 minutes by car. ⊠ *Victoria Rd., Box 32117, Camps Bay* ☎ *021/437–9000* ⊕ *www.12apostleshotel.com* 🔊 *46 rooms, 24 suites* & *In room: safe, DVD, Internet, Wi-Fi. In-hotel: 2 restaurants, room service, bars, pools, gym, spa, laundry service, Internet terminal, Wi-Fi* 🖹 *AE, DC, MC, V* ⏁ *BP.*

$$ 🖬 **Winchester Mansions Hotel.** This seafront hotel scores high with travelers for good value for money. Overlooking a green belt, popular promenade, and onward to the sea, the views and proximity to all visitor activities are key here. Upgraded rooms are comfortable and unfussy, while those that still need to be upgraded have a floral scheme. Sunday jazz brunches are legendary (and have to be booked in advance), and the elegant sea-facing terrace is always popular for tea and afternoon drinks. However, it's the Mediterranean-style courtyard with ivy and bougainvillea that's the real appeal. It's an elegant refuge from the blazing sun, offering tea and fine dining around a beautiful wrought-iron fountain. **Pros:** heated pool; lots of dining options within walking distance; good service; locals love it. **Cons:** Internet fees are costly. ⊠ *221 Beach Rd., Sea Point* ☎ *021/434–2351* ⊕ *www.winchester.co.za* 🔊 *76 rooms* & *In-room: safe, DVD (some), Internet, Wi-Fi. In-hotel: restaurant, room service, bar, pool, gym, spa, beachfront, laundry service, Internet terminal, Wi-Fi, parking (paid)* 🖹 *AE, DC, MC, V* ⏁ *BP.*

SOUTHERN SUBURBS

$ 🖬 **Alphen Hotel.** Built in the mid-1700s in Cape Dutch style, this former manor house is now a national monument and one of the Cape's historic treasures. The owners are descendants of the distinguished Cloete family, which has farmed the land around Constantia since 1750.

Cloete paintings and antiques, each with a story to tell, adorn the public rooms. Rooms range in size from compact to rather large. A small drawback is the slight traffic noise from the nearby highway in rush hour, but a health-and-wellness center on the grounds just might help you forget about it. Only luxury rooms have air-conditioning. Many rooms have been recently updated bringing them up to par with 2010 stylings, including velvet couches and silver-leafed side tables. The Boer 'n' Brit bar is wonderfully atmospheric with its huge wood-burning fireplace, leather club chairs, and historic mementos. It's very popular with locals who come for a beer, to watch the Saturday afternoon rugby match, and enjoy pub fare like fried hake and chips. The elegant Cloete restaurant had a face-lift in July 2009, and the new menu is offering white tomato soup, salmon *gravadlax*, and roasted duck with duck spring rolls. **Pros:** beautiful setting and landscaped gardens; great pool even though it's unheated; airport shuttle available. **Cons:** no gym; no elevator. ⊠ *Alphen Dr., Box 35, Constantia* ☎ *021/794–5011* ⊕ *www. alphen.co.za* ⮑ *21 rooms* ⚒ *In-room: DVD (some) Wi-Fi. In-hotel: restaurant, room service, bar, pool, laundry service, parking (free), Wi-Fi* ⊟ *AE, DC, MC, V* ⭤ *BP.*

$$$ ⛱ **Bishop's Court.** Nestled in the exclusive suburb of Bishopscourt, where the bishop of the Anglican Church still has his residence, this boutique hotel with unrivaled views over Kirstenbosch and Table Mountain is a good combination of class and homey comfort. Thanks to a friendly and attentive staff, you may end up feeling as though you're staying with wealthy cousins. After browsing through the private library, you can retreat to your gorgeous room. The decor is classical, and fine touches include fluffy robes, luxurious toiletries, and wonderful baths. Groups can even rent the entire establishment. Breakfast is served, but lunch and dinner are only available on request. **Pros:** mountain views from all rooms; within walking distance of Kirstenbosch gardens; airport shuttle available. **Cons:** no dining options on foot so far a car is recommended; no gym. ⊠ *18 Hillwood Ave., Bishopscourt* ☎ *021/797–6710* ⊕ *www. thelastword.co.za* ⮑ *5 rooms* ⚒ *In-room: safe, DVD, Internet, Wi-Fi. In-hotel: bar, tennis court, pool, laundry service, Internet terminal, Wi-Fi, parking (free), no kids under 12* ⊟ *AE, DC, MC, V* ⭤ *BP.*

$$$ ⛱ **Cellars-Hohenort Hotel & Spa.** It's easy to forget the outside world at
★ this idyllic getaway in Constantia. Set on acres of gardens on the slopes of the Constantiaberg, this luxury hotel commands spectacular views across Constantia Valley to False Bay. The 18th-century cellars of the Klaasenbosch wine estate and the Hohenort manor house form the heart of the hotel. Guest rooms are large and elegant, furnished in English-country style with brass beds, flowery valances, and reproduction antiques, while others have a fresh, new, pared-down, contemporary look. Rooms in the manor house have the best views of the valley. The Presidential Suite sleeps six. **Pros:** exquisite gardens; incredible cellar selection; friendly but gracious service. **Cons:** expensive bar prices; need a car to get around. ⊠ *93 Brommersvlei Rd., Box 270, Constantia* ☎ *021/794–2137* ⊕ *www.cellars-hohenort.com* ⮑ *52 rooms, 1 suite* ⚒ *In-room: safe, DVD, Internet. In-hotel: 2 restaurants, room ser-*

2

vice, bar, tennis court, pool, gym, spa, bicycles, laundry service, Wi-Fi, parking (free), no kids under 12 ☰ *AE, DC, MC, V* ⧫◎❙ *BP.*

$ ★ ⊡**Constantia Uitsig Hotel.** This 200-acre winery has an enviable setting, backed by the magnificent mountains of the Constantiaberg and overlooking the vineyards of Constantia Valley. You might be 25 minutes from the center of town, but this is a little slice of rural paradise, with horses grazing just a few hundred yards away. Rooms, in whitewashed farm cottages set on manicured lawns and gardens, are luxurious and inviting. Brass bedsteads, timber ceilings, and sophisticated check-and-floral patterns evoke an upscale farmhouse feel. The two restaurants near the original farmhouse, La Colombe and Constantia Uitsig, are just a few paces from the hotel and draw diners from all over the Cape, and the River Café, a lighter breakfast and lunch spot, is located at the gatehouse at the entrance to the estate. The manicured cricket pitch is the perfect place for a summer game. A stay includes a complimentary wine tasting. **Pros:** steps away from two of the Cape's finest restaurants; wood-burning fireplaces in the rooms; charming, home-style service that makes it hard to leave. **Cons:** activities beyond the estate require a car, but the hotel will arrange transport for you. ⊠ *Spaanschemat River Rd., Box 32, Constantia* ☎ *021/794–6500* ⊕ *www.constantiauitsig.co.za* ⊅ *16 rooms* ♿ *In-room: safe, DVD. In-hotel: 3 restaurants, room service, bars, pool, spa, laundry service, Internet terminal, parking (free)* ☰ *AE, DC, MC, V* ◎❙ *BP.*

$ ⊡**Palm House.** Towering palms dominate the manicured lawns of this peaceful guesthouse straddling the border of Kenilworth and Wynberg, a 20-minute drive from the city. The house is an enormous, stolid affair, built in the early 1920s by a protégé of architect Sir Herbert Baker and filled with dark wood paneling, wood staircases, and fireplaces. Bold floral fabrics and reproduction antiques decorate the large guest rooms. Upstairs rooms benefit from more air and light. Guests often meet for evening drinks in the drawing room. **Pros:** there's a stately feel about the 1920s proportions of this beautifully restored historic building; helpful management and staff make you feel nothing is too much trouble for them; airport shuttle available. **Cons:** breakfast is served only until 10 AM, making lie-ins difficult. ⊠ *10 Oxford St., Wynberg* ☎ *021/761–5009* ⊕ *www.palmhouse.co.za* ⊅ *10 rooms* ♿ *In-room: safe. In-hotel: bar, pool, laundry service, Wi-Fi, parking (free), Internet terminal* ☰ *DC, MC, V* ◎❙ *BP.*

$ ⊡**Red House.** Once the hunting lodge of Lord Charles Somerset, this house, dating from 1729, is one of Cape Town's oldest surviving buildings. It's been lavishly restored, but the walls remain their signature red, the result of a former, eccentric owner who chose the bold color to "ensure protection against the elements." You won't have to worry much about the elements here, as the elegant rooms are extremely comfortable and decorated with heavy drapes, dark mahogany furniture, chandeliers, and bold gilt-frame mirrors. What's more, the guesthouse is nestled in the leafy suburb of Newlands, just five minutes from Kirstenbosch and 10 minutes from the city center. The terrace is a good place to relax after a busy day, and you can even get an on-site massage in the garden or near the pool. **Pros:** owners speak English and Dutch;

beautiful mountain views from mountain-facing, first-floor rooms; airport shuttle available. **Cons:** sun sets earlier here, so there are fewer daylight hours than a property on the west side of the mountain; high winter-rainfall area. ✉ *4 Hiddingh Ave., Newlands* ☎ *021/683–8000* ⊕ *www.redhouse.co.za* ⇆ *5 rooms, 1 cottage* & *In-room: Internet, Wi-Fi. In-hotel: room service, pool, spa, laundry service, Wi-Fi, parking (free), no kids under 12* ☰ *AE, DC, MC, V* ⍩⊘*BP.*

$$$
Fodor's Choice
★

⊡ Steenberg Hotel. One of the area's oldest estates, the former Swaaneweide aan den Steenberg was granted to four-time widow Catherina Ras in the late 17th century by her lover, Simon van der Stel, then governor of the Cape, making her the first woman to own land in South Africa. She was, by all accounts, wild, and legend has it that she was given to riding her horse naked around the grounds, which might explain van der Stel's generosity. The original buildings on this working wine estate have been painstakingly restored, the gardens manicured to perfection, and the vineyards replanted on the slopes of the Constantiaberg. The original vineyards are now a championship 18-hole golf course. The buildings and contemporary guest rooms are all furnished with antiques. The three Heritage Suites offer exceptional accommodations on two levels. The Khoi Khoi suite, for example, is 1,710 square feet of custom-designed furniture and artifacts that hint at what life could be like if the original hunter-gatherer people of the Cape lived in luxury today. All suites have fully equipped kitchens. The estate's Catharina's restaurant *(➪ Where to Eat)* is most famous for its Sunday jazz brunches where people spill outside to eat under the giant oak trees. Don't leave without buying some sauvignon blanc. **Pros:** high security; on-site Eduardo Villa abstract sculpture collection; surrounded by mountain views. **Cons:** not protected from wind; Cape Colonial Suite pool visible from road. ✉ *Steenberg and Tokai Rds., Tokai* ⊡ *Net Suite 150, Private Bag, X26, Tokai 7966* ☎ *021/713–2222* ⊕ *www.steenberghotel.com* ⇆ *21 rooms, 3 suites* & *In-room: safe, refrigerator (some), DVD (on request), Internet, Wi-Fi. In-hotel: restaurant, room service, bar, golf course, pools, gym, spa, laundry service, Wi-Fi, Internet terminal, parking (free)* ☰ *AE, DC, MC, V* ⍩⊘*BP.*

$
⊡ Vineyard Hotel & Spa. On six acres of rolling gardens overlooking the Liesbeek River in residential Newlands, this comfortable hotel was built around the 18th-century weekend home of Lady Anne Barnard. The views of the back of Table Mountain are spectacular, but for a better rate ask for a courtyard-facing room. Children's programs are available December–January. The hotel is 15 minutes by car from the city but within walking distance of the Newlands sports arenas and the shops of Cavendish Square. On-site Myoga restaurant serves innovative and deconstructionist cuisine and is very well regarded. On the Square restaurant, in the original courtyard, is popular with locals for its sushi bar and family-style fare. Be sure to ask for a recently updated room as others are old-fashioned. **Pros:** superlative Angsana Spa; beautiful garden setting; airport shuttle available. **Cons:** construction noise and dust; first-generation rooms are old-fashioned. ✉ *Colinton Rd., Box 151, Newlands* ☎ *021/657–4500* ⊕ *www.vineyard.co.za* ⇆ *173 rooms* & *In-room: safe, Internet, Wi-Fi. In-hotel: 2 restaurants, room service, bar,*

pools, gym, spa, children's programs (ages infant–11), laundry service, Internet terminal, Wi-Fi, parking (free) ⊟ AE, DC, MC, V ⭑⭑ BP.

FALSE BAY

2

$ ⊞ **Boulders Beach Lodge.** Just a few steps from beautiful Boulders Beach— one of the best swimming beaches in Cape Town and penguin colony— this comfortable guesthouse is a winner. The understated rooms are decorated with elegant, black, wrought-iron furniture and snow-white linen, creating a restful, minimalist feel. The adjacent restaurant is excellent. **Pros:** access to penguins without the zillions of other tourists; great, friendly staff. **Cons:** no TV; noisy penguins during mating season; insufficient cupboard space in the rooms. ⊠ *4 Boulders Pl., Simon's Town* ☎ *021/786–1758* ⊕ *www.bouldersbeach.co.za* ⟿ *12 rooms* ⟁ *In-room: no TV. In-hotel: restaurant, bar, laundry service, Wi-Fi, parking (free)* ⊟ *AE, DC, MC, V* ⭑⭑ *BP.*

$ ⊞ **De Noordhoek.** Although it may take an hour to get here from Cape Town in busy traffic, once you get here you won't want to leave, as it's situated in a farm village with wonderful restaurants such as the Food Barn and Café Roux as neighbors and funky shops selling things like organic horse shampoo and collectible children's toys. Rooms are very comfortable, and if you're concerned about your carbon footprint, you'll like that water is heated through solar panels and that there's an indigenous, water-wise courtyard garden. All staff live within 7 mi of the hotel to reduce their carbon footprint. The hotel uses biodegradable cleaning materials and bathroom amenities, and recycled items, such as the tables in the dining area, which are locally made from reused timber. It's one of the very few hotels to have four wheelchair friendly rooms where beds, mirrors, and bathrooms are at a lower level. Despite the environmental considerations the hotel is very comfortable and affordable. **Pros:** eight rooms are connected, making them suitable for families. **Cons:** when Chapman's Peak Drive is closed (much of the time), access is via the Atlantic seaboard, on the other side of the peninsula and far to drive. ⊠ *Noordhoek Farm Village, Corner Chapman's Peak Dr. and Village La., Noordhoek* ☎ *021/789–2760* ⊕ *www.denoordhoek. co.za* ⟿ *20 rooms* ⟁ *In-room: safe, Internet. In-hotel: restaurant, room service, bar, laundry service, Internet terminal, parking (free)* ⊟ *AE, DC, MC, V* ⭑⭑ *BP.*

¢   ⊞ **Inn at Castle Hill.** The fishing village of Kalk Bay is a vacation destination in itself. From the inn you can stroll down to the beach, walk to the restaurants, or explore the antiques shops that this bohemian village is known for. The carefully restored Edwardian villa has a wonderful view over False Bay, and the spacious rooms are individually decorated. Be sure to ask for a room that opens onto the veranda. There's a communal TV lounge, and braai facilities are available on request. **Pros:** good value at a great location. **Cons:** location on top of a steep hill might hinder walking around the area; limited on-site parking. ⊠ *37 Gatesville Rd., Kalk Bay* ☎ *021/788–2554* ⊕ *www.castlehill.co.za* ⟿ *5 rooms* ⟁ *In-room: no phone, no TV. In-hotel: bar, laundry service, Internet terminal, parking (free), no kids under 12* ⊟ *AE, DC, MC, V* ⭑⭑ *BP.*

$$$ ★ **Rodwell House.** Luxury living in a converted historic mansion belonging to Randlord J.B. Taylor, a diamond baron. Walls are adorned with an impressive local art collection, and the wine cellar contains 15,000 bottles, including many vintages from every claret first growth from the Bordeaux estates, claimed to be unique in South Africa. There's even a professional wine-tasting facility on-site. The swimming pool is fed by mountain water. St. James is where the English aristocrats holidayed, and the air of moneyed elegance hasn't dissipated. Emphasis is on space, light, and comfort. All but one room have open-plan bathrooms, although toilets are always fully enclosed. **Pros:** live like the rich for less; beautiful indigenous gardens; great swimming beach and tidal pool nearby. **Cons:** train noise in the early morning might wake you up; upper balcony is shared with two other rooms, and other guests and staff can peer into yours while cleaning the rooms. ⊠ *Rodwell St., St. James* ☎ *021/787–9880* ⊕ *www.rodwellhouse.co.za* ⊅ *8 rooms* ♿ *In-room: safe, DVD (some), Wi-Fi. In-hotel: restaurant, room service, pool, gym, spa, beachfront, laundry service, Internet terminal, Wi-Fi, parking (free), no kids under 7* ═ *AE, DC, MC, V* ⫶⊙⫶ *BP.*

¢ **Simon's Town Backpackers.** Don't expect designer linen or glam furnishings at this backpackers' lodge. It's simple, cheap, cheerful, and spotlessly clean, and offers fantastic views from the upstairs balcony. Simon's Town is a great place to station yourself. It's under an hour by car from Cape Town, on the railway line, and within driving proximity of Boulders Beach and the penguin colony. You can also choose from plenty of nearby restaurants, serving everything from sushi to Nepalese fare. The historic building has been many things in its lifetime, including a brothel. A TV is available in the communal lounge. **Pros:** you can't beat the room rates; helpful German-speaking owner; airport shuttle available. **Cons:** not much to do at night in Simon's Town; many locals are part of the area's naval community and can be cliquey. ⊠ *66 St. George's St., Simon's Town* ☎ *021/786–1964* ⊕ *www.capepax.co.za* ⊅ *6 rooms, 4 dormitories* ♿ *In-room: no phone, no TV. In-hotel: bar, bicycles, laundry service, Internet terminal* ═ *AE, DC, MC, V.*

$ **Simon's Town Quayside Hotel.** On Jubilee Square, part of the Simon's Town Waterfront, this hotel is right in the action and has wonderful views over Simon's Town Bay, the harbor, and the yacht club. Almost all rooms have sea views, and all are light and airy, combining lime-washed wood with white walls and pale-blue finishes. Room service can be arranged from the adjacent restaurants. **Pros:** Jubilee Square is town's epicenter; amazing views of fishing boats and naval fleet from sea-facing bedrooms; airport shuttle available. **Cons:** noisy room fridge; no nightlife in Simon's Town; breakfast voucher allowance not very generous. ⊠ *Jubilee Sq., St. George's, Box 555, Simon's Town* ☎ *021/786–3838* ⊕ *www.relaishotels.com* ⊅ *26 rooms* ♿ *In-room: safe, Wi-Fi. In-hotel: room service, laundry service, Wi-Fi, parking (free)* ═ *AE, DC, MC, V* ⫶⊙⫶ *BP.*

NIGHTLIFE AND THE ARTS

NIGHTLIFE

There's plenty to do in Cape Town after dark. The city's nightlife is concentrated in a number of areas, so you can explore a different one each night or move from one hub to another. That said, walking from one area to another isn't advisable, as there are some parts of the city that are completely deserted and unsafe. Women, in pairs or singly, and couples should not walk alone. One of the safest places to start is the Waterfront, where you can choose from movies, restaurants, bars, and pubs and walk between them quite happily, as there are plenty of security guards and other

PINK AND PROUD TO PARTY

A key event on Cape Town's social calendar is December's **MCQP** (*Mother City Queer Party* ⊕ *www. mcqp.co.za*), which started in 1993. Party animals should definitely add this to their must-do list. It's part Mardi Gras, part Gay Pride March, and one enormous fancy-dress party. Each year the party is themed, and everyone goes all out to dress up in fantastic outfits. All are welcome!

people walking around. The top end of Long Street is probably the city's best nightlife area. Here you'll find several blocks of bars, restaurants, and backpacker lodges that are open late. The area bounded by Loop, Long, Wale, and Orange streets is the best place to get a feeling for Cape Town's always-changing nightclub scene, but ask around for the latest on the current flavor of the month. De Waterkant in Green Point is also very busy at night and is home to many of Cape Town's gay venues; if you're in the area, you can take in the Green Point strip, where restaurants and bars open out onto the streets. On weekends these bars are packed, and you'll get a good idea of how Capetonians let down their hair. Heritage Square, in the city center, hosts an ever-changing mix of bars and restaurants generally catering to a more discerning (think wine bars and microbrewery) crowd. Mouille Point's Platinum Mile is an excellent place for evening cocktails, though it's less of a late-night spot. The views over the Atlantic and onto Robben Island are breathtaking, and this is where the ultracool set hangs out after a hard day at the beach or gym. Be prepared to line up to get in to places, especially on a Friday night.

BARS AND PUBS

For a fab evening on Mouille Point's Platinum Mile, plan to have drinks at **Wakame** (⊠ *1st fl., Beach Rd. and Surrey Pl., Mouille Point* ☎ *021/433–2377* ⊕ *www.wakame.co.za*) and then head to the downstairs restaurant for sushi and champagne. You'll have great views of the Atlantic and Robben Island.

Built right on the water's edge adjacent to the yacht marina, **Bascule Whisky Bar and Wine Cellar** (⊠ *Cape Grace Hotel, West Quay Rd., Waterfront* ☎ *021/410–7238*) is a fancy watering hole for well-heeled, cigar-

Jazz It Up

Music, especially jazz and local African music, was an extremely potent instrument for social change during the oppressive apartheid regime. Consequently, South Africans are passionate about music, and they celebrate their love of jazz with the **Cape Town International Jazz Festival** (⊕ *www. capetownjazzfest.com*), usually held in March or early April. Started in 1999, this event is arguably the best weekend of the year in Cape Town. There's an even mix of local and international stars, and past festivals have included the likes of Randy Crawford, Abdullah Ibrahim, Hugh Masekela, Ismael Lo, and Ladysmith Black Mambazo.

It's a tradition for jazz festival performers to play the Monday night jam at **Swingers** (✉ *1 Wetwyn Rd., near Wetton station* ☎ *021/762–2443*), a well-known but out-of-the-way jazz club in Wynburg. Dance music is played Friday and Saturday (cover R30), but Monday (no cover charge) is the night for jazz aficionados. There's also a full restaurant serving traditional Cape curries, seafood, and steaks. On any old night, the **Green Dolphin Jazz Restaurant** (✉ *Victoria & Alfred Arcade, Pierhead, Waterfront* ☎ *021/421–7471*) attracts some of the best mainstream jazz musicians in the country, as well as a few from overseas. The cover charge is R30–R35.

puffing locals. Its 450 whiskies are reputed to be the biggest selection in the Southern Hemisphere.

Caveau Wine Bar & Deli (✉ *Heritage Square, 92 Bree St., Cape Town Central* ☎ *021/422–1367*) is a hip yet unpretentious wine bar where you can sample a dizzying array of fabulous local wines by the glass while munching on excellent tapas or entrées. Extra seating is available in an inner courtyard.

★ Out of town in the quaint fishing village of Kalk Bay, **Polana** (✉ *Kalk Bay Harbour, off Main Rd., Kalk Bay* ☎ *021/788–7162*) has jaw-dropping views across the bay. You can see all the way to Cape Hangklip, and when the weather is good the open windows allow sea breezes to further cool a glass of South Africa's best. There's live music and DJs on Friday and Sunday.

LIVE MUSIC

Among the clubs with live African music, a good spot is **Mama Africa** (✉ *178 Long St., Cape Town Central* ☎ *021/426–1017*). It has a live marimba band Monday through Saturday, as well as authentic African food, music, and pulse. **The Assembly** (✉ *161 Harrington St., District 6, Cape Town Central* ☎ *021/465–7286* ⊕ *www.theassembly.co.za*) is one of Cape Town's best and hottest live music venues, featuring everything from South African indie-rock to Afro-Brazilian electronica.

★ From late November to early April, enjoy the best in South African music, from African to classical to electronica, at outdoor concerts on Sundays at **Kirstenbosch Summer Sunset Concerts** (✉ *Kirstenbosch National*

Botanic Gardens, Rhodes Ave., Newlands ☎ *021/799–8783* ⊕ *www. nbi.ac.za* ✉ *R50–70).* It's a Cape Town summer institution.

THE ARTS

FILM

The Waterfront and Cavendish Mall both have movie houses: respectively, the NuMetro, which plays mainstream fare, and the Cinema Nouveau theater, which concentrates on foreign and art films. Check newspaper listings for what's playing.

The **Labia** (✉ *68 Orange St., Gardens* ✉ *50 Kloof St., Gardens* ☎ *021/424–5927* ⊕ *www.labia.co.za*) is an independent art house and Cape Town institution that screens good-quality mainstream and alternative films. There are four screens at the Labia on Orange and two at the Labia on Kloof, just up the road. A small coffee bar serves snacks and wine at both venues.

THEATER

The **Baxter Theatre Complex** (✉ *Main Rd., Rondebosch* ☎ *021/685–7880* ⊕ *www.baxter.co.za*), part of the University of Cape Town, hosts a range of productions from serious drama to satirical comedies, as well as some rather experimental stuff. The complex includes a 666-seat theater, a concert hall, a smaller studio, and a restaurant and bar.

During the summer, when the weather's good, Cape Town has its own version of New York City's Central Park's Shakespeare in the Park at the excellent **Maynardville Open-Air Theatre** (✉ *Wolfe and Church Sts., Wynberg* ☎ *083/909–0909 Computicket* ⊕ *www.artscape.co.za*). Theatergoers often bring a picnic supper to enjoy before the show.

SPORTS AND THE OUTDOORS

Cape Town is the adventure capital of the universe. Whatever you want to do—dive, paddle, fly, jump, run, slide, fin, walk, or clamber—this is the city to do it in.

For spectator sports, it's easy to get tickets for ordinary club matches and interprovincial games. Getting tickets to an international test match is more of a challenge; however, there's always somebody selling tickets—at a price, of course.

BIKING

Downhill Adventures (☎ *021/422–0388 or 021/422–1380* ⊕ *www.downhilladventures.com*) offers great cycling trips around the peninsula. You can opt for a full day at the nature reserve at Cape Point, including a picnic lunch, or a leisurely cycle through the Constantia Winelands, stopping for wine tasting along the way. Those wanting something more hard-core might like mountain biking in the Tokai Arboretum. Expect to pay R600–R7,000 per trip. **Baz Bus** (☎ *021/439–2323* ⊕ *www. bazbus.com*) tours the south peninsula with a trailer full of bikes. You cycle the fun parts and sit in the bus for the rest. It costs about R425 for the whole day.

BIRDING AND WILDLIFE

Specialized birding walks can be organized through **Brians-Birding** (☎ 021/919–2192 ⊕ *www.brians-birding.co.za*), which offers birding walks that cost R2,200–2,600 for a full day. Prices are per group, usually with a max of about five people.

★ For a unique wildlife encounter, head out with **Baboon Matters** (☎ 021/782–2015). For R275, you'll follow trained guides as they track resident troupes of baboons on the peninsula. The guides will also explain baboon behaviors and conservation concerns.

CLIMBING

Cape Town has hundreds of bolted sport routes around the city and peninsula, ranging from an easy 10 to a hectic 30. (To give you some idea of difficulty, a route rated a 10 in South Africa would be equivalent to a 5.5 climb in the United States. A 20 climb would register around 5.10c, while the hardest you'll find in South Africa is probably a 34, which American climbers would know as a 5.14b. The toughest climb up Table Mountain rates about 32, which is a 5.14a.) Both Table Mountain sandstone and Cape granite are excellent hard rocks. There are route guides to all the major climbs and a number of climbing schools in Cape Town. A few favorite climbs include Table Mountain (from various angles), Lion's Head, Du Toit's Kloof, and Muizenberg Peak. ⇨ *For more information, see Hiking and Canyoning, below.* **High Adventure** (☎ 021/689–1234 ⊕ *www.highadventure.co.za*) specializes in climbing in the Cape Town area but also organizes trips farther afield.

FISHING

If you're keen to take to the open ocean for some deep-sea fishing, you'll have plenty of choices, as South Africa has excellent game fish, such as dorado, yellowfin tuna, and broadbill swordfish. **Hooked on Africa** (☎ 021/790–5332 ⊕ *www.hookedonafrica.co.za*) charters a 32-foot catamaran for a full day of deep-sea fishing (R10,000 to charter the whole boat).

In the mountains, just an hour or so away from Cape Town, you'll encounter wild and wily fish in wild and wonderful rivers. The season runs September–May. **Inkwazi Fly-Fishing Safaris** (☎ 083/626–0467 ⊕ *www.inkwaziflyfishing.co.za*) offers escorted tours, all the equipment you'll need, and plenty of good advice.

GOLF

Most golf clubs in the Cape accept visitors, but prior booking is essential. Expect to pay R250–400 for 18 holes and R200–350 to rent golf clubs. Most clubs offer equipment rental. You can also rent golf carts for around R200, but you are encouraged to employ a caddie instead, as this offers valuable employment to local communities. Expect to pay around R150 plus a tip of 10%–20% for good service. Founded in 1885, **Royal Cape Golf Club** (☎ 021/761–6551 ⊕ *www.royalcapegolf.co.za*) is the oldest course in Africa and has hosted the South African Open many times. Its beautiful setting and immaculate fairways and greens make a round here a must for serious golf enthusiasts. The challenging and scenic **Steenberg Golf Estate** (☎ 021/715–0227 ⊕ *www.steenberggolfclub.co.za*) is the most exclusive and expensive course on the peninsula. A round costs more than R500 per person unless you're staying at the hotel. Dress codes are strictly enforced here.

HIKING AND CANYONING

Cape Town and the surrounding areas offer some of the finest hiking in the world. Take some of the mystery out of Table Mountain with a guide who will share information on the incredible diversity of flora and fauna you'll come across. Join walking (R600 half day) and climbing tours (R750 half day) with **Venture Forth International Travel** (☎ 086/110–6548 ⊕ www.ctsm.co.za). Longer walking tours (four days and longer) outside Cape Town can be arranged through **Active Africa** (☎ 021/788–6083 ⊕ www.active-africa.com).

Kloofing, known as canyoning in the United States, is the practice of following a mountain stream through its gorge, canyon, or kloof by swimming, rock hopping, and jumping over waterfalls or cliffs into deep pools. There are some exceptional kloofing venues in the Cape. **Abseil Africa** (☎ 021/424–4760 ⊕ www.abseilafrica.co.za) runs a kloofing and abseiling (rappelling) trip (R695) on the Steenbras River, better known as Kamikaze Kanyon. **Table Mountain Walks** (☎ 021/715–6136 ⊕ www.tablemountainwalks.co.za) offers various hikes, including options at Table Mountain and Silvermine Nature Reserve, with a well-informed guide (R400–R650). ⇨ For more information on the Hoerikwaggo Trail, see Table Mountain, above.

HORSEBACK RIDING

Cantering down one of the Cape's long white-sand beaches or riding through the fynbos-covered dunes at sunset is a unique and tranquil pleasure, and Noordhoek is the place to do it, whatever your level. **Sleepy Hollows Horse Riding** (☎ 021/789–2341 ⊕ www.sleepyhollow-horseriding.co.za) has three guided rides a day. A two-hour ride costs around R350.

KAYAKING

You don't have to be a pro to discover Cape Town by kayak. **Coastal Kayak Trails** (☎ 021/439–1134 or 083/346–1146 ⊕ www.kayak.co.za) has regular sunset and sunrise paddles off Sea Point. A two-hour paddle costs around R250. **Real Cape Adventures** (☎ 021/790–5611 ⊕ www.seakayak.co.za) offers regular scenic paddles off Hout Bay and from Simon's Town around to Boulders. Expect to pay R250.

PARAGLIDING AND SKYDIVING

Para-pax Tandem Paragliding (☎ 082/881–4724 ⊕ www.parapax.com) will take you flying off landmarks such as Lion's Head, Signal Hill, and Table Mountain, depending on the wind and weather conditions; packages start at R950. You can do a tandem sky dive (no experience necessary) and have a video taken of you hurtling earthward with Table Mountain in the background with **Skydive Cape Town** (☎ 082/800–6290 ⊕ www.skydivecapetown.za.net). A tandem fall costs around R1,450; add on R570 if you want a video of your madness.

Cape Town Spas

Arabella. Breathtaking 360-degree views and ambrosial aromas (courtesy of Anne Sémonin and St Barth products) greet you at this streamlined 19th-floor spa with huge glass windows and floors of pressed pebbles. On arrival, you're offered Jing tea and use of the infinity lap pool and sauna—both with fantastic city views—and steam room. The Truly Precious Face and Body Experience, which includes a body exfoliation, Phyto-aromatic massage (using warmed, detoxifying essential oils), and brightening facial is pure indulgence. Don't miss a post-treatment lie-down in the heated water beds. Power Plate classes and personal trainers are also available.

Treatments Massage: Phyto-aromatic, hot stone, black sand, reflexology. **Exfoliation:** aromatic salt. **Wraps/baths:** oil wrap, anti-cellulite therapy, spirulina, pink kaolin. **Beauty:** Facials, waxing, manicure, pedicure, eye lifting, eye brightening, eyelash tinting, eyebrow grooming.

Prices Body Treatments: R390–R980. **Facials:** R495–R950. **Manicure/pedicure:** R395.

✉ *Westin Grand Arabella Quays, Lower Long St., 19th fl., Cape Town Central* ☎ *021/412–8200* ⊕ *www.westin.com/grandcapetown* ⊟ *AE, DC, MC, V* ⊙ *Treatments daily 9–5; sauna/gym facilities daily 6 AM–10 PM.*

Equinox. In the Cape Royal Hotel, Equinox resembles the interior of a beautiful lacquered box, with dark parquet lit by oil lamps, a smattering of orchids, and a few pieces of Edwardian furniture. Complimentary teas, nuts, and fruit are available in the relaxation room; the changing room is redolent of Charlotte Rhys products.

The chakra balance candle massage, using heated, essential-oils-scented mineral oil, leaves you in a state of balanced bliss. Treatments are great value, including the more medical skin treatments (e.g., micro-dermabrasion). You can relax at the rooftop pool deck and sky bar—well worth a visit for the views of the mountains and ocean. Tai chi and Pilates classes are held weekdays at 6 AM.

Treatments Massage: chakra balance candle, Indian head, Swedish, aromatherapy, hot stone, lymphatic drainage, Thai, mom-to-be. **Exfoliation:** body polish, body scrub. **Wraps:** full body. **Beauty:** Facial, chemibrasion, glycolic, exfoliating peel, micro-needling, micro-dermabrasion, Lumi 8 LED light therapy, waxing, lash/brow tinting, manicure, pedicure, reflexology, bio-sculpture nail treatment (natural nail enhancement), sunless tanning.

Prices Body treatments: R280–R620. **Facials:** R290–R580. **Manicure/pedicure:** R200–R330.

✉ *Cape Royale Hotel, 47 Main Rd., Green Point* ☎ *021/430–0500* ⊕ *www.equinoxspa.co.za* ⊟ *AE, DC, MC, V* ⊙ *Weekdays 8–8, Sun. 9–6.*

Klein Genot Spa. Just the drive to this spa through the Franschhoek Mountains makes a visit worthwhile. On the grounds of a boutique hotel and wine estate, the spa is modest in dimension and style, but equal to big-city spas in its personalized service. Matis, Environ, Africology, and Moya products are stocked, and the facials are fantastic. Themed collections—unwind, awakening, quietude—group complementary treatments together and include extras like cheese and wine or lunch.

2

The restaurant is excellent, and you can use the pool or do a wine tasting.

Body Treatments Massage: back, neck, and shoulder; hot stone; deep tissue; scalp; Swedish, lymphatic drainage, pressure point. **Exfoliation:** full body. **Wraps:** full body. **Beauty:** Facials, eye treatment, anti-aging, manicure, pedicure, lash/brow tinting, waxing, body bronzing.

Prices Body treatments: R238–R598. **Facials:** R258–R728. **Manicure/pedicure:** R198–R248.

✉ *Klein Genot Wine & Country Estate, Green Valley Rd., Franschhoek* ☎ *021/876-2738* ⊕ *www.kleingenot. com* 🚘 *AE, DC, MC, V* ⊘ *Daily 9–6.*

Librisa. An oasis of elegant calm in the Mount Nelson Hotel's bucolic English gardens, this spa has a glassed-in relaxation room with stunning views of Lion's Head. Many treatments feature local ingredients like *marula* (a fruit) and South African geranium. The therapeutic massage relieves travel stress and the decadent Rekindle Spa Experience combines an aromatic massage and facial followed by the hotel's legendary afternoon tea. Teen and kids' treatments are available, and you are welcome to use the hotel's family pool.

Body Treatments Massage: jet-lag, hot stone, aroma-touch, prenatal, therapeutic, reflexology. **Exfoliation:** grape seed, earth salt. **Wraps/baths:** green clay, marula, and mint wrap; ocean wrap (seaweed cellulite treatment); green tea detox; rooibos and lavender clay wrap. **Beauty:** Facial, manicure, pedicure, lash/brow tinting, waxing, body bronzing.

Prices Body treatments: R400–R800. **Facials:** R400–R800. **Manicures/pedicure:** R250–R300.

✉ *Mount Nelson Hotel, 76 Orange St., Gardens* ☎ *021/483-1550* ⊕ *www. mountnelson.co.za* 🚘 *AE, DC, MC, V* ⊘ *Daily 9–8.*

Spa at Cape Grace. Impeccable service and professionalism are the hallmarks of this spa, whose paprika-and-saffron-hued spice-route motif is vibrant yet elegant. An exclusive range of locally produced teas is available. A salon next door offers hairstyling. Drawing on Khoi-San healing customs, the African Cape massage includes a full-body massage with a shea butter and snowbush flower infusion. Facial therapies and body treatments using the Africology range are excellent and use essential oils and local plant extracts like rooibos and African potato. The relaxation and hot spa area (mineral spa bath, sauna, steam room, rain showers) has spectacular views of Table Mountain.

Treatments Massage: jet-lag, hot stone, Aromasoul, Swedish, back cleanse, deep tissue, fusion therapy. **Exfoliation:** marula scrub. **Wraps:** D-Age repairing (with *kamani* oil), body strategist nutritional (with vegetable and rice protein), Monticelli detoxifying. **Beauty:** Facials, waxing, manicure, pedicure, haircuts, highlights, eye treatments, body bronzing.

Prices Body treatments: R455–R1,185. **Facials:** R720–R965. **Hair/salon services:** R210–R695. **Manicure/pedicure:** R300–R485.

✉ *Cape Grace hotel, West Quay, Waterfront* ☎ *021/418-0495* ⊕ *www.capegrace.com* 🚘 *AE, DC, MC, V* ⊘ *Daily 8–8.*

RAPPELLING

Abseil Africa (☎ *021/424–4760* ⊕ *www.abseilafrica.co.za*) offers a 350-foot abseil (rappel) off the top of Table Mountain for about R500, not including the cable car. Another excursion takes you over a waterfall in the Helderberg Mountains, an hour's drive away, for about R700, including transportation and lunch.

SAILING

Drum Africa (☎ *021/785–4775* ⊕ *www.drumafrica.co.za*) launches catamarans (and you) on Langebaan lagoon (one hour from Cape Town). Before you know it you'll be in a trapeze harness leaning over the side of a Hobie Cat (R395 per hour) like an old pro. This is the only company in South Africa that offers both instruction (half- and full-day courses) and chartering of Hobie Cats.

SCUBA DIVING

The diving around the Cape is excellent, with kelp forests, cold-water corals, very brightly colored reef life, and numerous wrecks. An unusual experience is a dive in the Two Oceans Aquarium. CMSA, NAUI, and PADI dive courses are offered by local operators; open-water certification courses begin at about R2,800 (all-inclusive). **Orca Industries** (☎ *021/671–9673* ⊕ *www.orca-industries.co.za*) offers dive courses, charters, and wreck dives. The friendly **Scuba Shack** (☎ *021/424–9368 Cape Town* ☎ *021/782–7358 Kommetjie* ⊕ *www.scubashack.co.za*) has two outlets: one in town and one near Kommetjie.

SHARK DIVING

Seeing great white sharks hunting seals around False Bay's Seal Island is one of the most exhilarating natural displays you're likely to witness. And if witnessing it all from a boat is not thrill enough, you can get in the water (in a cage). Run by marine biologists, **Apex Predators** (☎ *082/364–2738* ⊕ *www.apexpredators.com*) runs small trips (R1,700) out of Simon's Town during season (April–September). If the great whites aren't around, try the Ocean Predator Trip, in which you free dive (no cage) with makos and blues.

SOCCER

Soccer in South Africa is much more grassroots than cricket or rugby and has been very big in the townships for decades (⇨ *Fields of Play [District Six Museum], in Exploring Cape Town*). Amateur games are played from March to September at many venues all over the peninsula. Professional games are played from October to April at Athlone Stadium, Newlands, and Cape Town stadiums.

SURFING

Cape Town has some great but cold surf, and conditions can be complicated by the winds. Though it's no J-Bay (Jeffreys Bay), Cape Town still has some killer spots.

☾ **Gary's Surf School** (☎ *021/788–9839* ⊕ *www.garysurf.com*) offers surfing lessons to youngsters and the young at heart in the relatively warm and gentle waters at Muizenberg. You can also rent boards and wet suits. Lessons last two hours and cost around R500 for adults, R400 for children, including suit and board; if you still feel strong after that,

CLOSE UP

Cape Town and the World Cup

Cape Town Stadium will hold 70,000 World Cup fans, is 15 floors high, and has 16 elevators, 135 VIP suites, and basement parking for 1,200 cars. The stadium footprint is equivalent to six city blocks. The facade is covered with an open mesh fabric that plays with natural light. The roof protects from weather, while also providing proper acoustics for future music concerts. The city also redeveloped the common around the stadium into an urban park and sports area with an additional 5,000 parking spaces.

Address: Fritz Sonnenberg Road, Cape Town

Fan Park: Grand Parade Fan Park, next to the central railway station and the end point of the 2-km Fan Walk leading to the stadium, will be the city's official fan park, a free public viewing area. From 10 AM to midnight, fans can watch matches on large-screen TVs and enjoy entertainment, food, and drink. Additionally, the Bellville Velodrome (Northern Suburbs), the Athlone Stadium (Southern Suburbs), and the Swartklip Sports Center (Cape Flats) will show the Cape Town matches, semifinals, and the final match. These will also be free, and will offer the same amenities.

Match Schedule: Cape Town will host eight matches, including a quarterfinal and semifinal game. Matches take place on June 11, 14, 18, 21, 24, and 29 (all at 8:30); July 3 (at 4), and the semifinal on July 6 (8:30).

Safety and Security: The stadium and surrounds will have extensive video surveillance. On match days, police will patrol on horseback, bicycle, scooter, and foot. Police presence will be increased throughout the city and its fan parks for the duration of the tournament and private security firms will aid the South African Police Services. The stadium will also have its own security in and around the venue and in the fan parks. Tourism Ambassadors will be located in the airport, central city, fan parks, stadium, and key tourism sites to provide information and report suspicious activity. All tickets are marked with the name, passport number, and seat number of the ticket holder so that wrongdoers can be identified, arrested, and banned from future games.

Transportation: An integrated (bus-and-rail) rapid-transit system (IRT) is being created for the city, which includes dedicated lanes for fast bus travel and a shuttle between the airport and city center. Park-and-ride services will be available on match days (locations TBD), with parking bays in the city center and at the V&A Waterfront. Shuttles and trains converge at or near Hertzog Boulevard, the city's main transport hub; from here stadium shuttle buses will transport spectators the little over a kilometer to the game venue and back.

Information: ☎ 080/065-6463 *Metrorail (transport), 021/487-6800 Cape Town Tourism ⊕ www.capetown. gov.za/en/2010 or www.capetown. travel/2010.*

⇨ *For more information, see World Cup 411, in Chapter 1.*

2

you can keep the equipment for the rest of the day. You do need to be aware, however, that you'll be sharing the ocean with plenty of sharks, but that never seems to stop anyone.

SHOPPING

When it comes to shopping, Cape Town has something for everyone—from sophisticated malls to trendy markets. Although African art and curios are obvious choices (and you will find some gems), South Africans have woken up to their own sense of style and creativity, and the results are fantastic and as diverse as the people who make up this rainbow nation. So in a morning you could bag some sophisticated tableware from Carrol Boyes, a funky wire-art object from a street vendor, and a beautifully designed handbag made by HIV-positive women working as part of a community development program.

Cape Town has great malls selling well-known brands, and the V&A Waterfront is an excellent place to start, followed by Cavendish Square in Claremont and Canal Walk at Century City, on the N1 heading out of town toward Paarl. But it's beyond the malls that you can get a richer shopping experience, one that will give you greater insight into the soul of the city and its people. Shopping malls usually have extended shopping hours beyond the normal 9–5 on weekdays and 9–1 on Saturdays. Most shops outside of malls (except for small grocery stores) are closed on Sunday.

MARKETS

Greenmarket Square. You can get good buys on clothing, T-shirts, and locally made leather shoes and sandals, and you can find a plethora of African jewelry, art, and fabrics here, too. It's one of the best places in town to purchase gifts, but it's lively and fun whether or not you buy anything. More than half the stalls are owned by people not from South Africa. Here you'll find political and economic refugees from Ethiopia, Eritrea, Zimbabwe, and the Democratic Republic of Congo trying to eke out a living. Bargain, but do so with a conscience. ⊠ *Longmarket, Burg, and Shortmarket Sts., Cape Town Central* ☎ *No phone* ☺ *Mon.– Sat. 9–4:30.*

☻ **Obs Holistic Lifestyle Fair.** For everything weird and wonderful, this market is an absolute winner. Cape Town is home to plenty of alternative-therapy practitioners, crystal gazers, and energy healers, and they congregate on the first Sunday of every month to sell their wares and trade spells. Food is abundant, healthful (of course), and vegetarian. Kids are not ignored; they run wild together with their parents. ⊠ *Station and Lower Main Rds., Observatory* ☎ *021/788–8088* ☺ *1st Sun. of month 10–4.*

V&A Craft Market. This indoor market contains an assortment of handcrafted jewelry, rugs, glass, pottery, and leather sandals, the majority of which are made in South Africa. There's also a wellness center where you can have a shiatsu massage or some reflexology to pep you up if you're shopped out. ⊠ *Dock Rd. (next to Aquarium), Waterfront* ☎ *021/408–7842* ☺ *Daily 9:30–6.*

Woodstock Neighbour Goods Market. Also known as the Biscuit Mill market, Woodstock is aimed at Cape Town's hip, organic types on their Vespas looking for artisan breads, pesto, home-cured olives, and produce imported from France. It gets frantically busy, which indicates just how popular it is, but if you want to rub shoulders with trendy design types and eat fabulous artisanal everything, this is the place to be. One of the stalls sells seared-tuna sandwiches and salads; it's worth standing in line. When you're done browsing at the market, head to some of the great stores in the same complex. ⊠ *373–375 Albert Rd. (Lower Main Rd.), Woodstock* ☎ *No phone* ☾ *Sat. 9–3.*

SPECIALTY STORES
ARTS AND CRAFTS
A number of stores in Cape Town sell African art and crafts, much of which comes from Zululand or neighboring countries. Street vendors, particularly on St. George's Mall and Greenmarket Square, often sell the same curios for half the price. Pick up the excellent "Not the Official Arts + Crafts Map" and "Cape Town Design Route" brochures available at Cape Town Tourism, for listings of excellent and cutting-edge galleries, boutiques, and designers.

Africa Nova. If you aren't crazy about traditional African artifacts, you might want to visit this store, which stocks contemporary African art that's quirky and interesting. Original African art is showcased for those looking for one-of-a-kind pieces. Come Christmastime, the store is transformed with beaded African Christmas decorations: gorgeous stars, divine angels, and brilliant nativity animals. Even if you aren't buying, it's worth visiting for the display. ⊠ *72 Waterkant St., Cape Quarter* ☎ *021/425–5123* ⊕ *www.africanova.co.za.*

African Image. Look here for contemporary African art and township crafts, colorful cloth from Nigeria and Ghana, plus West African masks, Malian blankets, and beaded designs from southern African tribes. ⊠ *Burg and Church Sts., Cape Town Central* ☎ *021/423–8385.*

Mnandi Textiles. Here you'll find a range of African fabrics, including traditional West African prints and Dutch wax prints. The store sells ready-made African clothing for adults and children, and you can also have garments made to order. ⊠ *90 Station Rd., Observatory* ☎ *021/447–6811.*

Pan-African Market. The market, extending over two floors of a huge building, is a jumble of tiny stalls, traditional African hairdressers, tailors, potters, artists, musicians, and drummers. There is also a small, very African restaurant. If you're not going to visit countries to the north, come here for an idea of what you're missing. ⊠ *76 Long St., Cape Town Central* ☎ *021/426–4478.*

★ **Streetwires.** You'll see street wire art everywhere in Cape Town, but this shop is a trove of the art form, which uses a combination of wire, beads, and other recycled materials to create bowls, lights, mobiles, and expressive sculptures. You might even want to buy a working wire radio. You won't find too many of those back home. ⊠ *77 Shortmarket St., Cape Town Central* ☎ *021/426–2475* ⊕ *www.streetwires.co.za.*

BOOKS AND MUSIC

★ **African Music Store.** The people who work here are passionate about African music and eager to pass on their love to anybody who lends them half an ear. You could easily spend a couple of hours listening to any and everything in the store. With a listening booth to sample any CD in the shop, you're bound to find something here that captures the heart of the country for you. ⊠ *134 Long St., Cape Town Central* ☎ *021/426–0857.*

The Book Lounge. Cape Town's best independent bookstore has a fantastic selection of titles, with many classics and contemporary must-haves on all things African. It also frequently hosts readings and book launches and has a nice café downstairs where you can enjoy a cappuccino while browsing. ⊠ *211 Long St., Cape Town Central* ☎ *021/423–5739.*

Exclusive Books. This is one of the best all-around bookshops in the country. The chain carries a wide selection of local and international periodicals and coffee-table books on Africa, and branches are found at all big malls and the airports. ⊕ *www.exclusivebooks.com.*

WINE

Most Capetonians wouldn't dream of having supper without a glass of wine, and most supermarket chains carry a good range of affordable local labels. A visit to Cape Town isn't complete until you've tasted and bought some of the wine the area is famous for. Your best bet is to buy directly from the vineyards, but if you don't manage to get out to the Winelands, head to one of the area stores that can fix you up with local or international wines. ⇨ *For information on how to ship wine back to the States, see Chapter 3, Winelands and Beaches: The Western Cape.*

Manuka Fine Wines. This store in the Southern Suburbs makes a point of stocking wines from the nearby Constantia Valley wine farms as well as those from the rest of the Cape. There are free wine tastings on Saturday morning and wine-tasting dinners once a month, at which winemakers introduce their product to appreciative imbibers. ⊠ *Steenberg Village Shopping Centre, Steenberg Rd. and Reddam Ave., Tokai* ☎ *021/701–2046* ⊕ *www.manuka.co.za.*

★ **Vaughan Johnson's Wine & Cigar Shop.** This wineshop has a terrific selection and staff members who know their stuff. It has specially designed boxes to take a few cases home with you. And who could blame you? ⊠ *Dock Rd., Waterfront* ☎ *021/419–2121.*

Winelands and Beaches

THE WESTERN CAPE

WORD OF MOUTH

"I got a private driver for the Winelands and asked to go to smaller wineries that would not export to Canada as I don't want to try wine I could try at home. It was fantastic and I didn't need to worry about driving or staying sober. Had a fantastic time and even tried some wineries the tour guide had never been to so she had fun exploring too."

—laughternlife

Updated by
Karena du
Plessis

The Western Cape is an alluring province, a sweep of endless mountain ranges, empty beaches, and European history dating back more than three centuries and anchored by Cape Town in the southwest. The cultures of the indigenous Khoekhoen and San people—the first inhabitants of this enormous area—also contribute to the region's richness. In less than two hours you can reach most of the province's highlights from Cape Town, making the city an ideal base from which to explore.

The historic Winelands, in the city's backyard, produce fine wine amid the exquisite beauty of rocky mountains, serried vines, and elegant Cape Dutch estates. Here farms have been handed down from one generation to another for centuries, and old-name families like the Cloetes and Myburghs have become part of the fabric of the region. Even first-time visitors may notice subtle differences between these Cape Afrikaners and their more conservative cousins in the hinterland. For the most part they are descendants of the landed gentry and educated classes who stayed in the Cape after the British takeover in 1806 and the emancipation of the slaves in 1834.

The region they stayed behind in was one truly blessed by nature. Wildflowers are one extraordinary element of this natural bounty. The Western Cape is famous for its fynbos (pronounced *fane*-boss), the hardy, thin-leaf vegetation that gives much of the province its distinctive look. Fynbos composes a major part of the Cape floral kingdom, the smallest and richest of the world's six floral kingdoms. More than 8,500 plant species are found in the province, of which 5,000 grow nowhere else on earth. The region is dotted with nature reserves where you can hike through this profusion of flora, admiring the majesty of the king protea or the shimmering leaves of the silver tree. When the wind blows and mist trails across the mountainsides, the fynbos-covered landscape takes on the look of a Scottish heath.

Not surprisingly, people have taken full advantage of the Cape's natural bonanza. In the Overberg and along the West Coast, rolling wheat fields extend to the horizon, while farther inland jagged mountain ranges hide fertile valleys of apple orchards, orange groves, and vineyards. At sea, hardy fisherfolk battle icy swells to harvest succulent crayfish (similar to lobster), delicate *perlemoen* (abalone), and line fish, such as the delicious *kabeljou*. Each June–November hundreds of whales return to the Cape shores to calve, and the stretch of coastline that includes Hermanus, now referred to as the Whale Coast, becomes one of the best places for land-based whale-watching in the world.

For untold centuries this fertile region supported the Khoekhoen (Khoikhoi) and San (Bushmen), indigenous peoples who lived off the land as pastoralists and hunter-gatherers. With the arrival of European settlers, however, they were chased off, killed, or enslaved. In the remote recesses of the Cederberg mountains and along the West Coast you can still see the fading rock paintings left by the San, whose few remaining clans have long since retreated into the Kalahari Desert. The population of the Western Cape today is largely "coloured," a term used to describe South Africans of mixed race and descendants of imported slaves, the San, the Khoekhoen, and European settlers (⇨ *"A Note on the Term 'Coloured'" box, below).*

ORIENTATION AND PLANNING

GETTING ORIENTED

The Winelands, just 45 minutes east of Cape Town, is the Napa Valley of Southern Africa. The region boasts some of South Africa's best restaurants and hotels, not to mention incredible wine. Running in a broad band from northeast to southeast is the beautiful Breede River valley, home to farms, vineyards, and orchards.

East of the Winelands and bordering the Atlantic Ocean, the Overberg is home to the small towns and villages of Gordon's Bay, Betty's Bay, Kleinmond, Hermanus, Stanford, and Gansbaai, and is usually referred to as the Overstrand. (*Strand* is Afrikaans for beach.) Inland, Overberg villages of Elgin, Greyton, Swellendam, and Elim embody a bygone age.

Heading north out of Cape Town is the drier, more windswept West Coast. Small fishing villages hunker down next to the sea and offer visitors plenty of space to roam.

The Winelands. This area fans out around three historic towns and their valleys. Founded in 1685, Stellenbosch's oak-lined streets, historic architecture, good restaurants, interesting galleries and shops, and vibrant university community make it an ideal base for wine travel. Franschhoek, enclosed by towering mountains, is the original home of the Cape's French Huguenots, whose descendants have made a conscious effort to reassert their French heritage. Paarl lies beneath huge granite domes, its main street running 11 km (7 mi) along the Berg River past some of the country's most elegant historic monuments.

Breede River Valley. Farms, vineyards, and orchards make up most of the Breede River valley. (So it should come as no surprise that one of the towns in the area is called Ceres, after the Roman goddess of agriculture.) Small-town hospitality, striking mountains, and wide-open spaces are hallmarks of this area. In summer the heat can be overwhelming, while in winter the mountain peaks are often covered with snow.

The Overberg. The genteel atmosphere of the southwestern Cape fades quickly the farther from Cape Town you go. The Overberg, separated from the city by the Hottentots Holland Mountains, presides over the rocky headland of Cape Agulhas, where the Indian and Atlantic oceans meet (officially) at the southernmost tip of the continent. Unspoiled

TOP REASONS TO GO

Land of Divine Wine. Few places in the world can match the drama of the Winelands, where mountains rise above vine-covered valleys and 300-year-old homesteads. Against this stunning backdrop you can visit scores of wineries, tour their cellars, relax under old oaks with a picnic basket, and dine at the many excellent restaurants in the area. You'll be hard-pressed to decide which wines to take home with you.

Whale of a Time. Come spring, when the winter rains are no longer lashing the Cape, the icy seas teem with Southern Right whales who come here to calve. Towns like Hermanus offer some of the best land-based whale-watching in the world, and you can also take a boat trip out to see these gentle giants. If it's adrenaline you're after, head to Gansbaai, where you can go diving amid great white sharks.

Flower Power. In summer, when the temperatures soar and the land is dusty, parched, and brown, it's hard to imagine the transformation that takes place each spring when millions of flowers carpet the West Coast hills. It's a photographer's dream, with the blue ocean in the background and swaths of yellow, white, and orange daisies.

Fabulous Food. South African food has come into its own. Boring *boer-ekos* (directly translated as "farmer's food"), characterized by meat and overcooked vegetables, has given way to an explosion of great cuisine. A new generation of chefs is making the most of the area's fabulous fresh produce, and restaurants in Franschhoek and Stellenbosch regularly get voted among the world's best.

The Great Outdoors. The Western Cape's real charm lies outdoors. Erinvale and the Western Cape Hotel & Spa, near Kleinmond, have some of the most spectacular golf courses in the world. In the Cederberg you can hike for days and explore ancient rock formations while learning about the leopard-conservation programs. You can also ride horses through the vineyards of the Winelands or go boating in the Klein River lagoon near Hermanus.

beaches, coastal mountains, and small towns are the lure of this remote area.

West Coast. North of Cape Town on the West Coast, civilization drops away altogether, save for a few lonely fishing villages and mining towns. Each spring, though, the entire region explodes in a spectacular wild-flower display that slowly spreads inland to the desiccated Namaqualand and the Cederberg mountains. For nature lovers, the West Coast provides some unique opportunities, including birding at the West Coast National Park at the Langebaan Lagoon and hiking in the remote wilderness areas of the Cederberg.

PLANNING

Many people come to the Western Cape after getting a big-game fix in Kruger. Although it's possible to explore Cape Town and the Winelands in three or four days—the area is compact enough to allow it—you need six or seven to do it justice. You can get a good sense of either

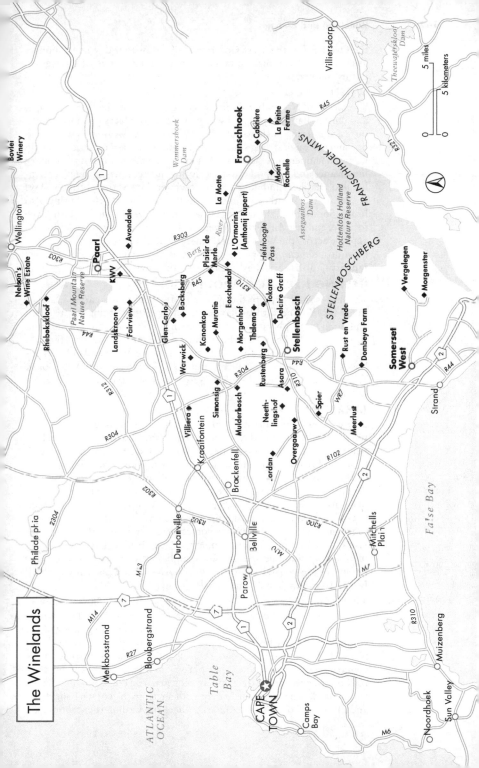

the Overberg or the West Coast on a three- or four-day jaunt, but set aside a week if you plan to tackle more than one or two of the regions in this chapter.

WHEN TO GO

Summer (late November–January) is high season in the Western Cape, and during that time you will seldom visit major places of interest without encountering busloads of fellow visitors. The weather is warm and dry, and although strong southeasterly winds can be a nuisance, they do keep the temperature bearable. If soaking up the sun is not of primary importance and you prefer to tour during quieter times, spring (September and October) and autumn–early winter (late March through May) are ideal. The weather is milder, and the lines are shorter. Spring also brings Southern Right whales close to the shores of the Western Cape to calve, and late August–October are the months to see the wildflowers explode across the West Coast. If the Winelands are high on your list of must-dos, remember that the busiest time in the vineyards and cellars is January–April, when they begin harvesting and wine making.

GETTING HERE AND AROUND

The best way to explore the Western Cape is to rent a car and take to the roads. You need to be flexible to enjoy all this region has to offer, and public transportation is too limited. Navigating your way around is not difficult. There are three main routes out of the city: the N1, N2, and N7. The N1 and N2 take you to the Winelands of Stellenbosch, Franschhoek, and Paarl, and the N7 heads up the West Coast. To reach the Overberg, take the N2 out of town and head up over Sir Lowry's Pass.

TAKE IT ALL IN

3 Days: You could devote a couple of days to touring the wineries, spending perhaps one day visiting Stellenbosch-area wineries such as Simonsig and Villiera, and another day around Franschhoek or Paarl. Consider breaking up your wine touring with horseback riding at one of the vineyards and a night in Franschhoek. A third day could be devoted to a long, scenic route back to Cape Town after lunch at one of Franschhoek's many good restaurants. Another option is to spend the first day wine tasting, and then drive over Sir Lowry's Pass through Elgin and on to Greyton, where you can wander around the village and visit the Moravian Mission complex in Genadendal. The last morning of your stay could be spent in Greyton before you head back to Cape Town via the coastal road, Clarence Drive, that passes Kleinmond, Betty's Bay, Pringle Bay, and Gordon's Bay.

5 Days: With five days, you can work in time to see the Winelands as well as Clanwilliam, at the edge of the Cederberg. (The drive to the Clanwilliam area will take you through the Swartland and the beginning of the wildflower route, which is best in spring.) If nature beckons, head into the Cederberg, where you can easily spend two nights in some of the country's most spectacular scenery. You can hike, swim in crystal-clear rock pools, and admire ancient San rock art. You could also combine a trip to the Winelands or Cederberg with a visit to the coast's Langebaan and the West Coast National Park, where the birding is exceptional.

7 Days: A week would allow you to comfortably visit the Winelands, Cederberg, and the coast. You could spend a few days in the Cederberg and then head through Riebeek Kasteel and Wellington and on to the Winelands towns of Paarl, Stellenbosch, and Franschhoek, where you can linger for the next two or three days. You could easily spend your last days in the beautiful Franschhoek valley. Or you could take a scenic back route on the R45 and then the R321 into the Overberg. You could spend a couple of days exploring the coast, overnighting in Hermanus or Arniston. If it's winter, watch whales, and if you're not sick of wine by this point, sample some of the Overberg wines. Drive back to Cape Town via the spectacular coastal road of Clarence Drive.

RESTAURANTS

The dining scene ranges from fine South African cuisine complete with silver service to local, laid-back, country-style cooking. Franschhoek restaurants attract some of the country's most innovative chefs, who aren't afraid to experiment with unusual ingredients or food-and-wine combinations, and offer up a very sophisticated dining experience in a gorgeous setting. West Coast fare is not as urban as what you find in the Winelands, and coastal towns usually concentrate on seafood, often served in open-air restaurants. Farther inland the cuisine tends to be less trendy and the portions more generous. Be sure to try some Cape Malay cuisine, characterized by mild, slightly sweet curries and aromatic spices. The only places you're likely to be disappointed in the food are in smaller agricultural towns in the Overberg or up the West Coast, where overcooked veggies and an uninspiring and indistinguishable roast are still the norm. But this is changing from month to month as weary city slickers are heading out of town to open lovely restaurants serving quality food.

Country restaurants tend to serve lunch from noon and dinner from 6, and do not cater to late diners except on weekends. Because these areas rely heavily on tourists and local day-trippers, most restaurants in the Winelands and seaside towns are open on weekends, especially for leisurely Sunday lunches, but may catch their breath on Sunday evenings or quieter Mondays. Dress codes vary as much as the dining experiences. Casual wear is acceptable during the day and at most restaurants in the evening. On the coast people pull shorts and T-shirts over their swimsuits before tucking into a plate of calamari and chips (fries), but some Winelands restaurants like their patrons to look as good as the cuisine they deliver. Even so, a nice pair of jeans or pants and a good shirt are usually enough; jackets and ties are rarely expected. If there's someplace you really want to eat, reserve ahead. In December and January, popular restaurants book up quickly, and reservations are advised at least a day or two in advance.

HOTELS

The Winelands are sufficiently compact that you can make one hotel your touring base. Stellenbosch and Paarl, situated close to dozens of wineries and restaurants as well as the major highways to Cape Town, offer the most flexibility. Here bed-and-breakfasts and self-catering (with cooking facilities) options are often less expensive than hotels,

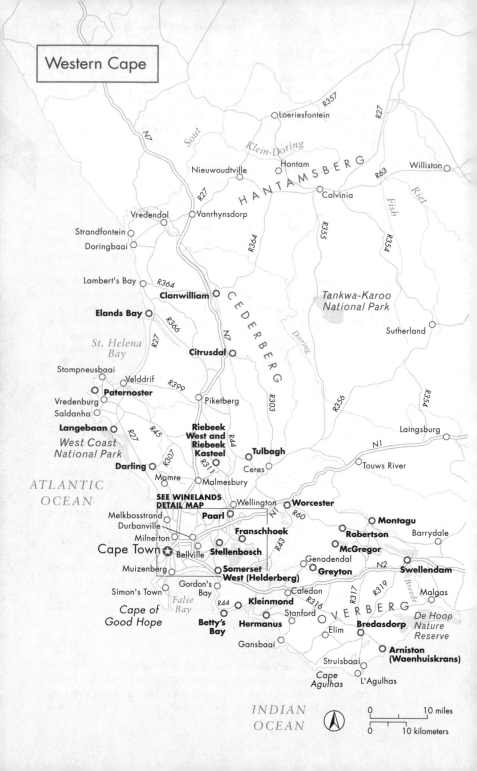

and provide a better taste of life in the country. Franschhoek is comparatively isolated, which many visitors consider a blessing. The West Coast, the Cederberg, and the Overberg are much more spread out, so you'll want to stay in one place for a day or two and then move on. During the peak season of December–January, book well in advance, and be prepared for mandatory two-night stays on weekends. Although the winter months of June–September are usually a lot quieter and bring negotiable rates, seaside towns get really busy (and booked up) when the whales arrive to calve. The same is true up the West Coast during flower season.

3

WHAT IT COSTS IN SOUTH AFRICAN RAND

	¢	$	$$	$$$	$$$$
Restaurants	under R70	R70–R100	R101–R150	R155–R200	over R200
Hotels	under R1000	R1,000–R1,500	R1,501–R2,500	R2,501–R3,500	over R3,500

Restaurant prices are per person for a main course at dinner, a main course equivalent, or a prix-fixe meal. Hotel prices are for a standard double room in high season, including 14% tax.

HEALTH AND SAFETY

If you plan to go hiking in the mountains, come prepared with the right clothing and the correct attitude—each year tourists get lost in the mountains. Cape weather is notoriously changeable, so you need something warm and preferably waterproof. Take at least two liters of water per person and something to eat. If possible, hike with somebody who knows the area well, but if you're walking alone, be sure to take a cell phone and program in some emergency numbers (but be aware that cell phones won't work in all areas). Let somebody know of your route and when you expect to return, and don't stray from the paths if the mist closes in.

VISITOR INFORMATION

You can get almost all the information you need about the Western Cape and Winelands from the very organized Cape Town Tourism offices, which are open weekdays 8–6, Saturday 8:30–1, and Sunday 9–1.

Tourist Offices Cape Town Tourism (⊠ *The Pinnacle, Burg and Castle Sts., Cape Town* ☎ *021/426–5639* ⊕ *www.tourismcapetown.co.za*).

THE WINELANDS

Frank Prial, wine critic for the *New York Times,* wrote that he harbored "a nagging suspicion that great wines must be made in spectacular surroundings." If that's true, then the Cape Winelands are perfectly poised to produce fantastic wines, because the setting of dramatic mountains and lush valleys is absolutely stunning.

Although the Winelands region is largely thought of as the wine centers of Stellenbosch, Franschhoek, and Paarl, today these areas make

CLOSE UP

A Note on the Term "Coloured"

South Africa has come a long way since the first democratic elections in 1994. Parts of the country are, in fact, just about unrecognizable. What hasn't changed, however, is the enormous complexity surrounding language, race classification, and cultural identity. While for many Americans the term *"colored"* is offensive, in South Africa the term (spelled *"coloured"*) is not considered offensive and is widely used to describe South Africans of mixed race, often descended from imported slaves, the San, the Khoekhoen, and European settlers. Over the years the term *"coloured"* has lost its pejorative connotations. Coloureds don't regard themselves as black Africans, and culturally they are extremely different. What is especially confusing to people just passing through South Africa is that many coloureds share so much in common with Afrikaners and are united in their love for and use of Afrikaans.

up only about 35% of all the land in the Cape under vine. This wine-growing region is now so vast you can trek to the fringes of the Karoo Desert, in the northeast, and still find a grape. There are around 18 wine routes in the Western Cape, ranging from the Olifants River, in the north, to the coastal mountains of the Overberg and beyond. There's also a well-established Winelands brandy route, and an annual port festival is held in Calitzdorp, in the Little Karoo.

The secret to touring the Winelands is not to hurry. Dally over lunch on a vine-shaded veranda at a 300-year-old estate, enjoy an afternoon nap under a spreading oak, or sip wine while savoring the impossible views. Of the scores of wineries and estates in the Winelands, the ones listed below are chosen for their great wine, their beauty, or their historic significance. It would be a mistake to try to cover them all in less than a week. You have nothing to gain from hightailing it around the Winelands other than a headache. If your interest is more aesthetic and cultural than wine driven, you would do well to focus on the historic estates of Stellenbosch and Franschhoek. Most Paarl wineries stand out more for the quality of their wine than for their beauty.

GETTING HERE AND AROUND

Driving yourself is undoubtedly the best way to appreciate the area. Each wine route is clearly marked with attractive road signs, and there are complimentary maps available at the tourism bureaus and at most wine farms. Roads in the area are good, and even the dirt roads leading up to a couple of the farms are nothing to worry about.

The best way to get to the Winelands is to take the N2 out of Cape Town and then the R310 to Stellenbosch. Outside of rush hour, this will take you around 45 minutes. Expect some delays during the harvest months (generally late January–late March), when tractors ferry grapes from farms to cellars on the narrower secondary roads. On your way back to Cape Town, stick to the R310 and the N2. Avoid taking the M12, as it gets very confusing, and you'll end up in suburbs that aren't on tourist maps.

The major car-rental agencies have offices in the smaller towns, but it's best to deal with the Cape Town offices. Besides, you'll probably want to pick up a car at the airport. If you're already in the Winelands and would like a car for the day, try Wine Route Rent-a-Car, based in Paarl, which will drop off a car at your hotel. Since driving yourself around limits the amount of wine you can taste, unless you have a designated driver, it's best to join a tour, take a taxi, or—do it in style—rent a limo. Limos cost about R400 per hour, so they're particularly cost-effective if you have a group of four or five.

Paarl Radio Taxis will transport up to three people at about R9 per kilometer (half mile). Waiting time is around R60 per hour. Larger groups can arrange transportation by minibus. Daksi Cab, based in Stellenbosch, works on a trip rate rather than a per-kilometer basis. A trip to a local restaurant costs around R70 regardless of the number of people. Daksi also provides shuttle service to the airport.

There's no regular bus service to the Winelands suitable for tourists. If you are based in Stellenbosch, however, and don't want to drive to the wineries, you can make use of the Vine Hopper, a minibus that follows a fixed route to six wine farms. Tickets cost around R150 for a one-day ticket and R260 for a two-day ticket, and you'll be given a timetable so that you can get on and off as you please.

Cape Metro trains run from Cape Town to Stellenbosch and Paarl, but owing to an increase in violent muggings the trains should be avoided.

SAFETY AND PRECAUTIONS
If you spend a day out in the Winelands and return at dusk or after dark, be on the lookout for pedestrians, especially on weekends, when people are likely to have been drinking. There is, unfortunately, a high incidence of pedestrian-related accidents on these roads. Also be sure to designate a driver to avoid the risks associated with drinking and driving.

TOURS
Most tours of the Winelands are operated by companies based in Cape Town, such as African Eagle Day Tours, Hylton Ross, iKapa, Springbok Atlas, Welcome Tourism Services, and Windward Tours. Most of these companies have half- or full-day tours, but they vary by company and might include a cheese tasting or cellar tour in addition to wine tasting. Expect to pay around R450 for a half day and R630 for a full day, including all tasting fees. Though you stop for lunch, it is not included. Most tour buses stop at Spier, as the cheetahs provide a magnetic pull.

Easy Rider Wine Tours has a great all-day tour that's very reasonably priced (around R350, including lunch in Franschhoek). You get picked up around Stellenbosch at about 10:30 for a visit to five estates in the three regions.

For those serious about wine, Vineyard Ventures offers the best of the Winelands tour companies. Sisters Gillian Stoltzman and Glen Christie are knowledgeable and passionate about wine and will tailor tours to your interests. The cost ranges from around R1,600 per person and includes all tastings, museum entries, and a fabulous lunch (with wine, of course). If there are two of you, you'll pay around R2,200 for a car and driver but then will pay for your own lunch. The rates come down, as the number of people increases, so it's good to team up with another couple for a great day out.

Lesley Cox from Amber Wine Tours is wildly enthusiastic about Cape wines, knows many of the Cape winemakers and wine-farm owners, and will personalize tours. Lesley prefers visiting boutique farms not on the tourist map, but she'll tailor tours to your tastes. So if you want to only sample sauvignon blancs, for instance, she'll know just where to take you. If you're not crazy about wine, but want to tour the Winelands, Lesley can tell you about Cape Dutch architecture and the history of the area. Gourmet Wine Tours will also tailor a trip to the Winelands to suit your tastes. Expect to pay around R2,000 a day for a personalized tour.

The Wellington Wine Walk is a great way to combine wine tasting with exercise. This three-day walking tour, which caters to groups of six to 12 people (they'll group you with other people if you're on your own or in a small group), leads you from one upscale guesthouse to the next through vineyards and indigenous fynbos in the picturesque Wellington Valley. Your guides and hosts know all there is to know about the history and culture of the area, as well as the wines. They're also passionate about good food, and each day you'll have a picnic lunch and a gourmet dinner paired with the appropriate wines. The walking isn't tough, but you cover around 18 km (11 mi) each day. Your luggage is transferred for you from place to place, so all you have to carry is a light day pack. Expect to pay around R3,600 per person (all-inclusive, except for evening drinks). The best times to go are in autumn (April–May) and then again in spring (October–November) before the temperatures soar.

ESSENTIALS

Bus Line Vine Hopper (☎ 021/882–8112 ⊕ www.vinehopper.co.za).

Emergency Services Ambulance (☎ 10177). **Police** (☎ 10111). **Police, fire, and ambulance** (☎ 107 from landline). **Vodacom emergency services** (☎ 112 from mobile phone).

Internet Access Fandango (✉ Drostdy Square, Bird St., Stellenbosch ☎ 021/887–7501 ⊕ www.fandango.co.za). **Stellenbosch Adventure Centre** (✉ 36 Market St., Stellenbosch ☎ 021/882–8112 ⊕ www.adventureshop.co.za).

Limousine Company Cape Limousine Services (☎ 021/785–3100).

Rental Companies Avis (☎ 021/424–1177, 021/934–0330 airport, 086/111–3748 reservations ⊕ www.avis.co.za). **Budget** (☎ 021/418–5232, 021/380–3140 airport ⊕ www.budget.co.za). **Europcar** (☎ 021/421–5190 rental, 082/305–0066 emergency ⊕ www.europcar.co.za). **Hertz** (☎ 021/410–6800 ⊕ www.hertz.co.za). **Wine Route Rent-a-Car** (☎ 021/872–8513 or 083/225–7089).

Taxis Daksi Cab (☎ 082/854–1541 ⊕ www.daksicab.co.za). **Paarl Radio Taxis** (☎ 021/872–5671 or 082/852–9856).

Tour Operators African Eagle Day Tours (☎ 021/464–4266 ⊕ www.daytours. co.za). **Amber Wine Tours** (☎ 083/448–7016 ⊕ www.ambertours.co.za). **Easy Rider Wine Tours** (☎ 021/886–4651 ⊕ wwwwinetour.co.za). **Gourmet Wine Tours** (☎ 021/705–4317 or 083/299–3581 ⊕ www.gourmetwinetours.co.za).

CLOSE UP

South African Wine

The South African wine industry is booming. Buried by sanctions during apartheid, South African wines were largely unknown internationally. But today there's enormous interest in South African reds *and* whites. While South Africa has a reputation for delivering good quality at the bottom end of the market, more and more ultra-premium wines are emerging. Good-quality wines at varied prices are readily available—even in supermarkets.

Currently white wine production outstrips red, but the quality continually improves for both, and they regularly win international awards. Particularly notable is Pinotage, South Africa's own grape variety, a cross between pinot noir and Cinsaut (formerly Hermitage). Chenin blanc is the country's most widely planted variety and is used in everything from blends to bubbly (known in South Africa as Méthode Cap Classique).

The industry is transforming itself slowly. The illegal *dop* (drink) or tot system, in which farmers pay some of laborers' wages in wine, is finally on its way out, and there's a concerted effort among producers to uplift their laborers' quality of life. Many international companies refuse to import wine from farms that don't secure their workers' rights, and many farms are working at black empowerment. Tukulu, Riebeek Cellars, Thandi Wines, and Ses'Fikile (which translated means "we have arrived"), M'hudi, and Freedom Road are just some of the pioneers. Tragically, South Africa has one of the highest incidences of fetal alcohol syndrome (FAS), a legacy left over from the dop system.

If you're serious about wine, arm yourself with *John Platter's Wine Guide* or *Wine* magazine, featuring local wineries. For an in-depth read and fantastic photos, pick up *Wines and Vineyards of South Africa* by Wendy Torein or *New World of Wine from the Cape of Good Hope: The Definitive Guide to the South African Wine Industry* by Phyllis Hands, David Hughes, and Keith Phillips.

Hylton Ross Tours (☎ 021/511–1784 ⊕ www.hyltonross.co.za). **iKapa Tours & Travel** (☎ 021/510–8666 ⊕ www.ikapa.co.za). **Springbok Atlas** (☎ 021/460–4700 ⊕ www.springbokatlas.com). **Stellenbosch on Foot** (☎ 021/887–9150 or 083/218–1310). **Vineyard Ventures** (☎ 021/434–8888 or 082/920–2825 ⊕ www.vineyardventures.co.za). **Welcome Tourism Services** (☎ 021/532–6350 ⊕ www.welcome.co.za). **Wellington Wine Walk** (☎ 083/313–8383 ⊕ www. winescapetours.co.za). **Windward Tours** (☎ 021/419–3475 ⊕ www.windward-tours.co.za).

SOMERSET WEST (HELDERBERG)

45 km (28 mi) southeast of Cape Town on the N2.

Somerset West, nestled at the foot of the Helderberg Mountains, is just 30 minutes from the center of Cape Town and close to Gordon's Bay and the Strand beaches. Once an important farming town, former dairy fields are now covered with dreary town houses and faux Tuscan villas. But, a few historic estates still remain and are worth visiting.

Just before you reach the center of town you'll see the turnoff to Lourensford Road, which runs 3 km (2 mi) to Vergelegen and Morgenster. If you're keen to stretch your legs, the Helderberg Nature Reserve overlooks the beautiful False Bay and is home to plenty of fauna and flora.

GETTING HERE AND AROUND

Somerset West is 30 minutes southeast of Cape Town on the N2 and 20 minutes from the airport. Public transport in these outlying towns leaves a lot to be desired. Your best bet is to rent a car and invest in a good map or GPS. Don't be tempted to catch trains out to the Winelands after dark—you run the risk of being mugged.

VISITOR INFORMATION

Cape Town Tourism's Helderberg branch is open weekdays 9–5 in winter (approximately March–October) and weekdays 9–6, Saturday 9–1 in summer (about November–February).

Tourist Offices Cape Town Tourism–Helderberg Branch (✉ *186 Main Rd., Somerset West* ☎ *021/840-1400* ⊕ *www.tourismcapetown.co.za*).

EXPLORING

Fodor'sChoice
★

Vergelegen was established in 1700 by Willem Adriaan van der Stel, who succeeded his father as governor of the Cape. His traditional Cape Dutch homestead, with thatch roof and gables, looks like something out of a fairy tale. An octagonal walled garden aflame with flowers surrounds it, and huge camphor trees, planted almost 300 years ago, stand as gnarled sentinels. The estate was purchased for Lady Florence Phillips by her husband, mining magnate Sir Lionel Phillips, in 1917, and she spent vast sums on the restoration of the homestead, library, and gardens. The homestead is now a museum and is furnished in period style. Other historic buildings include a magnificent library and the old stables, now the reception area and interpretive center. Behind the house, the Lady Phillips Restaurant serves lunch and tea, and the Rose Terrace café looks onto a formal rose garden.

Although Vergelegen still buys grapes from neighboring farms, the vineyards that were planted in 1989, during what is described as the renaissance of the farm, are beginning to give an inkling of some very good wines to come. Vergelegen's flagship wine is its Vergelegen Red, an alluring blend of cabernet sauvignon, merlot, and cabernet franc. The 2004 vintage is well worth taking home, as is the farm's other favorite—the Vergelegen White 2007. If you aren't mad about blends, try the 2005 merlot, which is rich in ripe, plummy flavors, or the 2008 chardonnay with touches of wood fermentation and a fresh citrus nose. Reservations are essential for the tours. ✉ *Lourensford Rd.* ☎ *021/847-1334/7* ⊕ *www.vergelegen.co.za* ✉ *Tastings R30 for six glasses* ☼ *Daily 9:30–5. Cellar tours Nov.–Apr., daily at 10:15; May–Sept., daily at 11:30 and 3.*

Nestled against the base of Helderberg Mountain and shaded by giant oaks, the peaceful **Rust en Vrede** winery looks over steep slopes of vines and roses. This is a comparatively small estate that specializes entirely in red wine—and produces some of the very best in South Africa. Rust en Vrede Estate is the flagship wine, a blend of predominantly cabernet sauvignon, Shiraz, and just over 10% merlot grapes. The 2004 vintage

Cape Dutch Architecture

As you travel around the region, the most visible emblems of settler culture you'll encounter are the Cape Dutch–style houses. Here 18th- and 19th-century manor houses share certain characteristics: thick whitewashed walls, thatch roofs curving around elegant gables, and small-pane windows framed by wooden shutters. It's a classic look—a uniquely Cape look—ideally suited to a land that is hot in summer and cold in winter. The Cape Dutch style developed in the 18th century from traditional long houses: simple rectangular sheds capped by thatch. As farmers became more prosperous, they added the ornate gables and other features. Several estates, most notably Vergelegen (near Somerset West) and Boschendal (on the Franschhoek wine route), have opened their manor houses as museums.

is the current hot-seller, having already won several awards both locally and abroad, but it would do well to mature in the bottle for another 10 years or more. Another interesting wine is the Shiraz, which has an inviting, spicy bouquet with a mellowness imparted by the American oak in which it is matured, but none of the characteristic cloying sweetness; it will age from five to eight years, and the 2004 vintage is currently available. ⊠ *1 Annandale Rd., off R44, between Somerset West and Stellenbosch* ☎ *021/881–3881* ⊕ *www.rustenvrede.com* 🏠 *Tastings R30 (refundable on purchase)* ☉ *May–Sept., weekdays 9–5; Oct.–Apr., weekdays 9–5.*

WHERE TO EAT AND STAY

$-$$
ECLECTIC
✕ **96 Winery Road.** This relaxed venue is always buzzing with folk from the wine industry, regulars, and up-country visitors. Inside, burgundy walls are cozy for winter, while outside terrace seating offers soothing mountain views. The menu changes regularly but tempts with such fresh and flavorful first courses as prawn tempura and salmon and line-fish sashimi. Steak lovers are treated well here; dry-aged cuts of prime beef are grilled and teamed with a variety of sauces. Vegetarians will find good choices, too, such as a salad of organic mixed leaves with grilled vegetables, feta, olives, Parmesan cheese, and toasted pine nuts. A good cheese board makes a savory—and many think, superior—option to rich desserts. The selection of wine is also impressive—in 2006 the restaurant won the Wine Spectator Grand Award for its comprehensive and innovative wine list. ⊠ *Zandberg Farm, Winery Rd., between Somerset West and Stellenbosch* ☎ *021/842–2020* ⊕ *www.96wineryroad. co.za* 🏠 *Reservations essential* ▤ *AE, DC, MC, V* ☉ *No dinner Sun.*

$$
ECLECTIC
✕ **Lady Phillips Restaurant.** In summer you need to reserve a table three weeks in advance at this idyllic country restaurant on the Vergelegen Estate. In pleasant weather ask for a table on the terrace, shaded by liquidambar trees. Consider starting with kudu carpaccio marinated in teriyaki sauce and served with a mustard-and-rosemary vinaigrette before moving on to homemade smoked-salmon pasta. The delicious lemon-thyme-marinated lamb rump is served with potatoes gratin and

CLOSE UP

From Soil to Oil

South Africans are beginning to produce extra-virgin olive oils that are as excellent as their wines. One place to learn about this fruit of the local fields is the historic estate **Morgenster** (Morning Star), which is part of Cape Governor Simon van der Stel's original 17th-century farm. In the mid-'90s the estate was restored to its original splendor, and olive trees were planted; it's now producing some of the best oils in the country. Five different olive cultivars—frantoio, leccino, favoloza, coratina, and peranzana—are pressed individually before they're blended. For R15 you can taste the olives, the oil, balsamic vinegar, and the delicious olive paste. Phone a day ahead if you're traveling in a group bigger than six. ⊠ *Vergelegen Ave., off Lourensford Rd., Somerset West* ☎ *021/852–1738* ⊕ *www.morgenster. co.za* ☜ *Wine or olive tastings R15, R30 combined* ⊙ *Daily 10–4.*

Kloovenburg Wine Estate. In addition to producing wine, this estate in the picturesque Riebeek Valley (⇨ *Riebeek West and Riebeek Kasteel,*

in West Coast, below) also makes olive oil and a delectable range of olive products that you can eat and rub on your body. Annalene du Toit, wife of the vineyard's owner, and one of her young sons took to the kitchen to come up with some of the olive concoctions, and they only sell what they like to eat. ⊠ *R46 just outside Riebeek Kasteel as you're coming down the pass into Riebeek Valley* ☎ *022/448–1635* ⊕ *www.kloovenburg.com* ☜ *Reservations essential* ☜ *Tastings free* ⊙ *Weekdays 9–4:30, Sat. 9–2.*

Fairview. This vineyard in the Suid-Agter-Paarl area has a range of olive oils it's proud of. You can taste single-cultivar oils and take home a bottle of your own particular blend. Or you can just buy the farm's oil, along with its excellent wines and goat's-milk cheeses. ⊠ *WR3, off R101 (Suid-Agter-Paarl Rd.), Suider-Paarl* ☎ *021/863–2450* ⊕ *www.fairview.co.za* ☜ *Wine and olive-oil tasting R15* ⊙ *Weekdays 8:30–5, Sat. 8:30–4, Sun. 9:30–4.*

baby vegetables in season. Of the wide dessert selection, sticky-date-and-macadamia-nut pudding with cream and maple sauce is noteworthy, calorie-packed, and hugely delicious. If you can't get a reservation, head to the estate's Rose Terrace during summer for light meals or a picnic underneath the camphor trees (around R165). ⊠ *Vergelegen Estate, Lourensford Rd.* ☎ *021/847–1346* ☜ *Reservations essential* ☰ *AE, DC, MC, V* ⊙ *No dinner.*

$ ⌂ **Willowbrook Lodge.** This lodge makes a good base for exploring the entire southwestern Cape, including the peninsula, the Winelands, and the Overberg. The lodge lies hidden among beautiful gardens that extend down to the Lourens River; in the distance the peaks of the Helderberg are visible. It's a very peaceful place, with large, airy, comfortable rooms and sliding doors opening onto the gardens. D'Vine Restaurant ($$) has equally high standards and is regularly voted onto the country's top-100 list. The menu changes seasonally, but how's this for a delectable starter: wild mushrooms and chicken molded in a poppy-seed crepe and served with a duo of port and foie gras jus. It sounds complicated, but it's absolutely delicious. A simpler starter might be baked goat cheese on walnut bread served with a honey-dressed salad of lemon, coriander, and green beans. For a main course, you'll be hard-pressed to choose between the likes of crispy aromatic duck or the springbok medallion served with berry compote, mushroom spaetzle, and sautéed green beans. **Pros:** close to top golf courses, beautiful beaches, and the Cape Winelands; away from the hustle of Cape Town. **Cons:** very few rooms available; only one restaurant on-site. ⊠ *Morgenster Ave., Box 1892* ☎ *021/851–3759* ⊕ *www.willowbrook.co.za* ⤵ *11 rooms, 1 suite* ⚒ *In-room: safe, refrigerator, Wi-Fi (some). In-hotel: restaurant, bar, pool, laundry service, Wi-Fi, parking (free), no kids under 12* ⊟ *AE, DC, MC, V* ⏐◎⏐ *BP.*

SPORTS AND THE OUTDOORS

The Gary Player–designed **Erinvale Golf Club** (⊠ *Lourensford Rd.* ☎ *021/847–1144* ⊕ *www.erinvalegolfclub.com*) is beautifully nestled beneath the Hottentots Holland Mountains. It costs R395 for 9 holes and R650 to play 18 holes, R210 (9 holes) or R350 (18 holes) to rent clubs, and R180 or R290 for a golf cart (there are no caddies). You can book only one week in advance during peak season (September–May); ask for availability when you phone. **Somerset West Golf Club** (⊠ *Rue de Jacquelin* ☎ *021/852–2925* ⊕ *www.somersetwestgolfclub.co.za*) is an easy course with plenty of leeway for errant tee shots, except when the wind blows. Greens fees run around R350 for 18 holes, R190 for 9 holes; club rental is around R150. Golf carts are available for about R180, but you are encouraged to make use of the caddies for around R150, excluding tip.

EN ROUTE

You can't drive down the R44 between Somerset West and Stellenbosch without noticing the remarkable scarecrows at **Mooiberge Farm Stall.** They're riding bicycles, driving tractors, and working in the strawberry fields, where you can spend a morning picking the luscious red fruit. The strawberry season varies from one year to the next but usually begins in October and runs to February. You pay for what you pick, and you can also buy jams, dried fruit, and other refreshments at the farm stall. Look for the interesting display of old farm implements at the side of the building. ⊠ *R44, between Somerset West and Stellenbosch* ☎ *021/881–3222* ⏐ *Free* ◎ *Daily 8–6.*

STELLENBOSCH

★ *15 km (9½ mi) north of Somerset West.*

You could easily while away a week in this small, sophisticated, beautiful, and absolutely delightful town. South Africa's second-oldest municipality, after Cape Town, Stellenbosch actually *feels* old, unlike so many other historic towns. Wandering the oak-shaded streets, which still have open irrigation furrows (known as the *lei water,* pronounced lay *vaa*-ter), you'll see some of the finest examples of Cape Dutch, Georgian, Victorian, and Regency architecture in the country. The town was founded in 1679 by Simon van der Stel, first governor of the Cape, who recognized the agricultural potential of this fertile valley. Wheat was the major crop grown by the early settlers, but vineyards now

Sip and Spoeg Like an Expert

South Africa currently has more growing areas than ever that yield a huge selection of very different wines. One of the best ways to find your way around the enormous selection is to buy one of the local magazines, such as the monthly *Wine* magazine (R25), devoted to the subject. Wine prices ex-cellar are significantly cheaper than most retail outlets, so if you're looking for a bargain, buy directly from the farm.

AH, BUT YOUR LAND IS BEAUTIFUL

When it comes to South African terroir, think sun, sea, and soil. While Northern hemisphere farmers work hard to get as much sunlight onto their grapes as possible, local viticulturists have to deal with soaring summer temperatures (this is why the cooling influence of the two oceans is so welcome). South Africa also has some of the world's oldest soil, and there's a mineral element to its wines, a quality that's most prominent in the top-end sauvignon blancs like those produced by Cape Point Vineyards, Steenberg, and Springfield.

YOU CAN'T LEAVE WITHOUT TRYING PINOTAGE

In 1920s, a professor at Stellenbosch University decided to create a truly South African varietal. He crossed pinot noir (a tricky grape to grow) with Cinsaut (a vigorous and very hardy grape)—he liked the idea of combining a drama queen with a pragmatic, no-nonsense type—and came up with Pinotage. Though it's had its ups and downs, including being accused by everyone from critics to connoisseurs of being bitter and rubbery, strides are being made to express the grape's character. One example is the coffee Pinotage. It's been on the market for just a few years and is hugely popular because it's a ballsy, bold wine. There's a distinct mocha flavor to the wine that's a combination of the soil and the winemaking technique. A good example of this is the Diemersfontein Carpe Diem Pinotage. Other Pinotages to keep an eye out for: Stellenzicht Golden Triangle Pinotage, Spier Private Collection Pinotage, and Kanonkop Pinotage.

HUNDREDS AND THOUSANDS TO CHOOSE FROM

Wines that have helped put South Africa on the map include chenin blanc, sauvignon blanc, and Bordeaux-style red blends of cabernet sauvignon, merlot, and cabernet franc. South African red blends have done well at international competitions, and the quality rivals some of the world's best producers. Until recently, chenin blanc was something of a Cinderella varietal. It accounts for the bulk of South African white wine plantings but, because of its versatility, was largely overlooked. Luckily, this has shifted, and there are now more than 100 chenin blancs out there demanding attention and commanding top prices.

■ Good Sauvignon Blancs: Alexanderfontein Sauvignon Blanc, Springfield Estate Life from Stone Sauvignon Blanc, and Cape Point Vineyards Sauvignon Blanc.

■ Great red blends: Stellenrust Timeless, Rustenberg John X Merriman, and Kanonkop Paul Sauer.

■ Great Chenin Blancs: Kleine Zalze barrel fermented chenin blanc, Rudera Robusto Chenin Blanc, and Ken Forrester FMC Chenin Blanc.

3

A ROSÉ BY ANY OTHER NAME

Though it legally can't be called champagne, Méthode Cap Classique, South Africa's version of the bubbly, is made in exactly the same way. You'd be unwise to pass on an offer of Graham Beck Brut Blanc de Blancs or Villiera Brut Tradition.

NAME-DROPPING

There are some iconic South African wines you really should try before you leave the country. Of course, the list of such wines varies depending on whom you talk to, but keep an eye out for:

■ Kanonkop Pinotage or Paul Sauer

■ Meerlust Rubicon

■ De Toren Fusion V

■ Vergelegen V

■ Steenberg Sauvignon Blanc Reserve

■ Hamilton Russell Chardonnay and Pinot Noir

■ Cape Point Isliedh

■ Jordan Chardonnay

■ Springfield Méthode Ancienne Cabernet Sauvignon

■ Boekenhoutskloof Cabernet Sauvignon

■ Boplaas Vintage Reserve Port

Potential future icons include Columella and Palladius, both made by Eben Sadie, and Raats Family Vineyard Cabernet Franc.

TO SHIP OR NOT TO SHIP

You're bound to want to take some great South African wine home with you, but it's not as easy as cramming your hand luggage with your favorite tipple. Travelers to the States can take only two bottles on board. Any more than that and it will need to be shipped to you by an agent. Each person is allowed two cases (or 24 bottles), but some states won't allow you to import a single bottle without an importer's license. Expect to pay around R1,500 per case of wine (East Coast destinations are usually cheaper than those on the West), and it will take anywhere from six to 18 days to reach you. Alternately, when you're wine tasting, ask the estate if they distribute in the United States, as you might find a local agent closer to home. The Vineyard Connection (⊕ www.vineyardconnection.co.za) is just one of the agents who could help you get your favorite bottle delivered to your door!

blanket the surrounding hills. Stellenbosch is considered the center of the Winelands, and many of the older and more established wineries are situated nearby. Wine routes fan out like spokes of a wheel, making excellent day trips if you're staying in town. The town is also home to the University of Stellenbosch, the country's first and most prestigious Afrikaner university.

GETTING HERE AND AROUND
The best way to explore this area is by renting a car. Expect to pay around R150 for an entry-level car per day and up to R700 for a Mercedes C Class. Avoid public transportation.

TOURS
The historic area of Stellenbosch is so pretty and compact that it's a pity just to drive through. Take a walking tour with Sandra Krige from Stellenbosch on Foot. Tours last around 1½ hours and take in all the well-known sights. Sandra is a mine of information about the town and even offers an evening ghost tour. Expect to pay around R80 per person if there are two of you for the evening tour. If you're alone, you'll pay around R170.

VISITOR INFORMATION
In summer Stellenbosch Tourism and Information Bureau is open weekdays 8–6, Saturday 9:30–5, Sunday 10–4; in winter it's open weekdays 8–5, Saturday 9:30–2, Sunday 10–2.

ESSENTIALS
Hospitals **Stellenbosch Medi-Clinic** (✉ *Saffraan Ave. and Rokewood Rd., Die Board* ☎ *021/861–2000* ⊕ *www.stellenboschmc.co.za*).

Late-Night Pharmacy **Die Boord Pharmacy** (✉ *14 Saffraan Ave., Die Boord Shopping Centre* ☎ *021/887–9400*).

Tourist Offices **Stellenbosch Tourism and Information Bureau** (✉ *36 Market St.* ☎ *021/883–3584* ⊕ *www.stellenboschtourism.co.za*).

Tour Operators **Stellenbosch on Foot** (☎ *021/887–9150 or 083/218–1310*).

EXPLORING
Start your tour of the town at the corner of Dorp Street and the R44, where you first enter Stellenbosch. Look for street names written in yellow on curbs; they're easy to miss, so remember to look down and not up.

Architecture buffs will be happy to know that there are still examples of 19th-century Stellenbosch design around. To check them out, turn left off Market Street onto Herte Street. The whitewashed cottages along this street were built by and for freed slaves after the Emancipation Act of 1834. Although they are no longer thatch, the houses on the left-hand side of the road are still evocative of this era.

TOP ATTRACTIONS
Dorp Street. Stellenbosch's most historic avenue is oak-lined Dorp Street. Almost the entire street is a national monument, flanked by lovely restored homes from every period of the town's history.

Oom Samie Se Winkel. Redolent of tobacco, dried fish, and spices, this 19th-century-style general store is one of Stellenbosch's most popular landmarks. In addition to the usual Cape kitsch, Oom Samie sells some genuine South African produce, including *witblitz* and *mampoer,* both Afrikaner versions of moonshine. The shop has a restaurant, too. ⊠ *84 Dorp St.* ☎ *021/887–0797* ⊙ *Weekdays 8:30–6, weekends 9–5.*

WORTH NOTING

Die Braak. Some of Stellenbosch's most historic buildings face the Braak, the grassy town square, which is a national monument. At the southern end of the square is the **Rhenish Mission Church** (⊠ *Bloem St.*), erected by the Missionary Society of Stellenbosch in 1823 as a training school for slaves and blacks. **St. Mary's Church** stands at the far end of the Braak. Built in 1852 as an Anglican church, it reflects the growing influence of the English in Stellenbosch. Across Bloem Street from St. Mary's is the **Burgher House,** built in 1797. Today it houses the offices of Historical Homes in South Africa. ⊠ *Bordered by Bloem, Alexander, and Bird Sts.*

D'Ouwe Werf. Possibly the country's oldest boardinghouse, d'Ouwe Werf first took in paying guests in 1802. To get here from Dorp Street, turn onto Andringa Street, and then a right onto Church (aka Kerk) Street; d'Ouwe Werf will be on your left. ⊠ *30 Church St.* ☎ *021/887–4608* ⊕ *www.ouwewerf.com.*

La Gratitude. This early-18th-century Dorp Street home was built in traditional Cape Dutch town-house style. The all-seeing eye of God molded on its gable was designed as a talisman to watch over the owner's property and keep him and his family safe from harm. ⊠ *95 Dorp St.*

Rhenish Complex. One of the most impressive restoration projects ever undertaken in South Africa, and a good example of what early Stellenbosch must have been like, this complex consists of an art center; the Leipoldt House, which melds elements of English and Cape architecture; and a two-story building that is typically English. Also part of the complex is the old Cape Dutch Rhenish parsonage (1815), which is now the **Toy and Miniature Museum** (☎ *021/887–9433* ☎ *R15* ⊙ *Weekdays 8:30–5*). The complex is just east of the Tourist Information Bureau on Market Street, on your left, facing a large lawn. ⊠ *Bordered by Herte, Market, Bloem, and Dorp Sts.*

Stellenbosch Village Museum. This museum comprises four dwellings scattered within a two-block radius. Dating from different periods in Stellenbosch's history, the houses have been furnished to reflect changing lifestyles and tastes. The oldest is the very basic Schreuderhuis, built in 1709. The others date from 1789, 1803, and 1850. ⊠ *18 Ryneveld St., at Church St.* ☎ *021/887–2948* ⊕ *www.museums.org.za/stellmus* ☎ *R20* ⊙ *May–Aug., Mon.–Sat. 9–5, Sun. 10–4; Sept.–Apr., Mon.– Sat. 9–5, Sun. 10–1.*

V.O.C. Arsenal. Next to the Burgher House, just across from the Braak on a traffic island in Market Street, stands the V.O.C. Arsenal, often called the **V.O.C. Kruithuis** (*kruithuis* means "powder house"). It took 91 years for the political council to decide that Stellenbosch needed its own magazine, and just six months in 1777 to complete the structure. Today the arsenal contains a wide selection of guns, gunpowder holders, and cannons. If the arsenal is closed, call or pop into the Toy and Miniature Museum *(⇨ Rhenish Complex, above)* and someone will open it up for you. ⊠ *Market St.* ☎ *021/886–4135* ▣ *By donation* ⊙ *Weekdays 9:30–3:30.*

Voorgelegen. This 19th-century home and the houses on either side of it form one of the best-preserved Georgian ensembles in town. ⊠ *116 Dorp St.*

WINERIES

Many wine estates are wheelchair friendly and you'll be able to access the tasting rooms without a problem. But, some don't have toilet facilities for the disabled. You might want to phone ahead so you know what to expect.

TOP ATTRACTIONS

Fodor's Choice **Kanonkop.** In the days when ships of the Dutch East India Company
★ used Cape Town as a refreshment station on the way to the East, a ship would fire a cannon as it entered the harbor to let farmers know provisions were needed, and a set of relay cannons, all set on hilltops, would carry the message far inland. One such cannon was on this farm, which was then called Kanonkop, Afrikaans for Cannon Hill. The beauty of Kanonkop today is not in its history or its buildings but in its wine. Winemaker Abrie Beeslaar has taken over from the legendary Beyers Truter (a very hard act to follow), but Kanonkop continues to reel in numerous awards and accolades. Paul Sauer, a blend of about 80% cabernet sauvignon with the balance made up of equal parts merlot and cabernet franc, rakes in awards year after year, and the winery won two golds and a silver at the Decanter World Wine Awards in May 2009. Check out the 2007 Pinotage and its 2005 cab sauv. You're going to wish you could take caseloads home with you. There are no guided cellar tours, but during harvest you can do a walkabout in the cellar to see all the action. An added attraction to this farm is the art gallery that opened in October 2008. The thinking behind the project was to bring fine South African art—and wine—to the people. It has succeeded! ⊠ *R44, between Paarl and Stellenbosch* ☎ *021/884–4656* ⊕ *www. kanonkop.co.za* ▣ *Tastings R10* ⊙ *Weekdays 8:30–5, Sat. 9–2.*

★ **Meerlust.** A visit to Meerlust, probably South Africa's most celebrated estate, provides an introduction to Cape history. In the same family for generations, the wine farm was bought by Johannes Albertus Myburgh in 1757. When Nicolaas Myburgh, eighth-generation Myburgh and father of Hannes (the current owner), took over the reins in 1959, he began restoring the farm's Cape Dutch buildings. The entire complex was declared a national monument in 1987. But Nico Myburgh did more than just renovate. He took a fresh look at red wines and broke with tradition by deciding to make a red blend. In the '70s, conventional wisdom had it that cabernet sauvignon was king, but Nico went against the grain and opted for a Bordeaux-style blend, planting both merlot and cabernet franc. The first wine, made in 1980 and released in 1983, was named Rubicon (an allusion to Julius Caesar) to symbolize the crossing of a significant barrier. Rubicon garners awards year after year and is rated as an international best seller. Meerlust's other wines—chardonnay 2007, pinot noir 2003, and merlot—are also notably good.

CLOSE UP

Stellenbosch Wine Route

ALONG R310

West of Stellenbosch, the R310 (also known locally as Baden Powell Drive) forks to the left, but go straight on the M12 (also known as Polkadraai Road); Asara is first up on your right, followed by **Neethlingshof.** Turn right on Stellenbosch Kloof Road, where **Overgaauw** is a merlot mainstay. Follow the winding road through pretty vineyards; at the end is **Jordan,** known for its whites. Double back to Stellenbosch and at the set of traffic lights, take the R310 to your right to the touristy but fun **Spier.** Next up this road is **Meerlust** with its submerged windmill.

If you drive east on the R310 from Stellenbosch, detour up the Idasvallei Road and follow a narrow lane through cattle pastures and oak groves to **Rustenberg,** which focuses on reds. Then it's up and over the scenic Helshoogte Pass to **Thelema Mountain Vineyards,** which has knockout reds and whites. Its neighbor, **Tokara,** is a great lunch spot,

while **Delaire Graff Estate,** over the road, has breathtaking views and an extensive face-lift.

ALONG R44

Some important wineries are on the R44 north of Stellenbosch. At **Morgenhof** you can sip chardonnay and Pinotage and linger for lunch. About 3 km (2 mi) farther along on the R44, turn right on Knorhoek Road to reach low-frills **Muratie,** with some good reds. Back on the R44, travel a short way and then turn left on Kromme Rhee Road to visit **Simonsig,** home to wonderful bubbly. On the R44 once more, continue to **Kanonkop,** which has won numerous awards, and **Warwick,** with great red blends.

ALONG R304

This road shoots northwest from Stellenbosch past several wine farms. Stop at **Mulderbosch** for its excellent white wines. Cross over Kromme Rhee Road and on to **Villiera,** known for sparkling wine and lush sauvignon blanc.

3

✉ *Off R310* ☎ *021/843–3587* ⊕ *www.meerlust.co.za* 🍷 *Tastings R20* ◉ *Weekdays 9–4, Sat. 10–2.*

Thelema Mountain Vineyards. On the slopes of the Simonsberg, just off the Helshoogte Pass, this is an excellent example of the exciting developments in the Cape Winelands since the early 1980s, when farmers began to eye land that hadn't traditionally been earmarked for wine farming. When Gyles and Barbara Webb started the farm in 1983, there was nothing here but very good soil and old fruit trees. It's a testament to their efforts that the winery has regularly won prizes for both its reds and whites ever since. To cap it all off, the view of the Groot Drakenstein mountains from the tasting room is unforgettable. Ever the pioneers, the Webbs have also bought Sutherland, an old fruit farm (not open to the public) in the Elgin area, an exciting new wine-growing region at the top of Sir Lowry's Pass. They had brilliant crops from here in 2009; keep an eye out for their pinot noir and rousanne, which we'll see in a few years. Be sure to taste Ed's Reserve, a dry white named after the late, legendary Edna McLean, Barbara's mother, who originally bought the Thelema farm and in later years was a stalwart in the tasting

Wine Goes Green

As romantic as vineyards seem, wine farming is a monoculture and generally not that eco-friendly. The Biodiversity & Wine Initiative (BWI) is a pioneering project in the Cape Winelands working with committed wine farmers to set aside highly threatened natural habitat on their farms for conservation, while ensuring that the members of the BWI farm in an environmentally sensitive and sustainable way. A label featuring a protea (the country's national flower) and a sugarbird identifies members.

Each month, more wine farms sign up, and to date the total land conserved among the BWI members is 279,542 acres—more than 100% of the current vineyard footprint in the Cape Winelands (the rest is set aside for future expansion). So, when you're wine tasting and buying, look for the BWI label. By supporting these farms, you'll be making a significant contribution to the long-term conservation of critical natural habitats and species in the Western Cape Winelands.

room. Also try the Thelema Sutherland Sauvignon Blanc, with its lovely mineral, grassy qualities. The 2006 mint cabernet sauvignon comes from a single block that produces a distinctively minty wine. For obvious reasons, it's been dubbed "The Full Minty." ⊠ *Off R310, between Stellenbosch and Franschhoek* ☎ *021/885–1924* ⊕ *www.thelema.co.za* ⊠ *Tastings free* ⊙ *Weekdays 9–5, Sat. 10–3.*

Fodor's Choice **Tokara.** Perched on the crest of the Helshoogte Pass between Stellenbosch
★ and Franschhoek, Tokara is the brainchild of banker G.T. Ferreira. For a city slicker with lots of money, he's done everything right by employing an excellent winemaker in the super-sexy Miles Mossop and paying careful attention to the quality of his vines. At the 2009 Decanter World Wine Awards, Tokara scooped two golds and five silver medals, which is testimony to his excellent wine making. The farm produces under two labels—Tokara and Zondernaam (meaning "without name" in Old Dutch)—and the reds are big and powerful. The flagship red, a blend of cabernet sauvignon, merlot, petit verdot, and cabernet franc, is well worth taking home. It also has farms in the cooler Elgin and Hemel-en-Aarde regions, which means it can produce a stunning sauvignon blanc with plenty of complexity. Tokara also produces its own premium olive oil, which you can buy from the Olive Shed on the farm. Tokara's restaurant is a foodie's delight. ⊠ *Off R310, between Stellenbosch and Franschhoek* ☎ *021/808–5900, 021/808–5959 restaurant* ⊕ *www.tokara. com* ⊠ *Tastings free* ⊙ *Weekdays 9–5, weekends 10–3.*

WORTH NOTING

Delaire Graff Estate. This has to be one of the most spectacular settings of any winery in the country. Sit on the terrace of the tasting room or restaurant and look past a screen of oaks to the valley below and the majestic crags of the Groot Drakenstein and Simonsberg mountains. It's an ideal place to stop for lunch, although at the time of writing the restaurant had just opened so hasn't stood the test of time. It's not designed for children under 12 so don't expect fish fingers and fries on the kids' menu. The range of wines is limited, but this has allowed it to focus on upping the quality. The Bordeaux blend Red Blend has a splash of Shiraz, which makes an interesting change, and the 2007 chardonnay is very elegant with fresh lime and creamy butterscotch flavors. There's a boutique hotel in the works. ⊠ *Helshoogte Rd., between Stellenbosch and Franschhoek* ☎ *021/885–8160* ⊕ *www.delaire.co.za* ✉ *Tastings R25 for 5 wines plus canapés* ☉ *Weekdays 9–5, Sat. 10–5:30, Sun. 10–4:30.*

Jordan. At the end of Stellenbosch Kloof Road, this meticulous winery, flanked by the Bottelary hills, overlooks rolling vineyards and jagged mountains. Husband-and-wife team Gary and Kathy Jordan studied at the University of California at Davis and worked at California's Iron Horse Winery. The family made its fortune producing practical shoes, and although it produced its first vintage only in 1992, it has already established a formidable reputation. The sauvignon blanc, with refreshing hints of asparagus, makes for good summer drinking, and the multi-award-winning dense but fruity chardonnay is extremely popular and has regulars stocking up on cases at a time. The two are combined in the versatile, flavorful, and well-priced Chameleon dry white. Other wines to try are the Cobblers Hill Bordeaux blend and the Sophia CWG (Cape Winemakers Guild) Auction Reserve 2005 vintage, which is laden with awards. ⊠ *Stellenbosch Kloof Rd.* ☎ *021/881–3441* ⊕ *www.jordanwines.com* ✉ *Tastings R15* ☉ *Weekdays 10–4:30, weekends 9:30–2:30; cellar tours by appointment.*

Morgenhof Wine Estate. This beautiful Cape Dutch estate, with a history stretching back 300 years, lies in the lee of a steep hill covered with vines and pine trees. In 1993 Morgenhof was acquired by Anne Cointreau of Cognac, France, who spared no expense in making this a showpiece estate with a lovely rose garden on top of the working underground cellar. The estate has a talented winemaker, Jacques Cilliers, and some distinguished wines. Try the chardonnay with a fresh coconut nose and hints of lime, or the smoky, somewhat Burgundian Pinotage. The estate's flagship wine is the wonderful Première Sélection, a Bordeaux blend. Morgenhof is an excellent place to stop for a simple lunch of homemade soup and freshly baked bread. Reservations are advisable in summer. ⊠ *R44, between Paarl and Stellenbosch* ☎ *021/889–5510* ⊕ *www.morgenhof.com* ✉ *Informal tastings R10, formal tastings R25* ☉ *May–Oct., weekdays 9–4:30, weekends 10–3, Nov.–Apr., weekdays 9–5:30, weekends 10–5; cellar tours by appointment.*

Mulderbosch Vineyards. It's widely accepted that this small estate (only 67 acres are under vine) produces some of the best white wines around, thanks to Mike Dobrovic, an extremely talented cellar master. The robust, barrel-fermented chardonnay (2006 available) has a complex nose and a smooth, velvety finish; a sip might have you tasting buttered toast, citrus, vanilla, and wild herbs. The 2008 sauvignon blanc is also delicious; it's packed with gooseberry, nettle, and a touch of citrus. The Faithful Hound red blend was named after a dog who, when the current owners bought the farm in the late 1980s, refused to leave the house where he lived. Faithful Hound 2005 is available and as good as ever. A huge portion of the farm has been left to indigenous vegetation and wildlife. ✉ *R304, between Stellenbosch and Paarl* ☎*021/865–2488* ⊕ *www.mulderbosch.co.za* ⊠ *Fees vary* ☉ *Mon.–Thurs. 8–5, Fri. 8–4; tastings by appointment.*

Muratie. Ancient oaks and a cellar that truly seems to be more concerned with the business of producing wine than with decor make this a refreshing change from the "prettier" wineries. It's a small estate, specializing in rich, earthy reds and full-bodied dessert wines. Muratie's port is an old favorite in the Cape, and the well-balanced amber is a fortified dessert wine of note, with pleasing citrus overtones to counter the sweetness. The cellar produces some fine red wines. Worth looking out for are the pinot noir, from some of the oldest vines of this cultivar in the Cape; and Ansela van der Caab, a dry red blend of cabernet and merlot, named after the freed slave who married the first owner of the farm, Laurens Campher, and helped set up the vineyards in the early 1700s. The Ronnie Melck Shiraz also comes highly recommended. Cellar tours are not offered. ✉ *Knorhoek Rd., off the R44, between Stellenbosch and Paarl* ☎ *021/865–2330* ⊕ *www.muratie.co.za* ⊠ *Tastings R20* ☉ *Weekdays 9–5, weekends 10–5.*

ⓒ **Neethlingshof.** A long avenue of pines leads to this lovely estate, which traces its origins to 1692. The magnificent 1814 Cape Dutch manor house looks out across formal rose gardens to the Stellenbosch Valley and the Hottentots Holland Mountains. There's even a large play area, complete with jungle gyms, for kids. The wines produced on this estate and those from its sister farm, Stellenzicht, are highly regarded, so be prepared for a rush of tour buses during high season. The gewürztraminer is an off-dry, very elegant wine with rose-petal and spice aromas, and the Weisser Riesling Noble Late Harvest is one of the best of its kind, having scooped up almost every local award since 1990. The farm's flagship wine, Lord Neethling Laurentius—a blend of cabernet sauvignon, cabernet franc, merlot, and Shiraz—is definitely worth stockpiling. Try the food and wine parings: you'll have traditional fast food (pizza, burgers, chicken nuggets) paired with its wines. You get a box with a small piece of each food to try with different wines. The whole idea is to show that wine goes with everything—not just fancy food! ✉ *Neethlingshof Estate, 7599 Polkadraai Rd. (M12)* ☎ *021/883–8988* ⊕ *www.neethlingshof.co.za* ⊠ *Tastings R30; food and wine pairings R70; cellar tours R5* ☉ *Weekdays 9–5, weekends 10–4 (may stay open about 2 hrs later Dec. and Jan.); cellar tours by appointment.*

Overgaauw. Among the established estates on Stellenbosch Kloof Road, Overgaauw definitely deserves a visit. You can admire the pretty Victorian tasting room while exploring the range of big red wines. In 1982 Overgaauw was the first South African estate to make a merlot, but it also experiments with other varietals, and you should too. Try the Cape Vintage made with Portuguese varietals such as *touriga*, *tintas*, *souzao*, and *cornifesto*. Confused? Don't be. The result is a wonderful richly balanced blend. The Tria Corda sells out faster than it can be released. The spicy, fruity sylvaner is named for a grape of the same name. To date, Overgaauw is the only Cape estate to grow this varietal, which comes from the Alsace region of France, so it's definitely worth exploring. ✉ *Stellenbosch Kloof Rd., Vlottenburg* ☎ *021/881–3815* ⊕ *www.* *overgaauw.co.za* 🍷 *Tastings R10* ☽ *Weekdays 8:30–5, Sat. 10–12:30.*

Rustenberg. This estate may date back to 1682, but it's been brought thoroughly up-to-date with a state-of-the art winery and underground vaulted maturation rooms. The estate is known for red wine, particularly its 100% cabernet Peter Barlow (named after the present owner's father), which is made from grapes from one lovely, well-tended vineyard. The Five Soldiers Chardonnay is delicious and also made from a single vineyard, which gives it its unique character. It's named for the five tall pine trees that stand guard on top of the hill above the chardonnay grapes. The farm's second label, Brampton, also makes excellent wines. The 2004 and 2006 cabernet sauvignon have won awards, but both are sold out, so scoop up some of the 2007 while it's still available and put it down for a couple of years. The 2007 Shiraz is also wonderful. The farm uses screw caps for quality and environmental reasons. ✉ *Off R310 (Rustenberg Rd.), Ida's Valley* ☎ *021/809–1200* ⊕ *www.* *rustenberg.co.za* 🍷 *Tastings free* ☽ *Weekdays 9–4:30, Sat. 10–1:30.*

☾ **Simonsig.** Sitting in a sea of vines is this estate with tremendous views back toward Stellenbosch and the mountains. Simonsig has more than a dozen white and red wines of impressive range, both in terms of taste and price. But quantity certainly doesn't mean that it has compromised on quality. This family-run farm produces exciting and consistent wines. Kaapse Vonkel was South Africa's first Méthode Cap Classique, and since 1971 this classic blend of chardonnay, pinot noir, and a touch of pinot meunier has been among the best. The 2003 Tiara is a great Bordeaux blend. The Pinotage demonstrates how well this varietal fares with no wood aging, but the Red Hill Pinotage, from old bush vines, shows just how much good oaking can improve it. This is a great place for kids. You can bring your own picnic to enjoy at tables by the small playground, there's a maze that takes about 10 minutes to walk through, and it has a small vineyard of all the grape varietals where you can see which grape is used for the different wines and taste grapes directly from the vine. The glam Cuvee restaurant, with its dark walls and Persian carpets, has a seasonal menu of South African dishes with French influences. ✉ *Kromme Rhee Rd., Koelenhof* ☎ *021/888–4900* ⊕ *www.simonsig.co.za* 🍷 *Tastings R25 for 5 wines* ☽ *Weekdays 8–5, Sat. 8:30–4; cellar tours weekdays at 10 and 3, Sat. at 10; restaurant open Tues.–Sun. 11–3, Fri. and Sat. 7–10* PM.

☾ **Spier.** Describing Spier as simply a wine estate is doing it an enormous disservice. The vast complex comprises a manor house, wine cellars, wine and farm shop, rose garden, restaurants, equestrian facilities, a conference center, an open-air amphitheater featuring a variety of performances during summer, and a cheetah park, where you can watch the animals being fed daily between 1 and 2. A "private encounter" or photograph with a cheetah costs around R80 per person for an adult cat and R180 for a cub. It's all designed in Cape-country style, with whitewashed walls and thatch roofs, set along the verdant north bank of the Eerste River. So, yes, it's seriously touristy, but still delightful. The Spier wines go from strength to strength. The latest flagship wine is the Frans K. Smit 2004, named after its winemaker. Also try

3

the cabernet sauvignon 2008 or the consistently good and well-priced 2008 chardonnay that's been highly rated by wine *fundis* (experts). ⚠ Be warned that this estate gets very busy during summer and on public holidays. ⊠ *R310 (Lynedoch Rd.)* ☎ *021/809–1100* ⊕ *www.spier.co.za* 🖃 *Informal tasting R10, educational tasting R20, reserve-wine tasting R20, cheese and wine tasting R35 for 3 wines and 3 cheeses* ⊙ *Daily 9–5, tasting 10–4:30.*

Villiera. Since it started wine making in 1984, the Grier family has notched numerous successes. As John Platter, one of South Africa's foremost wine writers, says: "Other winemakers might jog or work out in the gym; Jeff Grier gets all the exercise he needs stepping up to the podium for wine industry awards." Try the Bush Vine Sauvignon Blanc, for which Grier was voted Winemaker of the Year in 1997, and you'll start to understand why it's become almost a cult wine. Then check out the range of Méthode Cap Classique sparkling wines—the Tradition Rosé Brut, for instance, is a delicate pink bubbly with soft, creamy overtones. This is one of the wineries that is, as much as possible, producing chemical-free wines, and it is registered as a bio-diversity farm. It is building a wildlife sanctuary on an adjacent farm. ⊠ *R101 and R304 (Old Paarl and Stellenbosch Rds.), Koelenhof* ☎ *021/865–2002 or 021/865–2003* ⊕ *www.villiera.com* 🖃 *Tastings free* ⊙ *Weekdays 8:30–5, Sat. 8:30–1; tours by appointment.*

Warwick. This Ratcliffe-family-run farm is all business. The tasting area is in a tiny cellar room cluttered with wine-making equipment, and the farm hubbub continues while you're tasting. Louis Nel, formerly from Neil Ellis estate, is the Warwick's winemaker. The previous winemaker, Norma Ratcliffe, spent a couple of vintages in France perfecting traditional techniques, which have influenced Warwick's reds. The first female winemaker in South Africa, Norma pioneered the way for a new breed of young women who are now making their mark in the industry. Trilogy is a stylish and complex red made predominantly from cabernet sauvignon, with about 20% merlot and 20% cabernet franc. The 2004 Trilogy was voted one of the top five wines in the world by *Wine Spectator*—no mean feat! It retails at just over R100 a bottle, making it a bargain. Another great red, the Three Cape Ladies, was named after the indomitable Ratcliffe women. It's been described as a "feminine" blend of around 50% cabernet sauvignon, 20% merlot, and 30% Pinotage. The cabernet franc is undoubtedly one of the best wines made from this varietal in the Winelands. There are no cellar tours. ⊠ *R44, between Stellenbosch and Klapmuts, Elsenburg* ☎ *021/884–3146* ⊕ *www.warwickwine.com* 🖃 *Tastings R25* ⊙ *Weekdays 10–5, weekends 10–4.*

WHERE TO EAT

$-$$

MEDITERRANEAN

✕ **Olivello.** Be sure to book a table outside near the lily pond at this relaxed restaurant that serves Cape-meets-Mediterranean-style food in a fabulous country setting. Though the menu is fairly small, you'll still be hard-pressed to make a choice between such tasty options as lamb *tagine* (stew) served with preserved lemon, venison shanks slow-cooked in red wine and flavored with juniper, and beef fillet dressed with a cracked-peppercorn-and-brandy sauce. If all that sounds too rich for a hot summer's day, try the chicken salad with a lightly curried mayonnaise

3

sauce, almonds, and apricots. On Sundays a Mediterranean buffet (R165) lets you choose from 20 tapas and four main courses; dessert is not included. There's a good kids' menu, and children can have fun in the boats on the nearby dam or play on the lawn while you keep a watchful eye on them. ⊠ *Marianne Wine Farm, Valley Rd., off the R44* ☏ *021/875-5443* ⊕ *www. olivello.co.za* ⊟ *MC, V* ☉ *Closed Mon. and Tues. No dinner.*

TASTING TIP

One of the funny things about small, family-owned farms is that they won't charge you for a tasting if they don't feel like it. But it's at the owners' discretion, and it all depends on whether or not they wake up in a good or bad mood. If they like you, you could end up with a tasting, tour, and lunch at their home. So be at your best and most charming. But don't tell them we told you.

$$$ ✕ **Pomegranate.** The busy road and
ECLECTIC the swathes of invasive alien trees
★ that need to be chopped down give
absolutely no indication of the gem that lies beyond the entrance to Vergenoegd wine farm. Pomegranate, formerly located in Johannesburg, is run by chef Mike Israel, who is known for his fresh, contemporary cuisine. You'll be hard-pressed to concentrate on the menu—the views are fantastic and the historic manor house wonderfully restored. Luckily, the menu is dead simple. Mike has gone for the less-is-more approach and simply lists fish, lamb, game, poultry, and vegetarian. This gives him plenty of scope to play with the fresh ingredients he has available. You could start with the famous Pomegranate tomato tart or opt for the beetroot carpaccio starter with goat cheese. There are field mushrooms served with rosemary and Gorgonzola in a poppy-seed crepe. Mains come with Mike's classic, flavor filled sauces. The wine list is clever and has an excellent selection of good wines divided into three price categories, the cheapest cheekily referred to as Bank Managers Choice. ⊠ *Vergenoegd Wine Estate, Baden Powell Dr. (R310), off the N2* ☏ *021/843-3248* ⊟ *AE, DC, MC, V.*

$$–$$$ ✕ **Terroir.** The setting on a golf estate and wine farm is pretty, but it's
ECLECTIC the excellent food and service that really stand out here. Chef Michael
Fodor's Choice Broughton does his best to honor the concept of *terroir* (from the French
★ *terre* for "earth") and get as many ingredients from the surrounding area as possible. The menu changes regularly to make use of the fresh produce. Earthy and nutty cèpe mushrooms lightly fried in butter, garlic, and parsley make great starters. Main courses might include braised pork belly with ginger, juniper, and soy on smoked mash with braising juices and cabbage purée, or the duck-confit pancake with fig jam. Try the pear and Frangelica crème brûlée for dessert. There's a jungle gym for small foodies but, interestingly, no separate menu. Though the wine list is small, you can sample several different (and delicious) wines by the glass. Try the barrel-fermented chenin blanc, one of the estate's best-kept secrets. To avoid disappointment, be sure to book well in advance. ⊠ *Kleine Zalze Residential Golf Estate, Strand Rd. (R44), between Somerset West and Stellenbosch* ☏ *021/880-8167* ⊕ *www. kleinezalze.com* ⚑ *Reservations essential* ⊟ *AE, DC, MC, V* ☉ *Closed June 29–July 17. No dinner Sun.*

$–$$

SOUTH AFRICAN

Fodor's Choice

★

✕ **Tokara.** At the top of the Helshoogte Pass with absolutely amazing views of the valley and mountains, Tokara is definitely a Winelands must-do. Chef Etienne Bonthuys is the acknowledged king of sauces—rich, slow reductions that you may be tempted to lick off your plate. His adventurous menu changes seasonally but could include such starters as chilled avocado soup with smoked salmon or warm oysters in a Cap Classique butter sauce (aah, therein lies his magic). For mains there are some unusual combinations that work brilliantly, such as grilled springbok served with a lobster sauce and mint oil, and the ostrich fillet accompanied by a mandarin-liqueur sauce and berries. The fantastic two-course kids' menu (R55) doesn't list greasy fried chicken and fries, but rather meals such as mini steak burgers, calamari-and-prawn kebabs with pasta, or grilled fish-and-chips. For added interest there's an art gallery, an olive oil cellar, and free wine and olive oil tastings. ⊠ *Off R310, between Stellenbosch and Franschhoek* ☎ *021/808–5959* ⊕ *www.tokara.co.za* ⊟ *AE, DC, MC, V* ☉ *Closed Sun. and Mon.*

WHERE TO STAY

$$$$

🏨 **Asara.** If you fancy picking your pillows off a pillow menu, then Asara, part of the prestigious Relais & Chateaux hotel group, is the place for you. The hotel on the outskirts of Stellenbosch might not have the most breathtaking setting that the Winelands has to offer, but what it lacks in location it more than makes up for in luxury and attention to detail. The rooms are classically decorated in creams, whites, and browns and have balconies overlooking the vineyards or hotel courtyard. There are two restaurants to choose from, and you're a hop and a skip away from Cape Town, the airport, and excellent wine farms. It is also producing excellent wines on the estate, so you don't have to travel if you don't feel like it. And, if you're exhausted after a day of wine tasting, staff can arrange a massage in the privacy of your room. **Pros:** you'll be treated like royalty; easy access to both Cape Town and the Winelands: highly rated wines produced on the estate. **Cons:** not far from the Stellenbosch municipal rubbish dump; lacks the gracious charm of some historic wine farms; you'll need a deep pocket. ⊠ *Polkadraai Rd. (M12), Vlottenburg* ☎ *021/888–8000* ⊕ *www.asara.co.za* ↩ *36 rooms* ↻ *In-room: refrigerator, DVD, Wi-Fi (some). In-hotel: 2 restaurants, room service, bar, pool, bicycles, laundry service, Internet terminal, Wi-Fi, parking (free)* ⊟ *AE, DC, MC, V* ❘◯❘ *BP.*

$

🏨 **D'Ouwe Werf Country Inn.** A national monument, this attractive 1802 inn is thought to be the oldest in South Africa. From the street, you enter the original living room, a beautiful space with a lofty beamed ceiling and elegant antiques. The hotel is divided into two parts: the old inn with luxury rooms on its Georgian second story and a new wing with more standard rooms. All luxury rooms are furnished with antiques, including four-poster beds, draped sash windows, and bronze bathroom fittings. The standard rooms have reproductions only. A lovely garden in a brick courtyard shaded by trellised vines is open for meals and drinks throughout the day. **Pros:** perfect location in the heart of Stellenbosch; landmark in-house restaurant; two family-sized, self-catering houses available; heated outside swimming pool. **Cons:** can get a bit noisy in the center of town; some rooms are dark. ⊠ *30 Church St.*

☎ *021/887–4608* ⊕ *www.ouwewerf.co.za* ⌨ *38 rooms ♿ In-room: safe, refrigerator, Wi-Fi. In-hotel: restaurant, room service, pool, bicycles, laundry service, Wi-Fi, parking (free)* ▤ *AE, DC, MC, V* ⦿ *BP.*

$$$–$$$$ 🛅 **Lanzerac Manor.** The sense of history is almost tangible at this large working wine estate dating from 1692. The sheer beauty of the setting has not changed: a classic Cape Dutch manor house flanked by the rolling vineyards and mountains of the Jonkershoek Valley. The staff at this luxurious hotel and winery are friendly, and guest rooms are individually decorated with plush carpets, heavy drapes, and antiques. Some rooms have a floral theme; others are more masculine with animal-print cushions and bold stripes. You can eat casual alfresco meals on the terrace (weather permitting; $$) or opt for fine dining at Governor's Hall ($$), where chef Stephen Fraser pulls out all the stops. Start your meal off with the "cappuccino" of porcini with white-truffle sauce and mushroom "biscotti." Main courses include Indian lamb curry and Karoo ostrich with fried banana, sweet potato, and other root vegetables. The legendary Lanzerac cheesecake is creamy, tangy, and utterly sublime. **Pros:** winery on-site; stunning location with views of the Helderberg Mountains; distinguished example of Cape Dutch architecture. **Cons:** not within walking distance of Stellenbosch; fairly formal atmosphere can be a turn-off for some. ⊠ *Jonkershoek Valley, Lanzerac Rd., 1 km (½ mi) from Stellenbosch* ☎ *021/887–1132* ⊕ *www.lanzerac.co.za* ⌨ *43 rooms, 5 suites ♿ In-room: safe, refrigerator, DVD (some), Internet. In-hotel: restaurant, room service, bars, pool, gym, spa, laundry service, Wi-Fi, parking (free)* ▤ *AE, DC, MC, V* ⦿ *BP.*

$$–$$$ 🛅 **Spier Hotel.** The innovative design of these two-story buildings grouped around six courtyards, each with its own pool and leisure area, makes this complex feel like a Mediterranean village, albeit a very luxurious one. Rooms and suites are elegantly appointed, with Indonesian furniture, gas fireplaces, and stylish detail evident in the cotton throws and wide choice of pillows. The surrounding orchards and shade trees make the complex and walkways both verdant and private. See review of Spier Winery, above. **Pros:** plenty of entertainment on hand; perfect for the whole family; very accessible and close to the N2. **Cons:** can get really busy in peak season; commercialized. ⊠ *Spier Estate, Lynedoch Rd.* ☎ *021/809–1100* ⊕ *www.spier.co.za* ⌨ *155 rooms ♿ In-room: safe, refrigerator. In-hotel: 4 restaurants, room service, bars, pool, children's programs (ages 2–12), laundry service, Wi-Fi, parking (free)* ▤ *AE, DC, MC, V* ⦿ *BP.*

¢ 🛅 **Stumble Inn Backpackers Lodge.** Stellenbosch's original backpackers' lodging is within easy walking distance of most major town sights and is a great place to stay if you're traveling on a limited budget. You can choose from simple double rooms, dorm beds, and even limited camping facilities in the gardens. Other amenities include shared kitchen facilities and an on-site travel agent. The folks here will even arrange budget-minded packages that include wine tours and cheese tastings. **Pros:** central location in town; helpful staff; camping site in the gardens. **Cons:** bunk beds (need we say more?); shared bathroom facilities. ⊠ *12 Market St.* ☎ *021/887–4049* ⊕ *www.jump.to/stumble* ⌨ *7 rooms, 5 dormitories ♿ In-room: no phone, no TV. In-hotel: bar, pool,* *laundry service, Internet terminal, parking (free), some pets allowed* ⊟ *AE, DC, MC, V.*

NIGHTLIFE AND THE ARTS
NIGHTLIFE

The **Dorp Street Theatre Café** (✉ *59 Dorp St.* ☎ *021/886–6107* ⊕ *www. dorpstraat.co.za*), usually open Tuesday–Saturday, always has a great lineup of local musicians. Take a stroll into the Church Street part of town, where shops stay open late, and bars and cafés spill onto the streets. A good place to start, the **Wijnhuis** (✉ *Church and Andringa Sts.* ☎ *021/887–5844* ⊕ *www.wijnhuis.co.za*) quickly fills up with trendy locals wanting to unwind.

THE ARTS

★ Each summer, performances ranging from African jazz to opera to ballet are staged at the **Oude Libertas Amphitheatre** (✉ *Corner of Adam Tas St. and Oude Libertas Rd.* ☎ *021/809–7473* ⊕ *www.oudelibertas. co.za*), a delightful open-air venue across from and run and owned by Distell. For bookings contact **Computicket** (☎ *083/915–8000* ⊕ *www. computicket.co.za*). The **Spier Arts Summer Festival** (✉ *Spier Estate, R310* ☎ *021/809–1100* ⊕ *www.spier.co.za*) runs from mid-November to mid-March and usually includes opera, classical music, and a host of other performances.

SPORTS AND THE OUTDOORS
GOLF

Stellenbosch Golf Club (✉ *R44 [Strand Rd.]* ☐ ☎ *021/880–0103* ⊕ *www. stellenboschgolfclub.com*) has long tree-lined fairways that will pose a problem if you don't hit the ball straight. Greens fees are R350 for 18 holes. A caddy costs R100, club rental R200, and a golf cart R200.

HORSEBACK RIDING

Spier Equestrian Centre (✉ *Spier Estate, R310* ☎ *021/881–3683 or 082/711–4945*) offers a gentle amble or a quick canter through the vineyards (R280 one hour, R450 two hours). If you don't fancy getting into a saddle, you can go on a horse-drawn wagon ride (for R400 the carriage that usually takes around four people for an hour).

▌ EN
  ROUTE

Little Wool Shop and Mama Joan's Farm Kitchen (✉ *R44, Delvera Farm, between Stellenbosch and Klapmuts* ☎ *021/884–4004* ▱ *Free* ⊙ *Daily summer 9–5, winter 10–4*)is one of the few places in the Western Cape to see spinning and hand weaving. The farm makes merino knitwear, cotton blankets, and has hand-dyed merino wool for sale The shop also sells knitting patterns and wool. A garden restaurant serves light lunches and snacks.

▌ EN
  ROUTE

From Thelema the **R310** runs down into the fruit orchards and vines that mark the beginning of the Franschhoek Valley. The R310 dead-ends at the R45. To the left is Paarl, to the right Franschhoek.

FRANSCHHOEK

★ *22 km (14 mi) northeast of Stellenbosch.*

Franschhoek (French Corner) takes its name from its first white settlers, French Huguenots who fled to the Cape to escape Catholic persecution in France in the late 1600s. By the early 18th century about 200 Huguenots had settled in the Cape; today their descendants—with names like de Villiers, Malan, and Joubert—number in the tens of thousands. With their experience in French vineyards, the early Huguenots were instrumental in nurturing a wine-making culture in South Africa.

Franschhoek is the most spectacular of the three wine centers: a long valley encircled by towering mountain ranges and fed by a single road that runs through town. As spectacular as the valley is today, it must have been even more so in the 17th century, when it teemed with game. In calving season herds of elephants would migrate to the valley via the precipitous Franschhoek Mountains. The last wild elephant in the valley died in the 1930s. Some leopards still survive high in the mountains, but you won't see them.

What you will see today is an increasingly upscale village with beautifully renovated cottages and gorgeous gardens. Although it can get very busy during the summer season, you will always be able to find a quiet spot with a view of the mountains, roses, and swathes of lavender, which do well here. Franschhoek has developed into something of a culinary mecca, with some of the country's best restaurants and cafés lining the pretty main street. In October the village hosts a music festival featuring many local and visiting artists, while in May there's the fabulous Franschoek Literary Festival—featuring local and international writers—to look forward to. The town is more touristy than agrarian, although you will see the occasional wine farmer steaming into town with his dogs on the back of his *bakkie* (pickup truck), looking for tractor tires or other essentials. It's a great place for lunch or for a couple of days, as there are excellent small hotels and guesthouses to choose from.

GETTING HERE AND AROUND
The best way to explore this area is by renting a car and braving the Cape's highways and byways. Be aware that drunken walking is a real hazard in wine-growing areas, and you need to keep a sharp eye out for staggering pedestrians, especially over the weekends.

VISITOR INFORMATION
Franschhoek Vallée Tourisme is open weekdays 9–6, weekends 9–5.

Tourist Offices Franschhoek Vallée Tourisme (⌂ 70 Huguenot Rd. ☎ 021/876-3603 ⊕ www.franschhoek.org.za)

EXPLORING
The **Huguenot Monument** stands at the end of the main road through Franschhoek. It was built in 1948 to commemorate the contribution of the Huguenots to South Africa's development. The three arches symbolize the Holy Trinity, the sun and cross from the Huguenots' emblem, and the female figure in front represents Freedom of Conscience. *⌂ Lambrecht and Huguenot Sts.* ☎ *No phone (contact Huguenot Memorial Museum at 021/876-2532)* ⊕ *www.museum.co.za* ⌂ *R10* ⊙ *Mon.–Sat. 9–5, Sun. 2–5.*

To trace the history of the Huguenot community here, visit the **Huguenot Memorial Museum.** Its main building is modeled after the Saasveld house, built in 1791 by renowned Cape architect Louis Thibault in Cape Town. Wall displays profile some of the early Huguenot families. Exhibits also focus on other aspects of the region's history, such as the development of Cape Dutch architecture and the relationship of the Huguenots with the Dutch East India Company. Displays in the annex cover the culture and life of the Khoekhoen, or Khoikhoi, once derogatorily known as Hottentots, as well as the role of slaves and local laborers in the development of the Franschhoek Valley. ⊠ *Lambrecht St.* ☏ *021/876–2532* ▭ *R10* ⊙ *Mon.–Sat. 9–5, Sun. 2–5.*

WINERIES

It should come as no surprise that the Franschhoek Valley produces excellent wines. After all, the original French settlers brought with them an extensive and intimate understanding of viticulture. Some of the country's oldest estates nestle at the base of the spectacular Groot Drakenstein mountains, and the wine farmers here are constantly trying to top themselves.

TOP ATTRACTIONS

Fodor'sChoice **Boschendal.** With a history that dates back three centuries, this lovely
★ estate is one of the Cape's major attractions. You can easily spend half a day here. Cradled between the Simonsberg and Groot Drakenstein mountains at the base of Helshoogte Pass, the farm—formerly called Bossendaal—was originally granted to Jean le Long, one of the first French Huguenot settlers in the late 17th century. Boschendal runs one of the most pleasant wine tastings in the region: you can sit inside at the Taphuis, a Cape Dutch *langhuis* (longhouse), or outside at wrought-iron tables under a spreading oak. In 1981 Boschendal was the first to pioneer a Cape blanc de noir, a pink wine made in a white-wine style from black grapes. The Boschendal Blanc de Noir remains the best-selling wine of this style. Of the farm's extensive range of wines, a recent addition is the Cecil John range named after Cecil John Rhodes, the late-19th-century Cape prime minister who owned Rhodes Fruit Farms, of which Boschendal was once a part. There are two premier wines under this label, an impressive Shiraz and an intense sauvignon blanc. From the Taphuis it's a two-minute drive through vines and fruit trees to the main estate complex. The excellent Boschendal Restaurant serves a buffet of Cape specialties, Le Café serves light meals at tables under the oaks leading to the manor house, and Le Pique Nique (October–May) provides picnic baskets that you can enjoy on the lawns. Reservations are essential for the restaurant and picnic services. Expect to pay around R150 for an adult picnic, while kids' hampers are R59. This excludes wine and other drinks. The estate is wheelchair-friendly. ⊠ *R310, between Franschhoek and Stellenbosch, Groot Drakenstein* ☏ *021/870–4210 or 021/870–4211 for winery, 021/870–4274 for restaurants* ⊕ *www.boschendal.co.za* ▭ *Tastings R15* ⊙ *Daily 10–4:30.*

★ **L'Ormarins (Anthonij Rupert Wines).** Dating from 1811, the archetypal Cape Dutch manor house is festooned with flowers and framed by majestic peaks, but instead of remaining in the past, this winery has embraced the future and pumped serious money into a major revamp. Two state-of-the-art cellars were launched in 2007 as part of the farm's long-term plans to produce exceptional wines. Chat with the

Franschhoek Wine Route

ALONG R310

The drive out of Stellenbosch up the Helshoogte Pass is spectacular. In winter you'll more than likely find snow on the mountain peaks; in summer, once you top the pass you enter a verdant valley of fruit trees and ordered vineyards. Be sure to stop in at **Hillcrest Berry Farm** (⊠ *R310, Dennesig* ☏ *021/885-1629* ⊕ *www. hillcrestberries.co.za*) for delicious tea and scones. Then head to **Boschendal,** one of the oldest and most established estates in the country.

ALONG R45

There are well more than 20 estates to choose from here, and there's something for everyone—from enormous farms covering hundreds of acres to smaller, boutique vineyards producing just a few hundred bottles each year. If you turn right on R45 from the R310, **L'Ormarins** is one of the first wine farms you'll come to (off the R45 through a tunnel of trees). It's a well-established estate that's undergone some interesting changes. Just outside town, **La Motte** is a sister farm to L'Ormarins. Closer to town the estates come thick and fast. Amid this flurry—Môreson (up the aptly named Happy Valley Road), Rickety Bridge, Agusta, Chamonix, and Dieu Donne—is **Mont Rochelle,** a relatively small producer of lovely wine and home to a boutique hotel. Outside town and up the Franschhoek Pass toward Villiersdorp, the fabulous **Cabrière,** at Haute Cabrière, is built into the mountain. **La Petite Ferme** is worth phoning ahead for (you can't just pop in).

If you turn left on the R45 from the R310, you'll find more outstanding wine farms, including **Plaisir de Merle,** which makes a distinctive cabernet and sauvignon blanc.

---

winemakers and they'll tell you that the farm has introduced revolutionary farming practices, from transporting the grapes to the cellar in cool trucks to hand-sorting and -stemming. The results are impressive. The sangiovese is a brilliant, light drinking wine, and the pinot grigio is always a pleasure. When you've had enough of the wine, you can visit the Franschoek Motor Museum on the estate. It's home to more than 80 cars of varying ages in mint condition. ⊠ *R45 (Franschhoek Rd.), Groot Drakenstein* ☏ *021/874-9000* ⊕ *www.rupertwines.com* ☒ *Tastings R30, Motor Museum R60* ☉ *Weekdays 9–4:30, Sat. 10–3.*

WORTH NOTING

Cabrière. Built in 1994 on the lower slopes of the Franschhoek Mountains, Cabrière is the brainchild of Achim von Arnim, one of the Cape's most colorful winemakers. To avoid scarring the mountain, the complex, which includes the fine Haute Cabrière restaurant, hunkers into the hillside. There are five Cap Classique sparkling wines under the Pierre Jordan label, and the fruity, mouth-filling Haute Cabrière pinot noir is consistently one of the best. Also delicious is the chardonnay–pinot noir blend, an ideal, extremely quaffable wine to enjoy at lunchtime. Take a Saturday-morning cellar tour with von Arnim or his son, Takuan, and watch him perform his trademark display of *sabrage*—the dramatic decapitation of a bottle of bubbly with a saber. ⊠ *R45 (Pass Rd.)* ☏ *021/876–8500* ⊕ *www.cabriere.co.za* ☒ *Tastings and cellar tour*

3

R40 ☺ *Weekdays 9–5, Sat. 10–4, Sun. 11–4; tours Sat. at 11.*

La Motte Estate. This estate is owned by a branch of the same Rupert family that owns L'Ormarins, and is a partner in Rupert & Rothschild, a vineyard closer to Paarl. The elegant and rather formal tasting room, with its long marble-top table at which you sample the wines, looks into the cellars through a wall of smoked glass. The 2007 La Motte Shiraz, which needs about five years

> **DINING UNDER THE STARS**
>
> What could be more romantic than dining under the stars? During the summer months, Boschendal hosts a formal full-moon dinner under the oak trees to the accompaniment of a string quartet. Doesn't it sound lovely? Make sure you call for a reservation.

to reach its peak, is one of the biggest and boldest you'll taste of this variety, full of rich flavors. The 2007 Pierneef Collection Shiraz-Viognier is being snapped up for its whiffs of dark chocolate, smoked beef, black cherry, and blackberry. This wine is named in honor of the famous South African artist J.H. Pierneef, who was well known for his stunning landscapes from the first half of the 20th century. There are no cellar tours. ⊠ *R45 (Huguenot Rd.)* ☎ *021/876–3119* ⊕ *www.la-motte.com* 🍷 *Tastings R20* ☺ *Weekdays 9–4:30, Sat. 10–3.*

La Petite Ferme. You'll have to phone ahead to arrange a tasting here, but it's worth it, because then you'll know what to have with your lunch if you decide to dine here. True to its name, this is a small, family-run estate producing just enough wine for the restaurant and to keep its faithful regular customers happy. Try the full-bodied chardonnay. ⊠ *R45 (Franschhoek Pass Rd.)* ☎ *021/876–3016/8* ⊕ *www.lapetiteferme.co.za* ☺ *Sales daily noon–4; tastings and tours by appointment at 11.*

Mont Rochelle. This picture-pretty estate overlooking Franschoek produces some excellent wines. The barrel-fermented chardonnay has made everybody sit up and take notice, but new to try is the Miko Chardonnay Sur Lie, named after former owner Miko Rwayitare who died unexpectedly in 2008. The Syrah 2004 is also noteworthy, and the sauvignon blanc reserve from 2007 is another winner. A swank hotel and Mange Tout restaurant are also on-site. For more informal meals, there's the Country Kitchen. Both come highly recommended. ⊠ *Dassenberg Rd.* ☎ *021/876–3000* ⊕ *www.montrochelle.co.za* 🍷 *Tastings R20; cellar tour R10* ☺ *Daily 9–6; cellar tours weekdays at 11, 12:30, and 3.*

Plaisir de Merle. The name means "Pleasure of the Blackbird" and has its origins with the original French owners of the farm. This huge estate (2,500 acres) is the showpiece of Distell, a huge wine and spirit producer. With its innovative architecture and conservation area, it truly feels different from the ubiquitous "oak and gable" wineries that you see all over the Cape. But forget all the frills—it really is about the wine. Don't miss the cabernet franc: 2006 is looking good but will benefit from a few years to mature. The 2008 sauvignon blanc is delicious—crisp, with plenty of hints of green asparagus. ⊠ *R45, Simondium* ☎ *021/874–1071 or 021/874–1072* ⊕ *www.plaisirdemerle.co.za* 🍷 *Nibbling tasting R50; cellar tour with tastings R30* ☺ *Apr.–Oct.,* *weekdays 9–5, Sat. 10–2; Nov.–Mar., weekdays 9–5, Sat. 10–4; cellar tours by appointment.*

WHERE TO EAT

$$
SOUTH AFRICAN

✕ **Boschendal Restaurant.** Reserve well in advance for the buffet lunch here at one of the Cape's most beautiful and historic wineries. A wide selection of soups, quiches, and pâtés prefaces a bewildering array of cold and hot main dishes, including pickled fish, roasts, and imaginative salads; traditional Cape dishes are well prepared. End with an excellent sampling of South African cheeses and preserves or a quintessentially Cape dessert such as malva pudding. Unobtrusive, professional, but friendly service complements the bounty, priced at R240 a head. ✉ *R310, between Franschhoek and Stellenbosch, Groot Drakenstein* ☎ *021/870–4274* ⚲ *Reservations essential* ▤ *AE, DC, MC, V* ⊗ *No dinner.*

$–$$
ECLECTIC
Fodor's Choice
★

✕ **Haute Cabrière.** Try to reserve a window table for views across the vine-clad valley at this restaurant atop a working winery built into the mountainside. The mix-and-match menu is intended to complement the estate wines maturing in the cellar beneath you. You can opt for half or full portions of renowned chef Matthew Gordon's mouthwatering seasonal fare. Selections might include prawn risotto with seared wild Alaskan scallop, or quail with an onion, pear, and saffron chutney served with brioche toast. Then there's the warm pork-belly terrine with *rooibos* (bush tea) glaze, parsnip mash, pickled red cabbage and crackling. If you don't like the pressure of choosing, you could opt for the chef's recommended tasting menu—four delicious courses for R275. ✉ *Franschhoek Pass Rd. (R45)* ☎ *021/876–3688* ⚲ *Reservations essential* ▤ *AE, DC, MC, V.*

$$
SOUTH AFRICAN

✕ **Mange Tout.** Be sure to ask for a window seat when you're making a reservation. The view onto the vines and Cape Dutch homesteads is breathtaking. As soon as your food arrives, however, the distraction will end. This is serious food that looks as spectacular as it tastes. There's a wide range to choose from and the restaurant offers two-, three-, four-, or five-course meals. For starters don't pass up on the celery root and truffle risotto with cappuccino of Parmesan and truffle. It's heavenly—creamy and rich and nuanced with flavor. Or there's the mouthwatering oxtail jam, red wine jus, baked bone marrow, and herb gratin. The springbok medallion and shank with quince puree, celery root, and grated chestnut is a perfect example of just how good game can be. If you have an inch of space left, the chocolate and praline slice with caramel ice cream is a good choice. You can have farm wine by the glass. It's not cheap, but it does mean you can try different wines with each dish. ✉ *Mont Rochelle Hotel and Mountain Vineyards, Dassenberg Rd.* ☎ *021/876–2770* ⚲ *Reservations essential* ▤ *AE, DC, MC, V.*

$$
ECLECTIC
★

✕ **Reuben's.** Reuben Riffel is one of a small band of talented homegrown chefs who are breaking culinary rules with passion, and, more important, delectable results. Riffel is flexing his wings and "cooking food he would like to eat." And so, it seems, people would like to eat along with him. Choose from a diverse range of dishes on the à la carte menu. Do you opt for the crisp pork belly, celery root, apple puree, chili, and ginger caramel, or pancetta wrapped around kudu with a potato fondant? The decor is minimalist but welcoming, with a roaring fire in winter, and the service impeccable. The waiters know their wine and are happy to make menu recommendations. Have a drink at the trendy bar, made from an airplane wing. ⊠ *19 Huguenot Rd.* ☎ *021/876–3772* ⊕ *www. reubens.co.za* ⚒ *Reservations essential* ▱ *AE, DC, MC, V.*

¢–$ ✕**Topsi & Company.** Chef Topsi Venter, doyenne of the Cape culinary
SOUTH AFRICAN   scene, is as renowned as a raconteur as she is for her innovative country fare. The decor is simple and rustic, and local art lines the white walls. Blackboard menus change daily, and only fresh, local ingredients are used. Venter concentrates on traditional and indigenous Cape food, saying, "If somebody arrives with goat, we'll do goat. If they come with a zebra, then we'll do zebra." The food is not that intimidating, however. The beetroot with goat cheese and a rich Pinotage syrup is a good start before you move on to the kudu fillet with pine-ring mushrooms. Mussel bobotie is an innovative take on the traditional South African dish, usually made with minced beef. The homemade ice cream is made from prickly pears, fresh figs, or tomatoes, depending on what's in season, and the old-fashioned apple-almond tart is sublime. In this valley of wonderful wines it's great to be able to BYOB. ⊠ *7 Reservoir St.* ☎ *021/876– 2952* ⚒ *Reservations essential in summer* ▱ *AE, DC, MC, V.*

WHERE TO STAY

$–$$ ▦**Klein Genot.** Guests visiting this house originally built as the private
★   home of owners Angie and Joey Diamond will certainly feel as if they are visiting a friend. The 74-acre estate is set just outside town, close enough to go to dinner but far enough away to feel as if you've escaped. In the house's main area, numerous seating areas with plush couches beckon weary travelers to rest their feet. Each suite has a private patio with views that take in the property's 360 fruit trees, the Franschhoek Mountains, or the vegetable and herb gardens that provide breakfast's fresh elements. On the inside, the suites encircle a babbling fountain complete with koi. The heated floors, rooibos-enhanced bathroom products, plush queen-size beds, and wood-burning fireplaces make each suite a cozy escape. If you don't feel like heading into town, Genot, the on-property restaurant, features the estate's delicious wine and locally grown produce in a weekly changing menu. **Pros:** on-site spa is a divine addition to your escape; private balconies are a great place to sip your morning coffee; 74 acres to stretch your legs. **Cons:** the location outside town may be inconvenient if you don't have a car. ⊠ *Green Valley Rd.* ☎ *021/876–2738* ⊕ *www.kleingenot.com* ⟿ *6 rooms, 1 suite* ⚒ *In-room: no phone, safe, DVD, Wi-Fi. In-hotel: restaurant, room service, pool, spa, laundry service, Wi-Fi, parking (free), no kids under 9* ▱ *AE, DC, MC, V* ⍾| *BP.*

$–$$ ▦**Le Ballon Rouge.** If you fancy being in the heart of the village, Le Ballon Rouge makes a good base. Here you're just a five-minute walk from galleries, restaurants, and the general buzz. The guesthouse—in a restored 1904 Victorian homestead—is both welcoming and relaxing. The rooms are individually decorated in a pleasing mix of traditional and contemporary; a brass bedstead sits in one room, a modern four-poster in another. The Owner's Suite, which can be yours despite the name, has a private deck and Jacuzzi with a mountain view—just the thing for a starry evening with a glass of Franschhoek's best. Private wine tours and safaris can be arranged. **Pros:** central location; personal and attentive service; airport shuttle can be arranged. **Cons:** few rooms available; children under 12 not allowed. ✉ *7 Reservoir St.* ☎ *021/876–2651* ⊕ *www.ballonrouge.co.za* ➲ *8 rooms, 2 suites* ⅋ *In-room: no phone (some), refrigerator (some). In-hotel: room service, bar, pool, laundry service, parking (free), no kids under 12* ⊟ *AE, DC, MC, V* ⦿ *CP.*

$$$$
Fodor'sChoice
★

🖾 **Le Quartier Français.** Part of the Relais & Châteaux group, this classy guesthouse exuding privacy and peace is a Winelands favorite. Rooms in two-story whitewashed cottages face a pool deck and central garden exploding with flowers. Decor is vibrant, with rustic furniture, sponge-painted walls, colorful drapes, and small fireplaces. Upstairs rooms have timber beams and mountain views, and suites have private pools. So which awards hasn't the restaurant won? None, by the looks of it, but chef Margot Janse and her team aren't resting on their laurels. You can eat at the Tasting Room, a formal restaurant, or the relaxed iCi ($–$$). Either way you won't likely be disappointed—unless you don't make reservations. Favorites from the iCi menu include the lamb burger with marinated tomatoes, pickled cucumber, and avocado, and the wild-mushroom-and-preserved lemon risotto. The Tasting Room ($$$$; no dinner Sunday) offers four-course meals (excluding wine) for R490, six courses for R610 and eight courses for R760. This is foodie territory—words like *ballotine* and *rillette* sprinkle the menu, but just ignore the complicated terminology and enjoy the creations on your plate. These could include inventive dishes like a roulade of sugar-cured tuna, salmon, and Alaskan snow crab; prawn tartare with horseradish cream; or crisp salmon trout with tomatoes, anchovy-and-basil terrine, and crushed potatoes. As you enter the boldly colored dining room, look for the exotic candelabras, made by iThemba, an organization providing employment for HIV-positive women. **Pros:** many children's activities; an in-house treatment room; screening room for moviegoers; cooking classes with Margot Janse. **Cons:** pricey; home will seem very dull; the food is so good you might leave a few pounds heavier. ✉ *16 Huguenot Rd., Box 237* ☎ *021/876–2151* ⊕ *www.lequartier.co.za* ➲ *13 rooms, 8 suites* ⅋ *In-room: safe, DVD, Wi-Fi. In-hotel: 2 restaurants, room service, bar, pools, bicycles, children's programs, laundry service, Internet terminal, Wi-Fi, parking (free)* ⊟ *AE, DC, MC, V* ⦿ *BP.*

$$$$

🖾 **Mont Rochelle.** With sweeping views over the valley and mountain range, you might choose to stay put at Mont Rochelle for a few days rather than explore all Franschoek has to offer. The hotel feels a bit like a family manor house, and you might be tempted to come to breakfast wearing the hotel's comfy slippers. The staff are friendly and more than attentive. Just squeak and they'll do their best to meet any request. The rooms are plush—there's lots of dark wood, crisp white linen, classic wing chairs and huge paintings to lend a luxurious feel. Two of the suites—which are enormous—have private plunge pools—a real luxury in summer when the temperatures soar. Children are welcome, but there aren't any dedicated children's programs or family rooms. **Pros:** two fantastic restaurants on-site; great walks on the farm; brilliant wine. **Cons:** pricey; pools are unfenced; some of the rooms and

suites are only accessible by two flights of stairs. ⊠ *Dassenberg Rd.*
☎ *021/876–2770* ⊕ *www.montrochelle.co.za* ☞ *16 rooms, 6 suites*
⚥ *In-room: safe, DVD. In-hotel: 2 restaurants, bar, pool, gym, spa,*
bicycles, laundry service, Internet terminal, Wi-Fi, parking (free) ⊟ *AE,*
DC, MC, V ⊺◎⎮ *BP.*

¢ ⊺⎮ **Résidence Klein Oliphants Hoek.** Originally built as the home of a British missionary, this lovingly restored guesthouse also once served as
a school. Now its rooms are decorated with rich fabrics and luxurious finishes. One has its own plunge pool, and others have generous
fireplaces. On arrival, you're automatically booked in at highly rated
Bouillabaisse, the sister seafood restaurant a five-minute stroll away,
but you're welcome to eat anywhere in the food lovers' paradise that is
Franschhoek. **Pros:** intimate setting with peaceful surroundings; a couple of the rooms have private splash pools. **Cons:** unsuitable for large
families or children; the upstairs loft rooms feel a bit cramped ⊠ *14*
Akademie St., Box 470 ☎ *021/876–2566* ⊕ *www.kleinoliphantshoek.*
com ☞ *8 rooms* ⚥ *In-room: no phone, safe, refrigerator (some), DVD.*
In-hotel: restaurant, room service, bar, pool, laundry service, Internet
terminal, parking (free) ⊟ *AE, DC, MC, V* ⊺◎⎮ *BP.*

PAARL

21 km (13 mi) northwest of Franschhoek.

Paarl takes its name from the granite domes of Paarl Mountain, which
looms above the town—*paarl* is Dutch for "pearl." The first farmers
settled here in 1687, two years after the founding of Stellenbosch. The
town has its fair share of historic homes and estates, but it lacks the
charm of its distinguished neighbor simply because it's so spread out.
Main Street, the town's oak-lined thoroughfare, extends some 11 km
(7 mi) along the western bank of the Berg River. You can gain a good
sense of the town's history on a drive along this lovely street.

GETTING HERE AND AROUND

As in the rest of the area, driving yourself is your best option in and
around Paarl. Estates are spread so there is distance between them, and
to really get the best out of the area you do need your own wheels.

VISITOR INFORMATION

The Paarl Tourism Bureau is open Monday–Thursday 8–5, Friday
8–4:45, weekends 10–1.

ESSENTIALS

Hospitals Paarl Medi-Clinic (⊠ *Berlyn St., Paarl North* ☎ *021/807–8000*
⊕ *www.paarlmc.co.za*).

Tourist Offices Paarl Tourism Bureau (⊠ *216 Main St.* ☎ *021/872–4842 or*
021/872–6737 ⊕ *www.tourismpaarl.co.za*).

EXPLORING

Most visitors to Paarl drive down the town's main street, take in the
historic buildings, and then head off to the Winelands, golf estates,
and restaurants. If you have the time, check out the Afrikaanse Taalmonument *(Afrikaans Language Monument)* and Jan Phillips Mountain

Drive. For some excellent examples of Cape Dutch, Georgian, and Victorian homes, head to Zeederberg Square, a grassy park on Main Street just past the Paarl Tourism Bureau.

Like the Voortrekker Monument in Pretoria, the concrete **Afrikaanse Taalmonument** *(Afrikaans Language Monument)*, set high on a hill overlooking Paarl, holds a special place in the hearts of Afrikaners, who struggled for years to gain acceptance for their language alongside English. The rising curve of the main pillar is supposed to represent the growth and potential of Afrikaans. When it was erected in 1973, the monument was as much a gesture of political victory as a paean to the Afrikaans language. Ironically, it may become the language's memorial. Under the new South Africa, Afrikaans has become just one of 11 official languages and is gradually losing its dominance, although attempts are being made to ensure that the rich culture isn't lost. The view from the top of the hill is incredible, taking in Table Mountain, False Bay, Paarl Valley, and the various mountain ranges of the Winelands. You can buy a picnic basket at the monument's restaurant and find a pretty spot to enjoy the wonderful view; a basket costs around R60 for two people and is crammed with cold meats, salad, cheese, breads, fresh fruit, and something sweet. A short, paved walking trail leads around the hillside past impressive fynbos specimens, particularly proteas. After the N1 bridge, a sign on your right points the way to the monument. ⊠ *Afrikaanse Taalmonument Rd.* ☎ *021/863-4809* ⌑ *R12* ☉ *Daily 8–5 (the monument sometimes stays open later in summer, but this varies).*

Halfway down the hill from the Afrikaans Language Monument is a turnoff onto a dirt road and a sign for the Paarl Mountain Nature Reserve. The dirt road is **Jan Phillips Mountain Drive**, which runs 11 km (7 mi) along the mountainside, offering tremendous views over the valley. Along the way it passes the **Mill Water Wildflower Garden** and the starting points for several trails, including hikes up to the great granite domes of Paarl Mountain. The dirt road rejoins Main Street at the far end of Paarl.

WINERIES
TOP ATTRACTIONS

★ **Avondale Wine.** Although the farm was established as early as 1693, current owners Johnny and Ginny Grieve have done some serious reorganizing in the vineyards and built a state-of-the-art cellar, which is dug into a dry river bed. Avondale started producing wines only in 1999, making it one of the newer kids on the block. No matter. The winery has hit the ground running, and its wines are winning one award after another. The reds are especially good, and the intense Paarl summers result in full-bodied grapes that deliver knockout flavors. Be sure to try the 2005 Les Pleurs Syrah and the new Jonty's Duck certified organic wine. Both are delicious. The Grieves are also farming as biodynamically as possible, and Avondale is now registered as biodiversity-compliant by both South African and Dutch authorities. The ducks the wine is named after patrol the vineyards looking for pests, while Jonty is the farmer and general manager. Many farms have absent owners, but the Grieve family takes a hands-on approach here. The casually dressed guy behind the wine-tasting counter is, in all likelihood, the owner.

Paarl Wine Route

Wineries here are spread far apart, so you might want to select only a couple or take a whole day to taste at leisure. Start in Paarl, home to the impressive **KWV**, with cellars covering 55 acres and a wide selection of wines.

Along R301/303. On its way to Franschhoek, the R301/303 runs past **Avondale Wine,** a relatively new farm with a state-of-the-art cellar, a gorgeous rose garden, and excellent wines.

Along WR1 between R44 and R45. On your way from Franschhoek to Paarl, take a quick detour down the WR1 (Simondium Road) to **Backsberg** and, a bit farther, **Glen Carlou.** Backsberg has more going on than Glen Carlou, but they both have wines that are worth tasting and buying. Continue on, and turn right on the R44. At a four-way stop, turn right onto the R101 and cross over the N1. Follow the goat signs to Suid Agter Paarl Road and Fairview.

Along Suid-Agter-Paarl and Noord-Agter-Paarl roads. Fairview is as famous for its goats and cheese as it is for its wines. Leave yourself plenty of time here. From Fairview, turn right onto the Suid-Agter-Paarl Road and make your way to **Landskroon,** known for full-bodied reds. Turn right on the R44 and, after about 10 km (6 mi), right onto the WR8 (Noord Agter Paarl Road), and then right again to **Rhebokskloof Private Cellar.** If you continue on the R44 toward Wellington, you'll pass Nelson Wine Estate (aka Nelson's Creek) on your left.

Once you've done your wine tasting and buying, be sure to visit Ginny's exquisite rose garden. ⊠ *Lustigan Rd., off R301* ☎ *021/863–1976* ⊕ *www.avondalewine.co.za* ⊠ *Tastings R25* ⊘ *Mon.–Sat. 10–4; cellar tours by appointment.*

★ **Fairview.** This is one of the few wineries that is good for families. Chil-
⊘ dren get a kick out of seeing peacocks roaming the grounds and goats clambering up a spiral staircase into a goat tower. In fact, Fairview produces a superb line of goat cheeses and olive oil, all of which you can taste. But don't let Fairview's sideshows color your judgment about the wines. Charles Back, a member of the family that runs Backsberg, is one of the most successful and innovative winemakers in the Cape, and the estate's wines are top-drawer and often surprising. Back doesn't stick to the tried-and-true Cape varietals. The zinfandel-Cinsaut blend is quite unusual, as is the Shiraz-mourvèdre-viognier blend. The winery also makes creative use of the farm's many Rhône varieties. Perhaps it's just because the pun was irresistible, but (as claimed by the label) goats are sent into the vineyard to personally select grapes for the Goats-do-Roam, which is indeed like a young Côtes du Rhône (infuriating French winemakers). Likewise, the very popular Goat-Roti sounds awfully like Côte-Rôtie. If you care to linger, you can have a light meal and freshly baked bread at the Goatshed restaurant for around R70. ⊠ *WR3, off R101 (Suid-Agter-Paarl Rd.)* ☎ *021/863–2450* ⊕ *www.fairview.co.za* ⊠ *Wine and cheese tastings: standard tasting R20, master tasting (with*

flagship wines) R60, cheese tastings R10 ☉ *Weekdays 8:30–5, Sat.*
8:30–4, Sun. 9:30–4; cellar tours by appointment.

WORTH NOTING

Backsberg. Framed by the mountains of the Simonsberg, this lovely
estate is run by the Back family, well known for producing great wines
of good value. Backsberg has a comprehensive range of red and white
wines and a very fine brandy made from chenin blanc. Among the
wines to look out for are the 2003 Babylons Toren Chardonnay, the
2003 Babylons Toren red blend, and the 2007 Special Late Harvest.
It also produces three kosher wines that are palatable: an unwooded
chardonnay, a merlot, and a Pinotage. The restaurant does a lamb spit
every lunch, so you can taste some excellent wines before digging in to
a typical South African meal. Breakfasts are now available from 9:30
onwards, and the estate has self-guided cellar tours. Concerned about
climate change and the environment, the Back family has put measures
in place to reduce the farm's carbon footprint. They've done a good job,
and Backsberg is the first carbon-neutral wine estate in South Africa.
Here's hoping others will soon follow suit. On the odd occasion—
and depending how busy everybody is—a tractor ride can be arranged
ahead of time for children. ✉ *WR1 (Simondium Rd.), between R44*
and R45 ☎ *021/875–5141* ⊕ *www.backsberg.co.za* ✆ *Tastings R15;*
cellar tours by appointment ☉ *Weekdays 8:30–5, Sat. 9:30–4:30, Sun.*
10:30–4:30.

Glen Carlou. What comes out of Glen Carlou is rather special. The
Quartzstone chardonnay 2007 is exceptional, the Shiraz is noteworthy,
and the Gravel Quarry Cabernet 2006 is making its mark. The cellar has
undergone a major overhaul, and an art museum that displays contemporary art has been added. There's a Zen garden to relax in after you've
stocked up on some seriously good wines, and you can always have a
light lunch at the restaurant. The prawn and avocado salad is lovely
in summer, while the slow-cooked springbok shanks are perfect when
the rain is belting outside. ✉ *WR1 (Simondium Rd.), between R44 and*
R45, Klapmuts ☎ *021/875–5528* ⊕ *www.glencarlou.co.za* ✆ *Tastings*
R15 ☉ *Weekdays 8:30–5, weekends 10–3.*

KWV. Short for Ko-operatieve Wijnbouwers Vereniging (Cooperative
Winegrowers' Association), KWV regulated and controlled the Cape
wine industry for decades. This is no longer the case, and KWV is seek-
ing to redefine itself as a top wine and spirit producer and has a number
of labels. Its brandies, sherries, and fortified dessert wines regularly
garner gold medals, and it produces an enormous selection of excellent wines. KWV's cellars are some of the largest in the world, covering
around 55 acres, and its cellar tours are the most popular and crowded
in the Winelands. Among the highlights is the famous Cathedral Cellar,
with a barrel-vaulted ceiling and giant vats carved with scenes from the
history of Cape wine making. In an adjoining cellar you can see the five
largest vats in the world under one roof. The tour begins with a short
audiovisual presentation and ends with a tasting of some of KWV's
products. Australian cellar master Richard Rowe is already making
his mark. Wines made in the heavy old-world style are spending less
time in old wood and getting a lighter touch. ✉ *André du Toit Bldg.,*

Kohler St. ☎ *021/807–3911* ⊕ *www.kwv.co.za* ✉ *Tastings R15; cellar tour with tastings R25* ⊗ *Mon.–Sat. 9–4:30; English tours Mon.–Sat. at 10, 10:30, and 2:15, and Sun. at 11.*

Landskroon. Landskroon means "crown of the land" in Afrikaans, and this venerable estate, run by the ninth generation of the de Villiers family, produces a lovely cabernet sauvignon—with hints of vanilla and oak—that's up there with the best. Look out for the premium-range 2007 Paul de Villiers Cabernet Sauvignon and the Landskroon 2007 Shiraz. For a little something to sip after a long, leisurely dinner, try the Murio Muscat Jerepico—a rich, velvety, fortified wine with a fresh finish. It also produces an excellent port made from tinta barocca, tinta roriz, souzao, and touriga nacionale. ⊠ *Suid-Agter-Paarl Rd., off R44, Suider Paarl* ☎ *021/863–1039* ⊕ *www.landskroonwines.com* ✉ *Tastings free* ⊗ *Weekdays 8:30–5, Sat. 9–1.*

Rhebokskloof Private Cellar. This winery sits at the head of a shallow valley, backed by hillsides covered with vines and fynbos. It's a lovely place for lunch on a sunny day, and you can also take horseback rides through the vineyards. The Victorian Restaurant serves à la carte meals and teas on an oak-shaded terrace overlooking the gardens and mountains; in inclement weather meals are served in the Cape Dutch Restaurant, which also has a Sunday buffet lunch. The Chardonnay Sur Lie 2007 is wonderful, with a lovely balance and fruity, toasty overtones, as is the flagship wine, the 2006 Syrah. The estate has a number of different wine tastings; the gourmet tasting includes a cellar tour and pairs six dishes with six wines for around R220 per person. ⊠ *WR8, Agter Paarl* ☎ *021/869–8386* ⊕ *www.rhebokskloof.co.za* ✉ *Tastings R15, formal tastings R70, gourmet tastings R220* ⊗ *Daily 9–5.*

WHERE TO EAT

$$$$
ECLECTIC
Fodor's Choice
★

✕ **Bosman's.** Set amid the heady opulence of the Grande Roche hotel, this elegant restaurant and Relais & Châteaux member ranks as one of the country's finest. The level of service is extraordinary, commensurate with that of the finest European restaurants. Once you overcome the hurdle of which menu to choose—seafood, tasting (six to eight dishes), Cape specialties, vegetarian, epicurean, or à la carte—you start with a complimentary *amuse-bouche* (literally, something to entertain your palate). A first course of baked goat-cheese dumplings served with a Mediterranean vegetable salad and smoked-tomato coulis could precede a main course of springbok with mushroom-apple brioche and port-wine jus. If you're looking to go big, try the four-course set menu for R580. ⊠ *Grande Roche, Plantasie St.* ☎ *021/863–5100* ▭ *AE, DC, MC, V* ⊗ *Daily noon–1:30, 7–9. Closed mid-May–July.*

$–$$
MEDITERRANEAN

✕ **Marc's Mediterranean Cuisine & Garden.** Chef-owner Marc Friederich is a foodie with an instinctive feel for what will work. And work his restaurant does. It's consistently full, consistently interesting, and always a pleasure to eat in. What to choose from? There's a Lebanese mezze for starters made up of mouthwatering dips, bite-size spinach and feta pies, and warm pitas for scooping, or you could opt for Marc's fish soup with a dash of ouzo and aioli crostini. For entrées there's organic beef done on a lava-stone grill, paella, or Franschoek trout with vegetables and a lemony sauce. Children are also well looked after—there's spaghetti with tomato sauce, a choice of burgers with fries and vanilla ice cream and chocolate sauce as part of the deal for a very reasonable R50. Marc also serves as a sommelier, so the wine list is comprehensive and he can help you with food-and-wine pairings. ☒ *129–131 Main St.7646* ☎ *021/863–3980* ⊕ *www.marcsrestaurant.co.za* ⊟ *AE, DC, MC, V* ☾ *Closed July. No dinner Sun.*

$–$$ ✕ **Pontac Manor.** Having established a popular small hotel in a striking
ECLECTIC Cape Victorian former farmstead, the owners added a restaurant that has become a Winelands favorite. The deep veranda is the place for lunch at Café du Pontac, except on very hot days, when the elegant dining room makes a cooler option. Diners are only too happy to tuck into such dishes as rack of lamb served with a potato-and-tarragon galette and thyme-and-honey jus. Finish with country cheeses or try the chocolate-truffle gâteau with whiskey sponge and a gooseberry topping. ☒ *16 Zion St.* ☎ *021/872–0445* ⊕ *www.pontacmanor.co.za* ⚠ *Reservations essential* ☾ *Daily 7–10 PM* ⊟ *AE, DC, MC, V.*

$$$ ✕ **Roggeland.** For an unforgettable Cape experience, make a beeline for
ECLECTIC this glorious Cape Dutch manor house on a farm outside Paarl. Meals are long, languid rituals, whether it's an alfresco lunch in the garden or a four-course dinner in the 18th-century dining room. The menu changes daily, but you might start with sweet-corn soup with cilantro cream followed by trout fillet on handmade pasta with a basil sabayon. A main course of lamb loin comes teamed with roasted butternut and shallots in muscadel, with an indigenous malva pudding with a *rooibos*-tea mousse as the finale. This feast is priced at R240 and includes a different wine with each course. ☒ *Roggeland Rd., Paarl North* ☎ *021/868–2501* ⊕ *www.roggeland.co.za* ⚠ *Reservations essential* ⊟ *AE, DC, MC, V.*

WHERE TO STAY

$$ ⌂ **Bartholomeus Klip Farmhouse.** For a break from a long bout of wine
Fodor'sChoice tasting, head to this Victorian guesthouse on a nature reserve and work-
★ ing farm. Its luxurious accommodations and excellent food come in the middle of 9,900 acres of rare *renosterveld* scrubland that is home to the endangered geometric tortoise. There's also plenty of eland, zebra, wildebeest, springbok, rhebok, bontebok, bat-eared fox, Cape buffalo, and birdlife in and around the mountains, streams, and plains, and the farm runs a growing Cape buffalo breeding program. Watch sheep shearing in action, hike, mountain bike, swim, or paddle. The farmhouse is decorated in old African colonial style, with plenty of floral fabrics, antique silver, and botanical art. Rooms have thick comforters and crisp linens. Ask for one that opens onto the veranda, especially in summer. Wild Olive House (R974 per person), a great self-catering option for families (though you can arrange to have your meals catered, too), is a five-minute walk from the farmhouse and has its own pool. High tea in the boathouse includes fabulous scones and cream and traditional *melktert* (cinnamon-sprinkled custard tart), a South African teatime institution. **Pros:** separate house available for self-catering families; very tranquil setting close to wine farms and small towns; rates include all meals, teas, and game drives. **Cons:** may be a bit intimate for some as all the rooms are in the manor house; this part of the Western Cape

can get unbearably hot in summer. ✉ *Off the R44, near Bo-Hermon* 🏠 *Box 36, Hermon 7308* 📠 *082/829–4131 or 022/448–1820* ⊕ *www. bartholomeus.co.za* ⇨ *4 rooms, 1 suite, 1 self-catering house* ⚙ *In-room: no TV, Wi-Fi. In-hotel: room service, bar, pool, water sports, bicycles, laundry service, Wi-Fi, parking (free), no kids under 16 in the main house* ▭ *AE, DC, MC, V* ⦿ *FAP.*

¢ 🏨 **Diemersfontein Wine & Country Estate.** Built in the 19th century, this historic farmstead is set in a lush garden with rolling lawns and abundant roses and azalea bushes. The farm has been transformed into a lifestyle estate—with private houses, a small school, and lovely cottages where you can stay. The rooms are comfortable and decorated in a relaxed country style with floral throws and fresh flowers. The farm produces a range of noteworthy wines, which you can taste; highlights include the flagship Carpe Diem Pinotage, the Carpe Diem Viognier 2006, and the Thokozani white blend of sauvignon blanc, chenin blanc, and viognier. Seasons restaurant ($) serves, appropriately enough, seasonal meals and is a wonderful venue for a late brunch or leisurely lunch. If you want something low-key, order a picnic basket to take onto the grounds. If you're feeling energetic, try your hand at bass fishing or horseback riding on the estate. **Pros:** lots to do including fishing, horse riding, wine tasting; lovely gardens; airport shuttle can be arranged. **Cons:** frequently used as wedding and conference venue so can get quite busy; setting pretty but not breathtaking. ✉ *Jan van Riebeek Dr. (R301), Wellington* 📠 *021/873–2671 lodging, 021/864–5060 restaurant, 021/864–5050 winery* ⊕ *www.diemersfontein.co.za* ⇨ *17 rooms* ⚙ *In-room: no phone (some), no TV. In-hotel: restaurant, bar, pool, laundry service, Wi-Fi, parking (free)* ▭ *AE, DC, MC, V* ⦿ *BP.*

$$$–$$$$　🏨 **Grande Roche.** A member of the prestigious Relais & Châteaux group,
Fodor's Choice　this establishment can stake a claim to being one of the best hotels in
★　South Africa. In a gorgeous Cape Dutch manor house that dates from the mid-18th century, the hotel sits amid acres of vines beneath Paarl Mountain, overlooking the valley and the Drakenstein Mountains. Suites are either in the historic buildings—slave quarters, stables, and wine cellar—or in attractive terrace buildings constructed in traditional Cape Dutch style. Rooms are a tasteful mix of the modern and the old: reed ceilings and thatch comfortably coexist with heated towel racks and air-conditioning. Offering a level of service extremely rare in South Africa, the employees, many of whom trained in Europe, outnumber the guests by two to one. **Pros:** estate declared a national monument in 1993; award-winning cuisine. **Cons:** not within easy walking distance from town; rarified atmosphere doesn't suit everybody. ✉ *Plantasie St., Box 6038* 📠 *021/863–5100* ⊕ *www.granderoche.co.za* ⇨ *5 rooms, 29 suites* ⚙ *In-room: safe, DVD (some). In-hotel: 2 restaurants, room service, tennis courts, pools, gym, laundry service, Wi-Fi, parking (free)* ▭ *AE, DC, MC, V* ⦿ *BP* ☾ *Closed mid-May–July.*

$　🏨 **Lemoenkloof Guest House & Conference Centre.** In the heart of Paarl, this national monument is decorated in sophisticated country style, with generous throws and flouncy curtains. The rest of the early-19th-century house is peppered with antiques and Oriental rugs. Modern accoutrements, such as television, air-conditioning, and tea- and coffee-making facilities in each of the guest rooms, make your stay comfortable. The swimming pool and art gallery add an element of fun, and the private garden is a great place to relax after some hectic wine tasting. **Pros:** declared a national monument in 1986; very reasonable rates and weekend specials; airport shuttle can be arranged. **Cons:** no children under 12 allowed; hosts many conferences so busy at times. ⊠ *396A Main St.* ☎ *021/872–7520 or 021/872–3782* ⊕ *www.lemoenkloof.co.za* ➳ *26 rooms* ⅙ *In-room: safe, refrigerator, Wi-Fi. In-hotel: pool, laundry service, Internet terminal, no kids under 12* ⊟ *AE, DC, MC, V* ⅠⓄⅠ *BP.*

$ ★ ⛫ **Roggeland Country House.** Dating from 1693, this farm is one of the most delightful lodgings in the Winelands. The setting in the Dal Josaphat valley is breathtaking, with stunning views of the craggy Drakenstein Mountains. Guest rooms in restored farm buildings have reed ceilings, country dressers, and mosquito nets (not just for effect). The 1779 manor house, which contains the dining room and lounge, is a masterpiece of Cape Dutch architecture. If you have kids in tow, contact Roggeland in advance to make arrangements, but it is a family-friendly atmosphere, with a big lawn out back and bats and balls for impromptu games. **Pros:** reasonable rates; excellent restaurant; nightly rate includes a four-course meal. **Cons:** no TVs in rooms; no air-conditioning and the summers can be blistering. ⊠ *Roggeland Rd., Box 7210, Paarl North* ☎ *021/868–2501* ⊕ *www.roggeland.co.za* ➳ *10 rooms* ⅙ *In-room: no TV. In-hotel: restaurant, pool, laundry service, parking (free)* ⊟ *AE, DC, MC, V* ⅠⓄⅠ *MAP.*

SPORTS AND THE OUTDOORS

BALLOONING

Wineland Ballooning (☎ *021/863–3192 or 083/983–4687* ⊕ *www.kapinfo.com*) makes one-hour flights over the Winelands every morning from about November through April, weather permitting. The balloon holds a maximum of five passengers, and the trip costs about R2,640 per person. After the flight there's a champagne breakfast at the Grand Roche.

GOLF

Paarl Golf Club (⊠ *848 Wemmershoek Rd.* ☎ *021/863–1140, 021/863–2828 pro shop* ⊕ *www.paarlgolfclub.co.za*) is surrounded by mountains, covered with trees, and dotted with water hazards. The greens fees are R440 for 18 holes for nonaffiliated members, golf-club rental is around R100, caddies cost around R150, and golf carts are approximately R220.

Pearl Valley Signature Golf Estate & Spa (⊠ *R301* ☎ *021/867–8000* ⊕ *www.pearlvalleygolfestates.com*) has a breathtaking setting in the valley, and the course, designed by Jack Nicklaus, has golfers in rapture. The greens fees are R765 for 18 holes, golf-club rental is around R495. Golf carts are included in the greens fee; there are no caddies. After your game you can relax at the great clubhouse, pool, or wellness center (which is also nice if some members of your party want to play while others want a bit of pampering).

HORSEBACK RIDING

Wine Valley Horse Trails (✉ *Rhebokskloof wine farm, WR8, off the R44* 📞 *083/226–8735 or 021/869–8687* ⊕ *www.horsetrails-sa.co.za*) offers scenic rides around the Rhebokskloof vineyards or up into the surrounding Paarl Mountain Nature Reserve. If horses aren't your thing, you can have fun on an all-terrain vehicle. It costs about R280 for one hour on a horse or all-terrain vehicle. A two-hour ride will cost you R400 while half-day wine tasting on horseback costs R650.

EN ROUTE

The **Bain's Kloof Pass Road,** built by engineer Andrew Geddes Bain and opened in 1853, links Wellington to Ceres and Worcester. The road (an extension of the R303 from Paarl through Wellington) winds north from Wellington, through the Hawekwa Mountains, revealing breathtaking views across the valley below. On a clear day you can see as far as the coast. The road has a good tar surface, but unlike many Western Cape passes, Bain's Kloof has not been widened much since it was built, so take your time and enjoy the views. There are places where you can park and walk down to lovely, refreshing mountain pools—great on a hot summer's day.

As you approach the initial slopes of Bain's Kloof, look out for the **Bovlei Winery,** on the right. Constructed in 1907 in traditional style, the building itself is not noteworthy, but it has a vast picture window offering a stupendous view of the undulating vineyards beyond. This winery celebrated its centennial in 2007, and its wines just keep getting better. Be sure to try the Centennial range Shiraz-mourvèdre blend, which promises great things. With plenty of well-priced, good-quality wines to choose from, you likely won't go away empty-handed. ✉ *Bain's Kloof Rd., Wellington* 📞 *021/873–1567* ⊕ *www.bovlei.co.za* 🍷 *Tastings free* ⊙ *Weekdays 8:30–5, Sat. 8:30–12:30.*

BREEDE RIVER VALLEY

The upper and central part of the catchment of the Breede River extends over a large area. It's a beautiful part of the country, with a combination of fantastic mountain scenery, fabulous fynbos, pretty bucolic farmlands, and small towns. A short drive over any one of the scenic mountain passes is sure to bring you into a secluded valley resplendent with the greens of spring, the grape-laden vines of summer, the myriad colors of autumn, or the snowcapped peaks and crisp misty mornings of winter.

A natural climatic combination of comparatively mild but wet winters followed by long, warm summers makes this area perfectly suited for the cultivation of deciduous fruit, especially viticulture. In the summer the intense sunshine allows the wine and table grapes to develop rich ruby colors. Virtually deprived of rain in summer, the vines nurture their precious crop, irrigated from the meandering Breede River and the huge Brandvlei dam, near Worcester.

GETTING HERE AND AROUND

Driving is definitely the way to go when exploring the Breede River valley, as it will give you the flexibility you need to discover interesting back roads or to linger at a lovely lunch spot. The roads in the Western Cape are generally good. Although you might have to navigate some dirt roads, they tend to be graded regularly and are in fine condition.

The major car-rental agencies have offices in some of the smaller towns, but it's best to deal with the Cape Town offices. An alternative is to pick up a car in Stellenbosch. ⇨ *For car-rental agencies, see The Winelands, above.*

The best way to get to this area is to take the N1 from Cape Town past Paarl. You can either go through the Huguenot toll tunnel (around R25 per vehicle) or over the spectacular Bain's Kloof mountain pass to Worcester. From there take the R60 to Robertson and Montagu.

Greyhound, Intercape Mainliner, and Translux provide daily service throughout most of the Western Cape, stopping at bigger towns such as Worcester and Robertson on their way upcountry. Although each company's timetable varies, most have approximately four trips a day from Cape Town. The journeys are not long. From Cape Town it takes about 1½ hours to Worcester and about two hours to Robertson. A one-way trip to Worcester costs around R250, and the drop-off spot is a service station on the side of the N1. It is a little way out of town, but shuttle buses will take you into town for a small fee.

EMERGENCIES

In the event of an emergency, you'll be able to track down medical professionals without too much trouble. Although Montagu and Robertson don't have any late-night pharmacies, small-town professionals are happy to open up after hours. Robertson and Montagu have small provincial hospitals, and Worcester has three, including the privately run Medi-Clinic.

INTERNET

You won't find a slew of Internet cafés in these smaller rural towns, but you won't be completely stuck without access either. Some hotels and guesthouses will let you send and receive mail, but if your hotel does not offer access, ask the local tourism bureau for suggestions. Rates vary, but expect to pay around R25 for 30 minutes and R50 for an hour.

TOURS

Instead of big tour companies, there are a couple of individual guides operating in Breede River towns. Because the guides are usually from the area, they provide rare insights about the towns. Your best bet is to ask at local tourism offices for names and numbers. If you wish to hike in the Montagu Mountain Reserve, where trails are not well marked, go with someone familiar with the area, such as Patti van Dyk. She charges around R150 per person and there are two hikes to choose from. There's a strenuous one of just over 15 km (9 mi), and an easier one of just over 11 km (7 mi). Best times to go are in spring or autumn, as it can get very hot in summer.

ESSENTIALS

Bus Lines Greyhound (✉ *1 Adderley St., Cape Town* ☎ *083/915–9000*
⊕ *www.greyhound.co.za).* **Intercape Mainliner** (✉ *1 Adderley St., Cape Town*
☎ *0861/287–287, 083/909–0909 for alternate booking through Computicket*
⊕ *www.intercape.co.za).* **Translux Express Bus** (✉ *1 Adderley St., Cape Town*
☎ *0861/589–282* ⊕ *www.translux.co.za).*

Emergency Services **Ambulance** (☎ *10177).* **Police** (☎ *10111).* **Police, fire,
and ambulance** (☎ *107 from landline).* **Vodacom emergency services** (☎ *112
from mobile phone).*

Tour Guide **Patti van Dyk** (☎ *023/614–1501 or 082/744–3655).*

TULBAGH

60 km (37 mi) north of Paarl.

Founded in 1743, the town of Tulbagh is nestled in a secluded valley
bound by the Witzenberg and Groot Winterhoek mountains. A devastating earthquake in September 1969 shook the city and destroyed
many of the original facades of the historic town. After this disaster,
well-known South African architect Gawie Fagan helped rebuild the
buildings in the style of an 1860s hamlet, and the result is a photographer's paradise. The 32 buildings that make up Church Street were all
declared national monuments and constitute the largest concentration
of national monuments in one street in South Africa. It's not all white
gables and brass doorknobs, however. The workaday side of town is
quite dreary, and unemployment is rife.

GETTING HERE AND AROUND

You won't be able to experience the beauty of this area unless you
can explore on your own terms, so be sure to rent a car. If you want
to travel on the back routes, do some asking around first—you might
need a 4x4 in winter after heavy rains when the gravel roads become
very slippery.

VISITOR INFORMATION

Tulbagh Tourism is open weekdays 9–5, Saturday 9–4, and Sunday
10–4.

ESSENTIALS

Tourist Offices **Tulbagh Tourism** (✉ *4 Church St.* ☎ *023/230–1348* ⊕ *tulbagh-
tourism.org.za).*

EXPLORING

Much of the town is unlovely, having simply been rebuilt, often prefab
style, on old foundations, but the real attraction of Tulbagh is **Church
Street,** parallel to the main Van der Stel Street, where each of the 32
buildings was restored to its original form and subsequently declared
a national monument.

The **Oude Kerk** *(Old Church)* museum stands at the entrance to Church
Street and is the logical departure point for a self-guided tour of the
area, which is well marked. The church has been extensively restored
and has an interesting collection of artifacts from the area, including
carvings made by Boer prisoners of war. A ticket includes admission

to another two buildings on Church Street, which operate as annexes of the main museum. These show a practical history of events before, during, and after the quake. The buildings have been painstakingly reconstructed. ⊠ *21 Church St.* ☎ *023/230–1041* 🖃 *R10* ☉ *Weekdays 9–1 and 2–5, Sun. 11–5.*

Want to lie under a shady tree for a few hours and do some navel-gazing? If so, head to Schoonderzicht Farm (⊠ *Off Steinthal Rd.* ☎ *023/230–0673 or 072/504–9592* ⊕ *www.schoonderzicht.com*). **Niki de Wolf puts together fantastic picnic baskets packed with quiches, marinated vegetables, gemsbok carpaccio, grilled chicken in chocolate-balsamic reduction, olives, smoked-salmon-and-cucumber rolls, a selection of cheese, wine, and chocolates. Phew! You may not be able to move after eating your way through this feast. Enjoy the food on the farm, which is high up in the Witzenberg Mountains, just five minutes out of Tulbagh, or at other venues in the area. Niki also makes fine Belgian-style chocolates and does chocolate and wine tastings.**

Just 3 km (2 mi) out of town, set on high ground commensurate with its status, is the majestic **Oude Drostdy Museum.** Built by architect Louis Thibault in 1804, the structure was badly damaged by fire in 1934 and later by the 1969 quake, but it has been carefully restored and is a fine example of neoclassical architecture. The building now houses an impressive collection of antique furniture and artifacts. Look for the gramophone collection and the Dutch grandfather clock that has a picture of Amsterdam harbor painted on its face. As the original magistrate's house, the Drostdy had a cellar that served as the local jail; it's now used for wine tastings and sales. ⊠ *4 Church St.* ☎ *023/230–0203* 🖃 *Museum R10 including wine tasting* ☉ *Weekdays 10–5, Sat. 10–2.*

If you stand in front of the church on Van der Stel Street, you will see a wine barrel indicating the road to **Twee Jonge Gezellen,** which is about 8 km (5 mi) from town. One of the finest and oldest wineries in the area, it's a family-run estate best known for its fantastic Cap Classique—Krone Borealis Brut. But many Capetonians are more familiar with the old, tried, and trusted TJ39, an easily drinkable, well-priced blend of *weisser* (white) Riesling, chardonnay, chenin blanc, and sauvignon blanc that has been making a regular appearance on local tables for years. The Krone Engeltjipipi (referring to—er—a certain body waste of little angels) is a blend made from grapes naturally infected with botrytis (a type of fungus) and considered a gift from the cherubs. The grapes are harvested by hand over a number of nights at the end of the season. ⊠ *Twee Jonge Gezellen Rd.* ☎ *023/230–0680* ⊕ *www.tjwines. co.za* 🖃 *Tastings free* ☉ *Weekdays 9–4, Sat. 10–2; cellar tours weekdays at 11 and 3, Sat. at 11.*

WHERE TO EAT AND STAY

$ **✕ Paddagang.** Though built as a private residence in 1809, by 1821 SOUTH AFRICAN Paddagang (Frog's Way) was already serving as one of South Africa's first tap houses (like a pub with wine on tap). Immaculately restored after the 1969 earthquake, it was turned into a restaurant and became a popular tourist destination. Although a little timeworn, the decor is authentic, as are the *riempie* (thong-upholstered) chairs. The vine-covered pergola makes a lovely place to eat in all but the hottest weather. Traditional Cape fare is your best bet here, from starters like *smoorsnoek* (local smoked fish braised with potato and onion) with grape jam on the side, to a main course of South Africa's national dish, bobotie. Though the establishment has much going for it, standards of both food and service aren't what they used to be. However, it remains popular with locals and visitors alike. ✉ *23 Church St.* ☎ *023/230–0394* ⊕ *www. paddagangs.co.za* ⊟ *AE, DC, MC, V* ⊘ *No dinner Sun.–Tues.*

$

ECLECTIC

★

✗ **Readers.** The historic residence of the former church reader makes a cozy setting for this restaurant with consistently high-quality food and service. Carol Collins's innovative fare offers sophisticated contrasts, although she keeps presentation simple and appetizing. Her small seasonal menu changes daily. Dinner could start with smoked chicken salad with papaw, nuts, and goat cheese, or a butternut-squash-and-zucchini soup. If the springbok fillet with gooseberry and Amarula sauce is listed, don't miss it. Any one of the dessert trio is sure to make a memorable finale. The carefully chosen and well-priced wine list reflects regional labels. ✉ *12 Church St.* ☎ *023/230–0087 or 082/894–0932* ⊟ *DC, MC, V* ⊘ *Closed Tues.*

$$–$$$

🛏 **Rijk's Country House.** This top-notch lodge is on the outskirts of the village, on a ridge overlooking a lake where you can enjoy sweeping views of the surrounding mountains. Each suite, decorated in a modern Cape-cottage style, has a private terrace leading to the poolside garden. High ceilings, good quality linen, and original art in each room contribute to the luxe atmosphere. Cottages across the river have two rooms that are great for families. There are nice touches such as DVD players in the family suites, so it's one less thing you'll need to pack. **Pros:** tranquil and remote location; fine dining on your doorstep; you can participate in night harvesting during summer. **Cons:** quite far from bigger towns; pool, dam, and river not fenced so kids need to be water safe. ✉ *Main Rd.* ☎ *023/230–1006* ⊕ *www.rijks.co.za* ⟿ *12 suites, 3 cottages* ♿ *In-room: refrigerator (some). In-hotel: restaurant, room service, bar, pool, laundry service, Internet terminal, Wi-Fi, parking (free)* ⊟ *AE, DC, MC, V* ⧖❘ *BP.*

$

🛏 **Tulbagh Country House.** Ginny Clarke, owner of this guesthouse with comfortable beds and hearty breakfasts, is warm, friendly, and open— just the sort of qualities you'd expect from somebody in a small country town. She's also a mine of information about the village. The house was built in 1809 and has been declared a national monument. There's even a resident ghost who appears periodically to make sure things are running as they should. If you don't feel like eating out, you can use the *braai* (barbecue) facilities, but there are a number of good restaurants within walking distance. Ginny will also pack you a picnic basket on request. **Pros:** lovely antiques, reasonable rates; braai facilities available. **Cons:** quiet nightlife; few rooms available; cold in winter. ✉ *24 Church St.* ☎ *023/230–1171* ⊕ *www.tulbaghguesthouse.co.za* ⟿ *3 rooms, 1 suite* ♿ *In-room: no phone, no TV (some). In-hotel: laundry service, parking (free)* ⊟ *MC, V* ⧖❘ *BP.*

WORCESTER

45 km (28 mi) southeast of Tulbagh; 50 km (31 mi) east of Paarl.

You're unlikely to linger in Worcester, by far the largest town in the Breede River valley. It's often termed the region's capital by locals, and with good cause. Much of the town's burgeoning commerce and industry is connected to agriculture—viticulture, in particular—and its brandy cellars produce the highest volume of the spirit in the country. But the town itself is unexciting and serves as a pit stop for prettier inland destinations. Pause to visit the Karoon National Botanical Garden or pop in at the Kleinplasie Living Open-air Museum.

GETTING HERE AND AROUND

Worcester is east of Paarl on the N1, on the other side of the du Toits Kloof Pass or tunnel; an 80-minute drive from Cape Town. Renting a car is the only way to get around.

VISITOR INFORMATION

The Worcester Tourism Bureau is open weekdays 7:45–4:30 and Saturday 7:45–12:30.

ESSENTIALS

Hospitals Worcester Medi-Clinic (✉ *67 Fairbairn St.* 🕾 *023/348-1500* ⊕ *www.worcestermc.co.za*).

Tourist Offices Worcester Tourism Bureau (✉ *23 Baring St.* 🕾 *023/348-2795* ⊕ *www.worcester.org.za*).

EXPLORING

The **Karoo National Botanical Garden** includes several hundred species of indigenous flora, including succulents, aloes, and trees; it's been billed as one of the most important such collections in the world. The Braille Garden is geared toward the visually impaired. If you phone ahead, you can arrange to watch a slide show and take a guided walk through the gardens and the collection houses for around R85 per person. Unfortunately, they won't do the tour unless there are at least seven people. The garden lies on the opposite side of the N1 highway from the town of Worcester but is easy to find if you follow the signs eastward from the last set of traffic lights on High Street. Follow the road from the entrance to the garden to the main parking area, the starting point of three clearly marked walks. ✉ *Roux Rd.* 🕾 *023/347-0785* 🗓 *Aug.–Oct. R14, Nov.–July free* ☉ *Daily 7–6.*

The **Kleinplasie Living Open-air Museum** is a welcome change from dusty artifacts in glass cases. The fascinating museum is actually a collection of original buildings from the area that have been re-erected around a working farmyard. Following a narrated slide show, venture into the farmyard and watch the museum staff, intent on keeping traditional skills alive, as they bake bread, twist tobacco, make horseshoes in a smithy, and distill witblitz. The museum also has a shop where you can buy produce from the farmyard. ✉ *Kleinplasie Agricultural Showgrounds, Traub St.* 🕾 *023/342-2226* ⊕ *www.kleinplasie.co.za* 🗓 *R12* ☉ *Mon.–Sat. 9–4:30.*

The **KWV Brandy Cellar** is the largest distillery of its kind in the world, with 120 pot stills under one roof. Informative guided tours, followed by a brandy tasting, will take you through the process of brandy making. The well-informed guide will give a layperson's rundown of the various methods used, the pros and cons of pot-still distillation as compared with the continuous-still method, as well as a description of the maturation process. In the cooperage you can watch traditional barrel making. ⊠ *Church and Smith Sts.* ☎ *023/342–0255* ⊕ *www.kwvhouseofbrandy.com* 🗐 *Tastings R25; tours R25 weekdays, R35 weekends* ☉ *Weekdays 8:30–4:30; English tours weekdays at 2.*

SPORTS AND THE OUTDOORS

RAFTING AND CANOEING

The Breede River has tiny rapids near Worcester, where it twists and turns between clumps of *palmiet* (river reeds) and overgrown banks. Using two-person inflatables, **River Rafters** (☎ *021/975–9727* ⊕ *www. riverrafters.co.za*) offers a one-day trip with wine tasting for R495 and a two-day, two-night trip for R1,150. **Wildthing Adventures** (☎ *021/556– 1917* ⊕ *www.wildthing.co.za*) runs one- and two-day canoe trips. The one-day Wine Route trip (R595) is the most popular and is more about food and drink than paddling. The highlight is the tasting of local wines during the extensive picnic lunch.

ROBERTSON

48 km (30 mi) southeast of Worcester.

Robertson was founded primarily to service the surrounding farms, and it retains its agricultural and industrial character. The town largely lives up to its mantra of "small town, big heart"—the townsfolk are welcoming and friendly, which makes up for the lack of action. Some effort has been made to beautify the town with tree-lined roads, but there is little reason for visitors to come here, other than to stop off for lunch on the way to McGregor or Montagu. If you are in the area, however, you might consider visiting one of the well-known local wine farms.

GETTING HERE AND AROUND

Robertson is less than a 30-minute drive from Worcester. Renting a car is the only way to get around in a reasonable amount of time.

VISITOR INFORMATION

The Robertson Tourism Bureau is open weekdays 8–5, Saturday 9–4, and Sunday 10–2.

ESSENTIALS

Hospitals **Robertson Hospital** (⊠ *Van Oudtshoorn St.* ☎ *023/626–3155*).

Internet Access **Rottó** (⊠ *Van Rheenen St.* ☎ *023/626–5468*).

Tourist Offices **Robertson Tourism Bureau** (⊠ *Reitz and Voortrekker Sts.* ☎ *023/626–4437* ⊕ *www.robertsonr62.com*).

EXPLORING

The Robertson cellar of **Graham Beck Wines,** on the road between Worcester and Robertson, is the sibling to a cellar of the same name in Franschhoek. Graham Beck has further extended his empire by acquiring the prestigious Steenberg Estate in the Constantia Valley. This country cousin produces some very sophisticated wines, and winemaker Pieter Ferreira is known as Mr. Bubbles for his wonderful sparkling wines. The Rhona Muscadel 2004 (named after Graham Beck's wife), a New Age muscat that's fruity but not cloying, and the excellent brut rosé are two favorites, but the reds are not to be ignored. Try the Ridge Syrah 2005, which is garnering rave reviews, as is the 2005 Coffeestone Cabernet. ⊠ *R60, about 10 km (6 mi) northwest of Robertson* ☎ *023/626–1214* ⊕ *www.grahambeckwines.co.za* ☜ *Tastings free* ☉ *Weekdays 9–5, Sat. 10–3, first Sun. of the month 10–3; cellar tours by appointment.*

Capetonians in the know have long considered **Rooiberg Winery,** between Worcester and Robertson, one of the best value-for-money wineries in the area. The red muscadel is reputedly one of the best in the world, and the Shiraz, Pinotage, chardonnay, and port are all good buys. A cabernet sauvignon–merlot blend, the Roodewyn (red wine) 2007 vintage is a good buy. The Bodega de Vinho deli serves light lunches, making this a good place to stop for something to eat. ⊠ *R60, about 10 km (6 mi) northwest of Robertson* ☎ *023/626–1663* ⊕ *www.rooiberg.co.za* ☜ *Tastings free, tours R10* ☉ *Weekdays 8–5:30, Sat. 9–3.*

Abrie Bruwer, winemaker and viticulturist at **Springfield Estate,** has a fan club, for good reason. Quality is assured, and if the wine doesn't meet Bruwer's stringent standards it isn't released. Although the cabernet has its loyal following, this innovative estate is best known for its unusual approach to white wines, especially chardonnay. The Méthode Ancienne Chardonnay is made in the original Burgundy style and is bottled only if it's perfect—which happens about two years in five. The creamy Wild Yeast Chardonnay, with its all-natural fermentation, is an unwooded version of the above and comes highly recommended. Everybody is raving about the Whole Berry Cabernet 2007 and the Life from Stone Sauvignon Blanc 2008. ⊠ *R317, to Bonnievale* ☎ *023/626–3661* ⊕ *www.springfieldestate.com* ☜ *Tastings free* ☉ *Weekdays 8–5, Sat. 9–4.*

Van Loveren Winery, between Robertson and Bonnievale, produces around 40 wines, so there's something to suit everybody's palate. The Noble Late Harvest 2006 and 2006 chardonnay reserve are both definitely worth mentioning. In addition to sampling the extensive wines, be sure to visit the unusual grounds of this family-owned and -run farm. An established garden of indigenous and exotic plants and trees surrounds a water fountain that supplies the entire farm. Weather permitting, instead of visiting the usual tasting room, sit out under the trees and the various wines are brought to you. It's very relaxed and friendly, and you may feel like part of the family before you know it. If you visit on a Saturday, you might also get to sample the farm's sweet-corn fritters with your wine. Delicious! ⊠ *Off R317, 15 km (9 mi) southeast of Robertson* ☎ *023/615–1505* ⊕ *www.vanloveren.co.za* ☜ *Tastings free* ☉ *Weekdays 8:30–5, Sat. 9:30–1.*

WHERE TO EAT

$–$$ ✕ **Fraai Uitzicht.** In a deeply rural setting between Robertson and Ashton,
ECLECTIC   this 200-year-old fruit and wine farm is home to a rustic restaurant
★   where chef Sandra Burchardt whips up impressively sophisticated fare.
Garden produce and herbs are transformed into a menu of culinary
joy, and serious food lovers can opt for the six- or seven-course tasting menu with matching wines for each course. You might start with
a bacon-wrapped salmon-trout fillet or the subtle smoked springbok
carpaccio. Main courses might include roast rack of lamb with rosemary pesto or the tagine of free-range chicken cooked with fresh herbs
and saffron and served with couscous and vegetables. Desserts are as
admirable, their sauces as stellar as those of the savory variety. Try the
"dream of Africa": a freshly baked mousse soufflé of Belgian chocolate
served with vanilla yogurt cream and a mixed-berry coulis. The wine
list does not disappoint, presenting a selection of the Robertson Valley's best, augmented with French champagne. ✉ *Off the R60, Klaas
Voogds East* ☎ *023/626–6156* ⊕ *www.fraaiuitzicht.com* ⚞ *Reservations essential* ▤ *AE, DC, MC, V* ⊗ *Closed June–mid-Aug. No lunch
Mon. and Tues.*

**EN
ROUTE**   On the R60 out of Robertson you can either take the clearly marked
turnoff to McGregor, which snakes between vineyards and farms—a
picture of bucolic charm—or continue on toward Montagu. Before
reaching the latter, you'll pass through the unlovely agricultural town
of Ashton. Keep left (don't turn off to Swellendam), and enter the short
but spectacular **Cogman's Kloof Pass.** On either side of the pass, which
runs in a river gorge, you can see the magnificent fold mountains, which
are ultimately the source for Montagu's hot springs.

MCGREGOR

20 km (12 mi) south of Robertson.

Saved from development as a result of a planned mountain pass that
never materialized, McGregor is the epitome of the sleepy country
hollow, tucked away between the mountains, and is one of the best-
preserved examples of a 19th-century Cape village. As you approach
McGregor from Robertson, farmsteads give way to small cottages
with distinctive red-painted doors and window frames. The McGregor
Wines, on the left, heralds your entry into the town with its thatch cottages in vernacular architecture.

McGregor has become popular with artists who have settled here permanently and with busy executives from Cape Town intent on getting
away from it all. Frankly, this is an ideal place to do absolutely nothing,
but you can take a leisurely stroll through the fynbos, watch birds from
one of several blinds on the Heron Walk, or follow one of the hiking or
mountain-bike trails if you are feeling more energetic. There is a great
hiking trail across the Riviersonderend Mountains to Greyton.

GETTING HERE AND AROUND

McGregor is a 10- to 15-minute drive from Robertson.

EXPLORING

The **McGregor Wines** is a popular attraction, with surprisingly inexpensive wines, considering their quality. Try the unwooded chardonnay; the 2006 and 2008 vintages have both won a Veritas Gold. The port is also exceptional and perfect for sipping near a log fire in winter, and the colombar gets rave reviews year after year. ⊠ *Main Rd.* ☎ *023/625–1741* ⊕ *www.mcgregorwinery.co.za* ✉ *Tastings free* ☾ *Weekdays 8–5, Sat. 10–3; cellar tours by appointment.*

Esletjiesrus Donkey Sanctuary is across the road from McGregor Wines. It provides a place of safety for neglected and abused donkeys and is a great place to visit with kids. They can meet the residents, there's a jungle gym, and you can get something to eat and drink at the coffee shop. ⊠ *Main Rd.* ☎ *023/625–1593* ⊕ *www.donkeysanctuary.co.za.*

WHERE TO STAY

¢ 🏨 **Green Gables Country Inn.** In the manor house that used to serve the mill, Green Gables is a good place to escape. It's a family-run affair and the Meyers are proud of their hospitality and food. The house was built in 1860 and is decorated with antiques and feels very much like an upmarket home. The self-catering unit is in a converted old barn with a freestanding Edwardian slipper bath, which is a great touch. Expect good linen, brass bedsteads, country-style decor, and friendly hosts. This family also runs the Miller's Pub and the Green Gables restaurant where all the locals hang out, which is always a good sign. **Pros:** amazing setting; good food; you'll soon feel part of the village. **Cons:** no pool, limited accommodation. ⊠ *Smith and Mill Sts.* ✆ *Box 362, 6708* ☎ *023/625–1626* ⊕ *www.greengablescountryinn.co.za* ⇋ *2 rooms* ♿ *In-room: no phone, no TV. In-hotel: restaurant, bar, laundry service, parking (free), some pets allowed* ═ *No credit cards* ⏚ *BP.*

SPORTS AND THE OUTDOORS

HIKING

The 19-km (12-mi) Rooikat Trail, through the **Vrolijkheid Nature Reserve** (⊠ *5 km [3 mi] outside McGregor* ☎ *023/625–1621*), takes about eight hours to complete. It's a strenuous, circular route winding up into the Eldandsberg Mountains, and an early start is recommended. There is basic self-catering accommodation at the reserve—eight *rondavels* (simple round huts) sleep four people each. There's a shared ablution block with showers and toilets. You need to get a permit (around R30 per person) at the entrance of the reserve. It's based on the honor system, and you put your money in a box on entry. If you don't want to hike, there are two bird hides and a mountain-bike trail.

MONTAGU

29 km (18 mi) northeast of Robertson.

Montagu bills itself as "the Gateway to the Little Karoo," and its picturesque streets lined with Cape Victorian architecture lend this some credence. Today the town's main attraction is its natural hot springs, and many of the Victorian houses have been transformed into B&Bs and guesthouses. You know you're in a special place when farmers drop off their produce at the Honesty Shop (an unmanned shop that operates on the honor system) and buyers leave money for what they owe. There are a number of resorts where you can stay and "partake of the waters."

GETTING HERE AND AROUND
Montagu is a 20-minute drive from Robertson.

VISITOR INFORMATION
The Montagu Tourism Bureau is open weekdays 8–6 and weekends 9–noon.

ESSENTIALS
Hospitals Montagu Hospital (⊠ *Church and Hospital Sts.* ☎ *023/614–8100*).

Internet Access Printmor (⊠ *59 Piet Retief St.* ☎ *023/614–1945*).

Tourist Offices Montagu Tourism Bureau (⊠ *24 Bath St.* ☎ *023/614–2471* ⊕ *www.montagu-ashton.info*).

EXPLORING
Popular **Avalon Springs,** the only resort open to day visitors, is not the most stylish, and the architecture leaves a lot to be desired. But if you look beyond this and the numerous signs carrying stern warnings and instructions, you'll get good insight into South African life and culture, as people float and splash around in the various pools. If you're not staying at the resort, you can rent bikes from the village and cycle to the springs, where you can spend a few hours before heading home again. ⊠ *Uitvlucht St., 3 km (2 mi) outside Montagu* ☎ *023/614–1150* ⊕ *www.avalonsprings.co.za* ☛ *R30 hot springs, R20 parking on weekends* ⊙ *Daily 8* AM–11 PM.

⟳ The popular three-hour **Langeberg Tractor Ride** takes you to the summit of the Langeberg (Long Mountain) and back. The tractor winds up some tortuously twisted paths, revealing magnificent views of the area's peaks and valleys. After a short stop at the summit, a similarly harrowing descent follows, but you won't be disappointed by the views or the driver's chirpy banter. If you're here in spring or summer when the flowers are in bloom, you might even get to pick some gorgeous proteas on the way down. Following your trip, you can enjoy a delicious lunch of *potjiekos* (traditional stew cooked over a fire in a single cast-iron pot) for R70 for the tractor ride, R80 for the lunch. Reservations are essential. ⊠ *Protea Farm, R318* ☎ *023/614–2471* ☛ *R150 for tractor ride and lunch* ⊙ *Wed. and Sat. at 10 and 2*.

WHERE TO EAT AND STAY
$–$$ ✕ **Jessica's Restaurant.** Housed in a Victorian building is a restaurant with
ECLECTIC   French colonial decor—with rich plummy colors, lots of candles, and dark wood—and pictures of the Staffordshire bull terrier for which the place is named. The crab and shrimp cakes, served with a creamy lime dressing, are a standout item on the starter menu, but you'll also be blown away by Thai prawns, marinated in lime, chili, ginger and garlic, served on a Thai green curry risotto. Follow that with the Karoo lamb noisettes with a rich cabernet and rosemary sauce.Classic highlights are the famous crispy duck and satiny lavender-infused crème brûlée. In

good weather, ask to sit in the garden. ⊠ *47 Bath St.* ☎ *023/614–1805* ⊕ *www.jessicasrestaurant.co.za* ⌖ *Reservations essential* ⊟ *AE, DC, MC, V* ⊙ *Closed Sun. and Tues. May–Sept., Dec., and Jan. No lunch.*

¢ 📷 **7 Church Street.** In the heart of the village sits this guesthouse in a lovingly restored Victorian home. Each room is individually and stylishly decorated with hand-embroidered cotton percale linens. The Honeymoon Suite, which is really more of a big room than a suite, has a big wrought-iron bed and a bathroom with a claw-foot tub. Ask for the Garden Suite if you want extra privacy. The pool is set in a magnificent garden and has stunning mountain views; it's the perfect place to relax with a book after a morning at the springs or exploring town. **Pros:** peaceful and secluded location; within easy walking distance of the hot springs. **Cons:** no young kids allowed; flagstone floors can be cold in winter. ⊠ *7 Church St., Box 43* ☎ *023/614–1186 or 084/507–8941* ⊕ *www.7churchstreet.co.za* ➳ *5 suites* ⅏ *In-room: no phone, refrigerator (some). In-hotel: pool, laundry service, no kids under 12* ⊟ *AE, MC, V* ⌾*BP.*

¢–$ 📷 **Montagu Country Hotel.** This salmon-color hotel was built in Victorian times but was extensively remodeled in the early 1930s. The present owner, Gert Lubbe, highlights its many art-deco features and collects furniture and artifacts from this era to complement the interior. A well-trained staff ensures efficient and personal service. The hotel has a wellness center and mineral pool. The Wild Apricot restaurant (¢–$) serves an excellent breakfast, satisfying no-frills lunch, and similarly straightforward dinner, with the addition of traditional country favorites like Karoo-lamb pie or Cape Malay bobotie. **Pros:** on-site spa and restaurant; centrally located; spacious luxury rooms. **Cons:** Sundays very quiet generally; avoid if you're not a fan of art deco. ⊠ *27 Bath St., Box 338* ☎ *023/614–3125 or 082/899–3670* ⊕ *www.montagucountryhotel.co.za* ➳ *34 rooms* ⅏ *In-room: refrigerator (some). In-hotel: restaurant, room service, bar, pools, laundry service, parking (free), some pets allowed* ⊟ *AE, DC, MC, V* ⌾*BP.*

THE OVERBERG

Overberg, Afrikaans for "over the mountains," is an apt name for this remote but beautiful region at the bottom of the continent, separated from the rest of the Cape by mountains. Before 19th-century engineers blasted a route over the Hottentots Holland mountain range, the Overberg developed in comparative isolation. To this day it possesses a wild emptiness far removed from the settled valleys of the Winelands.

It's a land of immense contrasts, and if you're planning a trip along the Garden Route, you would be well advised to add the Overberg to your itinerary. The coastal drive from Gordon's Bay to Hermanus unfolds a panorama of deserted beaches, pounding surf, and fractured granite mountains. Once you pass Hermanus and head out onto the windswept plains leading to Cape Agulhas, you have to search harder for the Overberg's riches. Towns are few and far between, the countryside an expanse of wheat fields, sheep pastures, and creaking windmills. The occasional reward of the drive is a coastline of sublime beauty. Dunes and unspoiled beaches extend for miles. Currently no roads run parallel to the ocean along this stretch, and you must repeatedly divert inland before heading to another part of the coast. But there are plans afoot for a major coastal highway, which has brought mixed reactions. It means economic growth for far-flung towns but threatens to destroy the peace and quiet that make these villages so attractive.

Unfortunately, the ocean's bounty has been the undoing of communities along this coastline. Perlemoen (abalone) poaching is an enormous problem. These sea mollusks are being illegally poached faster than they can reproduce and are then shipped to the East, where they are considered a powerful aphrodisiac. Violent Western Cape gangs are involved in perlemoen trafficking, and children as young as 11 are used as runners in exchange for drugs.

Naturally, the coast also has plenty of good on tap. Hermanus is one of the best places in South Africa for land-based whale-watching during the annual migration of Southern Right whales between June and November. Spring is also the best time to see the Overberg's wildflowers, although the region's profusion of coastal and montane fynbos is beautiful year-round. The raw, rugged beauty of Africa's southernmost coastline can be found at De Hoop Nature Reserve. The Whale Trail, a five-day hike mapped out through De Hoop, might just oust the Garden Route's Otter Trail as South Africa's most popular. In fact, walking is one of the Overberg's major attractions, and almost every town and nature reserve offers a host of trails.

The upper part of the Overberg, north of the N2 highway, is more like the Winelands, with 18th- and 19th-century towns sheltered in the lee of rocky mountains. Here the draws are apple orchards, inns, and hiking trails that wind through the mountains. The historic towns of Swellendam and Greyton are good places to spend a night before moving on to your next destination. Stanford, a tiny hamlet just outside of Hermanus, is also a lovely place to stay if you want to avoid the crowds that clog the streets of Hermanus on holidays.

GETTING HERE AND AROUND

Driving yourself is undoubtedly the best way to appreciate this lovely and diverse area. The roads here are generally good. They are signposted, and major routes are paved. For the most part, you'll come across gravel roads only around Elim and Napier and from Swellendam to Malgas, and they may be a bit rutted and bumpy. A two-wheel-drive vehicle is fine, but take it easy if it's been raining, as gravel roads can get slippery. You'll need a 4x4 only if you're planning to tackle some of the more remote back roads or want to do a 4x4 route.

The major car-rental agencies have offices in the bigger towns, such as Hermanus and Swellendam. However, it's best to deal with the Cape Town offices; you'll probably want to pick up a car at the airport anyway. ⇨ *For car-rental agencies, see The Winelands, above.*

The Overberg stretches over an enormous area, so you need to decide where you're heading before planning your route. If you want to enjoy the beauty of the coast, then take the N2 from Cape Town, but, instead of heading up Sir Lowry's Pass, turn off to Gordon's Bay and follow the R44, also known as Clarence Drive, along the scenic route. Just after Kleinmond the road becomes the R41 and turns inland to bypass the Bot River lagoon. It becomes the R43 as it makes its way toward Hermanus. If you want to explore inland, however, take the N2 over Sir Lowry's Pass and past Caledon and Swellendam. To get to the pretty hamlet of Greyton, take the R406 to your left just before Caledon.

Intercape Mainliner, Greyhound, and Translux have daily service throughout most of the Western Cape, especially to the bigger towns on the N2. Swellendam is a major hub and a good transit point, but to enjoy smaller towns such as Greyton or those along the coast, you'll need your own transportation.

EMERGENCIES

There are doctors and dentists in every town, as well as provincial hospitals in all but the smallest villages. Hermanus has a private hospital. Late-night pharmacies are a rarity in these small towns, but all pharmacies have emergency and after-hours numbers.

INTERNET

You won't find an Internet café on every corner, though you will find some in the more touristy destinations, such as Hermanus. First inquire at your hotel or B&B, as many allow guests access for a small fee. Print shops also often have an Internet station. Expect to pay around R15 for 10 minutes, but this varies from shop to shop.

TIMING

Touring the whole area would take three to four days, but you could easily spend a week in the Overberg. For a shorter trip, focus on the splendors of the coastal route from Gordon's Bay to Hermanus, and then head north toward Greyton and Swellendam.

TOURS

There are a number of individuals and small companies offering customized tours. A day trip, which should cost R800 per person per day, could involve an excursion to De Hoop Nature Reserve, with plenty of time to admire the birds, fynbos, and whales; a ride on the ferry at Malgas; and time at Bontebok National Park. Or, you could start in Swellendam and then head over picturesque Tradouw Pass through the spectacular Cape Fold Mountains to Barrydale, where you could do some wine tasting before heading on to Robertson. Other tours concentrate on the historic fishing village of Arniston (Waenhuiskrans), Bredasdorp, and Elim.

Stephen Smuts (a distant relative of the famous South African prime minister General Jan Smuts) is passionate about fynbos and will be able to give you an insiders' guide to the amazing flora of the area. He owns a private nature reserve, and you can organize a day walk with him as well.

Ex-pilot and navy man Louis Willemse is an experienced and accredited nature and culture guide, who can offer you a varied day tour. He'll cover everything from Elim, the southernmost tip of Africa to the archeological sites at de Kelders, as well as share lots of information about the local birds, flora, and fauna. You could also explore De Hoop with him. If he can't help you out, he'll refer you to other specialists in the area. Expect to pay around R1,500 a day for an experienced guide, excluding transport.

Wilson Salukazana, a former Hermanus whale crier, now conducts land-based whale-watching tours in the town. He's got all the experience in the world and can spot a Southern Right from miles away. When the whales aren't blowing in the bay, he conducts township tours. On a guided walk through the nearby township of Zwelihle, you can have a Xhosa meal, visit a traditional African healer, and meet local residents.

SAFETY AND PRECAUTIONS
Keep in mind that on Sunday afternoons and in early evenings traffic returning to the city via Sir Lowry's Pass can be very congested. Expect delays as you enter Somerset West, and be very careful if it is misty (which it often is on the pass), as this stretch of road sees numerous accidents each year. Leaving Cape Town on a Friday afternoon can also take time, so try to leave by lunchtime to avoid traffic jams.

ESSENTIALS
Bus Lines Greyhound (☎ 083/915–9000 ⊕ www.greyhound.co.za). **Intercape Mainliner** (☎ 0861/287–287, 083/909–0909 for alternate booking through Computicket ⊕ www.intercape.co.za). **Translux Express Bus** (☎ 0861/589–282 or 011/774–3333 ⊕ www.translux.co.za).

Emergency Services Ambulance (☎ 10177). **Police** (☎ 10111). **Police, fire, and ambulance** (☎ 107 from landline). **Vodacom emergency services** (☎ 112 from mobile phone).

Tour Operators Louis Willemse (☎ 028/423–3317). **Stephen Smuts** (☎ 028/423–3049). **Wilson Salukazana** (☎ 073/214–6949 or 083/212–1074).

Tourist Offices Overberg Tourism (✉ 22 Plein St., Caledon ☎ 028/214–1466 or 083/448–1664 ⊕ www.tourismcapeoverberg.co.za).

EN ROUTE

Gordon's Bay, 70 km (43½ mi) southeast of Cape Town, is built on the steep mountain slopes of the Hottentots Holland Mountains over-looking the vast expanse of False Bay. You can often see whales and their calves in the bay in October and November. This is a good point to start on the fantastic coastal route known as **Clarence Drive** (R44). This is one of the country's most scenic drives, particularly if you take the time to follow some of the dirt roads leading down to the sea from the highway. There are numerous paths down to the seashore from the road between Gordon's Bay and Rooiels. It's worth walking down to watch the waves pounding the rocky coast, but take care. If there are no other people around and the waves are quite big, stay a few yards back from the water, as this section of coast is notorious for freak waves in certain swell and wind conditions. Note the many crosses on the side of the road—each one denotes somebody who has been swept off the rocks and drowned at sea.

The road passes the tiny settlement of **Rooiels** (pronounced *roy*-else), then cuts inland for a couple of miles. A turnoff leads to **Pringle Bay,** a collection of vacation homes sprinkled across the fynbos. The village has little to offer other than a beautiful wide beach (check out the sign warning of quicksand). If you continue through Pringle Bay, the tar road soon gives way to a gravel road, now closed by shifting sand dunes, that used to lead to Betty's Bay (you now have to backtrack and take the inland route to get to Betty's Bay).

BETTY'S BAY

30 km (19 mi) southeast of Gordon's Bay.

Betty's Bay, or Betty's, as the hamlet is fondly known, is worth visiting for its penguins and botanical garden. The village is made up of retirees and weekenders wanting to escape the city hustle. The scenery is wild and untamed and the settlement unfussy, but don't go unless you're happy to hunker down inside when the summer wind is howling or when the winter rains set in.

If you're in the area, the colony of African penguins at Stony Point is definitely worth exploring. They are one of only two mainland colonies in southern Africa (the other is at Boulders Beach on the Cape Peninsula, where it is much easier to see these endangered seabirds). The Stony Point colony lies about 600 yards from the parking area along a rocky coastal path. Along the way you pass the concrete remains of tank stands, reminders of the days when Betty's Bay was a big whaling station. The African penguin is endangered, so the colony has been fenced off for protection but this still doesn't stop leopards making forays into the colony

To get to the penguins from Pringle Bay, return to Clarence Drive (the R44) and continue 1½ km (1 mi) to the turnoff to Stony Point, on the edge of Betty's Bay. Follow Porter Drive for 3 km (2 mi) until you reach a sign marked MOOI HAWENS and a smaller sign depicting a penguin.

GETTING HERE AND AROUND
Head out of Cape Town on the N2 toward Somerset West. Once you've made your way through the town (the traffic can be torturous on a Friday afternoon) take the R44 turnoff to Gordon's Bay. From there the road hugs the coast. It takes 45 minutes from Cape Town to get to Gordon's Bay if there are no traffic jams and then about 30 minutes to Betty's Bay, but this will vary depending on the traffic and weather—and how often you stop to admire the view.

VISITOR INFORMATION
The Hangklip-Kleinmond Tourism Bureau has information on Betty's Bay and is open weekdays 8:30–5, Saturday 9–2, and Sunday 10–2.

ESSENTIALS
Tourist Offices **Hangklip–Kleinmond Tourism Bureau** (✉ *14 Harbour Rd.* ☎ *028/271–5657* ⊕ *www.ecoscape.org.za*).

EXPLORING
★ **Harold Porter National Botanical Garden** is a 440-acre nature reserve in the heart of the coastal fynbos, where the Cape floral kingdom is at its richest. The profusion of plants supports 78 species of birds and a wide range of small mammals, including large troops of chacma baboons. You couldn't ask for a more fantastic setting, cradled between the Atlantic and the towering peaks of the 3,000-foot Kogelberg Range. Walking trails wind through the reserve and into the mountains via Disa and

Leopard's kloofs, which echo with the sound of waterfalls. Back at the main buildings, a pleasant restaurant serves light meals and teas. Book ahead for a volunteer guide to take you around the gardens, for which a donation is welcome. To get to the garden from the penguin colony, return to Porter Drive and turn right to rejoin the R44. Drive another 2 km (1 mi) to get here. ⊠ *R44* ☎ *028/272–9311* 🔊 *R15* 🕓 *Weekdays 8–4:30, weekends 8–5.*

WHERE TO EAT AND STAY

$ ✗**Hook, Line and Sinker.** Owners Jacqi and Stefan Kruger can be a bit
SEAFOOD   gruff, though well-meaning. Only the most obedient diners will escape unscathed, but the trial, like all heroes' journeys, makes survival and the meal that much sweeter. Expect fish—which is fresher than you'll find just about anywhere else—prepared simply, usually with salsa verde or a bourbon-and-mustard sauce. The dishes, all cooked on a wood fire, come only with fries. Start with either the rich and fragrant crab bisque or mussels in a tomato-based soup. Try the prawn gumbo, if it's available. Steak is served Wednesday and Sunday nights. Beer-battered fish-and-chips (made with hake) is a lunch option. The restaurant is small, the waiting list long. ⊠ *382 Crescent Rd., Pringle Bay* ☎ *028/273–8688* ⊕ *www.hooklineandsinker.co.za* ⚓ *Reservations essential* ▤ *AE, DC, MC, V* 🕓 *Usually closed Mon.*

¢   🏠**Waterlilly Lodge.** Nestled in the little village of Betty's Bay and just a 10-minute stroll from the beach, Waterlilly Lodge is a great option if you don't want to take out a second mortgage on your house. The look is clean, modern, and devoid of the tacky knickknacks that often curse beachside guesthouses. Restful shades of cream, gray, and black decorate the stylish rooms. Your host, Bryan Charlton, has worked in the hospitality industry for years and knows how to make guests feel at home. Bryan is also a whiz in the kitchen, so you'll start your day with a hearty breakfast; he can put together picnic baskets on request. There's even an honesty bar. Arrangements must be made in advance for children under 14. **Pros:** inside the Kogelberg Biosphere Reserve with its penguins, beaches and rocky coastline; prime site for whale-watching from June to November. **Cons:** very wet and cold area during winter (May–September); you must phone ahead if you want to bring children. ⊠ *Porter and Angler Drs., Box 326* ☎ *028/272–9378* ⊕ *www.waterlillylodge.co.za* 🛏 *5 rooms* ⚬ *In-room: no phone, refrigerator. In-hotel: bar, laundry service, parking (free)* ▤ *AE, DC, MC, V* ⦿|*BP or CP.*

KLEINMOND

25 km (15½ mi) southeast of Gordon's Bay.

The sleepy coastal town of Kleinmond (Small Mouth) presides over a magnificent stretch of shoreline, backed by the mountains of the Palmietberg. It's a favorite among retirees, but more and more city-weary folks are moving here pre-retirement as well. A harbor development near the old slipway is bustling with restaurants and shops.

GETTING HERE AND AROUND

Kleinmond is about 45 minutes from Gordon's Bay, depending on the weather and traffic on the R44.

VISITOR INFORMATION

The Hangklip-Kleinmond Tourism Bureau has information on Kleinmond and is open weekdays 8:30–5, Saturday 9–2, and Sunday 10–2.

ESSENTIALS

Tourist Offices **Hangklip–Kleinmond Tourism Bureau** (⌷ *14 Harbour Rd., Kleinmond* ☎ *028/271–5657* ⊕ *www.ecoscape.org.za*).

EXPLORING

NEED A BREAK?

Alive Alive-O-Shellfish Bar (⌷ *35 Harbour Rd.* ☎ *028/271–3774*) is one of the places where you can try abalone quite legally. At the big abalone factory the mollusks are cultivated, harvested, and packaged for local restaurants and overseas markets.

Close to town, on the Cape Town side and clearly marked with signs from the main street, is the **Kogelberg Nature Reserve**, a 66,000-acre area of fynbos that extends from the mountains almost to the sea, and includes most of the course of the Palmiet River. Take one of the well-marked nature walks through the reserve and you are sure to see some of the area's magnificent flora and birdlife. ☎ *028/271–5138* ⊕ *www. capenature.org.za* ⌷ *R25* ☉ *Daily 7–4.*

About 10 km (6 mi) of sandy beach fringes the impressive **Sandown Bay**, at the eastern edge of town. Much of the beach is nothing more than a sandbar, separating the Atlantic from the huge lagoon formed by the Bot River. Swift currents make swimming risky, although there is a sheltered corner near the rocks close to the old Beach House hotel, which burned down a few years ago. Keep an eye out for the famous Bot River horses that live on *vlei* (pronounced flay), or marsh. There are lots of theories about just how the horses got here. One has it that they were turned loose during the Boer War to save them from being killed and ended up on the vlei for safety. DNA tests show that these horses are descendants of the Kaapse Waperd (Cape wagon horse), a sturdy breed used to help settle the wild regions of the Overberg.

WHERE TO STAY

$$$$
Fodor's Choice
★

The Arabella Western Cape Hotel & Spa. Gone are the days when heading out into the country meant staying in pokey hotels with dodgy beds. The Arabella Western Cape Hotel & Spa is luxurious lodging in the most amazing setting—on the edge of the Bot River lagoon. There's plenty to boast about. The 18-hole golf course is in the top five in South Africa, and the AltiraSPA is highly regarded. Need any more prompting? The interior design is contemporary African, and bright bed throws and interesting signature pieces of furniture and art give each spacious room a unique feel. If you really want to splurge, the Presidential Suites, which include 24-hour butler service, will cater to your every need. For all the luxury, the hotel is also very child-friendly, with extensive child-care programs during the holidays. **Pros:** plenty of activities to keep both adults and children entertained; world-rated golf course. **Cons:** might stretch your budget; windy during summer months. ⌷ *Arabella Country Estate, R44* ☎ *028/284–0000* ⊕ *www.westerncapehotelandspa.co.za* ⌦ *117 rooms, 28 suites* ☖ *In-room: safe, refrigerator, Wi-Fi. In-hotel: 2 restaurants, room service, bars, golf course, tennis court, pool, gym,* *spa, children's programs (ages 4–12), laundry service, Wi-Fi, parking (free)* ☐ *AE, DC, MC, V* ⍟⍾ *BP.*

SPORTS AND THE OUTDOORS
GOLF
The setting of the **Arabella Golf Club** (☒ *R43* ☏ *028/284–0000* ⊕ *www. westerncapehotelandspa.co.za*) is so beautiful that you'd do well to take time to admire the views at the 8th hole, with the lagoon, the mountains, and the sea in the distance. This is Ernie Els's favorite spot and the most photographed hole on the course. Don't lose your head to the views—the course is fairly challenging. It's also expensive. Greens fees are R720 for 18 holes. A caddy costs R120, plus a recommended tip of R80 going directly to him; club rental is R295 and a golf cart R250.

RAFTING
The Palmiet River is a low-volume, technical white-water river of about Grade III. In high water in summer and winter, **Gravity Adventures** (☒ *21 Selous Rd., Claremont* ☏ *021/683–3698 or 082/574–9901* ⊕ *www. gravity.co.za*) offers rafting trips in two- or four-seater inflatable rafts. In low water it does the same trip but on specially designed one-person inflatable crafts called "geckos." A full-day rafting trip (including a light breakfast and lunch) costs R495. Tubing costs R355 for a full day; you can order lunch for an extra R55 or bring your own. Remember to take along plenty of sun protection.

EN ROUTE The R44 becomes the R41 and cuts inland around the Bot River lagoon. About 10 km (6 mi) past Kleinmond is the junction with the R43. Hermanus is to the right, but take a quick detour to the left through the sleepy town of Bot River to the big, old white gates of **Beaumont Wines.** This is a fabulous family-run winery. It's just sufficiently scruffy to create an ambience of age and country charm without actually being untidy. But, charm aside, it's the wine you come here for, and it really is worth the detour. Beaumont produces a range of dependable, notable wines, like the juicy Pinotage and the first mourvèdre to be bottled in South Africa. ☒ *R43, Bot River* ☏ *028/284–9194* ⍾ *Tastings free* ⊙ *Weekdays 9:30–12:30 and 1:30–4:30, Sat. 9:30–1:30.*

Head back toward Kleinmond, continuing on the R43 toward Hermanus and across the Bot River. The R43 swings eastward around the mountains, past the not particularly attractive fishing village of Hawston, one of the Overstrand communities hardest hit by abalone poaching and drug peddling, and the small artists' colony of **Onrus.** The Onrus lagoon is a great swimming spot for children. The water is always a couple of degrees warmer than the sea and is safe for the newly waterborne. When you're done with the beach, you can visit the artists in their homes.

The Milkwood (☒ *Atlantic Dr., Onrus* ☏ *028/316–1516*), overlooking the lagoon in Onrus, is a great place for a languid lunch. You can sit on the deck after a quick dip and eat some fresh fish (what kind of fish depends on the day's catch), grilled and served with a lemon or garlic-butter sauce, or a hearty Mediterranean lasagna.

HERMANUS

34 km (21 mi) southeast of Kleinmond.

Pristine beaches extend as far as the eye can see, and the Kleinriviersberg provides a breathtaking backdrop to this popular resort, the Overberg's major coastal town. Restaurants and shops line the streets, and Grotto Beach was awarded Blue Flag status (an international symbol of high environmental standards as well as good sanitary and safety facilities) in 2003 and is still going strong. Though the town has lost much of its original charm—thanks to the crowds and fast-food joints—it is still most definitely worth a visit.

GETTING HERE AND AROUND
Hermanus is about a 40-minute drive from Kleinmond on the R41 and the R43.

VISITOR INFORMATION
The Hermanus Tourism Bureau is open in summer weekdays 8–6, Saturday 9–5, and Sunday 10–3, and in winter Monday–Saturday 9–5.

ESSENTIALS
Hospitals Hermanus Medi-Clinic (⊠ *Hospital St.* 🕾 *028/313–0168* ⊕ *www. hermanusmc.co.za*).

Internet Access Maxitec (⊠ *155 Main Rd.* 🕾 *086/123–4111* ⊕ *www.maxitec. co.za*).

Tourist Offices Hermanus Tourism Bureau (⊠ *Lord Robert and Mitchell Sts.* 🕾 *028/312–2629* ⊕ *www.hermanus.co.za*).

EXPLORING
Hermanus sits atop a long line of cliffs, which makes it one of the best places in South Africa for land-based whale-watching. The town is packed during the Whale Festival in late September as well as over Christmas vacation. The 11-km (7-mi) Cliff Walk allows watchers to follow the whales, which often come within 100 feet of the cliffs as they move along the coastline. Keep an ear and an eye out for the whale crier, Pasika Nobobawho, who makes his rounds during the season. Using horns made from dried kelp, he produces different codes indicating where to catch the best sighting of these mighty giants of the deep. A long note followed by a short one signals the new harbor, for instance.

Originally, Hermanus was a simple fishing village. Its Old Harbour, built in 1904 and the oldest original harbor in South Africa that is still intact, has been declared a national monument. The **Old Harbour Museum** bears testimony to the town's maritime past. A small building at the old stone fishing basin displays a couple of the horrific harpoons used to lance whales and sharks, as well as some interesting whale bones. There are also exhibits on fishing techniques, local marine life, and angling records. The white building next to the harbor parking lot on Market Square is **De Wet's Huis,** which houses the Old Harbour Museum Photographic Exhibition. Here are photos of old Hermanus, and many of the town's fishermen proudly displaying their catches of fish, sharks, and dolphins—yes, dolphins. The museum's third component is the

Whale House with an interactive display. Although the exhibit is still only 75% complete, the touch screens, submarine, and a skeleton of a whale makes it a great place for kids. A whale movie runs twice a day, at 10 AM and 3 PM. A craft market every weekend outside De Wet's Huis is fun for browsing. ⊠ *Old Harbour, Marine Dr.* ☎ *028/312–1475* ✉ *R15* ◎ *Weekdays 9–4:30, Sat. 9–4, Sun. noon–4.*

On the outskirts of town a pair of white gateposts set well back
★ from the R43 signal the start of **Rotary Way.** This scenic drive climbs along the spine of the mountains above Hermanus, with incredible views of the town, Walker Bay, and the Hemel-en-Aarde (Heaven and Earth) Valley, as well as some of

> ## WONDER OF WHALES
>
> Whale sightings off South African shores weren't always so frequent, but each year it seems whales are arriving earlier, and leaving later. In the 1960s, whale populations, especially Southern Right whales, showed an increase around the coast. The population was probably around 1,000 in the '80s, and in 1984 the Dolphin Action and Protection Group, an organization campaigning to stop whaling, finally won year-round protection for the giants of the deep. Today, there are around 7,000 Southern Right whales that call SA waters home.

the area's beautiful fynbos. It's a highlight of a trip to Hermanus and shouldn't be missed. The entire mountainside is laced with wonderful walking trails, and many of the scenic lookouts have benches.

West of town off the R43, the R320 (Hemel-en-Aarde Valley Road) leads through the vineyards and orchards of the scenic Hemel-en-Aarde Valley and over Shaw's Pass to Caledon. The gravel road has some potholes and washboards but nothing terrifying. A short way down the road in a thatch building overlooking a small dam, **Hamilton Russell Vineyards** produces some excellent wines. The pinot noir won loud acclaim from wine critic Frank Prial of the *New York Times*, and is one of the best produced in the country; it's served in two of the world's top restaurants, El Bulli in Spain and The Fat Duck in England. The chardonnay comes closer to the French style of chardonnay than any other Cape wine, with lovely fruit and a touch of lemon rind and butterscotch. Both were selected to be served at former president Mandela's 2007 fund-raiser in Monaco hosted by Prince Albert, quite an honor. ⊠ *Off Hemel-en-Aarde Valley Rd. (R320), Walker Bay* ☎ *028/312–3595* ⊕ *www.hamiltonrussellvineyards.co.za* ✉ *Tastings free* ◎ *Weekdays 9–5, Sat. 9–1.*

With only 44 acres under vine, **Bouchard Finlayson** nevertheless thrills critics and wine lovers year after year. Winemaker Peter Finlayson makes good use of the cool sea breeze and unique terroir of the estate to create some fantastic deep-south wines. Try the French-style Galpin Peak Pinot Noir. Finlayson, who has a great voice, maintains that pinot noir "is like opera. When it's great it is pure seduction, almost hedonistic. There is no middle road." You might wish to lay down a few bottles of the limited-release, much-lauded Tête de Cuvée Galpin Peak Pinot Noir, which gives off an exciting whiff of truffles; the 2007 vintage is available. Bouchard is a short distance farther along the Hemel-en-Aarde

Valley Road past Hamilton Russell Vineyards. ⊠ *Off Hemel-en-Aarde Valley Rd.* *(R320)* ☎ *028/312–3515* ⊕ *www.bouchardfinlayson.co.za* ⊠ *Tastings free* ۩ *Weekdays 9:30–5, Sat. 9:30–12:30.*

WHERE TO EAT

$–$$
SEAFOOD
✕ **Burgundy.** In one of the village's original stone-and-clay fisherfolk cottages, the cozy Burgundy is one of Hermanus's oldest and best-loved restaurants. Not surprisingly, there's plenty of fish to be had on the extensive menu, from prawns and line fish to the specialty of the area—abalone, also known as perlemoen. The jury is out about just how tasty abalone is by itself, so it's usually served minced and highly flavored with other ingredients. Start with the delicate, delicious abalone with creamy mushrooms before you move on to succulent tiger prawns or the fantastically fresh line fish served with lemon risotto, seasonal vegetables, and a lemon-dill sauce. The menu also includes a large choice of meat dishes, ranging from duck to venison, and a good vegetarian selection—something of a novelty in smaller towns. A creamy theme seems to run through the impressive dessert menu. The tiramisu is delicious, and you can even pretend it's good for you, as the menu describes it as "a nourishing dish to be eaten when feeling low." ⊠ *Marine Dr.* ☎ *028/312–2800* ⊕ *www.burgundyrestaurant.co.za* ⊟ *AE, DC, MC, V.*

$–$$
ECLECTIC
✕ **Heaven.** If you're keen to escape the crush in Hermanus, Heaven is a good place to head for lunch. It's up the picturesque Hemel-en-Aarde Valley Road, where vines and fynbos cover the slopes and where you may wish you owned a country home. The view is wonderful, the service is attentive, and there's a good selection of local wines. The small, eclectic menu changes weekly but always emphasizes the best seasonal produce. Starters could include a salad of poached pears, greens, Brie, crispy bacon, fresh strawberries, pecan nuts, and pumpkin seeds. A main course might be substantial Mexican steak topped with a salsa of chopped avocado, red onion, tomato, and chilies, served with potato wedges and a side salad. ⊠ *Hemel-en-Aarde Valley Rd.* *(R320)* ☎ *072/905–3947* ⊟ *MC, V* ۩ *Closed Mon. and May–Aug. No dinner.*

¢–$
ECLECTIC
★
✕ **Mariana's.** Mariana and Peter Esterhuizen started out selling organic vegetables at the Hermanus farmers' market before converting a house in the little village of Stanford, just 10 minutes away, into a restaurant. In just a few years they made their mark, and today Capetonians regularly make the trip for one of their memorable meals. What's the attraction? Excellent food, local wines, a relaxed setting, friendly hosts, and seasonal organic produce grown behind the restaurant. Mariana and Peter pick their ingredients moments before you arrive. You're welcome to wander around the garden, which is as much a tapestry as it is a veggie patch. The food is Mediterranean with a South African twist. The Gruyère soufflé is a sublimely light, cheesy concoction served in a pool of tomato cream. There's usually a warm trout or chicken salad, but if you're really hungry, go for the *skaap en dinge* (sheep and things), an enormous lamb shank served with mashed potatoes and seasonal vegetables. No children under 10 are permitted. The kitchen closes at 2 PM, so don't be late. ⊠ *12 du Toit St., Stanford* ☎ *028/341–0272*

⚐ *Reservations essential* ▤ *No credit cards* ☉ *Closed Mon.–Thurs. and June–Sept. No dinner.*

$–$$

MEDITERRANEAN

✕ **Mediterrea Seafood Restaurant.** You can't go wrong with excellent food and sweeping bay views, and Mediterrea regulars know to ask for a window seat. In whale season you can hear the giants blow just below you. The restaurant's owner is Greek and together with the chef strives to combine the best of Mediterranean cuisine with all that South African food has to offer. Favorite starters include baby calamari tubes flamed with vodka, capsicums, and fresh herbs and served on *tsatsiki* (Greek-style yogurt-cucumber-garlic dip), and prawns *lemoni*—tiger prawns simmered in a heavenly, creamy, garlic sauce and served with lightly toasted Mediterranean bread. For a main course, the lamb stuffed with garlic, rosemary, and apricots and slow-roasted in red wine and fresh herbs is out of this world, as are the medallions of ostrich fillet topped with a sweet-onion-and-chili marmalade. Or you could go straight for the ice-cream halvah (layers of phyllo and vanilla ice cream infused with pistachio halvah and drizzled with honey). ✉ *83 Marine Dr.* ☏ *028/313–1685* ▤ *AE, DC, MC, V* ☉ *No lunch Mon.*

$

ECLECTIC

✕ **Mogg's Country Cookhouse.** Don't be put off by the bumpy dirt road heading up the Hemel-en-Aarde Valley. This restaurant on a fruit farm at the top of the valley is worth any amount of dust and corrugations. The converted laborer's cottage is as pretty as a picture in a tumble-down, overgrown kind of way, and the food is excellent in a relaxed and friendly setting. The seasonal menu is scribbled on a chalkboard. For starters you could expect beef carpaccio with a caper-and-olive dressing and pecorino cheese, or avocado-pear salad with hot walnut dressing and a sprinkle of blue cheese. Main courses might include chicken breast stuffed with tomatoes, olives, and feta and wrapped in phyllo, or homemade slow-roasted lamb shank accompanied by parsnip-potato mash with a mint-and-rosemary sauce. For dessert, homemade vanilla or Cointreau ice cream is served with a hot chocolate sauce. You're welcome to take your own wine, and it doesn't charge corkage, an added bonus. ✉ *Nuwe Pos Farm, off the Hemel-en-Aarde Valley Rd. (R320)* ☏ *028/312–4321* ⊕ *www.moggscookhouse.com* ▤ *No credit cards* ☉ *Closed Mon. and Tues. No dinner Sun.–Fri.*

WHERE TO STAY

If you want to avoid the crowds of Hermanus, consider lodging in the nearby tiny hamlet of Stanford.

$

🛏 **Auberge Burgundy Guesthouse.** If you want to be in the center of the village, this stylish guesthouse is an excellent choice. You're a stone's throw from the famous whale-watching cliffs and the market, and three minutes from the Old Harbour Museum. When Hermanus took off as a tourist destination, this well-run and friendly operation was one of the first lodgings to take off with it. The rooms are comfortably decorated in French provincial style. Larger rooms with sleeper couches cost about a third more, but they're great for families or friends traveling together. Ask for a room with a balcony overlooking the bay or a suite that opens onto the pool. **Pros:** close proximity to everything Hermanus has to offer; very friendly staff; less than 200 feet from the sea. **Cons:** central town location and some suites facing the street are noisy; no children under 12. ⊠ *16 Harbour Rd.* ☎ *028/313–1201* ⊕ *www.auberge.co.za* ⇔ *18 rooms* ☖ *In-room: safe, kitchen (some), refrigerator. In-hotel: pool, parking (free), no kids under 12* ▭ *AE, DC, MC, V* ⎩⊙⎭ *BP.*

$–$$ ⊡ **Blue Gum Country Estate.** Husband-and-wife team Nic and Nicole Drupper run a top-notch establishment on the banks of the Klein River just 10 minutes from Stanford and 30 minutes from Hermanus. Blue Gum is a world away from the Hermanus crowds and a wonderful place to relax. The rooms are individually decorated in a style best described as English country house meets colonial African. Mosquito nets, fluffy white pillows, crisp white linen, and dark wood will make you feel a little like a 21st-century Karen Blixen of *Out of Africa* fame. The emphasis is on comfort, and the hotel seems like an extension of the Drupper's upscale home. The food (dinner only) is exceptional—Nicole is a trained chef, with a critical eye for detail—and you'll likely be only too happy to head back to Blue Gum at the end of a busy day exploring. The menu for the prix-fixe candle-lighted dinners ($$$$) changes daily to make the most of seasonal ingredients, but you might start with chicken-tikka salad, followed by a tender beef fillet with spicy potatoes, roasted beetroot, and butternut squash. Weather permitting, you can have a predinner drink outside around the open fire. On the estate you can fish for trout or wander around the small vineyard with the family dog—or give in to the luxury and just laze near the pool. The Country Villa caters to families and can sleep up to 10 people. The villa has its own swimming pool, and there are lots of board games when the family needs a break from quad biking, hiking, or shark diving off Gansbaai. **Pros:** brilliant base to explore the area from; feels like home away from home with added luxury. **Cons:** you'll need to drive a distance to get to the busier areas; pitiful nightlife in Stanford. ⊠ *Off R326, Box 899, Stanford* ☎ *028/341–0116* ⊕ *www.bluegum.co.za* ⇔ *12 rooms* ☖ *In-room: safe, refrigerator. In-hotel: restaurant, room service (by request), bar, tennis court, pool, bicycles, laundry service, Wi-Fi, parking (free)* ▭ *DC, MC, V* ⎩⊙⎭ *BP.*

$$$$ ⊡ **Grootbos Private Nature Reserve.** Only a 15 minute drive from Her-
Fodor's Choice manus and two hours from Cape Town, this private nature reserve is
★ on 2,500 acres of Western Cape landscape overlooking Walker Bay. Here you can observe protea, fynbos, milk-wood forests, and tropical rain forests, as well as aquatic life: penguins, dolphins, seals, and Southern Right whales in early spring. Hiking trails, horseback riding, beaches, and children's programs are close by. Privacy is paramount in the luxurious suites, which have fireplaces, sunken bathtubs, and private sundecks opening onto fynbos, sea, and mountains as far as the eye can see. Go for the newer Forest Lodge suites that seamlessly meld nature and modern amenities. The reserve's foundation works to educate and employ the community with conservation, research, and sustainable-living projects. The cuisine is exquisite, enhanced by vegetables and herbs grown on the premises. **Pros:** certified green property; secluded natural surrounds; whale-watching. **Cons:** confining for longer stays; expensive. ⊠ *R43, Gansbaai* ☎ *028/384–8000* ⊕ *www.grootbos.com* ⇔ *27 suites* ☖ *In-room: safe. In-hotel: restaurant, room service, bars, pools, spa,*

water sports, children's programs (ages 3–16), laundry service, Internet terminal, Wi-Fi, parking (free) ☰ *AE, MC, V* ⭘ᴵ *FAP.*

$$$$
Fodor's Choice
★

⛯ **The Marine.** In an incomparable cliff-top setting, this venerable hotel has sumptuously decorated rooms. The decor is a tad conventional. There are four-poster beds, and the creams and beiges with touches of blue and white give the hotel a very refined, gentrified air. But the sea-facing rooms, some with private balcony and all with underfloor heating, provide whale-watchers with grandstand views over Walker Bay. The Sun Lounge feels a whole lot more contemporary than the hotel, and you can linger over tea or drinks, and the two restaurants tempt with sophisticated menus. The Pavilion ($$$$), with wonderful views of Walker Bay, serves up-to-the-minute fare. Smoked snoek, calamari, prawn, and herb ravioli is a delicious first course, as is the potato gnocchi with wild mushrooms, cured ham, and celeriac velouté. Mains include roast rack of Karoo lamb with forest-mushroom mille-feuille, roasted beetroot, and lamb jus. Desserts are stunning, making many diners wish they'd left room for more. Make time to visit the hotel's wine cellar, as it specializes in wines from the Walker Bay region. **Pros:** wonderful views of the ocean; old-world service excellence and attention to detail. **Cons:** you'll need a tony wardrobe to blend in; not a super-relaxed environment. ⊠ *Marine Dr., Box 9* ☎ *028/313–1000* ⊕ *www.marine-hermanus.co.za* ⌕ *43 rooms* ⚒ *In-room: safe, refrigerator, DVD (some). In-hotel: 2 restaurants, room service, bar, pools, spa, laundry service, Internet terminal, Wi-Fi, parking (free), no kids under 12* ☰ *AE, DC, MC, V* ⭘ᴵ *BP.*

$

⛯ **Whale Cottage, Hermanus.** Decorated in restful shades of blue and white, this is a great base from which to take long whale-watching walks. Ask for a room with a view and put your feet up while you watch the Southern Right whales splashing in the bay below. Alternatively, take a stroll along the nearby whale-watching cliffs. An honor bar and tea and coffee are available throughout the day. **Pros:** swimming beach within walking distance; children welcome. **Cons:** Southern Rights make a lot of noise when they're having a whale of a time; only three rooms are sea facing, so book early if you want to see the whales. ⊠ *38 Westcliff Dr.* ☎ *021/433–2100* ⊕ *www.whalecottage.com* ⌕ *6 rooms* ⚒ *In-room: no phone, safe, Wi-Fi. In-hotel: bar, pool, Wi-Fi, parking (free)* ☰ *AE, DC, MC, V* ⭘ᴵ *BP.*

$

⛯ **Windsor.** If you come to Hermanus anytime from July to November, consider staying at this hotel in the heart of town. It's a family-run hostelry that offers comfort but little pretense. Rooms are outdated, so the real reason to stay here its position atop the cliffs, making it a great place to view the annual whale migration. Request one of the second-floor, sea-facing rooms, with sliding-glass doors and unbeatable views. During holidays, a games room with a pool table and table tennis is set up for older children. Breakfasts are ample. **Pros:** world-class views of Walker Bay; in the heart of Hermanus; reasonable rates. **Cons:** tired decor needs a revamp; no pool. ⊠ *49 Marine Dr.* ☎ *028/312–3727* ⊕ *www.windsorhotel.co.za* ⌕ *60 rooms* ⚒ *In-room: refrigerator. In-hotel: room service, bar, laundry service, Internet terminal, parking (free)* ☰ *AE, DC, MC, V* ⭘ᴵ *BP.*

SPORTS AND THE OUTDOORS

East of Hermanus the R43 hugs the strip of land between the mountains and the Klein River lagoon. The lagoon is popular with water-skiers, boaters, and anglers.

BOATING

You can take a sunset cruise up the Klein River with **Walker Bay Adventures** (✉ *Prawn Flats, off R43* ☎ *082/739–0159* ⊕ *www.walkerbayadventures.co.za*). The cost is around R250 for the cruise and a braai afterward.

KAYAKING

For a really fun outing, join a gentle paddling excursion from the Old Harbour operated by **Walker Bay Adventures** (✉ *Prawn Flats, off R43* ☎ *082/739–0159* ⊕ *www.walkerbayadventures.co.za*). You paddle in safe, stable double sea kayaks accompanied by a guide, and you pay around R300 for a two-hour morning trip. From July to December, Walker Bay is a whale sanctuary, and this is the only company with a permit to operate here.

WHALE-WATCHING AND SHARK DIVING

Although Hermanus is great for land-based whale-watching, you get a different perspective on a boat trip into Walker Bay. Boats leave on 2½-hour whale-watching trips (around R900) from both Hermanus and Gansbaai. **Dyer Island Cruises** (☎ *082/801–8014* ⊕ *www.dyer-island-cruises.co.za*) is a good bet for whale-watching.

Shark diving is extremely popular (even Brad Pitt took the plunge), and Gansbaai has a number of operators working from the small harbor, including **White Shark Diving Company** (☎ *082/559–6858*). A 4½-hour trip (with plenty of adrenaline) costs around R1,000, including breakfast and snacks on the boat. If you don't want to take the plunge (which you do in a cage, to keep you safe from the sharks), you can just stay in the boat and watch the sharks from the deck.

SHOPPING

Wine Village (✉ *R43 and R320* ☎ *028/316–3988* ⊕ *www.wine-village.co.za*) carries a good selection of South African wines, including wines from neighboring vineyards Hamilton Russell and Bouchard Finlayson as well as Southern Right.

BREDASDORP

89 km (55 mi) east of Hermanus, 60 km (37 mi) east of Stanford.

This sleepy agricultural town has a certain charm, as long as you don't catch it on a Sunday afternoon, when everything's closed and an air of ennui pervades the brassy, windswept streets. Each spring, however, the usual lethargic atmosphere is abandoned, and a radical sense of purpose takes its place when Bredasdorp hosts the Foot of Africa Marathon. Don't be lulled by the small-town country setting into thinking that this race is a breeze; word has it that the undulating landscape has the fittest athletes doubting their perseverance.

GETTING HERE AND AROUND

Travel time from Hermanus is around 45 minutes and from Stanford 30 minutes. From Hermanus you travel on the R43 to Stanford, then you take the R326 and then the R316. The route is well signposted.

VISITOR INFORMATION

The Cape Agulhas Tourism Bureau has information for Bredasdorp. It's open weekdays 8–5 and Saturday 9–12:30.

ESSENTIALS

~~Hospitals~~ **Otto du Plessis Hospital** (⊠ *Dorpsig and van Riebeek Sts.* ☎ *028/424–1167*).

~~Tourist Offices~~ **Cape Agulhas Tourism Bureau** (⊠ *Dr Janson St.* ☎ *028/424–2584*).

EXPLORING

Housed in a converted church and rectory, the **Bredasdorp Museum** has an extensive collection of objects salvaged from the hundreds of ships that have gone down in the stormy waters off the Cape. In addition to the usual cannons and figureheads, the museum displays a surprising array of undamaged household articles rescued from the sea, including entire dining-room sets, sideboards, china, and phonographs. ⊠ *6 Independent St.* ☎ *028/424–1240* ≊ *R10* ☉ *Weekdays 9–5, weekends 11–4.*

OFF THE BEATEN PATH

Little has changed in the last hundred years in the Moravian mission village **Elim,** founded in 1824. Simple whitewashed cottages line the few streets, and the settlement's coloured residents all belong to the Moravian Church (⇨ *"A Note on the Term 'Coloured'" box, above*). At the Sunday 10 AM church service, which you're welcome to attend, just about the whole town turns out in their Sunday best, and voices soar in the white church at the top of the main street. The whole village has been declared a national monument, and it's the only town in the country that has a monument dedicated to the freeing of the slaves in 1838. It's also home to the country's oldest working clock and biggest wooden waterwheel. Elim is 36 km (22 mi) west of Bredasdorp and accessible only by dirt road. The easiest access is via the R317, off the R319 between Cape Agulhas and Bredasdorp.

De Hoop Nature Reserve is a huge conservation area covering 88,900 acres of isolated coastal terrain as well as a marine reserve extending 5 km (3 mi) out to sea. It's a World Heritage Site and well-deserving of this status. Massive white-sand dunes, mountains, and rare lowland fynbos are home to eland, bontebok, and Cape mountain zebra, as well as more than 250 bird species. Though the reserve is only three hours from Cape Town, it feels a lifetime away. Access is via the dirt road between Bredasdorp and Malgas. This is a fantastic place to watch whales from the shore—not quite as easy as in Hermanus but much less crowded. You can also hike the enormously popular **Whale Trail,** which runs through this reserve. A shuttle service takes your bags to each new stop, so all you have to carry is a small day pack and some water between overnight stops. You need to book up to a year in advance to enjoy the Whale Trail, or you might get lucky and snag a last-minute cancellation. In fact, this hike is now so popular that it's beginning to appear in online auctions. Self-catering cottages sleep up to four people and range from basic to fully equipped. The trail costs R950 per person but there's a minimum of six people each time so you'll have to drum up other happy hikers. ✉ *Private Bag X16, 7280* ☎ *028/542–1114 or 021/659–3500* ⊕ *www.capenature.org.za* ☉ *Sat.–Thurs. 7–6, Fri. 7–7.*

Past De Hoop Nature Reserve on the dirt road from Bredasdorp is the small hamlet of **Malgas,** a major port in the 19th century before the mouth of the Breede River silted up. In addition to a tiny village, you will find the last hand-drawn car ferry in the country (R30 round-trip). It's fascinating to watch the technique, as the ferry operators "walk" the ferry across the river on a huge cable, leaning into their harnesses.

■ OFF THE
BEATEN
PATH

Cape Agulhas. From Bredasdorp it's just 41 km (25½ mi) through rolling farmland to the Cape Agulhas lighthouse. Although the cape is not nearly as spectacular as Cape Point, it's a wild and lonely place—rather fitting for the end of a wild and wonderful continent.

ARNISTON (WAENHUISKRANS)

★ *25 km (15½ mi) southeast of Bredasdorp.*

Although its official name is Waenhuiskrans, and that's what you'll see on maps, this lovely, isolated vacation village is almost always called Arniston—after a British ship of that name that was wrecked on the nearby reef in 1815. Beautiful beaches, water that assumes Caribbean shades of blue, and mile after mile of towering white dunes attract anglers and vacationers alike. Only the frequent southeasters that blow off the sea and the chilly water are likely to put a damper on your enjoyment.

For 200 years a community of local fisherfolk has eked out a living here, setting sail each day in small fishing boats. Today their village, **Kassiesbaai** (translation: "suitcase bay," supposedly for all the suitcases that washed ashore from the frequent shipwrecks), is a national monument. It's fascinating wandering around the thatch cottages of this still-vibrant community, although declining fish stocks have left many families vulnerable. Abalone poaching is also a problem here. The adjacent village of Arniston has expanded enormously in the last two decades, thanks to the construction of vacation homes. Unfortunately, not all of the new architecture blends well with the whitewashed simplicity of the original cottages.

Waenhuiskrans is Afrikaans for "wagon-house cliff," a name derived from the vast cave 2 km (1 mi) south of town that is theoretically large enough to house several wagons and their spans of oxen. Signs point the way over the dunes to the cave, which is accessible only at low tide. You need shoes to protect your feet from the sharp rocks, and you should wear something you don't mind getting wet. It's definitely worth the trouble, however, to stand in the enormous cave looking out to sea.

GETTING HERE AND AROUND
It'll take drivers about 20–30 minutes to get here from Bredasdorp. Don't bother with public transport. Rent a car and you'll have the freedom to explore this vast area.

VISITOR INFORMATION
The Cape Agulhas Tourism Bureau has information for Arniston. It's open weekdays 8–5 and Saturday 9–12:30.

ESSENTIALS
Tourist Offices **Cape Agulhas Tourism Bureau** (✉ *Dr. Janson St., Bredasdorp* ☎ *028/424–2584*).

WHERE TO STAY

$$ ▦ **Arniston Spa Hotel.** You could easily spend a week here and still need
★ to be dragged away. The setting, a crescent of white dunes, has a lot to do with Arniston's appeal, but the hotel also strikes a fine balance between elegance and beach-vacation comfort. Request a sea-facing room, where you can enjoy the ever-changing colors of the horizon and have a grandstand view of the large concentration of cow-and-calf pairs found here during the whaling season, between June and November. The à la carte menu ($) offers substantial variety, with few surprises, but the grilled catch of the day is as fresh as you can get. Oenophiles rejoice at the quality of the deservedly renowned wine list. Lunch, which is included in the rate along with a full breakfast, is served on the patio in fine weather. ■**TIP→** **Pool-facing rooms are cheaper. Pros:** great views of the beach; located on a safe beach, which is brilliant if you have children. **Cons:** windy in summer; bit noisy during high season. ✉ *Beach Rd., Arniston* ✆ *Box 126, Bredasdorp 7280* ☎ *028/445–9000* ⊕ *www.arnistonhotel.com* ⟿ *60 rooms* ⚭ *In-room: safe, refrigerator, Internet. In-hotel: restaurant, room service, bar, pool, spa, beachfront, laundry service, parking (free)* ▤ *AE, DC, MC, V* ⏐⊚⏐ *BP.*

SWELLENDAM

★ *72 km (45 mi) north of Arniston (Waenhuiskrans).*

Beautiful Swellendam lies in the shadow of the imposing Langeberg. Founded in 1745, it is the third-oldest town in South Africa, and many of its historic buildings have been elegantly restored. Even on a casual drive along the main street you'll see a number of lovely Cape Dutch homes, with their traditional whitewashed walls, gables, and thatch roofs.

GETTING HERE AND AROUND
Swellendam is about an hour's drive from Arniston. Rent a car to get around.

VISITOR INFORMATION
The Swellendam Tourism Bureau is open weekdays 9–5, weekends 9–1.

ESSENTIALS
Hospitals **Swellendam Hospital** (✉ *18 Drostdy St.* ☎ *028/514–1142*).

Tourist Offices **Swellendam Tourism Bureau** (✉ *Oefeningshuis, Voortrek St.* ☎ *028/514–2770* ⊕ *www.swellendamtourism.co.za*).

EXPLORING

The centerpiece of the town's historical past is the **Drostdy Museum,** a collection of buildings dating from the town's earliest days. The Drostdy was built in 1747 by the Dutch East India Company to serve as the residence of the *landdrost,* the magistrate who presided over the district. The building is furnished in a style that was common in the mid-19th century. A path leads through the Drostdy herb gardens to Mayville, an 1855 middle-class home that blends elements of Cape Dutch and Cape Georgian architecture. Across Swellengrebel Street stand the old jail and the Ambagswerf, an outdoor exhibit of tools used by the town's blacksmiths, wainwrights, coopers, and tanners. ⊠ *18 Swellengrebel St.* ☎ *028/514–1138* ✎ *info@drostdymuseum.com* ✉ *R15* ☉ *Oct.–Apr., daily 9–4:30; May–Sept., daily 10–4.*

Swellendam's **Dutch Reformed Church** is an imposing white edifice built in 1911 in an eclectic style. The gables are baroque, the windows Gothic, the cupola vaguely Eastern, and the steeple extravagant. Surprisingly, all the elements work together wonderfully. Inside is an interesting tiered amphitheater with banks of curving wood pews facing the pulpit and organ. ⊠ *7 Voortrek St.* ☎ *028/514–1225* ✉ *R5; services free* ☉ *Weekdays 8–4; services (in Afrikaans) Sun. at 9:30.*

If you'd like to stretch your legs, take a hike in the **Marloth Nature Reserve** in the Langeberg above town. Five easy walks, ranging from one to four hours, explore some of the mountain gorges. An office at the entrance to the reserve has trail maps and hiking information. There is a five-day trail, which costs about R55 per person per day in addition to the park entrance fee. If you're doing a day walk, park outside the entrance boom. Although you can stay in the reserve until sunset, the gates close at the time advertised. ⊠ *1½ km (1 mi) from Voortrek St. on Andrew White St. to golf course, and follow signs* ☎ *028/514–1410* ⊕ *www.capenature.org.za* ✉ *R25* ☉ *Weekdays 7–4.*

Covering just 6,880 acres of coastal fynbos, **Bontebok National Park** is one of the smallest of South Africa's national parks. Don't expect to see big game here—the park contains no elephants, lions, or rhinos. What you will see are bontebok, graceful white-face antelope nearly exterminated by hunters in the early 20th century, as well as red hartebeest, Cape grysbok, steenbok, duiker, and the endangered Cape mountain zebra. ⊠ *Off the N2, 5 km (3 mi) from Swellendam* ☎ *028/514–2735* ⊕ *www.sanparks.org* ✉ *R16* ☉ *May–Sept., daily 7–6; Oct.–Apr., daily 7–7.*

WHERE TO STAY

¢ ♨ **Coachman Guesthouse.** Dating to the 18th century and declared a national monument in 1983, this guesthouse is in the historic heart of Swellendam, within easy walking distance of all the major sights and restaurants. A lovely garden surrounds the house; the rooms have entrances that open onto a courtyard, and two thatch garden cottages have their own verandas and great views over the Langeberg Mountains. Rooms are charmingly furnished with brass beds and comfortable throws. The pool is an absolute necessity in summer, when temperatures soar. **Pros:** tranquil and secluded for a real getaway; children are welcome. **Cons:** swimming pool is unfenced; not much nightlife. ⊠ *14*

Drostdy St. ☎ *028/514–2294* ⊕ *www.coachman.co.za* ⟐ *4 rooms, 2 cottages* ⚬ *In-room: no phone, safe, kitchen, refrigerator, no TV, Wi-Fi. In-hotel: room service, bar, pool, laundry service, Wi-Fi, parking (free), some pets allowed* ⊟ *AE, DC, MC, V* ⍾ *BP.*

¢–$ ⊡ **The Hideaway.** The Victorian homestead and its three luxury cot-
★   tages are set in a peaceful garden with literally hundreds of rosebushes. Although the setting and beautifully appointed cottages are excellent reasons to stay here, it's the level of hospitality that sets this place above the rest. The owners' dedication extends to providing lifts, planning routes, and presenting the best breakfast (complete with homemade jams) for many miles around. **Pros:** huge breakfasts; ideally situated in the historic part of town, around the corner from the museum, and in walking distance of good restaurants; special winter rates. **Cons:** small plunge pool. ⊠ *10 Hermanus Steyn St.* ☎ *028/514–3316* ⊕ *www.hide-awaybb.co.za* ⟐ *4 suites* ⚬ *In-room: no phone, safe, refrigerator, no TV. In-hotel: pool, bicycles, laundry service, Internet terminal, parking (free), some pets allowed* ⊟ *AE, MC, V* ⍾ *BP.*

$$ ⊡ **Klippe Rivier Country House.** Amid rolling farmland 3 km (2 mi) out-side Swellendam, this guesthouse occupies one of the Overberg's most gracious and historic country homes. It was built around 1825 in tra-ditional Cape style, with thick white walls, a thatch roof, and a distinc-tive gable. Guests stay in enormous rooms in the converted stables. The three downstairs rooms are furnished with antiques in Cape Dutch, colonial, and Victorian styles. Upstairs, raw-wood beams, cane ceilings, and bold prints set the tone for less expensive Provençal-style rooms with small balconies. Some public rooms have trouble supporting the sheer volume of antique collectibles, which gives them a museumlike quality. The delectable three-course dinners ($$$$) are table d'hôte and prepared with fresh herbs, vegetables, fruit, and cream from sur-rounding farms. **Pros:** historic architecture; walking distance to the Breede River. **Cons:** no small children allowed; resident dog could be a problem if you're allergic. ⊠ *On dirt road off R60 to Ashton, Box 483* ☎ *028/514–3341* ⊕ *www.klipperivier.com* ⟐ *6 rooms, 1 cottage* ⚬ *In-room: no TV (some). In-hotel: restaurant, room service (by request), pool, laundry service, Wi-Fi, parking (free), no kids under 8* ⊟ *AE, DC, MC, V* ⍾ *BP.*

$$–$$$ ⊡ **Mardouw Country House.** The old Cape Georgian farmhouse on this working wine-and-olive farm has been beautifully converted into a luxury guesthouse with stunning views of the Langeberg mountains. Among the amenities are an infinity pool, wide verandas, under-floor heating, and an attentive staff. Clean, contemporary lines decorate the tasteful rooms. The estate produces its own Pinotage and chenin blanc, which you can enjoy at Mardouw's sumptuous four-course dinners. The country house has its own herb-and-vegetable garden, so the emphasis is on fresh, seasonal food. The menu changes daily but might include a prawn starter and a main course of succulent beef medallions served with beetroot couscous and fresh ribbon vegetables. The chef's olive ice cream is a favorite on the dessert menu, and the cheese platter includes cheeses from a neighboring farm together with homemade preserves—figs in syrup, tomato jam, and marrow marmalade. Special

arrangements must be made in advance for children. **Pros:** great bird-watching on the property; great walks and mountain biking if you're feeling energetic. **Cons:** 20 minutes' drive to Swellendam; no spa facilities. ✉ *R60, between Ashton and Swellendam* ☐ *Box 625, Swellendam 6740* ☏ *023/616–2999* ⊕ *www.mardouw.com* ⤳ *3 rooms, 2 suites* ♿ *In-room: safe, refrigerator, DVD. In-hotel: room service, bar, golf course, pool, bicycles, laundry service, Wi-Fi, parking (free)* ☐ *MC, V* ⊙ *Closed July* ⎢○⎢ *BP.*

SPORTS AND THE OUTDOORS

HORSEBACK RIDING

You can take just a little trot or a longer excursion through the Marloth Nature Reserve on horseback with **Two Feathers Horse Trails** (✉ *Koloniesbos Hut* ☏ *082/494–8279*). Expect to pay between R200 for an hour and R1,200 for a full-day ride, including a packed lunch.

EN ROUTE From Swellendam return to the N2 and turn right toward Cape Town. The road sweeps through rich, rolling cropland that extends to the base of the Langeberg. A few kilometers after the town of Riviersonderend (pronounced riff-*ear*-son-der-ent), turn right onto the R406, a good gravel road that leads to the village of Greyton, in the lee of the Riviersonderend Mountains.

GREYTON

★ *32 km (20 mi) west of Swellendam.*

The charming village of Greyton, filled with white thatch cottages and quiet lanes, is a popular weekend retreat for Capetonians, as well as a permanent home for many retirees. The village offers almost nothing in the way of traditional sights, but it's a relaxing place to stop for a meal or a night, and a great base for walks into the surrounding mountains. There are plenty of small B&Bs and guesthouses to stay in, but no large hotels.

GETTING HERE AND AROUND

If you're driving from Swellendam, take the N2 west. Expect the trip to take an hour to an hour and a half.

VISITOR INFORMATION

The Greyton Tourism Bureau is open daily 9–5.

ESSENTIALS

Tourist Offices Greyton Tourism Bureau (✉ *29 Main Rd.* ☏ *028/254–9414 or 028/254–9564* ⊕ *www.greyton.net*).

EXPLORING

After Greyton the R406 becomes paved. Drive 5 km (3 mi) to the turnoff to **Genadendal** *(Valley of Grace)*, a Moravian mission station founded in 1737 to educate the Khoekhoen and convert them to Christianity. Seeing this impoverished hamlet today, it's difficult to comprehend the major role this mission played in the early history of South Africa. In the late 18th century it was the second-largest settlement after Cape Town, and its Khoekhoen craftspeople produced the finest silver cutlery and woodwork in the country. Some of the first written works in

Afrikaans were printed here, and the coloured community (⇨ *"A Note on the Term 'Coloured' " box, above*) greatly influenced the development of Afrikaans as it is heard today. None of this went down well with the white population. By 1909 new legislation prohibited coloured ownership of land, and in 1926 the Department of Public Education closed the settlement's teachers' training college, arguing that coloureds were better employed on neighboring farms. In 1980 all the buildings on Church Square were declared national monuments (it's considered the country's most authentic church square), but despite a number of community-based projects, Genadendal has endured a long slide into obscurity and remains impoverished. In 1995, then-president Nelson Mandela renamed his official residence Genadendal. You can walk the streets and tour the historic buildings facing Church Square. Ask at the Genadendal Mission Museum (⇨ *below*) for somebody to show you around. With luck you'll meet up with Samuel Baatjes, a fourth-generation Genadendal resident. Phone him at ☎ 028/251–8582 if you want a guided tour, which can last from one to three hours; prices vary depending on length, number of participants, and other variables.

Of particular note in Genadendal is the **Genadendal Mission Museum**, spread through 15 rooms in three buildings. The museum collection, the only one in South Africa to be named a National Cultural Treasure, includes unique household implements, books, tools, and musical instruments, among them the country's oldest pipe organ, which arrived in the village in 1832. Wall displays examine mission life in the Cape in the 18th and 19th centuries, focusing on the early missionaries' work with the Khoekhoen. Unfortunately, many of the displays are in Afrikaans only. ⊠ *Off R406* ☎ *028/251–8582* ⊕ *www.museums.org.za/ genadendal* ⊡ *R10* ⊙ *Mon.–Thurs. 9–1 and 2–5, Fri. 9–3:30.*

SPORTS AND THE OUTDOORS
HIKING
In addition to day hikes and short walks, you can take the 32-km (20-mi) **Boesmanskloof Trail** through the Riviersonderend Mountains between Greyton and the exquisite hamlet of McGregor (⇨ *Breede River Valley, above*). In the good old days, youngsters used to walk from Greyton to McGregor for an energetic game of tennis before walking home again the same evening. Accommodations, in hiking huts on a private farm (R50 per person excluding bedding), can be booked through **Barry Oosthuizen** (☎ *023/625–1794 or 072/240–0498*), who will also buy groceries and leave them at the hut, charging you only what he pays. Hikers often book the following night's accommodation at a local B&B and have a good meal and a good night's sleep before heading home. In McGregor the trailhead is a ways from the town, but most guesthouses will pick you up and drop you off. Note that cell-phone coverage is sporadic on the trail.

EN ROUTE
To head back toward Cape Town, follow the R406 to the N2. After the town of Bot River, the road leaves the wheat fields and climbs into the mountains. It's lovely country, full of rock and pine forest interspersed with orchards. **Sir Lowry's Pass** serves as the gateway to Cape Town and the Winelands, a magnificent breach in the mountains that opens to

reveal the curving expanse of False Bay, the long ridge of the peninsula, and, in the distance, Table Mountain.

WEST COAST

The West Coast is an acquired taste. It's dry and bleak, and other than the ubiquitous exotic gum trees, nothing grows higher than your knees. But it's a wild and wonderful place. An icy sea pounds long, deserted beaches or rocky headlands, and the sky stretches for miles.

Historically, this area has been populated by hardy fisherfolk and tough, grizzled farmers. Over the years they have worked out a balance with the extreme elements—responding with a stoic minimalism that is obvious in the building styles, the cuisine, and the language.

Unfortunately, minimalism became fashionable, and urban refugees started settling on the West Coast. The first lot wasn't bad—they bought tattered old houses and renovated them just enough to make them livable. Then came those who insisted on building replicas of their suburban homes at the coast. And then—worst of all—came the developers. They bought up huge tracts of land and cut them into tiny little plots, popping horrid little houses onto them. Or perhaps they'd turn a whole bay into a pseudo-Greek village. As a result, the austere aesthetic that makes the West Coast so special is fast disappearing. But it's not gone—at least not yet.

Just inland from the West Coast is the Swartland (Black Ground, a reference to the fertile soil that supports a flourishing wheat and wine industry). Rolling wheat fields extend as far as the eye can see to mountains on either side. In summer the heat is relentless, and there's a sea of golden-brown grain, but in winter the landscape is a shimmery green, and when there's snow on the mountains, it's as pretty as can be. The Swartland includes Piketberg, Malmesbury, Darling (also considered part of the West Coast), and the twin towns of Riebeek West and Riebeek Kasteel.

To the north, the Cederberg is an absolutely beautiful and rugged range of mountains, most of which is a designated wilderness area. In South Africa that means you may hike there with a permit, but there are no laid-out trails and no accommodations or facilities of any kind. Fantastic rock formations, myriad flowering plants, delicate rock art, and crystal-clear streams with tinkling waterfalls and deep pools make this a veritable hiker's paradise.

A loop around the West Coast, Swartland, and the Cederberg, starting from Cape Town, will take a minimum of three days, but the distances are long, so plan to spend more time here if you can.

EN ROUTE As you head out of Cape Town on the N1 or R27 on your way up the coast, it's easy to whiz past the tiny whitewashed settlement of Mamre on the R304. But it's worth turning off here to check out the old thatch buildings that made up the **Moravian Mission Station**, founded in 1808. The church here is almost always open, but phone ahead to make sure. All the buildings dating from this period have been restored and declared national monuments. Unfortunately, the rest of the town is unlovely and crippled with the usual ills of unemployment and poverty. ⊠ *Church St.* ☎ *021/576–1134.*

GETTING HERE AND AROUND

The roads up the West Coast are generally good, but some dirt roads are rutted and bumpy. If you plan to head into the Cederberg mountains rather than just sticking to the small towns, consider renting a 4x4, especially in winter, when roads become muddy and you run a small risk of being snowed in.

The major car-rental agencies have offices in the smaller towns, but it's best to deal with the Cape Town offices; you'll probably want to pick up a car at the airport anyway. ⇨ *For car-rental agencies, see The Winelands, above.*

To get up the West Coast and to the Cederberg, take the N1 out of Cape Town. Just before Century City shopping center, take Exit 10, which is marked GOODWOOD, MALMESBURY, CENTURY CITY DR. AND SABLE RD. and leads to the N7, the region's major access road. Though the highway is well marked, get yourself a good map from a bookstore or tourism office and explore some of the smaller roads, which offer surprising vistas or a glimpse into the rural heart of the Western Cape. The Versveld Pass, between Piketberg and the hamlet of Piket-Bo-Berg, at the top of the mountains, has views that stretch for miles.

Intercape Mainliner heads up the N7 daily, which is the main route up to the Cederberg. The bus stops at Citrusdal, and Clanwilliam, but not coastal towns such as Langebaan and Elands Bay. Expect to pay around R260 to Citrusdal and R250 to Clanwilliam. The journey to Clanwilliam from Cape Town takes about four hours.

Although there's public train service to major West Coast towns, it's not recommended as there have been regular on-board muggings.

EMERGENCIES

There are doctors and dentists in every town, as well as provincial hospitals in Citrusdal, Clanwilliam, Malmesbury (near the Riebeek Valley), and Vredenburg (near Paternoster). The closest private hospital is at Milnerton, a Cape Town suburb that has developed along the N7. Late-night pharmacies are a rarity in these small towns, but all pharmacies have emergency and after-hours phone numbers. If there isn't a pharmacy, head for the hospital.

INTERNET

There's public Internet access in several West Coast towns. For instance, you can have a cup of coffee or glass of wine while catching up on your e-mail at Saint du Barrys Country Lodge in Clanwilliam. Rates are reasonable and will depend on your host's mood and the time you spend there.

TOURS

To see the exceptional rock art in the Cederberg, it's recommended that you take a tour so that you can fully appreciate and understand this ancient art form, about which experts still have questions. The community-driven Clanwilliam Living Landscape Project has trained locals to act as guides. Expect to pay around R60 for a one-hour tour that includes a visit to two sites, and R100 for five sites, which takes about four hours. If you don't have your own vehicle, the guide can pick you up, but you'll be charged a little extra for gas.

Rooibos tea is a big part of this region's economy, and a rooibos tour with Elandsberg Eco-Tourism should fill you in on all you need to know. The shorter tour, around 1½ hours, costs R60, and the 2½- to 3-hour tour costs around R100. Because the tour is out on a farm, they will arrange to pick you up in town.

For something completely out of the ordinary, try a Donkey Cart Adventure, which starts at the top of the Pakhuis Pass and ends a couple of hours later in the tiny hamlet of Heuningvlei in the heart of the Cederberg Wilderness Area. The donkey-cart route is windy and takes you through some spectacular scenery and flora. It's best to plan this trip for spring, when the fynbos is at its best, or in autumn. In summer, temperatures soar in the Cederberg.

During the orange-harvest season (April–September), you can gain insight into the fruit industry with an hour-long tour through the packing sheds at Goede Hoop Citrus. These tours meet at the Citrusdal Tourism Bureau.

VISITOR INFORMATION

There are tourist offices in most small towns along the West Coast, but the West Coast Regional Tourism Organization has information on the entire area. Visit its Web site to get a good overview of the area.

The Flowerline is a central hotline that provides details about where the flowers are best seen each day. You can call 24 hours a day July–September.

ESSENTIALS

Bus Line Intercape Mainliner (✉ *1 Adderley St., Cape Town* ☎ *0861/287-287, 083/909-0909 for alternate booking through Computicket* ⊕ *www.intercape. co.za*).

Emergency Services Ambulance (☎ *10177*). **Police** (☎ *10111*). **Police, fire, and ambulance** (☎ *107 from landline*). **Vodacom emergency services** (☎ *112 from mobile phone*).

Hospital Milnerton Medi-Clinic (✉ *Racecourse and Koeberg Rds., Milnerton* ☎ *021/529-9000, 021/529-9299 for 24-hour emergency services* ⊕ *www.milnertonmc.co.za*).

Tour Operators Clanwilliam Living Landscape Project (☎ *027/482-1911 or 071/482-1765* ⊕ *www.cllp.uct.ac.za*). **Donkey Cart Adventure** (☎ *021/659-3500* ⊕ *www.capenature.org.za*). **Elandsberg Eco-Tourism** (☎ *027/482-2022* ⊕ *www.africandawn.com*). **Goede Hoop Citrus** (☎ *022/921-8100* ⊕ *www. ghcitrus.com*).

Tourist Information Flowerline (☎ *083/910-1028*). **West Coast Regional Tourism Organization** (✉ *Box 242, Moorreesburg 7310* ☎ *022/433-8505* ⊕ *www.capewestcoast.org*).

DARLING

82 km (51 mi) north of Cape Town.

Darling is best known for two draws: its sensational wildflowers and its sensational performer, Pieter-Dirk Uys, otherwise known as Evita Bezuidenhout. The wildflowers are usually at their best August–October, and there's an annual Wildflower and Orchid Show held in September. Evita is at her best all year-round (⇨ *Nightlife and the Arts, below*). When driving into Darling, ignore the rather unattractive new houses on the Cape Town side of the village, and head straight through to the Victorian section of town, where pretty period houses line up amid lush gardens.

GETTING HERE AND AROUND

Darling is an easy hour's drive from Cape Town along the N7 north and then west on the R315. Alternately, you could go north on the R27 out of town, then east on the R315.

VISITOR INFORMATION

The Darling Tourism Bureau, based at the Darling Museum, is open Monday–Thursday 9–1 and 2–4, Friday 9–1 and 2–3:30, and weekends 10–3.

ESSENTIALS

Internet Access **Evita se Perron** (✉ *Darling Station* ☎ *021/492–2831 or 022/492–3930* ⊕ *www.evita.co.za*).

Tourist Offices **Darling Tourism Bureau** (✉ *Pastorie and Hill Sts.* ☎ *022/492–3361* ⊕ *www.darlingtourism.co.za*).

EXPLORING

During the flower season the **Tienie Versfeld Wildflower Reserve** is just fantastic: a wonderful, unpretentious, uncommercialized little gem, boasting a range of uniquely South African veld types, like renoster-, strand-, riet- and sandveld. This variation has produced some amazing flowers. Look out for the Geophytes (bulbous plants), which are striking in their diverse sizes and colors. ✉ *R315, 12 km (7½ mi) west of Darling* ⊕ *www.darlingwildflowers.co.za* ⊠ *Free* ⊙ *Daily 24 hrs.*

A more formal flower experience than Tienie Versfeld Wildflower Reserve, **Rondeberg Nature Reserve** is justly proud of the more than 900 species found here, including rare disas (a type of orchid), which you aren't likely to find elsewhere as easily. All visits are via guided tours of the grounds, so you must call ahead to reserve a tour. ✉ *R27, 25 km (15½ mi) outside Darling* ☎ *022/492–3435* ⊕ *www.rondeberg.co.za* ⊠ *R70* ⊙ *Aug. and Sept. (flower season).*

Former dairy farmer Peter Pentz had enough of getting up at 4 AM to milk his cows, so together with his son, Nick, he turned instead to wine farming at **Groote Post Vineyard.** Groote Post fans couldn't be happier. The large, environmentally sensitive winery got off to a fantastic start when its maiden 1999 sauvignon blanc was judged one of the best in the Cape, and Groote Post has been garnering awards ever since. Try the delicate 2008 sauvignon blanc, or the 2008 merlot with hints of chocolate and berries. There are no cellar tours. The restaurant,

Hilda's Kitchen, is a really excellent choice for lunch. Regulars have been known to want to punch the chef if the Old Man's Steak Roll with its secret sauce isn't on the menu! A large portion of the farm has been left uncultivated and is covered with endangered *renosterveld* (literally, "rhino vegetation" in Afrikaans), which is found only in this area. These scrubby bushes might not look like much, but in the past they used to support large herds of game. Because the vegetation grows in fertile soil, a lot of renosterveld has been lost to agriculture. It's also very susceptible to fire and is the most endangered vegetation type in the Cape floral kingdom. Groote Post has introduced game drives through this unique vegetation for groups of 6 to 10 people. The drives are usually run by the charismatic owner, Peter, and last between one and two hours. Advanced bookings are essential for these drives and cost R100 per person. ✉ *Off R307* ☎ *022/492–2825* ⊕ *www.grootepost. com* ✍ *Tastings free* ☉ *Weekdays 8–5, weekends 10–4.*

Large **Darling Cellars** produces wines under a number of labels. In the Onyx range, look for the 2006 cabernet sauvignon and the 2008 noble late harvest. Other suggestions include the 2005 Pinotage and the 2009 sauvignon blanc. The DC range has some pleasing reds, including the nice, spicy Black Granite Shiraz and the 2008 Terra Hutton Cabernet Sauvignon. The newer Flamingo Bay range is proving that it can produce more than pleasant quaffs. In keeping with the West Coast, try the flamingo-pink 2008 Pinotage Rosé. ✉ *R315* ☎ *022/492–2276* ⊕ *www. darlingcellars.co.za* ✍ *Tastings free* ☉ *Mon.–Thurs. 8–5, Fri. 8–4, Sat. 10–2; cellar tours by appointment.*

WHERE TO STAY

¢ 🏠 **Darling Lodge.** You'll soon be made to feel at home at this pretty Victorian B&B set in a lovely garden in the heart of the village. It was one of the first guesthouses in Darling and prides itself on offering guests a great time. The three individually decorated rooms in the main house are all named after local artists whose prints hang on the walls, and all have en suite Victorian bathrooms. There are also three pool-deck rooms. There's plenty going on in the area, and you'll probably be ready for a refuge at the end of the day, perhaps in one of the claw-foot tubs or with a drink from the honesty bar. The breakfasts, groaning with homemade bread and jam and yogurt from the local dairy, are a highlight **Pros:** centrally located in Darling; perfect accommodation for families; only 15 minutes from the coast. **Cons:** limited number of rooms; dinner only on request. ✉ *22 Pastorie St.* ☎ *022/492–3062* ⊕ *www.darlinglodge.co.za* ⇆ *6 rooms* ⚬ *In room: no phone, no TV, Wi-Fi. In-hotel: bar, pool, laundry service, parking (free), some pets allowed* ▭ *No credit cards* ❢⊙| BP.*

¢ 🏠 **Trinity Guest Lodge and Restaurant.** This old Victorian house has been elegantly transformed into a stylish and comfortable guest lodge. White linen and subtle furnishings create a restful atmosphere. Some bathrooms have Victorian claw-foot tubs. Regularly voted one of South Africa's top-100 dining establishments, the restaurant ($) will likely have you coming back for more, especially for dishes such as roast beef fillet with a verjuice-hollandaise sauce. The menu changes daily, and there are also interesting food-and-wine-pairing dinners that are worth inquiring about. For the lodge, arrangements must be made in advance for children. **Pros:** in-house group cooking classes offered; fabulous on-site restaurant. **Cons:** close quarters; prior arrangements need to be made if you're bringing the kids. ⊠ *19 Long St.* ☎ *022/492–3430 or 083/325–4148* ⊕ *www.trinitylodge.co.za* 🛏 *6 rooms* 🔔 *In-room: no phone, safe. In-hotel: restaurant, room service, pool, laundry service, Internet terminal, parking (free), some pets allowed* ⊟ *DC, MC, V* ⅋❙*BP.*

NIGHTLIFE AND THE ARTS

Fodor's Choice
★

One of Darling's main attractions is **Evita se Perron** (⊠ *Darling station* ☎ *022/492–2831 or 022/492–3930* ⊕ *www.evita.co.za*), the theater and restaurant started by satirist and drag-artist Pieter-Dirk Uys. The theater is on the platform of the Darling station (*perron* is the Afrikaans word for "railway platform"). Pieter-Dirk Uys has made his alter ego, Evita Bezuidenhout, a household name in South Africa. Performances cost R100 and take place Saturday afternoon and evening, and Sunday afternoon. Come early to enjoy a buffet meal in the restaurant. In the same complex, **Evita's A en C** (get the pun on the name of the ruling party, the ANC?) is the gallery of an arts-and-crafts collective and skills-development center. Here you can see and buy works from West Coast artists. It's open daily 10–4.

LANGEBAAN

50 km (31 mi) northwest of Darling.

Probably the most popular destination on the coast, Langebaan is a great base from which to explore the region, and the sheltered lagoon makes for fantastic water sports, especially windsurfing, kite surfing, and sea kayaking. The town has a truly laid-back, beachy feel. To quote a local: "There is nowhere in Langebaan you can't go barefoot." Lots of Capetonians have weekend houses and head here on Friday afternoons with boats, bikes, and boards in tow. If you're not into water sports and serious tanning, however, Langebaan doesn't have that much to offer. The town grew up around a slipway, yacht club, and cluster of brick-faced beach houses, and the main drag is unexciting. Though the town comes alive in summer as youngsters crowd the beach and flex their muscles, during the off-season Langebaan quickly reverts to a quiet settlement where people retire to fish and mess about on boats.

GETTING HERE AND AROUND

It's about 30 minutes by car from Darling to Langebaan.

VISITOR INFORMATION

The Langebaan Tourism Bureau is open weekdays 9–5 and weekends 9–2.

ESSENTIALS

Internet Access Friends (⊠ *Marra Square, Bree St.* ☎ *082/447–4528*).

Tourist Offices Langebaan Tourism Bureau (⊠ *Municipal Bldg., Bree St.* ☎ *022/772–1515* ⊕ *www.langebaaninfo.co.za*).

Pieter-Dirk Uys: Everyone's Darling

It's fitting that Pieter-Dirk Uys (⊕ *www.pdu.co.za*) and his alter ego, Evita Bezuidenhout, live in a village called Darling. He's the darling of South African satire, and his speech is peppered with dramatic and warm-hearted "dahlings." *Tannie* (Auntie) Evita is as much a South African icon as braais and biltong.

But let's backtrack. Evita Bezuiden-hout debuted in a newspaper column written by playwright Pieter-Dirk Uys in the 1970s. He dished the dirt as though he were an insider at the Nationalist Party. His mysterious source's voice grew so strong that she was soon nicknamed the "Evita of Pretoria." She hit the stage in the early 1980s, when apartheid was in full swing and the ruling Nationalist Party was short on humor.

Uys's first production, *Adapt or Dye*, was performed at a small venue in Johannesburg at 11 PM, a time when he hoped the censors would be in bed. The titles of his shows and some characters (all of which he plays himself) are intricately wound up with South African politics and life. *Adapt or Dye*, for instance, was based on a speech by former prime minister P.W. Botha, who said, "South Africans have to adapt to a changing world or die." For a country ripped apart by politics based on color, it was a play on words Uys couldn't resist.

Every performance shows an intricate understanding of the country and her people. Over the years, Uys's richest material has come from the govern-ment. Most politicians were happy to be lampooned; in an inhumane society, laughing at themselves made them seem more human. If there's any criticism leveled at Uys, it's that for

all his biting remarks, he played court jester to the apartheid government and held back when he could have gone in for the kill. He would argue that shows need a balance between punches and tickles. Too many punches don't put bums on seats; too many tickles can be vacuous.

Uys is not just about comedy and satire, however. He's deeply commit-ted to transforming society. Before the first democratic elections in 1994, he embarked on self-funded voter-education tours. He's now channeling his considerable energy into tackling HIV/AIDS, which he believes the government is ignoring. He talks at schools, where he uses humor and intelligence and pulls no punches. During his talk he demonstrates how to put a condom on a banana. This he swiftly replaces with a rubber phallus, "because," he explains with a twinkle, "men and boys don't have bananas between their legs. A condom on a banana on the bedside table is not going to protect you!" Of course the kids shriek with laughter.

In 2002, Uys was nominated a national living treasure by the South African Human Sciences Research Council. Tannie Evita also has more than a few fans. She received the Liv-ing Legacy 2000 Award in San Diego by the Women's International Center for "her contribution to the place of women in the last century." In 2005 Pieter-Dirk Uys wrote his autobiog-raphy, *Between the Devil and the Deep—A Memoir of Acting and React-ing*. The book is good but can only go so far in portraying a man and his alter ego, both of whom are larger than life. Here's to you, dahling.

—Karena du Plessis

3

EXPLORING

Even if you don't stop in **West Coast National Park,** consider driving the scenic road that runs through it rather than the R27 to Langebaan. The park is a fabulous mix of lagoon wetlands, pounding surf, and coastal fynbos. On a sunny day the lagoon assumes a magical color, made all the more impressive by blinding white beaches and the sheer emptiness of the place. Birders can have a field day identifying water birds, and the sandveld flowers are among the best along the West Coast. Postberg, the little mountain at the tip of the reserve where ships would drop off their mail on their trip around the Cape, is open only in flower season, which changes from year to year but usually falls between August and October, when the flowers are at their very best. It's easy to run out of superlatives when describing West Coast flowers, but imagine acres of land carpeted in multicolored blooms—as far as the eye can see. If you're lucky, you may catch glimpses of zebra, wildebeest, or bat-eared fox. Accommodation in the park is rarer than hen's teeth, and families book cottages at the little village of Churchhaven here for years at a time. If you really want to spend time in the area, contact **Langebaan Houseboats** (☎ *021/689–9718 or 082/258–0929* ⊕ *www.houseboating. co.za*) to inquire about the houseboats moored in Kraalbaai. Some are superluxurious; others are simpler affairs. Either way, it's a great way to escape. ⊠ *Off the R27, 11 km (7 mi) north of the R315* ☎ *022/772–2144* ⊕ *www.sanparks.org* 🖃 *R66 in flower season, roughly ½ price other times* ☉ *Park: daily 7* AM–*6:30* PM. *Postberg: flower season (usually Aug.–Oct.), daily 9–5.*

WHERE TO EAT AND STAY

$

ECLECTIC

★

✕**Froggy's.** The food at this attractive and unpretentious establishment would be impressive even in a smart city restaurant, but in a town where most people consider steak, egg, and fries to be the height of culinary achievement, it really does stand out. The owner, Froggy, doesn't put on airs. The menu is eclectic—basically it's what Froggy likes to cook and eat. The caramelized-onion-and-Brie tart is a masterpiece, and the Mediterranean salad with grilled vegetables is a Langebaan institution. Other standouts are the Moroccan lamb shank—slow baked with cinnamon, coriander, cumin, ginger, and garlic—and the Thai curries. ⊠ *29 Main Rd.* ☎ *022/772–1869* ☐ *No credit cards* ☉ *Closed Mon. No lunch Tues., no dinner Sun.*

$–$$

SOUTH AFRICAN

✕**Geelbek.** Passionate about food and history, Elmarie Leonard created this restaurant to preserve the area's fast-disappearing old recipes. It's her way of paying homage to the different nationalities that helped shape the West Coast. The restaurant is in an old homestead dating to 1761, when it served as an outpost for people making the hard trip inland. Today the trip is a lot easier, but diners are still thrilled to tuck into Geelbek's venison carpaccio, fragrant Malay curry, and venison pie. If the stuffed harders (mullet) are on the menu, don't hesitate. These fish are filled with cheese, onions, and breadcrumbs, then wrapped in bacon and grilled. The combination is fantastic. If you're adventurous, try the snoek roe, which is deep-fried in beer batter. It's a local delicacy, commonly known as West Coast caviar. This is also a great place for tea. The lemon-meringue pie stands a mile high, and the chocolate cake is delicious. You can sit in the garden or on the veranda and watch the weaver birds go crazy in the nearby trees. ✉ *West Coast National Park, Box 520* ☎ *022/772–2134* ⊕ *www.geelbek.co.za* ✉ *MC, V* ☾ *Daily 9–5*

$–$$ ☶ **The Farmhouse Hotel.** Centered on a restored farmstead built in the 1860s, this hotel has thick white walls, tile floors, and timber beams. Rustic pine furniture and bright floral fabrics decorate the rooms, some of which have fireplaces and views of the lagoon. The hotel's à la carte menu focuses on seafood and Cape cuisine, which is served in the attractive dining room ($) notable for its Oregon-pine furniture, fireplace, and high ceiling. Breakfast is said to be the best in town—an enormous buffet of cheeses, cold meats, homemade breads and croissants, kippers, omelets, good coffee, and a view to die for. **Pros:** great views over the lagoon; relaxed atmosphere. **Cons:** avoid rooms above the kitchen area as they can be noisy; only two of the 18 rooms have air-conditioning; area is very windy—expect a few bad hair days. ✉ *5 Egret St., Box 160* ☎ *022/772–2062* ⊕ *www.thefarmhouselangebaan.co.za* ⟿ *18 rooms* ⚲ *In-room: refrigerator, Wi-Fi. In-hotel: restaurant, bar, pool, laundry service, Wi-Fi, parking (free)* ✉ *AE, DC, MC, V* ⏚ *CP or BP.*

¢   ☶ **Friday Island.** If you like water sports or cycling or are generally active, then this guesthouse is a great choice. It's bright, airy, and right on the beach. Rooms are, not surprisingly, decorated in blue and white and have an outside shower for wet suits, boards, and such. Sea-facing rooms are ideal for families, with two beds downstairs and two in a loft. To top it off, the property is connected to the Cape Sports Centre complex. But Friday Island also has a lovely beachfront bar and restaurant and is a good place to stay even if you don't take to water in a big way. **Pros:** perfect for family holidays; fall out of bed onto the beach. **Cons:** no pets allowed; sports center next door can get noisy during the flower season in spring and the summer holidays over Christmas and New Year. ✉ *Main Rd., Langebaan Lagoon, Box 280* ☎ *022/772–2506* ⊕ *www.fridayisland.co.za* ⟿ *12 rooms* ⚲ *In-room: no phone, safe, kitchen, refrigerator, no TV (some), Wi-Fi. In-hotel: restaurant, bar, Wi-Fi, parking (free)* ✉ *DC, MC, V* ⏚ *BP.*

¢   ☶ **Langebaan Beach House.** On the beach with uninterrupted views of the lagoon and close to the nightlife of Langebaan (such as it is), this comfortable, friendly place even has dogs you can take for walks on the beach. Both self-catering suites are sea-facing and are simply and tastefully furnished, with pine headboards and neutral comforters. There's a clean, unfussy feeling to each suite and a great outdoor area with a built in barbecue. **Pros:** you can't get any closer to the beach; great to be able to do your own thing. **Cons:** each suite sleeps only two people; people can smoke outside so it's not an entirely smoke-free environment. ✉ *44 Beach Rd.* ☎ *022/772–2625* ⊕ *www.langebaanbeachhouse.com* ⟿ *2 suites* ⚲ *In-room: no phone, safe, refrigerator. In-hotel: pool, beachfront, parking (free), no kids under 12* ✉ *AE, DC, MC, V* ⏚ *BP.*

SPORTS AND THE OUTDOORS

The sheltered Langebaan Lagoon is a haven for water-sports enthusiasts, but you don't have to be energetic all the time. There are expansive stretches of beach that are good for walking, sunbathing, and kite flying.

Be warned, however: the water might look calm and idyllic, but it's still cold, and the wind can blow unmercifully for days at a stretch. It's great for windsurfing, but not so great if you want to spend a peaceful day under your umbrella with a book.

Cape Sports Centre (⊠ *Main Rd.* ☎ *021/772–1114* ⊕ *www.capesport. co.za*) has everything you need if you want to kite surf, windsurf, kayak, or canoe or even learn how. You can rent gear or take lessons from qualified instructors, including packages consisting of a week of intensive lessons. Cape Sports Centre also rents mountain bikes.

EN ROUTE

About 20 minutes from Langebaan on the R45 on the way to Paternoster is the **West Coast Fossil Park,** one of the richest fossil sites in the world. It was discovered by chance while the area was being mined for phosphates in the 1950s. Since then, more than 200 kinds of fossilized animals have been collected, including the Africa bear, which used to roam this area. The park has been declared a national monument, and the curators have done much to make the park and information about the fossils as accessible as possible. There are interactive guided tours, cycle trails through the areas, and interesting archaeological workshops for all ages. There's also a children's play park. ⊠ *R27* ☎ *022/766–1606* ⊕ *www.iziko.org.za/iziko/partners/wcfp.html* ☞ *R10 entrance fee, R50 tour tariff* ☉ *Weekdays 8–4, weekends 9–noon; tours daily at 11:30.*

PATERNOSTER

47 km (29 mi) northwest of Langebaan.

Paternoster is a mostly unspoiled village of whitewashed thatch cottages perched on a deserted stretch of coastline. The population here consists mainly of fisherfolk, who for generations have eked out a living harvesting crayfish and other seafood. Despite the overt poverty, the village has a character and sense of identity often lacking in larger towns. It helps if you turn a blind eye to the rather opulent houses on the northern side of the village.

GETTING HERE AND AROUND

Paternoster is about a half-hour drive from Langebaan. Take Langebaanweg out of town until you reach the junction with the R45. Turn left and head northwest toward Paternoster. At Vredenburg the road name changes to the R399.

ESSENTIALS

Hospitals **Vredenburg Hospital** (⊠ *Voortrekker St., Vredenburg* ☎ *022/709–7200*).

EXPLORING

Along the coast just south of Paternoster, the **Columbine Nature Reserve** is a great spot for spring wildflowers, coastal fynbos, and succulents. Cormorants and sacred ibis are common here, and the population of the endangered African black oystercatcher is growing each year. You can walk anywhere you like in the 692-acre park (map provided); a round-trip through the reserve is 7 km (4 mi). It's very exposed, however, so don't plan to walk in the middle of the day, or you'll end up with some serious sunburn. Die-hard anglers and their families camp here during the Christmas holidays and revel in the isolation and abundant fish. The dusty road has no name, but head south out of town and ask directions of anybody along the way—it's impossible to get lost. There aren't that many roads to choose from. ⊠ *8 km south of Paternoster* ☎ *022/752–2718* ⊠ *R9* ☉ *Daily 7–7.*

WHERE TO EAT AND STAY

¢–$

SEAFOOD

★

✕ **The Noisy Oyster.** The seaside shack ambience is a perfect foil for the relaxed beach fare and easy banter from the owners. The menu changes daily depending on what's available, but you could enjoy calamari prepared with Moroccan spices, fish cakes with a zesty pawpaw salsa, and the fresh oysters are legendary. If you don't feel like fish, there are hearty burgers and good pizzas. The wine list is small but adequate, and you're welcome to bring your own without being charged corkage. ⊠ *St. Augustine Rd.* ☎ *022/752–2196.*

$–$$

SEAFOOD

★

✕ **Voorstrand.** A little West Coast gem, this old corrugated-iron shack on the beach stood empty for years, then suddenly metamorphosed into a truly innovative seafood restaurant. It's literally set on the sand, so you can almost hear the ones that got away. Voorstrand serves all the expected seafood and fish, but the Malay-style fish curries and fresh local crayfish are favorites. You could also splash out and try the seafood platter, which has a little bit of everything. Although it's designed to serve two people, there's always some left over. Expect to dish out over R200 when crayfish are in season. ⊠ *Strandloper St.* ☎ *022/752–2038* ▭ *MC, V.*

¢

⌷ **Paternoster Lodge & Restaurant.** This lodge makes the most of the sweeping views of the Atlantic Ocean. The rooms are simply decorated, but who needs artwork when at every turn you catch glimpses of the azure sea and pretty bay? At any rate, the rooms are comfortable, with good linens and firm beds, and—a big plus—they all open onto verandas. The lodge has a restaurant that caters to just about every taste, as well as a bar so you can sip cocktails while watching one of the sunsets the West Coast is so famous for. **Pros:** easy stroll to the beach; kids under six stay free. **Cons:** hold your hat during summer as the wind can blow; rooms are close together. ⊠ *64 St. Augustine Rd.* ☎ *022/752–2023* ⊕ *www.paternosterlodge.co.za* ➴ *7 rooms* ⚄ *In-room: safe, refrigerator. In-hotel: restaurant, room service, bar, beachfront, laundry service, parking (free)* ▭ *DC, MC, V* ⟟◎| *BP.*

ELANDS BAY

75 km (46½ mi) north of Paternoster.

Mention eBay auctions here, and most people will stare at you blankly. But mention the E'bay left-hand break, and you'll get nods of approval and instant admission into the inner circle of experienced surfers, who make the pilgrimage to Elands Bay to experience some of the Western Cape's best surfing.

This lovely destination is at the mouth of the beautiful Verlorenvlei Lagoon. Verlorenvlei (Afrikaans for "lost wetland," a testimony to its remoteness) is a birder's delight; you're likely to see around 240 species, including white pelican, purple gallinule, African spoonbill, African fish

3

eagle, and the goliath and purple herons. Nearby are some fantastic walks to interesting caves with well-preserved rock art that dates back to the Pleistocene era, 10,000 years ago.

GETTING HERE AND AROUND

Elands Bay is an hour's drive from Paternoster. To get here double back on the R399 to Vredenburg, then take the R399 North to Velddrif. You'll join the R27 at a junction just outside Velddrif. Follow the signs to Elands Bay through town and continue on to what looks like a secondary road. It may not seem to have a number, but it's still the R27.

WHERE TO EAT

$$ ✕ **Muisbosskerm.** For the true flavor of West Coast life, come to the origi-
SEAFOOD   nal open-air seafood restaurant, on the beach south of Lambert's Bay. It consists of nothing more than a circular *boma* (enclosure) of packed *muisbos* (a local shrub) and haphazardly arranged benches and tables. You'll watch food cook over blazing fires. Snoek is smoked in an old drum covered with burlap, bread bakes in a clay oven, and everywhere fish sizzles on grills and in giant pots. Prepare to eat as much as you can of the prix-fixe meal (R175), using your hands or mussel shells as spoons. Be sure to try some of the local specialties like *bokkems* (dried salty fish) and *waterblommetjiebredie* (water-flower stew). Crayfish costs extra (R35 for a half order, R70 for a whole one), but don't order it unless you have an enormous appetite. The only drawback is high-season crowding: when the restaurant operates at full capacity, your 150 fellow diners can overwhelm the experience. ■ **TIP→ Ask about the quaint Farm Cottage if you're looking for a place to stay.** ⊠ *Elands Bay Rd., 5 km (3 mi) south of Lambert's Bay* ☏ *027/432–1017* ⊕ *www. muisbosskerm.co.za* ⚒ *Reservations essential* ⊟ *AE, DC, MC, V.*

CLANWILLIAM

46 km (28½ mi) northeast of Elands Bay.

Although the town itself is uninspiring, it's no surprise that half the streets are named after trees or plants. Clanwilliam is at the edge of one of the natural jewels of the Western Cape—the Cederberg Wilderness Area, which takes its name from the cedar trees that used to cover the mountains. In spring the town is inundated with flower-watchers. Clanwilliam is also the center of the rooibos-tea industry.

Clanwilliam was home to Dr. Christiaan Louis Leipoldt, poet and Renaissance man. He is buried in a lovely spot in the mountains a little way out of town; you can visit his grave, which is on the way to the Pakhuis Pass (R364; there's a small signpost). You could also pop into the Clanwilliam Museum *(⇨ below)*, which houses a room devoted to Leipoldt.

GETTING HERE AND AROUND

Driving to Clanwilliam takes close to three hours from Cape Town without stopping, but half the fun is checking out what local farm stands have to offer and stopping to admire the scenery. In spring this trip will take much longer, as you'll likely want to stop to photograph the flowers that carpet the countryside.

VISITOR INFORMATION
In the flower season (approximately August–October), the Clanwilliam Tourism Bureau is open daily 8:30–6. During the rest of the year it's open weekdays 8:30–5 and Saturday 8:30–12:30.

ESSENTIALS
Hospitals Clanwilliam Hospital (✉ *35 Main Rd.* ☎ *027/482-2166*).

Internet Access Saint du Barrys Country Lodge (✉ *13 Augsburg Rd.* ☎ *027/482-1537* ⊕ *www.saintdubarrys.com*).

Tourist Offices Clanwilliam Tourism Bureau (✉ *Main Rd.* ☎ *027/482-2024* ⊕ *www.clanwilliam.info*).

3

EXPLORING
A scenic dirt road that heads south out of town, past the tourism bureau and museum, winds for about 30 km (18 mi) into the Cederberg to **Algeria,** a Cape Nature campsite set in an idyllic valley. Algeria is the starting point for several excellent hikes into the Cederberg. The short, one-hour hike to a waterfall is great, but it's worth going into the mountains for a day or two, for which you will need to book and obtain a permit through **Cape Nature** (☎ *021/659-3400* ⊕ *www.capenature.org.za*) or from one of the local farms, many of which have simple, self-catering cottages on their land.

Fodor's Choice Clanwilliam is close to the northern edge of the **Cederberg,** a mountain
★ range known for its San paintings, its bizarre rock formations, and, once upon a time, its cedars. Most of the ancient cedars have been cut down, but a few specimens still survive in the more remote regions. The Cederberg is a hiking paradise—a wild, largely unspoiled area where you can disappear from civilization for days at a time. About 172,900 acres of this mountain range constitute what has been declared the Cederberg Wilderness Area, and entry permits are required if you wish to hike here.

The Cederberg might be the last place you'd expect to find a vineyard, but that's what makes **Cederberg Private Cellar** so unusual. It's been in the Nieuwoudt family for five generations. When old man Nieuwoudt, known to everyone as "Oom Pollie," planted the first vines in the 1970s, all his sheep-farming neighbors thought he had gone mad. Today, however, winemaker David Nieuwoudt and his viticulturist father, Ernst, are laughing all the way to the award ceremonies. At an altitude of around 3,300 feet, this is the highest vineyard in the Western Cape, and consequently is almost completely disease-free. They don't have to spray for the mildew and mealybugs that are the bane of wine farmers in the Winelands and Constantia. The chenin blanc wins one award after another, and the bukettraube is a perfect accompaniment to South African curries. The exciting CWG Auction Reserve Teen die Hoog Shiraz is made from the upper portion of the best vineyard and coaxed to maturity in new oak, but, unfortunately, this is not for sale on the farm. The farm has self-catering accommodations and is near the Wolfberg Cracks (cracks in the mountain that lure hikers) and Malgat (a huge rock pool), both well-known Cederberg attractions. The Cederberg Observatory also operates on this farm on Saturdays. It's an open-air wonder run by

San Rock Art

The Cederberg has astonishing examples of San rock art and there is a concerted effort to find ways of managing these sites. On your explorations you'll come across paintings of elephant, eland, bees, people, and otherworldly beings that seem to be half-human and half-beast. Some examples are in pristine conditions, while others are battered and scarred from a time when hikers saw nothing wrong with scribbling their names across the art, or lighting fires in the caves and overhangs where the paintings occurred. Luckily, this carelessness has shifted. So, too, has our understanding of the art. For centuries, people believed the rock art was simply a record of what happened during the daily lives of the San, but, post-1970, this began to shift. There's now a belief that the art is much richer and carries enormous spiritual meaning that tells us of the inner lives of the San. The art is riddled with metaphors, and it's unpacking the rich symbolism that poses a real challenge. Drawings of an eland, for instance, are not simply depictions of animals the San have seen or hope to hunt. Rather the eland serves as an intermediary between the physical and spiritual worlds.

passionate stargazers, who give a slide presentation when the weather permits and then help you spot faraway galaxies on their superpowerful telescopes. ■TIP→ **Make sure you call ahead to reserve your space. Tastings occur for no fewer than five people.** ⊠ *Dwarsrivier Farm, Algeria turnoff from the N7* ☎ *027/482–2827* ⊕ *www.cederbergwine.com* 🔖 *Tastings R20* ☻ *Mon.–Sat. 8–noon and 2–4.*

The display is old-fashioned and not particularly well curated at the **Clanwilliam Museum** but still gives a sense of the remarkable Dr. Christiaan Louis Leipoldt. You'll also get a sense of early settler life in the mountains. The wagons, carts, and rudimentary household equipment speak of much harder times when pioneers headed into the high country wanting to farm or escape colonial control in the cities. ⊠ *Main Rd.* ☎ *027/482–1619.*

East of Clanwilliam the R364 becomes a spectacularly scenic gravel road called **Pakhuis Pass.** Fantastic rock formations glow in the early morning or late afternoon. There's even a mountain range called the Tra-Tra Mountains, a completely fantastical name for a suitably fantastical landscape. A steep, narrow road to the right leads to the mission town of **Wuppertal,** with its characteristic white-thatch houses. You can drive this road in an ordinary rental car, but be very careful in wet weather. There are no guided tours, but there is a factory where you can see and buy sturdy handmade leather shoes and boots. Another way of seeing Pakhuis Pass is to take a Donkey Cart Adventure (⇨ *Tours, West Coast, above*) trip down to the tiny remote village of Heuningvlei, a former Moravian mission station. Currently only 20 families live here—making a modest living as subsistence farmers.

The **Ramskop Wildflower Garden** is at its best in August. (This is also when the Clanwilliam Flower Show takes place at the old Dutch Reformed

Leopard (and Sheep) Conservation

Sheep farming in the Cederberg is a precarious business. Not only are the winters harsh, but valuable sheep may be killed by the leopards that live in the mountains. Farmers have resorted to using gin traps to keep their flocks safe, but with devastating consequences for any animals caught in them. Two researchers, Quinton and Nicole Martins, in conjunction with the farmers in the area, were keen to find a solution to this problem. They established the **Cape Leopard Trust** (☎ 027/482-9923 or 073/241-4513 ⊕ www.capeleopard.org.za). The trust aims to track the movement of the predators to see exactly how many cats remain in the Cederberg and to pinpoint which farmers are most at risk. The trust is also working to introduce Anatolian Shepherds—dogs that are bred to bond with sheep and act as their protectors against leopards. Several farmers have already had great success with these dogs. Their flocks are safe, and the leopards aren't at risk of dying an agonizing death in a trap.

church, and almost every available space in town is filled with flowers.) It's a wonderful opportunity to see many of the region's flowers all growing in one place. Even in other seasons the gardens are still quite attractive, but spring is orders of magnitude prettier. ⊠ *Ou Kaapseweg* ☎ *027/482-8000* ⊴ *R12* ⊙ *Daily 7:30–5:30.*

WHERE TO STAY

$$$$
Fodor's Choice
★

⌘ **Bushmans Kloof Wilderness Reserve & Retreat.** Bushmans Kloof is in an area of rich cultural significance and a South African National Heritage site. The stark beauty of the mountains, the incredible rock formations, and the waterfalls, pools, and potholes probably were as attractive to the San of long ago as they are to visitors today. More than 130 San rock-art locations can be seen on a tour with a trained guide, and you can also go hiking, mountain biking, fishing, and canoeing. The reserve used to be an overgrazed stock farm, and every attempt is being made to restore the land to a more pristine state. Only game endemic to the area has been reintroduced, including wildebeest, Cape mountain zebra, eland, genet, mongoose, blesbok, brown hyena, and the endangered bontebok (an antelope species). Freestanding thatch double cottages have all the modern conveniences, and the luxurious suites in the manor house are spacious and stylish. The food is exceptional, including the legendary springbok loin. The attention to detail (flowers floating in the toilet bowl, for example) is astonishing. Koro Lodge is the property's only unit that allows children under 10; it caters to families, sleeps 10, and has children's program's (ages 3–12). **Pros:** guests are able to fly in to the reserve from Cape Town, which takes about an hour; many outdoor activities on offer; stunning rock art on the property; malaria-free. **Cons:** no small kids allowed at the lodge; very expensive. ⊠ *Off Pakhuis Pass* ☏ *Reservations: Box 38104, Pinelands 7430* ☎ *021/685-2598* ⊕ *www.bushmanskloof.co.za* ⇙ *13 rooms, 3 suites* ☕ *In-room: safe, refrigerator, no TV (some), Internet. In-hotel: restaurant, room service,* *bar, pools, gym, spa, bicycles, laundry service, Wi-Fi, parking (free), no kids under 10 (except Koro Lodge)* ☰ *AE, DC, MC, V* ⦿ *FAP.*

$-$$ 🔲 **Clanwilliam Lodge.** In an area known more for its magnificent landscape than its fine lodging, Clanwilliam Lodge is something of an anomaly. Creams and taupe decorate the contemporary, sophisticated rooms, with nary a dried flower or knickknack in sight. The rooms at this lodge, which in its previous life was a drab girls' hostel, range from basic to luxurious. There's a simple hiker's room for those just wanting to crash for the night, as well as family suites and the Presidential Suite, with a four-poster bed and huge bathtub. When the temperatures rise in summer, the pool area, with its bedouin-style daybeds, is a great place to lounge with a cold drink in hand. There's also a treatment room, so after some hard days roughing it in the mountains you can freshen up with a facial and massage. The restaurant has a pizza oven and a nightly buffet that can satisfy even the hungriest hiker. **Pros:** toy box provided for children in the rooms; easy walk into town and to other sites. **Cons:** lodge has an international feel and you could be anywhere in the world; summer heat is a killer. ⊠ *Graafwaterweg* ☎ *027/482–1777* ⊕ *www.clanwilliamlodge.co.za* ⮌ *29 rooms, 3 suites* ⚭ *In-room: no phone (some), safe, refrigerator, DVD (some). In-hotel: restaurant, bar, pool, spa, laundry service, Wi-Fi, parking (free)* ☰ *AE, MC, V* ⦿ *BP or MAP.*

$$ 🔲 **Karu Kareb.** Frans and Beneta Bester are old hands (and some of the best hands) at the guesthouse business. Rooms are in a 100-year-old farmhouse surrounded by high mountains, a crystal-clear stream, and fantastic rock art. Guests can also stay in luxurious tents overlooking the river. The Besters have mastered the art of excellent local cuisine, so guests are in for a real treat; nonguests are welcome as well. Frans does incredible things with a braai or a *potjie* (slow-cooked meat-and-vegetable stew), and Beneta is surprisingly creative with dietary restrictions. She cooks for vegetarians, diabetics, and lactose-intolerant people without batting an eyelid—a rarity in this part of the world. Beneta is also something of a mini–tourism bureau, with tons of information at her fingertips. **Pros:** quiet, cozy, and great for families; in-house restaurant serves delicious food. **Cons:** can get extremely cold and rainy in winter months (June–September); there's a 12-km (7-mi) unpaved road to get to the guesthouse. ⊠ *Boskloof Rd., 13 km (8 mi) from Clanwilliam, Box 273* ☎ *027/482–1675* ⊕ *www.karukareb.co.za* ⮌ *5 rooms, 5 safari tents* ⚭ *In-room: no phone, safe, kitchen, refrigerator, no TV. In-hotel: restaurant, bar, pool, gym, bicycles, laundry service, Internet terminal, parking (free), no kids under 12* ☰ *No credit cards* ⦿ *MAP.*

¢ 🔲 **Traveller's Rest.** If you're on a tight budget, this farm is the place to stay. There are no frills at these basic but comfortable cottages, but the surrounding mountain scenery is just as spectacular as it is at the expensive lodge next door. You can take a guided tour or explore on your own with a booklet (R30) that describes all the rock art on the farm. Owner Haffie Strauss is a mine of information and a force to be reckoned with. During the flower season in spring, Haffie opens her restaurant, Khoisan Kitchen, where she serves typical boerekos, including curried offal, robust stews, *roosterbrood* (bread cooked on the coals),

Rooibos Tea

Chances are you will either love or hate *rooibos* (red bush) tea, which South Africans drink in vast quantities. It has an unusual, earthy taste, and is naturally sweet. People drink it hot with lemon and honey or with milk or as a refreshing iced tea with slices of lemon and a sprig of mint. It's rich in minerals, such as copper, iron, potassium, calcium, fluoride, zinc, manganese, and magnesium; contains antioxidants; and is low in tannin. Best of all, it has no caffeine. Trendy chefs are incorporating it into their cooking, and you might see rooibos-infused sauces or marinades mentioned on menus. Rooibos leaves are coarser than regular tea and look like finely chopped sticks. When they're harvested they're green; then they're chopped, bruised, and left to ferment in mounds before being spread out to dry in the baking summer sun. The fermentation process turns the leaves red—hence the name.

oxtail, and lamb cooked on the spit. Her rich malva pudding is perfect for cool Cederberg evenings, and her ice cream made with homegrown granadilla is sublime. If you want in on Haffie's fabulous cooking, make sure to book well in advance. **Pros:** guided tours of nearby rock art available; cottages have self-catering facilities; very reasonable rates; the owner is a real character. **Cons:** credit cards are not accepted; this is not the Four Seasons. ⊠ *Off Pakhuis Pass* ☎ *027/482–1824* ⊕ *www.travellersrest.co.za* ↯ *16 cottages* ⚒ *In-room: no phone, kitchen, refrigerator, no TV. In-hotel: tennis court, pool* ⊟ *No credit cards.*

SHOPPING

Veldskoen, or *Vellies,* as they're fondly known, are something of a South African institution. All you have to do is think of the singer David Kramer and his signature red shoes to understand the place they hold in most South Africans' hearts. Vellies used to be the preserve of hardy farmers, who would wear these sturdy shoes with socks and shorts in winter, and without socks and shorts in summer. Thankfully, the styles have changed somewhat, and now you can get the softest shoes made to order from the **Strassberger Shoe Factory** (☎ *027/482–2141* ⊕ *www.strassberger.co.za*). The shoemakers you see working here come from generations of craftspeople dating back to when the Moravian missionaries first started shoemaking in Wupperthal.

CITRUSDAL

53 km (33 mi) south of Clanwilliam.

As you might guess from the name, Citrusdal is a fruit-growing town. It sits by the Olifants River valley, surrounded by the peaks of the Cederberg, and is known as the gateway to the Cederberg. For the most part it's a sleepy farming town, but in spring the smell of fruit blossoms as you come over the Piekenaarskloof Pass (also known as the Piekenierskloof Pass) is incredible.

GETTING HERE AND AROUND
It's 45 minutes on the N7 from Clanwilliam to Citrusdal.

VISITOR INFORMATION
The Citrusdal Tourism Bureau is open weekdays 8:30–12:30 and 1–5 and Saturday 9–12:30.

ESSENTIALS
Hospitals **Citrusdal Hospital** (✉ *Vrede St.* ☎ *022/921–2153*).

Tourist Offices **Citrusdal Tourism Bureau** (✉ *39 Voortrekker St.* ☎ *022/921–3210* ⊕ *www.citrusdal.info*).

EXPLORING
After a grueling hike in the Cederberg, there's no better way to relax than at the **Baths,** where hot mineral water gushes from a natural spring. The waters' curative powers have been talked about for centuries, and although the formal baths were established in 1739, there's little doubt that indigenous San and Bushmen spent time here as well. In 1903 the hot springs were bought by James McGregor, and his great-grandchildren run them today. On-site are self-catering facilities and a restaurant. You can also go as a day visitor, but you must book ahead as it limits the number of people at the baths. ✉ *16 km (10 mi) outside Citrusdal; follow signs* ☎ *022/921–8026* ⊕ *www.thebaths.co.za* 🖪 *Weekdays R30, weekends R60* ☉ *Daily 8–5.*

EN ROUTE
Once over the Piekenaarskloof Pass, you'll head toward the small town of Piketberg and enter the Swartland, the breadbasket of the Western Cape. On your left are the Groot Winterhoek Mountains and a road leading to the small town of Porterville. On your right is the village of Piketberg, where you can turn off for **Excelsior Farm** (✉ *Tar road off Versveld Pass* ☎ *022/914–5853* ⊕ *www.excelsiorfarm.com*), a small farm on top of the Piketberg Mountains. It offers day and overnight horseback rides (R300 for two hours, R500 for a full day with picnic lunch, overnight R1,000 for two days' ride and an overnight stay) through the orchards and fynbos-clad mountains, and two simple, inexpensive, self-catering cottages.

RIEBEEK WEST AND RIEBEEK KASTEEL

104 km (65 mi) south of Citrusdal.

Drive through the small agricultural town of Malmesbury and over the Bothman's Kloof Pass to these twin towns named after Jan van Riebeeck, the 17th-century Dutch explorer of the Cape. The towns developed only a few miles apart because of a disagreement about where to build a church. In the end, two separate places of worship were built, and two distinct towns grew up around them.

Riebeek West is the birthplace of Jan Christiaan Smuts, one of the country's great politicians and leader of the United Party in the 1940s. D.F. Malan, prime minister of the Nationalist Party in 1948, was born on the farm Allesverloren, just outside Riebeek Kasteel. This wine estate produces some great red wines, an exceptional port, and world-class olives and olive oil. The *kasteel*, or castle, in question is the Kasteelberg (Castle Mountain), which stands sentinel behind the towns.

Disenchanted city dwellers have been buying up cottages here to use as weekend getaways, and others are moving out to the small towns and commuting into the city. It's not hard to understand why. Children play in the street and people keep sheep in their huge gardens—a far cry from Cape Town life. There are numerous restaurants, some galleries, and plenty of olive products to buy, including excellent olive oils and bottled olives. Huge groves in the area do well in the Mediterranean climate. *(For more on the production of olive oil in South Africa, see the "From Soil to Oil" box, near the beginning of the chapter.)*

You'll hear the distinctive, rolling accent of the Swartland here. Known as the "Malmesbury *brei*," it's characterized by long "grrrr" sounds that seem to run together at the back of the throat. In Afrikaans, *brei* means "to knit" or "temper," both of which make sense when listening to somebody from the Swartland.

GETTING HERE AND AROUND

The Riebeek Valley is just over an hour from Citrusdal via the N7 and R311.

VISITOR INFORMATION

The Riebeek Valley Information Centre is open Monday–Saturday 9–4 and Sunday 9–1.

ESSENTIALS

Hospitals Malmesbury Hospital (✉ *P. G. Nelson St., Malmesbury* ☎ *022/482–1161*).

Tourist Offices Riebeek Valley Information Centre (✉ *Church St., Riebeek Kasteel* ☎ *022/448–1584* ⊕ *www.capewestcoast.org/Towns/RiebMiddel.htm*).

WINERIES

Translated from Afrikaans, **Allesverloren** means "all is lost." The bleak name derives from a story from the early 1700s, when the widow Cloete owned this farm. Legend has it that she left the farm for a few weeks to attend a church gathering in town, and in her absence the resentful indigenous tribespeople set her homestead alight. When she came back to a smoldering ruin, she declared, "Allesverloren," and the name stuck. Today the farm's prospects are a lot brighter. It has been in the Malan family for generations. The infamous D.F. Malan, regarded as one of the architects of apartheid, gave up the farm for politics. Happily, his descendents are doing a better job at wine making than he did at shaping a country's destiny, and their reds are big, bold, and full of flavor. Delicious and packed with rich, pruney, nutty flavors, the port is perfect for cool winter evenings. A restaurant on the premises means you can dine in a beautiful setting. ✉ *R311, between Riebeek Kasteel and Riebeek West* ☎ *022/461–2320* ⊕ *www.allesverloren.co.za* ✉ *Tastings free* ⊙ *Weekdays 8:30–5, Sat. 8:30–2.*

You have to move fast if you want to snap up any wines from the **Kloovenburg Wine Estate.** This family-run farm has many awards under its belt and is probably best known for its excellent Shiraz. In 2005 *Decanter* magazine awarded the 2002 vintage the only five-star "outstanding" honor among 95 other South African Shiraz wines. The extravagant, full-bodied chardonnay is also wonderful, and you may want to nab some of the 2008 vintage while it's still available. The 2006 Eight Feet cabernet sauvignon–merlot blend is a fun but very drinkable testimony to the generations of du Toits who have worked the land: it alludes to the eight grape-stomping feet of the owners' four sons. Don't miss out on Annalene du Toit's olive products. Her young son Daniel is chief taster, and the results are brilliant. It also hosts a quarterly market day when everybody from the area displays their products and you can get a real taste of local produce and home-crafted goods. ⊠ *R46, just outside Riebeek Kasteel as you come down the pass into Riebeek Valley* ☎ *022/448–1635* ⊕ *www.kloovenburg.com* 🖾 *Tastings free* ☉ *Weekdays 9–4:30, Sat. 9–2.*

OFF THE BEATEN PATH

Swartland Winery. Because of its location in the less fashionable part of the Winelands, this large cellar a few miles outside Malmesbury has had to work hard for its place in the sun. Previously a well-kept secret among local cost- and quality-conscious wine experts, it's slowly garnering an international reputation. It is particularly proud of its Indalo range, and the cabernet sauvignon 2007 can hold its own in any company. ⊠ *R45, Dooringkuil, Malmesbury* ☎ *022/482–1134* ⊕ *www. swwines.co.za* 🖾 *Tastings free* ☉ *Weekdays 8–5, Sat. 9–2; cellar tours by appointment.*

WHERE TO STAY

$ 🔝 **Riebeek Valley Hotel.** At the top of town, with a great view over vine-yards and mountains, this small luxury hotel in a converted farmhouse is an oasis from the sweltering Swartland summer heat as well as a winter getaway. Each room has a different color palette: refreshing lavender, peaceful cream, warm rose, and bold red, to mention just a few. In addition to a regular pool, there's an indoor pool so you can swim even if the weather is iffy. A number of spa treatments such as massage and reflexology are also available. The Sunday buffet (R110 per head), every first Sunday of the month, draws crowds of day-trippers. **Pros:** in-house spa treatments available; indoor heated pool. **Cons:** avoid room 8 as it's near the kitchen and can get noisy; entrance hall and reception desk need an upgrade. ⊠ *4 Dennehof St., Riebeek West* ☎ *022/461–2672* ⊕ *www.riebeekvalleyhotel.co.za* 🛏 *23 rooms, 5 suites* ⚒ *In-hotel: restaurant, room service, bar, pool, laundry service, Internet terminal, parking (free)* ☰ *AE, DC, MC, V* ⦿|*BP.*

The Garden Route and the Little Karoo

WORD OF MOUTH

"Don't miss Ronnie's Sex Shop in the Little Karoo. The place is an icon in the area and has nothing to do with sex. Ask at the shop and find out more . . ."

—Selwyn

"I would spend two nights in Knysna versus all the time in Plett. The sanctuary is a must see, and the town is fun to walk around, the views spectacular, and the food was great everywhere we went!"

—Egbentx

"We actually did whale-watching from Plettenberg and had a fab time. We saw many Southern Right whales—some very close—and for me was one of the highlights."

—Allyb

Updated by
Claire Melissa
Baranowski

This region is a study in contrasts. The Outeniqua and Tsitsikamma mountains, forested ranges that shadow the coastline, trap moist ocean breezes, which then fall as rain on the verdant area known as the Garden Route. Meanwhile, these same mountains rob the interior of water, creating the arid semideserts of the Little and Great Karoo. Even within these areas, however, there is significant variety.

The Garden Route, the 208-km (130-mi) stretch of coastline from Mossel Bay to Storms River, encompasses some of South Africa's most spectacular and diverse scenery, ranging from long beaches and gentle lakes and rivers to tangled forests, impressive mountains, and steep, rugged cliffs that plunge into the wild and stormy sea. It's the kind of place where you'll have trouble deciding whether to lie on the beach, lounge in a pretty pastry shop, or go on an invigorating hike. For most people the Garden Route is about beaches, which are among the world's best. Though the ocean may not be as warm as it is in KwaZulu-Natal, the quality of accommodations tends to be far superior, and you can take your pick of water sports.

A trip into the Little Karoo, on the other hand, offers a glimpse of what much of South Africa's vast hinterland looks like. This narrow strip of land wedged between the Swartberg and Outeniqua ranges, stretching from Barrydale in the west to Willowmore in the east, is a sere world of rock and scrub. The area is most famous for its ostrich farms and the subterranean splendors of the Cango Caves, but there is much more for the discerning visitor to see. However, unlike those found on the classic safari destinations, these treasures are not handed to you on a plate. You have to really look. Scour the apparently dry ground to spot tiny and beautiful plants. Or spend time walking in the sun to discover some of the many bird species. A fairly energetic hike into the hills will reward you with fascinating geological formations, numerous fossils, and extensive rock art. You can also just stand still and enjoy the space and the silence. Even if all this leaves you cold, it is still worth the effort to explore spectacular passes that claw through the mountains into the desert interior.

■TIP→ The national parks of Wilderness, Knysna, and Tsitsikamma, once separate entities, are now part of the Garden Route National Park. Each area is a section of the Garden Route National Park by name, but continues to be administered as before.

ORIENTATION AND PLANNING

GETTING ORIENTED

Although it *is* possible to get from place to place by bus, the best way to explore this region is by car. There are two practical routes from Cape Town to Port Elizabeth. You can follow the N2 along the Garden Route, or you can take Route 62, which goes through the Little Karoo. These two roads are separated by the Outeniqua Mountains, which are traversed by a number of scenic passes. So it is possible—even desirable—to hop back and forth over the mountains, alternating between the lush Garden Route and the harsher Little Karoo. The inland border of the Little Karoo is formed by the Swartberg Mountains, which cover much of the interior of South Africa.

Garden Route. This beautiful 208-km (130-mi) stretch of coast takes its name from a year-round riot of vegetation. Here you'll find some of the country's most inspiring scenery: forest-cloaked mountains, rivers and streams, and golden beaches. This area draws a diverse crowd, from backpackers and adventure travelers to family vacationers and golfers. Major resort towns here are Mossel Bay, George, Wilderness, Knysna, and Plettenberg Bay.

Little Karoo. Presenting a striking contrast to the Garden Route is the semiarid region known as the Little Karoo (also known as the Klein Karoo). In addition to a stark kind of beauty that comes with its deep gorges and rugged plains, the Little Karoo has ostrich farms, the Sanbona Wildlife Reserve, the impressive Cango Caves, and even some vineyards.

PLANNING

WHEN TO GO

There's no best time to visit the Garden Route, although the water and weather are warmest November through March. From mid-December to mid-January, however, the entire Garden Route is unbelievably crowded and hotel prices soar, so try to avoid visiting at this time. Between May and September the weather can be very cold and even rainy. But—and it's a big but—it makes all the more cozy the huge, blazing log fires and large bowls of steaming soup that local hostelries provide. And, of course, there are fewer tourists. Even in these colder months it's rarely cold for more than two or three days at a stretch, after which you'll get a few days of glorious sunshine. Wildflowers bloom along the Garden Route from July to October, the same time as the annual Southern Right whale migration along the coast.

The Little Karoo can be scorchingly hot in summer and bitterly cold at night in winter, but winter days are often warm and sunny. It really doesn't rain much in the Little Karoo.

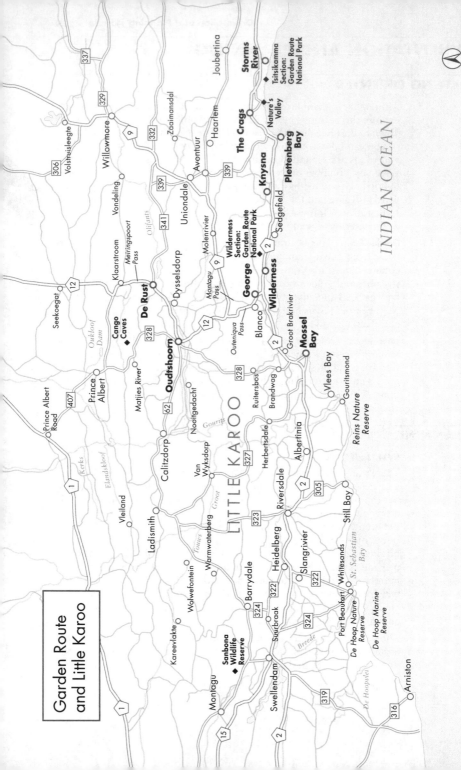

Garden Route
and Little Karoo

TOP REASONS TO GO

Cetacean Central Some of the best boat-based whale- and dolphin-watching in the world can be found at Plettenberg Bay. And although Plett is the best, there are also good trips to be had at Mossel Bay. You can often watch these friendly cetaceans frolicking from the shore, as well. If you really want to feel part of the ocean, your best bet is a kayaking trip in Plett, which might let you get up close and personal with these fascinating creatures.

Turning Wheels One unique way to enjoy the striking scenery of the Garden Route is to take a trip on the Outeniqua Choo-Tjoe, an authentic narrow-gauge steam train that runs between the Transport Museum in George and the Bartolomeu Dias Museum Complex in Mossel Bay. This is the last scheduled passenger steam train still operating in South Africa.

Animal Crackers The Crags area, just outside Plettenberg Bay, is a great place to spend the day with the animals. Visit with rescued primates at Monkeyland, amble through the world's largest free-flight aviary next door at Birds of Eden, and finish off the day interacting with an elephant—and perhaps taking a ride on one—at the Elephant Sanctuary just down the road. Other spots for animal watching include the ostrich farms and Cango Wildlife Ranch at Oudtshoorn and—for big game—the Sanbona Wildlife Reserve.

Soar Through the Air If you just can't keep your feet on the ground, you've come to the right place. Start off with a leap of faith via a bungee cord at the Gouritz Bridge at Mossel Bay, or try a bridge swing instead. If those prove too tame for you, move on to the highest bungee jump in the world (at 700 feet) at Bloukrans Bridge. If you must go higher, leap out of a plane with Skydive Plett. For something a little bit closer to the ground, nothing beats the canopy tour at Tsitsikamma, where you fly through the trees (via cables and a harness) with the greatest of ease.

Hike in Style Enjoy the best of nature in comfort on an escorted, guided, portered, and catered hike, locally called "slackpacking." Try the Dolphin Trail in the Tsitsikamma section of the Garden Route National Park for remote and rugged coastal terrain and indulgent accommodation. The Oystercatcher Trail in Mossel Bay lets you explore a wide range of coastal scenery, from cliff-top paths to long beaches, and the food emphasizes traditionally cooked local seafood. The Garden Route Trail combines long and short day hikes with some paddling through the wonderful wetlands of the Wilderness section of the Garden Route National Park.

4

GETTING HERE AND AROUND

AIR TRAVEL

The only true airport serving the Garden Route and the Little Karoo is George Airport, 10 km (6 mi) southwest of town. George is well served by SA Airlink, South African Airways (SAA), Kulula, and 1time. Flights take approximately two hours from Johannesburg and one hour from Cape Town. SA Airlink sometimes runs one flight a day between Johannesburg and the little airfield in Plett, 6 km (4 mi) west of town. African Ramble runs charters from Plett to Johannesburg and Cape Town, or anywhere you may wish to go that has a landing strip, but more commonly to the Eastern Cape game reserves. These particularly scenic trips start by flying over Robberg and out over the bay (where you may see whales or dolphins) and then hugging the coast up to Nature's Valley before heading inland.

⇨ *For additional airline contact information, see Air Travel, in the Travel Smart South Africa chapter.*

Airport George Airport (*GRJ* ☎ *044/876–9310* ⊕ *www.acsa.co.za*).

Airlines African Ramble Air Charter (⊠ *Plettenberg Bay Airport* ☎ *044/533–9006* ⊕ *www.aframble.co.za*).

BUS TRAVEL

Intercape Mainliner and Greyhound offer regular service between Cape Town and Port Elizabeth, stopping at all major Garden Route destinations on the N2, although they often don't go into town but drop passengers off at gas stations along the highway. Neither of these services accesses out-of-the-way places like Oudtshoorn, Storms River, and De Rust, however. For them you need the Baz Bus, which does go to Storms River and also meets a shuttle in George that will get you to Oudtshoorn. The bus stops at all backpacker hostels along the Garden Route, so you don't have to arrange transportation from a bus station.

Bus Lines Baz Bus (☎ *021/439–2323* ⊕ *www.bazbus.com*). **Greyhound** (☎ *083/915–9000* ⊕ *www.greyhound.co.za*). **Intercape Mainliner** (☎ *021/380–4400* ⊕ *www.intercape.co.za*).

CAR TRAVEL

Most of the towns in this chapter can be found along the N2 highway. The road is in good condition and well signposted. A few words of warning, however: there is a wide shoulder along most of the route, but pull onto it to let faster cars overtake you *only* when you can see a good few hundred yards ahead.

■**TIP**➡ An alternative to the N2 is the less traveled—some say more interesting—inland route, dubbed Route 62, even though some of it is on the R60. From Worcester, in the Breede River valley (⇨ *Chapter 2*), traveling on the R60 and R62 to Oudtshoorn provides a great view of the Little Karoo.

TRAIN TRAVEL

⇨ *For the Outeniqua Choo-Tjoe train that runs between George and Mossel Bay, see George.*

The Premier Classe train line runs a luxury overnight service between Port Elizabeth in the Eastern Cape and Cape Town via Oudtshoorn; you can take the journey as far as Oudtshoorn if you wish. Trains depart once a week. No more than two guests inhabit a four-berth compartment; the train has a dining car and lounge cars. Passengers can also use the Blue Train VIP lounge at Cape Town Station.

Train Line Premier Classe (☎ *086/000–8888 or 021/449–2252* ⊕ *www. premierclasse.co.za*).

TAKE IT ALL IN

3 Days: Choose a home base in the Garden Route: either Mossel Bay, Knysna, or Plettenberg Bay (Plett). You'll encounter wonderful crafts shops and studios in all these towns, so keep your credit card handy. On your first day, take a half-day walk through Plett's Robberg Nature Reserve; along the Cape St. Blaize Trail, part of the larger Oystercatcher Trail, in Mossel Bay; or at Knysna's Garden of Eden. Devote the afternoon to a boat or kayak trip; you may see dolphins, seals, and/or whales, particularly around Plett. Dedicate the second day to whatever activity suits your fancy—lounging on the beach, paddling, horseback riding, or abseiling (rappelling). If you're staying in Plett, you could drive out to Storms River on the third day to do the treetop canopy tour or, for the less adventurous, a tractor tour of the forest. If you're staying farther west, head over one of the scenic passes to Oudtshoorn, visit the Cango Caves, and take a different scenic drive back.

5 Days: Start with the three-day itinerary above. Then spend the next two days at the Little Karoo's Sanbona Wildlife Reserve, where you can take in the big game and lovely flora. Alternatively, you could spend some extra time at any of the Garden Route destinations from the first itinerary; you may want to linger, for example, in Storms River, which will put you right near the spectacular Tsitsikamma section of the Garden Route National Park.

8 Days: Spend the first day or two at Sanbona Wildlife Reserve. Then head east along the R62, stopping for lunch at the Joubert-Tradauw winery, or the Rose of the Karoo, in Calitzdorp, and ending up in Oudtshoorn. The next day, drive a long scenic loop, stopping at wineries and visiting the Cango Caves. Then head over either the Robertson, Montagu, or Outeniqua pass to Mossel Bay, Plettenberg Bay, Knysna, or Wilderness, where you'll have no trouble filling the rest of your time with shopping, beach lounging, kayaking, whale-watching, or any combination thereof. If you have an adventurous bent, spend the last two or three days at Storms River, where you can take the treetop canopy tour, hit a mountain-bike trail, or go for a long walk in the Tsitsikamma section of the Garden Route National Park from Storms River Mouth. Want still more adventure? En route to Storms River, make the world's highest bungee jump at the Bloukrans River Bridge.

HEALTH AND SAFETY

The whole area is malaria-free, the climate is salubrious, and the water is safe to drink. Be careful of sunburn, and take care when swimming in the sea, as tides in some areas can be strong. Don't ever feed wild animals, even cute little dassies (hyraxes) or vervet monkeys.

Most towns have late-night pharmacies, and if they don't, pharmacies usually have an emergency number on the door. Call the general-emergencies number for all emergencies. If you break down while driving, call your car-rental company or the company's designee. You can also call the Automobile Association (AA) for assistance.

Emergency Services Automobile Association (☏ *083/84322*). General Emergencies (☏ *10111 from landline, 112 from mobile phone*).

MONEY MATTERS

There are ATMs all over, except in De Rust and Storms River; the closest ATMs to these towns, respectively, are in Oudtshoorn and at the fuel complex at the Storms River Bridge on the N2. Banks are open weekdays from 9 to 3 or 3:30 during the week and on Saturday mornings.

RESTAURANTS

Most medium-size towns along the Garden Route offer a decent selection of restaurants, and the smaller towns of the Little Karoo usually have one or two good restaurants and a handful of lesser eateries. If you look around in the region, you'll find some fabulous places to eat; usually the emphasis will be on seafood in general and oysters in particular. (Knysna has an oyster festival in July.) The farms of the Little Karoo provide fresh ostrich meat and organic mutton or lamb, which stand up to South African red wines. Ostrich biltong (jerky) is widely considered the best variety of this national treat.

HOTELS

The region would not have such allure if it weren't for its exclusive seaside getaways and colonial manor houses, as well as its more rustic inland farms and national-park log cabins. Many of the better establishments are set on little islands of well-tended gardens within wild forests. Breakfast is included in most lodgings' rates, and if your guesthouse serves dinner, eating the evening meal in situ often has a welcome intimacy after a day of exploring. On the flip side, some cottages are self-catering (with cooking facilities); pick up some local delicacies and make yourself a feast.

Note that the prices listed are for high season, generally October–April. In some cases these prices are significantly higher than during low season, and they may go up higher still for the busiest period—mid-December to mid-January. (If you're traveling during South Africa's winter, don't let high-season prices put you off before inquiring about seasonal specials.)

Keep in mind that although mailing addresses are provided for most of the lodgings below, you'll have a much easier time securing a reservation if you phone or, in some cases, book via the lodging's Web site.

WHAT IT COSTS IN SOUTH AFRICAN RAND				
	¢	$	$$	$$$	$$$$
Restaurants	under R50	R50–R75	R76–R125	R126–R175	over R175
Lodging	under R250	R250–R500	R501–R1,000	R1,001–R2,500	over R2,500

Dining prices are per person for a main course at dinner, a main course equivalent, or a prix-fixe meal. Lodging rates are for a standard double room in high season, including 14% tax.

VISITOR INFORMATION

Most local tourism bureaus are very helpful. In peak season (generally October to April), you may find them open longer than their off-season hours, which are typically weekdays 8 or 8:30 to 5 or 5:30, Saturday

8 or 8:30 to 1 or 1:30. In very quiet periods the staff may close up shop early.

GARDEN ROUTE

The Garden Route means different things to different people. The backpacking crowd loves it for the great beaches, exciting adventures, and parties, whereas more sophisticated visitors revel in the fantastic seafood, scenery, golf courses, and guesthouses and hotels—many with attached spas—where pampering is the name of the game. The Garden Route is also a fabulous family vacation destination, where little ones can frolic on the beach, visit Monkeyland and the Elephant Sanctuary or go exploring in the forest. And almost no one passes up the opportunity to see whales and dolphins. With numerous guided, catered, and portered multiday hikes and loads of pretty day walks, the Garden Route is ideal for keen walkers and hikers.

EN ROUTE

The small town of Albertinia, about 40 km (25 mi) west of Mossel Bay, is an interesting place to break your journey into the Garden Route from Cape Town or the Winelands. It's the center of the aloe ferox industry. The gel of this indigenous aloe has even greater therapeutic benefits than the better known aloe vera. Two factories in Albertinia make cosmetics and health-care products from this interesting plant. **Alcare House of Aloes** manufactures and sells a range of aloe products and offers free tours of the factory on request. There's also a coffee shop. ⊠ N2 ☎ 028/735–1454 ⊕ www.alcare.co.za ☉ Weekdays 8–5, weekends 8–4.

MOSSEL BAY

384 km (238 mi) east of Cape Town.

Mossel Bay's main attractions are an excellent museum complex; several beautiful historic stone buildings, some of which date back hundreds of years (the central part of Mossel Bay is exceptionally well preserved); some of the best oysters along the coast; golf; and good beaches with safe, secluded bathing. The area has most of the very few north-facing (read: sunniest) beaches in South Africa, but be warned: as it's very popular with local families, it is a writhing, seething mass of juvenile humanity every December. Dolphins—sometimes hundreds at a time—frequently move through the bay in search of food, and whales swim past during their annual migration (July–October). You could take a cruise out to Seal Island, home to a breeding colony of more than 2,000 Cape fur seals or, if you're feeling brave, a cage dive to view the numerous white sharks (blue pointers) that hang around the seal colony.

GETTING HERE AND AROUND

Mossel Bay, at the western end of the Garden Route, lies 384 km (238 mi) east of Cape Town along the N2 highway. It usually takes about four hours to drive from Cape Town to Mossel Bay—unless you stop to look at a view, have lunch, or browse in a roadside produce or crafts store.

Of all the buses servicing the Garden Route, only the Baz Bus goes into the town; the others stop at the Shell Voorbaai Service Station, at the junction of the highway and the road into town.

ESSENTIALS

Emergency Services National Sea Rescue Institute (☎ *082/990–5954*).

Rental Cars Avis (☎ *044/695–3060*).

Tourist Information Mossel Bay Tourism (✉ *Church and Market Sts.* ☎ *044/691–2202* ⊕ *www.visitmosselbay.co.za*).

EXPLORING

★ Named for the 15th-century Portuguese navigator, the **Bartolomeu Dias Museum Complex** concentrates on the early history of Mossel Bay, when it was a regular stopover for Portuguese mariners en route to India from Europe. Probably the most interesting exhibit is the full-size (340-foot-long) replica of Dias's ship (a caravel), which was sailed to Mossel Bay from Lisbon as part of the quincentenary celebrations in 1988. If you pay the extra fee to board it, you'll find it all pretty authentic, except for the modern galley and heads. Also here is the Post Office Tree. In the 15th century a few sailors decided that the tree—then a lone tree on a deserted beach on an unexplored coast—stood out sufficiently and left some letters here in an old boot, under a stone, in the hope they would be found and delivered. They were. Pop a postcard into the shoe-shape mailbox and see if the service is still as good. Your mail will arrive with a special postmark. This museum is a terminus for the Outeniqua Choo-Tjoe train (↦ *George, below*). ✉ *Church and Market Sts.* ☎ *044/691–1067* ⊕ *www.diasmuseum.co.za* 🖽 *R10, caravel additional R15* ۞ *Weekdays 9–4:45, weekends 9–3:45.*

WHERE TO EAT AND STAY

$$–$$$ ✕ **Café Gannet.** Tour-bus crowds occasionally descend on this popular
SEAFOOD   spot, located right next to the Dias Museum and Old Post Office Tree, but don't let that put you off. Justly renowned for its seafood—the oysters are extremely fresh and totally wild, not cultivated—it also has good general and vegetarian menus. Try a pizza, or something a bit more exotic, such as deep-fried Camembert coated in cashew nuts served with figs and drizzled with wild-forest-berry coulis, followed by skewered tuna cubes in a curry-infused arugula-and-mango yogurt sauce. The inevitable ostrich is here, served up skewered with port-soaked, sun-dried apricots, caramelized onion jus, and savory rice. In summer sit outside on the shaded terrace or in the refurbished and stylish interior. ✉ *Church and Market Sts.* ☎ *044/691–1885* ▭ *AE, DC, MC, V.*

¢–$ ✕ **Delfino's Espresso Bar and Pizzeria.** Good coffee, yummy pizzas and
ITALIAN   pastas, tables on the lawn right next to the beach, and a fantastic view of the bay and the Cape St. Blaize lighthouse make this a great place to spend a sunny afternoon. ✉ *2 Point Village* ☎ *044/690–5247* ▭ *AE, DC, MC, V.*

$$$ 🖽 **Point Hotel.** Situated next to the Cape St. Blaize lighthouse and over-
★   looking a huge, linear tidal pool, the Point Hotel has incredible views over the ocean and the rugged coastline stretching west. In season (July–October), you may see whales from your private balcony. A neutral

palette in the spacious, comfortable rooms means there's nothing to detract from the spectacular view. The start of the scenic and fragrant cliff-top Cape St. Blaize Trail is yards away from the front door, and the ocean is a stone's throw from your balcony. The tidal pool is public, but it's a short stroll from the hotel. One disadvantage of the location is that on foggy nights the lighthouse emits an aural rather than visual signal; this doesn't happen often, however, and when it does the noise is not that loud and can't be heard at all if you close the door to the balcony. (Most people, of course, leave the door open for the sound of the sea.) ■TIP➔ Ask for a room with a sea view when you book. Pros: unbeatable location; rooms have large balconies; good breakfast. Cons: hotel's decor needs a bit of a revamp; no a/c in the entire hotel; far from town, so restaurant choices are limited. ✉ *Point Rd., Point Village* ✉ *Box 449, 6500* ☎ *044/691–3512* ⊕ *www.pointhotel.co.za* ⤴ *52 rooms* ⚅ *In-room: safe. In-hotel: restaurant, room service, bar, laundry service, Internet terminal, Wi-Fi, parking (free)* ▭ *AE, DC, MC, V* ⦿*BP.*

4

$$$ ▦ **Protea Hotel Mossel Bay.** Just yards away from the museum complex, this stylish hotel, which was refurbished at the beginning of 2009, is close to most of what's happening in Mossel Bay. You can take in the great view of the harbor, beach, and sea while relaxing at the Blue Oyster Pool Lounge. Strange nooks and crannies and yard-thick stone walls testify to the building's status as the third oldest in Mossel Bay (built in the mid-19th century), but rooms are bright and spacious, with exposed-brick walls and decor in tasteful shades of creams and greens. Standard rooms have showers only. Self-catering apartments are as gorgeous as the hotel rooms with two balconies that overlook the water. Pros: location very central for museums, restaurants, and the beach; stylish and modern rooms. Cons: swimming pool is small and overlooked by the terrace; street-facing rooms can be noisy.✉ *Market St.* ✉ *Box 349, 6500* ☎ *044/691–3738* ⊕ *www.oldposttree.co.za* ⤴ *23 rooms, 1 suite, 7 apartments* ⚅ *In-room: safe, refrigerator, Wi-Fi. In-hotel: restaurant, room service, bar, pool, laundry service, Wi-Fi, parking (free)* ▭ *AE, DC, MC, V.*

$ ▦ **Santos Express Train Lodge.** And now for something completely different. In an old train parked on the beach, this lodging uses real train compartments for accommodations. Though the place is not exactly luxurious, the location is hard to beat. Book way ahead to secure the Caboose, which has its own bathroom and a private deck, or if you're on a really tight budget, there's a 16-bed dorm with a self-catering kitchen. The restaurant (¢–$) is almost always busy and serves the usual fish, steak, and burgers. You'll also find a good range of traditional South African dishes, such as *bobotie* (a dish of spicy ground meat with savory custard topping) and *waterblommetjiebredie* (water-flower stew)—don't knock it till you've tried it. Pros: all the cabins face the sea; town center is a 10-minute walk away. Cons: compartments are a bit cramped; you need to supply your own towel and soap; rooms near the bar are noisy. ✉ *Munro Rd., Santos Beach* ☎ *044/691–1995* ⊕ *www. santosexpress.co.za* ⤴ *29 rooms, 1 with bath; dormitory* ⚅ *In-room: no phone, no TV. In-hotel: restaurant, bar, beachfront, laundry service, Internet terminal, parking (free)* ▭ *AE, DC, MC, V* ⦿*CP.*

SPORTS AND THE OUTDOORS
BOATING

For a closer look at the Cape fur seals lounging around on Seal Island or to check out whales and dolphins, take a trip with **Romonza Boat Trips** (☎ *044/690–3101 or 082/701–9031* ⊕ *www.mosselbay.co.za/ romonza*) on a 54-foot sailing yacht. Seal Island trips cost R100 and whale-watching trips R550.

From a convenient location near the harbor entrance, **Waverider Adventures** (☎ *076/335–1515* ⊕ *www.waverider.co.za*) rents kayaks and Jet Skis and arranges parasailing (school holidays only) and various boat trips. Prices range from R80 for a half-hour kayak rental to R300 to R450, depending on how many people, for parasailing.

BUNGEE JUMPING AND BRIDGE SWINGING

The Gouritz Bridge is about 35 km (22 mi) from Mossel Bay. It's only 220 feet high, but it provides a range of wacky adrenaline opportunities. **Face Adrenalin** (☎ *044/697–7001* ⊕ *www.faceadrenalin.com*) offers bungee jumps for R220 and tandem swings for R200. **Wildthing Adventures** (☎ *021/556–1917* ⊕ *www.wildthing.co.za*) operates a bridge-swinging operation. You jump from one bridge with climbing ropes and swing from the adjacent bridge. The first jump costs R180 for a single (tandems cost R280 and triples cost R420). The popular Superman, where your harness is fixed behind you so you start the jump as if you are skydiving, costs R220. The next time you jump, you pay half price if you bring a friend paying full price.

HIKING

The spectacularly scenic cliff-top **Cape St. Blaize Trail** affords memorable views of the crashing waves below. The trail starts at the Cape St. Blaize Lighthouse, at the Point, and then meanders through fynbos and past an interesting cave once inhabited by the San. These caves are considered to be one of the most important archaeological discoveries made in the past 100 years, but you can access them only with a guide as part of the Oystercatcher Trail.

Fodor's Choice ★ The guided, catered **Oystercatcher Trail** (☎ *044/699–1204* ⊕ *www.oyster-catchertrail.co.za*) offers the best of both worlds, providing a multiday hiking experience along the beach and over rocky shorelines while you carry only a day pack. The trail starts in Mossel Bay, with the first day spent on the lovely cliff-top Cape St. Blaize Trail, and continues to the mouth of the Gouritz River. At midday you'll be provided with a delicious picnic lunch. Nights are spent in a guesthouse or a thatched cottage, where delicious traditional food is prepared for you on open fires. Knowledgeable guides point out birds and plants and discuss local history and customs. Walking on the beach can be hard if the tide is in, but most people of average fitness should manage. A typical trip is four days and five nights and starts at R35,450 per person (for 6 to 12 people), but shorter hikes of one or two days can be arranged.

GEORGE

45 km (28 mi) northeast of Mossel Bay, 50 km (31 mi) southeast of Oudtshoorn.
About 11 km (7 mi) from the sea, George is the largest town and the de facto capital of the Garden Route. Although the surrounding countryside is attractive and there is a thriving farming and crafts community on its outskirts, George itself is not particularly appealing unless you are a golfer or are interested in steam trains.

> ## BEER AND CHEESE
>
> If you're into country life, pick up a map from George Tourism at 124 York Street and follow the **Outeniqua Hop**, a fun country route to hop farms (hops are used in beer making), strawberry farms, cheese farms, and numerous crafts outlets.

GETTING HERE AND AROUND

The only true airport serving the Garden Route and the Little Karoo is George Airport, 10 km (6 mi) southwest of town. Most people who arrive by plane rent a car to continue their journey on the Garden Route. Kulula, 1time, and South African Airways all fly to George from most major destinations in the country.

It takes about half an hour to get to Mossel Bay and Oudtshoorn from George, and the roads are good.

Greyhound and Intercape buses stop at George Train Station, and the Baz Bus stops at the McDonald's on Courtenay Street (at Symons Lane).

⚠ The area between George and Wilderness is notorious for speed traps, especially in the Kaaimans River Pass, just west of Wilderness.

Avis, Budget, Europcar, and Hertz all have car-rental offices at George Airport. Europcar rentals include a cell phone.

ESSENTIALS

Airport George Airport (*GRJ* ☎ *044/876–9310* ⊕ *www.acsa.co.za*).

Hospitals George Medi-Clinic (✉ *York St. and Gloucester Rd.* ☎ *044/803–2000*).

Rental Cars Avis (☎ *044/876–9314* ⊕ *www.avis.co.za*). Budget (☎ *044/876–9204* ⊕ *www.budget.co.za*). Europcar (✉ *0861/131–000* ⊕ *www.europcar.co.za*). Hertz (☎ *044/801–4700* ⊕ *www.hertz.co.za*).

Tourist Information George Tourism Information (✉ *124 York St.* ☎ *044/801–9295* ⊕ *www.georgetourism.co.za*).

EXPLORING

The **Outeniqua Transport Museum** is a huge hangarlike building with old steam trains on display. It's a real attraction for steam-train enthusiasts, as South Africa has a particularly good collection of preserved steam-driven rolling stock. This museum is a terminus for the Outeniqua Choo-Tjoe train. ✉ *2 Mission Rd.* ☎ *044/801–8289* ⊕ *www.online-sources.co.za* ☎ *R20* ☉ *Weekdays 8–4:30, Sat. 8–2.*

Fodor's Choice The **Outeniqua Choo-Tjoe,** an authentic narrow-gauge steam train, is the
★ only scheduled passenger steam train still in operation in South Africa.
This aged workhorse used to travel between George and Knysna until
floods in 2006 temporarily closed the Kaaimans River Pass. Early in
2007 a new, more scenic, and infinitely more interesting route was
started and looks set to remain the only route in place. The train now
travels the two hours between the Outeniqua Transport Museum in
George and the Bartolomeu Dias Museum Complex in Mossel Bay (you
can also take the trip in the opposite direction). You may end up with a
soot-blackened face if you succumb to the temptation of sticking your
head out of the window to admire the beautiful Gwaing and Maalgate
rivers as you cross them or the crashing waves on the beaches stretching miles west of Mossel Bay, but it's so hard to resist. It's also fun to
wave at bystanders who gather to watch the immense billows of steam
as the driver obliges keen photographers with an extra blast when the
train passes particularly scenic sections. When weather and vegetation
conditions are very dry, the steam engine poses a fire threat, so a diesel
locomotive is used. Reservations are essential and should be made at
least a day in advance. ⊠ *Mission Rd.* ☎ *044/801–8289* ⊕ *www.online-
sources.co.za/chootjoe* ⊠ *R140 one way, R180 round-trip* ☉ *Mon.–Sat.
Departs George at 10 AM; departs Mossel Bay at 2:15 PM.*

WHERE TO EAT AND STAY

¢–$ ✕ **The Conservatory at Meade House.** This light and airy restaurant is
open only for breakfast and lunch. It serves the usual sandwiches and
salads but is also locally renowned for some unusual combinations.
The omelet with Chinese-style chicken, snap peas, and hoisin sauce is
a new twist on an old breakfast favorite. You'll also find teas, coffees,
and cakes, plus freshly squeezed juices. ⊠ *Donerail Square, 91 Meade
St.* ☎ *044/873–3850* ▭ *AE, MC, V* ☉ *Closed weekends. No dinner.*

$–$$ ✕ **Leila's Arms.** Intended to be an example in sustainable living, this
ECLECTIC friendly and informal restaurant serves fabulous lunches—made mostly
★ from organic ingredients—at a great price. The classic is a baked sweet
potato smothered with creamy chicken, cheese, olive oil, spinach, salsa,
dates, and fresh herbs. There is always a slow-cooked lamb dish, either
curry or *bredie* (stew). The crockery is from a local potter—and you
won't find two matching plates. Leila's is on a farm just outside George;
the turnoff is signposted on Montagu Street about 1 km (½ mi) on
the airport side of Fancourt. Lunch is only served weekdays Tuesday–
Friday. There's also a three-course Sunday lunch. ⊠ *Off Montagu St.,
Blanco* ☎ *044/870–0292 or 084/844–7996* ⊕ *www.leilas.co.za* ▭ *No
credit cards* ☉ *Closed Mon. and Sat. Dinner by appointment.*

$$ ⊡ **Ambleside Country House.** One of the more reasonably priced options
in town, this is a great base from which to play golf. The owner, a keen
golfer himself, can book courses, arrange transportation, and gener-
ally make sure you play as much golf as you can handle. The lodge is
unpretentious without compromising on comfort. The casual lounge,
large garden with attractive pool area, and honor bar create a great
home away from home for weary golfers. Although no dinner is served,
many guests make use of the breakfast room and have food delivered.
Pros: lovely, large swimming pool; all rooms have sundecks. **Cons:**

no a/c in the hotel; no dinner is served. ⊠ *Upper Maitland St., Blanco* ☎ *044/870–8138* ⊕ *www.ambleside.co.za* ⟿ *12 rooms, 2 suites* ♿ *In-room: no phone. In-hotel: bar, pool, Internet terminal, parking (free)* ⊟ *AE, DC, MC, V* ⊺⊙⊺ *BP.*

$$$$ **Fancourt Hotel and Country Club Estate.** If you're one of those people who believe that we were created with opposable thumbs solely in order to hold a golf club, you'll *love* Fancourt. In the shadows of the Outeniqua Mountains, this luxury resort resembles a country club with numerous sports, leisure, and business facilities. Rooms, which were refurbished in 2008, are either in an old 1860 manor house or in villas nestled in landscaped gardens. Whereas the rooms in the manor house have a classical air, the newer rooms are sleek and modern, with cream walls and pale stone finishes. There's an excellent Kids Club, with cold and heated pools, a cinema, and a lounge for teens. Golf widows are well cared for with a luxury spa on the premises and a well-equipped gym and boutique. Of the five restaurants, Sansibar ($$–$$$), with its Africa-theme menu, is the most popular. **Pros:** hotel has excellent green credentials; kids' program will keep them out of your hair. **Cons:** modern estate lacks character; if you don't play golf you'll feel out of place. ⊠ *Montagu St., Blanco* ⌂ *Box 2266, Blanco 6530* ☎ *044/804–0000* ⊕ *www.fancourt.com* ⟿ *92 rooms, 57 suites* ♿ *In-room: safe, refrigerator, Wi-Fi. In-hotel: 5 restaurants, room service, bars, golf courses, tennis courts, pools, gym, spa, bicycles, children's programs (ages 3–10), laundry service, Internet terminal, Wi-Fi, parking (free)* ⊟ *AE, DC, MC, V* ⊺⊙⊺ *BP.*

$$–$$$ **Hoogekraal.** About 16 km (10 mi) outside George, this historic farm
★ sits on a grassy hill with panoramic views of the Outeniqua Mountains and the Indian Ocean. The public rooms are filled with antiques, heirlooms, and some impressive art. Accommodations are in two sections, a building dating from 1760 and a newer one built in 1820. The buildings are full of character and have many lovely old pieces of furniture, but the bathrooms need updating, and some of the rooms are a little musty. Try to get the 1820 Suite, which is roomier than the others. The service is laid-back and friendly, so staying here is more like visiting distant relatives in the country than lodging at a hotel. The owner/manager Colin Bryan is more than happy to discuss the building's history and the antiques that have been collected over the years. Most guests choose to stay for a home-cooked five-course dinner ($$$$), hosted by Bryan and served on fine porcelain at a communal table in the dining room (the price includes wine and after-dinner port or brandy). Nonguests may dine here if there's room but must reserve at least a day in advance. **Pros:** friendly owner and manager; antiques and artwork. **Cons:** bathrooms need upgrading; short on creature comforts. ⊠ *Glentana Rd., off N2 between George and Mossel Bay* ⌂ *Box 34, 6530* ☎ *044/879–1277 www.hoogekraal.co.za* ⟿ *3 rooms, 3 suites* ♿ *In-room: no phone, no TV. In-hotel: restaurant, laundry service, Internet terminal, parking (free), no kids under 13* ⊟ *DC, MC, V* ⊺⊙⊺ *BP.*

4

SPORTS AND THE OUTDOORS

GOLF

Fancourt's Links, Montagu, and Outeniqua golf courses and the public George Golf Club are all regularly featured among South Africa's top 10 courses, and are never out of the top 20. You have to stay at **Fancourt Hotel and Country Club Estate** (⊠ *Montagu St.* ☎ *044/804–0000* ⊕ *www.fancourt.com*) to play on its Gary Player–designed championship courses, Montagu and Outeniqua. The Links, which is open to residents and members, is particularly challenging and was the venue of the 2003 Presidents Cup. Outeniqua and Montagu cost R795 per person per day—but you can play both on one day for that price. The Links is expensive: R1,500. There is also an on-site golf academy.

Expect to pay about R420 in greens fees and R200 for a golf cart or R100 for a caddy at the top-rated public **George Golf Club** (⊠ *Langenhoven St.* ☎ *044/873–6116*). You can rent clubs (R150–R200 for 18 holes) and pull carts (R25) from the **George Golf Shop** (⊠ *George Golf Club, Langenhoven St.* ☎ *044/874–7597*).

EN ROUTE

From George the N2 descends steeply to the sea through a heavily forested gorge formed by the Kaaimans River. Look to your right to see a curved railway bridge spanning the river mouth. This is one of the most photographed scenes on the Garden Route (and was especially popular with shutterbugs when the Outeniqua Choo-Tjoe steam train used to puff over it). As you round the point, a breathtaking view of mile upon mile of pounding surf and snow-white beach unfolds before you. There is an overlook from which you can often see dolphins and whales frolicking in the surf, and if you look up, you may see a colorful paraglider floating overhead.

WILDERNESS

12 km (7 mi) southeast of George.

Wilderness is a popular vacation resort for good reason. Backed by thickly forested hills and cliffs, the tiny town presides over a magical stretch of beach between the Kaaimans and Touw rivers, as well as a spectacular system of waterways, lakes, and lagoons strung out along the coast, separated from the sea by towering vegetated dunes.

GETTING HERE AND AROUND

The Greyhound and Intercape bus services drop you off at the Caltex Garage, on the corner of the N2 and South Street, and the Baz Bus will drop you off at any backpacker accommodation. Many hotels offer a transfer from George airport, but your best bet is to drive yourself, as the roads are good and you'll be able to see a lot more of the country.

ESSENTIALS

If you arrive in Wilderness without having booked any accommodation, the tourist office is an excellent resource. It has binders with photographs and full details of accommodation in the area. Staff will even phone ahead to make a reservation for you at the lodging of your choice.

Tourist Information Wilderness Tourism (✉ *Milkwood Village, Beacon Rd.*
☎ *044/877-0045* ⊕ *www.visitgeorge.co.za*).

EXPLORING

Much of the area now falls under the control of the **Wilderness section
of the Garden Route National Park,** a 299,000-acre reserve that stretches
east along the coast for 31 km (19 mi). This wetlands paradise draws
birders from all over the country to its two blinds. Walking trails wend
through the park, including the circular 10-km (6-mi) Pied Kingfisher
Trail, which covers the best of what Wilderness has to offer: beach,
lagoon, marsh, and river. ✉ *Off N2* ☎ *044/877-1197* ⊕ *www.sanparks.
org* 🎫 *R16.*

WHERE TO EAT AND STAY

$-$$ ✗ **Pomodoro.** Friendly service, great food, and good value are the high-
ITALIAN lights of this Italian eatery conveniently located in the middle of town.
The emphasis is on crispy thin-crust pizzas—the butternut squash, feta,
and rocket (arugula) is a favorite with locals—pastas, and other Italian dishes. Try the slow-roasted lamb shanks or line fish cooked in a
parcel with shrimp and mussels in a creamy fennel sauce. ✉ *George St.*
☎ *044/877-1403* 🖃 *DC, MC, V.*

$$ ✗ **Serendipity.** Start your evening at this award-winning restaurant with
SOUTH AFRICAN predinner drinks on the patio overlooking the river, and then move
inside to a candlelit table to feast on a fabulous five-course menu. The
menu, which changes daily, is imaginative, taking classic South Afri-
can ingredients and giving them an original, modern twist; chef Lizelle
Stolze's passion is evident in the creative combination of flavors and
attention to detail in presentation. Dishes could include perfectly cooked
venison medallions served with a wild mushroom "lasagna" made of
thin slices of *mieliepap* (a kind of polenta) or Cape salmon served with
sautéed niçoise vegetables and hollandaise sauce. Desserts also have a
South African touch, such as Amarula crème brûlée or saffron-infused
milk tart. There are also four luxurious guest rooms upstairs ($$$),
all with river views and a large communal balcony. ✉ *Freesia Ave.*
☎ *044/877-0433* 🖃 *AE, DC, MC, V* ⊙ *No lunch. Closed Sun.*

$-$$ ✗ **Zucchini.** The focus here is on free-range, organic, fresh, and seasonal
SOUTH AFRICAN food. Chances are the salad on your plate has been freshly picked from
Fodor's Choice the organic garden outside. The result is tasty, imaginative, healthy
★ fare that's served in generous portions. Vegetarians won't know where
to start. The menu changes regularly, but think roasted vegetables of
the day served with sweet potato fries, a garden salad, and a veggie
cigar (a golden phyllo-pastry tube stuffed with vegetables and feta) or
the lasagna, layers of grilled vegetables with herb and egg fritters and
mozzarella. There are also homemade pastas, soups, sandwiches, and
a range of salads served either roasted or raw. Meat eaters take heart,
you have not been neglected. Venison *frikkadells* (meatballs) are served
with a buttery potato mash and beetroot chutney, and there are steaks
served with potato wedges or dishes like slow-cooked lamb shanks with
potato mash and roasted vegetables. The setting is a charming, rustic
wooden cottage, and guests are encouraged to linger over their meal.
Zucchini's is part of Timberlake Farm Stall, which has a range of artisan

4

and organic shops and a kiddies' playground. There's a market every Saturday morning, too. ✉ *Timberlake Farm Stall, off the N2 halfway between Sedgefield and Knysna* ☎ *044/882–1240* ▤ *AE, DC, MC, V.*

¢–$ ⛺ **Ebb and Flow Restcamp, Wilderness section of the Garden Route National Park.** This rest camp is divided into the North and South sections. The South section is larger and consists of brick family cottages, which sleep up to six, as well as log cabins and forest huts, both of which sleep up to four. The log cabins are prettier than the cottages, but both are bright and pleasant, furnished in a plain but adequate manner with floral or geometric curtains and upholstery; both have bedrooms, kitchens, and bathrooms with balconies. Forest cabins are smaller but cute. Campsites, some of which directly overlook the river, are set on a wide lawn under trees. The much smaller North section has a few grassy campsites and a dozen *rondavels* (round huts). Two of the rondavels don't have their own bathrooms, but the communal bathroom areas for the campsite are well maintained, clean, and adequate. You can fish, hike, and boat here. **Pros:** central location that's easy to get to; lots of activities on offer. **Cons:** accommodation options are clustered together; rondavels not particularly attractive. ✉ *Off N2* ☖ *Box 746, 6560* ☎ *044/877–1197* ⊕ *www.sanparks.org* ☛ *5 cottages; 8 log cabins; 10 2-bed and 10 4-bed forest cabins; 12 rondavels, 10 with bath; 100 campsites* ⚙ *Inhotel: laundry facilities, parking (free)* ▤ *AE, DC, MC, V.*

$ ⛺ **The Wild Farm.** Horses and cows in the field, a huge vegetable garden, and endless views over the ocean create a sense of space and abundance at this friendly, squeaky-clean hostel set high on a farm above Wilderness. Brothers Riaan and Theo Barnard, both qualified tour guides, offer excursions all over the Garden Route, as well as surfboard rentals and regular shuttles to and from Wilderness and the surrounding beaches. You're welcome to use the well-equipped kitchen or barbecue, though you might want to start the day off with a big farm breakfast for R35. **Pros:** you can pick your own vegetables; there's a fantastic volunteer program run by the Farm, for the benefit of disadvantaged children in the community. **Cons:** Internet access isn't free; you need to be young at heart and adventurous to get the most out of your stay. ✉ *291 Whites Rd., Uitsig* ☖ *Box 366, 6560* ☎ *044/877–070 or 082/838–5944* ⊕ *www.wildfarm.co.za* ☛ *2 doubles, 1 twin, 2 dormitories* ⚙ *In-room: no phone, no TV. In-hotel: bar, Internet terminal, parking (free)* ▤ *No credit cards.*

$$$–$$$$ ⛺ **Xanadu.** Deep-pile carpets, double-volume spaces, spectacular floral arrangements, and voluminous drapes framing the sea-view windows add to the sense of opulence at this beachfront establishment. The classic, over-the-top style—with dramatic shades of terra-cotta and rich vibrant fabrics—tells you you're about to be pampered. Rooms are individually decorated, and all have balconies. The beach is just a short hop from the lawns or the saltwater pool. A small kitchenette means you can prepare a small snack or call for delivery. **Pros:** just a short walk to the beach; bathrooms are modern and large. **Cons:** too far to walk into town; breakfast is eaten communally with other guests. ✉ *43 Die Duin* ☖ *Box 746, 6560* ☎ *044/877–0022* ⊕ *www.xanaduwilderness.co.za* ☛ *6 rooms* ⚙ *In-room: no phone, safe, Wi-Fi, DVD.*

In-hotel: room service, pool, beachfront, laundry service, Internet terminal, Wi-Fi, parking (free) ☰ *MC, V* ⍩⦶ *BP.*

SPORTS AND THE OUTDOORS

Wilderness section of the Garden Route National Park and environs provide opportunities for lovely walks, fantastic paddling, and fishing.

CANOEING

★ Based inside the Wilderness section of the Garden Route National Park, **Eden Adventures** (☎ *044/877–0179* ⊕ *www.eden.co.za*) offers a canoeing and mountain-biking trip (R345), a *kloofing* (canyoning) excursion (R450), and abseiling (rappelling) in Kaaimans Gorge (R345). These are all half-day trips and include refreshments and exclude lunch, but they can be combined to form a full-day trip (R750 with lunch). You can also rent a two-seater canoe for exploring the wetlands (R180 per day). Eden Adventures also runs a two-and-a-half-day guided canoeing and hiking trip in the park. It's fully catered, and accommodation is in either a tented camp or chalets (prices on request). Custom tours can also be arranged.

HIKING

On the five-day guided **Garden Route Trail** (☎ *044/883–1015 or 082/213–5931* ⊕ *www.gardenroutetrail.co.za*) you start in the Ebb and Flow Restcamp and then head east along the coast, taking in long beach walks and coastal forest before ending in Brenton on Sea. The emphasis is on the natural environment, and knowledgeable guides provide commentary along the way. The trip is catered and portered, and you do some canoeing in addition to hiking. The five-day trail costs from R4,600 depending on the number of people; a three-day trail is also available for R3,600. There are also a number of popular day walks, such as a guided forest canoe and walking trail (R220) and a Moonlight Meander on the beach at full moon (R60).

PARAGLIDING

★ Wilderness is one of the best paragliding spots in the country. You can ridge-soar for miles along the dune front, watching whales and dolphins in the sea. If you've never done it before, don't worry: you can go tandem (R450) with an experienced instructor from **Cloudbase Paragliding** (☎ *044/877–1414* ⊕ *www.cloudbase-paragliding.co.za*).

KNYSNA

40 km (25 mi) east of Wilderness.

Knysna (pronounced *nize*-nuh) is one of the most popular destinations on the Garden Route. The focus of the town is the beautiful Knysna Lagoon, ringed by forested hills dotted with vacation homes. Several walking and mountain-bike trails wind through Knysna's forests, many offering tremendous views back over the ocean. With luck you may spot the Knysna turaco, a brilliantly plumed and elusive forest bird also known as the Knysna loerie, or the even more outrageously colored and more elusive Narina trogon.

Towering buttresses of rock, known as the Heads, guard the entrance to the lagoon, funneling the ocean through a narrow channel. The sea approach is so hazardous that Knysna never became a major port, which may explain why it developed instead into the modern resort town it is today, with the attendant hype, commercialism, and crowds, especially in summer. About the only aspect of the town that hasn't been modernized is the single-lane main road (the N2 goes straight through the middle of town), so traffic can be a nightmare. Walking is the best way to get around the town center, which is filled with shops, galleries, restaurants, and coffeehouses. Knysna's main claims to fame are edible and drinkable. The former are its famous—and abundant—cultivated oysters, and the latter is locally brewed Mitchell's beer, on tap at most bars and pubs.

GETTING HERE AND AROUND
If you're traveling by public transport, Greyhound and Intercape buses stop in the center of town, and the Baz Bus will drop you off at any backpacker accommodation. The main N2 highway travels straight through the center of Knysna, so the road can get rather busy in the high season.

ESSENTIALS
Emergency Services **National Sea Rescue Institute** (☎ *044/384–0211 or 082/990–5956*).

Hospitals **Knysna Private Hospital** (✉ *Hunters Estate Dr., Knysna* ☎ *044/384–1083*).

Rental Cars **Avis** (☎ *044/382–2222*).

Tourist Information **Knysna Tourism** (✉ *40 Main St.* ☎ *044/382–5510* ⊕ *www.visitknysna.com or www.tourismknysna.co.za*).

EXPLORING
Knysna Art Gallery is in the Old Gaol, a structure that dates to 1859. As well as constantly changing exhibitions of a high standard, there is a semipermanent exhibit of works by local artists, of which Knysna seems to produce an inordinate number. ✉ *Queen and Main Sts.* ☎ *044/382–7124* 🎟 *Free* ⊙ *Weekdays 9:30–4:30, Sat. 9:30–1.*

★ You can't come to Knysna without making a trip out to the **Heads,** at the mouth of the lagoon. The rock sentinels provide great views of both the sea and the lagoon. Only the developed, eastern side is accessible by car, via George Rex Drive off the N2. You have two options: to park at the base of the Head and follow the walking trails that snake around the rocky cliffs, just feet above the crashing surf, or drive to the summit, with its panoramic views and easy parking.

Unlike its eastern counterpart, the western side of the Heads, part of the **Featherbed Nature Reserve** (☎ *044/382–1693* ⊕ *www.knysnafeatherbed. com*), is relatively unspoiled. In addition to a bizarre rock arch and great scenery, the reserve is home to various small mammals, more than 100 species of birds, and 1,000 plant species. There are two standard trips here, plus more in high season (generally October–April). The morning trip costs R375, leaves at 10, and lasts four hours. It consists of a ferry ride across the Lagoon to the Western Head, a 4x4 tractor ride onto the reserve, and a guided 2.2-km (1.3-mi) downhill walk through the

Reserve and along the coastline. After this there's a buffet lunch under the trees. The afternoon trip leaves at 2:30, costs R260, takes three hours, and is identical except that it does not include lunch.

One of the most interesting buildings in the area stands across the lagoon from Knysna, in the exclusive community of Belvidere. The Anglican **Holy Trinity Church,** built in 1855 of local stone, is a lovely replica of a Norman church of the 11th century. The interior is notable for its beautiful stinkwood and yellowwood timber and stained-glass windows. ⊠ *N2 west out of Knysna to Belvidere turnoff just after bridge; then follow signs* 🕾 *No phone* ⊡ *Free* ⊙ *Daily 8:30–5, except during services.*

BEACHES

Although Knysna is very much a seaside destination, there are no beaches actually in the town—unlike in Plett or Mossel Bay—but there are some fabulous ones nearby. **Leisure Isle,** in the middle of the lagoon, has a few tiny strands.

The beach at **Brenton on Sea,** past Belvidere, is a beautiful, long, white-sand beach on which you can walk for 6 km (4 mi) to Buffalo Bay. It's about a 10-minute drive; the turnoff from the N2 is about 12 km (7½ mi) west of Knysna. ☞ *Lifeguard, toilets, showers, parking lot.*

Buffalo Bay Beach is a wonderful little secret spot, with great walks in either direction—toward Brenton on Sea or into the Goukamma Nature Reserve. The surfing is great, and you can go horseback riding here. ☞ *Toilets, food concession, grills/fire pits, parking lot.*

WHERE TO EAT

Of course there are restaurants that don't serve seafood, but very few of them are in Knysna. It's what the town's all about.

$$ ✕**34° South.** Right on the water's edge in what appears to be a dolled-up
SEAFOOD warehouse, this place gives off a sense of abundance, with shelves, bas-
★ kets, and display stands overflowing with all kinds of delicious goodies. Defying convention, 34° South manages to combine elements of a fish-monger, a bar, a bistro, a deli, a coffee shop, and a seafood restaurant. Choose from the huge array of fresh fish, including sushi, and enjoy your feast while sitting on the jetty looking at the boats. You could also opt for a delicious sandwich laden with avocados and *peppadews* (spicy pickled peppers). Or just fill a basket with delicious breads, pickles, cheeses, meats, and other delights. There's also a good selection of wines and a gift-shop section. ⊠ *Knysna Quays* 🕾 *044/382–7331* ▤ *AE, DC, MC, V.*

¢–$ ✕**Ile de Pain.** Almost every South African you will meet on the Garden
ECLECTIC Route will tell you to visit Ile de Pain. Its stellar reputation is well
Fodor's Choice deserved; owners Liezie Mulder and Markus Farbinger have an uncom-
★ promising attitude to quality that shows in their wonderful bread and pastries, as well as on the short, perfectly executed menu. Local and organic suppliers are used wherever possible, the menu changes seasonally, and everything is made on the premises. For breakfast try a rolled frittata with herbs, leeks, smoked salmon, horseradish sauce, cream cheese, and capers, or brioche French toast with caramelized pineapple, frozen yogurt, and passion-fruit syrup. Lunch favorites include a slice of ciabatta bread with sirloin steak, balsamic caramelized onions,

and mustard butter. Not all the menu items are bread-based; the duck confit with accompanying grain and nut salad is outstanding. There's a smaller branch on Grey and Gordon streets called Mon Petit Pain, which focuses on handheld pocket breads with fillings such as scrambled eggs and salmon. ⊠ *Boatshed, Thesen Island* ☎ *044/302–5707* 🖃 *AE, MC, V* ⊗ *Closed Mon. No dinner.*

$$–$$$ ✕ **Lush.** Depending on how you spent the '60s and '70s, you may think
ECLECTIC you're having an acid flashback as you walk into this stylish, retro-chic eatery with a red, black, and white pop-art vibe. But don't worry: the decor may hark back to a different age, but the food is right here and now, and just a little bit different. The prawn tempura is fried in a pale-green batter made with cilantro and sesame seeds, and dipped in a sweet plum sauce; rose-petal-glazed duck breast is accompanied by goji berry basmati rice, chiffonade vegetables and cherry compote. If you have a really sweet tooth, you may like the chocolate fondant with iced double cream. ⊠ *Sawtooth La., Thesen Harbour Town* ☎ *044/382–7196* 🖃 *AE, DC, MC, V* ⊗ *No lunch.*

$$$–$$$$ ✕ **Zachary's.** Knysna is starting to gain a reputation as a gourmet desti-
SOUTH AFRICAN nation, and Zachary's, at the Pezula Resort Hotel and Spa, about a 10- to 15-minute drive from Knysna, is helping to cement that reputation. Head chef Geoffrey Murray, former wunderkind of New York's dining scene, cites the availability of quality organic and seasonal produce from farms in the surrounding areas as one of the best things about living here. The dining room is stylish and luxurious, with gold, cream, and splashes of orange, amber, bronze, and copper. The food is fine dining with a local flavor, and the menu changes seasonally. Entrées could include dishes like natural, farmed *charmoula* (Moroccan-spiced) Karoo lamb loin with eggplant puree and pine nut and pistachio lemon rice, or grilled prawns with vegetable noodles, lime, chili *sambal* (a spicy chutney-like sauce), and Malaysian *laksa* (fish-and-coconut broth). The Friday night Gourmand set menu is the best way to sample the range of Murray's expertise. There's also a brunch menu and lighter lunch menu. With so much amazing food on offer, you have the perfect excuse to come and eat here at any time of the day, and after your first visit you'll want to. As expected, there's an excellent wine list and a sommelier on hand to make recommendations. ⊠ *Pezula Resort Hotel and Spa, Lagoon View Dr., Eastern Head* ☎ *044/302–3333* ⊕ *www.zacharys. co.za* ⌨ *Reservations essential* 🖃 *AE, DC, MC, V.*

WHERE TO STAY

There are more bed-and-breakfasts than you can possibly imagine, as well as some fantastic guesthouses, self-catering resorts, and hotels, so you will not be short of choices.

$$$ ▦ **Belvidere Manor.** There are lovely views across the lagoon to Knysna,
★ some 6½ km (4 mi) away, at this attractive establishment. Airy cottages face each other across a lawn that slopes down to a jetty. Choose from one- and two-bedroom units, all with dining areas, sitting rooms with fireplaces, and fully equipped kitchens. The manor house, a lovely restored 1849 farmstead, contains a restaurant and guest lounge. In summer, breakfast is served on the veranda overlooking the lagoon. Sizable discounts are offered for long stays. **Pros:** there's a British-style

pub, beautiful views of Knysna. **Cons:** you'll need a car to get around; cottages don't have a/c. ✉ *169 Duthie Dr., Belvidere Estate* ⬧ *Box 1195, 6570* ☎ *044/387–1055* ⊕ *www.belvidere.co.za* ⇝ *30 cottages* ⏚ *In-hotel: restaurant, room service, bar, pool, Internet terminal, Wi-Fi, parking (free), no kids under 7* ⊟ *AE, DC, MC, V* ⎮⚬⎮ *BP*.

$$ ⬚ **Brenton on Rocks.** It's unusual to find a self-catering establishment that is quite this sophisticated and understated with clean lines, black granite, and stainless-steel finishes. The suites and public rooms are spacious, and all share breathtaking ocean views. The two double rooms don't have a direct sea view, though you can see the water from the balconies, and they have only showers, whereas the suites have roomy showers and tubs. A steep, twisty path leads to a small beach that is easily seen from all the suites. All the accommodations have kitchenettes, but there are also two well-equipped communal kitchens (plus barbecues) for preparing meals, which you can then serve in the big sea-view dining room or on the veranda. It's a bit like having your own beach house. The house next door, which has been redecorated and has almost as good a view, is a great bargain for families. **Pros:** close proximity to the sea, with private beach; a restaurant nearby for convenience. **Cons:** standard double rooms have limited views and no bathtubs; no Wi-Fi. ✉ *276 Steenbras St., Brenton on Sea* ⬧ *Box 951, 6570* ☎ *044/381–0489 or 083/249–3644* ⊕ *www.brentononrocks.co.za* ⇝ *2 rooms, 5 suites, 1 4-bed house* ⏚ *In-room: safe, kitchen. In-hotel: pool, beachfront, laundry facilities, Internet terminal, parking (free)* ⊟ *AE, DC, MC, V*.

$$ ⬚ **Cuningham's Island Guest House.** This casual beach house—okay, it's not actually on the beach, but it feels like it is—gets many return guests. Decorated with light lime-washed pine and wicker furnishings, it has an easy flow from the breakfast room to the sunny pool area. Owner Tim Cuningham will help make arrangements for golf and can provide plenty of advice on other activities, too. Bathrooms don't have tubs, but the generously proportioned shower stalls make up for that. **Pros:** you can go for walks on Leisure Island, a lovely well-established garden on the property. **Cons:** small pool; no bathtubs. ✉ *Kingsway Rd. and Church St., Leisure Isle* ⬧ *Box 3420, 6570* ☎ *044/384–1319* ⊕ *www.islandhouse.co.za* ⇝ *7 rooms* ⏚ *In-room: no phone. In hotel: bar, pool, laundry service, Wi-Fi, parking (free), no kids under 10* ⊟ *AE, DC, MC, V* ⎮⚬⎮ *BP*.

$$ ⬚ **Lightleys Holiday Houseboats.** For a sense of freedom and adventure,
Fodor's Choice rent one of these fully equipped houseboats and cruise the lagoon.
★ The inside is compact, light, and bright, and outside there's an ever-changing vista of lagoon, forest, and mountain. This is self-catering at its very best. A four-berth boat costs R985 per day for two people and R1,895 for four; a six-berth boat costs about R2,695 per day. The longer you stay the cheaper it gets. If you don't require fancy cooking, you can arrange to pick up meals or picnic baskets from the base or have them delivered to you at a mooring of your choice. Or you can just hop on a jetty and take your pick of Knysna's restaurants. **Pros:** barbecue facilities on each boat; bathrooms at the marina are good. **Cons:** you have to return to the marina every morning to repower the

4

boat; where you can go in the lagoon depends on the tides. ⬧ *Box 863,
6570* ☎ *044/386–0007* ⊕ *www.houseboats.co.za* ⬧ *9 4-berth boats, 5
6-berth boats* ⬧ *In-room: kitchen* ⊟ *MC, V.*

$$$$
Fodor's Choice
★
⬧ **Phantom Forest Lodge.** On a private 450-acre nature reserve, this stunning lodge is built from sustainable natural materials. Accommodations are in luxury tree houses, and the living areas are joined by wooden walkways to protect the undergrowth. Though the original suites have natural tones and wood with coir (coconut fiber used to make doormats, etc.) finishes, newer rooms are decorated in a vibrant North African style. Of the two restaurants, the funky, colorfully decorated Chutzpah ($$$$) focuses on North African/Moroccan food, with tasty *tagines* (meat stews) and couscous in a variety of guises. Forest Boma ($$$$) is a more romantic setting and produces contemporary classical cuisine with a local flavor, such as peppered springbok loin with asparagus, garlic mashed potatoes, and berry jus, or roasted butternut-squash tortellini with apple, asparagus, and fennel salad. Desserts might include a fig, passion-fruit, and browned-butter pie with chili and vanilla ice cream. Service is outstanding. Nonguests can book a table at either place for dinner. **Pros:** spacious and luxurious bathrooms, with underfloor heating; lodge has a secluded feel although it's in the center of Knysna; food and service are excellent. **Cons:** lodge is up a steep hill so you need to be driven back and forth by jeep; not all the rooms have views of the lagoon as there are trees in the way.⬧ *Phantom Pass, Box 3051* ☎ *044/386–0046* ⊕ *www.phantomforest.com* ⬧ *14 suites* ⬧ *In-room: no TV, refrigerator, safe. In-hotel: 2 restaurants, bar, pool, gym, spa, bicycles, laundry service, Wi-Fi, parking (free), no kids under 12* ⊟ *AE, DC, MC, V* ⦿*MAP.*

$$$–$$$$
★
⬧ **St. James of Knysna.** This elegant lodging is right on the edge of Knysna Lagoon. Outdoors you can enjoy a landscaped formal garden with tranquil koi ponds and a private pier with free use of canoes or fishing equipment. Indoors the setting is light and bright, with some lovely antiques. Most of the individually decorated rooms have uninterrupted views of the water. Bathrooms range from Victorian fantasies to a bricktone retreat with a glass wall that leads to a private leafy garden with an outside shower. **Pros:** some rooms are enormous, and all are decorated individually; views of the lagoon are stunning; rooms have a/c, which you'll appreciate in February. **Cons:** old-fashioned decor; swimming pool is on the small side. ⬧ *The Point, Main St.* ⬧ *Box 1242, 6570* ☎ *044/382–6750* ⊕ *www.stjames.co.za* ⬧ *2 rooms, 13 suites* ⬧ *In-room: safe, refrigerator. In-hotel: restaurant, room service, bar, pools, laundry service, Internet terminal, Wi-Fi, parking (free), no kids under 12* ⊟ *AE, DC, MC, V* ⦿*BP.*

SPORTS AND THE OUTDOORS
BOATING
In addition to running the ferry to the nature reserve, the **Featherbed Company** (⬧ *Ferry Terminus, Remembrance Ave.* ☎ *044/382–1693* ⊕ *www. knysnafeatherbed.com*) operates sightseeing boats on the lagoon (trips start at R75 per person), as well as a Mississippi-style paddle steamer that does lunch and dinner cruises.

★ **Springtide Charters** (✉ *Knysna Quays* ☎ *082/470–6022* ⊕ *www.spring-tide.co.za*) operates a luxury 50-foot sailing yacht for scenic cruises on the lagoon and through the Heads (weather permitting). You can have breakfast, lunch, or a romantic dinner on board—or even spend the night. The boat takes a maximum of 12 passengers, and dinner and overnight trips are limited to one party with a maximum of four people. Rates start at about R390 per person for a two-hour sail or R590 for a three-hour trip with snacks.

GOLF

Perched on the cliff top of the Eastern Head, the challenging 18-hole **Pezula Championship Golf Course** (✉ *Lagoon View Dr., Eastern Head* ☎ *044/302–5300* ⊕ *www.pezula.com*) is one of South Africa's most scenic courses, designed by Ronald Fream and David Dale. It costs R695–R795 per person, including a compulsory golf cart. Also available are a comfortable clubhouse with a great restaurant and lessons from resident pros.

HIKING

The two-day **Harkerville Trail** (✉ *N2, 15 km [9 mi] east of Knysna*) passes through the indigenous forests, pine plantations, and "islands" of fynbos, as well as fairly taxing sections on the coast. (This is not a beginner's trail.) Homesick Californians can hug a familiar tree in a small stand of huge redwoods (*Sequoia sempervirens*), planted as part of a forestry experiment years ago. Overnight accommodation is in a hut with beds and mattresses, water, and firewood, but you'll need to bring your own bedding and food provisions. The trail costs R100 per person. For more information, contact **SANParks** (☎ *044/302–5600*).

If you'd like to sample the Harkerville Forest but don't want to commit to a strenuous, two-day hike, try the easy stroll in the **Garden of Eden.** The short trail goes into the forest on a wheelchair-friendly wooden boardwalk. You'll see some big old trees, plus tables where you can picnic. The kiosk at the Garden of Eden is open daily 7:30–4, and entry is R6 per person. Contact **SANParks** (☎ *044/302 5600*) for more information.

Diepwalle Elephant Walk (✉ *Off N2, Uniondale Road, Diepwalle Forest Estate, 24 km [15 mi] east of Knysna*) is a lovely forest walk that's about 20 km (12 mi) long. It takes six to seven hours to walk but has been split up into three shorter routes of about two to three hours each. Entrance is free, except on school holidays when it is R14. For more information, contact **SANParks** (☎ *044/302–5600*).

If you don't fancy heading off on your own, take a guided walk through the area with **Knysna Forest Tours** (☎ *044/382–6130* ⊕ *www.knysna-foresttours.co.za*). Prices are about R350 for a half day and R450 for a full day including lunch.

MOUNTAIN BIKING

★ The Garden Route is ideal for mountain biking. There are four circular trails of varying length and difficulty at **Harkerville** (✉ *N2, 15 km [9 mi] east of Knysna*), starting and ending at the Garden of Eden if you bring your own bike; at the Outeniqua Biking Trail office if you rent one. All the trails are great, but the last 6 km (4 mi) of the Petrus se Brand

Trail is widely considered to be the most fun (but not challenging) piece of single track in South Africa. Unlike the others, Petrus se Brand is not circular; it can be done either way between Diepwalle and Garden of Eden. It's tight and twisty, and you'll zip downhill (if you start at Diepwalle) over the springy forest floor, dodging enormous trees. You can rent bikes (R125) from **Outeniqua Biking Trails** (⊠ *Harkerville* ☎ *044/532–7644 or 083/252–7997*), which is conveniently located right on the forest edge and close to the trails. The SANParks entrance fee is R25.

PLETTENBERG BAY

32 km (20 mi) east of Knysna.

Plettenberg Bay is South Africa's premier beach resort, as the empty houses on Beachy Head Road (known as Millionaires' Mile) during the 11 months when it's not beach season will attest. But in December the hordes with all their teenage offspring arrive en masse. Even then you can find yourself a stretch of lonely beach if you're prepared to walk to the end of Keurboomstrand. Plett, as it is commonly known, is one of the best places in the world to watch whales and dolphins. Boat-based trips are run from Central Beach, as are sea-kayaking trips, which, although loads of fun, are not quite as efficient as the big motorboats.

GETTING HERE AND AROUND

There is an airport in Plett, but it's not currently in operation. There's no public transport to and around Plett, so your best bet is renting a car and driving yourself.

The Greyhound and Intercape bus services will drop you off at the Shell Ultra City gas station, just off the N2 in Marine Way, 2 km (1.2 mi) from the city center. The Baz Bus will drop you off at backpacker accommodation in the area.

ESSENTIALS

Emergency Services **National Sea Rescue Institute** (☎ *082/990–5975*).

Hospitals **Plettenberg Bay Medi-Clinic** (⊠ *Muller St., Plettenberg Bay* ☎ *044/501–5100*).

Rental Cars **Avis** (☎ *044/533–1315*). **Budget** (☎ *044/533–1858*).

Tourist Information **Plettenberg Bay Tourism Association** (⊠ *Shop 35, Melville's Corner, Marine Dr. and Main St.* ☎ *044/533–4065* ⊕ *www.plettenbergbay. co.za*).

EXPLORING

It's fun to take a tour of the **Jacks Jungle Juice** *mampoer* (moonshine) distillery, located at the Buffalo Hills Game Reserve and Lodge. You can see how mampoer is made, and taste several mampoer-based liqueurs. ⊠ *Stofpad, Wittedrif* ☎ *044/535–9739* ☜ *Free* ☉ *Weekdays 9–3.*

BEACHES

Plett presides over a stretch of coastline that has inspired rave reviews since the Portuguese first set eyes on it in 1497 and dubbed it *bahia formosa* (the beautiful bay). Three rivers flow into the sea here, the most spectacular of which—the Keurbooms—backs up to form a large lagoon. For swimming, surfing, sailing, hiking, and fishing you can't do much better than Plett, although the water is still colder than it is around Durban and in northern KwaZulu-Natal.

Sadly, Lookout Beach, Plett's flagship Blue Flag beach (indicating high environmental standards) disappeared when the mouth of the lagoon shifted.

⚠ **Keep in mind that the beach facilities (i.e., lifeguards, food concession, etc.) are available only during the summer months (November–April).**

All the dolphin-watching boats and kayak trips leave from **Central Beach.** A constant stream of tenders going out to the fishing boats moored in the bay makes this area quite busy, but it's still a great spot. Just keep away from the boat-launching area and swim in the southern section. ☞ *Lifeguard, toilets, showers, food concession, grills/fire pits, parking lot.*

Just on the other side of the Beacon Isle, the unmissable hotel at the end of the tombolo (a sand spit linking the island to the mainland), is **Robberg Beach,** a great swimming beach that continues in a graceful curve all the way to Robberg Peninsula. You can get pretty good sightings of dolphins and whales just behind the back break. ☞ *Lifeguard, toilets, showers, food concession, parking lot.*

Keurboomstrand is about 10 km (6 mi) from Plett—right on the eastern edge of the bay. If you're fit, you can walk all the way from here to Nature's Valley, but you need to watch both the tides and the steep, rocky sections. It's best to ask locals before tackling this. Even if you're not fit, you can still walk about a mile down the beach, relax for a while, and then walk back. ☞ *Lifeguard, toilets, showers, food concession, grills/fire pits, parking lot.*

WHERE TO EAT

Plett has plenty of fabulous places to eat and overnight, although dining options are better in Knysna.

$–$$ ✕ **Cornuti Al Mare.** The blue and white tiles on the facade of this popu-
ITALIAN lar, casual Italian eatery—a favorite with locals that's usually pretty full—give the place a beach-house feel. Try the pastas or the thin crust wood-fired pizzas; the potato pizza is so much tastier than it sounds. Salads, seafood, and steaks round out the menu. In summer, get here early to get a seat on the veranda. ⊠ *Oddlands and Perestrello Sts.* ☎ *044/533-1277* ⚱ *Reservations not accepted* ▤ *DC, MC, V.*

$–$$ ✕ **Fushi & BoMa.** Plett's slickest, sleekest eatery is all clean surfaces and
ASIAN classical lines. Start with a cocktail and Asian snacks at BoMa, the alfresco terrace, then move into the main restaurant for dinner. In addition to sushi, there are some fabulously named fusion main courses, such as the Angry Samurai (slow-braised chili-and-garlic lamb with lentil pilaf and cucumber yogurt), Sideways into the Sea (tempura-style softshell crab), or Field of Enchantment (Nepalese-style vegetable curry). The wasabi crème brûlée is a new twist on an old favorite. Service is slick, there's a good wine list, and prices are surprisingly reasonable. The BoMa also serves light meals and a popular brunch on Sundays, and the Chef's Bar downstairs is open until late. ⊠ *Upper Deck, Marine Dr.* ☎ *044/533-6497* ▤ *AE, DC, MC, V.*

¢–$ ✕ **Plett Ski Boat Club.** Want to know a secret? Plett fisherfolk, ski-boat
SEAFOOD   skippers, surfers, kayak operators, and other locals frequent this very, very casual eatery. It's right on the beach where the ski boats launch, so there's a great view—especially from the outside tables. It offers really good value for the money: well-cooked, fresh but not fancy seafood, the usual burgers and fries, and full breakfasts. Many locals can be reliably tracked down to the popular bar on weekday afternoons—especially if there is a rugby match on TV. ⊠ *Central Beach* ☎ *044/533–4147* ⚴ *Reservations not accepted* ☰ *AE, DC, MC, V* ⊗ *No dinner.*

WHERE TO STAY

$$ 🏨 **Bitou River Lodge.** Some places just seem to get everything right. This
Fodor's Choice   lovely, quiet, restful B&B has a wonderful location on the bank of
★   the Bitou River, about 3 km (2 mi) upstream from the lagoon. Rooms overlook a pretty garden and a quiet bird-rich and lily-filled pond. The decor is understated and soothing, with neutral pastels dominating. Breakfasts are delicious affairs with freshly baked breads, muffins, and other goodies, in addition to the usual fruit, cereal, and eggs. Bitou feels like it's in the middle of nowhere, but it's only a 10-minute drive from the center of town. Don't pass up the opportunity to explore the river in one of the available canoes. **Pros:** beautiful river running past the property; owners are friendly and helpful. **Cons:** no a/c in the rooms; it's a 10-minute drive to the nearest restaurant. ⊠ *About 3 km (2 mi) on the R340 to Wittedrif (off the N2)* ⊡ *Box 491, 6600* ☎ *044/535–9577 or 082/978–6164* ⊕ *www.bitou.co.za* ⟿ *5 rooms* ⚹ *In-room: no phone, refrigerator. In-hotel: pool, laundry service, Wi-Fi, parking (free), no kids under 12* ☰ *MC, V* ⦿ *BP.*

$$$ 🏨 **Buffalo Hills Game Reserve and Lodge.** Pockets of indigenous bush and tracts of fynbos alternate with old farmland on this fun property about 15 minutes outside Plett. It's not Mpumalanga—or even the Karoo or Eastern Cape—but it's a great place to see a variety of game, including buffalo and rhino. In this warm, friendly place, evening meals are taken around an enormous table, and outrageous stories are told. Try the game walk or even a multiday hike into the hills. Even little ones can do short game walks near the lodge at this child-friendly establishment. The rooms are in an old farmhouse, and there are also en suite safari-style tents scattered around—some near the farmhouse and others across the river. The price includes game drives and walks but not lunch, as most guests choose to spend the middle of the day in Plett, where there are loads of restaurants. For R3,950, the fabulous three-day special includes lodging, breakfast and dinner, game drives, walks, a tour of the on-site Jacks Jungle Juice distillery, and four activities from a list of 26 of the most fun things to do in and around Plett. **Pros:** you can watch animals from the veranda; it's sociable. **Cons:** rooms don't have a/c; range of animals is not on the same scale as the larger reserves. ⊠ *Stofpad, Wittedrif* ⊡ *Box 1321, 6600* ☎ *044/535–9739* ⊕ *www.buffalohills.co.za* ⟿ *6 rooms, 9 tented rooms, 1 cottage* ⚹ *In-room: no phone, no TV. In-hotel: bar, pool, laundry service, Internet terminal, parking (free)* ☰ *AE, DC, MC, V* ⦿ *MAP.*

$$$ 🏨 **The Grand Café and Rooms.** Although the entrance is on the town's main street, walking into the Grand is like walking into a different

world. The owner describes the decor as "monastery meets bordello," and this seems apt: think dark, smooth walls with rounded arches, large black-and-white prints on the walls, dim lighting, mismatched boho-chic leopard print–and-brocade sofas, ornate fireplaces, fresh flowers everywhere, and huge silver candelabra. And that's just the reception areas. The rooms are just as fabulous. All have private entrances, and the beds are extra high and extra large, with percale cotton linen and goose-down pillows. Bathtubs placed in front of French windows have amazing views of the ocean and mountains. It doesn't get more eclectic and stylish than this. The restaurant ($$$), which is open to nonguests, serves bistro classics and seafood. It's on the expensive side, but you really come here for the atmosphere. **Pros:** central location; unique, quirky decor. **Cons:** rooms can be a bit dark; it's expensive. ⊠ *27 Main Rd. 6600* ☎ *044/533–3301* ⊕ *www.thegrand.co.za* ⇨ *7 rooms* ⌂ *In-room: no phone, safe, DVD, Wi-Fi. In-hotel: restaurant, pool, laundry service, Internet terminal, parking (free), no kids under 16* ⊟ *AE, DC, MC, V* ⦿ *CP.*

$$$–$$$$
★
🖽 **Hunter's Country House.** Just 10 minutes from town, this tranquil property is set amid gardens that fall away into a forested valley. The heart of the lodge is an old farmstead, a lovely thatch building with low beams and large fireplaces. Guest rooms are in individual white thatch cottages, each with its own fireplace and veranda. Three suites have private plunge pools. Tasteful antiques grace the rooms, and claw-foot tubs are the centerpiece of many of the gigantic bathrooms. Service is outstanding. Most guests eat at the hotel's excellent table d'hôte restaurant ($$$$), which brings a French touch to local South African produce. Reservations are essential for nonguests. There's also the option of eating at Zinzi's ($$), a separate restaurant on the grounds. It's part of Tsala Treetop Lodge, but it's open to Hunter's Country House guests, too. The Summer House, in the garden, is open for teas and lunches in summer. The lodge is very child-friendly, with facilities for both little ones and teens, making it one of the few places where you don't have to sacrifice sophistication for family accommodations. **Pros:** you have a choice of three excellent restaurants; breakfasts are sublime; complimentary wine is a nice touch. **Cons:** atmosphere is quite formal; 10-minute drive from town. ⊠ *Off N2, between Plettenberg Bay and Knysna* ⌂ *Box 454, 6600* ☎ *044/501–1111* ⊕ *www.hunter-hotels.com* ⇨ *18 suites* ⌂ *In-room: safe. In-hotel: 2 restaurants, bar, pool, children's programs, laundry service, Internet terminal, Wi-Fi, parking (free)* ⊟ *AE, MC, V* ⦿ *BP.*

¢–$
🖽 **Nothando Backpackers.** This always-buzzing, warm, friendly hostel with some private rooms is light and bright and conveniently located near the middle of town. It's easy to find a sunny or shady spot in the garden to just relax with a book, and the lively bar is a great place to share adventures come evening. All in all, it's an excellent value and the private rooms offer a touch of affordable luxury. There's an information desk, and staff is happy to make recommendations and reservations, as well as drop you off at adventure activities like bungee jumping or attractions such as Monkeyland. **Pros:** it's great value in a great location; staff is helpful. **Cons:** Internet access is not free; it's a 20-minute

4

walk to the beach. ⊠ *5 Wilder St.* ☎ *044/533–0220* ⊕ *www.nothando. com* ↘ *8 rooms, 6 with bath; 1 dormitory* ♿ *In-room: no phone, no TV (some). In-hotel: bar, laundry service, Internet terminal, parking (free)* ▤ *MC, V*

$$$$ ☆ **Plettenberg.** High on a rocky point in Plettenberg Bay, this luxury hotel has unbelievable views of the bay, the Tsitsikamma Mountains, and Keurbooms Lagoon; miles of magnificent beach; and, in season, whales frolicking just beyond the waves. Built around an 1860 manor house, the hotel is light and bright, decorated in shades of white and blue. Service is wonderfully attentive, with a front-desk staff that tries to anticipate your every need. Even if you don't stay here, treat yourself to lunch on the hotel terrace. Diners sit under large fabric umbrellas and look out over a pool that seems to extend right into the incredible views. The lunch menu offers light meals, salads, and sandwiches. Dinner in The Sand ($$; reservations essential) is a fancier affair, focusing on local meat and seafood, and you can have a romantic dinner for two in the private dining room in the cellar for no extra charge. Villas are self-catering. **Pros:** watch dolphins frolicking from your room; walk down to the beach in minutes; the view from the breakfast terrace is incredible. **Cons:** standard rooms are small; some rooms look out onto the car park. ⊠ *Lookout Rocks* ✉ *Box 719, 6600* ☎ *044/533–2030* ⊕ *www. plettenberg.com* ↘ *24 rooms, 12 suites, 2 villas* ♿ *In-room: kitchen (some), refrigerator, Wi-Fi. In-hotel: restaurant, bar, pools, spa, laundry service, parking (free), no kids under 12* ▤ *AE, DC, MC, V* ¶◎¶ *BP.*

$$$$ ☆ **Plettenberg Park.** The setting of this stylish, minimalist lodge—in splendid isolation on a cliff top in a private nature reserve on the western (wild) side of Robberg Peninsula—is one of the best anywhere, and the view of the open ocean across fynbos-clad hills is spectacular. Rooms are decorated in understated creams, blues, and browns; those that face the sea have dramatic views, and the others overlook a tranquil lily pond. A steep path leads to a private beach and natural tidal pool. **Pros:** rooms are spacious; the restaurant is good; there's a private beach. **Cons:** pool has no view; no a/c in the rooms. ⊠ *Off Robberg Rd.* ✉ *Box 167, 6600* ☎ *044/533–9067* ⊕ *www.plettenbergpark.co.za* ↘ *10 rooms* ♿ *In-room: safe, refrigerator, DVD. In-hotel: restaurant, room service, pool, spa, beachfront, laundry service, Wi-Fi, parking (free), no kids under 12* ▤ *AE, DC, MC, V* ¶◎¶ *BP.*

$$$$ **Fodor's Choice** ☆ **Tsala Treetop Lodge.** Built on the same property as Hunter's, and also run by the Hunter family, this lodge combines the best of sleek design with spectacular natural surroundings. Fabulous glass, stone, metal, and wood chalets are built on stilts overlooking a steep forested gorge and, in some cases, extending into the forest canopy. Suites have plunge pools with fantastic views, verandas, and fireplaces, and the unusual decor includes specially manufactured oval baths, hand-beaten brass plumbing fittings, and loads of glass. There are also beautiful African antiques in the reception areas. Suites are connected by raised timber walkways. The restaurant is open to nonguests, and there's the further option of dining at Zinzi's ($$), a reasonably priced and gorgeous restaurant on the same property. **Pros:** beautiful infinity plunge pools; vegetarians are looked after. **Cons:** emphasis is on privacy and romance—it's not

for the sociable; suites don't have valley views as trees are in the way. ✉ *Off N2, between Plettenberg Bay and Knysna* ☎ *Box 454, 6600* ☎ *044/532–7818* ⊕ *www.hunterhotels.com/tsalatreetoplodge* ➪ *10 suites* ⚒ *In-room: safe. In-hotel: restaurant, pool, room service, bar, laundry service, Internet terminal, Wi-Fi, parking (free), no kids under 10* ☰ *AE, MC, V* ⦿ *BP.*

SPORTS AND THE OUTDOORS
HIKING
★ **Robberg Nature Reserve** (✉ *Robberg Rd., near the airport* ☎ *044/533–2125*), open daily 7:30–6, has three fabulous walks. The shortest takes about a half hour and offers great views of the ocean. A longer walk (1½ hours) passes above a seal colony and connects to the "island" via a tombolo. At 2½ hours or more (up to 3½ if you are leisurely), the longest walk goes right to the end of the peninsula. You need to watch the tides on this one. In addition to great sea views, dolphins, whales, birds, and seals, there are fantastic flowers and swimming beaches (make sure to consult the map as to which beaches are safe for swimming, however). Admission is R25, and it's worth taking a picnic. A fascinating archaeological excavation at Nelson's Bay Cave has a display outlining the occupation of the cave over thousands of years.

KAYAKING
★ Kayaking on **Plettenberg Bay** is a great way to see the sights and possibly enjoy a visit from a whale or dolphin. Though you aren't likely to see as many animals as the people on the big boats will, it's a far more intimate and exciting experience if you do. You also get to paddle past the Cape fur seal colony on Robberg. Trips cost about R250 for three hours. **Dolphin Adventures** (✉ *Central Beach* ☎ *083/590–3405* ⊕ *www.dolphinadventures.co.za*) offers regular trips in sleek but stable tandem kayaks. **Ocean Blue** (✉ *Hopwood St., Central Beach* ☎ *044/533–5083* ⊕ *www.oceanadventures.co.za*) runs regular paddling trips on which you may see whales and dolphins.

SKYDIVING
If you want your views with a bit of adrenaline thrown in, consider a tandem skydive with **Skydive Plett** (✉ *Plettenberg Bay Airport* ☎ *082/905–7440* ⊕ *www.skydiveplett.com*). Tandem jumps cost about R1,600, and it's worth the extra R400 to get the DVD so you can show your friends back home. You get nearly half a minute of free fall, during which you get to see Robberg and the whole of the Tsitsikamma coast. If you think you might get serious about this sport, you can take an Accelerated Free Fall (AFF) course.

WHALE-WATCHING
Plettenberg Bay is one of the very best locations worldwide for boat-based whale- and dolphin-watching. Most days, visitors see at least two cetacean species and Cape fur seals, as well as a variety of seabirds, including Cape gannets and African penguins. On some days people have seen up to six cetacean species in the course of a few hours.

Two similar operators have you board an open vehicle outside a shop and from there step directly onto a boat at the beach. Boats are fast, safe, and dry. Both operators offer similar trips, and boats are licensed

Fodor's Choice
★

to come as close as 164 feet to the whales. These trips are limited in season to one trip per company per day in order to minimize disturbance to the whales. **Ocean Blue** (⊠ *Hopwood St., Central Beach* ☎ *044/533–5083* ⊕ *www.oceanadventures.co.za*) has a 1½-hour whale-watching trip that costs R400. **Ocean Safaris** (⊠ *Hopwood St., Central Beach* ☎ *044/533–4963 or 082/784–5729* ⊕ *www.oceansafaris.co.za*) runs regular whale-watching trips from the beach area. These last 1½ to two hours and cost R650. Trips to see dolphins and seals only cost R400.

SHOPPING

Plenty of shops in and around town sell casual beachwear and various crafts, but for a good concentration in a small place, you can't beat **Old Nick** (⊠ *N2, just east of town* ☎ *044/533–1395*). Originally just a pottery and weaving studio, it has grown to include a host of other crafts—so many that you could spend a whole day here. Included are a weaving museum, a shop selling lovely woven goods, a crystal shop, and a few galleries. A handmade-soap factory beckons with the scent of essential oils and fruits, and the **Country Kitchen** competes for your olfactory attention with the heady aroma of freshly brewed espresso.

THE CRAGS

16 km (10 mi) northeast of Plettenberg Bay.

Although technically part of Plett, the Crags is very different. It's rural and forested and is home to primate and elephant refuges, plus a free-flight aviary. Although there's no beach, the Crags region is close to the lovely beach at Nature's Valley. There are loads of fantastic accommodation options and exciting activities, most of which belong to a great little marketing initiative called Cruise the Crags.

GETTING HERE AND AROUND

The Crags is part of Plett, so the same travel information applies. There's no public transport to and around Plett, so renting a car and driving yourself is your best option.

The Greyhound and Intercape bus services will drop you off at the Shell Ultra City gas station, just off the N2 in Marine Way, 2 km (1.2 mi) from the city center, and you can arrange to be picked up by your hotel. The Baz Bus will drop you off at the backpacker accommodation in the area.

ESSENTIALS

Tourist Information **Cruise the Crags** (☎ *044/534–8386* ⊕ *www.cruise-thecrags.co.za*).

EXPLORING

☾ **Monkeyland** is a refuge for abused and abandoned primates, most of which were once pets or laboratory animals. They now roam in a huge enclosed area of natural forest and are free to play, socialize, and do whatever it is that keeps primates happy. There are lemurs, gibbons, spider monkeys, indigenous vervet monkeys, howler monkeys, and many more. Guided walks are run throughout the day, and the tamer "inmates" often play with guests. ⊠ *16 km (10 mi) east of Plettenberg Bay along the N2, just before Nature's Valley turnoff* ☎ *044/534–8906*

⊕ *www.monkeyland.co.za* ⬙ *R120, combined ticket with Birds of Eden R200* ⊙ *Daily 8–5.*

Ↄ Built over a natural valley in the forest, **Birds of Eden** is the largest free-flight aviary in the world, spanning five dome-enclosed acres. A stream, waterfalls, ponds, paths, benches, and rest areas make it a great place to spend the day. About 200 species of birds, some of which are quite tame, fly freely in the huge space. ⊠ *16 km (10 mi) east of Plettenberg Bay along the N2, just before Nature's Valley turnoff* ☎ *044/534–8906* ⊕ *www.birdsofeden.co.za* ⬙ *R125; combined ticket with Monkeyland R200* ⊙ *Daily 8–5.*

Ↄ If you want to see an elephant, your best bet is the **Elephant Sanctuary.** Knysna Forest once harbored large herds of elephants, but hunting and habitat encroachment almost put an end to the wild population. At one time it was thought that there was only one old matriarch left, so a few young elephants were relocated from Kruger to keep her company and—with luck—breed. The new ellies couldn't cope with the forest, however, and after they wandered into farmland, the project was abandoned. Since then, more elephants, including a few young ones, have been found deep in the forest, but since they're not venturing near the more-traveled areas, it's extremely unlikely that you'll see one. Still it's nice to know they're there. At the Elephant Sanctuary you can go on a guided forest walk with these amazing animals, touch them, learn more about them, and take a short ride. ⊠ *N2, 16 km (10 mi) east of Plettenberg Bay, just before Nature's Valley turnoff* ☎ *044/534–8145* ⊕ *www.elephantsanctuary.co.za* ⬙ *R295; additional R375 for elephant ride* ⊙ *Daily 8–3:30; tours on the hr (on the ½ hr 1:30–3:30).*

WHERE TO STAY

$$$$ ⊞ **Hog Hollow Country Lodge.** Vistas stretch into the misty green distance
Fodor's Choice at this lovely lodge set among gardens on the edge of a forested gorge.
★ Rooms are decorated in a modern African motif, with cast-iron furniture, white linen, and African artwork. In summer the private verandas with hammocks are as popular as the fireplaces are in winter. The food (for lodge guests only) is great, and meals are sociable affairs, taken around a huge table in the main house; breakfasts are taken on the patio, from where you can watch vervet monkeys play in the trees. Local seafood and ostrich are well represented on the menu, but vegetarian food is handled with flair. An energetic one-hour walk through the forest will bring you to Monkeyland, Birds of Eden, and the Elephant Sanctuary. The lodge is very conscientious about environmental issues. Pros: lodge hires its staff from the surrounding community and trains them; breakfasts are great, especially the breakfast trifle. Cons: dining is communal, although you can opt to have a separate table. ⊠ *Askop Rd.* ✉ *Box 503, Plettenberg Bay 6600* ☎ *044/534–8879* ⊕ *www.hoghollow.com* ➳ *16 suites* ⌂ *In-room: no phone, refrigerator, no TV, safe. In-hotel: bar, pool, laundry service, Internet terminal, Wi-Fi, parking (free)* ⊟ *MC, V* ⊖ *BP.*

$$$$ ⊞ **Kurland.** On the road out of Plett toward Tsitsikamma, this mag-
★ nificent 1,500-acre estate is centered on a lovely historic Cape Dutch homestead. Spacious guest suites are in separate buildings, and the huge

bathrooms, antique furniture, book-filled shelves, fireplaces, and private balconies give you the feeling you're staying in your own country home. A view of horse-filled paddocks makes it seem even more opulent. Ten rooms have staircases leading to charming children's attic rooms. The food in the restaurant ($$$$) is exactly what you might expect in such a refined atmosphere: well cooked, beautifully presented, and made from whatever's fresh. Guests have the use of a complimentary all-terrain quad bike and mountain bikes for exploring the estate. There are free pony rides for kids, plus children's programs during Easter and summer school holidays. **Pros:** 10 of the villas have attic rooms that kids will love; rooms are individually decorated. **Cons:** you need your own transport as it's about a 15-minute drive out of Plettenberg Bay; not for those who want an adults-only hotel. ⊠ *N2* ⌂ *Box 209, The Crags, 6602* ☏ *044/534–8082* ⊕ *www.kurland.co.za* ⇆ *2 rooms, 10 suites* ⚐ *In-room: safe. In-hotel: restaurant, room service, bar, tennis court, pool, gym, spa, Wi-Fi, parking (free), children's programs (ages 1–6)* ⊟ *AE, DC, MC, V* ⦿ *BP, MAP.*

EN ROUTE

As you travel on the N2 east from Plett, you cross a flat coastal plain of fynbos, with the forested Tsitsikamma Mountains on your left. Just after The Crags, turn off onto the R102, an alternative to the toll road and a far more interesting and scenic route. The road passes through farmland before dropping suddenly to sea level via the Groot River Pass. It's a great descent, with the road worming back and forth through a tunnel of greenery, impenetrable bush pressing in on either side. At the bottom of the pass, turn right into **Nature's Valley,** where the Groot River forms a magnificent lagoon hemmed in by bush-cloaked hills before crossing a long, beautiful beach to enter the sea. An almost fairy-tale settlement nestles beneath the trees. This is the end point of the Otter Trail. At a small restaurant-cum-shop near the beach, weary hikers give their boots a solemn resting place if they're not fit for another hike. A walk to Salt River is another great way to spend the day, and there is a reasonable chance of spotting an otter.

From Nature's Valley the R102 climbs out of the Groot River valley and crosses the N2. Here you can choose to take the N2 or stay on the R102 through the incredibly scenic Bloukrans Pass and rejoin the N2 13 km (8 mi) farther on. From this point it's another 9 km (5½ mi) to the turnoff to Tsitsikamma section of the Garden Route National Park and the Storms River Mouth. The pretty and rather remote Storms River village is another 4 km (2½ mi) farther east on the N2.

TSITSIKAMMA

31 km (19 mi) east of Nature's Valley, 42 km (26 mi) east of Plettenberg Bay.

GETTING HERE AND AROUND

The Intercape, Greyhound, and Baz buses stop at the Caltex gas station at Storms River Bridge, on the N2, which is about 25 minutes from the park. Pickup can be arranged with most lodges. There's no public transport in this area, so your best bet is renting a car and driving yourself. The roads are in good condition.

EXPLORING

The **Tsitsikamma section of the Garden Route National Park** (which is administered as its own park) is a narrow belt of coastline extending for 80 km (50 mi) from Oubosstrand to Nature's Valley, encompassing some of the most spectacular coastal scenery in the country, including deep gorges, evergreen forests, tidal pools, and beautiful empty beaches. The best way to see the park is on the five-day Otter Trail, South Africa's most popular hike, or the somewhat easier and more comfortable Dolphin Trail. A less strenuous highlight is the Storms River Mouth, in the middle of the park. The river enters the sea through a narrow channel carved between sheer cliffs. Storms River was aptly named: when gale winds blow, as they often do, the sea flies into a pounding fury, hurling spray onto the rocks and whipping spume high up the cliffs. From the Tsitsikamma section's visitor center, a trail descends through the forest (different tree species are all labeled) and over a narrow suspension bridge strung across the river mouth. It's a spectacular walk, a highlight of any trip to the Garden Route. On the other side of the bridge a steep trail climbs to the top of a bluff overlooking the river and the sea—the turning point of the Storms River MTB (mountain bike) Trail, which starts and finishes in Storms River village. Other trails, ranging from 1 to 3.2 km (½ to 2 mi), lead either to a cave once inhabited by hunter-gatherers or through the coastal forest. A pleasant, ordinary restaurant with great views of the river and the ocean serves breakfast, lunch, and dinner at the park. ⊠ *Off N2* ☎ *042/281–1607* ⊕ *www.sanparks.org* ✆ *R80.*

WHERE TO STAY

$–$$ 🖫 **Storms River Mouth Rest Camp.** The lodgings here are pretty basic but are clean and comfortable, and the setting, almost within soaking distance of the pounding surf, is spectacular. Log cabins sleep either two or four people, forest huts are the cheapest option and are very basic, "oceanettes" are attractive seaside apartments with fully outfitted kitchens, and the freestanding chalets are the closest to the sea. **Pros:** you can't beat the waterside location; good facilities for such a basic place; everything is well cared for and clean. **Cons:** you have to pay the daily SANParks conservation fee on top of accommodation rates; restaurant is not great. ⊠ *Off N2* ☎ *012/428–9111* ⊕ *www.sanparks.org* ✆ *21 cottages, 20 huts, 17 oceanettes, 16 chalets, 6 cabins ⚭ In-room: no phone, no TV. In-hotel: restaurant, beachfront, diving, water sports, laundry facilities* ☰ *AE, DC, MC, V.*

SPORTS AND THE OUTDOORS

BOATING

For a really good look at the gorge, take a boat trip (R60) on the **Spirit of Tsitsikamma** (☎ *042/281–1607* ⊕ *www.sanparks.org*). The boat departs every 45 minutes between 9:30 and 2:45 from the jetty below the suspension bridge.

HIKING

Fodor's Choice The **Dolphin Trail** (☎ *042/280–3588* ⊕ *www.dolphintrail.co.za*) is the ★ perfect marriage between exercise and relaxation, rugged scenery and comfort. Starting at Storms River Mouth, the trail continues east along the coast, with scenery similar to the Otter Trail's. Though the Dolphin is quite hard going, it covers just 20 km (12 mi) over two days, and the best part is that you carry only a day pack (your luggage is transported by vehicle to the next spot). Accommodations on the first night are in very comfortable cabins with private baths at Storms River Mouth. The next two nights are spent in lovely guesthouses with awesome views and great food. It costs R4,200 per person, which includes a guide, all meals, transportation, and three nights' accommodation.

★ The most popular of South Africa's hiking trails, the **Otter Trail** (☎ 012/426–5111 ⊕ *www.sanparks.org*) runs along the coast from the mouth of Storms River to Nature's Valley, passing rocky cliffs, beaches, fynbos, rivers, and towering indigenous forest. The trail is only 42 km (26 mi) long, but there are a lot of steep uphills and downhills. It's billed as a five-day hike to give you time to swim and hang out. Accommodations are in overnight huts equipped with sleeping bunks, *braais* (barbecues), and chemical toilets. You must carry in all food and carry out all trash. Only 12 people are allowed on the trail per day, making it vital to book at least a year in advance. However, because people sometimes book all 12 slots and then arrive with only four or five others, there are often cancellations. If you really want to hike this trail but can't get a reservation, you can try hanging around for a few days to see if a spot opens up. The trail costs R595 per person, plus an R80 conservation fee per person per night.

STORMS RIVER

★ *4 km (2½ mi) east of Tsitsikamma section of the Garden Route National Park.*

Although it's a small, isolated village, Storms River absolutely buzzes with activity. A hotel, a couple of guesthouses, and a smattering of backpackers' lodges all cater to the numerous adrenaline junkies and nature lovers who frequent this hot spot for adventure and ecotourism activities. Bear in mind that Storms River Mouth, the SANParks camp in the Tsitsikamma section of the Garden Route National Park, and Storms River village are not the same place.

GETTING HERE AND AROUND

Greyhound and Intercape buses stop at the Caltex Garage on the N2, at Storms River bridge. Storms River Mouth is 18 km (11 mi) south of the bridge. There's no public transport around the area, so you will need your own transport. The Baz Bus will drop you off at your backpacker accommodation.

WHERE TO EAT AND STAY

¢ ✕ **Trees Fine Foods.** Don't expect anything fancy, but do expect good value for the money at simple Trees Fine Foods, which is part of a CAFÉ poverty-alleviation and employment program. Conveniently located in the heart of Storms River village, it serves vegetarian and beef burgers, a small range of toasted sandwiches, and breakfasts. ⊠ *Main Rd.* ☎ *042/281–1836* ▭ *MC, V.*

$$ ▥ **At the Woods Guest House.** Built with care and attention to detail, this ★ lovely owner-managed guesthouse is a winner. The decor is understated,

and most of the finishes are natural: stone tiles in the bathrooms, reed ceilings, and lots of woodwork, including some charming old wooden doors. All rooms have king-size beds, huge shower stalls, and roomy balconies with a mountain view. It's right in the village, so it's close to all the wonderful activities in Storms River. Hostess Bev Coetzee is a mine of information on the local area as well as the whole Garden Route. ■ TIP→ Ask for an upstairs room facing the mountain. Pros: rooms are spacious; there's a comfortable guest lounge. Cons: swimming pool is small; dining options in the area are limited. ⊠ *Formosa St.* ⌓ *Box 92, 6308* ☎ *042/281–1446* ⊕ *www.atthewoods.co.za* ⇡ *8 rooms* ♿ *In-room: safe, refrigerator. In-hotel: pool, laundry service, Internet terminal, Wi-Fi, parking (free)* ▤ *AE, DC, MC, V* ⍣ *BP.*

$$ 🏨 **Protea Hotel Tsitsikamma Inn.** The guest rooms here are in pretty, color-
ECLECTIC ful buildings that are neatly arranged around a village green, and the public rooms are in an old hunting lodge built in 1888. The inn is well known for its restaurant—De Oude Martha ($$)—which was named after the hotel's first cook; though she has retired, her influence lingers. Food is mostly dependable standbys such as grilled line fish, calamari, chicken, steaks, and pastas. Pros: good restaurant; gardens are a lovely place to stroll; a wide range of accommodation options. Cons: fee for Internet; it's also a conferencing center so it can get noisy. ⊠ *Main Rd.* ⌓ *Box 53, 6308* ☎ *042/281–1711* ⊕ *www.tsitsikammahotel.co.za* ⇡ *49 rooms,* ♿ *In-hotel: restaurant, bar, pool, Internet terminal, Wi-Fi, laundry service, parking (free)* ▤ *AE, DC, MC, V* ⍣ *BP.*

$ 🏨 **Tsitsikamma Backpackers.** This small, tidy hostel is a bit quieter than most, so it's a good place to stay if you're on a budget. The lovely garden has great mountain views. If you don't feel like making use of the communal kitchens, you can book meals (Continental breakfast and dinner only) in advance. You can rent bicycles, shoot pool, and use the barbecue facilities. There's also a self-catering cottage that sleeps four. Pros: huge garden; it's as environmentally friendly as possible. Cons: shuttle to take you to nearby activities is not free; the tented accommodation can get hot in summer. ⊠ *54 Formosa St.* ☎ *042/281–1868* ⊕ *www.tsitsikammabackpackers.co.za* ⇡ *4 rooms, 2 dormitories, 6 tents* ♿ *In-room: no phone, no TV. In-hotel: bar, laundry facilities, Internet terminal, Wi-Fi, parking (free)* ▤ *MC, V.*

SPORTS AND THE OUTDOORS
BUNGEE JUMPING

Fodor's Choice If you do only one bungee jump in your life, do it from the Bloukrans
★ River bridge with **Face Adrenalin** (⊠ *N2* ☎ *042/281–1458* ⊕ *www. faceadrenalin.com*). At 700 feet, it's the highest commercial bungee jump in the world. The span is the third-highest bridge in the world and the highest in the Southern Hemisphere. The jump costs R620, and the DVD to show your friends back home is an extra R120. A photo CD with about 30 images is another R60. If you want to see what it's all about but have no intention of flinging yourself off the bridge, you can do a walking tour for R90, but even that's not for the faint of heart, as it is pretty high, exposed, and scary. The flying fox—a cable on which you slide under the bridge and above the bridge arch to the jump-off

spot—costs R170 for a single, and R260 for a tandem ride. The combo of fox and jump costs R750.

CANOPY AND FOREST TOUR

Fodor's Choice ★ Want a turaco's-eye view of the treetops? **Storms River Adventures** (⊠ *Main Rd.* ☎ *042/281–1836* ⊕ *www.stormsriver.com*) will take you deep into the forest, where you don a harness, climb up to a platform, clip in, and "fly" on long cables from platform to platform. You can even control your speed. The cost is R450, and the DVD with video and download-able photos costs an extra R145.

Storms River Adventures also offers a gentle, open-vehicle tour of the forest and the old Storms River Pass. Knowledgeable guides expand on the flora and fauna, as well as the interesting history of the region. You end it all with lunch or tea at a beautiful picnic site next to the Storms River, where wagons would stop more than a century ago. The tea trip costs R125, and the lunch trip R175.

MOUNTAIN BIKING

The **Storms River Mountain Bike Trail** is a scenic, circular 22-km (14-mi) trail administered by the Department of Water Affairs and Forestry. It's free, and you don't need a reservation. Just go to the starting point, near the police station at Storms River, and fill out a form in a box at the gate to issue yourself a permit. **Tsitsikamma Backpackers** (⊠ *54 Formosa St.* ☎ *042/281–1868* ⊕ *www.tsitsikammabackpackers.com*) rents out mountain bikes for R20 per hour.

LITTLE KAROO

The landscape of the Little Karoo—austere, minimal, and dry—stands in stark contrast to the Garden Route. In summer it resembles a blast furnace, whereas winter nights are bitterly cold. In its own way, how-ever, it is absolutely beautiful. The Little Karoo, also called the Klein Karoo (*klein* is Afrikaans for "small"; *karoo* derives from the San [Bush-man] word for "thirst"), should not be confused with the Great Karoo, a vast semidesert scrub on the other side of the Swartberg Mountains. Everything here is a little surreal—giant birds soar overhead, huge caves stretch for miles underground, and bright-green vineyards contrast with intricately eroded, deep red hills.

EN ROUTE Set between Montagu and Barrydale on the R62, the Op-de-Tradouw region, named after a pass through the mountains, is best known for its excellent wines. **Joubert-Tradauw** (⊠ *R62, 12 km [7½] mi west of Barry-dale* ☎ *028/572–1619* ⊕ *www.joubert-tradauw.co.za* ⊠ *Free* ⊙ *Week-days 9–5, Sat. 9–2*) is a great place to stop for a wine tasting or for lunch or tea. Owner Meyer Joubert makes wine in the age-old French tradition—unfiltered and unrefined. His chardonnay is sublime, and he has publicly stated that it is his ambition to make the best Syrah in the world. (Try it; he's definitely on the right track.) While he works his magic in the winery, his wife Beate waves her star-spangled wand over the small deli–coffee shop, where you can sit under the pergola and spend ages over a superb cheese platter or Gruyère salad, or just have a quick coffee and cheesecake. It's tapas alfresco with a traditional

Afrikaner touch. For a more adventurous dining experience, you can combine lunch or tea with a quad-bike (all-terrain-vehicle) tour. **Tradouw Quads** (✉ *R62* ☎ *082/055–4096* ⊕ *www.tquads.co.za*) has great tours ranging from gentle rides to a hectic mountain adventure All tours can be combined with a picnic if arranged in advance.

If you're heading down the R62 toward Oudtshoorn and you get a little peckish, stop at **Rose of the Karoo on Route 62** (✉ *Voortrekker St., Calitzdorp* ☎ *044/213–3133* ⊕ *www.roseofthekaroo.co.za*). Options range from a light sandwich to a lamb- or ostrich-based Karoo specialty, and breakfast and tea are served here, too. And it's one of the few places in town where you can get really good coffee. Out back there's a lovely vine-covered patio, and a small deli section sells home-baked goods and local preserves. An added bonus in summer: it's air-conditioned.

4

OUDTSHOORN

85 km (53 mi) north of Mossel Bay.

Oudtshoorn has been famous for its ostriches since around 1870, when farmers began raising them to satisfy the European demand for feathers to adorn women's hats and dresses. In the years leading up to World War I, ostrich feathers were almost worth their weight in gold thanks to the continuing demands of fashion, and Oudtshoorn experienced an incredible boom. Many of the beautiful sandstone buildings in town date from that period, as do the "feather palaces," huge homes built by prosperous feather merchants and buyers. Although feathers are no longer a major fashion item, these huge birds are now bred for their tough and distinctive leather and almost completely fat- and cholesterol-free red meat. Almost as much of a moneymaker, though, is the tourist potential of these weird and wonderful birds. In addition to visiting an ostrich farm, you can buy ostrich products ranging from the sublime—feather boas— to the ridiculous—taxidermic baby ostriches emerging from cracked eggs. Several farms compete for the tourist buck, offering almost identical tours and a chance to eat an ostrich-based meal. Be warned—these can be real tourist traps: glitzy, superficial, and filled with horrendous crowds. As well as watching local "jockeys" racing on ostriches, you'll be offered the opportunity to ride one. This is pretty cruel; although the birds are incredibly strong, their legs are very thin, and many birds suffer broken legs when ridden. If this concerns you, visit instead the Cape Town ostrich farms, which do not allow this practice.

Note that most of the restaurants, guesthouses, and attractions listed below are on Baron van Reede Street. This street becomes the R328, which heads north from Oudtshoorn to the Cango Caves, the Swartberg Pass, and Prince Albert.

GETTING HERE AND AROUND

As there's no public transport in this area, the most convenient and efficient way of getting around is driving yourself. The roads are good and parts are very scenic. Intercape and Greyhound buses don't go to Oudtshoorn. The Baz Bus does come from George and will drop you off at backpacker accommodation or in town. Most of Oudtshoorn's

What the . . . ?

No, your eyes are not playing tricks on you. That sign definitely says **Ronnie's Sex Shop** (☎ *028/572-1153*). And no, it's not a country brothel, nor does it purvey rubber garments and toys of an adult nature. It's actually a Route 62 icon that started out as a joke. Ronnie (a real person) returned to his farm one day to find his friends had decorated the disused laborer's cottage near the road, painting on it in big red letters RONNIE'S SEX SHOP. It stayed like that for years—a local landmark—until Ronnie thought he would cash in on the unintentional marketing, and opened a pub in it. It's a far cry from a sophisticated venue, but it's a great place to meet the less productive members of the local farming community, many of whom spend a large proportion of the day here. It's also a mandatory stop on most motorcycle rallies. It's open from 10 in the morning until the last person leaves at night, which is usually pretty late. You can't miss it—it's right on Route 62, just on the Ladysmith side of Barrydale. You may not want to go in, but you'll probably want to photograph it.

museums and restaurants are located on the main road, Baron van Reede Street, which also leads to the Cango Caves.

ESSENTIALS

Rental Cars Avis (☎ *044/272-4727*).

Tourist Information Oudtshoorn Tourism Bureau (✉ *12 Baron van Reede St.* ☎ *044/279-2532* ⊕ *www.oudtshoorn.com*).

EXPLORING

The **C. P. Nel Museum** focuses on the ostrich and Oudtshoorn's boom period at the beginning of the 20th century. The section on fashions of the feather-boom period are by far the most picturesque. The display that depicts the contribution of Lithuanian Jews to the economic development of Oudtshoorn and the feather industry contains a reconstruction of the town's first synagogue. ✉ *Baron van Reede St.* ☎ *044/272-7306* ⊕ *www.cpnelmuseum.co.za* ✉ *R12 (includes admission to Le Roux's Town House)* ⊙ *Weekdays 8–5, Sat. 9–1.*

The most interesting remnants of the glory of the boom period are the magnificent palaces built by successful farmers. Most are private homes, but you can visit the sandstone **Le Roux's Town House,** built in 1909 and furnished in period style, to see just how good they had it in those heady days. ✉ *High and Loop Sts.* ☎ *044/272-3676* ✉ *Free with ticket to C. P. Nel Museum* ⊙ *Weekdays 9–noon and 2–5.*

The name **Cango Wildlife Ranch** is a bit misleading, as this is really just a glorified zoo, crocodile farm, and cheetah-breeding center, but it is great fun—especially for children. As well as the crocodiles and cheetahs, you may see white Bengal tigers and lions in large pens. Other attractions include a snake park, pygmy hippos, a tropical house with birds and giant fruit bats: in short, loads of different animals that will keep the little ones amused for ages. You can even do a croc cage dive (R220), which isn't as bizarre as it sounds: it's not really diving, as you are separated from the croc by glass and can stand up for a breath of air whenever you feel the need. For an extra fee (R145 to R300), you can cuddle one of the resident beasts (cheetahs, lions, pythons). The price, which includes a photograph, depends on the species you choose. ⊠ *Caves Rd.* ☎ *044/272–5593* ⊕ *www.cango.co.za* 🖃 *R95* ⊘ *Daily 8–5.*

♺ **Cango Ostrich Farm** is probably the least commercialized of the ostrich show farms. Guides explain the bird's extraordinary social and physical characteristics, and there are lots of interactive opportunities, including feeding and petting the ostriches and posing on one for a photograph. People who weigh less than 75 kilograms (165 pounds) are permitted to ride the ostriches. Many people consider this to be cruel, but the farm complies with strict regulations, meaning that you can ride for no longer than 30 seconds and not more than four people can ride per tour. The farm is conveniently located en route to the Cango Caves from town. From September to February, you may see babies hatching. ⊠ *R328, 14 km (9 mi) north of Oudtshoorn* ☎ *044/272–4623* ⊕ *www.cangoostrich. co.za* 🖃 *R56* ⊘ *Daily 8:30–4:30.*

★ Between Oudtshoorn and Prince Albert, the huge and stunningly beautiful **Cango Caves**, filled with weird and wonderful stalactite and stalagmite formations, are deservedly one of the most popular attractions in the area. Only a small fraction of the caves, which extend for several miles through the mountains, is open. Unfortunately, due to short-sighted tourism schemes in the 1960s and vandalism, there's some damage, especially to the first chamber, but they are still very impressive and get more magnificent the more the tour progresses. One of the highlights is "Cleopatra's Needle," which is 29 feet high and at least 150,000 years old. You can choose between two tours: the hour-long standard tour and the aptly named adventure tour, which lasts 1½ hours. Think long and hard before opting for the latter if you're overweight, very tall, claustrophobic, or have knee or heart problems. It's exhilarating, but the temperature and humidity are high, there's not much oxygen, and you'll be shimmying up narrow chimneys on your belly, wriggling your way through tiny tunnels, and sliding on your bottom. Wear old clothes and shoes with a good tread. Standard tours leave on the hour, adventure tours on the half hour. ⊠ *Off R328, 29 km (18 mi) north of Oudtshoorn* ☎ *044/272–7410* ⊕ *www.cango-caves.co.za* 🖃 *Standard tour R55, adventure tour R70* ⊘ *Daily 9–4.*

NEED A BREAK?
♺ At the turnoff to the Cango Caves, **Wilgewandel Coffee Shop and Country Farmstall** (⊠ *R328, 2 km (1 mi) from the caves* ☎ *044/272–0878*) serves well-cooked simple food such as hamburgers, toasted sandwiches, ostrich steaks, and sweet treats. Shady outdoor tables overlook a big lawn and duck-filled pond. Trampolines and camel, pony, and boat rides are offered for children.

WHERE TO EAT

$-$$ ✕ **Jemima's Restaurant.** Named after the mythical guardian angel of love, ECLECTIC good taste, and good cooking, this restaurant would not disappoint its ★ muse. All the ingredients are sourced locally from farmers in the district,

CLOSE UP

Back and Forth

Part of the beauty of the Garden Route and Little Karoo is found in the spectacular passes that connect the two and in those between the Little and Great Karoo. Be sure to see at least one.

Between Oudtshoorn and George, choose the Outeniqua Pass (via the paved N12) or the more historic Montagu Pass (off the N9, after it diverges from the N12, on a narrow gravel road built in 1843 by Henry Fancourt White). The latter offers excellent views, picnic sites, and examples of Victorian road building, including a five-span arch bridge, railway viaduct, and expertly laid dry-stone embankments. An old tollhouse still sits at the bottom of the pass.

The Robertson Pass, between Oudtshoorn and Mossel Bay, is an easy tarred road with some fabulous views. One of the most interesting things about this route (especially if you're traveling from Mossel Bay) is that you can see the abrupt change of vegetation as you crest the ridge and drive over into the rain shadow.

For a great loop between the Great and Little Karoo, drive counterclockwise from Oudtshoorn through De Rust and the spectacularly scenic Meiringspoort. The road runs along the bottom of a deep gorge, crossing the pretty Meirings River 25 times as it cuts through red cliffs. Halfway through the pass is a rest area, where a path leads to a 200-foot waterfall. Head west on the R407 to Prince Albert; then head south through the Swartberg Pass on the R328 back to Oudtshoorn. (The views are more dramatic from this direction.) The road through this pass was built between 1881 and 1886 by the legendary engineer Sir Thomas Bain. At times the road barely clings to the mountainside, held only by Bain's stone retaining walls. From the top, at 5,230 feet, you can look out toward the hot plains of the Great Karoo and the distant mountains of the Nuweveldberg or down at the huge gorge and sheer walls of deep-red rock.

---

and the menu focuses on such local delicacies as olives, Karoo mutton, and, of course, ostrich. Meat lovers often opt for the Three Tenors—medallions of beef, ostrich, and venison fillet. Herbivores love the spinach and brown mushroom cheesecake. There's an extensive list of local wines. ⊠ *94 Baron van Reede St.* ☎ *044/272–0808* ⊕ *www.jemimas. com* ⚹ *Reservations essential* ⊟ *AE, DC, MC, V* ☉ *No lunch Sun.*

$$–$$$ ✕ **Kalinka Restaurant.** Set in a lovely old stone house with a small but
ECLECTIC   tranquil garden and a glass conservatory, this is a pleasant option for
Fodor'sChoice   dinner. Try the African trio: gemsbok, kudu, and ostrich served on a
★   warm vegetable terrine; or wildebeest served on spiced sweet-potato gratin with roasted vegetables and monkey-gland sauce (a spicy tomato and onion sauce). Of course there has to be an ostrich meal—it's served with a warm beetroot salad, baby potatoes, and a mustard sauce and is a firm favorite. ⊠ *93 Baron van Reede St.* ☎ *044/279–2596* ⊟ *MC, V* ☉ *No lunch.*

WHERE TO STAY

$ ⊞ **Backpackers Paradise.** A communal kitchen, pool table, swimming pool, bar, and TV lounge combine to create that typical hostel vibe where everyone becomes friends in half an hour. The dorms are on the small side; some have en suite bathrooms, as do some of the doubles. The double en suite rooms have tea- and coffee-making facilities, towels, and soap, and the lounge has cable TV and a library. Breakfast is available every day (R35), and every night there's an ostrich barbecue (R90). Backpackers Paradise is conveniently located on Baron van Reede Street, just on the caves side of town. **Pros:** inexpensive; bar located away from the hostel; spacious grounds. **Cons:** small pool; dorms are on the small side; no Wi-Fi. ⊠ *148 Baron van Reede St.* ☎ *044/272–3436* ⊕ *www.backpackersparadise.net* ⤴ *11 rooms, 5 with bath; 3 dormitories* ⚴ *In-room: no TV, no phone. In-hotel: bar, pool, laundry service, Internet terminal, parking (free), no kids under 5* ▭ *AE, DC, MC, V* ⏺ *BP.*

$$ ⊞ **Hlangana Lodge.** Conveniently situated on the edge of town on the road out to the caves, this great option is warm and friendly and has a lovely garden surrounding a swimming pool. "Superior" rooms have baths and showers, whereas standard rooms have either showers or baths. Though only breakfast is served on the premises, you can arrange for a plan that includes a free shuttle to dinner at any restaurant in town. In case you're wondering, the lodge's name is pronounced *shlung-gah-na.* **Pros:** Superior rooms have huge bathrooms; staff is friendly and helpful. **Cons:** rooms not very private; service at breakfast can be slow. ⊠ *Baron van Reede and North Sts.* ☎ *51 North St., 6625* ☎ *044/272–2299* ⊕ *www.hlangana.co.za* ⤴ *18 rooms, 1 suite* ⚴ *In-room: safe, DVD (some), Wi-Fi. In-hotel: bar, pool, laundry service, Internet terminal, Wi-Fi, parking (free)* ▭ *AE, DC, MC, V* ⏺ *BP.*

$–$$ ⊞ **Kleinplaas.** The name means "small farm," and although it isn't really a farm, there are sheep, goats, ostriches, ducks, and other animals in small pens where children can gaze at them in wonder. Comfortable, well-appointed chalets with fully equipped cooking facilities are neatly arranged in a huge, shady lawn area. There's also a pretty campsite with laundry facilities. Prices are per chalet for a maximum of four or six people (depending on the chalet). Extra people can be accommodated on sleeper sofas. **Pros:** chalets serviced daily; a private patio area for each chalet. **Cons:** not all rooms have a/c; no Wi-Fi. ⊠ *171 Baron van Reede St.* ☎ *044/272–5811* ⊕ *www.kleinplaas.co.za* ⤴ *54 chalets, 40 campsites* ⚴ *In-room: no phone. In-hotel: pool, laundry facilities, Internet terminal, parking (free)* ▭ *AE, DC, MC, V.*

$$ ⊞ **La Plume Guest House.** This stylish guesthouse is set on a working
★ ostrich farm on the Calitzdorp side of Oudtshoorn. The rooms are all individually decorated with beautiful antiques, and all of the bathrooms have Victorian claw-foot tubs. Guests meet for predinner drinks in the elegant lounge or on the veranda overlooking the valley. If you're keen on seeing what ostrich farming is all about, you can do an informal and informative tour with the owner of the farm—so much better than all the hype you'd get at the show farms. The turnoff to the farm is 7 km (4 mi) west of Oudtshoorn and is well marked from the R62. **Pros:**

beautiful views of the valley from the patio; spacious bedrooms and en suite bathrooms; terrific attention to detail (candles in bathrooms, sprigs of lavender on the pillow, etc.). **Cons:** a 10-minute drive out of town; no room phones. ⊠ *Volmoed, 14 km (9 mi) west of Oudtshoorn* ☎ *Box 1202, 6620* 🖷 *044/272–7516 or 082/820–4373* ⊕ *www.laplume.co.za* 🛏 *7 rooms, 3 suites, 1 2-bedroom cottage* 🔥 *In-room: no phone, refrigerator, Wi-Fi. In-hotel: restaurant, pool, bicycles, laundry service, Internet terminal, parking (free)* ▭ *AE, DC, MC, V* 🍽 *BP.*

$$ 🏨 **Le Petit Karoo.** Perched high on a hill just off the R328, three en suite tents with spa-baths on the veranda have fabulous views of the hills and pass. The tents are small and basic, but you feel like you're in your own little private paradise. There are also four family rooms: two of them sleep four people, and the other two sleep three. There's a campsite, and some families choose to bring a small tent for the kids while Mom and Dad enjoy the romance of the permanent tents. Dinner, which is by arrangement, usually has a French flair, and a full breakfast is R40 per person. There's a labyrinth for walking and musing, and you can also go horseback riding or hiking. This is not a good choice if you like to spend time in your room during the day, as the tents can get quite hot. Camping is R130 per site, which can hold up to four people. **Pros:** breakfasts are great; the Jacuzzis in the tents are wonderful; the owner/hosts are charming. **Cons:** it's rustic; tents can get hot in summer; if you want to have dinner at the restaurant it needs to be booked at breakfast. ⊠ *Off the R328, about 14 km (9 mi) north of Oudtshoorn* ☎ *Suite 39, Private Bag 680, 6620* 🖷 *044/272–7428* ⊕ *www.lepetitka-roo.za.net* 🛏 *3 tents, 4 rooms, 10 campsites* 🔥 *In-room: no phone, no TV, Wi-Fi. In hotel: restaurant, pool, laundry facilities, Wi-Fi, parking (free)* ▭ *No credit cards.*

$$$$ 🏨 **Rosenhof.** For luxury and indulgence in the heart of Oudtshoorn, look no further than Rosenhof. Rooms, in garden cottages with patios facing a pretty stone fountain, are spacious and elegantly furnished in shades of cream, with black-and-white tiled bathrooms. Suites have a separate sitting room and private pool. The reception is located in an old farmhouse dating from 1852, with polished tile floors, exposed beams, Persian carpets, and low-lit lamps. The restaurant has a five-course set menu (R270) of well-executed classic dishes, such as ostrich with red wine sauce and steak fillet béarnaise. You'll also find a full room-service menu, a spa, pool, and all other amenities you'd expect of a luxury hotel. Nothing is too much trouble for the warm and friendly staff. The breakfast, served under a garden gazebo in summer, has to be the best in Oudtshoorn. **Pros:** gardens are lovely, with many places to sit and relax; on-site art gallery. **Cons:** outside areas of rooms are not private; small pool area. ⊠ *264 Baron van Reede St.* 🖷 *044/272–2232* ⊕ *www.rosenhof.co.za* 🛏 *12 rooms, 2 suites* 🔥 *In-room: Wi-Fi. In-hotel: restaurant, room service, bar, pool, gym, spa, laundry service, Internet terminal, Wi-Fi, parking (free), no kids under 12* ▭ *AE, DC, MC, V* 🍽 *BP.*

SPORTS AND THE OUTDOORS

BALLOONING

Oudtshoorn Ballooning (☎ *082/784–8539* ⊕ *www.oudtshoornballooning. co.za*) offers a scenic balloon flight over the town and neighboring farms at dawn. Flights are R2,100 per person and include tea and coffee on arrival, sparkling wine on landing, and breakfast.

HORSEBACK RIDING

Horse rides from **Le Petit Karoo** (☎ *044/272–7428* ⊕ *www.lepetitkaroo. za.net*) range from a gentle one-hour walk for beginners to three-hour rides on the veld. Rates start at R150 for the one-hour ride.

MOUNTAIN BIKING

★ **Joyrides** (☎ *044/272–3436* ⊕ *www.backpackersparadise.net*), based at Backpackers Paradise, runs a fabulous mountain-biking trip. You get transported to the top of the Swartberg Pass, where you (and your fellow cyclists) are left with a mountain bike, helmet, and water. It's pretty much downhill all the way back to town, and the route passes Cango Caves (it's a bit of a steep uphill detour to get there), Wilgewandel coffee shop, Cango Ostrich Farm, Cango Wildlife Ranch, and Le Petit Karoo and then back to Backpackers Paradise. So you've got all day to visit the main tourist attractions. The tour costs R250, plus a R100 bike deposit.

SHOPPING

Oudtshoorn has loads of stores selling ostrich products, but it pays to shop around, as prices vary significantly. The smartest shops strung out along Baron van Reede Street have a great variety but are a tad pricey. **Lugro Ostrich** (☎ *044/272–7012 or 082/788–7916* ⊕ *www.lugro-ostrich. co.za*) is a small factory on a farm 10 km (6 mi) south of Oudtshoorn (8 km [5 mi] off the R62). Here you'll find great ostrich handbags and wallets, as well as belts and smaller items such as key rings. The **Klein Karoo Co-op** (☎ *044/203–5270* ⊕ *www.kleinkaroo.com/showroom*), which coordinates the marketing of ostrich products, has a boutique on its premises near the airport, on the western side of town. (This is really just an airfield, but it's called the airport.) Here you can purchase bags, feather boas, shoes, and other smaller items. It can be a little tricky to find, so it's best to phone for directions or ask for help at your hotel.

DE RUST

40 km (25 mi) northeast of Oudtshoorn.

De Rust is a sleepy Little Karoo village. The main road is lined with crafts stores, coffee shops, restaurants, and wineshops.

GETTING HERE AND AROUND

There's no public transport here. You will need your own vehicle to travel around, but the roads are good, and the scenery is very beautiful.

ESSENTIALS

Tourist Information **De Rust Tourism Bureau** (✉ *2 Schoeman St.* ☎ *044/241–2109* ⊕ *www.derust.org.za*).

EXPLORING

★ **Domein Doornkraal** sells a superb range of fortified wines and a fantastic, inexpensive chardonnay-sémillon blend, but the red wines are what it's really all about—particularly the cabernet sauvignon–merlot blend, which you sometimes have to fight for. You may be lucky and find a few jars of homemade olives, but the small stock usually sells out pretty quickly. ✉ *R62, about 10 km (6 mi) southwest of De Rust* ☎ *044/251–6715* 🎫 *Free* ⏲ *Weekdays 8–5, Sat. 8–1).*

Mons Ruber Estate is named after the Red Hills, which dominate the landscape and whose soil creates the perfect environment for growing grapes with a high sugar content. So it's not surprising that this winery specializes in dessert wines as well as a fine brandy. There is a lovely restored 19th-century kitchen, and an easy hiking trail stretches 1½ hours into the fascinating Red Hills. ✉ *N12, about 15 km (9 mi) southwest of De Rust* ☎ *044/251–6550* 🎫 *Free* ⏲ *Weekdays 9–5, Sat. 9–1.*

WHERE TO STAY

$$$ ★ **Oulap Country House.** Oulap is an eclectic mix of textures and colors, winding staircases and little book-filled nooks, antiques, and impressive contemporary South African art. Guest rooms are individually decorated with original artwork, and the owners grow their own olives and fruit, which they preserve. But what steals the show is the almost unbelievable star-studded Karoo sky; you haven't seen stars until you've spent a night in the Karoo. Four-course farmhouse suppers—Karoo lamb, hearty soups, and regional produce—are wonderful, and conversation around the huge dining table, which often carries on until late in the evening, is possibly even better. The owners are very sociable, and staying here feels more like being a guest in a home than staying in a hotel. A large percentage of the money earned by this lodge has gone into building a village school, complete with school meals and 32 computers; even more community projects are planned. **Pros:** small and intimate; you can go hiking in the forest or relax in the library. **Cons:** no a/c in rooms; fairly remote location. ✉ *15 km (9 mi) from De Rust on R341* 📫 *Box 77, 6650* ☎ *044/241–2250* 🌐 *www.classicafrica.com/portfolio/oulap.htm* *5 rooms* *In-room: no TV, Internet. In-hotel: bar, pool, laundry service, parking (free), some pets allowed* 💳 *AE, DC, MC, V* 🍽 *MAP.*

The Eastern Cape

WORD OF MOUTH

"We were met at Port Elizabeth airport by the owner of Hitgeheim Country Lodge. It is truly a family business; the rooms and food were outstanding and the level of personal attention we received was tremendous."

—MisterAviator

Updated by
Claire Melissa
Baranowski

The Eastern Cape is South Africa's most diverse province and has some of its best vacation destinations, yet it is perhaps the most glossed over by overseas visitors. Starting where the Garden Route stops, it includes much of the Great Karoo—a large, semidesert region of ocher plains, purple mountains, dramatic skies, and unusual, hardy vegetation—and abuts KwaZulu-Natal in the northeast and Lesotho's mountain lands in the north. But a glance at a map will reveal the region's main attraction: its coastline, largely undeveloped and running for some 640 km (400 mi) from temperate to subtropical waters.

The climate is mild across the region and throughout the year, with temperatures at the coast ranging between winter lows of 5°C (41°F) and summer highs of 32°C (90°F). It has many of the country's finest and least crowded beaches, African montane forests and heathlands, an ever-increasing number of fantastic malaria-free game reserves, and some of the most interesting cultural attractions in South Africa.

There are a few areas of note. Frontier Country, formerly known as Settler Country, stretches from the outskirts of Port Elizabeth to Port Alfred in the east, Grahamstown in the northeast, and the Zuurberg Mountains in the north. It was here that the early-19th-century immigrants (colloquially called the 1820 Settlers) tried to set up farms, some successfully, some not. Toward the end of the last century, many of the unprofitable farms were bought up and redeveloped as game reserves, thus adding superb game-viewing to the already existing cultural attractions.

Another noteworthy region on the Eastern Cape is the Wild Coast, which is aptly but perhaps a little unfairly named. Sure, it does get some monumental storms, when huge waves crash into the beach and cliffs, but it also has a gentler face.

Unfortunately, during the political uncertainty of the 1980s the Wild Coast lost a lot of its allure—more due to the perceived threat of violence than anything else. Hotels went out of business, the overnight huts on the fantastic Wild Coast Hiking Trail fell into disrepair, and the Transkei sank further into economic depression. For many years it was only die-hard locals with strong emotional ties and hordes of backpackers who frequented these still-lovely and little-known places. Today the area is going through a revival. Coastal hotels are being renovated one by one, and community projects are being put in place to ensure that the tourist dollar goes where it is intended. In addition to long, lovely beaches, the Wild Coast has crystal-clear turquoise lagoons, some of which can be paddled for miles. The area is still virtually unspoiled, and the people who live here are mostly subsistence farmers and fisherfolk. It's not uncommon for a family who can't afford a loaf of bread to dine (reluctantly) on oysters and lobster. It's just another of the Eastern Cape's contrasts and seeming contradictions.

ORIENTATION AND PLANNING

GETTING ORIENTED

The Eastern Cape is a big space with many tiny gems. The towns, and even the cities, of the province are relatively small, often quaint, and the distances between them are fairly large. Since the only airports are in Port Elizabeth, East London, and Mthatha (previously Umtata), the best way to experience the region is on a driving tour, leaving yourself plenty of time to explore (but be prepared for some poorly maintained roads traveling east of Grahamstown on the N2 and in some regions of the Transkei).

Frontier Country. Formerly known as Settler Country, the area stretches from the outskirts of Port Elizabeth to Port Alfred in the east, Grahamstown in the northeast, and the Zuurberg Mountains in the north. The area also encompasses Addo Elephant National Park and the game reserves at Shamwari and Kwandwe, as well as Grahamstown itself.

Wild Coast. Lovely, long beaches stretch as far as the eye can see, with only a few cows and a small herder to break the isolation. Strictly speaking, the Wild Coast originally stretched from the Kei River mouth to Port Edward (which were the borders of the then nominally independent Transkei), but today it has spread almost to the outskirts of East London.

PLANNING

WHEN TO GO

Although winters are pretty mild, especially farther north along the Wild Coast, summer—from September to April—is the most popular time to visit, especially for sun worshippers. (The beaches are best avoided at Christmas and New Year's, as they become severely overcrowded with hordes of reveling locals.) But even winter has its attractions. The sardine run, usually in June or early July (⇨ "The Food Chain Up Close" box, in Wild Coast), is becoming a major draw, and July's (sometimes late June's) National Arts Festival draws thousands of cultural pilgrims to the delightful university town of Grahamstown.

TAKE IT ALL IN

3 Days: Fly in to Port Elizabeth in the morning and head straight out to Grahamstown. Do a historical tour in the afternoon followed by dinner at your guesthouse or one of the restaurants in town. The next morning, drive out to Shamwari, Kwandwe, or Addo; plan to spend two days in one of these reserves (staying at one of the private luxury lodges or, at Addo, at an inexpensive SANParks camp) and then drive back to Port Elizabeth to fly out. Alternatively, you could spend two

TOP REASONS TO GO

Take a Walk on the Wild Side The Wild Coast is a fabulous "slackpacking" destination. You can walk all day on long, lovely beaches, past turquoise lagoons, and through unspoiled villages. Wonderful day-hiking opportunities include the 37-km (23-mi) walk between Bulungula and Coffee Bay—which takes you along beaches, cliff tops, and rolling hills—plus guided hikes run by many of the lodges.

Take a Look at the Wildlife With its rich and varied topography and flora, the Eastern Cape supports a wide range of game, much of which was once hunted to near extinction by farmers and settlers. Initiatives to reclaim this area for its original inhabitants include Addo Elephant National Park, Shamwari Game Reserve, and Kwandwe Private Game Reserve. Most of the terrain here is hilly with thick bush, so you won't see vast herds of animals wandering across open plains, and some areas bear visible scars from farming. But the game is here: elephants, antelope, rhinos, buffalo, and much more. And best of all—it's malaria-free.

Take a Dive on the Wild Side If you've cage-dived with great whites, plumbed the depths of dark and narrow caves, and dived under ice, you probably think you've done it all. Wrong. Diving with a "baitball"— fish herded together by dolphins

for dining purposes—in the sardine run off the Wild Coast is the ultimate adrenaline dive. Sharks, Cape gannets, Bryde's whales, and even humpbacks have all been known to join in the feast.

Take in the Culture and History From unsullied Xhosa villages— where women paint their faces with ocher clay and boys undergo circumcision rites of passage—to colonial mansions, the range and depth of the Eastern Cape's cultural heritage is amazing. Since the early 19th century, the Eastern Cape has been a frontier and focus of black resistance. In almost every town you'll find fascinating museums and art galleries and a good tour operator who can expose you to the history and culture of this heterogeneous society. The cultural highlight of South Africa is the annual National Arts Festival, which runs for 10 action-packed days every late June and/or July in Grahamstown.

See the Other Side The Transkei is the real Africa. Taking a tour will allow you to interact with locals while traversing the spectacular Wild Coast on foot, horse, bicycle, or ATV. If you're more interested in culture than adventure, a visit to Bulungula will let you meet locals and generally interact on a far more personal level.

days in Port Elizabeth—soaking up the sun, playing a round of golf, taking a cultural tour, and just relaxing—and a third day on a day trip to Addo for an animal fix.

5 Days: With five days you could fly in and out of East London to join the Wild Coast Meander tour with Wild Coast Holiday Reservations *(⇨ East London)*—your days filled with walking this wonderful coastline, and each night spent at a different beach hotel. For a glimpse of Africa not on the usual tourist route, fly to Mthatha from Johannesburg;

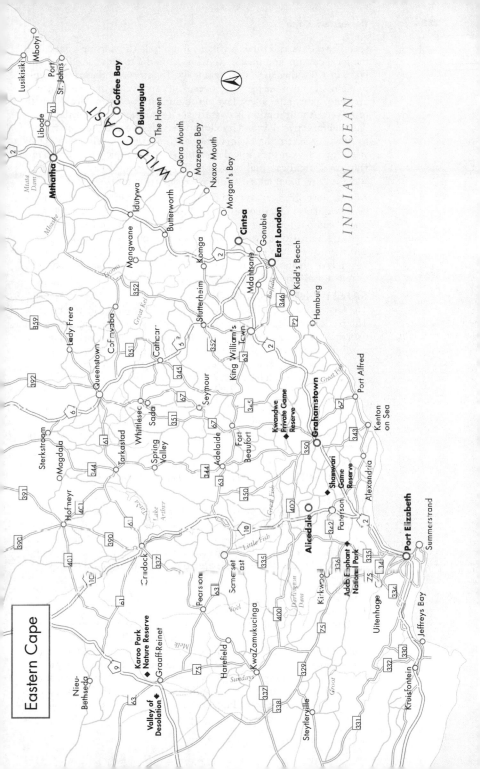

spend two days and three nights at Bulungula, immersing yourself in the local culture, and then drive from Mthatha to either Addo, Shamwari, or Kwandwe for a good game fix. If you spend these last couple of nights at one of the private lodges, you can revel in the indulgence of absolute luxury after a few days of roughing it. Return to Port Elizabeth to fly out. A third option is to start in Grahamstown, as for the three-day itinerary; two days in Grahamstown will give you the opportunity to fully appreciate the history and culture of this lovely town. Then spend two days at the game destination of your choice—Addo, Shamwari, or Kwandwe—and one more day in Port Elizabeth soaking up some culture, lounging on the beach, or playing golf.

7 Days: Start off as you would for the three-day itinerary but spend at least two days in Grahamstown and three days at your game destination. Then opt for some beach time at Port Elizabeth, Coffee Bay, or Cintsa. Alternatively, fly into East London to join the Wild Coast Meander; then spend two days at Addo, Shamwari, or Kwandwe. Head to Port Elizabeth and try to work in time to relax on the beach, play golf, or join a tour before flying out.

SAFETY AND PRECAUTIONS

The Eastern Cape is malaria-free, and the climate is generally healthy. The tap water in the deep rural areas may be a bit dicey, but it's fine in the cities and towns. Avoid driving east of Grahamstown at night: the roads are unfenced and animals wander onto—or even sleep on—the warm tarmac, which is a serious hazard. Be sure to bring protection against sunburn, and be careful swimming in the sea. The Wild Coast beaches don't have lifeguards.

In case of an emergency, call the general emergencies number. For vehicle breakdown, call your car-rental company. If your car is not a rental, call the Automobile Association (AA). If you need an emergency pharmacist, ask at your hotel.

Emergency Services Automobile Association (☎ 083/84322). **General Emergencies** (☎ 10111 from landline, 112 from mobile phone).

RESTAURANTS

Generally speaking, the restaurants of the Eastern Cape are good but not great. Of course there are always a few serendipitous exceptions to every rule, but for really good food choose a great guesthouse—some of which are noted for their cuisine. Not surprisingly, most restaurants are reasonably casual, and there are none where men would be expected to wear a tie.

HOTELS

Most hotels along the coast get booked up over summer vacation (December–January), and the Wild Coast hotels are even busy over the winter school vacation, usually around June. Most establishments run winter specials, but there are exceptions. Grahamstown is packed in late June and/or early July for the National Arts Festival; every guesthouse is full, the campsite bulges, and even school and university dorms rent out rooms. Hotels on the Wild Coast often offer packages for the sardine run, usually in June or early July, but it's always a bit of a gamble. The sardines are just not as reliable as the artists of the Grahamstown festival.

Note that although mailing addresses are provided for most of the lodgings below, you'll have a much easier time securing a reservation if you phone or, in some cases, book via the lodging's Web site. Another thing to keep in mind is that many of the lodgings on the Eastern Cape are in a state of flux in terms of Internet service provided for guest use: some have limited service, others offer high-speed connections, and still others are planning to expand their service. In the facilities lists for the lodgings in this chapter, we've specified when a lodging has an Internet terminal, which means there is a computer available for guest use, or Wi-Fi, for which you will need your own laptop. If the ability to connect to the Web is important to you, be sure to clarify the type of service available when you make your reservation.

WHAT IT COSTS IN SOUTH AFRICAN RAND					
	¢	$	$$	$$$	$$$$
Restaurants	under R40	R40–R75	R76–R125	R126–R175	over R175
Hotels	under R250	R250–R500	R501–R1,000	R1,001–R2,500	over R2,500

Restaurant prices are per person for a main course at dinner, a main course equivalent, or a prix-fixe meal. Hotel prices are for a standard double room in high season, including 14% tax.

MONEY MATTERS
You will find ATMs even in really small towns—but not tiny villages like Coffee Bay or Alicedale—and full-service banks in Port Elizabeth, East London, and Grahamstown. Some of the smaller businesses do not accept credit cards, and some of the medium-sized ones do not accept American Express and/or Diners Club.

FRONTIER COUNTRY

PORT ELIZABETH

770 km (477 mi) east of Cape Town.

Port Elizabeth, or PE, may not have the range of attractions found in Cape Town or on the Garden Route, but it's a pleasant town that's worthy of a few days' exploration. There are some beautiful beaches (although you'll need to visit them early in the day in summer as the wind tends to pick up by midday) and some wonderfully preserved historic buildings in the older part of the city, called Central. A large part of the town's charm lies in its small size and quiet environment, but PE is not a total sleepy hollow. If you feel the need for a bit of nightlife, head to the Boardwalk complex near the beach, for its restaurants, cafés, theater, and casino, or to Parliament Street in Central, which has recently been pedestrianized and has a vibrant restaurant and nightlife scene.

PE is a good base for exploring some other fantastic destinations, both wild and cultural, including Addo Elephant National Park. If you are traveling to any of the luxury game reserves east of Port Elizabeth (such as those in Addo, Shamwari or Kwandwe), it may be a good idea to spend the night before in PE, as many places advise you to check in before lunch and it could be a scramble to get there if you're driving or flying in that morning.

Port Elizabeth's suburbs can be a little confusing. Humewood and Summerstrand are PE's two main coastal suburbs, with Humewood closer to the city center. The Humewood Golf Course, one of South Africa's best, is in Summerstrand, not Humewood, however (just to keep you on your toes).

GETTING HERE AND AROUND

Port Elizabeth (PLZ) airport, small and easy to navigate, is served daily by South African Airways and SA Airlink. Kulula and 1time, two no-frills budget airlines, also offer a good service but usually have only one or two flights a day. You can fly here from Cape Town (1 hour), Johannesburg (1½ hours), and most other major cities; there are no international flights. There's a minibus shuttle at the airport that will drop you off at your hotel (R60 one way, much less than a metered taxi), but you'll need to book in advance.

Greyhound and Intercape Mainliner have pretty reliable and reasonably priced bus services, but the distances are long. Both services depart and arrive at Greenacres shopping complex, in the Newton Park suburb 3 km (1.8 miles) from the city center. This area is perfectly safe during the day, but you do need to arrange to be picked up in advance. If you are concerned about your budget, consider saving money by staying at a backpackers' lodge and spending a bit more on the Baz Bus (which travels door-to-door); an added benefit is that you won't have to wander around town with your luggage.

Traveling by car is the easiest and best way to tour this area. The major rental agencies have offices at the airport and in downtown PE. One-way rentals are available. Roads are generally in good shape, but east of Grahamstown the N2 is a single-lane road with no shoulders, few fences, and quite a few potholes.

SAFETY AND PRECAUTIONS

One thing to keep in mind is that although most of the Central area of PE is safe, a few parts of it can be dicey. The lower section along Govan Mbeki is lively and vibrant and the upper section is quiet and peaceful, but the bits in between have seen some crime. The area is slowly improving, but it's still best to get advice from your hotel or the tourism office before wandering around.

TOURS

★ **Calabash Tours** offers the best cultural, township, and shebeen tours in Port Elizabeth. In recognition of its commitment to community development, this operator has been awarded a Fair Trade in Tourism, SA accreditation—one of only a few. Calabash offers a tour of the local townships (R350), which usually includes a visit to the spectacular Red Location Museum or, for the more adventurous, an evening shebeen tour (R400) that includes visits to a couple of township taverns, dinner, and, almost certainly, some good music. Calabash also has multiday tours to Addo Elephant National Park, as well as three- to five-day African heritage tours.

From a short city or township tour to an all-day game-viewing excursion or an elephant ride, **Highwinds Adventure and Travel** offers a variety of tours in and around Port Elizabeth.

VISITOR INFORMATION
Port Elizabeth's Nelson Mandela Bay Tourism is open weekdays 8–4:30 and weekends 9:30–3:30.

ESSENTIALS
Airports Port Elizabeth Airport (☎ 041/507-7319 ⊕ www.acsa.co.za).

Airlines 1time (☎ 0861/345-345 ⊕ www1time.aero). **Kulula** (☎ 0861/585-852 ⊕ www.kulula-air.com). **SA Airlink** (☎ 0861/359-722 ⊕ www.saairlink.co.za). **South African Airways** (☎ 0861/359-722 ⊕ www.flysaa.com).

Airport Shuttle Blunden Minibus Shuttle (☎ 041/582-3720 ⊕ www.blunden.co.za).

Bus Lines Baz Bus (☎ 021/439-2323 ⊕ www.bazbus.com). **Greyhound** (☎ 083/915 9000 ⊕ www.greyhound.co.za). **Intercape Mainliner** (☎ 021/380-4400 ⊕ www.intercape.co.za).

Car Rentals Avis (☎ 041/363-3014 ⊕ www.avis.co.za). **Budget** (☎ 041/581-4242 ⊕ www.budget.co.za). **Europcar** (☎ 0861/131-000 ⊕ www.europcar.co.za). **Hertz** (☎ 041/508-6600 ⊕ www.hertz.co.za).

Emergency Services Automobile Association (☎ 083/84322). **General Emergencies** (☎ 10111 from landline, 112 from mobile phone). **National Sea Rescue Institute** (☎ 041/374-8315).

Hospitals Greenacres Hospital (✉ Rochelle and Cape Rds., Greenacres ☎ 041/390-7000).

Pharmacies Blooms Nu Pharmacy (✉ 323 Cape Rd. ☎ 041/365-2070).

Tours Calabash Tours (☎ 041/585-6162 ⊕ www.calabashtours.co.za). **Highwinds Adventure and Travel** (☎ 041/586-3721 ⊕ www.highwinds.co.za).

Visitor Information Nelson Mandela Bay Tourism (✉ Donkin Reserve, Belmont Terr., Central ☎ 041/585-8884 ⊕ www.nmbt.co.za).

EXPLORING
South End was once the most vibrant part of Port Elizabeth, until it was flattened by the apartheid-era government to "tidy up" the city and put everything and everyone in their places. At the **South End Museum** a map, photographs, and paintings give you an idea of what the old South End was like in its heyday. ✉ Humewood Rd. and Walmer Blvd., Summerstrand ☎ 041/582-3325 ⛫ Donations welcome ⊙ Weekdays 9–4, weekends 10–3.

Red Location Museum won the inaugural World Leadership Award in the Architecture and Civil Engineering category for 2005. Innovative displays, including multimedia memory boxes exploring the experiences of individuals under apartheid, depict the history of forced resettlement in the area. The museum, on the outskirts of town, is well signposted and safe to visit, but you may be more comfortable viewing it as part of a guided tour. ⊠ *Olaf Palme and Singaphi Sts., Red Location, New Brighton* ☎ *041/408–8400* ⊠ *R12* ⊘ *Tues.–Fri. 10–4, Sat. 9–3.*

BEACHES

The beaches listed here are lined with restaurants, shops, and coffee bars, and there are flea markets on weekends. Beyond Hobie Beach the seafront is still built up with houses and apartments, but the frenetic commercialism is missing.

> **DID YOU KNOW?**
>
> Port Elizabeth is the first South African city to supply off-road wheelchairs for use on the beach (either King's or Humewood). You can swap your regular street-legal chair for a "four-wheel-drive" model—and even get a lifeguard to help you in and out of the water. And, yes, it's free. Book the chairs through **PE Beaches** (☎ *041/584-0584*).

★ Within the bay and starting closest to the city center and harbor (which is best avoided), the first beach you come to is **King's Beach,** so named because King George VI slept in the Royal Train here during a visit to the city before World War II. You may want to avoid the far end of King's Beach, as it can get pretty crowded. ↻ *Lifeguard, toilets, showers, parking lot.*

The section of beach near **McArthur Baths** (☎ *041/582–2282*) is great for swimming and very popular. If you'd rather swim in flat water, head for the bath complex (R30, open September–April), which has a range of pools, two of which are heated to a few degrees above sea temperature. There's no natural grass here, however, so you will need to rent a lounge chair (R6) to be comfortable. ↻ *Lifeguard, toilets, showers.*

Humewood Beach runs from King's Beach to Shark Rock Pier. It's a great place for families, with shaded areas supplied by an overhead promenade. There's a convenient parking lot behind the beach (behind Buffalo Bills Steakhouse) and excellent facilities, plus lifeguards on duty during peak times. There are some grassy areas that lead into Happy Valley, but it's not recommended that you walk into the valley as it's often completely deserted and you may be in danger of being mugged. ↻ *Lifeguard, toilets, showers, picnic tables, parking lot.*

★ The pier marks the beginning of **Hobie Beach,** where sailing catamarans and Jet Skis launch. The section of beach closest to the pier is great for swimming. ↻ *Lifeguard, toilets, showers, food concession, parking lot.*

★ **Pollock Beach,** adjacent to the suburb of Summerstrand, is one of the better swimming beaches, with a lovely small natural tidal pool. It also offers great surfing. (Generally the surfing in PE is not too challenging, unlike at Jeffreys Bay, just over an hour's drive to the west, which has some pretty exciting waves.) The far end of Pollock Beach is best avoided, as it can get crowded with somewhat boisterous, picnicking, partying crowds. ↻ *Lifeguard, toilets, food concession, parking lot.*

CLOSE UP

Hanging Ten at Jeffreys Bay

When a right-hand break in St. Francis Bay was immortalized in the '60s cult surf classic *Endless Summer,* surfers from around the world made the pilgrimage to check it out for themselves. They soon discovered that the wave was not so perfect after all and began scouring the area only to stumble upon the right-hand break in Jeffreys Bay, which is now considered to be one of the top three surf spots in the world. At that point, Jeffreys Bay consisted of little more than some sand dunes and farms, but today it has become overdeveloped and rather tacky, and it gets extremely busy over the summer holidays.

WHERE TO STAY
If you're after a more tranquil, upmarket feel, St. Francis Bay is a better place to stay, although both towns have lovely beaches.

WHEN TO GO
Winter is the best season for surfing. The Billabong Pro, an annual competition, takes place every July.

SURF LESSONS
If you're a novice, it's pretty easy to rent a wet suit and find someone to give you some lessons.

5

For a truly fantastic beach experience, very little can beat Sardinia Bay Beach, outside the bay and about a 20-minute drive from the main beaches. Here, miles and miles of deserted, snow-white sand are great for long walks. It's best to come on weekends, however, as during the week it can be isolated and there have been a few incidents of muggings. On weekends there are plenty of people, and you will be perfectly safe. ☞ *Lifeguard, toilets, food concession, grills/fire pits, parking lot.*

WHERE TO EAT
The beachfront is lined with reasonably priced hotels and restaurants, as well as a few higher-quality ones.

$-$$
SEAFOOD
✕ **34° South.** Sibling to the fabulous deli-restaurant-fishmonger of the same name in Knysna, this popular restaurant at the well-frequented Boardwalk has a relaxed, nautical theme inside and outside seating on a terrace overlooking the lake. The line fish is always fresh, and the best way to try it is as a line fish *espatada*—skewered chunks of firm, white fish grilled with roasted peppers and onions and drizzled with lemon butter. For an equally fishy experience, fill a huge platter from the seafood meze. Try one of the raspberry cheesecakes for dessert. ⊠ *Boardwalk, Marine Dr., Summerstrand* ☎ *041/583–1085* ▤ *AE, DC, MC, V.*

$$
SOUTH AFRICAN
Fodor's Choice
★
✕ **Ginger.** This is Port Elizabeth's fine-dining option, and a welcome addition to the beachfront dining scene. It's located in the Beach Hotel opposite the pier. Glass doors open onto a terrace, with sea views, or you can sit inside at tables placed around the bar, which is located in the center of the restaurant. Cuisine is contemporary with local flavors; highlights include ostrich fillet with a tangy ginger-and-beer sauce and whole grilled crayfish with béarnaise sauce and buttered herb rice. There's also a large selection of steaks and game meats. For dessert try

a Spice Route ice-cream plate, with four different flavors of ice cream: ginger, cinnamon, fennel, and honey. Or, order the crêpe suzette, which is served from a flambé trolley that is brought to your table. The wine list is excellent, and there's a small but good selection of wines available by the glass. Prices are reasonable, especially considering the size of the portions. A lighter lunch menu features warm salads, sandwiches, burgers, and pastas, as well as some seafood and steak dishes. ⊠ *The Beach Hotel, Marine Dr., Summerstrand* ☎ *041/583–1229* ⊕ *www. ginger-restaurant.co.za* ⊟ *AE, DC, MC, V.*

WHERE TO STAY

$$$$
★
🏨 **Hacklewood Hill Country House.** For superbly comfortable and gracious lodgings, try this inn set in English-style gardens in the leafy suburb of Walmer. Beautiful antiques, such as four-poster beds, furnish the spacious rooms—some of which are downright enormous, with sofas and huge wardrobes. The Victorian baths are also huge, with separate showers and marble-top vanities. All rooms except one have balconies. The hotel restaurant offers some of the best dining in town, and nonguests will be accommodated if there's space; booking in advance is essential. Food is French-style cuisine with a South African twist, and the four-course set menu is R215. Light meals are available during the day, and there's a four-course set menu at night. **Pros:** it has a great air of tranquility; service is excellent. **Cons:** decor is a bit old-fashioned; it's not in walking distance of the beachfront; no a/c. ⊠ *152 Prospect Rd.* ⓓ *Box 5108, Walmer 6065* ☎ *041/581–1300* ⊕ *www.hacklewood.co.za* 🛏 *8 rooms* ⚴ *In-room: safe, refrigerator. In-hotel: restaurant, room service, bar, tennis court, pool, laundry service, Internet terminal, Wi-Fi, parking (free), no kids under 8* ⊟ *AE, DC, MC, V* ⑩ *BP.*

¢
🏨 **Jikeleza Lodge.** In a quiet part of the Central neighborhood, this hostel tends to attract mature backpackers who are more interested in culture and adventure activities than partying. Rooms are clean, comfortable, and basic, the communal kitchen is well-appointed, and the managers are friendly and helpful. There's a lovely garden looking over the valley, which has visiting *dassies* (a guinea pig–like animal unique to South Africa). **Pros:** within walking distance of restaurants and bars in less touristy area than the beachfront; tables in the garden make dining (either brought in or cooked in the communal kitchen) a pleasure. **Cons:** you will need to take a taxi to the beachfront; Internet access is not free. ⊠ *44 Cuyler St., Central Hill* ☎ *041/586–3721* ⊕ *www.jikelezalodge. co.za* 🛏 *6 rooms, 2 dormitories* ⚴ *In-room: no phone, no TV. In-hotel: bar, laundry service, Internet terminal, parking (free)* ⊟ *AE, MC, V.*

$$–$$$
★
🏨 **King's Tide Boutique Hotel.** In a quiet part of Summerstrand, this hotel feels cocooned, but it's close to the Boardwalk and Humewood Golf Course and within easy walking distance of Pollock Beach. The rooms are richly furnished with heavy fabrics and dark wood (which is not as overpowering as it sounds). Most bathrooms have enormous tubs and triple-head showers in roomy stalls, though four rooms have showers only. **Pros:** has a comfortable communal lounge with reading material; Wi-Fi in all the rooms; barbecue facilities are available. **Cons:** small swimming pool; no garden (only a patio). ⊠ *16 10th Ave., Summerstrand* ☎ *041/583–6023* ⊕ *www.kingstide.co.za* 🛏 *10 rooms*

In-room: a/c (some), Wi-Fi. In-hotel: room service, bar, pool, laundry service, Internet terminal, Wi-Fi, parking (free), no kids under 16 ☰ AE, DC, MC, V ⍾ BP.

$$$ ★ 🏨 **La Provence Country House.** Rooms look out over lovely gardens, rolling lawns, and horse-filled paddocks on this large property. It's a quiet, restful place to stay, and the garden suites, which were once very roomy stables, are particularly soothing. The rooms, in shades of white and beige with wicker furniture, are monastically understated, although white percale cotton linen and underfloor heating in the bathrooms adds a luxurious touch. A quick drive will bring you to the lovely Sardinia Bay Beach, where you can go for a long, leisurely walk of up to 8 km (5 mi). It's worth staying for the delicious three-course dinners ($$–$$$), as this establishment is a member of the Good Cooks and Their Country Houses. The menu changes daily, and nonguests are accommodated if there is room. **Pros:** gourmet dining, including light lunches; attentive service. **Cons:** it's a bit of a drive to town and to the airport; Wi-Fi is in public areas only. ⍟ *Old Seaview Rd., Lovemore Heights ⍟ Box 15777, Emerald Hill 6011 ☎ 041/368–1911 ⊕ www.laprovence.co.za ⟱ 10 rooms ⍾ In-room: a/c (some), safe, refrigerator. In-hotel: restaurant, tennis court, pool, laundry service, Internet terminal, Wi-Fi, parking (free), no kids under 10 ☰ AE, DC, MC, V ⍾ BP.*

$$ 🏨 **Summerstrand Hotel.** Two major attractions of this hotel are its good prices and its location—close to the beach on the quieter side of the bay and virtually on top of the excellent Humewood Golf Course. But it's the deeply entrenched culture of service that sets this large, comfortable, owner-managed hotel apart from the many other city hotels it otherwise resembles. Sea-facing rooms have lovely bay views, and golf course–facing rooms have excellent views of the fourth and fifth holes, plus a generous glimpse of sea. Rooms are spacious; singles have king-size beds, whereas doubles have two double beds. Ask for a sea view when you book. Original artwork decorates the public rooms and suites. **Pros:** free shuttle to the Boardwalk Complex; excellent on-site travel office will help you arrange tours and onward travel. **Cons:** exterior looks a bit bleak and dilapidated; it's a popular conference venue so can get a bit noisy. ⍟ *Marine Dr., Summerstrand ⍟ Box 204, Port Elizabeth 6000 ☎ 041/583–3131 ⊕ www.summerstrandhotel.co.za ⟱ 136 rooms, ⍾ In-room: safe, refrigerator (some). ⍾ In-hotel: restaurant, room service, bar, pool, laundry service, Internet terminal, Wi-Fi, parking (free) ☰ AE, DC, MC, V.*

SPORTS AND THE OUTDOORS
GOLF

★ Consistently listed as one of the country's top 10 courses, the challenging championship **Humewood Golf Course** (⍟ *Marine Dr., Summerstrand* ☎ *041/583–2137* ⊕ *www.humewoodgolf.co.za*) is set in undulating dunes on the edge of Algoa Bay, making it one of South Africa's few natural links courses. The late South African golfer Bobby Locke considered it the finest course in the country and compared it favorably to the best of British links courses. At 7,030 yards and exposed to stiff sea breezes, it's not for the fainthearted. Greens fees are R515, cart fees R200, caddies R100–120, and club rental R245.

ALICEDALE

5 km (3 mi) north of edge of Shawmari, 60 km (37 mi) west of Grahamstown.

A tiny settlement west of Grahamstown, Alicedale was once an important railway town. The demise of the steam train, however, sent Alicedale into decline, turning it into a virtual ghost town populated by a depressed band of unemployed wraiths subsisting on meager railway pensions and funds sent home from family members working elsewhere. The development of a major golf course, hotel, and game reserve, however, has brought life back to Alicedale: property prices have risen, unemployment is down, and a sense of relative prosperity is slowly settling on the town.

GETTING HERE AND AROUND

The road that connects Alicedale to the N10 road from Port Elizabeth is currently being paved. There's no public transport besides local minibus taxis, which are cheap and convenient but not always safe; they are best suited to the adventurous traveler. The Bushman Sands Hotel can arrange transfers from Port Elizabeth through Avis, but your best bet is to rent a car, especially if you want to visit sights in the surrounding areas.

WHERE TO STAY

$$ ⊞**Bushman Sands Hotel.** Built around a demanding Gary Player–designed, links-style golf course and adjacent to the Bushman Sands Game Reserve, this hotel offers a number of leisure options—including golf, game drives, and sunset cruises on the nearly 500-acre New Year's Dam. Rooms are in separate structures that echo the style of the original Victorian school building, which forms the hotel's center. The decor is understated and classical, with black-and-white-tile bathroom floors and claw-foot tubs. The suites, which are renovated railway cottages, have fabulous bathrooms, with shower stalls just big enough for you and your favorite baseball team. The food served at the restaurant is nothing special, but the golf course setting makes this a pleasant enough place to eat. The smart-casual dress code means that men are not allowed to wear T-shirts, jeans, or open-toed shoes. **Pros:** luxurious health and spa facilities; there is the opportunity to fit in a game drive at the adjacent Bushman Sands Game Reserve. **Cons:** service can be erratic; there isn't much for children. ⊠ *Main St.* ⌂ *Box 39, 6135* ☎ *042/231–8000* ⊕ *www.bushmansands.com* ⤴ *34 rooms, 5 suites* ⚿ *In-room: safe, refrigerator. In-hotel: restaurant, room service, bar, golf course, pools, gym, spa, laundry service, Internet terminal, parking (free)* ⊟ *AE, DC, MC, V* ⎮⊚⎮ *BP.*

SPORTS AND THE OUTDOORS
GOLF

The challenging, links-style 6,599-yard championship **Bushman Sands Golf Course** (☎ *042/231–8000* ⊕ *www.bushmansands.com*), designed by South African golfer Gary Player, undulates along the banks of the Bushman's and New Year's rivers. Greens fees are R275 (R135 for hotel guests), cart fees are R160, and club rental costs R175.

GRAHAMSTOWN

60 km (37 mi) east of Alicedale, 120 km (75 mi) northeast of Port Elizabeth.

Although billed as a city, Grahamstown looks more like an English village than anything else—if you discount that alter ego of most South African towns, the desperately poor contiguous shanty townships. These are a big part of Grahamstown, and they contribute to the city's wealth of cultural history. Established as a garrison town to enforce the arbitrarily assigned border of the British Cape Colony, Grahamstown was the center of several battles during the last couple of centuries.

It's worth spending a day or two to explore the sights and to perhaps take two different tours—just to reinforce the fact that history, no matter how accurately portrayed, is always subjective.

GETTING HERE AND AROUND

It's easiest and best to tour this area by car. Roads are generally in good shape, but there's a distinct difference in road conditions east and west of Grahamstown. To the west (that is, on the PE side) roads are wide, often dual lane, and well maintained. East of Grahamstown the N2 is a single-lane road with no shoulders, few fences, and quite a few potholes.

From PE, the drive is approximately 1½ hours, and half an hour from Alicedale. Bus services (Greyhound, Intercape) stop in the center of town. There's also Minilux, a minibus shuttle that runs from PE Airport to Grahamstown most days of the week and then on to East London.

Grahamstown is small enough that you can easily walk around on foot, although you should take a taxi at night.

TOURS

One of South Africa's most seminal historical incidents was the 1819 Battle of Grahamstown, when the Xhosa prophet Makana tried to rid his area of British colonizers. Makana was arrested and sent to Robben Island, where he died trying to escape. You can relive this battle from the point of view of young Xhosa historians with the Grahamstown-based Egazini Tours. The cost varies according to the number of people on the tour, but should be about R200 if you have a rental car and are prepared to drive the guide around. The tour usually includes a visit to the Egazini Outreach Project, where you can see and buy local artworks, screen-printed fabric, T-shirts, and bags.

Fodor'sChoice Spirits of the Past, run by Grahamstown oral historian Alan Weyer, has
★ fascinating and informative full- and half-day tours of the surrounding countryside, including visits to local forts, a balanced but emotive relation of the Battle of Grahamstown, and a visit to the Valley of the Ancient Voices, which is rich in rock art (and is best appreciated with a knowledgeable guide like Weyer). Prices range from about R600 to R1,500 per person.

VISITOR INFORMATION

In Grahamstown, Makana Tourism is open weekdays 8–5 and Saturday 9–1.

ESSENTIALS

Bus Service Minilux (☎ 043/741–3107).

Pharmacy RET Butler Pharmacy (✉ *Bathurst St.* ☎ 046/622–7305).

Rental Cars Avis (☎ 046/622–2235 ⊕ *www.avis.co.za*).

Tours Egazini Tours (☎ 046/637–1500). **Spirits of the Past** (☎ 046/622–2843 ⊕ *www.spiritsofthepast.co.za*).

Visitor Information Makana Tourism (✉ 63 *High St.* ☎ 046/622–3241 ⊕ *www.grahamstown.co.za*).

EXPLORING

Home to Rhodes University and some of the country's top schools, Grahamstown is considered by many to be the seat of culture and learning in South Africa.

The 10-day **National Arts Festival** (☎ *046/603–1103* ⊕ *www.nafest.co.za*), which takes place in late June and/or early July and is purported to be second in size only to the Edinburgh Festival in Scotland, is the country's premier cultural event.

TOP ATTRACTIONS

The **Cathedral of St. Michael and St. George** is Grahamstown's most prominent landmark, as much by virtue of its steeple—the highest in South Africa at 176 feet—as the strict geometry of the town. High Street runs in a straight line from the cathedral doors through the Drostdy Arch to the doors of the administration buildings of Rhodes University. The cathedral's eight bells, which you can hear ringing out on Sundays, were the first and still are the heaviest in Africa. Though construction on the cathedral started in 1824, it wasn't completed until 1952. ✉ *108 High St.* ☎ *046/622–2445* 🎫 *Free* ☉ *Weekdays 9–3, Sat. 9–noon.*

The **Observatory Museum** is an intriguing study of Victorian-era cutting-edge science. The building was constructed by a watchmaker and amateur astronomer, H. C. Gulpin, who built a cupola above his shop to house his instruments. The museum contains a two-story pendulum and the only genuine Victorian camera obscura in the Southern Hemisphere. You can stand in the tower and watch what's happening in the town below—pretty useful if you've lost your companions. ✉ *10 Bathurst St.* ☎ *046/622–2312* 🎫 *R10* ☉ *Weekdays 9–4:30, Sat. 9–1.*

WORTH NOTING

The statue of the **Winged Angel of Peace** commemorates the dead of the Second South African War (1899–1902), also called the Boer War. The site was chosen as one that was "in the midst of our daily work," so it would be seen often and would serve as an inspiration for peace. Irreverent students can't help pointing out that it looks as though the angel is supporting a drunk (not dying) soldier and pointing accusingly at one of the local pubs. ✉ *Bathurst St.*

The **National English Literary Museum** houses a comprehensive collection of books, articles, and press clippings on South African writers in the English language, including some unpublished works. There is also a bookshop. ✉ *87 Beaufort St.* ☎ *046/622–7042* 🎫 *Free* ☉ *Weekdays 8:30–4:30.*

CLOSE UP

Grahamstown's Arts Festival

The National Arts Festival (⊕ www. nafest.co.za) began in 1974 with some 60-odd performances, and now offers a staggering variety of entertainment. Besides theaters, every conceivable kind of venue is utilized, including churches, school halls, museums, and pubs. There is a formal program, an official fringe festival, and even a fringe of the fringe that gets seriously alternative. Some offbeat productions have included families of giant puppets and stilt workers roaming the streets and a theater ensemble who create hair installations on its audience. Others are more thought-provoking and challenging, such as a walk through the streets of the town with homeless children, highlighting the inequality of wealth in South Africa. You can also see local and international music, theater, ballet and modern dance performances. There's a Children's Festival and a large outdoor market with vendors selling everything from hand-painted T-shirts to local crafts.

The large festival events and the film festival are staged at the **1820 Settlers National Monument,** a concrete edifice on Gunfire Hill, next to the old garrison, Fort Selwyn. Sundowner concerts at 5 PM in the monument's foyer give previews of the various shows.

TICKETS
Tickets are available via Computicket (⊕ www.computicket.com) up to two months before the festival.

GETTING TO AND AROUND THE FESTIVAL
If you are flying into Port Elizabeth, you can rent a car to make the hour-long journey to Grahamstown, or you can take the festival minibus that meets passengers at the airport (until 8 PM, R150 per person). Check out the festival Web site for booking information.

In Grahamstown, the Hopper Bus travels between the monument and various venues throughout the day. Timetables and booking information for all festival-related events are on the comprehensive Web site.

WHERE TO STAY
A wide variety of accommodations is available, ranging from rooms in university halls to private-home stays. It's advisable to plan your trip three months in advance or more, but it's still possible to find something at the last minute. Many overseas visitors stay in surrounding towns or on game farms in the area (which often have special packages) and make day trips into the town.

BE PREPARED
The festival takes place in midwinter, and it's always very cold at night. Days can be hot and sunny, so it's advisable to wear layers, and to bring a coat and scarf.

When Grahamstown was a garrison town, the **Drostdy Arch,** erected in 1841, was the original entrance to the military parade ground. Now it is the gateway through which thousands of Rhodes students pass when leaving campus for town. There is a small crafts market "under the Arch" on weekdays 9–5 and Saturday 9–1. ⊠ *High St.*

The **International Library of African Music** is a teaching and research center for indigenous music. It has a collection of more than 200 traditional African musical instruments, including *djembes* (drums), *mbiras* (thumb pianos), and marimbas (xylophones). ⊠ *Rhodes University, Prince Alfred St.* ☎ *046/603–8557* ⊠ *Free* ⊙ *Weekdays 8–12:45 and 2–4:30.*

> ## THE ELASTIC CITY
>
> Most of the year Grahamstown is pretty small, but around festival time (late June/early July) this elastic city expands to accommodate the tens of thousands of festival goers. Come December, it shrinks to a mere ghost of itself as the students and scholars go home.

WHERE TO EAT AND STAY

You won't find a great choice of dining establishments here, particularly when it comes to fine dining, as Grahamstown is largely a student town. There are a number of cafés on High Street that are reasonable.

Your best bet for help with lodging, especially at festival time, is the **Grahamstown Accommodation Bureau** (⌂ *Box 166, 6140* ☎ *046/622–3261 or 074/148–7146* ⊕ *www.grahamstownaccom.co.za*).

¢–$ ✕ **137 High St.** Conveniently located right on High Street, this warm, friendly coffee shop is popular with students, and there's outside seating in a pretty, sunny courtyard. It serves the usual pastas, sandwiches, and salads—and arguably the best coffee in town. The seven-room bed-and-breakfast ($$) upstairs has fabulous yellowwood floors in the residents' lounge. One room has a tub; the others have showers only. There's a self-catering one-bedroom flat, too. ⊠ *137 High St.* ☎ *046/622–3242* ⊕ *www.137highstreet.co.za* ⊟ *MC, V* ⊙ *No dinner Sun.*

$$$ ⊞ **7 Worcester Street.** Built in 1888, this magnificent dressed-stone man-
★ sion has been meticulously restored and beautifully decorated with a mix of local, Thai, and Indonesian artifacts. Rooms are elegantly proportioned and have high ceilings and large bathrooms. There are also attractive garden rooms next to the swimming pool. Dinner is by arrangement. As befits an establishment of this nature, the service is friendly and discreet, and no request seems too much trouble for the staff. You can arrange cultural and historical tours and activities through the inn. **Pros:** fine-dining restaurant; front patio is a wonderful place to have breakfast. **Cons:** no air-conditioning in the hotel, although the rooms do stay cool in summer; it's not in easy walking distance of town. ⊠ *7 Worcester St.* ☎ *046/622–2843* ⊕ *www.worcesterstreet.co.za* ↵ *10 rooms* ↺ *In-room: safe, refrigerator. In-hotel: bar, pool, laundry service, Internet terminal, Wi-Fi, parking (free)* ⊟ *MC, V* ⊠ *BP.*

$$ ⊞ **Cock House.** Over the years, this charming building, a National Monument built in 1826, has been the home of distinguished citizens, most notably academic and novelist André Brink, so it's fitting that the

individually decorated rooms are named after previous owners. The small hotel suffers from (or is blessed by, depending on how you look at it) the rather haphazard improvements that have been made over time. The spacious reception rooms have beautiful wooden floors. The dining room ($–$$) is large and somewhat gloomy, but the food is fantastic, and it's worth staying here just for that. You can also book a table for breakfast, lunch, or dinner if you're staying elsewhere. Try the delicious lamb shank, served in a thyme-and-rosemary sauce, or feta-cheese soufflé with *peppadews* (a cross between a sweet pepper and a chili). Dinner is usually a set menu, but à la carte is available. The next-door building has four self-catering apartments, which are good value for a longer stay, though they are cold and lack atmosphere. The rooms in converted cottages in the garden are the most attractive. **Pros:** a small, lovely garden in the back; good restaurant. **Cons:** rooms are on the small side; no air-conditioning in the hotel. ⊠ *10 Market St., at George St.* ☎ *046/636–1295* ⊕ *www.cockhouse.co.za* ☞ *7 rooms, 2 suites, 4 apartments ⚹ In-hotel: restaurant, bar, laundry service, Internet terminal, Wi-Fi, parking (free)* ▤ *AE, DC, MC, V* ⊺⊙⊺ *BP.*

WILD COAST

As the name suggests, the Wild Coast is a haven of unspoiled wilderness. While other areas of the country have become tourist playgrounds, the Coast's lack of infrastructure has resulted in the large undeveloped swathe of country east of Cintsa. The coastline consists of more than 280 km (174 mi) of desolate white-sand beaches, ragged cliffs, and secluded bays. Inland it's green and forested, with abundant birdlife. With mild year-round weather, this is a great destination for the adventure traveler.

To many though, this part of the Eastern Cape is a glimpse into the "real" South Africa. The mostly Xhosa population farm the land communally, domestic animals roam free, and traditional thatched *rondawel* huts dot the landscape. This is also one of South Africa's poorest regions, but the introduction of responsible tourism is helping to raise employment levels.

East London, the largest city in the area, has excellent transport links with the rest of the country and is a good starting point for visiting the region.

EAST LONDON

150 km (93 mi) east of Grahamstown.

The gateway to the Wild Coast, East London was built around the mouth of the Buffalo River, which forms South Africa's only river port. Although fairly urban, East London is still close to the rural heartland, so it retains a pleasantly small-town air. There's a great museum here, and you can take a half-day city tour, an escorted visit to a local township, or a full-day tour of a rural village (➪ *Tours, below*). Although the beaches on the outskirts of the city are wonderful, those within the central business district are crowded and not very pleasant.

GETTING HERE AND AROUND

The small and easy-to-navigate East London (ELS) airport is served daily by South African Airways and SA Airlink. The budget airline 1time flies here from both Johannesburg and Cape Town. The airport has all the expected facilities. There's also an airport shuttle service called the Little Red Bus, which will drop you off at your hotel, but you'll need to book it in advance.

> **DID YOU KNOW?**
>
> East London is part of Buffalo City, the name given to the towns clustered in this area: East London, King William's Town, and Bhisho, the administrative center of the province.

Greyhound and Intercape Mainliner have pretty reliable and reasonably priced bus services from the country's major cities, including Johannesburg and Cape Town, but the distances are long. The Minilux minibus service also travels from Port Elizabeth to East London via Grahamstown. All the buses stop and depart from the coach terminal in town. A more convenient option is the Baz Bus, which travels to East London, Cintsa, and Coffee Bay and will drop you off at your lodgings.

It's easiest and best to tour this region by car. The major rental agencies have offices at East London's airport and in the city's downtown section. One-way rentals are available. Roads are wide, often dual lane, and well maintained. Northeast of East London there are long sections of road that are relatively broad and well maintained, but they are all unfenced—meaning livestock can wander onto the road—and some stretches have potholes.

TOURS

Based in East London, Imonti Tours runs a three- to four-hour tour through the local township, including a visit to a *sangoma* (traditional healer) and a local shebeen where you can enjoy a *braai* (barbecue) lunch and drinks with the locals, and listen to some awesome jazz (R220). On Sundays, the tour includes a church visit. A tour of a rural village takes the whole day and costs R390. Imonti's full-day Nelson Mandela Freedom Trail takes in Mandela's childhood home in Qunu and the Nelson Mandela Museum in Mthatha. The price ranges from R650 per person for groups of four (two people minimum) and includes lunch.

The Wild Coast has been a favorite hiking destination for years, but the overnight huts have practically disintegrated. Perhaps they will be repaired, but until then you can take advantage of some good options—perhaps better than the original—offered by the East London–based Wild Coast Holiday Reservations. ■TIP→ These Wild Coast Holiday tours are highly recommended. The Wild Coast Meander and the Wild Coast Amble are five- or six-day guided hikes during which you walk between hotels and/or resorts on the southern section of the coast. Farther north, the Hole-in-the-Wall and Wild Coast Pondo walks traverse more remote and less densely populated terrain. The Pondo Walk is a series of treks to and from a comfortable base camp over far more spectacular, but also much steeper, terrain than what you'll find on the other hikes. The trips are all catered, and you can arrange to have your luggage driven or portered. Costs start at R3,900 per person. Shorter walks can be organized by request. This really is the best of both worlds. You walk on deserted beaches during the day and stay in comfy hotels with all the modern conveniences at night.

VISITOR INFORMATION

Tourism Buffalo City, in East London, is open weekdays 8–4:30, Saturday 9–2, and Sunday 9–1.

ESSENTIALS

Airlines 1time (☎ 0861/345–345 ⊕ www1time.aero). **SA Airlink** (☎ 0861/359–722 ⊕ www.saairlink.co.za). **South African Airways** (☎ 0861/359–722 ⊕ www.flysaa.com).

Airports East London Airport (☎ 043/706–0306 ⊕ www.acsa.co.za).

Airport Shuttle Little Red Bus (☎ 082/569–3599).

Bus Lines Baz Bus (☎ 021/439–2323 ⊕ www.bazbus.com). **Greyhound** (☎ 083/915–9000 ⊕ www.greyhound.co.za). **Intercape Mainliner** (☎ 021/380–4400 ⊕ www.intercape.co.za). **Minilux** (☎ 043/741 3107).

Emergency Services Automobile Association (☎ 083/84322). **General Emergencies** (☎ 10111 from landline, 112 from mobile phone). **National Sea Rescue Institute** (☎ 043/700-2100, 043/700-2142, or 082/990-5972).

Hospitals St. Dominic's Hospital (✉ 15 St. Mark's Rd., Southernwood ☎ 043/707-9000).

Pharmacies Berea Pharmacy (✉ 31 Pearce St., Berea ☎ 043/721-1300).

Rental Companies Avis (☎ 043/736–1344 ⊕ www.avis.co.za). **Budget** (☎ 043/707–5300 ⊕ www.budget.co.za). **Europcar** (☎ 043/736–3092 ⊕ www.europcar.com). **Hertz** (☎ 043/736–2116 ⊕ www.hertz.co.za).

Tours Imonti (☎ 083/487–8975 ⊕ www.imontitours.co.za).

Wild Coast Holiday Reservations (☎ 043/743–6181 ⊕ www.wildcoast-holidays.co.za).

Visitor Information Tourism Buffalo City (✉ 91 Western Ave., Vincent ☎ 043/721-1346 ⊕ www.tourismbuffalocity.co.za).

EXPLORING

There's definitely something fishy going on at the **East London Museum.** In addition to a whole section on the discovery of the coelacanth, the museum has a large display of preserved fish, including an enormous manta ray. For a different kind of fishy, check out what is claimed to be the world's only surviving dodo egg. *Jurassic Park,* here we come! Probably the most worthwhile exhibit, though, is the extensive beadwork collection; it's culturally interesting and just plain beautiful. ✉ 319 Oxford St. ☎ 043/743–0686 ☎ R10 ⊙ Weekdays 9–4:30, Sat. 10–1, Sun. 10–3.

BEACHES

East London is just far enough north of PE that the water and the weather are a bit warmer, but the inner-city beaches are not that great and would appeal more to surfers than to general loungers.

Gonubie Beach is at the mouth of the Gonubie River, about half an hour northeast of the city. The riverbank is covered in dense forest, with giant *strelitzias* (wild banana trees) growing right to the water's edge. A lovely beach, tidal pools, and a 500-yard-long wooden walkway make this a fantastically user-friendly beach. ☞ *Lifeguard, toilets, showers, food concession, picnic tables, grills/fire pits, playground, parking lot.*

Nahoon Beach, at the mouth of the Nahoon River, about a 20-minute drive from the city, has some fantastic surf—but only for people who know what they're doing. It's also just a lovely beach for sunbathing and watching surfers, and the lagoon is great for swimming and snorkeling. ☞ *Lifeguard, toilets, food concession, picnic tables, grills/fire pits, playground, parking lot, camping.*

WHERE TO STAY

$$ 🏨 **Blue Lagoon Hotel.** Overlooking the mouth of the beautiful Nahoon
☺   River and within easy reach of Nahoon Beach, this is a great place for a low-key family beach break. The standard rooms are quite ordinary and lack views, but the family suites have magnificent views of the lagoon, the sea, or both. Each suite has two bedrooms, one bathroom with tub and shower, a well-appointed kitchen, a living room, and a spacious balcony. The restaurants (¢–$$) are popular with locals—as much for the fabulous views as for the large menu of pastas, steaks, and fish dishes, plus a few interesting innovations thrown in. **Pros:** staff are friendly and warm; there's an airport shuttle. **Cons:** it's a conference venue so can get noisy; only the suites have river or sea views. ✉ *Blue Bend Pl.* 🏠 *Box 2177, Beacon Bay 5205* 🖀 *043/748–4821* ⊕ *www.bluelagoonhotel.co.za* 🛏 *67 rooms, 36 suites* ♿ *In-room: kitchen (some), Wi-Fi. In-hotel: 2 restaurants, bars, pool, spa, beachfront, laundry service, Internet terminal, Wi-Fi, parking (free)* ☰ *AE, DC, MC, V* ⍾ *BP.*

$$ 🏨 **Meander Inn.** In the leafy suburb of Selborne, Meander Inn is close to the East London Museum, restaurants, and shops. It's a convenient place to stay on either side of a Wild Coast hike, but it's also great for business travelers, thanks to its business services. Of the older rooms in the main house, one is not en suite, but it does have its own bathroom across the hall. All rooms are predominantly white, with a different color accent in the soft furnishings. The newer rooms have wood accents and stylish bathrooms with black-granite finishes. All rooms have showers but no tubs. Dinner is available by request. **Pros:** pool and gardens are lovely; good business facilities are available; there's an airport shuttle. **Cons:** groups about to embark on the Wild Coast Meander stay here the night before, so it could get noisy; rooms don't have air-conditioning or telephones. ✉ *8 Clarendon Rd., Selborne* 🏠 *Box 8017, Nahoon, East London 5210* 🖀 *043/726–2310* 🛏 *10 rooms* ♿ *In-room: no phone. In-hotel: bar, pool, laundry service, Internet terminal, parking (free)* ☰ *AE, DC, MC, V* ⍾ *BP.*

$$ 🏨 **Stratfords Guest House.** It's worth staying at this friendly, stylish guest-
★   house just to see the building. A masterpiece of design, it makes excellent use of space and utilizes unusual materials like corrugated iron, bare concrete, wood, and glass in incredibly innovative ways to create a comfortable, stimulating environment. It received a merit award from the SA Institute of Architects. Loft suites have microwaves, fridges, and combination tub-showers, whereas the other rooms have only showers. Centrally situated in the suburb of Vincent, Stratfords is close to the

East London Museum, shops, and restaurants. It's particularly popular with business travelers. **Pros:** the building is unusual and was designed by the owner; the garden is sheltered from the elements. **Cons:** there's no Internet access if you don't have your own laptop; it's also a conferencing venue so could get noisy. ⊠ *31 Frere Rd., Vincent* ☎ *043/726–9765* ⤴ *12 rooms, 4 suites* ♿ *In-room: refrigerator (some). In-hotel: bar, pool, laundry service, Wi-Fi, parking (free)* ▭ *MC, V* ⊙ *BP.*

¢ 🖼 **Sugarshack Backpackers.** The numerous wet suits and surfboards lying around make it clear that this fun, casual hostel is the place to go if you're after some waves. It's right on Eastern Beach in Quigney, a suburb of East London; the big open-air deck, which leads off the communal kitchen-lounge, is a great place to sit and watch the waves. Double rooms, which share bathrooms with dorm residents and campers, are in cute but tiny wooden cabins with their own sea-view verandas. There are loads of restaurants and pubs within walking distance. Like most hostels, this place can get quite lively; drumming evenings are a regular occurrence. All kinds of adventure tours (such as paddling and sandboarding) are on offer, along with surfing lessons. Reasonably priced beauty treatments can also be arranged off-site. It's next door to the Buccaneers Pub and Grill, and you get free beer if you're staying at Sugarshack. **Pros:** in easy walking distance of the bus station, or the Baz Bus will drop you off here; prices are very reasonable. **Cons:** no on-site restaurant; camping spaces are limited. ⊠ *Eastern Beach, Quigney* ⓓ *Box 18312, Quigney 5201* ☎ *043/722–8240* ⊕ *www.sugarshack.co.za* ⤴ *5 rooms without baths, 4 dormitories, 4 camping spaces* ♿ *In-room: no phone, no TV. In-hotel: bar, beachfront, laundry service, Internet terminal* ▭ *No credit cards.*

CINTSA

40 km (25 mi) northeast of East London.

This lovely, quiet little seaside town a half-hour's drive from East London is a winner. A nice long beach, pretty rock pools, and a beautiful lagoon on which to paddle make this a coastal paradise. Not much happens here, which is its main attraction. The town—if it can be called a town—is divided by the river mouth into an eastern and a western side. It's a drive of about 10 km (6 mi) between them, although you can walk across the river at low tide (most of the time). The town has a couple of restaurants and small shops, plus a good choice of accommodations.

GETTING HERE AND AROUND

It's best to tour this area by car, and the road from East London to Cintsa is paved and in good condition. The Baz Bus drops passengers off in Cintsa. Greyhound buses go as far as East London, but do not continue any farther up the coast; they veer inland to Bloemfontein and then rejoin the coast in Durban. Greyhound buses go from East London to Mthatha, but they do not make any stops along the way except at Butterworth, a town inland on the N2.

5

TOURS

■ **TIP**➜ African Heartland Journeys arranges excellent tours into the Transkei and Wild Coast. They cost anywhere from R700 to R2,000 daily, depending on the nature of the trip and the number of guests. Tours generally focus on the people and culture but all include an element of adventure and are tailor-made to suit the needs, interests, and fitness levels of participants. You can choose to travel by vehicle, ATV, horse, canoe, mountain bike, on foot, or a combination thereof. Overnight accommodation may be in a village or at hotels—again, usually a combination of the two. The company also offers working holidays and volunteering programs focusing on education, conservation, and social betterment.

ESSENTIALS

Tours African Heartland Journeys (☎ 043/738–5523 or 082/269–6421 ⊕ www.ahj.co.za).

WHERE TO STAY

$ 🏨 **Buccaneers Lodge and Backpackers.** Half hostel, half B&B, this very casual establishment is a shirts-and-shoes-optional sort of place, and it does get quite lively. The dorms are what you'd find at any hostel, but there are also pretty chalets scattered across a wooded slope leading to the beach. They all have cooking facilities, and most have fantastic views over the lagoon and ocean. The platformed safari tents are small and basic, containing not much more than a bed and without private baths, but the privacy and views make them a good budget option. There's something happening at 4 o'clock every afternoon—a volleyball game, free sundowner cruise, or some other spur-of-the-moment activity, with free wine included. It's a great base from which to undertake a whole range of reasonably priced cultural tours and excursions, which can be booked from here. Breakfast is about R15–R45, lunch (usually served at the pool bar in summer) costs about R15–R50, and a hearty supper will set you back R45–75. Children are permitted, and the self-catering cottages are family-friendly. But be warned: this is a PG-13 option, as backpackers can be very casual, and the language might not be what you'd hear in church. **Pros:** has an airport shuttle; sociable environment; restaurant can cater for dietary restrictions. **Cons:** most activities are not run from the lodge itself; accommodations can be very basic. ⊠ *From the N2 toward Durban take the Cintsa West turnoff and follow signs for the lodge on the left* ⌂ *Box 13092, Vincent 5217* ☎ *043/734–3012* ⊕ *www.cintsa.com* ⟿ *5 chalets, 5 safari tents without bath, 4 dormitories, 20 camping sites* ♿ *In-room: no phone, no TV. In-hotel: restaurant, bars, pool, beachfront, laundry service, Internet terminal* ▭ *AE, MC, V.*

BULUNGULA

295 km (183 mi) northeast of East London.

Bulungula is a tiny community near the mouth of the Bulungula River, about a 25-km (16-mi) walk from Coffee Bay's Hole-in-the-Wall. There are no shops, no banks, and no post office. There isn't even a decent road. The one lodge is run in partnership with the local community,

The Food Chain Up Close

Hailed by locals as "the greatest shoal on earth," the sardine run is, in terms of biomass, the world's largest animal migration. Cold water traveling up the coast moves closer to shore and brings with it untold millions of sardines (actually pilchards). These tiny fish are, of course, highly edible, so they have quite a following. Cape gannets, Cape fur seals, common and bottlenose dolphins, sharks, and Bryde's whales all follow this movable feast. The run coincides with the northern migration of the humpback whales, so the sea is teeming with life. Local fishing folk revel in the huge catches to be had simply by wading into the shallows with makeshift nets, and sightseers can watch for the bubbling water and attendant cloud of seabirds that signal shoals moving past.

There are boat trips aplenty to take you out for a closer look, but the real thrill is in diving the run. It's awesome just being amid all those fish, but you often are also among a thousand common dolphins. What everyone is really hoping for is a "baitball"— when dolphins herd a big school of sardines into a circle, keep them there by swimming around them, and pick them off at will. Sharks almost always join in, and an acrobatic seal or two might take advantage of the free lunch. Bryde's and even humpback whales have been known to take a (rather large) passing bite out of the ball, and the sight of Cape gannets from underwater as they dive-bomb the fish is memorable.

making it a completely different destination for adventure travelers. This is the *real* Africa. Bulungula is a great place to just chill out on the beach, but there are also loads of great activities—all owned and run by members of the community in conjunction with the lodge. You can choose from a horseback ride, a canoe or fishing trip, an educational walk through the bush with an herbalist, a visit to a local restaurant, or a day spent with the women of the village, learning how they live. You might learn to carry water and firewood on your head, harvest wild foods and cook them for your lunch, make mud bricks, work in the fields, or weave baskets.

This is a really worthwhile destination, but it's not for everyone. But because Bulungula is such a small, isolated community, crime is practically nonexistent and it is very safe.

GETTING HERE AND AROUND

You'll need to travel on unpaved roads to get to Bulungula. The driving time from East London is 4½ hours. Only 4x4 vehicles can make it all the way to the lodge. The lodge will provide you with a detailed map if you're driving yourself. Your best bet is to leave your car in the secure parking provided by the lodge at a small grocery store about 1½ km (1 mi) away, from where you can walk to the lodge (downhill for 45 minutes) or be picked up. If you arrive after 5 PM, leave your vehicle at the larger grocery store 15 km (9 mi) away and arrange for a pickup, as it's not advisable to drive the dirt road in the dark. In both instances, the owners of the stores will look after your vehicles for

R15 per night. The lodge also runs a shuttle service to and from the bus stop at Mthatha.

WHERE TO STAY

¢

Fodor's Choice

★

▣ **Bulungula Lodge.** Even though it is relatively isolated, Bulungula's one lodge is, in spirit, just an extension of the village. The fair-trade lodging is partly owned by the local community, which is not an uncommon thing on the Wild Coast. What makes it different, though, is that in contrast to what you'll find at smarter hotels, the local people are fully integrated in the running of the lodge. Accommodations are in traditional *rondavels* (round thatched huts) overlooking the lagoon and ocean. Furnishings are simple: a bed, a table, and a stick suspended from the roof on which to hang clothes. The eco-friendly, odor-free composting toilets and paraffin-fired hot showers are communal and situated in beautifully decorated colorful thatched buildings. Meals are served in a large lounge-cum-bar, where you can engage in a long discussion with one of the villagers or the other guests. You can use the cooking facilities, but it's far nicer to take advantage of the generous, simple, but well-cooked meals on offer ($). Lunches are usually a traditional dish or toasted sandwiches; breakfast and dinner are also available and all meals include a good vegetarian option. Bed linen is supplied, but you need to bring a towel and toiletries (including soap and shampoo). Babysitting is available. The lodge is inaccessible to all but 4x4s, but a shuttle is available from Mthatha and from closer destinations (where there is safe parking). If you are self-driving, the lodge will e-mail you a detailed map with distances when you book. Guided trips (R30–R140) include canoeing, cultural tours, and horseback riding. You can also have a massage (R50–R100). A 37-km (23-mi) guided walk to Coffee Bay via Hole-in-the-Wall costs R70 one way, and you can arrange to have your luggage transported; keep in mind that it's only for the relatively fit. You can also do the trip in reverse, from Coffee Bay to Bulungula. **Pros:** interaction with local Xhosa people means you learn a lot about their culture; eco-friendly credentials; warm and friendly staff. **Cons:** accommodation is simple and low on creature comforts; not much privacy or solitude. ✉ *Bulungula River Mouth, Nqileni Village ⌂ Box 52913, Mthatha 5099 ☎ 047/577–8900 or 083/391–5525 ⊕ www.bulungula.com ⇆ 7 rooms without bath, 3 dormitories, 3 safari tents, camping ⚿ In-room: no phone, no TV. In-hotel: restaurant, bar, beachfront, laundry service, parking (free)* ▤ *MC, V.*

COFFEE BAY

★ *295 km (183 mi) northeast of East London.*

The village of Coffee Bay is a bit run-down, but the beaches and the scenery are great. (The surf is fantastic, but don't head out alone if you don't know what you're doing.)

You can do a fabulous 37-km (23-mi) hike from Coffee Bay to Bulungula (or vice versa) via Hole-in-the-Wall, across the cliff tops, and along the beach. It's best to take a guide, who can cut about two or three hours from the journey by taking a shortcut through rolling hills dotted with thatched huts. Arrange for a guide through Bulungula Lodge *(⇨ above)*, where you should plan to overnight at the end of your hike; the lodge can transport your luggage while you walk. The cost for the guide and luggage transfer is R70 (R50 going from Bulungula to Coffee Bay).

GETTING HERE AND AROUND

Coffee Bay is about 1½ hours from Mthatha. Greyhound buses and the Baz Bus stop at the Shell Ultra City just outside the town. The Coffee Shack (⇨ *below*) will pick guests up from Mthatha airport or the Shell Ultra City (R60 each way). Local minibus taxis also run from Mthatha to Coffee Bay for about R40 one way. They leave from the taxi stand in the center of town and change at Mqanduli, a small town on the way. They are a cheap and convenient way of getting around but are not always the safest option.

If you are driving take the N2 to Viedgesville (about 20 km [12 mi] south of Mthatha) and then follow signs for Coffee Bay road. The coastal road is paved, but there are lots of potholes and you're advised to travel only during daylight. The drive takes about 3½ hours from East London.

Coffee Bay itself is small, so you can walk to most places or take local minibus taxis to get around.

EXPLORING

What makes Coffee Bay stand out from all the other lovely destinations, though, is its proximity—only 9 km (5½ mi)—to the spectacular **Hole-in-the-Wall**, a natural sea arch through a solid rock island. You can go here on a rather adventurous road from Coffee Bay, and it's included on almost any tour of the Wild Coast. The Xhosa name, Esikaleni, means "place of the water people," and it is believed to be a gateway to the world of our ancestors. If you try swimming through it in rough seas, it certainly will be, but some intrepid souls have made it on calm (very calm) days.

WHERE TO STAY

$ 🖫 **Coffee Shack on the Beach.** The main (but certainly not the only) attraction of this vibey backpackers' lodge are the surfing lessons (R40 for two hours, including surfboard and wet suit)—possibly from former world pro-am surfing champion Dave Malherbe, who moved here so he could surf the perfect wave whenever he wanted—at least when he isn't running one of the better backpackers' lodges on the coast. You need to book pretty far ahead to secure the rooms with private bathrooms, although the shared facilities are decent. Accommodation is in private single or double rooms, dormitories or camping, and there are traditional thatched huts across the river offering double en suite and dorm accommodations. As at all backpacker lodges, you don't need to be young to stay here, but an open mind and a sense of fun are prerequisites. The kitchen serves three meals a day at reasonable prices, and there are two well-equipped kitchens for self-catering. Guided trips include abseiling (R85), cultural tours (R80), and hikes, including one to Hole-in-the-Wall (R60–R100). **Pros:** surf lessons are great value; stay for four nights and get the fifth free throughout the year. **Cons:** can have a noisy, party atmosphere, although quieter accommodation is located across the river; you need to book ahead. ⊠ *Bomvu Beach,*

5

Coffee Bay ☎ *Box 687, Mqanduli 5080* 📞 *047/575–2048* 🌐 *www. coffeeshack.co.za* 🛏 *9 rooms, 6 dormitories, 10 campsites* ♿ *In-room: no TV. In-hotel: beachfront, laundry service, Internet terminal, parking (free)* ▤ *AE, DC, MC, V.*

$$$ 🎦 **Ocean View Hotel in Coffee Bay.** This old Wild Coast hotel is light and

★ bright, with white walls and blue fabrics with marine motifs. Some rooms overlook the sea. A resident tour operator can arrange day walks, gentle cruises, and canoeing. A 4x4 trip to Hole-in-the-Wall and a cultural visit costs R160. Like all Wild Coast resorts, it's child-friendly. The food ($$) is good, well cooked, and unpretentious—just keep in mind that lobster and other seafood are considered unpretentious in this region, and you may well find wild coastal oysters offered as bar snacks. Nonguests may book for dinner if the hotel is not full (R90 for a three-course set menu). Like some other Wild Coast properties, this hotel is partly owned by the local community. **Pros:** child-friendly; there are tons of adventure activities to participate in; the hotel is close to the beach. **Cons:** rooms are basic but comfortable; it's a family resort, so there may be children around. ⊠ *Main Beach, Coffee Bay* ☎ *Box 566, Umtate 5100* 📞 *047/575–2005 or 047/575–2006* 🌐 *www.oceanview. co.za* 🛏 *30 rooms* ♿ *In-room: no phone, safe, no TV. In-hotel: restaurant, bar, pool, beachfront, children's programs (ages 3–12), laundry service, Internet terminal, parking (free)* ▤ *AE, DC, MC, V* 🍽 *MAP.*

MTHATHA

295 km (183 mi) northeast of East London, 100 km (62 mi) northwest of Coffee Bay.

Mthatha is poor and run-down. Most people don't stay here beyond making a travel connection elsewhere. However, if you're traveling on your own and have some free time, be sure to make a detour to see the Nelson Mandela Museum, which is 19 km (12 mi) outside of town. The museum can arrange a tour for you, which is advised.

GETTING HERE AND AROUND

SA Airlink flies between the tiny airport at Mthatha (UTT)—for travel to the Wild Coast—and Johannesburg. There are three flights a day, which take about one hour 40 minutes. Because Mthatha is a really small airport, it doesn't have all the expected facilities. Greyhound and Baz Bus drop passengers off at the Shell Ultra City just outside Mthatha.

ESSENTIALS

Airports Mthatha Matanzima Airport (☎ 047/536–0023).

Airlines SA Airlink (☎ 0861/359–722 🌐 www.saairlink.co.za).

Rental Cars Avis (☎ 047/536–0066 🌐 www.avis.co.za). **Budget** (☎ 047/536–0917 🌐 www.budget.co.za).

EXPLORING

The **Nelson Mandela Museum** stands as evidence of the love and respect that this awesome statesman has inspired in people all over the world, from rural schoolchildren to royalty. The many gifts Mandela has

★ received through his life say more about the givers than the receiver, and the Long Walk to Freedom display shows the political and personal journey of this beloved politician. In addition to the building in Mthatha, there are two other sites. **Qunu,** where Mandela spent his childhood and where he now has his permanent residence, is on the N2, 32 km (20 mi) south of Mthatha (on a tarred road); you can see his home, a rather ordinary brick house, from the highway. A beautifully designed museum combines natural stone and unfinished wattle branches to create an interesting pattern of light and shade that complements the black-and-white photographs documenting Mandela's early life and his period of activism and incarceration. There's also a reconstruction of his prison cell on Robben Island. Huge glass windows overlook the fields where Madiba (an affectionate sobriquet for Mandela) herded cattle as a boy, and his present house can be seen in the distance. **Mvezo** was the birthplace of Mandela. Although the foundations of the house in which Mandela was born are visible and there is a small open-air museum, Mvezo is more a place of pilgrimage than a museum (since there isn't very much to see here). It's best to visit Mvezo as part of a tour—both because it's hard to find and because you'll get much more out of it with a knowledgeable guide—which you can arrange through the museum. But you can get directions from the museum in Mthatha if you want to go on your own. You'll need to travel down a 19 km (12 mi) gravel road, but a 4x4 is not required. ■ TIP→ It's possible to visit the Nelson Mandela Museum on Saturday afternoons and Sundays if you make an arrangement in advance. ✉ *Owen St. and Nelson Mandela Dr. (N2) 5100* ⌂ *Box 52808, 5099* ☏ *047/532–5110* ⊕ *www.mandelamuseum. org.za* ⌨ *Free* ☉ *Weekdays 9–4, Sat. 9–noon.*

Durban and KwaZulu-Natal

WORD OF MOUTH

"Durban is like any big town near the sea, but to the north and South Coast it is definitely worth a visit if you want warm seas and beautiful beaches."
—Andrew1963

"An area you might consider visiting is where the Zulus and the British battled. Isandlwana, Rorke's Drift, Blood River, and Ulundi are fascinating places, if you are interested in Zulu history and British imperialism. The region is pretty, too."
—Zambezi

Updated by
Tracy Gielink

Durban isn't slick or sophisticated, but 320 days of sunshine a year entices visitors and locals alike to the vast stretches of beautiful beach that hug the coastline. The close proximity to the beach has given the province's largest city a laid-back vibe that makes it a perfect holiday destination and the ideal springboard from which to visit the diverse beauty of the rest of the province of KwaZulu-Natal.

As one of the few natural harbors on Africa's east coast, Durban developed as a port city after the first European settlers landed in 1824 with the intention of establishing a trading post. It's the busiest port in South Africa as it exports large volumes of sugar and is home to the country's largest import and export facility for the motor industry. The port also has a passenger terminal for cruise liners that mostly operate between November and May.

The city's "Golden Mile" (an area much larger than the name implies) consists of high-rise hotels flanked by a popular promenade and beaches, and the colonial-inspired suburbs of Berea and Morningside that overlook the city offer boutique hotels and packed restaurants.

Residential and upmarket commercial development has seen coastal spots like Umhlanga to the north earn cult status with tourists, and collections of small villages along both the north and south coasts have access to pristine beaches. Add to the mix two World Heritage Sites (Drakensberg and St. Lucia Wetland Park), and KwaZulu-Natal itself embodies South Africa's mantra: the world in one country. More importantly, it's truly representative of South Africa's rainbow nation.

KwaZulu-Natal (commonly referred to as KZN) is a premier vacation area for South Africans, despite being a comparatively small province (which, perhaps surprisingly, has the country's largest province population at more than 10 million people). It's all but impossible to resist the subtropical climate and the warm waters of the Indian Ocean. In fact, the entire 480-km (300-mi) coastline, from the Wild Coast in the south to the Mozambique border in the north, is essentially one long beach, attracting hordes of swimmers, surfers, and anglers.

KwaZulu-Natal's two-part moniker is just one of the many changes introduced since the 1994 democratic elections. Previously the province was known simply as Natal (Portuguese for "Christmas"), a name bestowed by explorer Vasco da Gama, who sighted the coastline on Christmas Day, 1497. KwaZulu, "the place of the Zulu," was one of the nominally independent homelands created by the Nationalist government (1948–94), but with the arrival of democratic South Africa the two were merged to form KwaZulu-Natal. The province is now defined as the Kingdom of the Zulu, and the local Zulu population (about 2.2 million) is characterized by warm hospitality and friendly smiles. The Indian population—originally brought here by the British in the late 1860s as indentured laborers to cut sugarcane—has also made an indelible mark and now represents about 1 million of Durban's total population of 3.5 million.

ORIENTATION AND PLANNING

GETTING ORIENTED

Hugging the country's east coast, Durban's requisite amount of sunshine has earned the city the nickname "South Africa's playground." Here you'll find the colonial-inspired suburbs of Berea and Morningside, the coastal village of Umhlanga, and the warm waters and vacation towns that populate the areas known as the Dolphin Coast and South Coast. Head inland to the KwaZulu-Natal Midlands and the dramatic Drakensberg Mountains for the antithesis of coastal beauty. Further north you'll find the Battlefields and Zululand that portray the province's bloody history, as well as the Big Five roaming in various game reserves. ⇨ *For more information on the safari parks and reserves in this area, including Hluhluwe-Imfolozi, Mkuze, Ithala, and Phinda game reserves, see Chapter 9, Safaris in South Africa.*

Durban. South Africa's third-largest city, Durban is southern Africa's busiest port (chiefly cargo). Durban's chief appeal to tourists is its long strip of high-rise hotels and its popular promenade—known as the Golden Mile (though it's actually several miles long)—fronting its beaches.

Umhlanga. The previously small vacation village has mushroomed with increased residential and business development but remains one of the most sought-after coastal holiday destinations in the country. It offers beautiful beaches flanked by a strip of hotels. Despite its expanding surroundings, the heart of Umhlanga has retained its village charm.

Side Trips from Durban. To find beaches unmarred by commercial development, you need to travel north to the Dolphin Coast or south to the aptly named South Coast. Moving inland takes you to the KwaZulu-Natal Midlands, just off the N3 between Durban and Johannesburg. Here racehorse and dairy farms stud rolling green hills and lush pastures that are reminiscent of England. The Midlands Meander (a series of routes set up by the local tourism board) is a great way to experience the area's farms and crafts shops

Zululand and the Battlefields. Zululand, the region north of the Tugela River and south of Swaziland and Mozambique, is the traditional home of the Zulu people. Prominent towns (though these are all relatively small) in this region are the industrial towns of Empangeni and Richards Bay, Eshowe, Pongola, and Ulundi. The farther north you go, the less populated and more rural the area becomes, with traditional Zulu huts and herds of long-horned brown-and-white and black-and-white Nguni cattle tended by boys or young men scattering over the hills.

The Battlefields (Anglo-Zulu and Anglo-Boer) are inland, to the north of the Midlands and northeast of the Drakensberg. The towns dotted among the Zululand battlefields tend to be a little ugly and dusty during

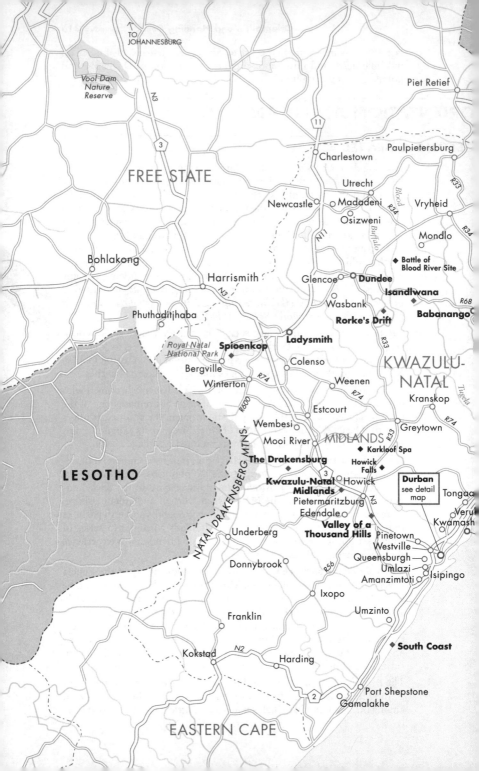

MOZAMBIQUE

SWAZILAND

KwaZulu–
Natal

N2

thala
Game
eserve

Phongola

Louwsburg
Amazulu
Private
Game
Reserve

Nongoma

ULULAND

Black Umfolozi

R66

White Umfolozi

Hluhluwe-Imfolozi
Game Reserve

R34

Ngwelezana
◆Shakaland

Gingindlovu

N2

◆ Dolphin Coast

Dukuza

Umhlanga
see detail
map

Phongola

Jozini

Mkuze

Mkuze
Game
Reserve

Msunduze

Thanda Private
Game Reserve

N2

Maputaland
Coastal
Reserve

Phinda
Private
Game
Reserve

Hluhluwe

ELEPHANT COAST

Greater St. Lucia
Wetland Park

Cape Vidal

St. Lucia

Mtubatuba

2

Empangeni

Richards Bay

Ezikhawini

INDIAN OCEAN

0   30 miles

0   30 kilometers

TOP REASONS TO GO

Beautiful Beaches Durban's beaches are some of the world's safest and most beautiful. The long, sandy beaches and inviting water temperatures extend all the way up the Dolphin (north) Coast and beyond, as well as south from Durban, down the Hibiscus Coast and into the Eastern Cape.

Reliving History Explore the battlefields of the Anglo-Zulu and Anglo-Boer wars, making sure you visit the legendary sites of Isandlwana, Rorke's Drift, and Blood River.

Game Viewing Although smaller than Kruger, the easily accessible Hluhluwe-Imfolozi Game Reserve,

Mkuze, Ithala (aka Itala), and Pongola game reserves are all teeming with game, including the Big Five.

Amazing Natural Wonders KZN has two World Heritage Sites—the Drakensberg and Greater St. Lucia Wetland Park—as well as numerous game reserves.

A Vibrant City Durban, Africa's busiest port, has a distinct feel, flavored by its diverse populations. In the city center, you'll find mosques, temples, and churches. Take a rickshaw ride along the Beachfront after browsing for Zulu beadwork, or try a local "bunny chow" (curry inside a hollowed-out loaf of bread).

the dry winter months, but this is an area to visit more for its historic than its scenic value.

PLANNING

WHEN TO GO

The height of summer (December and January) brings heat, humidity, higher prices, and crowds, who pour into "Durbs," as it's fondly known, by the millions. Locals know never to brave the beach on holidays or over the Christmas season except for an hour or two from 6 AM—one of the nicest times there. June and July are Durban's driest months, and while you can never predict the weather, expect warm, dry days and cool nights.

The best time to tour KwaZulu-Natal is early autumn through winter and into spring (April to October), with the coast particularly pleasant in winter—you'll see people swimming. April is a lovely time to visit the city (avoid Easter weekend if you can), though most of this time is pleasant enough, with warm air and sea temperatures.

Some facilities in the Zululand game reserves close in summer because of the extreme and unpleasantly high temperatures.

TAKE IT ALL IN

2 Days: If you have just two days, spend it in Durban. Start with an early morning walk along the Golden Mile to watch the surfers. ⚠ **Always leave jewelry and valuables in your hotel safe.** Spend three or four hours on a guided walking tour of the Indian District or downtown Durban. Tours (reservations are a must) leave from the Tourist Junction (Old Station Building). Wilson's Wharf, which overlooks the Durban harbor, and Morningside's trendy Florida Road offer great options for lunch or

Durban and the World Cup

Moses Mabhida Stadium is in the heart of the multisport Kings Park Sporting Precinct, which has been developed looking toward a bid for the 2020 Olympics. With the capacity to seat 70,000 fans during the 2010 World Cup, it can also expand to 85,000 seats.

The stadium design was inspired by the South African flag, which is visible in the Y-shaped grand arch. The two legs on the southern side of the stadium come together to form a single footing on the northern side symbolizing the uniting of a once-divided nation. A high-tech cable car will transport visitors to a viewing platform 348 feet above the field, where they'll have panoramic views of the ocean and city. If it rains, 95% of stadium seating is covered.

Address: Isaiah Ntshangase Road, Durban

Fan park: On the Beachfront, close to the Kings Park Sporting Precinct, Durban's official fan park will be outfitted with giant screens and entertainment, food, and beverage facilities. Admission to the fan park is free, and transportation facilities and other entertainment options will be easily accessible.

Match Schedule: June 13, 16, 19, 22, 25, 28, and July 7

Safety and Security: The stadium and surrounds will have extensive video surveillance to identify and handle any problems. In addition, all tickets will be marked with the name, passport number, and seat number of the ticket holder so that any bad behavior can be pinpointed to individuals. Those identified will be arrested and banned from future games. There will be horse- and foot-patrol police on match days, and additional policing will be deployed throughout the city and its fan parks for the duration of the tournament. The stadium will have its own security personnel, augmented by volunteer security officers, to provide additional security in and around the stadium and the fan parks. Volunteers will also act as tourism ambassadors at strategic locations such as the beach, where they will provide information to visitors and alert police to any suspicious activity.

Transportation: In addition to Durban International Airport (DUR), which is 16 km (10 mi) south of town, the new King Shaka Airport, in La Mercy, 32 km (20 mi) north of Durban, also offers domestic and international flights. The People Mover bus offers a safe, reliable, and convenient mode of public transportation from the city and beachfront to Durban's Moses Mabhida Stadium on match days. There's also a new stadium railway station that allows fans to travel by rail to the event. Park-and-ride facilities allow fans to leave their cars at designated parking areas and take the regular shuttle services to the stadium. A new pedestrian walkway will link the Moses Mabhida Stadium to the beachfront.

Information. 031/311-4720 visitor center fifaworldcup.durban.gov.za.

⇨ *For more information, see World Cup 411, in Chapter 1.*

6

Durban's Annual Events

January: The **Dusi Canoe Marathon** (⊕ www.dusi.org.za) is a 120-km kayak race that runs between Pietermaritz-burg and Durban along the Msunduzi (Duzi) River. It's regarded as one of the toughest canoe events in the world and takes place over three days.

April: Splashy Fen (⊕ www.splashy-fen.co.za), South Africa's longest-running and most renowned annual music festival, turns 22 in 2010. It takes place outdoors on a Midlands farm and the lineup includes some of SA's top bands.

May: The **Comrades Marathon** (⊕ www.comrades.com) is the world's oldest and largest ultra-marathon—approximately 90 km between Pieter-maritzburg and Durban. The race route changes annually, and the 2010 mara-thon on May 30 (the 85th running of the race) will see runners doing the "down" run ending in Durban.

June/July: Dubbed "The Greatest Shoal on Earth," the **Sardine Run** (⊕ www.sardinerun.co.za) is regarded as one of nature's most amazing migrations. Starting along the South Coast and moving up to Durban, sardine shoals of 20–30 km (12–18 mi) are followed by some 20,000 dol-phins, birds, and sharks. The spectacle can be viewed from the beach or at various dive spots. From the end of June to the beginning of July, surfing fans head to Ballito for **Mr Price PRO** (⊕ www.mrpricepro.com), one of the longest-running professional surfing events in the world; it was established in 1969.

July: The **Durban July** (⊕ www.voda-comdurbanjuly.co.za) is South Africa's most prestigious horse race. Tens of thousands descend on Greyville Race-course to partake in one of the year's biggest social events and to watch the ponies run.

dinner. If you dine on Florida Road, make sure you stop by the African Craft Market for beautiful Zulu beadwork, baskets, prints, and other crafts and curios. You can also spend the afternoon strolling around Mitchell Park, which is known for its colorful flowerbeds at the top of Florida Road (also be sure to visit the small zoo here). On your second day, visit the aquarium at uShaka Marine World, one of the largest and best in the world, perhaps lunching on seafood at Cargo Hold, adjacent to the shark tank. In the afternoon, visit the Natal Sharks Board for a show and fascinating shark dissection—yes, they actually do a dissection (Tuesday–Thursday, and Sunday only). You could also visit the Umgeni River Bird Park, whose live bird shows are a must-see (11 and 2 daily).

5 Days: Spend at least one day in Durban (see above) before or after you explore KwaZulu-Natal following the Zululand and the more northern section option, which takes in the coastal strip and some of the northern game parks and private lodges. Start out with a tour of the battlefield sites of Isandlwana, Rorke's Drift, and the Talana Museum, at Dundee. Afterward, travel north and take the R103 to pick up the Midlands Meander, which stretches north all the way to Mooi River, through the tranquil KZN Midlands.

If you decide to head up the north coast, spend a night at Shakaland or Simunye Zulu Lodge (⇨ *"Seeing Shaka Zulu" box at the end of this chapter)* to get the total Zulu cultural experience. Then schedule at least two days in Hluhluwe-Imfolozi Game Reserve or Phinda Private Game Reserve to see the game that

> **WARNING**
>
> It is essential that visitors to the northern parts of the province, including Zululand, take antimalarial drugs, particularly during the wet summer months.

these reserves are known for. A trip to Greater St. Lucia Wetland Park to see hippos and crocodiles in the wild is another great experience.

7–10 Days: Spend a day or two exploring Durban and Umhlanga and then head up to Zululand to start your grand loop. Visit Greater St. Lucia Wetland Park on your way to the incredible wildlife of Hluhluwe-Imfolozi Game Reserve or Phinda Private Game Reserve. A three-day trek in the wilderness of Imfolozi could be the high point of your trip. For something more sedate, spend three days at Rocktail Bay Lodge in the Maputaland Coastal Reserve, close to the Mozambique border; it's especially interesting during turtle-breeding season, from November to early March. Another distant park near the edge of the province is the delightful, less-visited Ithala Game Reserve. On your way back to Durban, drive through the battlefields.

⇨ *For more information on any of the reserves mentioned in the above itineraries, see Chapter 9, Safaris in South Africa.*

RESTAURANTS

Durban's dining public is fickle by nature, and restaurants tend to change hands fairly often. But don't be discouraged—Durban offers some superb dining options, provided you eat to its strengths. Thanks to a huge Indian population, it has some of the best curry restaurants in the country.

Durbanites eat lunch and dinner relatively early because they're early risers, particularly in summer, when it's light soon after 4. They're also generally casual dressers—you'll rarely need a jacket and tie, and jeans are rarely frowned upon.

HOTELS

Many of Durban's main hotels lie along the Golden Mile, but there are some wonderful boutique hotels and B&Bs (especially in the Berea, Morningside, and Umhlanga) that offer a more personalized experience.

In northern Zululand and Maputaland, game reserves and lodges—both publicly and privately owned and managed—are smaller than what you'd find in Mpumalanga, but offer delightful game-viewing experiences. Many are all-inclusive (or nearly so), though some have self-catering options.

■**TIP➜** Prices, especially along the coast, tend to rise with the summer heat.

WHAT IT COSTS IN SOUTH AFRICAN RAND				
	¢	$	$$	$$$	$$$$
Restaurants	Under R50	R51–R75	R76–R100	R101–R125	over R125
Hotels	Under R500	R501–R1,000	R1,001–R2,000	R2,001–R3,000	over R3,000

Restaurant prices are per person for a main course at dinner, a main-course equivalent, or a prix-fixe meal. Hotel prices are for a standard double room in high season, including 14% value added tax (VAT).

DURBAN

Durban has the pulse, the look, and the complex face of Africa. It may have something to do with the summer heat, a clinging sauna that soaks you with sweat in minutes. If you wander into the Indian District or drive through the Warwick Triangle—an area away from the sea around Julius Nyerere (Warwick) Avenue—the pulsating city rises up to meet you. Traditional healers tout animal organs, vegetable and spice vendors crowd the sidewalks, and minibus taxis hoot incessantly as they trawl for business. It is by turns colorful, stimulating, and hypnotic.

It's also a place steeped in history and culture. Gandhi lived and practiced law here, and Winston Churchill visited as a young man. It's home to the largest number of Indians outside India; the massive Indian townships of Phoenix and Chatsworth stand as testimony to the harsh treatment Indians received during apartheid, though now thousands of Indians are professionals and businesspeople in Durban.

⚠ Street names have all been updated, but the old ones remain in brackets as some maps and locals still refer to streets by the old names.

GETTING HERE AND AROUND
AIR TRAVEL
Durban's new international airport, the King Shaka International Airport, at La Mercy, on the north coast, will take over operations from Durban International Airport (DUR) in 2010, prior to the World Cup. (At this writing, it plans to open on May 1, 2010.) The airport—three times the size of the current airport—is about 17 km (11 mi) from Umhlanga and about 32 km (20 mi) from Durban. Durban International Airport (DUR), which is 16 km (10 mi) south of town along the Southern Freeway, will be decommissioned once the new airport opens. For updates on the new airport, contact Airports Company South Africa.

South African Airways (SAA) flies to Durban via Johannesburg. Domestic airlines serving Durban include SAA, BA/Comair, Kulula, 1Time, SA Airlink, and Mango. Perhaps the easiest way to book a ticket to or from Durban is online. Kulula and 1Time are the more comfortable of the budget-priced airlines, as their seats are a little larger, but Mango is also well worth considering. If you're flying one of these three airlines, you'll be expected to buy your own snacks and drinks on board. SAA is usually the more expensive option, unless you're looking for a ticket at short notice (next day or two), when it may turn out to be cheapest.

The most inexpensive transfer into Durban and back is the Airport Shuttle Service, which costs R50 and departs a half hour after incoming flights arrive and leaves the city center every hour. Its drop-off points are flexible within the city and include the Hilton Hotel and South Sun Elangeni, but it's likely to drop you anywhere central if you request it first. Call ahead and the bus will pick you up at any hotel in the city; there's no need to reserve for the trip into Durban. If you want to go farther afield, call the Magic Bus or catch a cab from outside the terminal building.

⇨ *For airline contact information see Air Travel, in the Travel Smart South Africa chapter.*

Airport **Airports Company South Africa** (☎ *011/921-6262* ⊕ *www.acsa. co.za*). **Durban International Airport** (☎ *031/408-1155*). **King Shaka International Airport** (☎ *011/921-6262*).

Airport Transfers **Airport Shuttle Service** (☎ *031/465-5573*). **Magic Bus** (☎ *031/263-2647*).

BUS TRAVEL

Greyhound and Translux Express offer long-distance bus service to cities all over South Africa from Durban. All intercity buses leave from New Durban Station off Masabalala Yengwa Avenue (N.M.R. Avenue), between Archie Gumede Road (Old Fort Road) and Sandile Thusi Road (Argyle Road). Bear in mind that you can often fly for much the same prices as traveling by bus, especially if you book well in advance or find a discount.

Small Mynah buses operate from 6 AM to 7 PM along set routes every hour through the city, along the beachfront, and on to the Berea. Bus stops are marked by a sign with a mynah bird on it. The main bus depot is on Monty Naicker Road (Pine Street) between Samora Machel (Aliwal) and Dorothy Nyembe (Gardiner) streets. It costs a couple of rand per ride, and you pay as you board; exact change isn't required. Route information is also available at an information office at the corner of Samora Machel Street and Monty Naicker Road.

The new People Mover buses service the Golden Mile and Central Business District (aka CBD) at a cost of R4 per ride or R15 for a day pass; buses arrive every 15 minutes between 6:30 AM and 11 PM. All of the fleet's 10 buses are air-conditioned and equipped with electronic ramps for disabled access and strollers. Buses also have security cameras, and each of the 17 stops is staffed by security people

Bus Lines **Greyhound** (☎ *083/915-9000*). **Mynah Bus and People Mover** (*Durban City Transport* ☎ *031/309-5942*). **Translux Express** (☎ *031/361-7670*).

CAR TRAVEL

Durban is relatively easy to find your way around because the sea is a constant reference point. Downtown Durban is dominated by two parallel one-way streets, Dr. Pixley Kaseme Street (West Street) going toward the sea and Anton Lembede Street (Smith Street) going away from the sea, toward Berea and Pietermaritzburg; together they get you in and out of the city center easily. Parking downtown is a nightmare; head for an underground garage whenever you can. As with the rest of South Africa, wherever you go you'll be beset by self-appointed car guards who ask if they can watch your car. The going rate for a tip—if you want to give one—is R2–R5, depending on how long you're away. The guards directly outside Joe Kool's, between North and South beaches, are said to be very trustworthy. ⚠ **Don't leave your keys with anyone.**

The M4 (Ruth First Highway), which stretches north up to the Dolphin Coast—from Umhlanga to Ballito, about 40 km (25 mi), and beyond—is a particularly pretty coastal road, offering many views of the sea through lush natural vegetation and sugarcane fields. It's much nicer than the sterile N2 highway, which takes a parallel path slightly inland and offers no views.

Avis, Budget, Europcar, and Tempest have rental offices at the airport. The cheapest car costs about R300 per day, including insurance and 200 km (125 mi) free, plus R1.50 per kilometer (per half mile), or about R400 for the weekend. Avis offers unlimited mileage to international visitors, as long as you can produce your return ticket as proof.

Rental Companies Avis (☎ *0861/102–1111* ⊕ *www.avis.co.za*). **Budget** (☎ *0861/016–622* ⊕ *www.budget.co.za*). **Europcar** (☎ *0861/131–000* ⊕ *www. europcar.co.za*). **Tempest Car Hire** (☎ *0861/836–7378* ⊕ *www.tempestcarhire. co.za*).

RICKSHAW TRAVEL

Colorfully decorated rickshaws are unique to Durban—you won't find them in any other South African city. Though their origins lie in India, these two-seat carriages with large wheels are all over the city and are pulled exclusively by Zulu men dressed in feathered headgear and traditional garb. The rickshaw runners ply their trade all day, every day, mostly along the Golden Mile section of the beachfront. The going rate is R20 for about 15 minutes per person, and R8 for a photo (don't assume you can take a picture without paying for the privilege). While it's worth doing because it will be memorable and you won't have the opportunity anywhere else—negotiate the rate before climbing on.

TAXI TRAVEL

Taxis are metered and start at R5, with an additional R9 to R10 per kilometer (per half mile); after-hours and time-based charges apply. Fares are calculated per vehicle up to four passengers. Expect to pay about R50 from City Hall to North Beach and R200 to Durban International Airport. The most convenient taxi stands are around City Hall, in front of the beach hotels, and outside Spiga d'Oro on Florida Road in Morningside. Some taxis display a "for-hire" light, whereas others you simply hail when you can see they're empty. Major taxi companies include Bunny Cabs, Eagle Taxi, Mozzies, Umhlanga Cabs, and Zippy Cabs. If you're headed to the Indian Market on a weekend, consider having your taxi wait for you, as it can be difficult to flag a taxi in this neighborhood.

There's no need to worry about contacting a taxi on your own. They will either be easy to find or your hotel or restaurant can call one for you. Once a driver has dropped you off, he/she will usually give you a card so you have contact details for the return trip.

MONEY MATTERS

There are plenty of ATMs in and around Durban—at shopping centers, large attractions like Suncoast and uShaka, and even some of the smaller supermarkets. Most bank branches exchange money, and the airport and uShaka have money exchanges, as do Rennies and the AmEx foreign-exchange bureau. Shops in the bigger malls like Gateway, Pavilion, Musgrave, and La Lucia often take traveler's checks. Though you will need cash at the markets, don't carry too much. Use credit cards where you can.

SAFETY AND PRECAUTIONS

Durban has not escaped the crime evident in every South African city. Particularly in the city center but also elsewhere, smash-and-grab thieves roam the streets, looking for bags or valuables in your car, even while you're driving, so lock any valuables in the trunk and keep your car doors locked and windows up at all times. While there's no need to be fearful, be observant wherever you go. Hire a guide to take you around Durban, don't wander around the city center or outside your hotel alone at night, and keep expensive cameras and other possessions concealed. The Durban Beachfront (with recently upgraded security features), Umhlanga, and the outlying areas are safe to explore on your own, though you'll need a taxi or car to get between them. If you plan on taking a dip while you're at the beach, ask a neighboring beachgoer or lifeguard to keep an eye on your belongings, or put them in a locker—available between North and South beaches and on Umhlanga Main Beach.

The best hospitals in central Durban are Entabeni and St. Augustine's, both private hospitals in the Glenwood area with 24-hour emergency rooms. Umhlanga Hospital is the best north of the city. Addington Hospital, a massive public hospital on the Beachfront, operates a 24-hour emergency room; though it's cheaper, it's not recommended.

Consulate U.S. Consulate (✉ *Durban Bay House, 333 Smith St., City Center, Durban* ☎ *031/305-7600*).

Emergency Services Ambulance (☎ *082-911 or 10177*). **Fire** (☎ *031/361-0000*). **General Emergencies** (☎ *10111*). **Police** (☎ *10111*).

Hospitals Entabeni Hospital (✉ *148 S. Ridge Rd., Glenwood, Durban* ☎ *031/204-1300*). **St. Augustine's** (✉ *4 Cato Rd., Glenwood, Durban* ☎ *031/268-5000, 031/268-5559 trauma*). **Umhlanga Hospital** (✉ *323 Umhlanga Rocks Dr., Umhlanga* ☎ *031/560-5500, 080/033-6961 trauma*).

TOURS

The city's tourism office, Durban Tourism, has a series of city walking tours for R40 per person. Tours depart from the Tourist Junction weekdays at 9:45 and return at 12:30, but you need to book in advance, as the tour guide only arrives if reservations have been made. The Oriental Walkabout explores the Indian District, including Victoria Market and several mosques. The Historical Walkabout covers the major historic monuments in the city. On a guided township tour you'll be exposed to social history, visit a shebeen (an informal township bar), and gain insight into the challenges facing today's townships. Durban Tourism offers other tour options as well; a comprehensive list of tour options is on its Web site.

Sarie Marais Pleasure Cruises and Isle of Capri offer sightseeing cruises around Durban Bay or out to sea. Tours, which range from 30 minutes to 75 minutes cost from R60 to R70 per adult, depart from the jetties next to the Natal Maritime Museum on the Margaret Mncadi Avenue.

Your accommodation should be able to assist in recommending tour companies, and most will tailor a trip for you, although there may be a minimum charge for small parties.

Tour Operators Durban Tourism (☎ *031/304–4934* ⊕ *www.zulu.org.za*). **Isle of Capri** (☎ *031/337–7751*). **Sarie Marais Pleasure Cruises** (☎ *031/305–2844*).

VISITOR INFORMATION

The Tourist Junction, in the restored Old Station Building, houses a number of tourist-oriented companies and services, where you can find information on almost everything that's happening in Durban and KwaZulu-Natal. Among the companies represented are Durban Tourism, the city's tourism authority; an accommodations service; a KwaZulu-Natal Nature Conservation Service booking desk; regional KwaZulu-Natal tourist offices; and various bus and transport companies. It's open weekdays 8–4:30 and weekends 9–2. Sugar Coast Tourism (covering the Umhlanga and nearby Umdloti areas), is open weekdays 8:30–4:45 and Saturday 9–1.

Tourist Offices Sugar Coast Tourism (✉ *Shop 1A Chartwell Centre, 15 Chartwell Dr., Umhlanga* ☎ *031/561–4257*). **Tourism KwaZulu-Natal** (☎ *031/304–4934* ⊕ *www.zulu.org.za*). **Tourist Junction** (✉ *160 Monty Naicker Rd. [Pine St.], City Center, Durban* ☎ *031/304–4934*).

EXPLORING DURBAN

By no means should you plan an entire vacation around Durban, because there is so much more to see beyond the city. Nevertheless, it's definitely worth a stopover. To get the most from your visit, get ready to explore the Central Business District (CBD), which includes the Indian District; the Beachfront; and Berea and Morningside. If you're concerned about safety within the CBD, book tours through Tourist Junction.

Numbers in the text correspond to numbers in the margin and on the Durban map.

CITY CENTER AND THE BAYFRONT

The center of the city is indicative of South Africa's third-world status and first-world leanings. Large office buildings dominate streets filled with African taxis and buses, while every so often you'll stumble across a building that speaks of an imperial past. It can get horribly humid from December through February, so if you visit then, avoid walking too much during the midday heat. Browse the air-conditioned museums when it's hot, and save walking outside for later in the afternoon, making sure you get to the museums and galleries before they close, around 4:30.

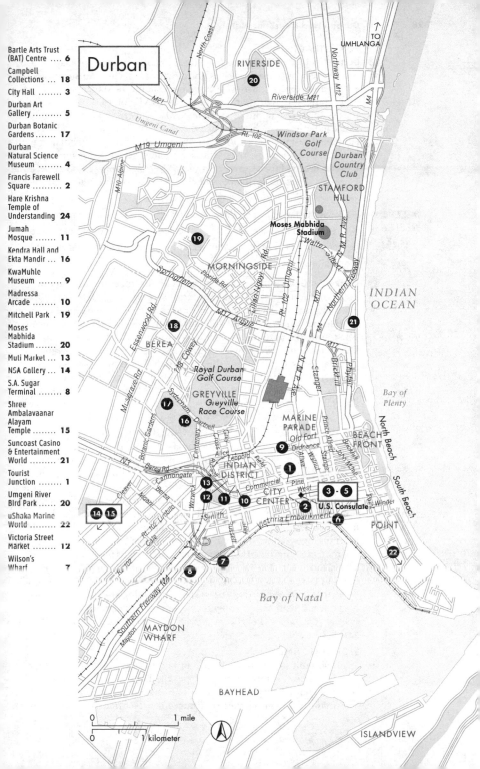

Durban

TOP ATTRACTIONS

6 **★** **Bartle Arts Trust (BAT) Centre.** The vibrant center (though perhaps a little on the seedy side these days) is abuzz with artists and musicians. Most days—and some nights—you can watch sculptors, dancers, musicians, and painters at work, and at night the BAT comes alive with plays, music, and African film or video festivals. The center is home to several small galleries, which showcase the work of local artists. The center contains a restaurant, a coffee bar overlooking the bay, a nightspot with live music, and shops that sell an excellent selection of high-quality African crafts, fabrics, and ceramics. ⊠ *45 Maritime Pl., Small Craft Harbour, Victoria Embankment* ☎ *031/332–0468* ⊕ *www.batcentre. co.za* ⊠ *Free* ⊙ *Daily 10–5.*

NEED A BREAK?

Walk over to the adjacent Wilson's Wharf (⊕ *www.wilsonswharf.co.za*), where you can have a cool cocktail or a meal on a deck overlooking the harbor at one of several restaurants ranging from an oyster bar to fast-food outlets.

5 **Durban Art Gallery.** The gallery presents a vibrant, contemporary mix of local, southern African, and international work, though the main focus is on work from KwaZulu-Natal. Exhibits have included the cultural diversity of South African handicrafts, forensic investigation, a project celebrating the paternal instinct, and a multimedia display highlighting Durban's annual events with work from Mozambique, Botswana, and Angola. Look out, too, for the traditional, patterned *hlabisa* baskets, regularly displayed at the gallery. Exhibits change every few months. ⊠ *City Hall, entrances in Anton Lembede (Smith) and Church Sts., 2nd fl., City Center* ☎ *031/311–2264* ⊕ *www.durbanet.co.za/exhib/ dag/dagmain.htm* ⊠ *Free* ⊙ *Mon.–Sat. 8:30–4, Sun. 11–4.*

9 **KwaMuhle Museum.** Pronounced kwa-*moosh*-le (with a light *e*, as in *hen*), this small museum, housed in what used to be the notorious Department of Native Affairs, tells of Durban's apartheid history. During apartheid the department was responsible for administering the movement of black people in and out of the city, dealing with the dreaded passes that blacks had to carry at all times, and generally overseeing the oppressive laws that plagued the black population. Ironically, the name means "place of the good one," Kwa meaning "place of" and "Muhle" meaning "good one" (after J.S. Marwick, the benevolent manager of the municipal native affairs department from 1916 to 1920). Exhibits provide the often heartbreaking background on this period through old photographs and documents, replicas of passbooks, and lifelike models of people involved in the pass system, including *shebeen* (an informal bar) queens, who had to apply for permits to sell alcohol. ⊠ *130 Braam Fischer (Ordnance) Rd., City Center* ☎ *031/311–2223* ⊠ *Free* ⊙ *Mon.– Sat. 8:30–4, Sun. 11–4.*

WORTH NOTING

3 **City Hall.** Built in 1910 in Edwardian neo-baroque style, the hall looks as if it has been shipped straight from the United Kingdom column by column—hardly surprising, since it's an exact copy of Belfast City Hall. The main pediment carries sculptures representing Britannia, Unity, and Patriotism, and allegorical sculptures of the arts, music, and literature adorn the exterior. City Hall still houses the mayor's parlor and other government offices, the Durban Art Gallery and Natural Science Museum, and the City Library. Ask the guard to let you in to see the huge theater's ornate molding and grand parterre boxes, or join an official tour run by Durban Africa. ⊠ *Dr. Pixley Kaseme (West) and Church Sts., City Center* ☎ *031/304–4934* ⊕ *www.cityofdurban.co.za* 🖃 *Free* ⊙ *Daily 8:30–3:30.*

NEED A BREAK?

The Royal Coffee Shoppe (⊠ *267 Anton Lembede [Smith] St., City Center* ☎ *031/304–0331*), in the Royal Hotel, is a popular meeting place for pre- and post-theater crowds. Crystal chandeliers, etched glass, formally dressed staff, and live piano music in the nearby lounge at lunchtime create a rich atmosphere of old-time colonial Durban. The café serves light breakfasts and lunch as well as coffees, teas, cakes, quiches, salads, and sandwiches.

4 **Durban Natural Science Museum.** Despite its small size, this museum provides an excellent introduction to Africa's numerous wild mammals (the displays include a stuffed elephant and leopard, as well as smaller mammals like wild dogs and vervet monkeys), plants, birds, reptiles, and insects. It's a great place to bring the kids or to familiarize yourself with the local wildlife before heading up to the game parks in northern KwaZulu-Natal. At one popular gallery, the KwaNunu Insect Arcade, giant insect replicas adorn the wall; another, the bird gallery, showcases a variety of stuffed birds, including flamingos, ostriches, eagles, and penguins. ⊠ *City Hall, Anton Lembede (Smith) and Church Sts., 1st fl., City Center* ☎ *031/311–2256* 🖃 *Free* ⊙ *Mon.–Sat. 8:30–4, Sun. 11–4.*

2 **Francis Farewell Square.** In the heart of Durban, the square is a lovely shady plaza bordered by some of the city's most historic buildings, like City Hall, the Central Post Office, and the Royal Hotel. Walkways lined with stately palms and flower beds crisscross the square and lead to monuments honoring some of Natal's important historic figures. The square stands on the site of the first European encampment in Natal, established by Francis Farewell and Henry Fynn in 1824 as a trading station to purchase ivory from the Zulus. A statue representing Peace honors the Durban volunteers who died during the Second South African War (1899–1902), also known as the Boer War or Anglo-Boer War. The Cenotaph, a large stone obelisk, commemorates the South African dead from the two world wars. Apart from the historic attractions, it's an energetic, bustling part of the city center, with inexpensive street stalls selling flowers, clothes, and food for the Durban locals. You'll really feel the vibe of the city here. ⚠ Pay attention to your valuables while walking in the square. ⊠ *Bounded by Anton Lembede (Smith), Dr. Pixley Kaseme (West), and Dorothy Nyembe (Gardiner) Sts. and the Church St. pedestrian mall, City Center.*

8 **S.A. Sugar Terminal.** Much of Durban's early economy was built on the sugar industry, and even today the hills and fields around the city and along the north and south coasts are covered with sugarcane. It's not surprising then that Durban's Sugar Terminal is the largest in southern

Africa and one of the most advanced in the world. A short video presentation provides background on the sugar industry, and then you'll be taken on a walking tour of the terminal. Together, the tour and video presentation take 45 minutes. It's extraordinary to see the terminal's three enormous silos piled high to the domed ceiling with tons of raw sugar. The architectural design of the silos has been patented and used in other parts of the world. ⊠ *25 Leuchars Rd., Maydon Wharf* 🕾 *031/365–8100 or 031/365–8153* 🖾 *R15* ✆ *Tours Mon.–Thurs. at 8:30, 10, 11:30, and 2; Fri. at 8:30, 10, and 11:30* 🖎 *Reservations essential.*

❶ Tourist Junction. The city's principal tourist information outlet occupies Durban's old railway station, an attractive brick building constructed in 1894 in Flemish Revival style. The NGR above the main entrance stands for Natal Government Railways. Durban Africa, the city's tourist authority, is here, and the KwaZulu-Natal tourism authority also has a large office here, so it's a good place to pick up pamphlets and information for the city and province, and book tours or trips to any of the province's game reserves. ⊠ *160 Monty Naicker Rd. (Pine St.), at Soldier's Way, City Center* 🕾 *031/304–4934* ✆ *Weekdays 8–4:30, weekends 9–2.*

❼ Wilson's Wharf. Near the BAT Centre and on the edge of the harbor, this pleasant, privately developed section of waterfront is a lovely place to while away a few hours, soaking up the atmosphere, admiring the harbor view, and maybe having a meal or drink at one of the open-air restaurants on the expansive wooden deck. In addition to restaurants and fast-food outlets, there are boat rentals and a market with 65 stalls, some selling classy local crafts, others selling cheaper trinkets from India and China. ⊠ *Boatman's Rd., Maydon Wharf* 🕾 *031/307–7841* ⊕ *www.wilsonswharf.co.za* ✆ *Market Mon.–Thurs. 10–6, some restaurants daily 8:30–midnight.*

▌**NEED A BREAK?**   The popular **Zack's** (⊠ Wilson's Wharf, Boatman's Rd., Maydon Wharf 🕾 031/305–1677) often hosts live music. It serves breakfast until late, as well as lunch and dinner.

INDIAN DISTRICT

The biggest Indian population outside of India resides in Durban, and you can feel the influence on the city from the architecture to the cuisine. Under apartheid's Group Areas Act that designated where various race groups could live and own businesses, Indian traders set up shop on Grey Street (recently renamed Yusuf Dadoo Street). Here you can eat vegetarian curry, bargain for goods, buy fabrics, or just browse shops whose ownership spans generations, and soak up the Eastern vibe. ⚠ **Watch your belongings closely.** In addition, this part of town can be quite grubby, and in the midday summer heat it can get unpleasantly humid.

TOP ATTRACTIONS

⓫ Jumah Mosque. Built in 1927 in a style that combines Islamic and colonial features, this is the largest mosque in the Southern Hemisphere. Its colonnaded verandas, gold-domed minaret, and turrets give the surrounding streets much of their character. Tours (the only way to visit) are free and can be arranged through the Islamic Propagation Center, in a room at the entrance of the mosque, or through the Durban Tourism offices at Tourist Junction. If you plan to go inside, dress modestly, as in most mosques around the world. Women should bring scarves to cover their heads out of courtesy, wear skirts below the knees, and cover their shoulders. Men should not wear shorts. A good idea is to keep a *kikoi* (a lightweight African sarong readily available in local markets) in your bag to use as a skirt or scarf. Men can use them, too, to cover bare legs. You'll have to take off your shoes as you enter, so wear socks if you don't want to go barefoot. No tours are offered during Islamic holidays, including Ramadan, which varies but lasts a whole month in the latter part of the year. ⊠ *Yusaf Dadoo (Grey) and Denis Hurley (Queen) Sts.* ☎ *031/306–0026* ⊠ *Free* ⊙ *Weekdays 8–12:30 and 1:40–4:30.*

🔟 **Madressa Arcade.** The thoroughfare has a Kiplingesque quality, recalling the bazaars of the East. Built in 1927, it's little more than a narrow, winding alley perfumed by spices and thronged with traders. You can buy everything from plastic trinkets to household utensils and recordings of Indian music. Bursts of color—from bright yellow material to dark red spices—create a refreshing and photogenic sight. You can buy striking costume jewelry that would cost three times more at major shopping centers, but be wary of pickpockets while browsing through the stores. ⊠ *Entrances on Denis Hurley (Queen) and Cathedral Sts.* ⊙ *Daily 9–5.*

⑬ **Muti Market.** For a uniquely African experience, hire a guide through Durban Tourism at Tourist Junction to take you to southern Africa's largest and most extensive *muti* (traditional medicine, pronounced moo-tee) market. The market also serves as a distinctive traditional-medicine facility, where *sangomas* (traditional healers) offer consultations to locals in a bustling, urban atmosphere. If you're feeling bold, you might wish to consult a sangoma on matters of health, wealth, or personal problems. ⚠ **Don't go without a guide.** ⊠ *Warwick Junction, Julius Nyerere Ave.* ☎ *No phone* ⊙ *Weekdays 8–6, Sat. 8–1.*

⑫ **Victoria Street Market.** Masses of enormous fish and prawns lie tightly
★ packed on beds of ice while vendors competing for your attention shout their respective prices. In the meat section, goat and sheep heads are stacked into neat piles (this spectacle is for those with iron stomachs), and butchers slice and dice every cut of meat imaginable. The noise is deafening. In an adjacent building—where all the tour buses pull up—you'll discover a number of curio shops whose proprietors are willing to bargain over wood and stone carvings, beadwork, and basketry. You'll also find shops selling spices, recordings of African music, and Indian fabrics. The current structures stand on the site of an original, much-loved market, a ramshackle collection of wooden shacks that burned down during the years of Nationalist rule. ⚠ **Watch your belongings closely. Ask your taxi to wait for you, or visit as part of a guided tour.** ⊠ *Denis Hurley (Queen) and Jospeh Nduli (Russell) Sts.* ☎ *031/306–4021* ⊙ *Weekdays 8–5, weekends 9–2.*

6

Bunny Chow

Contrary to what you might think, bunny chow is not about lettuce and carrots. This Durban specialty, prevalent in the Indian District, is a hollowed-out loaf of bread traditionally filled with bean curry, although mutton and sometimes beef and chicken are also used. The dish was popularized in the 1940s, during apartheid, when blacks were prohibited from entering Kapitan's Restaurant, in the city center, where traditional Indian beans in *roti* (pancakelike bread) were sold. The manager, known fondly as Bhanya, started offering takeout on the pavement, but the rotis often fell apart. So he started using a hollowed-out quarter loaf of bread as a small pot for the beans, and the soft bread was used to soak up the gravy. "Bhanya's chow" became bunny chow, and meat was soon added as filling.

Good bunnies can be found at several Indian District eateries. **Patel Vegetarian Refreshment House** (✉ *Rama House, 202 Yusaf Dadoo [Grey] St.* ☎ *031/306–1774*), founded in 1912, has built a family legacy of good traditional food. **Victory Lounge** (✉ *Yusaf Dadoo [Grey] and Bertha Mkhize [Victoria] Sts.* ☎ *031/306–1906*) puts meat in its bunny chow and is usually very busy. In a quieter part of town, the vegetarian **Little Gujarat** (✉ *43 Dr. Goonam Rd. [Prince Edward St.]* ☎ *031/305–3148*) has simple wood decor.

BEACHFRONT

Either you'll hate the Durban Beachfront for its commercial glitz, or you'll love it for its endless activity. It extends for about 12 km (7½ mi) from uShaka Marine World, at the base of Durban Point, all the way past North Beach and the Suncoast Casino to Blue Lagoon, on the southern bank of the Umgeni River. The area received a R150-million upgrade that included creating a 65-foot-wide uninterrupted promenade and an additional pedestrian walkway linking the Beachfront to the Moses Mabhida Stadium. There are refreshment stands and places to relax every 980 feet. The section of Beachfront between South Beach and the Suncoast Casino is particularly safe, as police patrol often, though don't walk there late at night. It's lovely to take a stroll along here early or late in the day when it's less busy. Walk out onto one of the many piers and watch surfers tackling Durban's famous waves. Of any place in Durban, the Beachfront most defines the city.

Depending on the weather, parts of the Beachfront can be quite busy, especially on weekends. There's always something to see, even in the early mornings, when people come to surf or jog before going to work.

TOP ATTRACTIONS

㉒
☾
★ **uShaka Marine World.** This aquatic complex combines the uShaka Sea World aquarium and the uShaka Wet 'n Wild water park. The world's fifth-largest aquarium and the largest in the Southern Hemisphere, **uShaka Sea World** has a capacity of nearly 6 million gallons of water, more than four times the size of Cape Town's aquarium. The innovative design is as impressive as the size. You enter through the side of a giant ship and walk down several stories, past the massive skeleton of Misty,

a Southern Right whale that died near Cape Town after colliding with a ship, until a sign welcomes you to the BOTTOM OF THE OCEAN. Here you enter a "labyrinth of shipwrecks"—a jumble of five different fake but highly realistic wrecks, from an early-20th-century passenger cruiser to a steamship. Within this labyrinth are massive tanks, housing more than 200 species of fish and other sea life and the biggest variety of sharks in the world, including ragged-tooth and Zambezi sharks (known elsewhere as bull sharks), responsible for more attacks on humans than any other species. Don't expect to see great whites, though; they don't survive in aquariums. While inside the aquarium, try to catch a fish feeding. The best is the open-ocean feed in the afternoon, when divers hand-feed the fish. Look out for the interesting bottom feeders, like rays and sand sharks.

On dry land, 20-minute dolphin and seal shows, held in adjacent stadiums two or three times a day, are worth attending (for the best views sit in the middle, toward the back). Watch for 30-year-old Gambit, the biggest dolphin in any dolphinarium in the world. Seals also strut their stuff in humorous, well-rehearsed shows.

Add-ons—available Wednesday–Sunday only—include a 20-minute shark dive in an acrylic capsule, with instruction (R130; no children under 12); a snorkeling experience in the fish tanks (R70 for 45 minutes; R160 day pass); and ocean walking (R140; no children under 12), where you don a helmet and descend into a fish tank, with the assistance of a guide.

The extensive **uShaka Wet 'n Wild** water fun park comprises slides, pools, and about 10 different water rides. The intensity ranges from toddler to adrenaline junkie. As you walk into uShaka Marine World, you'll see people lazily floating on giant red tubes in the Duzi Adventure River, a ride that circles the aquarium, descends down a long slide, and runs under waterfalls and past fish tanks in a nearly 1,500-foot loop that takes about 15 minutes. The giant, almost vertical Plunge is the most exciting slide, and the Zoom-Zoom, a five-lane racer, is also popular. The Drop Zone is one of the highest slides in Africa. You can easily spend the better part of a day here, and a combo ticket with Sea World lets you go back and forth between the two. Durban's moderate winter temperatures make it an attraction pretty much all year round, though it's especially popular in summer. ∎ TIP➔ **Avoid it on public holidays and call ahead during the winter as hours can change.**

✉ *1 Bell St., Point* ☎ *031/328–8000* ⊕ *www.ushakamarineworld.co.za* 🖥 *Sea World R92, Wet 'n Wild R70, combo ticket R135* 🕙 *Weekdays 9–5, weekends 9–6.*

WORTH NOTING

㉑ **Suncoast Casino & Entertainment World.** Part of the rejuvenation of Durban's Golden Mile, this casino is done in the art-deco style for which Durban is famous. Colorful lights make it a nighttime landmark, but it's established itself as a daytime hot spot as well. There are deck chairs beneath umbrellas on a grassy sundeck and a pretty beach (R5). A paved walkway dotted with benches is a pleasant place to sit and watch cyclists, inline skaters, and joggers. There's often a band playing directly in front of the complex on weekends, which you can listen to from the stairs. ✉ *20 Suncoast Blvd., Beachfront* ☎ *031/328–3000* ⊕ *www.suncoastcasino.co.za* ✉ *Pedestrians free, cars R5, sundeck R5* ⊘ *24 hrs.*

NEED A BREAK?

Of the 20 or so restaurants, fast-food outlets, and coffee shops at Suncoast Casino, Mozart's (☎ 031/332–9833) offers a respite from Durban's balmy days. You can choose from 39 flavors of smooth ice cream including mint chocolate chip and blueberry.

BEREA AND MORNINGSIDE

Durban's colonial past is very much evident in these two suburbs that overlook the city. Built on a ridge above the sea, both are characterized by old homes with wraparound balconies, boutique hotels, and strips of fashionable restaurants.

TOP ATTRACTIONS

⑱ ★ Campbell Collections. In the middle of bustling, suburban Berea, Muckleneuk is a tranquil Cape Dutch home in a leafy garden. It's much as it was when it was built in 1914 upon the retirement of Sir Marshall Campbell, a wealthy sugar baron and philanthropist who lived here with his wife, Ellen, and daughter, Killie. Today Muckleneuk houses a museum administered by the University of KwaZulu-Natal, including the **William Campbell Furniture Museum.** (William was the son of Sir Marshall.) The house is furnished similarly to when the Campbells lived here, and contains some excellent pieces of Cape Dutch furniture that belonged to them, an extensive collection of works by early European traveler artists, such as Angas, as well as paintings by prominent 20th-century black South African artists, including Gerard Bhengu, Daniel Rakgoathe, and Trevor Makhoba. The **Mashu Museum of Ethnology** displays the best collection of traditional Zulu glass beadwork in the country; African utensils, like tightly woven wicker beer pots; weapons dating from the Bambatha Uprising of 1906, during which blacks in Natal rebelled against a poll tax and were brutally put down; carvings; masks; pottery; and musical instruments. Paintings of African tribespeople by artist Barbara Tyrrell, who traveled around South Africa from the 1940s to 1960s capturing people in their traditional costumes and gathering valuable anthropological data, add vitality to the collection. The **Killie Campbell Africana Library,** which is open to the public, is a treasure trove of historical information on KwaZulu-Natal. It includes the papers of James Stuart, a magistrate and explorer during the early 20th century; the recorded oral tradition of hundreds of Zulu informants; a collection of pamphlets produced by the Colenso family in their struggle for the recognition of the rights of the Zulu people; and a good collection of 19th-century works on game hunting. ✉ *220 Gladys Mazibuko (Marriott) Rd., at Stephen Dlamini (Essenwood) Rd., Berea* ☎ *031/207–3432 or 031/260–1722* ⊕ *campbell.ukzn.ac.za* ✉ *Muckleneuk tours R250, library free* ⊘ *Muckleneuk tours daily at 11 and 2:30; library weekdays 9–noon and 2–4:30, Sat. 9–noon* ⚜ *Tour reservations essential.*

WORTH NOTING

⑰ **Durban Botanic Gardens.** Opposite the Greyville Racecourse, Africa's oldest surviving botanical garden is a delightful 150-year-old oasis of greenery interlaced with walking paths, fountains, and ponds. The gardens' orchid house and collection of rare cycads are renowned. The Garden of the Senses caters to the blind, and there's a lovely tea garden where you can take a load off your feet and settle back with a cup of hot tea and cakes—the crumpets (similar to flapjacks) are the best in town! On weekends it's a popular place for wedding photographs, so you'll be sure to see retinues of colorfully clad bridesmaids. Look out for Music at the Lake, which happens on some Sundays. Various musical acts perform in the gardens (there is an additional entrance fee), and people take along picnics to while away the afternoon. ⊠ *70 St. Thomas Rd., Berea* ☏ *031/201–1303* ⊕ *www.durbanbotgardens.org. za* ⊠ *Free* ☉ *Daily 7–5.*

⑲ **Mitchell Park.** The magnificent rose garden, colorful floral displays, and leafy lawns here are real treats on a hot summer day. Attached to the park is a small zoo, named after Sir Charles Mitchell, an early governor of Natal. It was opened at the turn of the 19th century, and the Aldabra tortoises that were donated to the park in the early 1900s, now massive, are still in residence. There are also a number of small mammals, reptiles, tropical fish, and birds in large aviaries. The park has a popular playground, and the leafy terrace of the park's Blue Zoo Restaurant is a great place for breakfast or a light lunch. ⊠ *Bordered by Innes Rd., Nimmo Rd., Ferndale Rd., and Havelock Crescent, Morningside* ☏ *031/312–2318* ⊠ *Gardens free, zoo R3* ☉ *Gardens daily 7:30* AM*–8* PM*, zoo daily 8–5.*

OUTLYING ATTRACTIONS

Directly west of the city center is Glenwood, an old leafy suburb with wide streets, big homes, the NSA Gallery, and some pleasant new restaurants. Farther west, over the ridge, is Cato Manor (home to the Shree Ambalavaanar Alayam Temple) and then Westville (and, if you keep heading northwest, Pietermaritzburg, the Midlands, and ultimately Johannesburg). To the east—toward the sea—are Greyville and the Kendra Hall & Ekta Mandir. Heading north on the other side of the Umgeni River, are Durban North and the Umgeni River Bird Park. (Even farther north you reach Umhlanga and eventually the Dolphin Coast and Elephant Coast.)

Surrounding Durban, many Indian and black townships are largely racially homogenous and mostly poor, a holdover from apartheid. Chatsworth, one such large Indian township, to the southwest, has the Hare Krishna Temple of Understanding.

TOP ATTRACTIONS

⑳ **Umgeni River Bird Park.** This bird park, ranked among the world's best, is built under high cliffs next to the Umgeni River and has various walk-through aviaries. The variety of birds, both exotic and indigenous, is astonishing. You'll be able to take close-up photographs of macaws, giant Asian hornbills, toucans, pheasants, flamingos, and eight species of crane, including the blue crane, South Africa's national bird. Try

6

CLOSE UP

The Florida Road Strip

From its intersection with Sandile Thusi (Argyle) Road to where it meets Innes Road, the Florida Road strip has been the social heart of the Berea and Morningside since restaurants and clubs started opening here a dozen years ago. The area has continued to grow and is known particularly for its bustling nightlife. These stops on the strip are listed in geographical order.

African Art Centre (⊠ *94 Florida Rd., Morningside* ☎ *031/312–3804 or 031/312-3805* ⊕ *www.afriart.org.za*) carries an outstanding collection of art and crafts from local artisans. It'll ship overseas. If you're looking for a bite, ✕ Bangkok Wok (⊳ *Where to Eat)*, serves delicious Thai dishes— duck entrées are particularly good. The small **Elizabeth Gordon Gallery** (⊠ *120 Florida Rd., Morningside* ☎ *031/303–8133*) carries a wide selection of work—including prints— by local and international artists and photographers. The Space (⊠ *150 Florida Rd., Morningside* ☎ *031/312-7565* ⊕ *thespace.co.za*) carries fashion from the best Durban designers, with a few quirky accessories and collectibles thrown into the mix.

Asian-fusion restaurant and bar/ lounge ✕ Society (⊠ *178 Florida Rd., Morningside* ☎ *031/312–3211)* is just that, a see-and-be-seen place for the mover and shakers, swathed in elegant-yet-funky South Pacific decor. ✕ Spiga d'Oro (⊳ *Where to Eat)* is a local institution. Open all day and into the early hours of every morning, it dishes up reasonably priced Italian food in an upbeat atmosphere. Super-stylish interiors store Cécile & Boyd's (⊠ *253 Florida Rd.* ☎ *031/303–1005* ⊕ *www.cecileandboyds.com*) cleverly combines the best of African and colonial design in a contemporary

space. ✕ Mo's Noodles (⊠ *Shop 5, Florida Centre, 275 Florida Rd.* ☎ *031/312–4193)* is for those who have a predilection for Eastern food. The decor is minimalist but unpretentious. Reservations aren't taken.

At the top of Florida Road (technically on Innes Road), Mitchell Park (⊳ *Worth Noting, below)* entices and invites with rolling green lawns and manicured gardens. ✕ Vida e Caffè (⊠ *Shop 2, Oakwood Centre, 465–471 Innes Rd., Morningside* ☎ *031/312–4606* ⊕ *www.caffe. co.za*), just across the street from Mitchell Park, sells perfect coffees in various forms (accompanied by a piece of Lindt chocolate), and freshly squeezed orange juice, muffins, rolls, and a few pastries. Mark Gold Jewels (⊠ *Oakwood Centre, 469 Innes Rd., Morningside* ☎ *031/303–4177* ⊕ *www.markgold.net*) sells contemporary handcrafted pieces, many featuring diamonds. Alongside Mark Gold is ✕ Harvey's (⊠ *Oakwood Centre, 465 Innes Rd., Morningside* ☎ *031/312–5706*), a chic restaurant with a fabulous wine list. Each dish is presented in four portions, which facilitates sharing. Think tapas, but bigger portions.

If you want to stay in the middle of the action, try one of two small hotels in the road: Quarters or The Benjamin (⊳ *Where to Stay)*.

to time your visit to take in the bird show, which is a delight for both children and adults, and afterward have your photo taken with Otis, a white-faced owl. Drinks and light lunches are served at the park's kiosk. ⊠ *490 Riverside Rd., off the M4, Durban North* ☎ *031/579–4600* ⊕ *www.umgeniriverbirdpark.co.za* ⊠ *R30* ☉ *Daily 9–5; bird shows daily at 11 and 2.*

WORTH NOTING

㉓ **Hare Krishna Temple of Understanding.** This magnificent lotus-shaped temple opened in 1985 is at the heart of activities run by the city's International Society for Krishna Consciousness. Gold-tinted windows adorn the outside of the temple, and the interior has floors made of imported Italian marble. Colorful laser drawings depicting the life of the Hindu god Krishna cover the ceiling, and statues of Krishna and his consort Radha are elaborately dressed in traditional Indian attire. You need to remove your shoes when entering the temple. ⊠ *50 Bhaktivedanta Swami Circle, off Higginson Hwy., Unit 5, Chatsworth* ☎ *031/403–3328* ⊠ *Free* ☉ *Mon.–Sat. 10–1 and 4:15–6:30, Sun. 10–9; traditional singing and dancing Sun. 1:30–5 PM.*

NEED A BREAK?

Govinda's (⊠ *Hare Krishna Temple of Understanding* ☎ 031/403–4600) is an inexpensive yet excellent vegetarian restaurant. Hare Krishna devotees do not use onions, garlic, or mushrooms in their food. The traditional Indian *biryani,* a rice dish, is a favorite.

⓰ **Kendra Hall and Ekta Mandir.** One of the most easily accessible and opulent temples in the city center, the Kendra, adjacent to the Durban Botanic Gardens, opened in 2001 after two years of intricate work by sculptors in India. The structure is unmistakably Eastern, with golden domes that tower above a palm tree supported by ornately decorated columns and arches that give the temple an East-meets-West look. Inside are two halls: a small one on the ground level and a larger one upstairs, which is a popular venue for weddings and leads to the temple. Huge statues of Hindu gods, notably Ganesha, Krishna, and Ram, are garlanded and clothed in exquisite Indian fabric. You can join an early morning or evening prayer daily at 6:30 AM and 6:30 PM. ⊠ *5 Sydenham Rd., Greyville* ☎ *031/309–1824* ⊠ *Free* ☉ *Daily 8:30–4.*

⓮ **NSA Gallery.** The National Society of the Arts' Gallery complex houses four exhibition areas, in addition to a crafts shop, the Durban Center for Photography, and a classy open-air restaurant. The center does not have a particular focus but is committed to promoting emerging talent in the province. Exhibition mediums range from photos and paintings to video installations. The center's clean architectural lines and leafy setting make this a popular venue with Durban's trendy set, and it's a lovely place to cool off after a hot morning touring the town. The gallery and crafts shop support and promote local art, so it's worth hunting for tasteful souvenirs. The daytime-only restaurant is wonderful child-friendly pit stop. ⊠ *166 Bulwer Rd., off the M8, Glenwood* ☎ *031/277–1700* ⊕ *www.kznsagallery.co.za* ⊠ *Free* ☉ *Tues.–Fri. 9–5, weekends 10–4.*

6

⑮ **Shree Ambalavaanar Alayam Temple.** One of Durban's most spectacular Hindu shrines is in Cato Manor. The temple's facade is adorned with brightly painted representations of the Hindu gods, notably Ganesha, Shiva, and Vishnu. The magnificent doors leading to the cellar were salvaged from a temple built in 1875 on the banks of the Umbilo River and subsequently destroyed by floods. During an important Hindu festival held annually in March, unshod fire walkers cross beds of burning, glowing coals. There are no set visiting hours. If the temple is open you'll be welcome to go inside; if not, the exterior of the building is still worth seeing. To get here, take the M13 (from Leopold Street) out of the city; at the major fork in road after Westridge Park and the high school, veer left onto Bellair Road. ✉ *890 Bellair Rd., Cato Manor* ☎ *No phone* 🖅 *Free* 🕐 *Hrs. vary.*

WHERE TO EAT
BEACHFRONT

$$-$$$
SEAFOOD
★

✕ **Cargo Hold.** You might need to book several months in advance to secure a table next to the shark tank here, but if you do it'll be one of your most memorable dining experiences ever. You can enjoy a trio of carpaccios—smoked ostrich, beef, and salmon—while 13-foot raggedtooth and Zambezi sharks drift right by your table. Aside from the array of fish dishes like sesame-seared tuna and kingklip à la Cargo (grilled kingklip topped with mussels poached in a passion-fruit-and-bourbon cream sauce), Cargo Hold also serves meat dishes like oxtail and rosemary-and-rock-salt leg of lamb. The restaurant is done up like a shipwreck; of three floors, two have tank frontage (the view of the shark tank from the bottom floor is best, so ask for this when booking). The restaurant is part of the building known as the Phantom Ship. Access to the ship costs R20, though this is refunded if you dine in Cargo Hold. ✉ *1 Bell St., Point* ☎ *031/328–8065* 🖎 *Reservations essential* ☰ *AE, DC, MC, V.*

$$ $$$
ECLECTIC
★

✕ **Havana Grill & Wine Bar.** The sea views and good food combine to make this one of Durban's finest restaurants. It offers spectacular sea vistas (ask for a table with a view when making your reservation) and minimalist Afro-Cuban decor, with richly upholstered chairs, some leather couches, and antelope horns on the walls. Steak—aged on meat hooks in a giant fridge—and seafood are both specialties. Try Havana's tasting platter for starters (minimum of two people sharing): nachos, jalapeño poppers stuffed with cheese, grilled calamari, and spring rolls. For mains, consider the Lamb Tanganyika, which is rubbed with toasted cumin and coriander and served with a rich gravy, or line fish (likely sailfish, dorado, or Cape salmon) served in five different ways: grilled with lemon butter, topped with fresh pesto and fettuccine, with a coriander dipping sauce and wasabi-infused mash, in a Thai green coconut curry, or in an Asian red curry. There's a good basic wine list as well as a walk-in cellar from which special bottles can be ordered. ✉ *Shop U2, Suncoast Casino & Entertainment World, Beachfront* ☎ *031/337–1304* ⊕ *www.havanagrill.co.za* 🖎 *Reservations essential* ☰ *AE, DC, MC, V.*

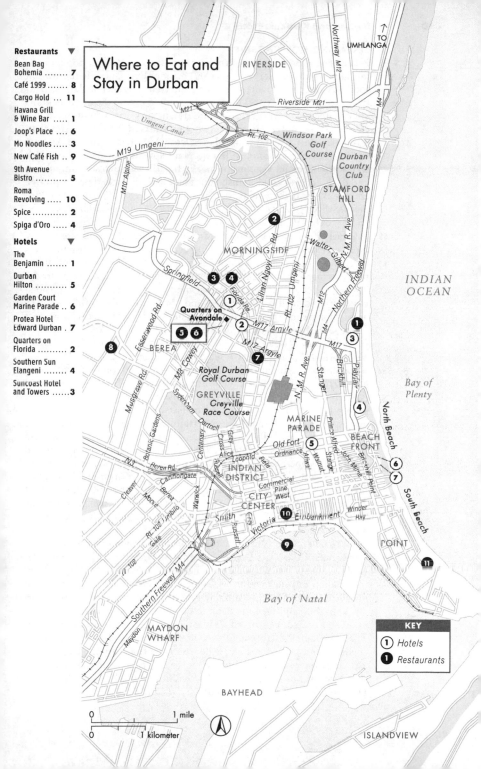

Where to Eat and Stay in Durban

RIVERSIDE

TO UMHLANGA

Riverside M21

Umgeni Canal

Windsor Park Golf Course

Durban Country Club

STAMFORD HILL

M19 Umgeni

MORNINGSIDE

INDIAN OCEAN

Springfield

Quarters on Avondale

BEREA

Royal Durban Golf Course

GREYVILLE
Greyville Race Course

MARINE PARADE

Bay of Plenty

BEACH FRONT

NORTH BEACH

Old Fort

INDIAN DISTRICT

CITY CENTER

Embankment

SOUTH BEACH

POINT

Bay of Natal

MAYDON WHARF

BAYHEAD

ISLANDVIEW

0   1 mile

0   1 kilometer

KEY

① Hotels

❶ Restaurants

BEREA AND MORNINGSIDE

$–$$

MEDITERRANEAN

✗ **Bean Bag Bohemia.** One of the city's most intimate and popular restaurants, Bean Bag serves a mix of cosmopolitan and Mediterranean food. It's abuzz with Durban's young and trendy, especially late at night when you can get a good meal after a movie or the theater. Cocktails and lighter meals are served at the downstairs bar, where live musicians often play jazz. Up rickety wooden stairs at the main restaurant, a popular starter is the meze platter, with Mediterranean snacks such as hummus, baba ghanoush (an eggplant spread), olives, and pita. It's well known for its vegetarian meals, but dishes such as lamb shank and duck are also good. Finish your meal with the baked pecan-praline cheesecake and then relax on the terrace. ⊠ *18 Lilian Ngoyi (Windermere) Rd., Greyville* ☎ *031/309–6019* ⊕ *www.beanbagbohemia. co.za* ▭ *AE, DC, MC, V.*

$–$$

MEDITERRANEAN

★

✗ **Café 1999.** Trendy this restaurant may be, but the food is infinitely more memorable than the shopping center setting. The husband-and-wife owners encourage you to celebrate taste with a menu of dishes that are meant for sharing, from the "titbits" (small servings) to the "bigbits." Let your fork and fingers wander between dishes like breaded olives stuffed with ricotta cheese and chicken kebabs with coriander-and-lemon pesto. The macadamia-nut-and-honey tart makes for a sweet finish. Café 1999 is a great place for lunch. ⊠ *Shop 2, Silvervause Centre, 117 Vause Rd., Musgrave* ☎ *031/202–3406* ⌂ *Reservations essential* ▭ *AE, DC, MC, V* ⊗ *Closed Sun. No lunch Sat.*

$$–$$$

STEAKHOUSE

★

✗ **Joop's Place.** No trip to South Africa would be complete without a good traditional steak, and without a doubt, Joop's (pronounced *yopes*) is the best and most popular steak house in Durban. It goes without saying that most customers are regulars. It has an intimate, homey atmosphere, though the decor is certainly nothing special. The food is the true focus, with Joop—a butcher by trade—himself selecting and preparing the steaks in an open kitchen. The specialty here is panfried steak; the pepper steak and Hollandse (Dutch-style) *biefstuk* (a center-cut fillet panfried in black butter and flambéed in brandy) are tasty favorites. The exceptionally hungry should try the 800-gram (about 21-ounce) T-bone. ⊠ *Shop 14, Avonmore Centre, 9th Ave., Morningside* ☎ *031/312–9135* ⌂ *Reservations essential* ▭ *AE, DC, MC, V* ⊗ *Closed Sun. No lunch Sat.–Thurs.*

$

THAI

★

✗ **Mo Noodles.** Don't let the name or mostly outside location fool you: this is one of the city's best restaurants, known for its huge portions, freshly prepared meals, and reasonable prices. The decor is chic and minimalist, but unpretentious and comfortable. Opt for a starter of prawn skewers in peanut dipping sauce or chicken teriyaki salad with a peanut dressing; then move on to chicken, prawn, and beef panfried noodles; a seared, marinated sesame fillet of beef; or any of the excellent Thai-style curries. Homemade ice cream comes in flavors like ginger, coconut, and honey cashew. It doesn't take reservations, so go early, especially on weekend nights. ⊠ *Shop 5, Florida Centre, 275 Florida Rd., Morningside* ☎ *031/312–4193* ⌂ *Reservations not accepted* ▭ *AE, DC, MC, V* ⊗ *Closed Sun. No lunch Sat.*

$$–$$$ ✕ **9th Avenue Bistro.** Chef-patron Carly Goncalves has a dedicated
ECLECTIC following, and deservedly so. While his dishes are based on classic
★ principles, he continues to interpret them with a modern twist. Think
pepper-seared tuna sashimi on Japanese radish and cucumber salad
with wasabi, soy, and pickled ginger, or crispy roasted free-range duck
served on a gingered sweet potato and butternut-squash mash, with
grilled asparagus and cinnamon-orange demi-glace. The food is decadent but the setting is less so, and a meal can be enjoyed without the
snobbery that accompanies five-star establishments as friendly waiters
work happily to indulge diners. The wine list contains a good choice
of South African wines, which your waiter can assist in choosing if
you're not yet familiar with local labels. ⊠ *Shop 2, Avonmore Centre,
9th Ave., Morningside* ☎ *031/312–9134* ⊟ *AE, DC, MC, V* ☉ *Closed
Sun. No lunch Mon.*

$$–$$$ ✕ **Spice.** Don't go expecting a curry restaurant, and you won't be disap-
ECLECTIC pointed. You can, however, expect the subtle use of spices to create aromatic dishes like roasted-coriander-and-rosemary-spiced rack of lamb on
a minted pea, potato, and onion mash (think funky potato concoction).
For dessert try a traditional milk tart with cinnamon, topped with preserved ginger and toasted almonds. If you really need a good curry fix,
there are a few options including the Oriental prawn version. Located
in a converted Victorian-style house that's typical of the area, the eclectic restaurant is serious in its approach to food but thankfully free of
pomp and ceremony. ⊠ *362 Lilian Ngoyi (Windermere) Rd., Morningside* ☎ *031/303–6375* ⚠ *Reservations essential* ⊟ *AE, DC, MC, V.*

¢–$ ✕ **Spiga d'Oro.** Located on the fashionable Florida Road, Spiga is some-
ITALIAN thing of a Durban institution, and it's not just because it named a dish
after regular client and convicted fraudster Shabir Shaik. That said, the
Linguine à la Shaik done with a tomato and basil sauce with a touch of
chili is perennially popular. Spiga, as it is known to locals, represents
the attitude and overall feeling of Durban—it's unpretentious with an
animated atmosphere that makes diners feel part of the crowd. The Italian menu is not always classical in its interpretation, but you can count
on it being delicious and a good value (pasta dishes come in medium or
large portions). And, if you enjoy taking your time when dining, there
are no over-zealous staff trying to turn your table. Open from breakfast, the kitchen doesn't close until the early hours of the next morning,
when it's constantly abuzz with a steady stream of hungry patrons. Be
prepared for a wait. ⊠ *200 Florida Rd., Morningside* ☎ *031/303–9511*
⚠ *Reservations not accepted* ⊟ *AE, DC, MC, V.*

CITY CENTER AND BAYFRONT

$$ ✕ **The New Café Fish.** This popular eatery juts out into the Durban Yacht
SEAFOOD Basin between the BAT Centre and Wilson's Wharf. Here, the city's
vertical lines—towering skyscrapers along the embankment and the
slender masts of vessels anchored beside the restaurant—tie sky and
sea together in a memorable setting. The food is tasty, with fish a spe-
cialty, as the restaurant's name suggests. Try the mild Thai prawn curry
or the pesto line fish, or order a seafood platter of special-order items
like extra-large crayfish and prawns according to seasonal availability
(but be prepared to pay quite a bit extra for seasonal specials). The bar

6

upstairs is pleasant for sundowners and serves light meals and snacks. ⊠ *31 Yacht Mole, Margaret Mncadi Ave., City Center* ☎ *031/305–5062 or 031/305–5063* ▤ *AE, DC, MC, V.*

$–$$

ITALIAN

✕ **Roma Revolving.** In business since 1973, this slowly revolving restaurant, which takes about an hour to do one full rotation, offers what has to be the most spectacular views of the city, especially the harbor. It's run by the original Italian owners, and the extensive menu runs the gamut from pasta to seafood. From old-school waiters to the hard-to-resist dessert trolley, there's something pleasingly old-fashioned about the Roma Revolving. While the restaurant is perched atop a high-rise building, its entrance is in an area that has become rather run-down over the years; the parking lot is fenced in. ⊠ *John Ross House, 32nd fl., Margaret Mncadi Ave., City Center* ☎ *031/368–2275* ⊕ *www.roma. co.za* ⌕ *Reservations essential* ▤ *AE, DC, MC, V* ⊗ *Closed Sun.*

WHERE TO STAY

BEACHFRONT

$$

⊡ **Garden Court Marine Parade.** You can't beat the location of this pleasant hotel midway between South and North beaches and only a five-minute drive from the city center. Rooms are attractive and modern, each with a small sitting area. All face the sea, but request an upper-floor room for the best views. Views from the pool deck on the 30th floor are superb. **Pros:** centrally located on Golden Mile; sea views; friendly staff. **Cons:** hotel lobby and bar area lack atmosphere; recommended restaurants a taxi ride away; inadvisable to walk in area after dark. ⊠ *167 Marine Parade, Box 10809, Beachfront* ☎ *031/337–3341* ⊕ *www.southernsun.com* ⌕ *348 rooms, 6 suites* ☖ *In-room: safe. In-hotel: restaurant, bar, pool, room service* ▤ *AE, DC, MC, V* ⌑ *BP.*

$$

⊡ **Protea Hotel Edward Durban.** Built in 1939 in classic colonial style, the Edward is one of Durban's oldest hotels. Although it's been restored almost to its former elegance, it seems to have lost a little of its soul in the process. Nevertheless, service is excellent, and the stylish cut-glass chandeliers, molded ceilings, and subtle art-deco details bring to mind a more refined past. Rooms are tastefully furnished; 10 have balconies overlooking the sea, and the others have bay windows with sea views. The hotel faces beautiful South Beach. **Pros:** don't be put off by the facade, the interior is old-world elegance; on Golden Mile; you can catch a rickshaw right outside hotel; 24-hour business center. **Cons:** recommended restaurants are a taxi trip away; inadvisable to walk around in the area after dark. ⊠ *149 Marine Parade, Box 105, Beachfront* ☎ *031/337–3681* ⊕ *www.proteahotels.com* ⌕ *101 rooms, 10 suites* ☖ *In-room: Wi-Fi, refrigerator, safe. In-hotel: restaurant, room service, bars, pool, Internet terminal* ▤ *AE, DC, MC, V.*

$$

⊡ **Southern Sun Elangeni.** One of the best hotels on the beachfront, this 21-story high-rise overlooks North Beach and is a two-minute drive from the city center. It attracts a mix of business, conference, and leisure travelers. Though all rooms have views of the water, request a room on an upper floor for a full ocean view. The hotel has one of the few Japanese restaurants in the city, as well as a first-class Indian restaurant. A minimum two-night stay is required. **Pros:** tour and travel desk; friendly staff; tastefully decorated rooms; great on-site restaurants; discounted weekend rates. **Cons:** not for travelers who prefer an intimate hotel experience; breakfast not included in price during peak times. ⊠ *63 Snell Parade, Beachfront* ☎ *031/362–1300* ⊕ *www.southernsun.com* ⇨ *449 rooms, 10 suites* ⚒ *In-room: Internet, refrigerator (some), safe. In-hotel: 3 restaurants, room service, bars, pools, gym* ≡ *AE, DC, MC, V.*

$$–$$$ ⊞ **Suncoast Hotel and Towers.** Situated adjacent to the Suncoast Casino, the hotel is a stone's throw from the beach. Like the casino, it's designed in the art-deco style of the 1930s, which is in keeping with some of Durban's architectural heritage (the city is still home to a few beautiful art-deco apartment buildings). The hotel is furnished in pastel shades and is elegantly minimalist, though the rooms are rather small. The sea views from the higher floors are spectacular (sea-facing rooms are slightly more expensive but worth it). The hotel mostly attracts businesspeople and gamblers. The 36 suites in the towers are a bit more luxe than those in the hotel. **Pros:** closest hotel to Moses Mabhida Stadium; fantastic spa; access to beautiful beach (albeit with a R5 fee). **Cons:** adjacent to casino; smallish rooms. ⊠ *20 Battery Beach, Beachfront* ☎ *031/314–7878* ⊕ *www.southernsun.com* ⇨ *165 rooms, 36 suites* ⚒ *In-room: safe, refrigerator, Wi-Fi. In-hotel: restaurant, room service, bar, pool, gym, spa* ≡ *AE, DC, MC, V* ⦿ *BP (suites only).*

BEREA AND MORNINGSIDE

$ ⊞ **The Benjamin.** In one of Durban's transformed historic buildings, this small hotel offers excellent value. Its location is ideal—perched on trendy Florida Road, with its excellent restaurants and nightlife, and approximately five minutes from both the beaches and the city center. The residents' lounge is quiet and elegant but still warm and comfortable, as are the stylish rooms. The breakfast room has big glass doors opening out onto a small pool. **Pros:** within walking distance to restaurants; covered swimming pool; historic building's charm has been retained. **Cons:** limited secure parking; no on-site restaurant; no elevator. ⊠ *141 Florida Rd., Morningside* ☎ *031/303–4233* ⊕ *www. benjamin.co.za* ⇨ *45 rooms* ⚒ *In-room: Internet, refrigerator, safe. In-hotel: pool* ≡ *AE, DC, MC, V* ⦿ *BP.*

$$$ ⊞ **Quarters on Florida.** Four converted Victorian homes comprise the
★   city's most intimate boutique hotel, on Florida Road; an additional, newer, 17-room property up the road is called Quarters on Avondale. Both are contemporary European-style properties, although the Florida Road hotel has a colonial African feel and the new sister hotel is more modern in its approach. Rooms have mahogany furniture, cream-colored, damask-covered beds, and sunken tubs in luxurious bathrooms. Many of the rooms have small verandas facing onto Florida Road, with its swaying palm trees and sometimes busy traffic, but double-glazed windows help to dull noise. **Pros:** tastefully appointed rooms; on-site restaurants; close to restaurants and nightlife of Florida Road. **Cons:** despite efforts, street-facing rooms are noisy; no pool; limited off-street parking. ⊠ *101 Florida Rd., Berea* ☎ *031/303–5246* ⊕ *www.quarters. co.za* ⇨ *25 rooms* ⚒ *In-room: Internet, refrigerator, safe. In-hotel: restaurant* ≡ *AE, DC, MC, V* ⦿ *CP.*

6

CITY CENTER AND BAYFRONT

$$$–$$$$ ⊡ **Durban Hilton.** This massive luxury hotel adjacent to the International Convention Centre is relatively close (short taxi trip) to the city center and beachfront and is favored by businesspeople and conference-goers. The rooms are small but tastefully decorated in light wood with cream-colored bedding and African touches and have either beach or city views. Executive floors have a small club room, where guests can get breakfast and free Internet access. Large public areas come complete with marble pillars and a pianist tinkling away on a baby grand. The Rainbow Terrace restaurant has an excellent buffet and a take-out à la carte menu. The Hilton also boasts impeccable service, making it one of the top hotels in this chain in Africa. Though expensive by Durban standards, rates can vary significantly based on how full the hotel is, which often relates to which conferences are being held at the convention center. **Pros:** close to the convention center; good gym; beauty salon offers unusual treatments such as the bamboo massage that utilizes different size pieces of bamboo. **Cons:** not within walking distance of restaurants; unsafe to walk outside hotel after dark. ⊠ *12–14 Walnut Ave., City Center* ☎ *031/336–8100* ⊕ *www.hilton.com* ⌁ *327 rooms, 16 suites* ⚬ *In-room: Internet, Wi-Fi, refrigerator, safe. In-hotel: 2 restaurants, bar, pool, gym, room service* ⊟ *AE, DC, MC, V.*

NIGHTLIFE

What's On in Durban, a free monthly publication put out by the tourism office and distributed at popular sites, lists a diary of upcoming events. **Billy the BUMS** (⊠ *504 Lilian Ngoyi [Windermere] Rd., Morningside* ☎ *031/303–1988*) hums from the early evening until late. It also serves tasty tidbits food, like jalapeño poppers. California-style **Joe Kool's** (⊠ *137 Lower Marine Parade, Beachfront* ☎ *031/332–9697*) is a popular nightclub and restaurant, right on the beach. A longstanding nightspot, Joe Kool's caters to a fairly upmarket crowd. You can sip a cocktail watching the sun go down over Durban's harbor at the **New Café Fish Bar** (⊠ *31 Yacht Mole, Margaret Mncadi Ave., Victoria Embankment* ☎ *031/305–5062 or 031/305–5063*), in the Durban Yacht Basin.

SPORTS AND THE OUTDOORS

BEACHES

The sea near Durban, unlike that around the Cape, is comfortably warm year-round: in summer the water temperature can top 27°C (80°F), whereas in winter 19°C (65°F) is considered cold. The beaches are safe, the sand is a beautiful golden color, and you'll see people swimming all year round. All of KwaZulu-Natal's main beaches are protected by shark nets and staffed with lifeguards, and there are usually boards stating the wind direction, water temperature, and the existence of any dangerous swimming conditions. Directly in front of uShaka Marine World, **uShaka Beach** is an attractive public beach. The **Golden Mile**, stretching from South Beach all the way to Snake Park Beach, is packed with people who enjoy the waterslides, singles' bars, and fast-food joints. A little farther north are the **Umhlanga beaches,** and on the opposite side of the bay are the less commercialized but also less accessible and safe beaches on **Durban's Bluff.** Another pretty beach and coastal walk, just north of the **Umhlanga Lagoon,** leads to miles of near-empty beaches backed by virgin bush. Please note: you should not walk alone on deserted beaches or carry any jewelry or other valuables, and you should never walk at night.

BOATING

It's easy to charter all manner of boats, from a paddleski (a flat fiberglass board that you paddle) for a few rand to a deep-sea fishing vessel for a few thousand. Inexpensive harbor tours lasting a half hour, booze cruises, and dinner cruises can all be booked from the quayside at Wilson's Wharf. Shop around to find something that suits your budget, taste, and time frame.

DOLPHIN-WATCHING AND DIVING

36 Degrees (☎ 082/553–2834 or 082/451–8578 ⊕ www.36degrees. co.za) operates various boat excursions on which you are likely to see dolphins. From June to November there's also a chance of spotting migrating humpback and Southern Right whales. The company also specializes in dives to various sites and offers equipment rentals. **Calypso Dive and Adventure Centre** (☎ 031/332–0905 or 083/263–7585 ⊕ www.calypsodiving.co.za) is a PADI five-star Instructor Development Center and a National Geographic dive center that organizes dives and rents equipment.

FISHING

Deep-sea fishing is a popular activity, as there's almost always something biting. Summer (November–May) brings game fish like barracuda, marlin, sailfish, and dorado, whereas winter is better for the bottom fishes, like mussel crackers, salmon, and rock cod.

Casea Charters (☎ 031/561–7381 or 083/690–2511 ⊕ www.caseacharters.co.za) offers trips on a ski boat from Granny's Pool, in front of Umhlanga's Cabana Beach, that run from three to five hours (R400–R550). Fish for dorado, yellowfin tuna, king and queen mackerel, garrick, rock cod, salmon, and other species. Bait and equipment are supplied, but bring your own food and drinks. You can keep the fish you catch. Booking is essential. **Lynski Charters** (☎ 031/539–3338 or 082/445–6600 ⊕ www.lynski.com) offers deep-sea fishing for barracuda, sailfish, marlin, shark, and reef fish out of Durban's harbor. Trips, in a 35-foot game-fish boat, cost R4,000 for up to six people fishing for a day trip, although the boat can take nine people altogether. The price includes equipment, tackle, bait, and cold drinks. **Swissroll Charters** (☎ 031/467–2185 or 082/451–6567 ⊕ www.swissroll.co.za) offers similar deep-sea fishing trips from the harbor. For R3,800, skipper-owner Ralph Nussbaumer takes a maximum of six people for a day on his 30-foot boat with a cabin. Sometimes he sets up a gas cooker and fries some fresh fish.

GOLF

Durban Country Club (☎ 031/313–1777 ⊕ www.dcclub.co.za) has hosted more South African Opens than any other course, and is regularly rated the best in South Africa. Tees and greens sit atop large sand dunes, and trees add an additional hazard. Visitors are welcome, but can't play Wednesday and Thursday afternoons or Saturdays; fees for the 18-hole, par-72 course are R560. Rental clubs are available. Inside the Greyville

Racecourse, the **Royal Durban Golf Club** (☎ *031/309–1373* ⊕ *www.royal-durban.co.za*) offers no protection from the wind, which makes hitting the narrow fairways very difficult, but the surroundings are attractive and the venue is central. Fees for the 18-hole, par-72 course are R300, rental clubs are available, and reservations are essential. The course is open every day, and the first tee-off is at 7 AM. **Zimbali Country Club** (☎ *032/538–1041* ⊕ *www.zimbali.org*) is built in and around one of the few remaining coastal forests in the province. The world-class 18-hole course was designed by Tom Weiskopf and lies amid sand dunes above a secluded beach, natural springs, and a lake. There is a fully stocked pro shop. Greens fees for 18 holes are R350 on weekdays and R400 on weekends. Compulsory cart rental is R200; rental clubs are available for R300 per set.

SURFING
Surfing has a fanatical following in Durban, and several local and international tournaments are staged on the city's beaches, at nearby Umhlanga, Ballito, or on the Bluff. Crowds of more than 10,000 are not unusual for night surfing competitions or the annual Mr. Price Pro championship (formerly the Gunston 500) held in Ballito, a top World Qualifying Series event on the world surfing circuit. When the conditions are right, New Pier is one of the best beach breaks in the world.

Just the other side of Durban's protected bay, Cave Rock, on the Bluff, offers a seething right-hander that can handle big swell. It can be a tough paddle and is not for amateurs. Farther down the South Coast, surfers head for Scottburgh, Green Point, Park Rynie, or Southbroom. North of Durban, popular spots include Umhlanga, Ballito, Richard's Bay, and Sodwana Bay.

The more popular spots can get crowded, and locals are known to be territorial about certain sections. Be sure to obey the laws of surfing etiquette. Usually the best waves are found at dawn and dusk. If the southwester blows, the Durban beaches are your best bet. In the winter months look out for an early-morning land breeze to set up good waves along the whole coastline.

SHOPPING
Durban offers a great array of shopping experiences, from the Beachfront, where you can buy cheap beadwork and baskets, to enormous Western-style malls such as Gateway in Umhlanga *(⇨ Top Attractions, in Umhlanga)*. In general, bargaining is not expected, though you might try it at the Beachfront or with hawkers anywhere. Look out for goods indigenous to the province: colorful Zulu beadwork and tightly handwoven baskets. ⇨ *For Florida Road shops, see "The Florida Road Strip" box, above.*

MARKETS
One of the nicest and most popular of Durban's many flea markets, the **Essenwood Flea Market** (✉ *Stephen Dlamini [Essenwood] Rd., Berea* ☎ *031/202–5632*) is held every Saturday until 2. Classy stalls sell handmade clothes and crafts, leatherwork, stained glass, and restored wooden furniture, among many other items, in a beautiful park setting. The **Stables** (✉ *Newmarket horse stables, Jacko Jackson Dr., next to*

the Absa Park Rugby Stadium ☎ 031/312–3752) carries cheap imports from the East, but also an interesting selection of local crafts, such as beaded and leather goods. It's open Wednesday and Friday evenings 6–10 for a moonlight market and Sunday 10–5, except for June and July. The most exciting market in the city is the **Victoria Street Market** (✉ Denis Hurley [Queen] and Joseph Nduli [Russell] Sts., Indian District ☎ 031/306–4021), where you can buy everything from recordings of African music to curios and curry spices. Bargaining is expected here, much as it is in India.

UMHLANGA

20 km (12½ mi) north of Durban

Also known as Umhlanga Rocks (meaning Place of the Reeds), this area used to be a small vacation village, but Durban's northward sprawl has incorporated it into a popular and upscale residential and business suburb, much like Sandton is to downtown Johannesburg. To the north are the nicest sea views; to the south is Umhlanga's lighthouse. Umhlanga's village charm and lovely beaches have entrenched it as one of the most sought-after vacation destinations for locals and foreigners, and it boasts many of Durban's top hotels.

6

GETTING HERE AND AROUND

Durban International Airport is 32 km (20 mi) south of Umhlanga and a transfer or taxi will cost R300 one way. The new King Shaka airport is closer at 17 km (11 mi) north and an added bonus is that you drive against traffic. A transfer or taxi to King Shaka Airport will cost about R170 one way.

Umhlanga is small enough to walk from hotels into the village although most would favor a taxi ride over the arduous uphill slog to the Gateway shopping center and the Sharks Board. Tourists can safely walk around during the day and taxis are readily available after dark. Street parking is a challenge during peak holiday times and, where necessary, be sure to put money in parking meters as the traffic police in the area are very officious! As with the rest of South Africa, wherever you go you'll be beset by self-appointed car guards, who ask if they can watch your car. The going rate for a tip if you want to give one is R2–R5, depending on how long you're away. ⚠ **Don't leave your keys with anyone.**

Taxis are metered and start at R5, with an additional charge of R9–R10 per kilometer (per half mile). Expect to pay R40 from the village to Gateway or the Sharks Board and R200 to the Berea or uShaka Marine World. Taxis are readily available in the village and at the Gateway shopping center.

ESSENTIALS

Airport Transfers Aqua Tours (☎ 082/410–7116). **Umhlanga Cabs** (☎ 031/561–1846).

Taxis Umhlanga Cabs (☎ 031/561–1846).

Visitor Information Sugar Coast Tourism (✉ Shop 1A, Chartwell Centre, 15 Chartwell Dr. ☎ 031/561–4257).

Numbers in the text correspond to numbers in the margin and on the Umhlanga map.

TOP ATTRACTIONS

㉕ **Gateway Theatre of Shopping.** The largest mall in the Southern Hemisphere, Gateway has been designed to let in natural light and is surprisingly easy to navigate. Shopping ranges from surfing paraphernalia and imported and local fashions to electronics and art and crafts. Gateway also has a large variety of entertainment options including an IMAX theater and the art-nouveau Barnyard Theatre, which hosts live music compilation shows in an informal "barn" environment; the largest indoor climbing wall in the world; and the Wavehouse, with artificially generated waves and a skate park. ⊠ *New Town Centre, 1 Palm Blvd.* ☎ *031/566–2332* ⊕ *www.gatewayworld.co.za* ⊘ *Mon.–Thurs. 9–7, Fri. and Sat., 9–9, Sun. 9–6.*

㉔ **Natal Sharks Board.** Most of the popular bathing beaches in KwaZulu-Natal are protected by shark nets maintained by this shark-research institute, the world's foremost. Each day, weather permitting, crews in ski boats check the nets, releasing healthy sharks back into the ocean and bringing dead ones back to the institute, where they are dissected and studied. One-hour tours are offered, including a shark dissection (sharks' stomachs have included such surprising objects as a boot, a tin can, and a car license plate!) and an enjoyable and fascinating audiovisual presentation on sharks and shark nets. An exhibit area and good curio shop are also here. You can join the early morning trip from Durban harbor to watch the staff service the shark nets off Durban's Golden Mile. Depending on the season, you will more than likely see dolphins and whales close at hand. Booking is essential for trips to the shark nets, and a minimum of six people is required; no one under age six is allowed. ■TIP→ **Book well in advance for this—it may turn out to be a highlight of your trip.** ⊠ *1a Herrwood Dr.* ☎ *031/566–0400* ⊕ *www.shark.co.za* ⊠ *Presentation R25, boat trips R250* ⊘ *Presentation Tues., Wed., and Thurs. at 9 and 2, Sun. at 2. Boat trips to shark nets, daily (weather dependent) 6:30–8:30* AM.

WORTH NOTING

㉖ **Hawaan Forest.** This 114-acre coastal forest grows on a dune that dates back 18,000 years and has 175 species of indigenous trees, fungi (during wet months), and various species of birds. Guided walks take two to three hours and are conducted on the first Saturday of every month (except in January or February), but if you call ahead you can be accommodated at another time. ■TIP→ **Be sure to wear closed-toe shoes.** ⊠ *Portland and Herald Drs.* ☎ *031/566–4018 or 031/562–0257* ⊠ *Donation appreciated* ⊘ *Daily 8–11* AM.

O'Connor Promenade. Join tourists and locals for a gentle stroll or vigorous run along the 3-km (1.8-mi) paved stretch that reaches from Durban View Park in the south to Umhlanga Lagoon Nature Reserve in the north. This is a great way to check out the local coastline and bathing areas, plus you'll come across Umhlanga's landmark lighthouse—closed to the public—and its newly built pier whose steel arches are designed to look like a whale's skeleton. ⊠ *Umhlanga Beach.*

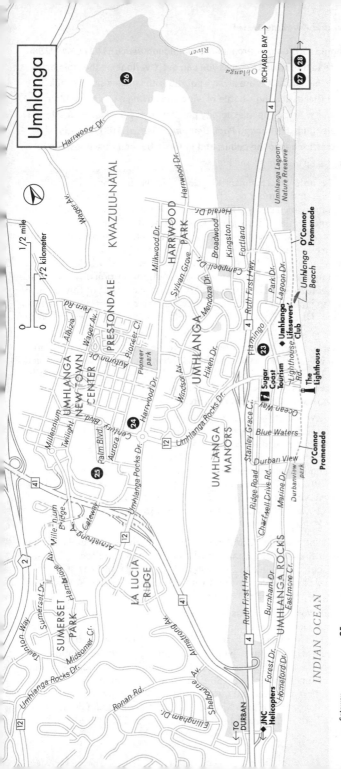

Umhlanga

KWAZULU-NATAL

Ohlanga River

RICHARDS BAY →

27 · 28

Umhlanga Lagoon
Nature Reserve

O'Connor
Promenade

Umhlanga
Beach

◆ Umhlanga Lifesavers
Club

i Sugar
Coast
Tourism

Lighthouse
Rd.

⚓ The
Lighthouse

Ocean Way

O'Connor
Promenade

Blue Waters

Durban View
park

INDIAN OCEAN

PRESTONDALE

HARRWOOD
PARK

Harrwood Dr.

Milkwood Dr.

Sylvan Grove

Campbell Dr.

Mendoza Dr.

Broadwood

Kingston

Fortland

Park Dr.

Lagoon Dr.

Flamingo

UMHLANGA

Hiken Dr.

Windsor Av.

Harrwood Dr.

Umhlanga Rocks Dr.

UMHLANGA MANORS

Stanley Grace Cr.

Ridge Road

Chartwell Drive Rd.

Marine Dr.

Durbanview Dr.

UMHLANGA
NEW TOWN
CENTER

Albizia

Autumn Dr.

Wager Av.

Pioneer Cr.

Pioneer
park

Century Blvd

Aurora

Palm Blvd

Millennium

Twilight

Umhlanga Rocks Dr.

Umhlanga Rocks Dr.

Fern Rd

LA LUCIA
RIDGE

Gateway

Armstrong

Mill-n-um
Bridge

SUMERSET
PARK

Summerset Dr.

Hambridge

Midsomer Cr.

Taunton Way

Umhlanga Rocks Dr.

Forest Dr.

Homeford Dr.

Armstrong Av.

Ronan Rd.

Shelbourne
Av.

Ellingham Dr.

**◆ JNC
Helicopters**

TO
DURBAN

UMHLANGA ROCKS

Burcham Dr.

Eastmone Cr.

Ruth First Hwy

Ruth First Hwy

Harrwood Dr.

Herald Dr.

Wager Av.

0   1/2 kilometer
0   1/2 mile

N

**NEED A
BREAK?**

La Spiaggia (✉ *O'Connor Promenade, Umhlanga Beach* ☎ *031/561–4388*) is as close to the Indian Ocean as you can get. Overlooking the main bathing beach, outside tables are always packed with families sipping milk shakes or friends sharing a bottle of wine and having a bite to eat off a menu that has broad appeal. Literally perched above the beach, **Umhlanga Lifesavers' Club** (✉ *Granny's Pool, Umhlanga Beach* ☎ *031/561–3519*) a local secret, is open to the public, and there's a bar and casual restaurant offering cheap breakfasts and lunches only.

㉘ Sibaya Casino & Entertainment Kingdom. Sibaya is expansive—in size, appearance, and number of activities—but is worth seeing for its grandiose, Zulu-themed design. The buildings themselves, for example, echo a giant and opulent Zulu *kraal* (compound/dwelling). Huge bronze statues of Zulu warriors and buffalos at the entrance provide a truly African welcome. Wherever you are at Sibaya, all 119 acres of it, a breathtaking view of the ocean is only a window or a balcony away. As you might expect, there are plenty of dining options. A 36-room, five-star hotel opened here in 2006. It's quite a way out of town, north of Umhlanga and about halfway between the city center and Ballito. ✉ *1 Sibaya Dr.* ☎ *031/580–5000 or 0860/742–292* ⊕ *www.sibaya.co.za* ☞ *Free* ⏱ *24 hrs.*

㉓ Souvenirs. For years a group of informal traders has sold its wares, ranging from woven baskets to straw hats, carvings, and various traditional beadworks, on the roadside. There are about eight stalls, open daily, and the vendors rarely change. Bring cash and a penchant for bargaining. ✉ *Opposite Cabana Beach Hotel, Lagoon Dr.*

㉗ Swallow View Site. If you're in the area from mid-October to mid-April, be sure to take in this amazing natural phenomenon that sees 3 million barn swallows returning to their nests at sunset. Arrive 45 minutes before sunset armed with something to sit on, binoculars, camera, sundowners, and some mosquito repellent. ✉ *From N2 take the Umdloti/ Verulam off-ramp and follow signs to Verulam Dr. for less than 1 km (600 yards) and turn at Umdloti Estate and follow signs to view site, Mount Moreland* ☎ *031/568–1671 or 031/568–1557.*

WHERE TO EAT

Despite being a village, Umhlanga is littered with eateries due to development in the area and year-round tourism. Most are located in and around Chartwell Drive in the center of Umhlanga and happy throngs of diners at neighboring restaurants make for a festive atmosphere, especially in peak holiday season.

$–$$ ✕ **Bangkok Wok.** Seafood has a strong presence here—think crispy cala-
THAI   mari or steamed fish with lemongrass—and the duck dishes are particularly good. Try the Bangkok duck, which is roasted, wrapped in a crepe, and topped with a honey, palm sugar, ginger, garlic, and lemongrass sauce. Noodle and egg-fried rice dishes are filling and budget-friendly. But it's the lunch specials at R30 that offer extraordinary value for the money and are best enjoyed outside while you soak up the sun and the friendly village atmosphere. ✉ *Shop 13, Lighthouse Mall, Chartwell Dr.* ☎ *031/561–2050* ⊕ *www.bangkokwok.co.za* ▭ *AE, DC, MC, V.*

$$ | ✕**Bel Punto.** Follow your stomach 15 minutes north of Umhlanga to
ITALIAN | Umdloti where you'll dine on Italian fare with a contemporary twist.
★ | The seafood is outstanding—think line fish baked in the wood-fired pizza oven and perfectly cooked calamari or prawns done in a garlic, white wine, tomato, cream, and chili sauce. And Italian staples like pastas, pizzas, and risotto hit the spot. The wine list is noteworthy and waiters are knowledgeable, although there are sometimes delays with food when the restaurant is busy. To make the most of the gorgeous sea views, book for lunch or an early dinner. ⊠ *Umdloti Centre, 1 South Beach Rd., Umdloti* ☎ *031/568–2407* ⚛ *Reservations essential* ▤ *AE, DC, MC, V* ☻ *Closed Mon. No lunch Tues.*

$$–$$$ | ✕**Butcher Boys.** This is mecca for red-meat lovers. Grain-fed beef comes
STEAKHOUSE | in all forms (think T-Bones to fillet), is aged for a minimum of 24 days, and can be cut on-site according to your preference. The cuts are served with a choice of sauces (mushroom and red wine, cheese, or garlic to name a few) and vegetable sides. There's also a good selection of fish and chicken dishes, and wine lovers will undoubtedly find something to delight their palate. ⊠ *Lighthouse Mall, Chartwell Dr.* ☎ *031/561–4106 or 031/561–4108* ⊕ *www.butcherboysgrill.co.za* ▤ *AE, DC, MC, V* ☻ *No lunch Sat.*

$$–$$$ | ✕**Ile Maurice.** One of Umhlanga's culinary gems, Ile Maurice is run by
FRENCH | the charming Mauvis family. The soft-hued interior and pretty veranda that overlooks the Umhlanga beach hark back to the area's colonial roots. On the menu you'll find classic French fare like escargot as well as aromatic Mauritian cuisine such as the *vindaye* (a pickled fish dish). Seafood is also a specialty: order the crab soup starter if it's on the menu. Those who aren't seafood fans are also taken care of, and a well considered wine list complements the menu. ⊠ *9 McCausland Crescent* ☎ *031/561–7609* ▤ *AE, DC, MC, V* ☻ *Closed Mon.*

$ | ✕**Kashmir.** The menu features mainly North Indian dishes that are so
INDIAN | large and filling that—take our word for it—appetizers are not needed. Standout curries include butter chicken, lamb *gosht pasanda* (done in an almond and cream sauce with saffron), and the *navratan korma* (mixed vegetables cooked in cashew gravy with fruit). The interior decor provides a sophisticated dining experience, but you'll get comfy wicker chairs and sea views on the balcony. There's a good, reasonably priced buffet on Friday and Saturday nights and Sunday lunch. Unfortunately the experience is sometimes clouded by sluggish service. ⊠ *11 McCausland Crescent* ☎ *031/561–7486* ⊕ *www.kashmir-restaurant. co.za* ▤ *AE, DC, MC, V.*

$$–$$ | ✕**Olive & Oil.** You can't go wrong here. Fantastic Mediterranean-
MEDITERRANEAN | inspired fare is good value for the money. The best way to start your meal is with a mezze platter to share among two or three people. Main courses range from melt-in-your-mouth calamari to steaks, pastas, and pizzas. The large restaurant is not suitable for a romantic night out, but it's great for families and offers consistently good food and service. If the weather's warm, try for a table on the veranda. ⊠ *19 Chartwell Centre, 15 Chartwell Dr.* ☎ *031/561–2618* ⚛ *Reservations essential* ▤ *AE, DC, MC, V* ☻ *No lunch Mon.*

6

$–$$ ✗ **Plaka.** Crisp white furnishings accented by striking shades of blue
GREEK   provide the perfect background for outstanding Greek fare. Start by
ordering lots of appetizers like pita with hummus, grilled baby octopus,
or *sheftalia* (a spicy sausage from Cyprus). Main course recommendations include traditional dishes such as *kleftico* (lamb shank slow
roasted on the bone) and moussaka (an eggplant and ground meat
dish), although the seafood options won't disappoint either. Efficient
service and a notable wine list round out a great experience. ⊠ *Gateway
shopping center, 7 Palm Blvd.* ☎ *031/566–7456* ⊕ *www.plaka.co.za*
⚓ *Reservations essential* ▭ *AE, DC, MC, V.*

¢–$ ✗ **So! Sushi.** The owners of So! Sushi were so intent on providing the
JAPANESE   freshest ingredients possible that they decided to open their own fish
shop. Sushi is the star here, though there are some supplemental East-
ern-inspired dishes available as well. You can sit at a conveyor belt
and simply pluck off what you like, though you may want to order
directly from the kitchen if it's a hot day. In warm weather, the small
shop space is expanded with pavement tables that allow you to soak up
the village vibe. ⊠ *3 Lighthouse Mall, Chartwell Dr.* ☎ *031/561–5393*
▭ *AE, DC, MC, V.*

¢–$ ✗ **Zara's.** A daytime-only eatery that, despite having a definite Medi-
CAFÉ   terranean influence, successfully manages to be all things to all people.
The pavement is prime real estate as tables are clustered under a large
awning, and a young, friendly team delivers everything with a smile.
Pop in for a cappuccino and cake (the carrot cake is inspirational), start
the day off right with a number of creative breakfast options, or simply
settle in at lunchtime over a salad or pasta and a glass of wine. ⊠ *4
Lagoon Dr.* ☎ *031/561–2511* ▭ *AE, DC, MC, V* ☉ *No dinner.*

WHERE TO STAY

$$$ ⌂ **Beverly Hills Hotel.** In a high-rise building right on the beach, this
upscale hotel is popular with both vacationers and businesspeople and
has a longstanding reputation as one of the best in town. The service is
excellent (although occasionally unreliable in the restaurants) and the
facilities superb. However, if you're the sort of beachgoer who likes to
loll about in a bathing suit, you may find this hotel too formal. The pub-
lic lounge, festooned with huge floral arrangements and yards of gath-
ered drapes, serves a full silver-service tea in the afternoon, and a pianist
plays in the evening. Guest rooms are fairly small, but all have terrific
sea views, particularly those on the upper floors. For a more open,
beachlike feel, take one of the cabanas—large rooms that open onto a
lovely pool deck. **Pros:** unbeatable sea views; hotel has its own demar-
cated piece of beach with lounge chairs; great cocktail bar. **Cons:** formal
atmosphere might put some people off; some rooms are smaller than
you might expect; prices increase dramatically in-season. ⊠ *54 Light-
house Rd.* ☎ *031/561–2211* ⊕ *www.southernsun.com* ⇆ *81 rooms, 6
suites* ⚐ *In-room: Internet, refrigerator, safe. In-hotel: 2 restaurants,
room service, bars, pool, beachfront* ▭ *AE, DC, MC, V* ⏽❙ *BP.*

$$ ⌂ **Breakers Resort.** This property enjoys an enviable position at the
northern tip of Umhlanga, surrounded by the wilds of the Hawaan
Forest and overlooking the unspoiled wetlands of Umhlanga Lagoon.
Of all the resorts in Umhlanga, this one suffers the least from crowds.

The disadvantage though is that you probably need a car to get into town, and you can't swim directly in front of the resort because the surf's too dangerous. The building is unattractive, with long, depressing corridors, but the rooms themselves are fine, with fully equipped kitchens and great views of the beach and lagoon. The lovely grassed pool area, where you can order light meals, has a beautiful view of the sea. **Pros:** babysitting services; sprawling gardens; great pool; family-friendly. **Cons:** taxi is required to get to local restaurants, especially at night; overrun with families in-season. ⊠ *88 Lagoon Dr.* ☎ *031/561–2271* ⊕ *www.breakersresort.co.za* ✍ *80 rooms* ⚐ *In-room: kitchen, safe, refrigerator. In-hotel: 2 restaurants, bar, tennis court, pool, laundry service* ⊟ *AE, DC, MC, V.*

$$ ⊡ **Cabana Beach.** Families who want a traditional beach vacation can't do better than this large resort, where children under 18 stay free. The bathing beach is directly in front of the hotel, and there are tons of activities to keep kids happy. Rooms are simple, but beach appropriate. Each cabana comes with a fully equipped kitchen, a dining-living area, and a veranda with great sea views. Request a tower or beachfront apartment for the most attractive and practical space configuration. Out of season, the rates can be reduced by up to about half. **Pros:** located at main swimming beach; adults-only pool; within walking distance to village. **Cons:** basic, no-frills, no-fuss decor; teeming with children in-season. ⊠ *10 Lagoon Dr., Box 10* ☎ *031/561–2371* ✍ *217 rooms* ⚐ *In-room: kitchen, safe, refrigerator. In-hotel: 4 restaurants, bar, tennis courts, pools, gym, laundry service, laundry facilities, children's programs (ages 3–6)* ⊟ *AE, DC, MC, V.*

$$$ ⊡ **Teremok.** Translated from Russian as "little hideaway" this eight-
★ bedroom boutique lodge is less than a mile from Umhlanga village and one block from the sea. Each of the individually decorated rooms offers a different sensory experience—its own specific body-product fragrance, mood CD, candy, etc.—and the three rooms on the top level have beautiful ocean views. Tea and coffee stations (with cappuccino machines and fresh biscotti) and an honesty bar can be found in each room. Delicious breakfasts are made to order, and, although this is the only meal offered, extra muffins and fruit are left out for guests during the day. Lunch or dinner can be ordered in from area eateries. Staff will gladly recommend and book restaurants and tours and the on-site spa offers international skin care and body treatments. **Pros:** personalized service; free Internet; free transfers to village; complimentary laundry service; extensive DVD library. **Cons:** 1 km from nearest restaurants; open-plan bathrooms in all but one room. ⊠ *49 Marine Dr., Box 1830 1320* ☎ *031/561–5848* ✍ *8 rooms* ⚐ *In-room: safe, DVD, Internet, Wi-Fi. In-hotel: bicycles, laundry service, pool, gym, spa, no kids under 16* ⊟ *AE, DC, MC, V* ⧠*BP.*

SPORTS AND THE OUTDOORS

HELICOPTER TOURS

JNC Helicopters. Flips (a short flight on a helicopter) are undertaken with a minimum of three people leaving from Virgina Airport. Take a scenic trip to Umhlanga (10 minutes), Umdloti (14 minutes), Durban harbor (14 minutes), or to Ballito (25 minutes) Seeing the coast from the air is quite breathtaking. ⊠ *Hangar 1, Virginia Airport, 220 Fairway, Virginia* ☎ *031/563–9513* ⊕ *www.choppers.co.za* ⊠ *R200–R900.*

SIDE TRIPS FROM DURBAN

VALLEY OF A THOUSAND HILLS

45 km (27 mi) northwest of Durban.

In the early part of the 19th century, before cars were introduced, wagons traveled from the port of Durban up along the ridge of this region of plunging gorges, hills, and valleys into the hinterland, where the mining industry was burgeoning. Today the Old Main Road (M103) still runs between Durban and Pietermaritzburg, winding through a number of villages and offering stunning views of hills and valleys dotted with traditional Zulu homesteads. It is along this route that the Comrades Marathon—South Africa's most famous road race—is run.

For purposes of exploring, the area has been organized into routes by the local tourism office. A favorite with Durbanites, the routes wind through villages and past coffee shops, art galleries, restaurants, quaint pubs, small inns, farms, and nature reserves. There are a number of excellent B&Bs, small inns, and lodges in the area, often with fantastic views of the gorges.

GETTING HERE AND AROUND

The main route is called the T1. It follows the M13 out of Durban, up Field's Hill, through the village of Kloof, and past Everton, Gillits, and Winston Park; it then joins the Old Main Road (M103) at Hillcrest. A number of small shopping centers along the M103 sell a variety of goods, from crafts to old furniture, and there are some excellent coffee shops, restaurants, and small hotels as well as cultural attractions. At the end of the M103 is the small town of Monteseel. Drive along the dirt roads to the signposted overlook for one of the best uninterrupted views of the Thousand Hills. Other well-marked routes in the area are the Kranzkloof, Assagay Averston, and Isithumba routes and the Shongweni Shuffle, all of which make for scenic drives.

ESSENTIALS

Visitor Information Thousand Hills Tourism Association (⊠ *Old Main Rd., Botha's Hill* ☎ *031/777–1874* ⊕ *www.1000hills.kzn.org.za*).

EXPLORING

Assagay Coffee. You can take a tour to see how this homegrown coffee, very popular with locals, is grown, roasted, and packaged. ⊠ *Off Old Main Rd., Botha's Hill* ☎ *031/765–2941* ⊠ *Tours R25* ⊗ *By appointment only.*

PheZulu Safari Park. Popular with big tour buses, PheZulu is the equivalent of fast-food tourism, good for people who want a quick-fix African experience. A tour of the cultural village with its traditional beehive huts gives some insight into African traditions, and there are performances of traditional Zulu dancing, but the operation is not as vibrant or professional as the cultural villages up north in Zululand. An old-fashioned crocodile farm and snake park is fairly interesting, if a little tacky. The curio shop is enormous; you can probably get just about any type of African memento or booklet imaginable. Impala and zebra are frequently spotted on the hour-long game drive (additional fee). ⊠ *Old Main Rd., Drummond* ☎ *031/777–1000* ⊕ *www.phezulusafaripark. co.za* ⊠ *Park R90, game drive R120* ☉ *Daily 8–4:30; shows daily at 10, 11:30, 2, and 3:30.*

DOLPHIN COAST

48 km (30 mi) northwest of Durban.

Located about an hour north of Durban, the Dolphin Coast (aka North Coast) lies along the warm waters of the Indian Ocean, making it a popular vacation spot for South Africans. The area's many beaches, protected by shark nets and lifeguards, are safe for swimming.

GETTING HERE AND AROUND

The only way to explore this area is in your own vehicle. You can take the N2, but it's better to follow the M4 north.

ESSENTIALS

Visitor Information Dolphin Coast (⊕ *dolphincoast.kzn.org.za*).

6

WHERE TO EAT AND STAY

$$
ECLECTIC
✕ **Gigi's.** Although it's located on the Hotel iZulu property, the restaurant is open to outside diners. Only the finest local ingredients are used in dishes whenever possible, like South African cheeses and lamb from the KZN Midlands; the presence of the national flag next to menu items indicates those dishes that contain local ingredients. The commitment to using local ingredients means that the menu changes seasonally and can include tempura prawns with goat-cheese ravioli on oven-roasted *peperonata* (slow-cooked peppers) and a prawn vichyssoise or roasted loin of springbok with potato slices that have been gently fried in butter and then roasted in the oven, creamed corn, and steamed broccolini topped with a deep-fried chocolate, chili, and walnut truffle. You might experience a "crocodile" menu, which offers the meat in various guises or a pumpkin-and-cinnamon tart served with a *koeksister* (sticky-sweet type of doughnut) and a *rooibos* (bush tea) and *buchu* (an African shrub) ice cream. A delicious but more casual menu is offered during lunch, which is best enjoyed poolside. ⊠ *3 Key's Place, Ballito* ☎ *032/946–3444* ⊕ *www.hotelizulu.com* ▤ *AE, DC, MC, V.*

$$$–$$$$
SEAFOOD
✕ **Mozambik.** Don't miss the opportunity to sample the authentic tastes of Mozambique without ever crossing the border at this unpretentious and vibrant restaurant. The eatery's rustic charm extends from the decor to the service to the food. Mozambiquan food is often, mistakenly, equated with Portuguese cuisine, but it also has Arab, Indian, and Goan influences. Not surprisingly, seafood and chicken are a specialty and appear in some irresistible combinations. The outstanding Cabo Delgado sees line fish paired with mango, green bananas, coriander, saffron, shallots, coconut milk, and limes, while prawns baked in the oven with a secret beer sauce are irresistible. Dining here is definitely a case of eat, mess, and be merry. ⊠ *Shops 4 and 5, Boulevard Centre, Jack Powell Rd., Ballito* ☎ *032/946–0979* ▤ *AE, DC, MC, V.*

$$$$ ★ 🏨 **Hotel iZulu.** The buildings—a disparate but harmonious mix of Tuscan and Balinese architecture—are the centerpiece of this intimate estate that's ensconced in lush, tropical gardens. Each of the 19 suites (one of which is the sprawling Royal Suite) has a neutral palate that's highlighted by a few tasteful African touches. Steps lead to a large sunken bath and walk-in shower, both of which could easily accommodate two people. Pamper yourself further with a restorative stress-relieving treatment at the in-house Impilo Spa—the 1½-hour Theranaka African Wood massage is recommended. **Pros:** one private Jacuzzi per two suites; only Relais & Chateaux property in KZN; hotel has various green initiatives in place. **Cons:** about 5 km (3 mi) by car to outside restaurants; the lack of on-site activities might bother more activity-minded guests. ✉ *3 Rey's Place, Ballito* ✉ *Private Bag X004, Ballito 4420* ☎ *032/946–3444* ⊕ *www.hotelizulu.com* ⇔ *19 suites* ⚲ *In-room: safe, refrigerator, DVD (some), Wi-Fi. In-hotel: restaurant, bar, pool, Internet* ☰ *AE, DC, MC, V* ⍐ *BP.*

★ 🏨 **Zimbali Lodge.** One of only two luxury lodges in the province with direct access to the beach, Zimbali's tranquil setting is in one of the few remaining coastal forests in the province. The decor is a stylish mix of African and Balinese, with lots of glass, dark wood, and rough woven fabrics. Rooms have an indulgently private and luxurious feel to them, with crisp white linen, wood carvings, large baths, and balconies that look out onto the forest, lake, and sea beyond. It's a wonderful place to laze around, enjoy afternoon tea, play a round of golf, or swim in the private Mauritian-style pool on the beach. The service is warm, friendly, and slick. **Pros:** access to unspoiled beach; professional service; good golf course. **Cons:** overly formal for some; isolated location. ✉ *M4, 20 km (12 mi) north of Umhlanga, Box 404, Ballito* ☎ *032/538–1007* ⊕ *www.suninternational.com* ⇔ *76 rooms, 10 suites* ⚲ *In-room: safe, refrigerator, DVD, Wi-Fi. In-hotel: restaurant, room service, golf course, tennis courts, pools, gym, spa, beachfront, bicycles* ☰ *AE, DC, MC, V* ⍐ *BP.*

SOUTH COAST

60 km (37 mi) northwest of Durban.

Vacation towns like Scottburgh, Margate, Ramsgate, Trafalgar, and Palm Beach dot KwaZulu-Natal's southern coast, which stretches for more than 200 km (125 mi) from Durban in the north to Port Edward in the south. The area has some of the country's best beaches, set against a tropical background of natural coastal jungle and palm trees. In fact, Blue Flag status has been conferred on the Marina (at San Lameer), Ramsgate, Lucien, and Hibberdene beaches.

The South Coast is also famous for the annual sardine run, which usually occurs in June or July. Colder currents in Antarctica at this time bring millions of sardines to local waters, and they often wash up right on the beach. Dolphins, seabirds, sharks, and whales follow in a feeding frenzy.

GETTING HERE AND AROUND

The best and really only way to explore this area is in your own transport. Main roads (the N2 and R61) are easy to navigate, and following the coastal road (turn off the R61 towards the coast) is picturesque.

If you're looking to explore the South Coast, the *Southern Explorer* magazine and Web site includes maps of the various tourist routes, along with details of restaurants, sights, and accommodation establishments.

BLUE FLAG STATUS
Blue Flag status, which is awarded to more than 3,700 "green" beaches and marinas in 37 countries by the Foundation for Environmental Education, changes every year. It's a good idea to check WESSA's (Wildlife and Environment Society of South Africa) Web site (⊕ www.wessa.org.za) to see who's on the list when you're planning a trip.

ESSENTIALS

Visitor Information **Southern Explorer** (⊕ www.southernexplorer.co.za). **Tourism South Coast** (☏ 039/682–7944 ⊕ www.tourismsouthcoast.co.za).

WHERE TO STAY

$$ ⚅ **San Lameer.** This exclusive self-catering resort is a great getaway from noisy city life for a group of friends or a family. Spacious one- to five-bedroom Tuscan-style villas, many with breathtaking views of the sea or the bird-filled lagoons, are set among gardens and indigenous forest. At night it's lit by hundreds of twinkling lights. Stroll down paved walkways to the private beach or meander through the woods and you'll likely see small antelope and monkeys. Golf enthusiasts enjoy the championship course, which hosts major tournaments, and there's also a mashie (tiny) course. **Helen Fouche** (☏ 011/896–3544 ✎ info@sanlameer.com) handles bookings for privately owned villas at reduced rates. If DIY is not your style, opt for the on-site **Mondazur Resort Estate Hotel**. **Pros:** good on-site golf course; located at a Blue Flag beach; abundant wildlife and indigenous flora. **Cons:** estate is very large; car ride away from outside restaurants; busy in-season. ✉ *Lower South Coast Main Rd., between Ramsgate and Palm Beach* ⌂ *Box 88, Southbroom 4277* ☏ *039/313–0011* ⊕ *www.sanlameer.com* ⟱ *40 rooms, 2 suites, 22 villas* ⌂ *In-room: safe, kitchen (some). In-hotel: restaurant, bar, golf course, tennis courts, pools, beachfront, bicycles, laundry service, Wi-Fi* ▭ *AE, DC, MC, V* ⟟❘*BP*.

6

THE KWAZULU-NATAL MIDLANDS

104 km (65 mi) northwest of Durban.

Set amid the rolling green foothills of the Drakensberg, the Midlands encompass waterfalls, lakes, reservoirs, forests, fields, Zulu villages, game reserves, and battle sites. The climate is pleasant most of the year, though summers tend to be hot. The area has long been an enclave for craftspeople—weavers, potters, woodcrafters, metalworkers, cheese makers, and beer brewers—who escaped the cities.

As a way to draw customers to the area, the crafters created four routes, called the Midlands Meander, in 1983, which include more than 160 shops, galleries, cultural activities, restaurants, and accommodations. Running through the towns of Curry's Post and Howick in the northeast and Nottingham Road, Mooi River, Balgowan, the Dargyle District, Lion's River, and Midmar in the southwest, the routes provide a great opportunity to shop for authentic South African arts and crafts while enjoying the tranquility and beauty of the countryside. The area is filled with top accommodations and dining options.

GETTING HERE AND AROUND

The only way to explore this area is in your own transport. Roads are easy to navigate, and all establishments are well marked. The N3 is the quickest route between places, but the R103 is a scenic route that passes through all areas.

TIMING

The most popular time to do the Meander is in the autumn (March to May), when it's not too hot or too cold. Many South Africans love the winters here; it often snows, particularly on the higher ground, and many establishments burn fires. Don't be surprised to experience four seasons in one day! No matter the time of year, though, there's always something to see and do, most of which involves shopping.

VISITOR INFORMATION

If you're looking to explore the area, contact the Midlands Meander Association for its magazine that includes maps of the routes and details of the various establishments. Members of the Association also stock the magazine.

Contact **Midlands Meander Association** (☎ 033/330–8195 ⊕ www.midlands-meander.co.za).

EXPLORING

Howick Falls. Though the area is mainly about dining, shopping, and the arts, this waterfall is definitely worth a 10-minute stop. Give yourself a little more time if you want to look at some arts and crafts or have a cup of tea. In the town of Howick, the Umgeni River plunges an impressive 300 feet into the gorge. There are numerous hikes of varying difficulty that provide different vantages of the falls. Contact or visit the Howick Tourism Office, which is just a few hundred yards from the falls, for information. ⊠ *Howick Tourism Office, 4 Fallview Dr., Howick* ☎ 033/330–5305.

Mandela Monument. The site itself is a small, unassuming brick monument, but it's really the magnitude of what happened here that's remarkable and noteworthy. After 17 months on the run, Nelson Mandela was arrested, despite being disguised as a chauffeur, on August 5, 1962, outside Howick, on his way from Durban to Johannesburg. He was convicted of incitement and illegally leaving the country and sentenced to five years in jail before being prosecuted in the Rivonia Trials that led to his incarceration on Robben Island. From the N3 take the Tweedie Interchange and get onto the R103; the monument is just outside Howick. ⊠ *R103, Howick.*

Nottingham Road Brewery. On the same premises as Rawdon's Hotel, this rustic microbrewery has developed a cult following. With names like Pickled Pig Porter, Whistling Weasel Pale Ale, Pye-Eyed Possum Pilsner, and Tiddly Toad Lager, you may have a tough time choosing which brew to taste first, so order a tasting paddle in the hotel's pub to sample them all. Call ahead if you would like to do a tour of the small brewery; otherwise just pop into the shop to stock up on beer, accessories, and clever merchandising. Guaranteed you'll head home with a PICKLED AS A PIG or I'M AS POSSED AS A PYE-EYED PISSUM T-shirt. ⊠ *R103, Nottingham Road* ☎ *033/330–5305* ⊕ *www.rawdons.co.za.*

The Stables Wine Estate. KwaZulu-Natal has been declared an official Wine of Origin area by the Wine and Spirits Board of South Africa (the Northern Cape and Western Cape are also official sites), and the Stables was the first estate to bottle a wine in the area. You'll find a wide range of wines on offer including a sparkling wine, a red blend and a port; visitors can choose up to five wines to taste (R20). Wines can be purchased from the farm, as can cheese plates if you feel like lingering and having a snack with your wine. ⊠ *R103, Nottingham Road* ☎ *033/266–6781* ⊕ *www.stableswine.co.za* ☉ *Daily 10–5.*

Swissland Cheese. Visitors to this family-run cheesery are greeted by goats grazing demurely in luscious green pastures. In the Swiss-chalet-style tasting room, you can sample a range of goat cheeses including *chevin*—similar to a cream cheese but a little crumblier—and a mild blue cheese, as well as learn about the cheese-making practices that the Vermaak family has been following for more than two decades. Witness the daily goat milking between 3 and 5 PM. ⊠ *R103, Nottingham Road* ☎ *033/234–4042* ☉ *Fri.–Wed., 9:30–4:30.*

WHERE TO STAY

$$$ ▦ **Fordoun.** Nestled in the heart of a dairy farm that dates back to the 1800s, original stone buildings have been converted into luxurious rooms and have been decorated in *nguni* (African cattle) skins and wooden furniture that help to create a warm, homely atmosphere. If your ideal vacation includes a few spa treatments, the on-site, award-winning Fordoun Spa is uniquely African. Dr. Elliott Ndlovu, a sangoma (traditional African healer), herbalist, and ethnobotanist, has assisted in developing a signature range of products for sale and use within the spa. We suggest trying the Inkomfe body wrap, which utilizes the African potato said to have anticancer and immunization properties, or the Nduku Nduku massage, which uses traditional Zulu *knobkierie* sticks on the back of the body. Skye Restaurant offers guests a great on-site dining option; call ahead for reservations. Menu items include a duck-leg tartlet with a maple butternut-squash puree, goat cheese, black cherry marmalade, and *dukkha* (a mixture of nuts, seeds, and Middle Eastern spices) dressing, and grilled squid stuffed with pork shank and chorizo, served with mushy peas, chunky chips, and an avocado-and-lemon-bush dressing. **Pros:** complimentary use of the sauna, steam room, and gym; good on-site restaurant; tranquil country setting; heated floors in the guest rooms. **Cons:** isolated; no on-site activities. ⊠ *R103, 3 km (1.9 mi) off the N3* ✉ *Box 17, Nottingham Road 3280* ☎ *033/266–6217* ⊕ *www.fordoun.com* ⇥ *17 suites* ⚒ *In-room:*

6

safe, refrigerator, DVD (some). In-hotel: restaurant, bar, pool, gym, spa ☰ *AE, DC, MC, V* �’⃝❙ *BP.*

$$ 📖 **Granny Mouse Country House.** One of the best-loved and oldest hotels on the Meander, Granny Mouse has cozy thatch rooms, all slightly different, with a river view, fireplace, and homey, though upmarket, atmosphere. Freestanding rooms offer privacy and peace, and the main hotel building—formerly an unusual farmhouse with doors and windows from an old church—offers conviviality and warmth in its several lounges. The on-site Mouse & Lion pub ($–$$) is locally famous for its lavish breakfasts and afternoon teas. Some of the best places on the Meander are within easy reach. **Pros:** cozy country-style bar; highly regarded restaurant; on-site spa. **Cons:** popular wedding venue; some might find decor a bit too quaint. ✉ *R103, 25 km (15½ mi) south of Nottingham Road exit off the N3* 🖭 *Box 22, Balgowan 3275* 📠 *033/234–4071* ⊕ *www.grannymouse.co.za* ➸ *20 rooms, 5 suites* ♨ *In-room: refrigerator. In-hotel: restaurant, bar, pools, spa, bicycles* ☰ *DC, MC, V* ❙⃝❙ *BP.*

$$–$$$
Fodor's Choice
★

📖 **Hartford House.** Built in 1875, this inn is steeped in history and misty beauty. High up on the Meander, in the foothills of the Drakensberg, and adjacent to the Summerhill racing stud, it's a deliciously luxurious, if rather formal, escape for the lucky few. A few of the suites are in the original house; others front an ethereal, lovely lake. Each suite is different, decorated in a gloriously eclectic collision of fabrics and furnishings from Africa, Europe, and the East. The food, which has garnered top honors, is just as rich and eclectically surprising. Dinner (R325 for a five-course set menu, reservations essential), which the chefs start preparing at dawn, is an unforgettable event with wines to match. Summerhill Stud, the neighboring thoroughbred racehorse stud farm, is a great place to visit if you have a few hours. **Pros:** gourmet getaway; beautiful English-styled garden; some suites have a fireplace and all have heated floors. **Cons:** all guests are required to eat dinner at the same time; common areas are rather formal. ✉ *Hlatikulu Rd., off road to Giant's Castle, Mooi River* 📠 *033/263–2713* ⊕ *www. hartford.co.za* ➸ *15 suites* ♨ *In-room: safe, refrigerator, DVD, Internet. In-hotel: restaurant, bar, tennis court, spa, bicycles, laundry service, no kids under 12* ☰ *AE, DC, MC, V* ❙⃝❙ *BP.*

SPORTS AND THE OUTDOORS
CANOPY TOURS
Karkloof Canopy Tours. Glide along steel cables through the treetops of the Karkloof Forest, the second biggest indigenous forest in South Africa. A 1-km (600-yard) long *foefie* (zip) slide is divided into eight slides— the longest is an exhilarating 574 feet long—that are interspersed with wooden platforms. Designed by a civil engineer, safety is paramount, and two trained guides (well versed in the forest and ecology) accompany each group; group size ranges from one to eight people. Tours (R395) take 2½ hours and leave every half hour in most weather conditions; call ahead to reserve your spot. Anyone from the ages of 7 to 70 can participate. Light refreshments, lunch, and a 4x4 trip up the mountain are included. ✉ *From Howick, take Karkloof Rd. for 19 km*

(12 mi) and follow signs to Canopy Tours for another 2 km (1¼ mi)
☎ *033/330–3415* ⊕ *www.karkloofcanopytour.co.za.*

SHOPPING

Though on the whole the route is known for its quality, you can also find some establishments that are not up to standards of others. If you've only a limited time, head for the concentration of crafts shops on the R103 between Nottingham Road and Lion's River. If you have a couple of days, base yourself at one of the hotels and explore the Meander using the large-format, free guide available at most Meander stops. Many of the better establishments offer shipping services for those unusual items large and small.

A great place to buy handmade leather goods, especially shoes and beautiful bags and briefcases, is **Groundcover** (✉ *Curry's Post Rd.* ☎ *033/330–6092* ⊕ *www.groundcover.co.za*). The **Rosewood Embroidery Shoppe** (✉ *9 km [6 mi] northwest of the Curry's Post/Lion's River exit off the N3, then 5 km [3 mi] on the Dargyle Rd.* ☎ *033/234–4386* ⊕ *www.rosewoodshoppe.co.za*) sells beautiful hand-stitched, pure cotton linens, upholstery, night wear, and gifts. The shop's signature is a pink-and-pale-green hand-stitched rose. At the **Woodturner** (✉ *6 km [4 mi] from Rosewood, down the Dargyle Rd.* ☎ *033/234–4548* ⊕ *www. sculpturalwood.co.za*), father and son Andrew and John Early specialize in making elegant bowls, modern wood sculptures, and one-of-a-kind furniture pieces using salvaged, exotic woods like jacaranda and local varieties like African mahogany and stinkwood. Their pieces are often snapped up by studios in New York and elsewhere. The studio is a delight; ask to see the Earlys at work in their workshop behind the sprawling farmhouse. Near the Woodturner is **Dargyle Valley Pottery** (✉ *1 km [½ mi] on the D666 off Dargyle Rd.* ☎ *033/234–4377*), where renowned potter Ian Glenny, whose work is in private collections and galleries worldwide, founded the Meander in 1983. Choose from porcelain, stoneware, or terra-cotta pots, bowls, and vases—or indulge in a fireplace.

Culamoya Chimes (✉ *3 km [2 mi] off the R103* ☎ *033/234–4503 or 083/627–6195*), in the Dargyle District, has a 13-foot chime as well as other chimes that boom the sounds of Big Ben and St. Paul's Cathedral down to gentle tinkles of fairy magic. Near Culamoya and Granny Mouse, **Mole Hill** (✉ *R103, 8 km [5 mi] south of Nottingham Road* ☎ *033/234–4352* ⊕ *www.millgate.co.za*) has a good reputation for high-quality men's and women's shirts with an African twist. Back toward Durban, the **Weaver's Hut** (✉ *4 km [2½ mi] from the Howick/ Midmar exit off the N3* ☎ *033/330–4026* ⊕ *www.weavershut.com*) in Howick has beautiful handmade rugs. Farther south, **Peel's Honey** (✉ *N3, below the Midmar Dam* ☎ *033/330–3762*) sells an assortment of honey, brittle, and other tasty treats.

6

THE DRAKENSBERG

240 km (150 mi) west of Durban

GETTING HERE AND AROUND

The main resort area of the Drakensberg is almost a direct shot along the N3 from Durban. A car is not strictly necessary for a trip to the Berg, although it is certainly a convenience, and though a 4x4 would be an advantage, it, too, is not a necessity. Gas stations can be found in Bergville, Winterton, and at the foot of Champagne Castle. Driving in this area is time-consuming. Trucks often slow up traffic, and you should watch for animals on and attempting to cross the road.

WHEN TO GO

If possible plan your visit to the Berg during the spring (September and October) and late autumn (late April–June), because although summer sees the Berg at its greenest, it's also the hottest and wettest time of the year. Vicious afternoon thunderstorms and hailstorms are an almost-daily occurrence. In winter the mountains lose their lush overcoat and turn brown and sere. Winter days in the valleys, sites of most resorts, are usually sunny and pleasant, although there can be cold snaps, sometimes accompanied by overcast, windy conditions. Nights are chilly, however, and you should pack plenty of warm clothing if you plan to hike high up into the mountains or camp overnight. Snow is common at higher elevations.

EXPLORING

Although you don't come here for big game, or much game at all, it's well worth visiting this World Heritage site, the first in South Africa to be recognized for both its natural and cultural attractions, with some of the finest rock art in the world.

Afrikaners call them the Drakensberg: the Dragon Mountains. To Zulus they are uKhahlamba (pronounced Ooka-hlamba)—"Barrier of Spears." Both are apt descriptions for this wall of rock that rises from the Natal grasslands, forming a natural fortress protecting the mountain kingdom of Lesotho. The Drakensberg is the highest range in southern Africa and has some of the most spectacular scenery in the country. The blue-tinted mountains seem to infuse the landscape, cooling the "champagne air," as the locals refer to the heady, sparkling breezes that blow around the precipices and pinnacles. It's a hiker's dream, and you could easily spend several days here just soaking up the awesome views.

The Drakensberg is not a typical mountain range—it's actually an escarpment separating a high interior plateau from the coastal lowlands of Natal. It's a continuation of the same escarpment that divides the Transvaal Highveld from the hot malarial zones of the lowveld in Mpumalanga. However, the Natal Drakensberg, or Berg, as it is commonly known, is far wilder and more spectacular than its Transvaal counterpart. Many of the peaks—some of which top 10,000 feet—are the source of crystalline streams and mighty rivers that have carved out myriad valleys and dramatic gorges. The Berg is a natural watershed, with two of South Africa's major rivers, the Tugela and the Orange, rising from these mountains. In this untamed wilderness you can hike

CLOSE UP

San Paintings

Besides the hiking opportunities and the sheer beauty of the mountains, the other great attraction of the Berg is the San (Bushman) paintings. The San are a hunter-gatherer people who once roamed the entire country from 8,000 years ago to the 1800s. With the arrival of the Nguni peoples from the north and white settlers from the southwest in the 18th century, the San were driven out of their traditional hunting lands and retreated into the remote fastnesses of the Drakensberg and the Kalahari Desert. San cattle raiding in Natal in the late 19th century occasioned harsh punitive expeditions by white settlers and local Bantu tribes, and by 1880 the last San had disappeared from the Berg. Today only a few clans remain in the very heart of the Kalahari Desert. More than 40,000 of their paintings enliven scores of caves and rock overhangs throughout the Berg in more than 550 known San rock-art sites—probably the finest collection of rock paintings in the country. They tell the stories of bygone hunts, dances, and battles as well as relating and representing spiritual beliefs and practices. Images of spiritual leaders in a trance state, their visions, and their transformation of themselves into animals have now been studied and written about, although some of the meanings are still not fully understood. ■TIP→ Be sure to bring binoculars with you For more information on viewing rock-art sites, contact **Ezemvelo KZN Wildlife** (☎ 033/845–1999 ⊕ www. kznwildlife.com), the province's official conservation organization.

6

for days and not meet a soul, and the mountains retain a wild majesty missing in the commercially forested peaks of Mpumalanga.

WHERE TO STAY

$ 🖫 **Cathedral Peak Hotel.** You'll get breathtaking views from almost every
☺   spot in this friendly, delightful hotel nestled among the mountains. Ideal
★   for families, the resort has something for everyone: you can amble along
a horse trail, go mountain biking, follow bird-watching trails, play a round of golf, or just soak up the heady mountain air. Accommodations run from basic singles to slightly bigger family units and various suites. Best for families is a deluxe suite with adjacent rooms and connecting door. You'll get excellent value here; prices include breakfast and hearty dinner buffets as well as most activities. And whether you're mildly active or a seasoned mountain hiker or climber, trained and experienced guides take you on daily walks and trails through the Berg. There's a children's dining room, plus babysitting service. **Pros:** numerous well-organized activities make it ideal for families; friendly, laid-back atmosphere. **Cons:** crowded in season; noisy kids at the holidays. ⊠ *Cathedral Peak Rd., 43 km (18 mi) from Winterton* ☎ *036/488–1888* ⊕ *www.cathedralpeak.co.za* ⇨ *104 rooms* ⚹ *In-room: safe. In-hotel: restaurant, room service, bars, golf course, tennis courts, pool, gym, spa, Wi-Fi* ⊟ *AE, DC, MC, V* ⏋⊚⏌ *MAP.*

$ 🖫 **Cleopatra Mountain Farmhouse.** It would be difficult to find better lodg-
Fodor's Choice   ing or dining anywhere in southern Africa than at this enchanting hide-
★   away tucked away at the foot of the Drakensberg Range. The lodge

overlooks a trout-filled lake and is encircled by mountains and old trees. Richard and Mouse Poynton, legendary South African chefs and hosts, have renovated the 1936 family fishing farm and created a perfect combination of comfort, tranquility, style, and exceptional food. Homemade biscuits, hand-painted and stenciled walls, lovingly embroidered cushions and samplers, fluffy mohair blankets, and heated towel racks are just a few of the details you'll find here. Don't even mention the word diet in a place where rich, natural, superb food rules the day. You'll eat truly sumptuous meals with ceremony but no pretension in an intimate dining room warmed on cold days by a blazing log fire. Pros: exclusive yet funky accommodations; food you'll write home about and dream about. Cons: if you have a cholesterol problem, stay away; overindulgence is guaranteed. ⊠ Off Kamberg Rd., near Rosetta ⬧ Box 17, Balgowan 3275 ☎ 033/267–7243 ⊕ www.cleomountain.com ⬧ 5 rooms, 4 suites ♿ In-hotel: restaurant, Internet terminal, no kids under 12 ▤ AE, DC, MC, V ⦿ MAP.

¢ 🏨 **Tendele Hutted Camp.** In a truly spectacular setting smack in the middle of Royal Natal National Park, which contains some of the most stunning mountain scenery in the Drakensberg, this very popular camp makes a great base for long hikes into the mountains. Accommodations are in a variety of bungalows, cottages, and chalets, each with excellent views of the Amphitheatre, a sheer rock wall measuring 5 km (3 mi) across and more than 1,500 feet high. You must bring all your own food, although you can purchase staples and frozen meat at the main visitor center. In the bungalows and cottages all food is prepared by camp staff, but you can do your own cooking in the chalets. There is one lodge, which accommodates six people. Pros: truly spectacular scenery; great views from every room; inexpensive rates. Cons: only for self-caterers; not for urban party animals. ⊠ Royal Natal National Park, west of Bergville ⬧ KwaZulu-Natal Nature Conservation Service, Box 13069, Cascades 3202 ☎ 033/845–1000 ⬧ 26 chalets, 2 cottages, 1 lodge ♿ In-room: kitchen (some) ▤ AE, DC, MC, V.

PARK ESSENTIALS

The Natal Drakensberg is not conducive to traditional touring because of the nature of the attractions and the limited road system. It's best to check into a hotel or resort for two or three days and use it as a base for hiking and exploring the immediate area. If you decide to stay at one of the self-catering camps, do your shopping in one of the bigger towns, such as Winterton or Harrismith for Tendele, and Bergville or Estcourt for Giant's Castle, Kamberg, and Injasuti. For more information on touring the area, visit the Drakensberg Tourism Association Web site (⊕ www. drakensberg.org.za).

ZULULAND AND THE BATTLEFIELDS

Zululand stretches north from the Tugela River all the way to the border of Mozambique. It's a region of rolling grasslands, gorgeous beaches, and classic African bush. It has also seen more than its share of bloodshed and death. Modern South Africa was forged in the fiery crucible of Zululand and northern Natal. Here Boers battled Zulus, Zulus battled Britons, and Britons battled Boers. The most interesting historic sites, however, involve the battles against the Zulu. Names like Isandlwana, Rorke's Drift, and Blood River have taken their place in the roll of legendary military encounters.

No African tribe has captured the Western imagination quite like the Zulus. A host of books and movies have explored their warrior culture and extolled their martial valor. Until the early 19th century the Zulus were a small, unheralded group, part of the Nguni peoples who migrated to southern Africa from the north. King Shaka (1787–1828) changed all that. In less than a decade Shaka created a military machine unrivaled in black Africa. By the time of his assassination in 1828, Shaka had destroyed 300 tribes and extended Zulu power for 800 km (500 mi) through the north, south, and west.

Fifty years after Shaka's death, the British still considered the Zulus a major threat to their planned federation of white states in South Africa. The British solution, in 1879, was to instigate a war to destroy the Zulu kingdom. They employed a similar tactic 20 years later to bring the Boer republics to heel and the rich goldfields of the Witwatersrand into their own hands.

Recently, interest in the battlefields has been growing, particularly since the Boer and Zulu War centenary celebrations in 2000. If you're not a history buff, the best way to tour the battlefields is with an expert guide, who can bring the history to life because many of the battle sites are little more than open grassland, graced with the occasional memorial stone.

WHEN TO GO
There is no bad time to visit Zululand and the battlefields.

GETTING HERE AND AROUND
Unless you're on a tour, it's almost impossible to see this part of the country without your own car. Your best bet is to rent a car in Durban and perhaps combine a trip to the battlefields with a self-drive tour of KwaZulu-Natal's game reserves. Roads are in good condition, although some of the access roads to the battlefields require more careful and slower driving, as dirt roads can be bumpy and muddy when wet.

MONEY MATTERS
There are plenty of banks and ATMs in all towns and at the larger filling stations. Ladysmith has branches of all the main banks.

SAFETY AND PRECAUTIONS
It is essential that visitors to the northern parts of the province, including Zululand, take antimalarial drugs, particularly during the wet summer months. Visitors should also wear comfortable shoes and plenty of sunblock, and don't forget the binoculars.

Ladysmith has two major hospitals. Elsewhere, call the general police number to be put in touch with the nearest hospital.

TOURS
The visitor information offices at Dundee's Talana Museum and in Ladysmith have lists of registered battlefield guides including John Turner of the Babanango Valley Lodge, Rob Gerrard of Isandlwana Lodge, and Pat Rundgren, who are experts on the Zulu battlefields. For ethnic and cultural tours, you'll want to look up Bethuel and Dudu Manyathi; for Berg, bush, and battlefield tours use the Dunbars, of Parker Tours. If you're interested in self-guided tours, stop by the Talana Museum to rent or buy cassette tapes and CDs that describe the events at Rorke's Drift and Isandlwana, including some narrated by the late David Rattray. Information about battlefield guides and guides specializing in authentic Zulu culture can be obtained at any information center or tourism office.

VISITOR INFORMATION
Battlefields Route is a good source for information on the battlefields. For a good overview covering this area, go to Tourism KwaZulu-Natal's Web site.

ESSENTIALS
Emergency Services **Police** (☎ *10111*).

Tour Operators **Fugitives' Drift** (☎ *034/271–8051 or 034/642–1843*). **Rob Gerrard** (☎ *034/271–8301*). **Ken Gillings** (☎ *031/702–4828*). **Tony Horn** (☎ *082/953–0737l* ⊕ *www.bushjunkies.co.za*). **Bethuel and Dudu Manyathi** (☎ *034/271–9710, 083/531–0061 cell*). **Parker Tours–Ken and Jane Dunbar** (☎ *082/679–0133 or 035/590–1576*). **Pat Rundgren** (☎ *034/ 212–4560*). **John Turner** (☎ *035/835–0062*).

Tourist Offices **Battlefields Route** (☎ *082/802–1643* ⊕ *battlefields.kzn.org.za*). **Tourism KwaZulu-Natal** (⊕ *www.zulu.org.za*).

LADYSMITH

160 km (99 mi) northwest of Pietermaritzburg.

Ladysmith, dating back to the middle of the 19th century, became famous around the world during the South African War, when it outlasted a Boer siege for 118 days. Nearly 20,000 people were caught in the town when the Boers attacked on November 2, 1899. Much of the early part of the war revolved around British attempts to end the siege. The incompetence of British general Sir Redvers Buller became apparent during repeated attempts to smash the Boer lines, resulting in heavy British losses at Spioenkop, Vaalkrans, and Colenso. Finally, the sheer weight of numbers made possible the British defeat of the Boers in the epic 10-day Battle of Tugela Heights and ended the siege of Ladysmith on February 28, 1900.

Today Ladysmith is a small provincial town with a haphazard mix of old colonial and newer buildings and the same inhospitable climate (scorchingly hot in summer, freezing in winter). Look out for the elegant, historic Town Hall built in 1893 and visit the gleaming white Soofie Mosque on the banks of the Klip River; this national monument

CLOSE UP

Boers, Brits, and Battlefields

The Boer War (1899–1902), now referred to as the South African War, was the longest, bloodiest, and costliest war fought by Britain for nearly 100 years. The Brits and the Boers, Afrikaner descendants of 17th-century Dutch settlers fighting for independence from Britain, engaged in numerous battles in which the little guys (the Boers) often made mincemeat of the great British colonial army sent out to defeat them. Britain marched into South Africa in the spring of 1899, confident that it would all be over by Christmas. However, the comparatively small bands of volunteers from the republics of the Transvaal and the Orange Free State were to give Queen Victoria's proud British army, as Kipling wrote, "no end

of a lesson." Today history has also revealed the part played by hundreds of thousands of black South Africans in the war as messengers, scouts, interpreters, and laborers—hence the renaming of the war.

The most famous—or infamous—battle was fought on top of Spioenkop, in KwaZulu-Natal, where the mass grave of hundreds of British soldiers stretches from one side of the hill to the other. Of interest is that three men who were to change the course of world history were there on that fateful day: Winston Churchill, Mahatma Gandhi (who was a stretcher bearer), and Louis Botha, the first prime minister of the Union of South Africa.

—Kate Turkington

6

is regarded as one of the most beautiful mosques in the Southern Hemisphere. On Murchison Street (the main street) is Surat House, a shop built in the 1890s, where Gandhi used to shop on his way through Ladysmith.

GETTING HERE AND AROUND
There are only two ways to get around the battlefields: with your own rental car or with an organized tour.

MONEY MATTERS
Ladysmith has branches of all the main banks, with ABSA, FNB, Standard Bank, and Nedbank ATMs on Murchison Street.

SAFETY AND PRECAUTIONS
If you need a hospital when you're in the area, choose Netcare's private Laverna Hospital. It has full emergency services and a pharmacy that's open 8–5.

VISITOR INFORMATION
The Ladysmith Information Bureau is open weekdays 9–4, Saturday 9–1, and Sunday by request.

ESSENTIALS
Emergency Services Police (☎ 036/638-3300).

Hospitals Laverna Hospital (✉ 1 Convent Rd. ☎ 036/631-0065).

Pharmacy Ladysmith Pharmacy (✉ 262 Murchison St. ☎ 036/631-0648).

Visitor Information Ladysmith Information Bureau (✉ Siege Museum, Town Hall, Murchison St. ☎ 036/637-2992).

EXPLORING

The **Ladysmith Siege Museum** brings the period of the siege skillfully to life, with the use of electronic mapping, artifacts from the period, and black-and-white photos. The museum can arrange guided tours, but it also sells two pamphlets that outline self-guided tours: the Siege Town Walkabout and the Siege Town Drive-About. ⊠ *151 Murchison St., next to town hall* ☎ *036/637–2992* ⊠ *R11* ⊙ *Weekdays 9–4, Sat. 9–1.*

In the courtyard of the Siege Museum stands a replica of a Long Tom, the 6-inch Creusot gun used by the Boers during the siege to terrify the inhabitants of Ladysmith. In front of the town hall are two howitzers used by the British and christened Castor and Pollux.

WHERE TO STAY

$ 🏨 **Royal Hotel.** This recently refurbished typical South African country hotel shares much of Ladysmith's historic past. The hotel was built in 1880, just 19 years before the town was attacked by the Boers during the war. Expect small rooms, although TVs and air-conditioning are standard features. The hotel serves a buffet for lunch and dinner at R100 a head and offers an à la carte menu on weekends. **Pros:** convenient, central location; great 1800s facade and front door; steeped in Anglo-Boer War history. **Cons:** undistinguished, bland rooms; hotel atmosphere is a bit lacking. ⊠ *140 Murchison St.* ☎ *036/637–2176* ⊕ *www.royalhotel.co.za* ⮢ *71 rooms* ⚹ *In-hotel: restaurant, bar* ⊟ *AE, DC, MC, V* �𝍌 *BP.*

SPIOENKOP

38 km (24 mi) southwest of Ladysmith.

The Second Anglo-Boer War (1899–1902) was the biggest, the longest, the costliest, the bloodiest, and the most humiliating war that Great Britain had ever fought. The **Battle of Spioenkop** near Ladysmith was a focal point, where the Boers trounced the British, who suffered 243 fatalities during the battle; many were buried in the trenches where they fell.

WHERE TO STAY

$ 🏨 **Three Trees Lodge.** In the lee of the famous hill, Spioenkop, where one of the bitterest battles of the Anglo-Boer War took place, lies the quaint little Victorian lodge of Three Trees. You'll feel as if you've stepped back in time when you stay in a cozy little en suite Victorian cottage with its own deck overlooking a secret game-filled valley, set against the magnificent backdrop of the Drakensberg Amphitheatre. In winter, candelabra aloes arch their fiery red arms to the sky, and the decor of the cottages picks up the theme—your bed linen, soft furnishings, furniture, rugs, and bath accessories all echo the green, golds, and scarlets of the indigenous vegetation. Inside the green cottages are cream and pale-green wooden walls, rich brown, polished, cement floors, and cow-skin rugs. Examine the pictures, photographs, and old advertisements on the walls in your cottage and in the comfortable main lodge where a crackling fire burns on cold nights. Most of these souvenirs are original—there's even a copy of one of Winston Churchill's paintings of the area when he was a war correspondent here and famously escaped his Boer captors. The homegrown and home-cooked food is a delight, and the owners, Sheryl and Simon Blackburn, immediately make you feel like part of the family, rather than a guest. Even if you're not into military history, a morning's visit to the top of Spioenkop and its mass grave with the knowledgeable Omri Nene, the resident guide, may well have you in tears. Go horse riding, mountain biking, take a trip into the adjacent game reserve, or take a full day's picnic into the mountains. There are over 270 bird species with a dazzling selection of sunbirds. **Pros:** owner-managed; charming authentic Victorian atmosphere; stunning Anglo-Boer War memorabilia. **Cons:** limited cell phone reception. ⊠ *D564, about 25 km (16 mi) northeast of Bergville* ⌂ *PO Box 3534, Ladysmith* ☎ *036/448–1171* ⊕ *www. threetreehill.co.za* ⋗ *6 suites, 1 family suite* ⚒ *In-room: no phone, no TV. In-hotel: restaurant, bar, pool* ▤ *AE, DC, MC, V* ¶⊙| *FAP.*

DUNDEE

74 km (46 mi) northeast of Ladysmith.

Once a busy coal-mining town, Dundee still has straight roads wide enough for the ox wagons of pioneer days to turn in, but today it's just a small commercial center in an area of subdued farming activity.

GETTING HERE AND AROUND

To get to Dundee from Ladysmith, take the N11 north and then the R68 east. For a more scenic route, take the R602 towards Elandslaagte from the N11 and then go east on the R68.

VISITOR INFORMATION

Dundee's Regional Information Tourism Office is open weekdays 7:30–4. The Talana Museum visitor information office is open weekdays 8–4:30 and weekends 10–4:30.

Tourist Offices **Regional Information Tourism Office** (⊠ *Main St. and Osborn Rd.* ☎ *035/473–3474* ⊕ *www.dundeekzn.co.za*). **Talana Museum** (⊠ *R33, 2 km [1 mi] east of Dundee* ☎ *034/212–2654*).

EXPLORING

The first-rate **Talana Museum,** set in a 20-acre heritage park, on the outskirts of Dundee, encompasses 10 buildings. Fascinating exhibits trace the history of the area, from the early San hunter-gatherers to the rise of the Zulu nation, the extermination of the cannibal tribes of the Biggarsberg, and, finally, the vicious battles of the South African War. The museum stands on the site of the Battle of Talana (October 20, 1899), the opening skirmish in the South African War, and two of the museum buildings were used by the British as medical stations during the battle. The military museum here is an excellent starting point for the Battlefields Route, along which you follow in the footsteps of the Zulus, Brits, and Boers as they battled it out for territory and glory. ⊠ *R33, 2 km (1 mi) east of Dundee* ☎ *034/212–2654* ⊕ *www.talana. co.za* ⋗ *R15* ⊙ *Weekdays 8–4, weekdays 10–4.*

NEED A BREAK?

The Miner's Rest Tea Shop, in a delightfully restored miner's cottage at the Talana Museum, serves refreshments as well as more substantial dishes like peri-peri chicken livers and spinach, feta, and chicken pie in phyllo pastry. The food is good and the atmosphere most welcoming. Alternatively, you can take advantage of the braai and picnic facilities on the museum grounds.

Off the R33 northeast of Dundee is the **site of the Battle of Blood River,** one of the most important events in the history of South Africa. This battle, fought between the Boers and the Zulus in 1838, predates the Anglo-Zulu War by more than 40 years. After the murder of Piet Retief and his men at Mgungundlovu in February 1838, Dingane dispatched Zulu impis to kill all the white settlers in Natal. The Voortrekkers bore the brunt of the Zulu assault. For the next 10 months their future hung in the balance: entire settlements were wiped out, and a Boer commando was smashed at the Battle of Italeni. By November a new commando of 464 men and 64 wagons under Andries Pretorius had moved out to challenge the Zulus. On Sunday, November 9, the Boers took a vow that should God grant them victory, they would forever remember that day as a Sabbath and build a church in commemoration. They repeated the vow every night for the next five weeks. On December 16 an enormous Zulu force attacked the Boers, who had circled their wagons in a strategic position backed by the Blood River and a deep *donga,* or gully. Armed with only spears, the Zulus were no match for the Boer riflemen. At the end of the battle 3,000 Zulus lay dead, but not a single Boer had fallen. The immediate effect of the victory was to open Natal to white settlement, but the long-term effects were far more dramatic. The intensely religious Voortrekkers saw their great victory as a confirmation of their role as God's chosen people. This deeply held conviction lay at the spiritual heart of the apartheid system that surfaced more than a century later, in 1948. Indeed, when you see the monument here, there's no mistaking the gravity and importance that the Nationalist government ascribed to its erection. The laager, a defensive circle of 64 wagons, has been reconstructed in exacting detail, made from a mix of cast steel and bronze. It's a truly haunting monument, made even more so by its position on empty grasslands that seem to stretch for eternity. ⊠ *Off R33, between Dundee and Vryheid* ☏ *072/088–3544* ⌨ *R20* ⊙ *Daily 8–4.*

WHERE TO STAY

¢ ⬚ **Lennox Cottage.** This active farm is owned and run by ex–South African National Team Springbok rugby center Dirk Froneman and his wife, Salomé. After a day touring the battlefields (they will recommend superb guides), if you've still got some energy left you can ride, swim in the large pool, play snooker, or go on an evening game drive around the farms before sinking into a comfortable bed in your country-style room. Salomé's home cooking is superb, and each evening she serves such traditional Afrikaans dishes as butternut soup, *bobotie* (a spicy ground-meat dish), and local venison on an antique dining table as guests discuss the day's doings over a *dop* (drink) or two (dinner R180). **Pros:** wonderful hosts and personal service; Salomé's truly South African food is superb. **Cons:** genuine retro '70s feel makes the locale a bit bleak in the winter; comfortable, but not cozy. ⊠ *R68, Box 197* ☏ *082/574–3032* ✍ *lennox@dundeekzn.co.za* ⇲ *12 rooms* ⚬ *In-hotel: bar, pool, Internet terminal* ⊟ *AE, DC, MC, V* ⊙ *MAP.*

RORKE'S DRIFT

★ *35 km (22 mi) southwest of Dundee.*

GETTING HERE AND AROUND
Rorke's Drift is southwest of Dundee on the R68.

EXPLORING
Rorke's Drift is by far the best of the Zulu War battlefields to see without a guide. An excellent museum and orientation center retells the story of the battle, with electronic diagrams, battle sounds, and dioramas. From the British perspective this was the most glorious battle of the Zulu War, the more so because it took place just hours after the disaster at Isandlwana. The British force at Rorke's Drift consisted of just 141 men, of whom 35 were ailing. They occupied a Swedish mission church and house, which had been converted into a storehouse and hospital. The Zulu forces numbered some 3,000–4,000 men, composed of the reserve regiments from Isandlwana. When a survivor from Isandlwana sounded the warning at 3:15 PM, the tiny British force hastily erected a stockade of flour bags and biscuit boxes around the mission. The Zulus attacked 75 minutes later, and the fighting raged for 12 hours before the Zulus faltered and retreated. To this day, historians cannot figure out why the Zulus failed to press their huge advantage. When the smoke cleared, 500 Zulus and 17 Britons lay dead. ⊠ *Rorke's Drift Rd., off the R68* ☎ *034/642–1687* ☜ *R15* ☽ *Weekdays 8–4, weekends 9–4.*

WHERE TO STAY
$$$ ⊞ **Fugitives' Drift Lodge.** Set on a 4,000-acre game farm, this attractive lodge lies just a couple of miles from the site of the famous engagement at Rorke's Drift and overlooks the drift where survivors of the British defeat at Isandlwana fled across the Buffalo River. The family of the late, legendary Anglo-Zulu War expert David Rattray, who owned and ran this lodge before his untimely death in January 2007, continues his lifelong commitment to Zululand, and the David Rattray Foundation has been established to carry on his community projects with the local people. Rooms, in individual cottages that open onto gardens, have fireplaces and wood furniture. You can rent a room in a cottage or the whole cottage, depending on your group size. The focal point of the lodge is the lounge and dining room, decorated with old rifles, British regimental flags, Zulu spears, and antique military prints. Battlefield tours cost R820 per person. **Pros:** cottages have lovely garden settings; you'll be contributing to the local communities through the lodge's David Rattray Foundation; fascinating battlefield and military memorabilia on display. **Cons:** pricey; can be full of groups of old military gentlemen. ⊠ *Rorke's Drift Rd.* ☝ *Rorke's Drift* ☎ *034/271–8051* ⊕ *www.fugitives-drift-lodge.com* ☜ *8 chalets, 1 cottage* ☖ *In-hotel: bar, pools* ☰ *AE, DC, MC, V* ☩ *FAP.*

$$ ⊞ **iSibindi Lodge.** This lodge within the iSibindi Eco Reserve combines game-viewing and Zulu cultural experiences with battlefield tours (R650) led by excellent local guides and historians. You'll see antelopes, giraffes, zebras, and wildebeests on your early-morning and evening game drives, and during cultural evenings you'll see traditional Zulu dancers and enjoy traditional delicacies. Another highlight will be a

visit to a traditional village across the river where the sangoma (traditional healer) will "throw the bones" for you and read your fortune. In summer, rafting is possible on the Buffalo River. Rooms, in elevated Zulu-style beehive huts with private decks, face glorious vistas of hill and valley. An attractive lounge and bar area shows off African prints and Zulu artifacts, and an outdoor bar and sunken pool look out at the view. **Pros:** situated in a lovely eco-reserve so you get game (not predators); exciting Zulu dancing plus an on-site sangoma to tell your future; great birding. **Cons:** avoid the summer months, as Zululand can get very hot and sticky and there's no a/c. ⊠ *9 km (4 mi) from Rorke's Drift* ⊅ *Box 275, Umhlali 4390* ☎ *034/642–1620* ⊕ *www.zulunet.co.za* ⊅ *6 huts* ⚲ *In-hotel: bar, pool* ⊟ *AE, DC, MC, V* ⦿l *MAP.*

SHOPPING

Rorke's Drift is still a mission station, run by the Evangelical Lutheran Church. The **Rorke's Drift ELC Art and Craft Centre** (⊠ *Rorke's Drift Rd., off R68* ☎ *034/642–1627*), at the mission, sells wonderful pottery, handwoven rugs, and linocuts, all created by mission artists.

ISANDLWANA

35 km (22 mi) southeast of Rorke's Drift on R68.

The Battle of Isandlwana, on January 22, 1879, was a major defeat for the British army. Coming as it did at the very beginning of the Zulu War, the defeat sent shudders of apprehension through the corridors of Whitehall and ultimately cost Lord Chelmsford his command. Chelmsford was in charge of one of three invasion columns that were supposed to sweep into Zululand and converge on Cetshwayo's capital at Ulundi. On January 20 Chelmsford crossed the Buffalo River into Zululand, leaving behind a small force at Rorke's Drift to guard the column's supplies.

Unknown to Chelmsford, the heart of the Zulu army—20,000 men— had taken up a position just 5 km (3 mi) away. Using Shaka's classic chest-and-horns formation, the Zulus swept toward the British positions. The battle hung in the balance until the Zulus' left horn outflanked the British. The fighting continued for two hours before the British fled the field, with the Zulus in triumphant pursuit. About 1,000 Zulus perished in the attack, as did 1,329 British troops. Today the battlefield is scattered with whitewashed stone cairns and memorials marking the resting places of fallen soldiers. The visitor center houses a small but excellent museum of mementos and artifacts, following the course of the battle in marvelous detail—a good place to start if you're here without a guide. Allow at least two or three hours for a visit. ⊠ *Off R68* ☎ *034/271–8165* ⊠ *R20* ⊙ *Weekdays 8–4, weekends 9–4.*

GETTING HERE AND AROUND

The site of the Battle of Isandlwana is halfway between Dundee and Babanango, just off the R68.

WHERE TO STAY

$$ ⚏ **Isandlwana Lodge.** It's said that during the Battle of Isandlwana, which was a major defeat for the British army, on January 22, 1879, the chief of the Zulu army stood on Nyoni Rock where this lodge is now built. With sweeping views of the battlefield, the building, shaped like a Zulu shield, commemorates Isandlwana. The comfortable rooms are named for Zulus significant in the war, and bathrooms contain shield-shape sink pedestals. Decor is modern yet Afrocentric, with African prints and wooden furniture. Picture windows in public areas make the most of the incredible battlefield views. Trips to the local battle-fields conducted by brilliant historian, lecturer, and fellow of the Royal Geographical Society Rob Gerrard, will be a highlight of your stay. **Pros:** you're literally on the edge of the Isandlwana battlefield; amazing views and funky architecture; battle tours on-site. **Cons:** area can look and feel a bit bleak if the weather's bad. ⊠ *Off R68* ⌂ *Box 30, 3005* ☎ *034/271–8301* ⊕ *www.isandlwana.co.za* ☜ *13 rooms* ⌂ *In-hotel: bar, pool, Internet terminal* ⊟ *AE, DC, MC, V* ⧆ *MAP.*

BABANANGO

33 km (20 mi) east of Isandlwana on R69.

The tiny hamlet of Babanango is a major agricultural center and a great place to base your exploration of the battlefields.

GETTING HERE AND AROUND

A dirt road connecting the R34 to Babanango passes through some of the most beautiful countryside in Zululand, with seemingly endless views over rolling grasslands. The road ends at the tarred R68. Turn right and drive less than 2 km (1 mi) into the pleasant hamlet of Babanango.

WHERE TO STAY

$ ⚏ **Babanango Hotel.** It's worth the trek from Isandlwana to stay in one of the country's most famous watering holes. This is where the cast of the movie *Zulu Dawn*, starring Sir Richard Attenborough and Michael Caine, rested up and relaxed in the late '70s. It's a tiny place decorated in country style, with lots of wood and earthy colors. Don't expect a gourmet meal, but the grilled rump steak and french fries are tasty and inexpensive. **Pros:** it's comfortable, homey, and has lots of history; if it's crowded at all, it will only be with locals. **Cons:** it's a bit off the beaten track, so is an extra journey to get here; if you're looking for five-star luxury stay away. ⊠ *10 Justice St.* ☎ *033/835–0029* ☜ *5 rooms* ⌂ *In-hotel: restaurant, bar* ⊟ *AE, DC, MC, V* ⧆ *BP.*

$$ ⚏ **Babanango Valley Lodge.** This tiny guest lodge lies at the end of a rut-ted dirt road on an 8,000-acre cattle farm. Obviously, it's not the sort of place where you constantly pop in and out, but that's okay—you probably won't want to leave anyway. The lodge sits at the head of a steep valley, far from any other buildings and with tremendous views of acacia-studded grasslands and hills. John and Meryn Turner, the charm-ing hosts, and their very hospitable team, go out of their way to make you feel at home. John is a registered guide, and many people stay at the lodge as part of his battlefield tour. Rooms are decorated in contem-porary style with fluffy white duvets and raw-silk lamp shades—simple,

CLOSE UP

Seeing Shaka Zulu

If you're interested in learning more about the fierce warrior Shaka Zulu or the Zulu culture, there are a few places of note that will give you a glimpse into this amazing culture.

Shakaland, a living museum of Zulu culture, is one of the most popular tourist stops in the region. Originally the movie set for *Shaka Zulu* (1987), Shakaland consists of a traditional Zulu kraal, with thatch beehive huts arranged in a circle around a central cattle enclosure. The emphasis here is on Zulu culture as it existed under King Shaka in the 19th century. You can watch Zulus dressed in animal skins or beaded aprons engaged in everyday tasks: making beer, forging spears, and crafting beadwork. Opt for a three-hour day tour or spend the night. A Zulu cultural adviser leads you through the kraal, explaining the significance of the layout and the roles played by men and women in traditional Zulu society. A highlight is a half-hour performance of traditional Zulu and other dances. Some critics have labeled this a Zulu Disneyland, but it's fun and you learn a great deal about Zulu culture. A buffet lunch is included in the tour. ⊠ *Off R66, 13 km (8 mi) north of Eshowe* ☎ *035/460–0912* ⊕ *www.shakaland.com* 🍽 *R265* ⊙ *Tours daily at 11 and noon.*

WHERE TO STAY

For a more in-depth exploration of the site, stay the night at the 55-room **Protea Shakaland** ($$). Overnight guests have access to additional cultural events and stay in a quasi-traditional Zulu dwelling. Rooms are attractive and luxurious Africa-inspired accommodations: enormous thatch beehive huts supported by rope-wrapped struts, decorated with African bedspreads, reed matting, and African art. All have modern bathrooms and superb views. Meals are included in the price: Western-style dishes and some Zulu specialties are served. ⊠ *Off R66, 13 km (8 mi) north of Eshowe* 🏠 *Box 103, Eshowe 3815* ☎ *035/460–0912* ⊕ *www.proteahotels.com.*

If Shakaland is too commercial for your tastes, consider **Simunye Zulu Lodge** ($), a small settlement in a remote valley of Zululand. Simunye's introduction to traditional Zulu culture extends to contemporary Zulu lifestyles, too. Leave your luggage, labels, and bling in Depart Point and just take an overnight bag for your trip to camp via ox wagon, horseback, or 4x4—the views are breathtaking. While here you'll watch Zulu dancing and visit a working kraal, where you'll meet the residents. Rooms, built of stone and thatch, are a classy mix of Zulu and pioneer cultures, with locally handmade wooden beds and chairs and decorated with Zulu cooking pots and cow-skin rugs. All the rooms have electricity and hot water. Try to book for two nights over a weekend and arrange to attend a wedding or coming-of-age ceremony in a neighboring village. These ceremonies are purely local affairs, and you won't experience a more authentic celebration of rural Zulu culture elsewhere. ⊠ *R68, 60 km (37 mi) from Babanango* 🏠 *Box 248, Melmoth 3835* ☎ *035/450–0101 or 035/450–0103.*

comfortable, and elegant. The four-course table d'hôte dinner focuses on traditional South African fare, including fresh farm produce. Battle-field tours, including a picnic lunch, cost R870. **Pros:** ultra-friendly, knowledgeable hosts; great personal service; delicious home-cooked meals. **Cons:** it's a long, bumpy road from the main road to the lodge. ⊠ *15 km (9 mi) off R68, near Babanango* ⊕ *Box 160, Dundee 3000* ☎ *035/835–0062* ☞ *9 rooms* ᕕ *In-hotel: pool* ⊟ *MC, V* ⓘ *MAP.*

6

Johannesburg

WORD OF MOUTH

"The arts and crafts market at Rosebank is terrific; the weekend is the best time to go. Loads of crafts with great Indian curries and other treats for sale."

—Bushwoman2002

"The South African Breweries downtown has a really great little museum that covers beer making and drinking from ancient times to today, with an authentic shebeen."

—Celia

Updated by
Tara Turkington
and Jade
Archer

Johannesburg, or Jo'burg, Egoli ("City of Gold"), or Jozi, as it is affectionately known by Jo'burgers, is the commercial heart of South Africa. Historically it is where money is made and fortunes found. It has been stereotyped as a cruel, concrete jungle, plagued by crime, but residents defend it fiercely as a city of opportunity and raw energy, the capital of "Can Do!"

Ask a *jol* (lively party) of Jo'burgers what they love about their home town and this is what you might hear: Highveld thunderstorms; Pirates vs Chiefs derby (the Orlando Pirates and Kaizer Chiefs are South Africa's most loved—and hated—soccer teams); the most cosmopolitan city in Africa; spectacular sunsets; jacaranda blooms carpeting the city in purple in October and November; great climate; the smell of jasmine in spring; open-air Sunday concerts at Emmarentia Dam; the fast-paced lifestyle and the can-do attitude of its people; the rich history; host city for the 2010 FIFA World Cup.

But Johannesburg may be best known for gold. The city sits at the center of a vast urban industrial complex that covers most of the province of Gauteng (the *g* is pronounced like the *ch* in Chanukah), which means "Place Where the Gold Is" in the Sotho language and is home to the world's deepest gold mines (more than 3.9 km [2.4 mi] deep). More than 100 years ago it was just a rocky piece of unwanted Highveld land. But in 1886 an Australian, George Harrison, officially discovered gold, catapulting Johannesburg into a modern metropolis that still powers the country's economy and produces nearly 20% of its wealth (though gold mining has been winding down in recent years).

With a population of more than 8 million—including outlying areas such as Soweto, Lenasia, and the West Rand—Jo'burg is a fairly big city by world standards (not much smaller in population than New York and Tokyo) and is by far the country's largest city. Despite its industrial past, Jozi remains a green city, with more than 10 million trees and many beautiful parks and nature reserves, which is all the more exceptional considering it is one of the few major cities in the world not built near a significant water source.

In the late 1980s many of central Johannesburg's big businesses fled north from crime and urban decay to the suburb of Sandton, now an upmarket commercial hub in its own right. But lately local government and business have been reinvesting in the inner city, particularly with an eye to the 2010 World Cup. The beautiful Nelson Mandela Bridge, which spans the railway tracks close to the Newtown Cultural Precinct, has been decorated with wonderful street sculpture. The streets in downtown Johannesburg have been beautified and renamed to reflect the country's cultural diversity: Miriam Makeba Street (formerly

TOP REASONS TO GO

Cradle of Humankind. Visit the Sterkfontein Caves and Maropeng Visitor Centre at this World Heritage Site, about an hour from Johannesburg, to view humankind's evolutionary pathway, fossils, and paleontology, presented in a fun, kid-friendly manner.

History in Your Lifetime. Do a self-guided tour of the Constitutional Court, built on the site of a prison whose inmates included Mahatma Gandhi and Nelson Mandela. The Apartheid Museum takes a holistic look at South Africa's road to democracy.

Iconic Soweto. Visit the site of some dramatic anti-apartheid struggles, as well as former homes of Nobel Peace laureates Nelson Mandela and Archbishop Desmond Tutu.

African Arts and Crafts. The African Craft Market in Rosebank showcases ornaments, masks, and fabrics from across Africa, ranging from the cheap and cheerful to one-off collector's items.

Bezuidenhout Street) is next to Dolly Rathebe Street, named for two of South Africa's jazz legends.

In addition, local government has invested in an extensive new public transport system that will serve the local working population (to be completed in mid-2010). This includes the Gautrain rapid rail system that will connect Johannesburg with Pretoria and the O. R. Tambo International Airport, moving Jo'burg steadily toward its goal of being—as the city council is eager to brand it—"a world-class African city."

ORIENTATION AND PLANNING

GETTING ORIENTED

South Africa's biggest city is in the middle of Gauteng, South Africa's smallest but wealthiest province. The greater metropolitan area is a massive 1,645 square km (635 square mi), most of which is made up of suburban sprawl. The M1, a major highway, runs centrally through the city and its suburbs. Two adjoining highways circle the city: the N3 to the east and the N1 to the west; the M1 bisects this circle.

Downtown Johannesburg. Jo'burg was born as a mining camp, and its downtown area—the oldest part—is a jumbled grid of one-way streets heading in opposite directions, reflecting its hasty start to life. A number of important attractions, such as the Johannesburg Art Gallery and Constitution Hill are found here.

Soweto and the South. About 20 km (12 mi) south of downtown Johannesburg, the vast township of Soweto is where the 1976 anti-apartheid student uprisings began. Take a township tour and visit the Hector Pieterson Memorial and Museum and former homes of Nelson Mandela and Desmond Tutu.

Northern suburbs. Most of the city's good hotels and major malls are in the northern suburbs: notably Sandton, the new financial center of South Africa, and Rosebank, a chic commercial center. Greenside and Parkhurst, close to Rosebank, are popular for eating out.

PLANNING

WHEN TO GO

Jo'burgers boast that they enjoy the best climate in the world: not too hot in summer (mid-September–mid-April), not too cold in winter (mid-April–mid-September) and not prone to sudden temperature changes. Summer may have the edge, though: it's when the gardens and open spaces are at their most beautiful.

GETTING HERE AND AROUND

It's virtually impossible to see anything of the Johannesburg area without a car. Your best bet is to rent one, decide what you want to see, and get a good road map or rent a GPS navigator. If you're reluctant to drive yourself, book a couple of day or half-day tours that will pick you up from where you're staying or from a central landmark.

AIR TRAVEL

O. R. Tambo International Airport (formerly Johannesburg International Airport) is about 19 km (12 mi) from Johannesburg and is linked to the city by a fast highway, which is always busy but especially before 9 AM and between 4 and 7 PM. Beginning in 2010, a high-speed train, the Gautrain, will connect Sandton (and eventually Johannesburg and Pretoria) directly with O.R. Tambo. Magic Bus offers private transfers to all major Sandton hotels (R350 per vehicle plus R40 per person). The journey takes 30 minutes to an hour. Airport Link will ferry you anywhere in Johannesburg in a Toyota Camry or Mercedes minibus for R335 per person. Wilro Tours runs from the airport to Sandton (R580 for three people, plus R200 if you arrive between 9 PM and 6 AM). In addition, scores of licensed taxis line up outside the airport terminal. By law they must have a working meter. Expect to pay about R250–R450 for a trip to Sandton. Negotiate a price before you get in a taxi.

Lines at the airport can be long: plan to arrive two to three hours before an international departure and at least an hour before domestic departures. The airport has its own police station, but luggage theft has been a problem in recent years. Keep your belongings close to you at all times.

If your hotel or guesthouse does not have a shuttle, ask it to arrange for your transportation with a reliable company. Most lodgings have a regular service they use, so you should have no problem arranging this in advance. If it's proving difficult, that is a red flag that you might want to choose a different establishment.

Prices vary, depending on where you are staying, but plan on R350–R400 ($35–$40) for a ride from the airport to Sandton hotels, and about R275 or R300 ($28–$30) for a hotel or guesthouse in Rosebank or Melrose. Most will allow you to add the charge to your bill, so you needn't worry about paying in cash.

Magic Bus runs shuttles from the airport to downtown or the suburbs. You save on price, but you will lose time on a shared ride. The fare is R350 to Sandton or Rosebank and other Jo'burg suburbs. Airport Link is a prebooked, private door-to-door service starting at R335 for one passenger, then an additional R55 for others going to the same destination, with slightly higher rates for Pretoria stops. Legend Tours and Transfers offers prearranged shared-ride transfers starting from R355 from O.R. Tambo.

⇨ *For airline contact information, see Air Travel, in the Travel Smart South Africa chapter.*

Airport O.R. Tambo International Airport (☎ 086/727-7888).

Airport Transfers Airport Link (☎ 011/792-2017 or 083/625-5090 ⊕ www. airportlink.co.za). **Legend Tours and Transfers** (☎ 021/704-9140 ⊕ www. legendtours.co.za). **Magic Bus** (☎ 011/548-0822 or 011/394-6902 ⊕ www. magicbus.co.za). **Wilro Tours** (☎ 011/789-9688 ⊕ www.wilrotours.co.za).

BUS TRAVEL

Intercity buses depart from Park Station in Braamfontein. Greyhound and Translux operate extensive routes around the country. Intercape Mainliner runs to Cape Town. The Baz Bus operates a hop-on, hop-off door-to-door service, stopping at backpackers' hostels between Johannesburg and Durban or Jo'burg and Cape Town on two routes—via the Drakensberg or via Swaziland. You can buy Greyhound, Intercape Mainliner, and Translux bus tickets through Computicket. Airfares with budget airlines in South Africa, such as 1Time, Mango, or Kulala (⇨ *Air Travel, in the Travel Smart South Africa chapter*) are often comparable to bus fares, particularly if you book a few weeks or more in advance.

Bus Lines Baz Bus (☎ 021/439-2323 ⊕ www.bazbus.com). **Computicket** (☎ 083/915-8003 or 011/340-8000 ⊕ www.computicket.com). **Greyhound** (☎ 083/915-9000 ⊕ www.greyhound.co.za). **Intercape Mainliner** (☎ 0861/287-287 ⊕ www.intercape.co.za). **Translux** (☎ 0861/589-282 ⊕ www.translux.co.za).

CAR TRAVEL

Traveling by car is the easiest way to get around Johannesburg, as the city's public transportation is not that reliable or extensive, though this is changing. The general speed limit for city streets is 60 kph (37 mph); for main streets it's often 80 kph (50 mph), and for highways it's 100 kph or 120 kph (62 mph or 75 mph). But be warned that Jo'burgers are known as the most aggressive drivers in the country, and minibus taxis are famous for ignoring the rules of the road, often stopping for passengers with little or no warning. Most city roads and main countryside road are in good condition, with plenty of signage. City street names are sometimes visible only on the curb, however. Avoid driving in rush hours, 7 to 8:30 AM and 4 to 6:30 PM, as the main roads become terribly congested. Gas stations are plentiful in most areas. (Don't pump your own gas though; stations employ operators to do that for you.)

Almost everywhere there are security guards who look after parked cars, as car burglaries are common. It's customary to give these guards a small tip when you return to your car. Most big shopping centers have parking garages (about R6 per hour).

If you plan to drive yourself around, get a *good* map of the city center and northern suburbs or buy or rent a GPS (available at the airport and most car-rental agencies). MapStudio prints excellent complete street guides, available at bookstores and many gas stations and convenience stores.

Major rental agencies have offices in the northern suburbs and at the airport. *(⇨ For information on roadside assistance or national car-rental companies, see Car Travel, in the Travel Smart South Africa chapter.)*

Rental Company Tempest Car Hire (✉ *O.R. Tambo International Airport* ☎ *011/394–8626* ⊕ *www.tempestcarhire.co.za*).

TAXI TRAVEL

Minibus taxis form the backbone of Jo'burg's transportation for ordinary commuters, but you should avoid using them since they're often not roadworthy, drivers can be irresponsible, and it's difficult to know where they're going without consulting a local. Car taxis, though more expensive, are easier to use. They have stands at the airport and the train station, but otherwise you must phone for one. Ask the taxi company how long it will take the taxi to get to you. Taxis should be licensed and have a working meter. Meters·start at R10 and are R10 per km. Expect to pay about R300 to the airport from town or Sandton and about R160 to the city center from Sandton.

Taxi Companies Maxi Taxi (☎ *011/648–1212*). **Rose Taxis** (☎ *011/403–9625 or 011/403–0000* ⊕ *www.rosetaxis.com*). **Safe Cab** (☎ *086/166–5566*).

TRAIN TRAVEL

Johannesburg's train station, Park Station, is in Braamfontein, at Leyds and Loveday streets. The famous, luxurious Blue Train, which makes regular runs to Cape Town, departs from here, as do Shosholoza Meyl trains to cities around the country, including the Trans-Karoo to Cape Town, the Komati to Nelspruit in Mpumalanga, and the Trans-Natal to Durban. Many of these trains have overnight service. They vary a lot in terms of comfort levels and price, and the more expensive ones such as the Blue Train are often booked up far in advance (though it's always worth a try if you want to make a reservation at short notice).

Train Lines Blue Train (☎ *012/334–8459* ⊕ *www.bluetrain.co.za*). **Shosholoza Meyl** (☎ *086/000–8888* ⊕ *www.shosholozameyl.co.za*).

TOURS
GENERAL-INTEREST TOURS

Springbok Atlas offers two- to three-hour tours (including self-drive tours) of Johannesburg to the city center, Soweto, the Apartheid Museum, Gold Reef City, and other points of interest. Other tours explore Tshwane, the diamond-mining town of Cullinan, Sun City, and Pilanesberg National Park. Tour fees start around R450 per person for half-day tours and R150 per person for five-hour game drives. Wilro Tours conducts various tours to Soweto, Johannesburg, and the Pilanesberg. The Johannesburg Tourism Company has a large database of tour operators for customized tours (golf, anyone?). JMT Tours and

Mining Diamonds

Anyone can go to a jewelry store and bring home South African diamonds, but how many people can say they got their sparkler from an actual mine? At **Cullinan Diamond Mine** (✉ *Mine: Oak Ave., west of Olienhout Ave.; Cullinan Tours: 95 Oak Ave., Cullinan* ☎ *012/734–0260*), not only can you buy diamonds, but you can get custom-made pieces from the resident jeweler, though don't expect your piece to include the world's largest diamond—the 3,106 carat Cullinan Diamond unearthed here in 1905 is now in the Crown Jewels in London. Mine tours are offered every day, ranging from the standard tour (R60; weekdays at 10 AM and 2:30 PM, weekends at 10 AM) to the four-hour underground tour (R440; daily at 8 AM). We suggest the underground tour— you experience what it's like being underground and see the miners' working conditions. You must reserve tours at least three days in advance; children under 16 are not permitted.

Cullinan has a series of delightful tea gardens to choose from. For pleasant outdoor dining, the Whispering Oaks Garden Café (✉ *94 Oak Ave.* ☎ *012/734–2496*) serves breakfast, lunches, and homemade sweets. Closed on Tuesday.

Safaris can arrange tailor-made trips for small groups to a number of destinations.

A hop-on, hop-off tour (R180; valid 12 hours) with Tour Network is a good way to see Johannesburg's main sights in a day, with plenty of stops along the way. Tours leave several times a day from Montecasino, Fourways. Africa Explore offers full-day and half-day tours of the Cradle of Humankind area; the full package (from R925 per person per day on a group tour to R1,125 per person for a single-person tour) includes the Kromdraai Gold Mine, Sterkfontein Caves, and the Rhino and Lion Park. Palaeo-Tours runs full- and half-day trips to local paleontological sites.

Tour Operators Africa Explore (☎ *011/917–1999* ⊕ *www.africa-explore. co.za*). **JMT Tours and Safaris** (☎ *011/980 6038* ⊕ *www.jmttours.co.za*). **Johannesburg Tourism Company** (☎ *011/342–4316* ⊕ *www.joburgtourism.com*). **Palaeo-Tours** (☎ *011/726–8788* ⊕ *www.palaeotours.com*). **Tour Network** (☎ *011/447–0432*). **Springbok Atlas** (☎ *011/396–1053* ⊕ *www.springbokatlas. com*). **Wilro Tours** (☎ *011/789–9688* ⊕ *www.wilrotours.co.za*).

DIAMOND AND GOLD TOURS

Mynhardts Diamonds, which sells diamonds and jewelry, gives audiovisual presentations by appointment. Schwartz Jewellers conducts one-hour tours of its workshops in Sandton by appointment. You can see stone grading, diamond setting, and gold pouring, plus get tips on what to look for when buying diamonds, as well as a brief history of South Africa's diamond industry. And, of course, you can buy the finished product. Tours are free and include refreshments; you need your passport for security reasons.

Tour Operators **Mynhardts Diamonds** (☎ *011/484–1717* ⊕ *www.mynhardts. com*). **Schwartz Jewellers** (☎ *011/783–1717* ⊕ *www.schwartzjewellers.com*).

TOWNSHIP TOURS

Tours of Soweto are offered by many of the above operators as well as Jimmy's Face to Face Tours. Information on Soweto tours can also be obtained from the Soweto Tourism Association and ⊕ *www.soweto. co.za*, a private initiative of tour operator KDR Travel.

Tour Information **Jimmy's Face to Face Tours** (☎ *011/331–6109* ⊕ *www.face-2face.co.za*). **Soweto.co.za** (☎ *011/326–1700* ⊕ *www.soweto.co.za*).

TAKE IT ALL IN

1 or 2 Days: If you have only one day in Jo'burg, take a tour of Soweto and visit the Apartheid Museum, then stop by Constitution Hill if you have a chance. Spend the evening having dinner at an African-style restaurant, such as Moyo. If you have a second day, focus on what interests you most: perhaps a trip to the Cradle of Humankind, where you can explore the sites of some of the world's most significant paleontological discoveries; a trip to Cullinan, where you can visit a working diamond mine; or a fun day or two at Sun City.

3 to 5 Days: Spend your first day touring Soweto and visiting the Apartheid Museum and Constitution Hill, followed by an African-style dinner. The next day, leave early and do Sterkfontein Caves and Maropeng in the Cradle of Humankind, then overnight at one of the establishments in the Magaliesberg, perhaps at the luxurious De Hoek Country House or Mount Grace Country House Hotel. For something beautiful but basic, stay one or two nights in a chalet at Mountain Sanctuary Park, in the Magaliesberg, then head out early to the Pilanesberg National Park *(⇨ Chapter 9)*, one of the finest parks in South Africa, where seeing a rhino and elephant is likely. Stay a night or two in one of the park lodges, and treat yourself to an early-morning balloon ride over the park.

SAFETY

Johannesburg is notorious for being a dangerous city—it's quite common to hear about serious crimes such as armed robbery and murder. Even South Africans fear it, regarding it as some Americans regard New York City: big and bad. That said, it's safe for visitors who avoid dangerous areas and take reasonable precautions. Do not leave bags or valuables visible in a car, and keep the doors locked, even while driving (to minimize the risk of smash-and-grab robberies or hijackings); don't wear flashy jewelry or carry large wads of cash or expensive equipment. ⚠ **Never, ever visit a township or squatter camp on your own.** Unemployment is rife, and foreigners are easy pickings. If you wish to see a township, check with reputable companies, which run excellent tours and know which areas to avoid. The Apartheid Museum and Cradle of Humankind are perfectly safe to visit on your own.

⚠ **It's inadvisable to drive yourself in and around the city, as certain areas are known carjacking spots.** Carjacking is so prevalent that there are permanent street signs marking those areas that are most dangerous.

Order a car service or transportation from your hotel for trips in and around the city.

EMERGENCIES

In the event of a medical emergency, seek help at one of the city's private hospitals. Among the most reputable are Milpark Hospital and Sandton Medi-Clinic. You'll find pharmacies all over the city, but when in doubt, there are pharmacies in every Clicks and Dis-Chem store located in shopping complexes citywide.

Embassy U.S. Embassy (✉ *877 Pretorius St., Arcadia, Tshwane* ☎ *012/431-4000*).

Emergency Services Ambulance (☎ *999 or 011/375-5911*). **General Emergencies** (☎ *10111 from landline, 112 from cell*). **Police** (☎ *10111*).

Hospitals Milpark Hospital (✉ *9 Guild Rd., off Empire Rd., Parktown* ☎ *011/480-5600*). **Sandton Medi-Clinic** (✉ *Main St. and Peter Pl., off William Nicol Dr., Lyme Park* ☎ *011/709-2000*).

MONEY MATTERS

You can exchange currency at O.R. Tambo International Airport or at the larger branches of South Africa's banks, such as ABSA, Standard Bank, First National Bank, and Nedbank's operations in Rosebank and Sandton. Look for the BUREAU DE CHANGE signs at these banks. ATMs are all over the city, especially at shopping centers. Be careful when using them: don't let anybody distract you, and avoid ATMs in quiet spots at night.

VISITOR INFORMATION

The helpful Gauteng Tourism Authority has information on the whole province, but more detailed information is often available from local tourism associations—for example, the Soweto Accommodation Association lists more than 20 lodgings. The Johannesburg Tourism Company has a good Web site, with information about Johannesburg and up-to-date listings of events happening around the city. The City of Johannesburg's Web site lists local events, news, service advisories, and more.

Contacts City of Johannesburg (⊕ *www.joburg.org.za*). **Gauteng Tourism Authority** (☎ *011/ 832-2780* ⊕ *www.gauteng.net*). **Johannesburg Tourism Company** (☎ *011/214-0700* ⊕ *www.joburgtourism.com*). **Soweto Accommodation Association** (☎ *011/936-8123*).

RESTAURANTS

Jo'burgers love eating out, and there are hundreds of restaurants throughout the city to satisfy them. Some notable destinations for food include Melrose Arch, Parkhurst, Sandton, the South (for its Portuguese cuisine), Greenside and Chinatown—a strip of restaurants and Asian grocery stores in Cyrildene, near Bruma Lake. Smart-casual dress is a good bet. Many establishments are closed on Sunday nights and Monday.

HOTELS

Most, if not all, of the good hotels are in the northern suburbs. Many of the hotels are linked to nearby malls and are well policed. Boutique hotels have sprung up everywhere, as have bed-and-breakfasts from Melville to Soweto. Hotels are quieter in December and January, and their rates are often cheaper. Generally the busy months in Jo'burg are from June to August. If there's a major conference, some of the smaller hotels can be booked months in advance.

WHAT IT COSTS IN SOUTH AFRICAN RAND					
	¢	$	$$	$$$	$$$$
Restaurants	under R50	R50–R75	R76–R100	R101–R125	over R125
Hotels	under R1,000	R1,000–R2,000	R2,001–R3,000	R3,001–R4,000	over R4,000

Restaurant prices are per person for a main course at dinner, a main course equivalent, or a prix-fixe meal. Hotel and lodging prices are for a standard double room in high season, including 12.5% tax.

EXPLORING JOHANNESBURG

Johannesburg epitomizes South Africa's paradoxical makeup—it's rich, poor, innovative, and historic all rolled into one. And it seems at times as though no one actually comes *from* Johannesburg. The city is full of immigrants: Italians, Portuguese, Chinese, Hindus, Swazis, English, Zimbabweans, Nigerians, Xhosa. And the streets are full of merchants. Traders hawk *skop* (boiled sheep's head, split open and eaten off newspaper) in front of polished glass buildings, as taxis jockey for position in rush hour. *Sangomas* (traditional healers) lay out herbs and roots next to roadside barbers' tents, and you never seem to be far from a woman selling *vetkoek* (dollops of deep-fried dough), beneath billboards advertising investment banks or cell phones.

The Greater Johannesburg metropolitan area is massive—more than 1,600 square km (635 square mi)—incorporating the large municipalities of Randburg and Sandton to the north. Most of the sights are just north of the city center, which degenerated badly in the 1990s but is now being revamped.

To the south, in Ormonde, are the Apartheid Museum and Gold Reef City; the sprawling township of Soweto is farther to the southwest. Johannesburg's northern suburbs are its most affluent. On the way to the shopping meccas of Rosebank and Sandton, you can find the superb Johannesburg Zoo and the South African Museum of Military History, in the leafy suburb of Saxonwold.

DOWNTOWN

Although the city center is experiencing a revival, it's not a place everyone will choose to visit. You'll find plenty to do downtown, including a visit to the impressive Standard Bank Gallery and Johannesburg Art Gallery. Diagonal Street runs—you guessed it—diagonally through the

Posing on a Gold Mine

In 1952, Dolly Rathebe, a young black woman who was to become a jazz-singing legend, and a white German photographer, Jürgen Schadeberg, scrambled to the top of a gold-mine dump for a *Drum* magazine photo shoot. The photograph looks like it was taken on some strange beach: Rathebe smiles, posing in a bikini. They were spotted by the police and arrested under the Immorality Act, which forbade intercourse between blacks and whites. This dump was at Crown Mines, and is now the site of the Crown Mines Golf Course. Today there's a street in Newtown named

after Rathebe, who died in 2004 at the age of 76. Schadeberg is still alive and lives in South Africa.

Today you can see gold-mine dumps along the edge of town marching east and west along the seam of gold. Some are close to 300 feet high. Many people are fond of them—they are one of the city's defining characteristics—but those who live nearby are blinded by the dust, and little vegetation grows on the dumps. Since they're also rich in minerals, they're slowly being chipped away and re-mined, and in years to come, they may be completely gone.

city center. The Hillbrow Tower is 883 feet, the tallest structure in Jo'burg, and is used for telecommunications, as is the 768-foot Brixton Tower in Auckland Park. The tall, round Ponte City apartment block near Hillbrow is another focal point that can be seen from almost all parts of the city.

Located in the western section of the city, Newtown, which is connected to Braamfontein via the Nelson Mandela Bridge, was once one of the city's most run-down neighborhoods. Today it is known as the city's cultural precinct, as it's the home of MuseuMAfricA, the SAB World of Beer, and the Market Theatre.

Braamfontein is home to Constitution Hill and the University of the Witwatersrand, one of South Africa's oldest and most respected universities.

Numbers in the margin correspond to numbers on the Downtown Johannesburg map.

TOP ATTRACTIONS

⑨ Constitution Hill Overlooking Jo'burg's inner city and suburbs, Constitution Hill houses the **Constitutional Court**, set up in 1994 with the birth of democracy, as well as the austere **Old Fort Prison Complex** (also called Number Four), where thousands of political prisoners were incarcerated, including South African Nobel Peace laureates Albert Luthuli and Nelson Mandela, and iconic Indian leader Mahatma Gandhi. The court decides on the most important cases relating to human rights, much like the Supreme Court in the United States. Exhibits in the visitor center portray the country's journey to democracy. You can walk along the prison ramparts (built in the 1890s), read messages on the We the People Wall (and add your own), or view the court itself, in which large, slanting columns represent the trees under which African

Fodor'sChoice
★

7

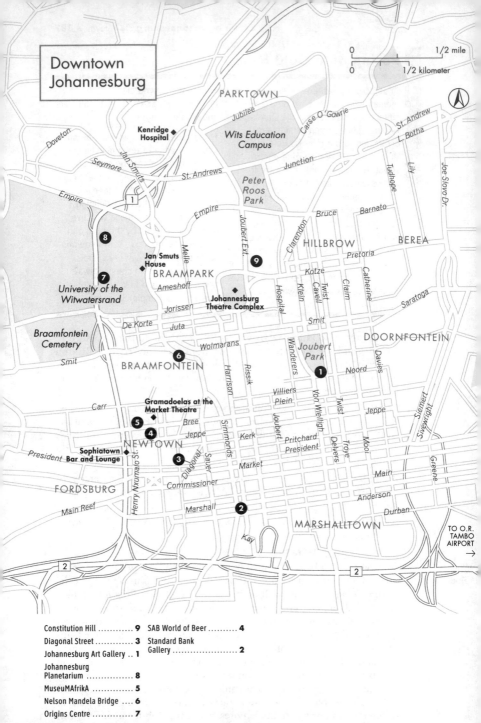

Downtown Johannesburg

PARKTOWN

Jubilee

Caise O'Gowrie

St. Andrew

L. Botha

Doveton

Seymore

Jan Smuts

St. Andrews

Junction

Joe Slovo Dr.

Kenridge Hospital

Wits Education Campus

Peter Roos Park

Empire

Empire

Joubert Ext.

Bruce

Clarendon

Barnato

Tudhope

Lily

HILLBROW

BEREA

Pretoria

Kotze

Twist

Catherine

Saratoga

8

Jan Smuts House

Melle

BRAAMPARK

Ameshoff

9

Klein

Cavell

Claim

7

University of the Witwatersrand

Jorissen

De Korte

Johannesburg Theatre Complex

Hospital

Smit

DOORNFONTEIN

Juta

Braamfontein Cemetery

Wolmarans

Joubert Park

Davies

Smit

6

BRAAMFONTEIN

Harrison

Rissik

1

Noord

Carr

Villiers Plein

Von Wielligh

Twist

Jeppe

Gramadoelas at the Market Theatre

5

Bree

Simmonds

Kerk

Joubert

Pritchard

Troye

Mooi

4

Jeppe

Devers

President

NEWTOWN

3

Diagonal

Sauer

Market

Main

Greene

Sophiatown Bar and Lounge

Henry Nxumalo St.

President

Commissioner

FORDSBURG

Marshall

Anderson

Durban

Main Reef

Kay

2

MARSHALLTOWN

TO O.R. TAMBO AIRPORT

2

2

0   1/2 mile
0   1/2 kilometer

villagers traditionally met to discuss matters of importance. If the court isn't in session, you can walk right into the courtroom, where many of the country's landmark legal decisions have been made in recent years and where the 11 chairs of the justices are each covered in a different cowhide, representing their individuality. A small but good shop carries interesting titles about South African history. Group tours of the Old Fort Prison Complex are given every hour on the hour from 9 to 4 and include a visit to the Women's Jail, where there are photographs and exhibits of how women were treated in the prison system and how they contributed to the struggle against apartheid. You can also take a private tour, which departs at any time. ⊠ *Joubert and Kotze Sts., entrance on Sam Hancock St., Braamfontein* ☎ *011/381–3100* ⊕ *www.constitutionhill. org.za* ⊠ *Court free; Old Fort group tour R22, private tour R40* ☉ *Court daily 9–5; last entry at 4. Old Fort group tours daily on the hr, 9–4; private tours by appointment.*

> **A JO'BURG BEACON**
>
> If there's a symbol of Johannesburg, it's **Ponte City** (⊠ *1 Lily St., Hillbrow*), a massive, hollow 54-story cylinder of apartments perched on the edge of the central business district. Built in 1975, and standing at a height of 568 feet with a flashing cell-phone ad at the top, it's the tallest residential building in the Southern Hemisphere.

⑤ ★ MuseuMAfricA. Founded in 1935, this was the first major museum to acknowledge black contributions to the city's development. The museum houses geological specimens, paintings, and photographs relating to South Africa's complex history. You can step into a re-creation of a 1950s shebeen or view the ever-changing exhibits of pottery, photography, and other arts and crafts. Seven permanent displays include a look at the history of gold mining in Johannesburg and a journey through the history of South African music, such as township jazz, *kwela* (pennywhistle street music), and *mbaqanga*, a form of driving township pop-jazz. Another display illustrates the life of Mahatma Gandhi, who once lived in Jo'burg. Upstairs, the Bensusan Museum examines the art, development, and technology of photography with fun, hands-on exhibits. ⊠ *121 Bree St., Newtown* ☎ *011/833–5624* ⊠ *Free* ☉ *Tues.–Sun. 9–5.*

⑦ ⟲ Origins Centre. This modern museum is dedicated to exploring human development over the past 100,000 years, and in particular the tradition

Fodor's Choice
★

of rock art—of which southern Africa has the oldest and some of the richest in the world. The center is complementary to Maropeng (⥲ *Cradle of Humankind, in Side Trips*), which details the past 5 million years or so of human evolution and the history of earth since its formation. The two experiences enhance each other rather than compete. Origins is spacious and elegantly designed, with multimedia displays and photographs catering to a range of tastes, from kids to visiting professors. The shop sells high-quality crafts and hard-to-source books on rock art in southern Africa, and the center's coffee shop, Café Fino, serves good, light meals. ⊠ *University of the Witwatersrand, Yale Rd., Braamfontein*

7

☎ 011/717–4700 ⊕ www.origins. org.za ☒ R60, including audio tour ⊙ Mon.–Sun. 9–5.

WORTH NOTING

❸ **Diagonal Street.** This street in the city center is lined with African herbalists' shops, where you can acquire a mind-boggling array of homeopathic and traditional cures for whatever ails you. If you're lucky, a sangoma (traditional healer) might throw the bones and tell you what the future holds. This is also the site of the old Johannesburg Stock Exchange building (the modern version is in Sandton).

❶ **Johannesburg Art Gallery.** This three-story museum hosts excellent local and international exhibitions in 15 halls and has collections of 17th-century Dutch art, 18th-century French art, and paintings by great South African artists such as Jacob Hendrik Pierneef, Ezrom Legae, Walter Battiss, Irma Stern, Gerard Sekoto, and Anton van Wouw. It exhibits 10% of its treasures at a time. You can also admire a large selection of traditional African objects, such as headrests, tree carvings, and beadwork. The parking and gallery itself are safe, but the area it's in is not, so don't walk around outside. ☒ King George and Klein Sts., Joubert Park ☎ 011/725–3130 ☒ Free ⊙ Tues.–Sun. 10–5.

❽ **Johannesburg Planetarium.** This planetarium, dating from 1960, has entertaining and informative programs on the African skies and presentations that range from space travel to the planets. Phone ahead to find out what's on. ☒ University of the Witwatersrand, Yale Rd., Braamfontein ☎ 011/717–1392 or 011/717–1390 ⊕ www.planetarium. co.za ☒ Varies by event, average R25 ⊙ Shows usually Fri.–Sun.

❻ **Nelson Mandela Bridge.** A symbol of the renewal process going on in the city, this modern, 931-foot-long bridge with sprawling cables spans the bleak Braamfontein railway yard, connecting Constitution Hill and Braamfontein to the revamped Newtown Cultural Precinct. The bridge is especially beautiful at night, when it is lit in white and blue. ☒ Take Queen Elizabeth St. from Braamfontein, or follow signs from central Newtown or from M1 South, Braamfontein and Newtown.

❹ **SAB World of Beer.** SABMiller is Africa's largest brewing company and its unusual museum is dedicated to that great South African favorite—beer. You can find out all about the history of beer brewing in South Africa and the process of beer making, including African brewing traditions. After a 90-minute tour you can enjoy two complimentary beers in the taproom. The World of Beer went through a major revamp in 2007. ☒ 15 President St., Newtown ☎ 011/836–4900 ⊕ www.worldofbeer. co.za ☒ R25 ⊙ Tues.–Sat. 10–6.

❷ **Standard Bank Gallery.** At the home of the Standard Bank African art collection you can admire contemporary South African artwork. The gallery hosts high-quality, ever-changing local and international exhibitions, including the annual traveling World Press Photo show. ⊠ *Frederick and Simmonds Sts., City Center* ☎ *011/631–1889* ⊕ *www. standardbankgallery.co.za* ☜ *Free* ⊘ *Weekdays 8–4:30, Sat. 9–1.*

SOWETO AND THE SOUTH

An acronym for South Western Townships, Soweto was founded in 1904, when city councilors used an outbreak of bubonic plague as an excuse to move black people outside the town. Today the suburb, which is 20 km (12 mi) south of the city, is home to about a million residents. What it lacks in infrastructure, it more than makes up for in soul, energy, and history. The largely working-class population knows how to live for today, and Soweto pulsates with people, music, and humor.

Other Soweto neighborhoods worth touring include old-town neighborhood Diepkloof, just beyond Orlando West, and its neighbor, the new Diepkloof Extension, which dates from the mid-1970s, when bank loans first became available to black property owners. The difference between the two is startling: the dreary prefabricated matchbox houses of Diepkloof next to what looks like a middle-class suburb anywhere. In nearby Dube, many of the evicted residents of Sophiatown—a freehold township west of the city and a melting pot of music, bohemianism, crime, and multiracialism that insulted Afrikaner nationalism—were resettled in 1959, bringing an exciting vibe to the dreary, homogenous dormitory town. The area remains a vibrant suburb, with an exciting mix of people and a festive atmosphere.

Between downtown Johannesburg and Soweto lie several suburbs less affluent than their northern counterparts, including Ormonde, where Gold Reef City and the Apartheid Museum are. Both attractions are well signposted from the N1 highway going both south and north and easy to find if you have hired a car, but many tour operators do include a stop at the Apartheid Museum in their Soweto tours.

Numbers in the margin correspond to numbers on the Johannesburg map.

GETTING HERE AND AROUND
■ **TIP➜ Take a guided tour** (⇨ *Township Tours, in Planning, at the beginning of this chapter*). **Soweto is a chaotic, virtually indistinguishable sprawl. Even if you found your way in, you'd struggle to find your way out—let alone around.** Various companies offer bus tours, but we suggest hiring a private guide or joining a smaller group tour because you'll get one-on-one attention and be able to ask any and all questions. You can also ask for a special-interest tour, such as art, traditional medicine, restaurants, nightlife, or memorials. Most tours start in Jo'burg, and you can arrange to be collected from your hotel.

TOP ATTRACTIONS
⓯ Apartheid Museum. The Apartheid Museum takes you on a journey
Fodor's Choice through South African apartheid history—from the entrance, where you
★ pass through a turnstile according to your assigned skin color (black or white), to the myriad historical, brutally honest, and sometimes shocking photographs, video displays, films, documents, and other exhibits.

7

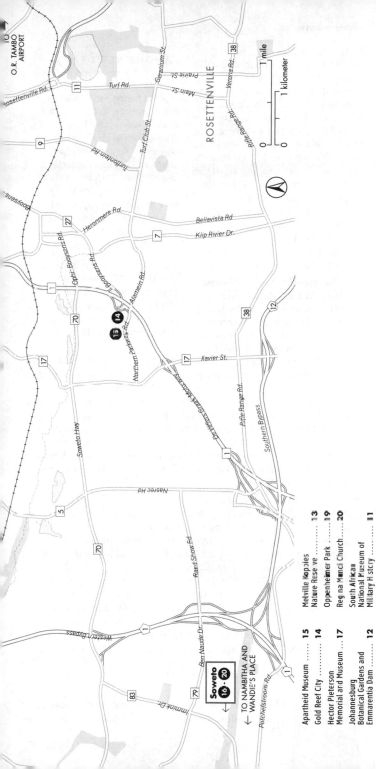

It's an emotional, multilayered journey. As you walk chronologically through the apartheid years and eventually reach the country's first steps to freedom, with democratic elections in 1994, you experience a taste of the pain and suffering with which so many South Africans had to live. A room with 121 ropes with hangman's knots hanging from the ceiling—one rope for each political prisoner executed in the apartheid era—is especially chilling. ✉ *Northern Pkwy. and Gold Reef Rd., Ormonde* ☎ *011/309–4700* ⊕ *www.apartheidmuseum.org* ⌖ *R40* ◷ *Tues.–Sun. 10–5.*

FAMOUS RESIDENTS

What other place on Earth can boast of having had two Nobel Peace laureates living within a block of each other? For most of his adult life Anglican Archbishop Desmond Tutu lived on Vilakazi Street, in Soweto's Orlando West neighborhood. For most of that time his close neighbor would have been an attorney named Nelson Mandela, had he not spent most of *his* adult life incarcerated on Robben Island (⇨ *Chapter 2*).

The archbishop's home is a gray, two-story building that is not open to the public, but you can visit the nearby Mandela house. It became a museum in 1997 and was revamped in 2009.

 Hector Pieterson Memorial and Museum. Opposite Holy Cross Church, a stone's throw from the former homes of Nelson Mandela and Archbishop Desmond Tutu on Vilakazi Street, the Hector Pieterson Memorial and Museum is a crucial landmark. Pieterson, a 12-year-old scholar, was the first victim of police fire on June 16, 1976, when schoolchildren rose up to protest their second-rate Bantu (black) education system. The memorial is a paved area with benches for reflection, an inscribed stone and simple water feature; inside the museum are grainy photographs and films that bring that fateful day to life. Small granite blocks in the museum courtyard are a tribute to the 350 children among the more than 500 people who died during this violent time. ✉ *Khumalo and Phela Sts., Orlando West* ☎ *011/536–2253* ⌖ *R15* ◷ *Mon.–Sat. 10–5, Sun. 10–4:30.*

WORTH NOTING

 Gold Reef City. This theme park lets you step back in time to 1880s Johannesburg and see why it became known as the City of Gold. One of the city's most popular attractions (avoid it on public holidays or weekends), it has good rides that kids will enjoy and is based on the real history of Jo'burg. In addition to riding the Anaconda, a scary roller coaster on which you hang under the track, feet in the air, you can (for an additional fee) descend into an old gold mine and see molten gold being poured, or watch a gumboot dance, a riveting dance developed by black miners. The reconstructed streets are lined with operating Victorian-style shops and restaurants. And for those with money to burn, the large, glitzy Gold Reef Village Casino beckons across the road. ✉ *Gold Reef Rd., 6 km (4 mi) south of city center, Ormonde* ☎ *011/248–6800* ⊕ *www.goldreefcity.co.za* ⌖ *R120* ◷ *Tues.–Sun. 9:30–5; mine tours 10–4 every hour.*

Mandela House. The former president lived in this small house until his arrest in 1961, with his ex-wife Winnie Madikizela-Mandela, who

CLOSE UP

Hector Pieterson and the Soweto Uprising

On June 16, 1976, hundreds of schoolchildren in Soweto marched to protest the use of Afrikaans as the primary language of education in the overcrowded, much neglected Bantu schools in the townships. This was a highly charged political issue. Not only was Dutch-based Afrikaans considered the language of the oppressor by blacks, but it also made it more difficult for students to learn, as most spoke an African language and, as a second language, English.

The march quickly turned nasty. The police started firing into the youthful crowd. One of the first people of more than 500 to die in what was the beginning of a long and protracted struggle was 12-year-old

Hector Pieterson. A picture taken by photographer Sam Nzima of the dying Pieterson in the arms of a crying friend, with Pieterson's sister running alongside them, put a face on apartheid that went around the globe.

Pieterson was just a schoolboy trying to ensure a better life for himself and his friends, family, and community. He and the many students who joined the liberation movement strengthened the fight against apartheid. Eventually Afrikaans was dropped as a language of instruction, and more schools and a teaching college were built in Soweto. Today, Hector Pieterson's name graces a simple memorial and museum about the conflict, and June 16 is Youth Day, a public holiday.

7

owns a high-security mansion higher up the street. The house is now a museum containing Mandela memorabilia from the 1960s. ✉ *Vilakazi St., Orlando West* ☎ *011/936–7754* 🎫 *Foreign tourists R60, South African citizens R40* ⊙ *Weekdays 9–5, weekends 9–4.*

⑲ Oppenheimer Park. Named after mining magnate Ernest Oppenheimer, who established the De Beers diamond mining company as a powerful global brand, this park is one of the few green spaces in Soweto and is rich in flora and birdlife. The park is dominated by a large tower built as a tribute to Oppenheimer, who helped resettle people displaced by the apartheid government in the 1950s. Here you can also see **Khayalendaba,** a cultural village built in the 1970s by South Africa's best-known traditional healer, artist, and oral historian, Credo Mutwa. Some of his statues here portray African gods, warriors, and mythical figures, even sculptures of prehistoric African animals. It's best to visit the park with a guide in the daytime for safety reasons. ✉ *Majoeng St., Central Western Jabavu* ☎ *No phone* 🎫 *Free* ⊙ *Daily 24 hrs.*

⑳ Regina Mundi Church. Central to the liberation struggle, this Catholic church was a refuge of peace, sanity, and steadfast moral focus for the people of Soweto through the harshest years of repression. Archbishop Desmond Tutu often delivered sermons in this massive church during the apartheid years. It has a black Madonna and Child painting inside and an art gallery upstairs. A few years ago, former U.S. President Bill Clinton and Hillary Clinton caused a stir here by accepting communion at a service, even though they are not Catholic. ✉ *1149 Khumalo St., Rockville* ☎ *011/986–2546* 🎫 *Donations requested* ⊙ *Weekdays 9–5.*

⑯ Walter Sisulu Square (formerly Freedom Square). In 1955 the Freedom Charter was adopted here by the Congress Alliance, a gathering of political and cultural groups trying to map a way forward in the repressive 1950s. The charter, the guiding document of the African National Congress, envisaged an alternative nonracial dispensation in which "all shall be equal before the law." Its significance in South Africa is similar to that of the Declaration of Independence in the United States, and it influenced South Africa's new constitution, adopted in 1995 and widely considered one of the best and most progressive in the world. ⊠ *Close to Union St. and Boundary Rd., Kliptown.*

NORTHERN SUBURBS

Johannesburg has dozens of northern suburbs, ranging in size from the huge and diverse Sandton, which includes the entire township of Alexandra, among other suburbs, to the smaller, leafy Saxonwold near the zoo. The northern suburbs highlighted here, in order from southernmost to northernmost, are by no means the only ones—they simply have the most attractions.

Numbers in the margin correspond to numbers on the Johannesburg map.

GREENSIDE
The suburb of Greenside has experienced a revival in the past 10 years, with a variety of restaurants and shops springing up in the area. It was once an average middle-class neighborhood but has become one of the hippest places around Johannesburg. Here you can eat at a variety of restaurants, from African to Portuguese to Thai, and enjoy an evening out at one of the vibey bars. Gleneagles Road has pleasant shops and sidewalk cafés.

⑫ Johannesburg Botanical Gardens and Emmarentia Dam. The large and beautiful botanical gardens here are five minutes from Greenside. This gigantic parkland, dotted with trees, statues, fountains, and ponds, is a wonderful haven. You can relax on benches beneath weeping willows surrounding the dam and lake, where canoeists and windsurfers brave the water, or wander across to the 24-acre rose and herb gardens. The gardens' flowers include an alpine collection and a cycad collection. On weekends bridal parties use the gardens as a backdrop for photographs. ⊠ *Thomas Bowler St., Roosevelt Park* 🕾 *011/782–7064* 🎫 *Free* ☉ *Daily sunrise–sunset.*

⑬ Melville Koppies Nature Reserve. A small nature reserve on the southern side of the Johannesburg Botanical Gardens, Melville Koppies has guided ecology walks, and many of the guides are members of the local botanical society and can introduce you to the rich diversity of Highveld flora found here. Bird-watching is also excellent: expect to see more than 200 varieties of grassland and Highveld birds, as well as suburban garden species and small mammals. An archaeological site contains a furnace dating from the Iron Age. The reserve is managed by volunteers, and you can take a three-hour tour with them by booking ahead. Don't go alone, as it isn't safe to do so. ⊠ *Judith Rd., Emmarentia*

Victorian Parktown

Parktown was once a gated community for the area's mining magnates, but most of its Victorian mansions fell victim to the wrecking ball long ago. Luckily, a few managed to survive. Perhaps the cream of the crop is **Northwards** (✉ *21 Rock Ridge Rd., near Oxford Rd.*), designed by Sir Herbert Baker. For many years it was the home of socialite Jose Dale Lace, whose ghost is said to still lurk in the minstrel gallery. Another gem is **Outeniqua** (✉ *St. David's Pl.*), a mansion built in 1906 for the managing director of Ohlssons Breweries. Today it's part of the Wits Business School Across the road you'll find **Eikenlaan**

(✉ *St. David's Pl.*), which was built in 1903 for James Goch, a professional photographer and the first to use flash photography in South Africa. In 1985 the home was turned into a rather garish franchise of the Mike's Kitchen steak-house chain.

Interested in checking out these architectural treasures? Most are closed to the public, but the **Parktown and Westcliff Heritage Trust** (☎ *011/482–3349* ⊕ *www.parktown-heritage.co.za*) organizes tours of the houses and gardens, which allow you a glimpse of turn-of-the-20th-century grandeur.

☎ *011/482–4797* ⊕ *www.mk.org.za* ✉ *R20 donation requested, guides R30 per person and an additional R100 per hr* ☽ *Sun.; times vary.*

PARKTOWN, PARKVIEW, AND SAXONWOLD

Perched on the Braamfontein Ridge, Parktown was once the address du jour for the city's early mining magnates. Most of the magnificent houses have since met their demise, but those that are left are worth a look. The small but picturesque suburbs of Parkview and Saxonwold are nearby.

⑩ Johannesburg Zoo. Smaller than its Pretoria counterpart but no less impressive, the city's zoo makes for a pleasant day trip, and with plenty of lawns and shade, it's a good place to picnic. The large variety of species (more than 250) includes rare white lions and highly endangered red pandas. The polar bear enclosure has a viewing tunnel where you can see the bears cavorting underwater (the zoo has the only polar bears in Africa). Perhaps the best way to see the zoo is to rent a golf buggy for about R120 per hour, as it's so large that walking around it can be very tiring. (Get there early on a weekend to reserve a buggy.) Afterward, stroll past Zoo Lake in the large, peaceful park across the road. ✉ *Opposite Zoo Lake, Jan Smuts Ave., Parkview* ☎ *011/646–2000* ⊕ *www. jhbzoo.org.za* ✉ *R41* ☽ *Daily 8:30–5:30.*

⑪ South African National Museum of Military History. In a park adjacent to the Johannesburg Zoo, this museum has two exhibition halls and a rambling outdoor display focusing on South Africa's role in the major wars of the 20th century, with an emphasis on World War II. On display are original Spitfire and Messerschmidt fighters (including what is claimed to be the only remaining ME110 jet night fighter), various tanks of English and American manufacture, and a wide array of artillery. Among the most interesting objects are the modern armaments South Africa used in its war against the Cuban-backed Angolan army during the 1980s, including French-built Mirage fighters and Russian tanks stolen by the South Africans from a ship en route to Angola. More recent exhibits include the national military art collection, memorabilia from the Anti-Conscription Campaign of apartheid days, and an exhibit on the history of Umkhonto we Sizwe (Spear of the Nation, or MK, the African National Congress's military arm). The tall, freestanding South African (Anglo-Boer) War memorial, which looks like a statue-adorned mini Arc de Triomphe, is the most striking landmark of the northern suburbs. ⊠ 22 *Erlswold Way, Saxonwold* ☎ *011/646–5513* ⊕ *www.militarymuseum. co.za* ✉ *R22* ⊙ *Weekdays 9–4:30, weekends 9:30–4:30.*

WHERE TO EAT

There's no way to do justice to the sheer scope and variety of Johannesburg's restaurants in a few pages. What follows is a (necessarily subjective) list of some of the best. Try asking locals what they recommend; eating out is the most popular form of entertainment in Johannesburg, and everyone has a list of favorite spots, which changes often. Smart-casual dress is a good bet. Many establishments are closed on Sunday nights and Monday.

DOWNTOWN

$$$ ✕ **Gramadoelas at the Market Theatre.** Crossing the threshold here is like
AFRICAN   stepping into a strange old museum: African artifacts and mirrors litter the huge room. Established in 1967, Gramadoelas has hosted an impressive list of guests including Nelson Mandela, Elton John, the Queen of England, Bill and Hillary Clinton, and many others. The restaurant specializes in South African fare, but does have a few dishes from farther north in the continent. Try *umngqusho* (beans and whole corn) or, if you're feeling adventurous, *mogodu* (unbleached ox tripe) or *masonja* (mopane worms, or large, edible caterpillars). Traditional Cape Malay dishes include *bredie* (lamb casserole in a tomato sauce) and *bobotie* (a spicy casserole of minced lamb with savory custard topping). Meat lovers will like the selection of game meats such as the kudu (antelope) panfried with dried fruit and spices. The popular buffet is available most evenings for R150. ⊠ *Market Theatre, Margaret Mcingana St., Newtown* ☎ *011/838–6960* ⊕ *www.gramadoelas.co.za* ✉ *AE, DC, MC, V* ⊙ *Closed Sun. No lunch Mon.*

$ ✕ **Sophiatown Bar and Lounge.** Although not in the same league as the
AFRICAN   more famous Nambitha and Wandie's traditional township restaurants in Soweto, the Sophiatown Bar and Lounge in Newtown is popular and much easier to get to. The restaurant is decorated with photos and murals of '50s musicians like Miriam Makeba, and patrons gather around braziers on chilly winter nights. Jazz music vies for attention with the rather boisterous crowd, and the place has the feel of a shebeen (township bar). The food is a good example of black South African cuisine. A specialty is pap-and-wors—a traditional South African maize-meal porridge (pap) that is white and stiff with boerewors, South African sausage. The restaurant serves other dishes popular in the townships such as mogodu (tripe) and samp and beans, as well as ostrich

BEST BETS FOR JOHANNESBURG DINING

With hundreds of restaurants to choose from, how will you decide where to eat? Fodor's writers and editors have selected their favorite restaurants by price, cuisine, and experience. In the first column, Fodor's Choice properties represent the "best of the best" in every price category. You can also search by neighborhood for excellent eats—just peruse our reviews on the following pages.

Fodor's Choice ★

La Cucina di Ciro, $$, p. 403
Linger Longer, $$$$, p. 404
Moyo (Melrose Arch), $$$$, p. 400
Moyo (Parkview/Zoo Lake), $$$$, p. 403

Best by Price

¢

Nice, p. 401

$

Doppio Zero, p. 404
La Rustica, p. 404
Trabella Pizzeria, p. 401

$$

The Attic, p. 401
La Cucina di Ciro, p. 403

$$$

Gramadoelas at the Market Theatre, p. 398
Wandie's Place, p. 400

$$$$

La Belle Terrasse at the Westcliff Hotel, p. 403
Le Canard, p. 403
Linger Longer, p. 404
Moyo (Melrose Arch), $$$$, p. 400
Moyo (Parkview/Zoo Lake), $$$$, p. 403

Best by Cuisine

PIZZA

Doppio Zero, $, p. 404
La Rustica, $, p. 404
Trabella Pizzeria, $, p. 401

MEDITERRANEAN

The Attic, $$, p. 401
La Cucina di Ciro, $$, p. 403

La Cucina di Ciro, $$, p. 403
La Rustica, $, p. 404
Linger Longer, $$$$, p. 404

Le Canard, $$$$, p. 403
Parea, $$, p. 400

SOUTH AFRICAN

Gramadoela's at the Market Theatre, $$$, p. 398
Nambitha, $, p. 400
Wandie's Place, $$$, p. 400

Best By Experience

GREAT VIEW

La Belle Terrasse at the Westcliff Hotel, $$$$, p. 403
Moyo (Melrose Arch), $$$$, p. 400
Moyo (Parkview/Zoo Lake), $$$$, p. 403

MOST ROMANTIC

La Belle Terrasse at the Westcliff Hotel, $$$$, p. 403

GOOD FOR GROUPS

The Attic, $$, p. 401
Doppio Zero, $, p. 404
La Rustica, $, p. 404
Moyo (Melrose Arch), $$$$, p. 400
Moyo (Parkview/Zoo Lake), $$$$, p. 403
Sophiatown Bar and Lounge, $, p. 398

CHILD-FRIENDLY

Doppio Zero, $, p. 404
Moyo (Parkview/Zoo Lake), $$$$, p. 403
Nice, ¢, p. 401
Trabella Pizzeria, $, p. 401

7

steaks or burgers. Simpler meals like steak and fresh salads are also served. ⊠ *Jeppe and Henry Nxumalo Sts., Newtown* ☎ *011/836–5999 or 073/598–8581* ⊟ *AE, DC, MC, V.*

SOWETO AND THE SOUTH

$
AFRICAN

✕ **Nambitha.** You can't actually see Nelson Mandela's old house from this popular restaurant, which means that you're less likely to run into a tour bus. Nambitha has evolved from a township restaurant catering only to African tastes into a more versatile establishment. It plays an eclectic selection of music—soul, jazz, R&B, and more traditional African—and is constantly buzzing with people. Meals include mutton curry served with pap, dumplings, rice, or samp, spinach and pumpkin; mogodu (tripe); marinated traditional chicken, lamb shank, and oxtail. Meals are relatively inexpensive, ranging from about R52 to R88, but food is less Nambitha's strength than its busy vibe. Many locals pop in just to chat and mingle. ⊠ *6877 Vilakazi St., Orlando West* ☎ *011/936–9128* ⊟ *DC, MC, V.*

$$$
AFRICAN
★

✕ **Wandie's Place.** Wandie's isn't the only good township restaurant, but it's the best known and one of the most popular spots in Jo'burg. The decor is eclectic township (a bit makeshift), and the walls are adorned with signatures and business cards of tourists that have crossed its path. The waiters are smartly dressed in bow ties, and the food is truly African. Meat stews, *imifino* (a leafy African dish), sweet potatoes, beans, corn porridge, traditionally cooked pumpkin, chicken, and tripe are laid out in a buffet in a motley selection of pots and containers. The food is hot, the drinks are cold, and the conversation flows. You may end up here with a tour bus, but it's big enough to cope, and Wandie's now has an on-site guesthouse in case the alcohol flows too much. It's not that difficult to find, and parking is safe, but it's probably better to organize a visit on a guided trip. ⊠ *618 Makhalamele St., Dube* ☎ *011/982–2796* ⊕ *www.wandies.co.za* ⊟ *AE, DC, MC, V.*

NORTHERN SUBURBS

DUNKELD, ILLOVO, AND MELROSE ARCH

$$$$
AFRICAN
Fodor's Choice
★

✕ **Moyo.** From the food and decor to the music and live entertainment, Moyo is strongly African in theme. The focus of the rich and varied menu is pan-African, incorporating tandoori cookery from northern Africa, Cape Malay influences such as lentil bobotie (a traditional South African baked minced lamb dish), Moroccan-influenced tasty *tagines* (stews with lamb, chicken, fish, or seven vegetables), and ostrich burgers and other dishes representing South Africa. Diners are often entertained by storytellers, face painters, and musicians. The restaurant has four locations (in Johannesburg at Melrose Arch in Melrose North and at Zoo Lake in Parkview, outside Cape Town at the Spier wine estate, and in Durban at the uShaka Pier). At night or in wintertime, Melrose Arch is the best bet of the two Jo'burg outposts. In summer and during the day, the Zoo Lake and Spier branches are nicest. ⊠ *Melrose Arch, Shop 5, High St., Melrose North* ☎ *011/684–1477* ⊕ *www.moyo.co.za* ⌲ *Reservations essential* ⊟ *AE, DC, MC, V.*

$$
GREEK

✕ **Parea.** Previously known as Plaka, this Greek taverna, grill, and meze café is the best of its kind in the city. Greek music floats above the buzz of conversation, a souvlaki spit turns slowly near the door, and a refrigerated case displays an array of meze (small appetizers). Most people sit on the roofed terrace or at the few street-side tables (in summer). Start with a meze platter of souvlaki, feta, olives, cucumber, and tomato, followed by the line fish, grilled on an open flame with olive oil and lemon, or *kleftiko* (lamb slow cooked in a clay oven) and a carafe of wine. On weekend evenings, belly dancers perform between the tables, and Greek dancers do the Zorba to a backdrop of "controlled" plate breaking—all while patrons find it hard to resist a glass of ouzo. Even the manager is known to let his hair down and perform for the patrons once in a while. The dress is casual and the atmosphere very relaxed. Choose the set menus, ranging from R110 to R180, or the à la carte menu. ✉ *3 Corlett Dr., at Oxford Rd., Illovo* ☎ *011/788–8777* ▤ *AE, DC, MC, V.*

$ ✗ **Trabella Pizzeria.** This intimate restaurant of 14 tables or so is on a
ITALIAN   busy street corner around the corner from Parea—an accessible but not attractive position. Trabella's strength is its designer pizza, some of the best you'll ever taste, whether it's with the Brie and cranberry topping; Parma ham, rocket (arugula), and Parmesan; or smoked salmon, sour cream, and caviar, sprinkled with spring onion. The pasta and gnocchi are good options as well. ✉ *Number 3, Galen House, Oxford Rd., at Corlett Dr., Illovo* ☎ *011/442 0113 or 011/442–0414* ▤ *AE, DC, MC, V* ☺ *Closed Mon. No lunch Sun.*

GREENSIDE AND PARKHURST

$$ ✗ **The Attic.** This intimate corner restaurant is filled with simple wooden
ECLECTIC   furniture, and the walls are decorated with an eclectic assortment of pictures and vintage advertisements. The Attic prides itself on serving organic and free-range foods, complemented by a good wine list. Try the duck, hoisin, and ginger spring rolls for starters, the crab linguine for your main course, and finish off with oven-baked hot-chocolate pudding with homemade vanilla ice cream. ✉ *24 4th Ave., at 10th St., Parkhurst* ☎ *011/880–6102* ⌐ *Reservations essential* ▤ *DC, MC, V* ☺ *No lunch Mon.*

¢   ✗ **Nice.** This easygoing, unpretentious café serves only breakfast and lunch but is always busy, mostly because the food is so fresh and good. Breakfast is a specialty, with wholesome breakfast baskets made from toast and piled with succulent tomatoes, bacon, and a poached egg. Fresh open sandwiches are also good, with a wide range of options on the frequently changing menu. It's open from 7:45 AM until 3 PM. ✉ *4th Ave. and 14th St., Parkhurst* ☎ *011/788–6386* ▤ *DC, MC, V* ☺ *Closed Mon. No dinner.*

$ ✗ **Ruby Sushi** This Japanese and Chinese restaurant is in the heart of
ASIAN   Parkhurst's restaurant hub and sports a red-and-white color scheme, Asian-inspired lanterns, and a large painting of Japanese women. It's most popular for its variety of sushi, including creations such as bacon and avocado or pecan and avocado pieces. Begin a meal with the miso soup or some crispy spring rolls with sweet chili sauce and end it with a relaxing herbal tea. ✉ *24C 4th Ave., Parkhurst* ☎ *011/880–3673* ⌐ *Reservations essential* ▤ *DC, MC, V.*

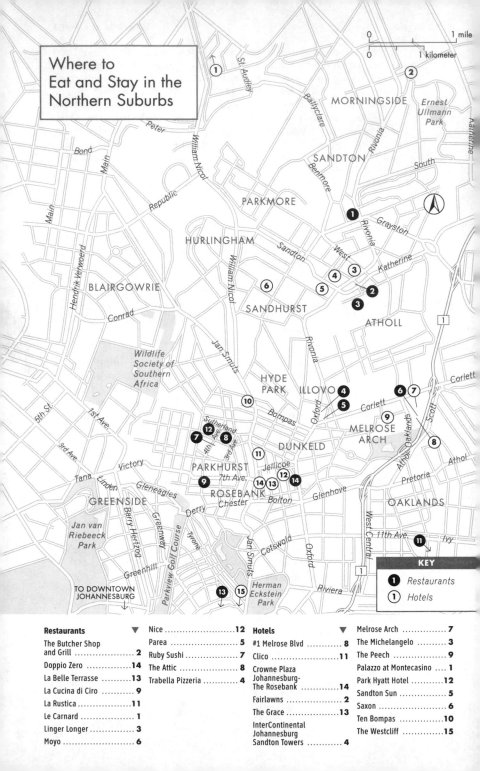

Where to Eat and Stay in the Northern Suburbs

KEY

- ● Restaurants
- ① Hotels

PARKTOWN, PARKVIEW, SAXONWOLD, AND WESTCLIFF

$$
ITALIAN
Fodor's Choice
★

✕ **La Cucina di Ciro.** This is one of the best Italian restaurants in Johannesburg. The owner and chef, Ciro, says the cuisine is "very much my own," which means you can find truly inventive dishes on his seasonally changing menu. The pasta is made on the premises. His most popular dishes are the duck and the variety of homemade pasta dishes, especially the seafood pasta. Be warned: Ciro will chat with complete strangers as if they've been friends for years. La Cucina di Ciro serves breakfast, lunch, and dinner. ⊠ *43 7th Ave., Parktown North* ☎ *011/442–5187* ⌕ *Reservations essential* ▤ *AE, DC, MC, V.*

$$$$
AFRICAN
Fodor's Choice
★

✕ **Moyo.** Of the two Moyo locations in Johannesburg (⇨ *Melrose Arch, above*) this Parkview branch, at Zoo Lake, is the nicest during the day, as you can dine with a view of the lake and take a stroll or a ride in a rowboat afterward. The branch retains the quintessential Moyo vibe, with the option to dine outside in the lush gardens or to enjoy the African decor indoors. The deck is a wonderful spot to enjoy a relaxing lunch or a late-afternoon drink. ⊠ *Zoo Lake Park, 1 Prince of Wales Dr., Parkview* ☎ *011/646–0058* ⊕ *www.moyo.co.za* ⌕ *Reservations essential* ▤ *AE, DC, MC, V.*

SANDTON

$$$$
STEAK

✕ **The Butcher Shop and Grill.** This is a good place for hungry meat lovers. It specializes in prime South African meat aged to perfection by Alan Pick, the butcher-owner. An operating butchery features prominently in the restaurant, and special cuts can be ordered for the meal or to take home. Kudu, springbok, ostrich, and other game are often on the specials list, and only the most tender cuts are served. For lighter choices, try the chicken or line fish. Jelly and custard pudding is a favorite with regulars. There's an excellent wine cellar. ⊠ *Nelson Mandela Sq., Sandton* ☎ *011/784–8676* ▤ *AE, DC, MC, V.*

$$$$
CONTINENTAL

✕ **La Belle Terrasse at the Westcliff Hotel.** Elegant furnishings and impeccable service complement a tasty, small menu in this upmarket establishment. Though it's based at the Westcliff Hotel, the majority of diners are not actually hotel guests—testimony to how good it is. Try the crocodile carpaccio for starters, followed by grilled kudu loin or sesame-encrusted salmon for your main dish, and finish off with a warm *malva* pudding, a traditional South African spongy apricot dessert. The restaurant has a superb view of the Johannesburg Zoo and the city, and it's particularly nice in summer (when making reservations, ask to sit outside on the veranda). Before dinner, indulge in a cocktail or two at the Polo Lounge just below the restaurant. Dozens of cocktails and delicious, spicy tapas are on offer here, all with the best view in Johannesburg in front of you; it's a particularly nice lunch venue. ⊠ *Westcliff Hotel, 67 Jan Smuts Ave., Westcliff* ☎ *011/481–6083* ⌕ *Reservations essential* ▤ *AE, DC, MC, V.*

$$$$
FRENCH

✕ **Le Canard.** In an old house off the busy arterial Rivonia Road, Le Canard provides a tranquil break from the hub of metropolitan Sandton. It has classically romantic touches—crystal glasses, small rose bowls, chandeliers—and the service is excellent. *Le canard* means "the duck" in French, and duck is the specialty. The French-Mediterranean food is rich in flavor with some unique twists, including a chocolate sauce for duck. Between courses expect little treats from the chef such as vegetable soup and duck-liver pâté. Le Canard has an extensive wine list of South African and international wines, champagnes, and liquors. ⊠ *163 Rivonia Rd., Morningside, Sandton* ☎ *011/884–4597* ⊕ *www.lecanard.co.za* ⌘ *Reservations essential* ▤ *AE, DC, MC, V* ◷ *Closed Sun.*

$$$$
CONTINENTAL
Fodor'sChoice
★

✕ **Linger Longer.** Set in the spacious grounds of a grand old home in Wierda Valley, in the business center of Sandton, Linger Longer has an air of gracious elegance. The wooden floors, colored walls, and striped curtains give this restaurant a Wedgewood-like quality. Though upscale, this restaurant has a warm atmosphere, and the hospitable staff and personal service of chef Walter Ulz attract local and international diners. The menu is varied and includes an array of seasonal specials. Start with the prawn firecracker, followed by the Asian split duck or the lamb rack cooked with crushed *chermoula,* a North African spice mix. The delicious porcini ravioli is the best choice on the vegetarian main menu, and the trio of sorbets is a nice finale. There's also a good wine list. ⊠ *58 Wierda Rd., Wierda Valley, Sandton* ☎ *011/884–0465* ⌘ *Reservations essential* ▤ *AE, DC, MC, V* ◷ *Closed Sun. No lunch Sat.*

ROSEBANK

$
MEDITERRANEAN

✕ **Doppio Zero.** This chain of restaurants is found across Johannesburg, but the Rosebank branch is well located if you are peckish after a morning shopping at the African Craft Market across the road. Doppio Zero serves wholesome, tasty Mediterranean-inspired meals. The sandwiches are excellent and contain ingredients like grilled *holoumi* (a salty mozzarella-texture Greek cheese), fresh tomato, arugula, avocado, and salmon. More substantial meals such as pastas and pizzas are also on the menu. ⊠ *Cradock Ave. and Baker St., Rosebank* ☎ *011/447–9538* ⊕ *www.doppio.co.za* ▤ *AE, DC, MC, V.*

HOUGHTON

$
MEDITERRANEAN

✕ **La Rustica.** Set in an old house, this popular family restaurant has outside covered areas that extend around a lovely garden with fountains. The weekend buffet (R195) is sumptuous, with meze-style starters like eggplant baked in a classic Italian Napoletana (tomato, onion, and garlic) sauce, Parma hams, salads, and calamari, followed by spit-braised meats including lamb and beef, and dessert items such as brandy snaps (a brittle, ginger-flavored, cone-shaped dessert often filled with cream), ice cream, crème brûlée, and cheesecake. During the week, dine from the à la carte menu. Try the *tagliolini panna e salmone,* thin ribbon noodles served with a smoked salmon and cream sauce, or the *fegato alla Veneziana,* calves' liver sautéed with caramelized onion, white wine, and sage, served with polenta. There's also a good wine list. Book early in the week for a table on the weekend. ⊠ *103 Houghton Dr., at Lloys Ellis Ave., Houghton* ☎ *011/728–2092* ⊕ *www.larustica.co.za* ⌘ *Reservations essential* ▤ *AE, DC, MC, V.*

WHERE TO STAY

You can find just about every type of lodging in Johannesburg, from the stately and classic Saxon to the fun and funky Ten Bompas. Although these varied options are all worthy places to lay your head, the truth is most travelers only stop here for an overnight before they head out to their safari destination. With that in mind, we have compiled a list of places that are easy to get to from the airport and are located in well-secured areas so that you will feel safe and comfortable.

All the hotels we list offer no-smoking rooms, and many have no-smoking floors.

DOWNTOWN

$$$ ☷ **InterContinental Johannesburg O.R. Tambo Airport.** A few paces from international arrivals and adjacent to the car-rental park, this is a good choice for those who have a one-night layover. Unlike other airport hotels in South Africa, the InterContinental is very comfortable and upscale, with a chic African interior of warm woods and granite. Although it's 40 minutes from Sandton City, those who spend a few nights here do so for the business and meeting facilities and proximity to industrial areas. Rooms are soundproof and have blackout curtains, and the eighth-floor heated pool, gym, and spa offers jet-lag-specific treatments. The Quills bar on the ground level serves meals 24 hours. **Pros:** ideal for those who want to bypass Johannesburg; excellent paid-access arrivals facility with Internet, showers, and pressing facilities free to Diners Club card holders; great runway views from gym and pool. **Cons:** at the airport; large and impersonal. ✉ *O.R. Tambo Airport, opposite Terminal 3, Kempton Park* ☎ *011/961–5400* ⊕ *www.intercontinental.com* ➲ *138 rooms, 2 suites* ⚐ *In-room: phone, safe, Internet, Wi-Fi. In-hotel: restaurant, room service, bar, pool, gym, spa, laundry service, Wi-Fi, parking (paid)* ⊟ *AE, DC, MC, V* ⏐⚈⏐ *BP.*

ROSEBANK

$ ☷ **Clico.** This small, upmarket guesthouse in central Rosebank is a 60-year-old Cape Dutch house with a gracious garden and offers perhaps the best value in an area known for expensive accommodation. It has an engaging mix of old and new—Oregon pine floorboards, antique inlaid-wood side tables from Morocco, custom-made couches, and modern, whimsical sculptures like one by Anton Smit, of a woman floating above water. The bedroom suites are luxurious and have heated floors; one has wheelchair access. The superb food has a strong French influence, though often with a local twist, and the chef adapts his menu daily to whatever fresh ingredients he can purchase. **Pros:** 24-hour manned security and CCTV cameras; free Wi-Fi throughout the hotel; the restaurant serves breakfast daily, and lunch and dinner are available upon request. **Cons:** constant noise and dust from construction of the nearby Gautrain rail network; some of the on-site parking spaces are difficult to negotiate; noise from the pool activity travels to the suites. ✉ *27 Sturdee Ave., at Jellicoe Ave., Rosebank* ☎ *011/252–3300* ⊕ *www.clicoguesthouse.com* ➲ *9 suites, including 1 room with kitchen* ⚐ *In-room: refrigerator, safe, Wi-Fi. In-hotel: pool, laundry service, Internet terminal* ⊟ *DC, MC, V* ⏐⚈⏐ *BP.*

BEST BETS FOR JOHANNESBURG LODGING

Fodor's offers a selective listing of quality lodging experiences in every price range, from the city's best budget beds to its most sophisticated luxury hotels. Here, we've compiled our top recommendations by price and experience. The very best properties—in other words, those that provide a particularly remarkable experience in their price range—are designated in the listings with the Fodor's Choice logo.

Fodor's Choice ★

The Grace, $$$, p. 407
The Saxon, $$$$, p. 411
The Westcliff, $$$, p. 412

By Price

$

Clico, p. 405
Crowne Plaza Johannesburg–The Rosebank, $, p. 407
The Peech, $, p. 408

$$

The Orient (Pretoria), p. 423
Palazzo at Montecasino, p. 412
Sandton Sun, p. 411

$$$

The Grace, p. 407
Melrose Arch, p. 408
The Michelangelo, p. 411

Ten Bompas, p. 412
The Westcliff, p. 412

$$$$

Park Hyatt Hotel, p. 407
The Saxon, p. 411

By Experience

BEST HOTEL BARS

Melrose Arch, $$$, p. 408
Park Hyatt Hotel, $$$$, p. 407
The Westcliff, $$$, p. 412

BEST GYM

Fairlawns Boutique Hotel & Spa, $$$, p. 409
InterContinental Johannesburg O.R. Tambo Airport, $$$, p. 409
Park Hyatt Hotel, $$$$, p. 407

BEST FOR ROMANCE

Fairlawns Boutique Hotel & Spa, $$$, p. 409
The Grace, $$$, p. 407
Palazzo at Montecasino, $$$, p. 412
Ten Bompas, $$$, p. 412
The Westcliff, $$$, p. 412

BUSINESS TRAVEL

The Grace, $$$, p. 407
InterContinental Johannesburg Sandton Towers, $$, p. 409
Melrose Arch, $$$, p. 408
Michelangelo, $$$, p. 411
Park Hyatt Hotel, $$$$, p. 407
Sandton Sun, $$, p. 411

HIPSTER HOTELS

Melrose Arch, $$$, p. 408

Crowne Plaza Johannesburg–The Rosebank, $, p. 407
Ten Bompas, $$$, p. 412

BEST INTERIOR DESIGN

Melrose Arch, $$$, p. 408
Crowne Plaza Johannesburg–The Rosebank, $, p. 407
The Saxon, $$$$, p. 411
Sandton Sun, $$, p. 411
Ten Bompas, $$$, p. 412

BEST-KEPT SECRET

Fairlawns Boutique Hotel & Spa, $$$, p. 409
The Peech, $, p. 408
Ten Bompas, $$$, p. 412

$ ⚏ **Crowne Plaza Johannesburg–The Rosebank.** Following a major upgrade in May 2009, this hotel now carries the Crowne Plaza insignia. Jazzed-up and quirky public spaces—Louis XVI reproduction armchairs, white shaggy rugs, and the very popular Circle Bar with its beaded booths—make this the newest "it" spot for late-night revelry. Standard rooms are small but perfectly formed, with white vinyl armchairs and side tables. Most will love the black-glass bathroom cube in the deluxe rooms (except those who enjoy privacy—this is not the room to share with a buddy). The so-called Heavenly beds are just that, and directional lighting means you can read while your partner sleeps. Sony Bravia LCD screens with 28 satellite-TV channels and iPod docking stations are standard in every room. Rooms also feature good work spaces, with back-supporting swivel chairs and multiple plug adaptors at eye level. **Pros:** hip nightspot; great spa and gym. **Cons:** popular with partying locals; toilets in deluxe suites lack privacy. ⊠ *Tyrwhitt and Sturdee Aves., Rosebank* 🕾 *021/448–3600* ⊕ *www.therosebank.co.za* ⇰ *318 rooms, 24 suites.* ⚸ *In-room: safe, Wi-Fi. In-hotel: 2 restaurants, room service, bar, pool, gym, spa, laundry service, Wi-Fi, Internet terminal, parking (paid)* ⊟ *AE, DC, MC, V* ⓄⓅ *BP.*

$$$
Fodor's Choice
★
⚏ **The Grace.** Most of the visitors to the Grace are businesspeople drawn to the old world elegance behind the towering brick façade and concrete columns. It's also in the center of Rosebank and linked to the nearby mall and African crafts market by a first-floor sky bridge. Travelers rave about the breakfast, and the restaurant, called simply the Dining Room, has established itself as one of Johannesburg's culinary centers. One of the hotel's finest features is the rooftop garden and pool area, which has sweeping views of the northern suburbs' greenery. Thoughtful extras include transportation within a 10-km (6-mi) radius and tea and cake served in the lounge. **Pros:** free Wi-Fi for in-house guests throughout the hotel; direct access to malls via sky bridge; free transportation within 6-mi radius to shopping and sights. **Cons:** major construction nearby makes lots of noise and dust; constant noise from the busy road; not on airport shuttle route, although hotel will collect you from airport for a fee. ⊠ *54 Bath Ave., Rosebank* 🕾 *011/280–7200* ⊕ *www.thegrace.co.za* ⇰ *60 rooms, 13 suites* ⚸ *In-room: safe, DVD (some), Wi-Fi. In-hotel: restaurant, bar, pool, gym, spa, laundry service, Internet terminal, Wi-Fi, parking (free)* ⊟ *AE, DC, MC, V* ⓄⓅ *BP.*

$$$$ ⚏ **Park Hyatt Hotel.** This Hyatt is trendy and opulent, with lots of black, gold, and glass. Enormous picture windows reveal stunning views of the northern suburbs. Local art lines the walls in discreetly lit passageways, and there's an ultramodern restaurant, a wine bar, and a solar-heated pool on the roof. Sunday brunch is a favorite with guests and local families, and the lobby serves coffee and light meals. The hotel is adjacent to Rosebank's major shopping malls. **Pros:** direct basement access to the adjoining malls; very cosmopolitan atmosphere; bustling lobby area is frequently used for meetings. **Cons:** questionable security, as the hotel has multiple access points; near major construction. ⊠ *191 Oxford Rd., Rosebank* ✆ *Box 1536, Saxonwold 2132* 🕾 *011/280–1234* ⊕ *www.johannesburg.park.hyatt.com* ⇰ *244 rooms* ⚸ *In-room: safe, Internet,*

DVD (some). In-hotel: 2 restaurants, room service, bar, pool, gym, laundry service Internet terminal, parking (paid) ⊟ *AE, DC, MC, V.*

$ ★ **The Peech.** The smart traveler stays here for the affordable rates; uncluttered, but comfortable interiors; and quality restaurant. Owner James Peech has something of a cult following as a result of his engaging London-advertising-boss-turned-hotelier personality with Cape Town–based folk from the film, TV, and advertising industries who make this their work-week home. You're likely to bump into an agency boss or TV executive at breakfast. Restaurant and meeting rooms are in the main house, with other suites in the garden. Those who care about their eco footprint will appreciate solar water heating, gray-water reticulation, and other green practices. The Peech is just a stone's throw from Melrose Arch and is adjacent to major Planet Fitness health club, which is available to guests for R100 per visit. The on-site bistro (with champagne bar) is open daily, serving breakfast, lunch, and dinner. There are monthly wine events and a seasonally changing menu. **Pros:** fabulous rain showerheads and Molton Brown toiletries in every bathroom; free Wi-Fi throughout the hotel and iPod docking stations in every room; every room has a private outdoor space. **Cons:** rooms and the neighboring gym overlook the pool; fee to use the gym. ⊠ *61 North St., Rosebank* ☎ *011/537–9797* ⊕ *www.thepeech.co.za* ⊅ *16 rooms* ♿ *In-room: safe, Wi-Fi. In-hotel: restaurant, room service, bar, pool, laundry service, parking (free)* ⊟ *AE, DC, MC, V* |◎| *BP.*

MELROSE ARCH

$$$ ★ **Melrose Arch.** This ultramodern hotel is within the shopping, dining, and residential enclave Melrose Arch. The eclectic decor mixes modern and traditional African influences, with high-tech colored lighting throughout and sculptures, baskets, and furnishings all highlighting the African locale. Even the elevators reflect this mix, with one representing the African day and the other, almost completely dark, suggesting the night. Mainly catering to businesspeople, the hotel has free Wi-Fi access in each room and in the public areas, including the warm, mahogany-clad library bar. The rooms are well equipped, and each has a view of the pool and garden. The pool area highlights the eccentric and modern taste that is echoed throughout the hotel, with trees planted in larger-than-life steel buckets, and tables and chairs set out in a few inches of water. Sip a cocktail here while soaking your feet in the heated pool, which has music piped underwater. Meals are offered at the stylish fusion restaurant, March. **Pros:** Melrose Arch is a high-security gated community with good dining and shopping options within safe walking distance; the Library bar is a favorite with well-heeled executives. **Cons:** hipster decor might not appeal to everyone; some might find it hard to relax in a high-energy environment; no on-site gym, but Virgin Active Gym is available at R20 per visit within walking distance. ⊠ *1 Melrose Sq., Melrose Arch* ☎ *011/214–6666* ⊕ *www.africanpridehotels.com/melrosearch* ⊅ *117 rooms, 1 suite* ♿ *In-room: safe, DVD, Internet, Wi-Fi. In-hotel: restaurant, room service, bars, pool, Internet terminal, laundry service* ⊟ *AE, DC, MC, V.*

$$$$ **#1 Melrose Blvd.** If you're going to be in town for a few days, or just like having your own space, then the apartments at #1 Melrose Blvd

are the perfect option; if you're traveling with a group there are three two-bedroom apartments, as well as one three-bedroom penthouse with a plunge pool. Because the hotel is located in the gated Melrose Arch community, you'll have no problem heading out at night for a bite to eat or a drink at one of the area's numerous bars and restaurants. There are also a number of shops, from pharmacies to stationery stores, in case you forgot to pack anything. The apartments are located on the third floor of an office building and overlook an inner courtyard with a serenely bubbling fountain. Each apartment has a balcony with *braai* (barbecue) facilities if you feel like entertaining, a full kitchen that includes a washer and dryer, and two bathrooms with Molton Brown products. Each guest receives complimentary breakfast vouchers that are redeemable at three restaurants (two are kosher) within walking distance, although a light breakfast (fruit, yogurt, milk, and muesli) is provided in the rooms. There's also a DVD library available for your perusal if you feel like staying in one night. **Pros:** safe area, walkable to numerous shops, restaurants, and bars; airport shuttles and tours can be arranged; breakfast vouchers are provided for three nearby restaurants. **Cons:** you do your own dishes and laundry; can be a bit lonely at night when the offices are closed. ⊠ *1 Melrose Blvd., Melrose Arch* ☎ *83/555-4793* ⊕ *www.1melrose.com* ➴ *6 apartments* ⚘ *In-room: safe, kitchen, refrigerator, DVD, Wi-Fi. In-hotel: laundry facilities, laundry service, Internet terminal, parking (free)* ⊟ *AE, MC, V* ❙◯❙ *BP.*

SANDTON

$$$ ▦ **Fairlawns Boutique Hotel & Spa.** Set in a residential area, this gracious boutique hotel was once a private home owned by the Oppenheimer family. Each individually decorated suite mimics classic European style (the honeymoon suite's canopied bed is a replica of one from Versailles), making guests feel like royalty. Large windows overlook the manicured gardens, and working fireplaces add to the romance. The large grounds with sweeping lawns and rose beds include a pool and a Balinese-themed spa. There's also well-equipped gym, an à la carte restaurant, and conference facilities. **Pros:** well-stocked library; complimentary shuttle service to Sandton City mall. **Cons:** service can be slow; property could use some updating. ⊠ *Alma Rd., Morningside Manor, Sandton* ☎ *011/804-2540* ⊕ *www.fairlawns.co.za* ➴ *19 suites* ⚘ *In-room: safe, DVD, Internet, Wi-Fi. In-hotel: restaurant, room service, bar, pool, gym, spa, laundry service, Wi-Fi, parking (free), no kids under 12* ⊟ *AE, DC, MC, V* ❙◯❙ *BP.*

$$ ▦ **InterContinental Johannesburg Sandton Towers.** Although it's not directly connected to Sandton City, Johannesburg's premier mall, the way some other hotels are, keen shoppers will love staying here for the proximity without presence. Smart and upscale in every way, this recently revamped hotel delivers an Afro-chic esthetic in the form of African art and sculpture and rooms decorated in earth tones. Despite its large size, the hotel's staff strives to deliver intimate service, which is especially useful for business travelers who form the main client base. **Pros:** free Wi-Fi throughout the hotel; free morning newspaper; international adaptors provided in the rooms; room windows open. **Cons:** easy to

7

Other Northern Suburbs Neighborhoods

While Saxonwold, Parkview, and Parktown are where you'll find most of the sights in the northern suburbs, the nearby suburbs of Rosebank, Greenside, Parkhurst, Sandton, and Melrose Arch are home to some of the best restaurants and hotels in Johannesburg. The Sandton, Melrose Arch, and Rosebank areas have seen massive growth in recent years in the number of top-quality hotels, and these suburbs provide the safest accommodation with easy access to the city's top restaurants and shopping options.

Originally a farm known as Rosemill Orchards, today **Rosebank** is home to upmarket shopping malls, restaurants, hotels, and art galleries. It's frequented by well-to-do locals and tourists. At the **Rosebank Rooftop Market,** in the Rosebank Mall's large parking lot and open every Sunday, everything and anything can be purchased, from crafts and jewelry to clothes and plants. The **African Craft Market,** open daily, is adjacent to the mall and is open every day. It is popular for its curios and African art. Clubs, bars, galleries, and an art-house cinema add flavor to this trendy area.

Close to Rosebank, the suburb of **Greenside** is filled with popular restaurants. **Gleneagles Road** is lined with small eateries, including Italian, Indian, Portuguese, and Japanese restaurants, along with those offering a more conventional range of meats, fish, and pasta. Over the weekend, cars fill the streets and people pack the sidewalks. The adjacent suburb of **Emmarentia** is also benefiting from Greenside's popularity, with small restaurants popping up. The **Emmarentia Dam** and gardens, a popular dog-walking and picnic spot, is also a draw.

Also near Rosebank, **Parkhurst,** a neighborhood full of freshly renovated homes and young couples, has some of the trendiest restaurants in Johannesburg. There are more than a dozen places to eat on **4th Avenue** alone. Antiques shops and boutique stores selling furniture and children's clothes also dot the street.

Close to both Rosebank and Sandton, **Melrose Arch** is an upmarket shopping, dining, and business district that features a handful of good restaurants and boutiques. This European-style lifestyle center offers pleasant accommodations, shopping and dining in a relaxed and safe setting.

Originally a residential area, **Sandton** is now home to the Johannesburg Stock Exchange and the enormous Sandton Convention Centre, which hosts large conferences and concerts.

In the large and expensive **Sandton City Shopping Centre** and adjacent open-air **Nelson Mandela Square** (also known as Sandton Square), you'll find trendy restaurants selling good but pricey food. There's also a small theater, Old Mutual Theater on the Square, which favors short, lightweight productions such as stand-up comedy. The convention center is next to the square.

But Sandton is not all glitz and glamour—a few miles from the Sandton City Shopping Centre and part of the large suburb is the township of **Alexandra,** home to an estimated 350,000 people, mostly living in overcrowded, squalid conditions in shacks and rented run-down houses.

get lost with the masses; public areas used extensively by locals for meetings. ⊠ *Maude and Fifth Sts., Sandton* ☎ *011/780–5555* ⊕ *www. intercontinental.com* ⟳ *293 rooms* ⚂ *In-room: safe, refrigerator, DVD, Internet, Wi-Fi. In-hotel: restaurant, room service, bar, pool, gym, spa, laundry service, Internet terminal, Wi-Fi, parking (paid)* ▤ *AE, DC, MC, V* ⑂ *BP.*

$$$ ⊡ **The Michelangelo.** As though taken from a street in Florence, this hotel forms the northern facade of much-touted piazza-inspired Nelson Mandela Square, also called Sandton Square. Although the hotel is unusually tasteful, even grand, the square lacks the authenticity of an Italian piazza. Still, this hotel has all the class, comforts, and facilities you'd expect from a top establishment. The atrium-style pool area is notable. The restaurant, Piccolo Mondo, focuses on Mediterranean cuisine and features plenty of seafood from Mozambique, such as rock cod, prawns, lobsters, langoustines, and mussels. **Pros:** great shopping (especially for designer labels and high-fashion items from Gucci and Louis Vuitton) in the Square and adjoining Sandton Sun Mall; high security is omnipresent. **Cons:** Nelson Mandela Square is very popular and never quiet; service can be inattentive at times. ⊠ *West St., Nelson Mandela Sq., Sandton* ⌖ *Box 784682, Sandton 2146* ☎ *011/282–7000* ⊕ *www. michelangelo.co.za* ⟳ *242 rooms* ⚂ *In-room: safe, DVD (some), Internet. In-hotel: restaurant, room service, bars, pool, gym, Internet terminal, Wi-Fi, parking (paid)* ▤ *AE, DC, MC, V.*

$$ ⊡ **Sandton Sun.** One of the first luxury hotels to open in Sandton, the Sun was updated in 2008 and the public areas have moved away from '80s glam to reflect a designer African feel. Elegant and luxurious, the new look draws inspiration from bold earth tones and sculptural baobab trees. Guest rooms are small but superbly laid out, with understated lighting and pared-down furniture, and have maintained all the functionality expected from a five-star property. The new spa on the mezzanine level includes eight treatment rooms and offers everything from massages and facials to waxing and manicures. **Pros:** linked to Sandton City, Johannesburg's premier mall, by a first-floor sky bridge; business suites have home-automation technology and video conferencing; excellent restaurants are within easy walking distance. **Cons:** shopping's the name of the game here—if conspicuous consumption bothers you, stay elsewhere; the service can be hit and miss. ⊠ *Sandton City, 5th St. and Alice La., Sandton* ☎ *011/780–5000* ⊕ *www.southernsun.com* ⟳ *334 rooms* ⚂ *In-room: safe, refrigerator, DVD (some), Wi-Fi. In-hotel: 2 restaurants, room service, pool, gym, spa, laundry service, Internet terminal, Wi-Fi, parking (paid)* ▤ *AE, DC, MC, V.*

SANDHURST

$$$$ ⊡ **The Saxon.** In the exclusive suburb of Sandhurst, adjacent to the
Fodor's Choice commercial and shopping center of Sandton, the Saxon has repeatedly
★ received awards for its excellence. Heads of state have stayed here, including Nelson Mandela, who came here after his release from prison and to work on his autobiography, *Long Walk to Freedom*. The butlers pride themselves on keeping files on their guests, right down to what they order from the bar. An azure pool adjoins the sleek, modern building. Inside, the feeling is calm and classical, and there's an extensive

7

African art collection on display throughout the hotel. Rooms are huge, with big bay windows overlooking the gardens or pool. Large-screen TVs, DVD players, surround sound, and a workstation with a fast Internet connection are standard. The delightful restaurant has a wonderful setting. **Pros:** possibly the most exclusive address in Gauteng; exceptionally high security; good for business travelers or high-profile folk who'd rather not see anyone else in the corridors. **Cons:** some might find the atmosphere a bit snooty; children under 14 not welcome in restaurant. ✉ *36 Saxon Rd., Sandhurst* ☎ *011/292–6000* ⊕ *www.thesaxon.com* ↺ *27 suites* ⚂ *In-room: DVD, Internet, Wi-Fi. In-hotel: restaurant, room service, bar, pools, gym, spa, laundry service, Internet terminal, Wi-Fi, parking (free)* ▤ *AE, DC, MC, V* ⦿ *BP.*

$$$ 🏨 **Ten Bompas.** This is a hotel-cum-restaurant and art gallery is small and
★ luxurious, and the decor is minimalist, with carefully chosen African art. Suites, each done by a different interior designer, have separate lounges and bedrooms, with fireplaces, complimentary minibars, and satellite TV. You can also peruse brochures for the hotel's partner game lodges in the far north of Kruger National Park. Sides, the restaurant, receives consistently good reviews. Its menu changes with the seasons. The food is exciting and fresh: roasted artichoke, mozzarella, and olive salad and roast-duck-and-orange risotto, for example. It also has a well-stocked wine cellar. **Pros:** sophisticated without being snooty; complimentary bar; complimentary same-day laundry service. **Cons:** a taxi-ride away from shopping or sightseeing. ✉ *10 Bompas Rd., Dunkeld West* ⌂ *Box 786064, Sandton 2146* ☎ *011/325–2442* ⊕ *www.tenbompas.com* ↺ *10 suites* ⚂ *In-room: safe, Internet, Wi-Fi. In-hotel: restaurant, room service, bar, pool, gym, laundry service, Internet terminal, Wi-Fi, parking (free)* ▤ *AE, DC, MC, V* ⦿ *BP.*

WESTCLIFF

$$$ 🏨 **The Westcliff.** This landmark hotel and Johannesburg icon was built
★ on a steep hill and has wide views of the northern suburbs and the Johannesburg Zoo. You're taken to your destination by a shuttle service, winding your way up twisting lanes. Bedrooms are in multistory villas, many with balconies. Enormous bathrooms have marble vanities and huge soaking tubs. The cuisine, service, and facilities are all top-notch. The Westcliff is known throughout the city for its lavish Sunday brunch for which reservations are recommended. **Pros:** Molton Brown bath products; sexy Polo lounge bar; stellar DVD collection of Academy Award winners; suites are very roomy. **Cons:** lots of stairs and no elevator; main pool is within public view of the restaurant and bar; there's nothing of note within walking distance; hefty room-service surcharge. ✉ *67 Jan Smuts Ave., Westcliff* ☎ *011/646–2400* ⊕ *www.westcliffhotel.orient-express.com* ↺ *104 rooms, 14 suites* ⚂ *In-room: DVD, Internet. In-hotel: restaurant, room service, bar, tennis court, pools, gym, spa, laundry service, Internet terminal, Wi-Fi, parking (free)* ▤ *AE, DC, MC, V.*

FOURWAYS

$$ 🏨 **Palazzo at Montecasino.** Built in the style of a Tuscan villa, the hotel is
★ set among formal herb gardens. Public rooms are on a grand scale, and the whole hotel is decorated in gilt, marble, and terra-cotta, with small

touches of trompe l'oeil. The rooms are spacious, with rich tapestry-style draperies, canopied beds, and gilt-framed mirrors and prints. Large picture windows and light terra-cotta tiles lighten the effect. The hotel is done with so much more style, attention to detail, and class than the adjacent casino and mall that it's almost impossible to believe they're connected. This is a good choice for a business stay, but be aware that its relatively northern location is closer to the business area of Bryanston and Sandton than downtown Johannesburg. Service is impeccable. **Pros:** neighboring casino complex has malls, cinemas, and major theater; the hotel's grounds contain great gardens and a pool. **Cons:** gridlocked traffic in the area means longer than usual traffic jams; as in the casino, the decor is faux-Tuscan. ⊠ *Montecasino Blvd., Fourways* ⬧ *Private Bag X125, Bryanston 2021* 🕿 *011/510–3000* ⊕ *www.southernsun.com* ⤵ *246 rooms, 12 suites* ⬧ *In-room: safe, DVD, Internet, Wi-Fi. In-hotel: restaurant, bar, pool, gym, laundry service, Internet terminal, Wi-Fi, parking (paid)* ▤ *AE, DC, MC, V.*

NIGHTLIFE AND THE ARTS

The best place to find out what's going on is in the "Tonight" section of the **Star** (⊕ *www.tonight.co.za*) , Johannesburg's major daily. For a comprehensive guide, read the "Friday" section of the weekly **Mail & Guardian** (⊕ *www.mg.co.za*). A useful Web site for event details is **JHBLive** (⊕ *www.jhblive.com*). Almost all major performances and many smaller ones can be booked through **Computicket** (🕿 *083/915–8000 or 011/340–8000* ⊕ *www.computicket.com*).

NIGHTLIFE

Johannesburg comes alive after dark, and whether you're a rebellious punk rocker or a suave executive, there's always something to do. Rivonia and the business district of Sandton have become trendy spots for young, hip professionals and their style-conscious friends, and the old neighborhood of Greenside still has streets filled with lively little bars and restaurants and a sprinkling of clubs. The Newtown Cultural Precinct, an old area that started as a produce market, has undergone a successful rejuvenation. Now clean and brightly lighted, it's home to the Market Theatre complex, which includes dance club Carfax and other entertainment venues. The suburb of Norwood also has a central street with a good selection of small restaurants and bars. To dine and dance in one go, you should venture to one of these suburbs or visit one of the casino complexes, such as the popular Montecasino in Fourways or Emperor's Palace next to the O.R. Tambo Airport.

BARS AND PUBS

★ Dress stylishly for **Café Vacca Matta** (⊠ *Montecasino, William Nicol Dr., Fourways* 🕿 *011/511–0511*), a trendy bar and restaurant where a sometimes-snobbish crowd dances to Top 40 hits.

★ **Capitol Music Café** (⊠ *Tyrwhitt and Keyes Aves., Rosebank* 🕿 *011/880–0033*) is a happening vinyl shop and bar, where DJs play what they have just bought and an eclectic crowd gathers.

Kwaito

Kwaito is a uniquely South African music genre, rooted in house, raga (a subgenre of reggae), hip-hop, and local rhythms. It emerged from the country's townships post-apartheid and gets its name, some say, from township slang for "cool talk." Its hard-pumping bass beats, lightly slowed down from a house rhythm, are topped with rambled-off lyrics in a style reminiscent of American rap. It's as much a lifestyle as it is a music genre, with its own ways of dancing and dressing.

The best-selling kwaito musicians (and kwaito DJs) have superstar status in South Africa, but they have a less unsavory reputation than their American hip-hop equivalents. Though some kwaito acts stand accused of sexism and vulgar lyrics, the kwaito attitude is generally quite respectable. Lyrics are often about banning guns or respecting women, or they comment on murder, rape, AIDS, and unemployment. One kwaito star, Zola—named after an impoverished Soweto community—has his own long-running TV series, in which he works to improve people's lives. His music is featured in the 2006 Academy Award–winning movie *Tsotsi*. Other chart-topping kwaito stars include Mandoza, whose catchy, powerful songs have earned him several awards and crossover appeal; Arthur Mafikizolo; Mdu; the Brothers of Peace; and Mzekezeke, an enigmatic masked singer.

—Riaan Wolmarans

★ Greenside's **Gleneagles Road** is a good place to go for a night of bar-hopping. **Gin** (⊠ *12 Gleneagles Rd., Greenside* ☎ *072/478–2592*) is a hip but relaxed spot that can get crowded. **Tokyo Star** (⊠ *Shop 1, Comtex House, 26 Gleneagles Rd., Greenside* ☎ *072/478–2592*) is a glitzy and trendy bar. The vibey **Fratelli's** (⊠ *12 Gleneagles Rd., Greenside* ☎ *011/646–9573*) is frequented by an energetic young crowd.

CLUBS

Jo'burg's clubs are usually not too expensive. On a normal club night, or for B-list local bands, you'll pay between R20 and R50 to get in. When dance parties or bigger events take place (or big-name DJs and musicians appear), expect to pay R60 to R150. Below are just some of the city's established clubs.

★ **Back 2 Basix** (⊠ *Perth and Lancaster Rds., Westdene* ☎ *011/726–6857*) is a laid-back restaurant and music venue with top local folk, pop, and rock musicians performing on weekends and most weeknights. **Back o' the Moon** (⊠ *Gold Reef City Casino, Ormonde* ☎ *011/496–1423* ⊕ *www.backofthemoon.co.za*) is a modern interpretation of an iconic 1950s bar in Sophiatown, a suburb destroyed during apartheid by forced removals. Vibey live entertainment every evening counters the clanging slot machines outside. The atmosphere is classy and the food good. It's closed Monday, and reservations are essential.

Fodor's Choice
★ Big parties happen at **Carfax** (⊠ *39 Pim St., Newtown* ☎ *011/834–9187*), a converted factory building. Performance art, dance events with guest DJs, and rock shows draw a selection of the town's more interesting people.

THE ARTS

THEATER

Joburg Theatre Complex (✉ *123 Loveday St., Braamfontein* ☎ *011/877–6800* ⊕ *www.showbusiness.co.za*) is Jo'burg's main cultural venue and the home of the South African Ballet Theatre. It contains the enormous Nelson Mandela Theatre and the smaller People's and Tesson theaters. Many international productions are staged here, but there's also a good balance of local material, such as the annual pantomime by Janice Honeyman, which satirizes South Africans uproariously.

Occupying an old produce market that dates from the early 1900s, the **Market Theatre** (✉ *Bree and Margaret Mcingana Sts., Newtown* ☎ *011/832–1641* ⊕ *www.markettheatre.co.za*) has a delightful vintage look. In the 1980s the Market played a key role in bravely staging protest theater against the apartheid regime—often to local and eventually critical acclaim. Plays like *The Island,* about Robben Island, and *Sarafina!,* denouncing the inferior Bantu education, made their debuts here. Today theater productions encompass everything from plays with an African focus by Athol Fugard and Gibson Kente to comedies imported from London's West End. The theater occasionally features traditional African music and jazz performances. Experimental plays test audience approval at the Market Theatre Laboratory, just across Bree Street. The complex also has a good bar and restaurant and an art gallery.

SHOPPING

Whether you're after designer clothes, the latest books or DVDs, high-quality African art, or glamorous gifts, Johannesburg offers outstanding shopping opportunities. Dozens of malls, galleries, and curio shops are scattered throughout the city, often selling the same goods at widely different prices. It's best to shop around.

MARKETS

At the city's several markets, bargaining can get you a great price, although it's not as expected here as in other countries. At the African Craft Market in particular, bargain hard by offering half the asking price, and then work your way up to about two thirds of the price if you're interested in the item. Take your time before you buy anything, as you will see similar crafts at different stalls, and the prices may vary considerably. Watch out for inferior goods, pirated DVDs and CDs, and fake designer clothes.

The **African Craft Market,** between the Rosebank Mall and the Zone, has a huge variety of African crafts from Cape to Cairo, all displayed to the background beat of traditional African music. ✉ *Cradock Ave. and Baker St., Rosebank* ☎ *011/880–2906* ⊙ *Daily 9–5.*

If you're into healthful living, visit the **Michael Mount Organic Market,** where homemade and organically grown food, flowers, handmade clothes and shoes, and other products clamor for your clean-living attention. Taste the cheeses. The quality of the products is probably the best you'll find at any market in the country, but the selection is relatively

Johannesburg and the World Cup

After years or preparation and planning, South Africa is ready to host the largest sporting event in the world, the World Cup, in 2010. The month-long tournament will be held at venues across South Africa, but Jo'burg will host the prestigious opening ceremony as well as the grand finale.

World Cup games will be played at the two main stadiums in Johannesburg (Soccer City and Ellis Park) and in two stadiums near the city (Loftus Versfeld and Royal Bafokeng). All have been upgraded for the tournament. The four stadiums will host 26 matches.

Soccer City, in Soweto, will host the opening ceremony and the final match. The stadium can seat more than 90,000 fans.

Address: Nasrec Road, Doornfontein, Johannesburg

Match Schedule: June 11, 14, 17, 20, 23, 27, and July 2 and 11

Ellis Park is the venue for additional matches. The stadium holds more than 60,000 people and is east of the city center.

Address: Staib Street, Doornfontein, Johannesburg

Match Schedule: June 12, 15, 18, 21, 24, 28, and July 3

Loftus Versfeld Stadium, a little farther afield in Pretoria, but still easily accessible from Johannesburg, seats 45,000 people.

Address: Kirknees Street, Sunnyside, Pretoria

Match Schedule: June 13, 16, 19, 23, 25, and 29

Royal Bafokeng Stadium, only two hours' drive from Johannesburg, has 42,000 seats.

Address: R565, Rustenberg

Match Schedule: June 12, 15, 19, 22, 24, and 26

Transportation: Fans will be required to use park-and-ride facilities so will not be able to use private vehicles or taxis to approach the stadiums. Public transport for the tournament has not been finalized at this writing; the FIFA Web site has up-to-date information.

Information: ☎ *011/375–5555 Johannesburg Tourism Company* ⊕ *www.joburg.org.za/fifaworldcup.*

⇨ *For more information, see World Cup 411, in Chapter 1.*

small. ✉ *Bryanston Dr. and Culross Rd., Bryanston* ☎ *011/706–3671* ⊗ *Thurs. and Sat. 9–3.*

Rosebank's **Rooftop Market** has become a Sunday tradition in the city. More than 600 stalls sell African and Western crafts, antiques, books, food, art, trinkets, CDs, jewelry and clothes. Frequently, African musicians, dancers, and other entertainers delight the crowds. ✉ *Rosebank Mall, 50 Bath Ave., Rosebank* ☎ *011/442–4488* ⊗ *Sun. 9–5.*

SPECIALTY STORES
AFRICAN ARTS AND CRAFTS

Art Africa brings together a dazzling selection of ethnic arts, crafts, and artifacts from across the continent and also sells funky items, such as tin lizards and wooden animals, that are produced in community empowerment projects that uplift and benefit the craftsmen and their communities. ✉ *62 Tyrone Ave., Parkview* ☎ *011/486–2052.*

The **Everard Read Gallery,** established in 1912, is one of the largest privately owned galleries in the world. It acts as an agent for several important South African artists. The gallery specializes in wildlife paintings and sculpture. ✉ *6 Jellicoe Ave., Rosebank* ☎ *011/788–4805.*

The highly successful, three-decade-old **Goodman Gallery** presents exciting monthly exhibitions by the stars of contemporary South African art, including Norman Catherine, William Kentridge, and Deborah Bell. ✉ *163 Jan Smuts Ave., Parkwood* ☎ *011/788–1113.*

GOLD AND DIAMONDS

Krugerrands, which carry images of President Paul Kruger and a springbok on either side, are among the most famous gold coins minted today. They lost some of their luster during the apartheid years, when they were banned internationally. Krugerrands are sold individually or in sets containing coins of 1 ounce, ½ ounce, ¼ ounce, and 1/10 ounce of pure gold. You can buy Krugerrands through most city banks, and several branches of First National Bank sell them over the counter. The most convenient branches are in the Sandton City Shopping Centre and in Rosebank.

South Africa is also diamond country. The world's biggest diamond, the 3,106-carat Cullinan, was found in the town of the same name (near present-day Tshwane) in 1905 and is now among the British crown jewels.

Charles Greig (✉ *Hyde Park Corner, Jan Smuts Ave., Hyde Park* ☎ *011/325–4477* ⊕ *www.charlesgreig.co.za*) sells a dazzling array of diamonds.

Schwartz Jewellers (✉ *Sandton City Shopping Centre, Sandton* ☎ *011/783–1717*) is a diamond wholesaler and manufacturing jeweler. It offers a large range of classical and ethnic African pieces and a custom design service.

SIDE TRIPS FROM JOHANNESBURG

About an hour north of Johannesburg (depending on the traffic—on a bad day it can take more than two hours), Pretoria, the country's capital, is within the larger metropolitan area of Tshwane (pronounced *chwa*-aah-neh). About an hour and a half from Johannesburg is the Cradle of Humankind, declared a World Heritage Site for its rich fossil record reflecting the history of humanity over the past 3 million years or so. To the north of Johannesburg, not far from the Cradle of Humankind, lies the Magaliesberg (pronounced muh-*xuh*-lees-berg," where the first *g* is pronounced like the *ch* in *Chanukah*), a gentle, ancient mountain range and leisure area, where you can get a restful break amid lovely mountain scenery, farmlands, and quiet country roads. Sun City, a multifaceted entertainment and casino complex comprising hotels, championship golf courses, and a water park, is about a two-hour drive from Johannesburg—well worth a visit if you have the time.

PRETORIA

The city of Pretoria, 48 km (30 mi) north of Johannesburg, lies within the Tshwane metropolitan area, which was formed in 2000 when Pretoria and its surrounding areas—Centurion, the townships of Atteridgeville, Mamelodi, and Shoshanguve, and neighboring areas—merged under a single municipal authority. The country's administrative capital and home to many senior politicians and diplomats, Pretoria is a pleasant city, with historic buildings and a city center that is easily explored on foot.

Founded in 1855, the city was named after Afrikaner leader Andries Pretorius, one of the Voortrekkers (pronounced *fooer*-treka) who moved from the Cape to escape British rule. In 1860 it became the capital of the independent Transvaal Voortrekker Republic. After the South African War of 1899–1902 (the Second Anglo-Boer War), the city became the capital of the then British colony, and in 1910 it was named the administrative capital of the Union of South Africa. In 1948, when the National Party came to power, Pretoria became the seat of the apartheid government. In 1964 the Rivonia Treason Trial (named for the Johannesburg suburb where 19 ANC leaders were arrested in 1963) was held here, and Nelson Mandela and seven of his colleagues were sentenced to life in prison.

In 2008 the Tshwane Metropolitan Council (*Tshwane* is a reference to the indigenous people who lived in the area before the Afrikaners arrived) announced its intention to change street names throughout the metropolitan area to reflect the country's cultural diversity, but this process has not yet begun.

GETTING HERE AND AROUND

There are a few options for getting to Pretoria. Beginning in 2010, the Gautrain will offer a high-speed connection between O.R. Tambo International Airport and Johannesburg and Pretoria. Alternatively, a rental car gives you the flexibility to explore the city at your leisure, and private transfers are offered by all of O.R. Tambo's airport transfer companies (⇨ *Air Travel, in Planning, at the beginning of the chapter*). It takes at least an hour to travel from Johannesburg to Pretoria in the Tshwane metropolitan area on the N1 (two hours if the traffic is bad, which happens quite regularly).

TIMING AND PRECAUTIONS

If you want to see everything, schedule an entire day here. A side trip to the Cullinan Diamond Mine will take at least half a day. Pretoria is not as notorious as Johannesburg for crime, but drive with your car doors locked and don't have bags or valuables visible or you could become a target of a "hit-and-grab."

VISITOR INFORMATION

Covering Pretoria, Centurion, Atteridgeville, Mamelodi, and surrounds, the Tshwane Tourism Information Centre has friendly staff, plenty of pamphlets and printed guides, and a 24-hour info line.

Visitor Information **Tshwane Tourism Information Centre** (☎ *012/358–1430* ⊕ *www.tshwane.gov.za*).

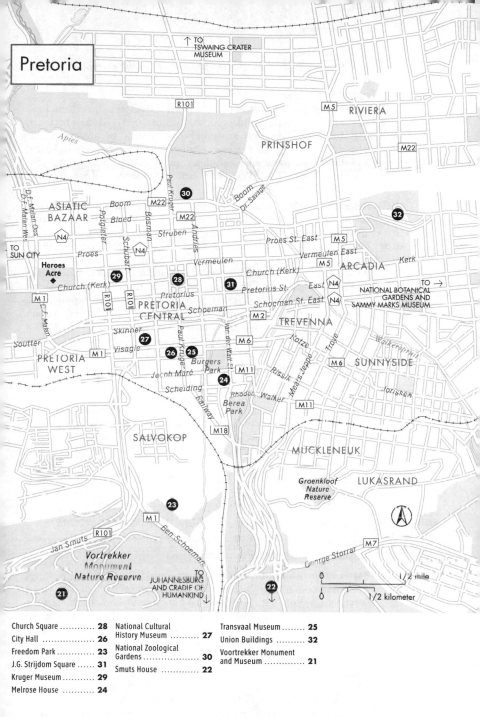

Pretoria

EXPLORING

Numbers in the text correspond to numbers in the margin and on the Pretoria map.

TOP ATTRACTIONS

㉗ ★ **National Cultural History Museum.** This museum offers an insightful look at the country's indigenous cultures. You can marvel at San rock art, African headdresses, clay sculptures, and several permanent collections of archaeological material dealing with Pretoria, South Africa, and the many people who call this country home. The museum also has a restaurant. ⊠ *149 Visagie St., between Bosman and Schubart Sts.* ☎ *012/324–6082* ⊠ *R20* ⊙ *Daily 8–4.*

㉚ ⓒ Fodor'sChoice ★ **National Zoological Gardens.** The city's zoo, covering nearly 200 acres, is considered one of the world's best, with about 9,000 animals from almost every continent (including rare Komodo dragons, the world's largest lizards). The animal enclosures here are much larger than those of most zoos. Like any modern zoo worth its name, this is just the public facade for a much larger organization that specializes in the research and breeding of endangered species. It includes an aquarium (with Africa's largest collection of freshwater fish) and reptile park, where the king crocodiles and the impressive collection of snakes don't fail to intimidate. A cable car transports you high above the zoo to a hilltop lookout, and it's a fun, worthwhile ride. It's also a good idea to rent a golf cart, so you can move more quickly between enclosures for the staggered feeding times each morning and afternoon. ⊠ *Boom St.* ☎ *012/328–3265* ⊕ *www.zoo.ac.za* ⊠ *R45* ⊙ *Daily 8:30–5:30.*

WORTH NOTING

㉘ **Church Square.** Anton van Wouw's statue of President Paul Kruger, surrounded by sentries, dominates this pleasant square, which is flanked by some of the city's most historic buildings: the Old Raadsaal (Council Chamber), designed by Dutch architect Sytze Wierda; the Palace of Justice (used as a military hospital during the South African War), built in early Italian Renaissance style; and the modern Provincial Administration Building. On Wednesday mornings you can watch a military parade and flag-raising. ⊠ *Bordered by Paul Kruger and Church Sts.*

NEED A BREAK? In a building dating from 1904, **Café Riche** (⊠ *Church Sq.* ☎ *012/328–3173*) is one of the better coffee shops in the center of town. It also serves *tramezzini* (toasted sandwiches) and salads.

㉖ **City Hall.** This imposing structure has a semi-Italian style that borrows freely from classical architecture. A tympanum on the front, by Coert Steynberg, one of South Africa's most famous sculptors, symbolizes the growth and development of the city. Statues of Andries Pretorius, the city's founder, and his son Marthinus, stand in the square fronting the building, and relief panels depict the founding in 1855. ⊠ *Visagie and Paul Kruger Sts.* ☎ *012/358–8949* ⊠ *Free* ⊙ *Weekdays 8–4.*

㉓ **Freedom Park.** Set to open in early 2010, the 129-acre Freedom Park will be a "one-stop-heritage-shop" for South Africa, dedicated to the struggle for freedom and humanity, as well as other aspects of South African heritage, including human evolution. At Salvokop, a prominent hill at the entrance to Pretoria on the highway from Johannesburg, and within view of the Voortrekker Monument (⇨ *below*), the site will comprise a memorial, interactive museum, archives, and a garden of remembrance. The park was launched in 2002 by President Thabo Mbeki, who said, "We dedicate this day to all the heroes and heroines in this country and the rest of the world who sacrificed in many ways and surrendered their lives so that we could be free." Individual South African, African, and global leaders who made significant contributions to the struggle against oppression, exploitation, racism, and other forms of discrimination will be honored, including Kwame Nkrumah, who led Ghana to become Africa's first independent country in 1957, and revolutionary icon Che Guevara. Call or check the Web site for up-to-date admission prices and hours. ⊠ *Glen Manor Office Park, Building 3, at Frikie de Beer St. and Glen Manor Ave.* ☎ *012/361–0021* ⊕ *www. freedompark.co.za.*

③ **J.G. Strijdom Square.** This square was once dominated by a huge bust of former pro-apartheid prime minister J.G. Strijdom. However, on May 31, 2001—exactly 40 years to the day after the government declared South Africa a republic—the supporting structure of the whole edifice crumbled, and Strijdom fell unceremoniously into the parking garage under the square. All that remains is a statue by Danie de Jager of charging horses atop a high column. ⊠ *Church and van der Walt Sts.*

㉙ **Kruger Museum.** This was once the residence of Paul Kruger, president of the South African republic between 1883 and 1902 and one of the most revered figures in South African history. The home, still fully furnished, is humble and somber, befitting this deeply religious leader who loved to sit on the front *stoep* (veranda) and watch the world go by. Exhibits in the adjoining museum trace Kruger's career, culminating in his exile by the British and eventual death in Switzerland in 1904. Of particular interest are the letters of support that Kruger received from all over the world, including the United States, when Britain instigated the South African War (1899–1902), also known as the Anglo-Boer War. Across the road is the Dutch Reformed Church, where Kruger's wife is buried. You need to book two days in advance for a guided tour. ⊠ *60 Church St. W, at Potgieter St.* ☎ *012/326–91/2* ☜ *R25, guided tours R30* ◷ *Weekdays 8:30–4:30, weekends 9–4:30.*

㉔ **Melrose House.** Built in 1886, this opulent structure is one of South Africa's most beautiful and best-preserved Victorian homes, furnished in period style. It has marble columns, mosaic floors, lovely stained-glass windows, ornate ceilings, porcelain ornaments, and richly colored carpets. On May 31, 1902, the Treaty of Vereeniging was signed in the dining room, ending the South African War. You can view a permanent exhibit on the war or arrange for a guided tour. ⊠ *275 Jacob Maré St.* ☎ *012/322–2805* ⊕ *www.melrosehouse.co.za* ☜ *R9, guided tour R50* ◷ *Tues.–Sun. 10–5.*

Sammy Marks Museum About 23 km (14 mi) east of Pretoria, this furnished, 48-room Victorian mansion, in a mixture of grand styles, and its outbuildings, surrounded by gardens, were built in 1884 for mining and industrial magnate Sammy Marks. Guided tours take place every

OFF THE
BEATEN
PATH

7

90 minutes on weekdays; there are ghost tours at night. A restaurant is on-site, and you can picnic on the grounds. ⊠ *Off N4 at Hans Strijdom Exit; follow signs* ☎ *012/802–1150* ⊞ *R30* ⊙ *Tues.–Sun. 10–4.*

㉒ Smuts House. This small wood-and-iron country house was the residence of three-time South African prime minister Jan Christian Smuts, who played active roles in the South African War and World Wars I and II and was instrumental in setting up the League of Nations (forerunner of the United Nations). Despite his military background, he was committed to working for peace and remains one of South Africa's most interesting historical characters. His home illustrates the simple manner in which he lived until his death in 1950. There's a tea garden on the large grounds, an adjacent campsite, and easy trails up a nearby hill. Ask about guided bird-watching and other tours. On the second and last Saturday of each month, a crafts market takes to the grounds. ⊠ *Off Nelmapius Rd., Irene* ☎ *012/667–1176* ⊞ *R10* ⊙ *Daily 9:30–4:30.*

㉕ Transvaal Museum. This massive natural-history museum has an extensive collection of land and marine animals from around the world, with an emphasis on African wildlife. The beautiful building also contains the Austin Roberts Bird Collection, the most comprehensive display of taxidermied African birds in southern Africa. Of particular interest are the Genesis exhibits, tracing the evolution of life on earth, and the geology section, with displays of weird and wonderful rocks and minerals. Mrs. Ples, the famous Australopithecus skull found at the Sterkfontein Caves in the Cradle of Humankind, resides here. ⊠ *Paul Kruger St., across from City Hall* ☎ *012/322–7632* ⊞ *R20, tours R3* ⊙ *Daily 8–4.*

OFF THE
BEATEN
PATH

Tswaing Crater Museum. This huge meteorite crater—recently declared a World Heritage Site—was formed about 220,000 years ago. Today it's home to 340 bird species and even more plant species. Browse through the crater's eco-museum to learn more about the area or explore an Ndebele cultural village. A three-hour guided tour (R80 per guide) includes a walk to the crater. ⊠ *Old Soutpan Rd. (M35), about 40 km (25 mi) north of Tshwane* ☎ *079/829–5464* ⊞ *R15* ⊙ *Daily 7:30–4.*

㉜ Union Buildings. Built in 1901, this impressive cream-sandstone complex—home to the administrative branch of government—was designed by Sir Herbert Baker, one of South Africa's most revered architects. It is his masterpiece and closely resembles the Parliament Buildings in New Delhi, where he went on to work. The complex incorporates a hodgepodge of styles—an Italian tile roof, wooden shutters inspired by Cape Dutch architecture, and Renaissance columns—that somehow works beautifully. Expansive formal gardens step down the hillside in terraces, which are dotted with war memorials and statues of former prime ministers. There's no public access to the building, but the gardens are perfect for a picnic lunch. ⊠ *Off Church St., Meintjeskop* ⊙ *Gardens open 24 hrs.*

㉑ Voortrekker Monument and Museum. This famous landmark is regarded as a symbol of Afrikaner nationalism and independence. Completed in 1949, the monument honors the Voortrekkers who rejected British rule and trekked into the hinterland to found their own nation. The Hall of Heroes traces in its marble frieze their momentous Great Trek, culminating in the Battle of Blood River (December 16, 1838), when a small force of Boers defeated a large Zulu army without losing a single life. The Voortrekkers considered this victory a special gift from God. An adjoining museum displays scenes and artifacts of daily Voortrekker life, as well as the Voortrekker Tapestries, 15 pictorial weavings that trace the historical high points of the Great Trek. The monument is in a nature reserve, which has a picnic area and hiking and biking trails. You can dine in the restaurant and tea garden if you don't like to rough it. Also on-site is **Fort Schanskop,** the best preserved of four area forts commissioned by President Paul Kruger in about 1897. The fort houses a South African (Anglo-Boer) War museum and gift shop. ⊠ *Eeufees Rd., Groenkloof* ☎ *012/326–6770* ⊕ *www.voortrekkermon. org.za* ⊠ *R32* ⊙ *May–Aug., daily 8–5; Sept.–Apr., daily 8–5:30.*

WHERE TO STAY

$$ ⊞ **The Orient.** This is an exquisite Asian-themed boutique all-suites hotel
★ aimed at the discerning traveler. Suites are large with equally large bathrooms that have deep soaking tubs and Oriental rugs on the marble floors. There are also shower cubicles with views over the surrounding hills and a separate toilet. All suites feature collectible objets d'art. The Constantinople suite has a 300-year-old Indian four-poster bed; others have a mix of antique and period reproduction pieces. Instead of bathrobes, guests will find in their wardrobes authentic galabayas, the all-in-one caftan worn in the East. Giant carved timber doors and reflecting pools are found throughout the property. All the rooms offer views over the surrounding hills. If walks in the conservancy (zebra and eland roam freely) don't appeal to you, there's an extensive library. Mosaic restaurant has been recognized for its superlative French cuisine. There's an on-site cinema and a museum of sculptor Tienie Prichard's work. **Pros:** superb cuisine; majestic surroundings; extraordinary service. **Cons:** no Wi-Fi; poor mobile phone reception; need a car to get around. ⊠ *Crocodile Valley Rd., Francolin Conservancy, Elandsfontein* ☎ *012/371–2902* ⊕ *www.the-orient.net* ⇆ *11 suites* ⚴ *In-room: safe, no TV. In-hotel: restaurant, room service, pool, spa, laundry service, Internet terminal, parking (free)* ⊟ *AE, DC, MC, V* ⍩ *BP.*

CRADLE OF HUMANKIND

This World Heritage Site stretches over an area of about 470 square km (181 square mi), with about 300 caves. Inside these caves, paleoanthropologists have discovered thousands of fossils of hominids and other animals, dating back about 4 million years. The most famous of these fossils are Mrs. Ples, a skull more than 2 million years old, and Little Foot, a skeleton more than 3 million years old. While the Cradle does not have the world's oldest hominid fossils, it has the most complete fossil record of human evolution of anywhere on earth and has produced more hominid fossils than anywhere else.

Archaeological finds at the Cradle of Humankind include 1.7-million-year-old stone tools, the oldest recorded in southern Africa. At Swartkrans, near Sterkfontein, a collection of burned bones tells us that our ancestors could manage fire more than 1 million years ago.

Not all the fossil sites in the Cradle are open to the public, but a tour of the Sterkfontein Caves and the visitor center provides an excellent overview of the archaeological work in progress, and a trip to Maropeng, a much larger visitor center 10 km (6 mi) from the Sterkfontein Caves, provides even more background. Special tours to fossil sites with expert guides can be booked at either of the visitor centers.

GETTING HERE AND AROUND

Public transport to the Cradle of Humankind area is limited, so using a rental car or transfer with a tour company is best, and some hotels in the area arrange transport on request. The Cradle of Humankind is about a 90-minute drive northwest of Johannesburg and is relatively well signposted once you get off the N1 highway at the 14th Avenue off-ramp.

VISITOR INFORMATION

The Maropeng Visitor Centre provides information about the various sites in the Cradle of Humankind. For further inquiries about the Cradle of Humankind and Magaliesberg areas—including suggestions for restaurants, small lodges, and routes to take—contact the Crocodile Ramble Information Centre.

Visitor Information Crocodile Ramble Information Centre (☎ 082/923–6120 ⊕ www.theramble.co.za). **Maropeng Visitor Centre** (☎ 014/577–9000 ⊕ www.maropeng.co.za).

EXPLORING

Ⓒ **Fodor's Choice** ★ It was in the **Sterkfontein Caves**, in 1936, that Dr. Robert Broom discovered the now famous Mrs. Ples, as she is popularly known—a skull of an adult *Australopithecus africanus* that is more than 2 million years old. The find reinforced the discovery of a skull of an *Australopithecus* child, the Taung Skull, by Professor Raymond Dart in 1924, which was the first hominid ever found. At the time, Dart was ostracized for claiming the skull belonged to an early human ancestor. Scientists in Europe and the United States simply didn't believe that humanity could have originated in Africa. Today, few disagree with this theory. Another important find was the discovery in the 1990s of Little Foot, a near-complete skeleton of an *Australopithecus*, embedded in rock deep inside the caves. Guided tours of the excavations and caves, which are spacious and not claustrophobic, last an hour. Wear comfortable shoes. Spend some time in the small but excellent **Sterkfontein Visitor Centre**, which has exhibits depicting the origins of the earth, life, and humanity. A small on-site restaurant is open Wednesday–Sunday. ⊠ *Sterkfontein Caves Rd., off R563, Kromdraai* ☎ *011/668–3200* ⊕ *www.maropeng.co.za* 🎟 *R95* ◷ *Tours daily 9–4 on the ½ hr; last tour departs at 4.*

Ⓒ **Fodor's Choice** ★ The impressive **Maropeng Visitor Centre** comprises displays, interactive exhibits, and even an underground boat ride (popular with kids) through the elements of water, air, wind, and fire. *Maropeng* means "returning to the place of origin" in Setswana, the area's main indigenous language. It's a one-stop tourist destination, with restaurants, a boutique hotel, an arts-and-crafts market, an interpretative center, and an amphitheater with cultural events. Exhibits are vast and are mostly housed in a giant underground chamber. A large area is dedicated to human evolution, and the lifelike models of human ancestors draw much attention. Download a map from the Web site. The excellent boutique hotel on the premises is known for its service and spectacular view of the Magaliesberg Mountains. ✉ *R24, off R563, Kromdraai* ☎ *014/577–9000* ⊕ *www.maropeng.co.za* 🎟 *R95* ⊙ *Daily 9–5; last boat ride at 4.*

For more recent history, tour the **Old Kromdraai Gold Mine,** one of the country's oldest gold mines, where gold was found in 1881. Frankly, it's a little spooky. You don a miner's helmet and wander into the mine's murky depths on one-hour guided tours. It's not a difficult walk, and if you're lucky, you'll see bats roosting. ✉ *Ibis Ridge Farm, Kromdraai Rd., Kromdraai* ☎ *073/147–8417 or 082/259–2162* ⊕ *www.oldkromdraaigoldmine.co.za* 🎟 *R60* ⊙ *Tours weekends 9–5, on the hr, last tour at 4; weekdays by appointment.*

☾ Rhinos, lions, wild dogs, cheetahs, hippos, and crocodiles are among the animals you can see at the **Rhino and Lion Nature Reserve.** You can spot about 600 head of game; visit the lion, wild dog, and cheetah enclosures (be careful of lions approaching vehicles) or vulture blind, or be thrilled by live snake shows on weekends and holidays. You can also visit the endangered-species breeding center and the magnificent white lions or cuddle a baby animal at the nursery for young orphaned animals. In addition to the self-driving tour, you can book an escorted game drive or horseback ride. The visitors' area has a pool, the Croc Pub and Diner, and a curio shop, as well as three basic chalets (no electricity) for overnights. ✉ *Kromdraai Rd., Kromdraai* ☎ *011/957–0109* ⊕ *www.rhinolion.co.za* 🎟 *R90* ⊙ *Weekdays 8–5, weekends 8–6.*

☾ The **Wonder Cave** is a huge single-chamber cave with a number of intact stalagmites and stalactites and formations up to 50 feet high. An elevator takes regular guided tours all the way down, but if you're feeling adventurous you can rappel down (by prior arrangement only). You can also book evening tours. ✉ *Kromdraai Rd., Kromdraai* ☎ *011/957–0106 or 011/957–0109* 🎟 *R50* ⊙ *Weekdays 8–5, weekends 8–6.*

WHERE TO EAT AND STAY

$$$$ ✕ **The Carnivore.** Don't come expecting a quiet romantic dinner, as the
AFRICAN huge space lends itself to a loud and sometimes frenetic scene. Game
★ meat such as warthog, impala, and crocodile vies with tamer fare such as pork and mutton for space around an enormous open fire in the center of the restaurant. Great hunks of meat are brought around to your table on Masai spears and carved directly onto your plate until you surrender by lowering the flag on your table. An excellent vegetarian à la carte menu features uniquely African dishes such as *aviyal* (a spicy mixed vegetable dish cooked in coconut milk). ✉ *Misty Hills Country Hotel, 69 Drift Blvd., Muldersdrift* ☎ *011/950–6000* 🖃 *AE, DC, MC, V.*

$–$$ ✕ **The Cradle.** Tables here overlook a 7,413-acre game reserve. The over-
SOUTH AFRICAN all impression is one of space and silence. The frequently changing menu is impressive, with sage pork chops, lamb shank, veal saltimbocca, and venison-and-pancetta stew. The extensive wine list has many local specialties. ✉ *Cradle of Humankind, Kromdraai Rd., Mogale*

City ☎ 011/659–1622 ⊕ www.the-cradle.co.za ⚑ Reservations essential ☱ AE, DC, MC, V ⊘ Closed Mon.–Thurs.

$$$ ⛶ **Forum Homini.** As its overriding theme, this boutique hotel in a game estate within the Cradle of Humankind aptly alludes to the mysterious and fascinating story of the development of humanity. Artworks of bygone years adorn the walls and the modern architecture takes into account the landscape. The windows have sweeping views and natural veld (pronounced *felt*)—long, African grasses—grows on the rooftops. Guests can visit the nearby Sterkfontein Caves and the Wonder Caves for an additional cost. The superb in-house restaurant, Roots, specializes in French cooking. There's also a gallery and wine cellar on the property. **Pros:** luxury accommodation; a daily changing menu. **Cons:** hotel can be overwhelmed with wedding parties on weekends; not suitable for children. ✉ *Letamo Game Estate, Bartlet Rd., Kromdraii, Mogale City* ☎ *011/668–7000* ⊕ *www.forumhomini.com* ⊷ *14 rooms* ⚬ *In-room: safe, DVD, Internet. In-hotel: pool, restaurant, room service* ☱ *AE, DC, MC, V* ⦿ *BP.*

$$ ⛶ **Maropeng Hotel.** The Maropeng Hotel offers peace and tranquility with magnificent views of the Magaliesberg and Witwatersberg mountain ranges and is just an hour and a half from Johannesburg. Rooms are beautifully decorated in warm, earthy tones that reflect the African setting, and every room has a small outdoor space where you can watch the sun set while sipping delicious cocktails. There is plenty to do in the area: the Maropeng Visitor Centre is a short walk from the hotel, the Sterkfontein Caves are just a few minutes' drive away, and for those looking to unwind, the deck and pool are the perfect spot to relax. Don't miss the once-per-month stargazing evening with an astronomer if the dates work out. The restaurant's tasty South African food might include roasted meat (lamb, beef, braaied chops and pap, curried chicken) with fresh-cooked veggies, such as pumpkin and roast potatoes. **Pros:** attentive service; easy access to the Maropeng Visitor Centre and Cradle of Humankind; delicious, fresh food. **Cons:** rooms on the small side; difficult to access without a car. ✉ *R400, off the R563 Hekpoort Rd., Kromdraai* ☎ *014/577–9100* ⊕ *www.maropeng.co.za* ⊷ *24 rooms* ⚬ *In-room: safe, refrigerator, Wi-Fi. In-hotel: restaurant, room service, bar, pool* ☱ *AE, DC, MC, V* ⦿ *MAP.*

THE CROCODILE RAMBLE

The **Crocodile Ramble** (☎ 082/923–6120 ⊕ www.theramble.co.za) is an arts, crafts, and restaurant route set up by local artists, potters, sculptors, and other craftspeople. It meanders through the Cradle of Humankind area on up to the Hartbeespoort Dam in the Magaliesberg. Whether you're shopping for jewelry, antiques, or art, or looking for a restaurant or pub, it's all on the Ramble. The Web site has a handy interactive road map.

THE MAGALIESBERG

The Magaliesberg Mountains (actually rolling hills) stretch 120 km (74 mi) between Pretoria and the town of Rustenburg. The South African War once raged here, and the remains of British blockhouses can still be seen. The region is most remarkable, however, for its natural beauty—grassy slopes cleft by ocher cliffs, streams running through the ferns, waterfalls plunging into pools, and dramatic rock formations. It's an outdoor lover's paradise: go hiking, mountain biking, or horseback riding; swim in crystal streams; picnic in one of the natural hideaways; or take a balloon flight at dawn followed by a champagne breakfast. It's also home to the large Hartbeespoort Dam, a water-sports hot spot.

GETTING HERE AND AROUND

Public transport to the Magaliesberg, about a 90-minute drive northwest of Johannesburg, is limited, so hiring a car or making use of private transfers are the best ways to get there and to get around when you are in the area. Some of the hotels and lodges in the area can arrange transfers on request.

TIMING AND PRECAUTIONS

The main areas and attractions become extremely crowded on weekends. On Friday evenings and Sunday afternoons there's always a wait—sometimes an hour or more—to cross the one-way bridge over the Hartbeespoort Dam. The area is relatively small, and two to three days is more than enough time to spend exploring.

VISITOR INFORMATION

The Cullinan Info Shop provides information about tours and attractions in and around Cullinan. Magalies Reservations covers accommodations and attractions in the Magaliesberg area.

Visitor Information Cullinan Info Shop (☏ 012/734–2170 ⊕ www.cullinan-meander.co.za). **Magalies Reservations** (☏ 014/577–1845).

EXPLORING

Fodor'sChoice
★
The **De Wildt Cheetah Centre** is respected for its conservation and breeding programs. It offers three-hour guided tours in vehicles (included in the price of admission); at an additional cost you can witness a cheetah run. A beautiful stone lodge has nine guest rooms. No children under six are permitted. Book visits to the center in advance. ⊠ R513, *near Hartbeespoort Dam* ☏ 012/504–1921 ⊕ *www.dewildt.co.za* ☑ R220, R310 *with a cheetah run* ☉ *Tours Tues. and Thurs. at 1:30, Wed. and Sun. at 8:30 and 1:30.*

The **Elephant Sanctuary** is home to 10 of the big mammals and has elephant rides. Visits are via prearranged interactive educational sessions only. As part of the session, you can groom and feed the elephants; learn about their habits, personalities, and anatomy; and ride one of Africa's largest mammals. A small on-site lodge sleeps up to 12. ⊠ *Rustenburg Rd. (R112), about 2 km (1 mi) from Hartbeespoort Dam* ☏ 012/258–0423 ⊕ *www.elephantsanctuary.co.za* ☑ *Sessions R375 (1 hr 45 mins) or R475 (2½ hrs), elephant rides R350* ☉ *Sessions daily at 8, 10, and 2.*

The **Snake and Animal Park** is not big (you can walk through in less than two hours) but has rare white lions, gray wolves, many primate species, and birds of prey. Its selection of reptiles is overwhelming. Snake cages line the walkways, containing anything from harmless little garden snakes to poisonous cobras and giant pythons. Keep an eye out for snake shows, especially on weekends. The park has a ferry restaurant on the dam and a tea garden. ✉ *1 Scott St., Hartbeespoort* ☎ *012/253–1162* ⊕ *www.hartbeespoortdam.com* 🎫 *R50* ⊙ *Daily 8–5.*

UP, UP, AND AWAY!

Flying Pictures (☎ *082/451–6731* ⊕ *www.flyingpictures.co.za*) offers hot-air balloon trips at sunrise. The flight costs R1,900, lasts about an hour, and includes sparkling wine and a full English breakfast on landing. **Bill Harrop's "Original" Balloon Safaris** (☎ *011/705–3201* ⊕ *www.balloon.co.za*) has one-hour flights daily at sunrise from a site close to the Hartbeespoort Dam. Flight costs vary and include breakfast and sparkling wine.

WHERE TO STAY

$$$ 🏨 **Budmarsh Private Lodge.** Surrounded by a lush garden in the heart of the Magaliesberg, this lodge has rooms with beautiful antique furniture. It's a good place for a river ramble or a mountain hike. ■**TIP→ Even if you don't stay overnight, drive through for dinner or a light lunch.** It's a beautiful drive, and the always-changing menu ($$$$) is prepared by a master chef, Zhan Steyn. Dinner (reservations essential) is a six-course set menu of French-influenced cuisine that changes daily. **Pros:** relaxing setting; peaceful library; rooms have Jacuzzis and outdoor showers. **Cons:** can be busy on weekends; inaccessible without a car. ✉ *T1 Rd., Magaliesberg* ✉ *Box 1453, Highlands North 2037* ☎ *011/728–1800* ⊕ *www.budmarsh.co.za* ⤺ *18 rooms* ⚬ *In-room: no phone, Wi-Fi. In-hotel: restaurant, pool, no kids under 10* ⊟ *AE, DC, MC, V* ⓜ*MAP.*

$$$ 🏨 **De Hoek Country House.** In France this exclusive establishment would be called an *auberge*, and the two-story stone-and-heavy-timber building along the river would not be out of place in Provence. De Hoek is in semi-indigenous gardens in the exquisite Magalies River valley. The quiet rooms have golden walls and dark mahogany furniture. Some of the superior suites have fireplaces, and all rooms have underfloor heating. Archery, croquet, lawn bowling, and mountain walks are some of the activities, but the restaurant ($$$$)—serving eclectic, classy cuisine such as homemade *tagliolini* with shredded crab meat in a chili, cream, and tomato sauce and roast rack of lamb rubbed with Moroccan-style spice and tamarind sauce—is what brings most people. Apart from Sunday lunch, the restaurant is open only to hotel guests. **Pros:** plenty of activities; attentive service; lovely setting; fabulous food. **Cons:** difficult to access with public transport; pricey. ✉ *Off R24, north of Magaliesberg, adjacent to Bekker School* 📮 *Box 117, Magaliesberg 1791* ☎ *014/577–9600* ⊕ *www.dehoek.com* ⤺ *4 rooms, 16 suites* ⚬ *In-room: DVD. In-hotel: pool, no kids under 12* ⊟ *AE, DC, MC, V* ⓜ*BP.*

$ ⊞ **Goblin's Cove.** You can find this delightful little hotel and restaurant, the creation of sculptor Charles Gotthard, amid trees next to a river. It's made up like a fantasy fairy world, with three stories of little rooms, winding passageways, and stairs leading to colorful private alcoves and balconies. The restaurant ($$) has tasty, creative cuisine, such as South African springbok carpaccio, Thai chicken salad, and lime-marinated chicken breasts. A set menu ($$$$) is offered on Sunday. Bookings are essential. A small shop sells dream catchers, small fairy statues, and the like, and the Gobble D'Gook coffee shop serves homemade cakes on weekends and holidays. There are three B&B units in a restored vintage train car and two forest cabins. Less than 10 km (6 mi) away and also operated by Gotthard are the smaller Out of Africa Guest Lodge, which has five two-story thatch cottages, and La Provence, which has seven suites, each with a lovely antique Victorian bath, in an old stone sculptor's studio. **Pros:** quaint train-coach accommodation; regularly updated menu. **Cons:** restaurant booking is essential. ⊠ *Off R24, Bekker School Rd., Box 98, Magaliesberg* ☎ *014/576-2143, 014/577-1126 Out of Africa and La Provence* ⊕ *www.goblins.co.za* ➹ *3 rooms, 2 cabins* ⚙ *In-room: no phone, no TV. In-hotel: restaurant* ⊟ *DC, MC, V* ⦿l *BP.*

¢   ⊞ **Green Hills.** This romantic B&B is just right for a break from the
★   city. Rooms are in three separate cottages in a lovely garden and have ceramic fireplaces. The bathrooms are spacious, with large showers and separate baths. Nothing is too much trouble for hosts Etaine and Sarah Hewitt, who make a delicious English breakfast every morning. **Pros:** warm hospitality; beautiful river views, hearty breakfasts. **Cons:** no Internet access; not much within walking distance. ⊠ *T1, 11 km (7 mi) from Magaliesberg, after Bekker School Rd.* ⓓ *Box 286, Magaliesberg 1791* ☎ *083/442-0967* ⊕ *www.greenhills.co.za* ➹ *3 cottages* ⚙ *In-room: no TV. In-hotel: laundry service* ⊟ *No credit cards* ⦿l *BP.*

$ ⊞ **Jameson Country Cottages.** These pretty, well appointed, self-catering cottages can sleep four or six people and have stoves, refrigerators, TVs, and a good selection of culinary appliances. Set in an attractive garden around a pool and adjacent to a cane-furniture factory and shop, they offer excellent value for the money. Breakfast and lunch are served in a tea garden. **Pros:** fully equipped with modern amenities; facilities to keep the kids entertained. **Cons:** additional cost for folding beds; difficult to reach without a car. ⊠ *R509 (Koster Rd.), 10 km (6 mi) from Magaliesberg* ⓓ *Box 96, Magaliesberg 1791* ☎ *014/577-1301 or 083/301-5791* ⊕ *www.westcamo.co.za* ➹ *6 cottages* ⚙ *In-room: kitchen. In-hotel: pool* ⊟ *MC, V.*

$ ⊞ **Lesedi Cultural Village.** This is not just a place to stay and eat; it's a place to learn about the cultures and history of South Africa's Basotho, Ndebele, Pedi, Xhosa, and Zulu nations. Daily shows of dancing and singing, tours of traditional homesteads, and a crafts market complement the dining, lodging, and conference facilities. The large Nyama Choma restaurant ($$–$$$$) serves food from all over the continent so you can taste North African fare, East African cuisine, or opt for a South African barbecue. Dishes include roast meats, porridge, and vegetables, often cooked in traditional African three-legged iron pots.

Most of the Africa-theme guest rooms have two beds. Packages can include breakfast, dinner, and the tours. **Pros:** rich cultural experience; tasty African fare; popular with kids. **Cons:** can be flooded with tour groups; rather trite and manufactured experience. ✉ *R512, 12 km (7½ mi) north of Lanseria* ⌖ *Box 699, Lanseria 1748* ☎ *087/940–9933* ⊕ *www.lesedi.com* ⤴ *38 rooms* ⚭ *In-room: no phone. In-hotel: restaurant, bar* ▤ *AE, DC, MC, V* ⅼ◎ⅼ *BP.*

$$$ ▦ **Mount Grace Country House Hotel.** This village-style bed-and-breakfast near the town of Magaliesberg has accommodations in a variety of delightful country-style buildings. All have glorious views of the mountains, valley, and the landscaped gardens. The Mountain Village is the most luxurious lodging, with sunken baths and heated towel bars. For more privacy, stay at Grace Village, which is farther down the mountain. The most reasonable lodging is the Thatchstone Village. The food is wholesome country fare with a Mediterranean influence, and the Mount Grace is famous for its Sunday lunches. **Pros:** luxury accommodation; top-rated spa facilities; complimentary Internet access. **Cons:** no children under 12; expensive. ✉ *R24 to Hekpoort, near Magaliesberg* ⌖ *Private Bag 5004, Magaliesberg 1791* ☎ *014/577–5600* ⊕ *www. africanpridehotels.com/mount-grace-country-house-and-spa.html* ⤴ *121 rooms* ⚭ *In-room: refrigerator. In-hotel: 2 restaurants, bar, tennis court, pools, spa, bicycles* ▤ *AE, DC, MC, V* ⅼ◎ⅼ *BP.*

¢ ▦ **Mountain Sanctuary Park.** Don't let the rather terse list of rules at the
Ⓒ entrance put you off; the owners are fiercely protective of their little
★ piece of paradise—and justly so. This is a simple campsite, with spotless bath facilities and comfortable self-catering cottages with electricity, hot water, and cooking facilities. The emphasis is on the surrounding 2,200 acres of mountains, pools, waterfalls, and streams, where you can hike a different route every day—each more beautiful than the last. Pets and radios are forbidden, but children are welcome. **Pros:** inexpensive; peaceful, rural setting; unspoiled nature reserve. **Cons:** rustic accommodation; self-catering experience not for those who don't enjoy camping. ✉ *40 km (25 mi) from Magaliesberg on dirt road, 15 km (9 mi) from N4* ☎ *014/534–0114 or 082/371–6146* ⊕ *www.mountain-sanctuary. co.za* ⤴ *4 chalets, 8 log cabins, 30 campsites* ⚭ *In-room: safe, kitchen, refrigerator. In-hotel: pool* ▤ *MC, V.*

$$$ ▦ **Valley Lodge.** Too big to be called a hideaway, this B&B has a bird sanctuary, 250-acre nature reserve, and a stream running through it. The lodge is popular with corporate groups, but it's big enough to find quiet (the Nature Rooms offer the most privacy). It's also one of few hotels in the area that accept small children. Rooms have small sitting areas, and some have four-poster beds and fireplaces; all have covered patios. **Pros:** well-stocked wine cellar; young children welcome; lots of outdoor activities on offer. **Cons:** private transport necessary to explore the area; no Internet access. ✉ *Jennings St.* ⌖ *Box 13, Magaliesberg 1791* ☎ *014/577–1301 or 014/577–1305* ⊕ *www.valleylodge.co.za* ⤴ *76 rooms* ⚭ *In-room: Internet. In-hotel: restaurant, bar, tennis courts, pool, gym* ▤ *AE, DC, MC, V* ⅼ◎ⅼ *BP.*

BALLOONING

A fun and fascinating way to start the day is with an early-morning balloon ride. **Bill Harrop's "Original" Balloon Safaris** (☎ *011/705–3201* ⊕ *www.balloon.co.za*) flies daily at sunrise from a site close to the Hartbeespoort Dam for about an hour, weather permitting. A flight costs R2,575, including breakfast and sparkling wine.

SHOPPING

The **Chameleon Village Lifestyle Junxion** (✉ *Hartbeespoort Dam* ☎ *012/253–1451* ⊕ *www.chameleonvillage.co.za*) has shops, fast-food outlets, and restaurants lined up alongside art studios. You can visit an ostrich show farm, a Bushman village, pet a pony (and put the kids on one), browse through the Crafters Junxion market, or enjoy live music on weekends. **Crystal Feeling** (✉ *Akasha Centre, 15 Rustenburg Rd., Magaliesberg* ☎ *014/577–2182*) has many fascinating decorative and healing crystals, dream catchers, books, and jewelry. The **Welwitschia Country Market** (✉ *R104 [Rustenburg Rd.], 2 km [1 mi] from Hart-beespoort Dam, at Doryn four-way stop* ☎ *083/302–8085* ⊕ *www. countrymarket.co.za*) sells arts and crafts among other goodies at 38 little shops and three restaurants. At **Western Cane Trading** (✉ *R509, 10 km [6 mi] from Magaliesberg* ☎ *014/577–1361* ⊕ *www.westcane. co.za*), you can browse through a huge warehouse of cane, wood, and iron furniture. There's a good tea garden and even a driving range.

SUN CITY

A huge entertainment and resort complex in the middle of dry bushveld in the North West Province, Sun City is popular with golfers and families, and South Africans and foreign tourists alike. Sun City's appeal is vastly enhanced by the Pilanesberg National Park (⇨ *Chapter 9*), which is only 10 km (6 mi) past Sun City, and by a full round of outdoor sports and activities, including two Gary Player–designed world-class golf courses, elephant-back riding, and archery.

GETTING HERE AND AROUND

Public transport to and from Sun City, 177 km (110 mi) northwest of Jo'burg, is limited. Ingelosi, the official Sun City shuttle, travels between Johannesburg and Sun City twice daily. The shuttle departs from O. R. Tambo Airport and the Sandton City Shopping Centre and tickets cost R500 round-trip. Otherwise, get to the area using private transfer or a rental car.

Within the Sun City complex there are shuttle buses that ferry visitors between the entertainment complex and the various hotels, and the Sky Train monorail transports day visitors from the parking lot to the entertainment complex.

TIMING AND PRECAUTIONS

There is plenty to keep you entertained in the area, so a few days are needed to do justice to the entertainment complex and adjacent national park.

VISITOR INFORMATION

Covering the entire North West Province (including Magaliesberg, Sun City, and the Pilanesberg National Park), the North West Tourism Information Web site offers plenty of useful information on what to do and where to stay in the province. The Sun International Web site also offers useful information on where to stay in Sun City.

Visitor Information **North West Province Tourism Information** (☎ 086/111–1666 ⊕ www. www.tourismnorthwest.co.za). **Sun International** (⊕ www.suninternational.com/destinations/resorts/suncity).

EXPLORING

Sun City was built in 1979, in the rocky wilds of the Pilanesberg Mountains. The area was in the then Bantustan of Bophuthatswana—one of several semi–self-governed areas during apartheid set aside for black ethnic groups. As such, it was exempt from South Africa's then strict anti-gambling laws. Today Sun City comprises four luxurious hotels; two casinos with slot machines, card tables, and roulette wheels; major amphitheaters that host international stars; and an array of outdoor attractions. The complex is split into two parts: the original Sun City, where the focus is on entertainment and gambling, and the Lost City, anchored by the magnificent Palace Hotel, which offers guests an opportunity to enjoy outdoor adventure at the Valley of the Waves.

In addition to its casinos, the original Sun City also stages rock concerts, major boxing bouts, the annual Sun City Golf Challenge, and the occasional Miss World pageant. At Lost City, painted wild animals march across the ceilings, imitation star-spangled skies glitter even by day, lush jungles decorate the halls, and stone lions and elephants keep watch over it all. ⊠ *R556, North West Province* ☎ *014/557–1000* ⊕ *www.suninternational.com/destinations/resorts/suncity.*

WHERE TO EAT AND STAY

There's a wide variety of dining options in and near Sun City (all of them pricey), from upmarket and glitzy to poolside cafés selling light meals like toasted sandwiches.

Accommodations in and around Sun City ranges from the luxurious **Palace of the Lost City** (☎ *014/557–3131, 011/780–7800 reservations)*, with suites decorated in a blend of African and Eastern styles, to the more affordable **Cabanas** (☎ *014/557–1000, 011/780–7800 reservations),* which have lovely views over the gardens and lakes. For information on all the hotels at Sun City, contact **Sun International** *(⇨ Visitor Information, above).*

Victoria Falls

WORD OF MOUTH

"This was a unanimous highlight of the trip!!! On previous trips to Africa we have always left off the Victoria Falls as too expensive, too out of the way, too difficult to arrange . . . This time we decided 'now or never.' Well, I can definitely say I hope to visit the falls again one day—they were beautiful!"

—PRICH

"Victoria Falls was truly breathtaking and a different, excellent experience from each side."

—MarnieWDC

Updated by
Sanja Cloete-
Jones

Roughly 750 mi from its humble origins as an insignificant spring, the Zambezi River has grown more than a mile wide. Without much warning the river bends south, the current speeds up, and the entire mass of water is forced into a single fissure. More than 1 million gallons of water disappear over a vertical, 300-foot-high drop in the time it takes an average reader to reach the end of this paragraph. The resulting spray is astounding, the brute force forming a cloud of mist visible 40 mi away on a clear day.

Dr. David Livingstone, a Scottish medical doctor and missionary, visited the area in 1855 and is widely credited with being the first European to document the existence of this natural wonder. He named it Victoria Falls in honor of his queen, although the Makololo name, Mosi-oa-Tunya (literally, "the Smoke that Thunders"), remains popular. Livingstone fell madly in love with the falls, describing them in poignant prose. Other explorers had slightly different opinions. E. Holub could not contain his excitement and spoke effusively of "a thrilling throb of nature," A. A. de Serpa Pinto called them "sublimely horrible" in 1881, and L. Decle (1898) expected "to see some repulsive monster rising in anger." The modern traveler can explore every one (or all) of these perspectives. There is so much to do around the falls that the only limitations will be your budget and sense of adventure or lack thereof.

The settlements of Livingstone, Zambia, and Victoria Falls, Zimbabwe, both owe their existence to the falls. Settled in different countries and intriguingly diverse in character, they nevertheless function like two sides of one town. Crossing the border is a formality that generally happens with minimum fuss. Although the Zimbabwean town of Victoria Falls continues to be perfectly safe, as it's far from the documented strife plaguing the country, Livingstone, on the Zambian side, is currently the favored destination. Visitors to Zambia are spoiled with an overabundance of top-class safari lodges along the Zambezi, and this strong competition places an emphasis on individualized service, which enables you to tailor your visit. The general mood in Zimbabwe is not always upbeat, and the shortage of basic necessities is starting to affect even the top hotels. However, the absence of large numbers of travelers is lovely, and this area currently provides excellent value for money. The region deserves its reputation as an adventure center and offers adrenaline-inducing activities by the bucketful. The backdrop for any of these is stunning and the safety record superb.

TOP REASONS TO GO

The Phenomenon. Not only can you experience Victoria Falls and the Batoka Gorge from up, down, and even inside—the sheer size of this wonder fosters the illusion of exclusivity.

Fundamental Adrenaline. Looking for an adventure to get your heart pounding? From bungee jumping to elephant-back riding and skydiving, Victoria Falls truly has it all.

Ultimate Relaxation. Massages are offered on the banks of the Zambezi River, sumptuous food is served wherever you turn, and there's nothing like having a gin and tonic at the end of the day while the spray of the Falls fades from rainbow to starlight.

Africa Intact. The heart of the Dark Continent proudly showcases a region governed by people who have lived here for centuries applying the very latest in ecotourism and benefiting from environmentally conscious development.

ORIENTATION AND PLANNING

GETTING ORIENTED

Victoria Falls is in southern Africa and literally provides a border between Zambia and Zimbabwe. Each country has a national park that surrounds the falls (Mosi-oa-Tunya National Park in Zambia and Victoria Falls National Park in Zimbabwe), as well as a town (Livingstone in Zambia and Victoria Falls in Zimbabwe) that serves as the respective tourist center. The fissure containing the falls stretches over a mile, roughly from southwest to northeast. Livingstone lies to the north and the town of Victoria Falls immediately to the south of the falls. The border between the countries is within walking distance of the compact town of Victoria Falls. The stretch between the falls border and town center on the Livingstone side should not be attempted, because of the dangers of wandering elephants, the African sun, and the occasional opportunistic thief.

Livingstone, Zambia. Named after the famous Dr. David Livingstone, the town was established in 1900, 10 km (6 mi) north of the falls. Its main street, Mosi-oa-Tunya Road, is lined with classic colonial buildings. The current unresolved political strife in Zimbabwe has caused many tourists to choose Livingstone as their base over Victoria Falls.

Victoria Falls, Zimbabwe. The town of Victoria Falls lies west of the falls on the Zambezi's southern bank. The view of the falls and the gorge is pretty spectacular from Zimbabwe. At one time, the town was the principal tourist destination for the area, but the lack of political stability has sent many tourists to the Zambia side. The town continues to be perfectly safe, but the atmosphere can be understandably negative.

PLANNING

WHEN TO GO

If you're at all sensitive to heat and humidity, visit from May through August, when it is dry and cool, with pleasant days and cool to cold nights. Although the bush can resemble a wasteland, with short brown stubble and bare trees, it does improve game-viewing, and most other adventure activities are more comfortable in the cooler weather. This is also the time when the mosquitoes are less active, although it remains a malaria area year-round, and precautions should always be taken.

The rainy season starts sometime around late October and generally stretches well into April. With the first rains also comes the "time of the bugs," with tsetse flies, mosquitoes, and the harmless but aptly named stink bug seemingly running the show for a couple of months. Of course, the abundance of insect life also leads to great bird-watching. Although the rain showers tend to be of the short and spectacular kind, they can interfere with some activities, especially if your visit is a short one. Try to arrange your activities for the early hours, as the rain generally falls in the late afternoon.

Peak flow is achieved in late April and May, when rafting and visiting Livingstone Island might not be possible. If your visit coincides with school vacations in South Africa, the area can become quite crowded.

HEALTH AND SAFETY

It's always a good idea to leave ample space in your luggage for common sense when traveling to Victoria Falls. Wild animals abound throughout this area and must be given a lot of room and respect. You must also remember that Zimbabwe and Zambia are relatively poor. Both countries have tourism police, but opportunistic thieving still happens occasionally. Although crime is generally nonviolent, losing your money, belongings, or passport will result in spending the remainder of your trip with various officials in stuffy, badly decorated offices instead of sitting back on the deck of your sunset cruise, drink in hand.

As for the water, it is always advisable to drink bottled water, although the tap water in Zambia is generally considered safe. Should you develop any stomach upset, be sure to contact a physician, especially if you are running a fever, in order to rule out malaria or a communicable disease.

Finally, confirm that your insurance covers you for a medical evacuation should you be involved in a serious accident, as the closest intensive-care facilities of international standard are in South Africa.

HOTELS

Lodge reservations can be made at any time, but flight availability can be a problem, especially traveling from and to South Africa on Friday and Sunday. Lodges tend to have inclusive packages; hotels generally include only breakfast. All hotels and lodges quote in U.S. dollars but accept payment in other currencies at unfriendly exchange rates. Though hotels in Zimbabwe have set rates, they are currently desperate for business, and you can bargain in many instances. It might be best to take an all-inclusive package tour because meals can be exorbitantly expensive. A 10% service charge is either included or added to the bill (as is the value-added tax) in both countries, which frees you to include an extra tip only for exceptional service. Although air-conditioning can be expected in the hotels, lodges tend to have fans. ■TIP→ **Travel with a sarong (locally available as a *chitenge*), which you can wet and wrap around you for a cooler siesta.**

RESTAURANTS

In Zimbabwe, game meat can be found on almost any menu, but it's something of a delicacy in Zambia; superior free-range beef and chicken are available everywhere. The local bream, filleted or whole, is excellent, and the staple starch, a thick porridge similar to polenta—*sadza* in Zimbabwe and *nsima* in Zambia—is worth a try; use your fingers to eat it (you'll be given a bowl for washing afterward). Adventurous? Try *macimbi* or *vinkuvala* (sun-dried mopane worms) and, in the flood season, *inswa* (flash-fried flying ants).

Meals are taken at regular hours, but during the week, restaurants close around 10. Dress is casual, although Africa easily lends itself to a little glamour, and you'll never be out of place in something more formal.

WHAT IT COSTS IN U.S. DOLLARS					
	¢	$	$$	$$$	$$$$
Restaurants	under $5	$6–$10	$11–$15	$16–$25	over $25
Hotels in Zambia	under $50	$51–$100	$101–$200	$201–$350	over $350
Hotels in Zimbabwe	under $100	$101–$400	$401–$700	$701–$1,000	over $1,000

Restaurant prices are per person for a main course at dinner, a main course equivalent, or a prix-fixe meal. Hotel prices are for a standard double room in high season, including 17.5% tax in Zambia and 15% tax in Zimbabwe and service charge.

LANGUAGES AND TIME ZONES

Zambia has more than 70 dialects, but there are only four main languages: Lozi, Bemba, Nyanja, and Tonga. English is the official language and is widely spoken, read, and understood.

Zimbabwe's official language is English. Both Chishona, Sindebele and their various dialects are also widely spoken.

Zambia and Zimbabwe operate on CAST (Central African Standard Time), which is two hours ahead of Greenwich Mean Time; it's the same as South Africa. That makes them seven hours ahead of North American eastern standard time (six hours ahead during eastern daylight saving time).

PASSPORTS AND VISAS

You'll need a valid passport and visa to enter **Zambia**, but it's simple to purchase a visa when you enter the country. The Zambian immigration department is currently revising its visa fees. At press time a standard U.S. single-entry visa costs US$50, and a single-entry and transit visa cost the same. Day-trip visas cost US$20 (often included in the cost of prebooked activities, so check with your booking agent). If you plan to leave Zambia and return, you'll need a multiple-entry visa or you'll have to buy another visa upon your return. Multiple-entry visas can only be purchased at Zambian Missions abroad and not on arrival.

It's possible to buy point-of-entry visas for **Zimbabwe** for US$35 for a single entry. If you leave Zimbabwe for more than 24 hours, you will need to buy another to reenter (unless you bought a double-entry visa for US$55), so think before you travel. To cross the border into Zambia for a day, you'll need to purchase a Zambian day visa for US$20, unless you have booked an activity that includes this cost. Visas can be purchased from an embassy before departure, but it will almost certainly be more trouble and generally cost more than buying them at the border.

> **WHEN IN ROME . . .**
>
> Fearing a few weeks without your Budweiser? No worries. There are a couple great local brews for you to try on both sides of the falls: Mosi in Zambia and Zambezi in Zimbabwe. Both are crisp, light, and thirst-quenching beers. What about after your meal? Order an Amarula on ice. Not unlike Baileys Irish Cream, this liquor is made from the fruit of the marula tree, a well-documented delicacy for elephants.

VISITOR INFORMATION

Although the Zambia National Tourist Board (next to the museum; open weekdays 8–1 and 2–5, Saturday 8–noon), is very helpful and friendly, you might be better off visiting Jollyboys (behind the Livingstone Museum; open daily 7–10) for comprehensive and unbiased advice.

In Zimbabwe, the Victoria Falls Publicity Association is fairly well stocked with brochures. It's open weekdays 8–1 and 2–4 and Saturday 8–1. It's also a good idea to seek advice from the many safari companies in town.

Contacts Victoria Falls Publicity Association (✉ *412 Park Way* ☎ *013/4–4202* ✐ *vfpa@mweb.co.zw*). **Zambia National Tourist Board** (✉ *Tourist Centre, Mosi-oa-Tunya Rd.* ☎ *213/32–1404* ⊕ *www.zambiatourism.com*). **Jollyboys** (✉ *34 Kanyanta Rd.* ☎ *213/32–4229* ⊕ *www.backpackzambia.com*).

LIVINGSTONE, ZAMBIA

This marvelous old town has a wealth of natural beauty and a surplus of activities. It used to be the old colonial capital, but after a few decades of neglect it has recently recast itself as Zambia's tourism and adventure capital. There's a tangible whiff of the past here: historic buildings outnumber new ones, and many inhabitants live a life not unlike the one they would have experienced 100 years ago. Livingstone handles the surge of tourists with equal parts grace, confidence, African mischief, and nuisance.

Many visitors to this side of the falls opt to stay in one of the secluded safari-style lodges on the Zambezi River. The Zambian experience sprawls out along the many bends of the large river and time ticks in a very deliberate African manner.

GETTING HERE AND AROUND

South African Airways and Comair/British Airways fly regularly from Johannesburg into Livingstone International Airport, 5 km (3 mi) out of town. The flight is a comfortable hop, just under two hours, and the airport is small and friendly, with helpful staff to speed you on your way. ■ TIP→ If at all possible, don't check your luggage in Johannesburg, and always lock suitcases securely, as luggage theft in South Africa is an everyday occurrence.

There's a perfectly reasonable traffic code in Zambia. Unfortunately, not many people have ever heard of it. You would do well to leave the driving to your guides or negotiate an all-inclusive rate with a taxi driver recommended by your hotel or lodge for the duration of your stay. Note that taxis are generally not allowed to cross the border, so if you want to visit Zimbabwe, you will have to book a tour that includes transfers. Once at the border, it is feasible to walk into and around Victoria Falls town or rent a bicycle.

If you insist on renting a car, you should know that some of the roads have more potholes than tar. You don't necessarily need a 4x4, but it's not a bad idea, especially if you want to off-road it a bit. Imperial Car Rental operates from the offices of Voyagers at the Day Activity Center near the Zambezi Sun lodge. Hemingways rents out Land Rovers, fully equipped with tents and other camping equipment—you can even hire a driver! Costs start from US$180 for an unequipped vehicle.

■ TIP→ If you plan to add the popular Kafue and Lower Zambezi camps to your trip, you should book your transfers together with your accommodation through a travel agent or with your camp reservations, as air transfer companies change hands or their minds quite often in Zambia. You will also be assured that the connection times work to your best advantage if they are responsible for the transfers.

MONEY MATTERS

Zambia's currency is the Zambian *kwacha*, which comes in denominations of ZK20, ZK50, ZK100, ZK500, ZK1,000, ZK5,000, ZK10,000, and ZK50,000 bills, necessitating carrying huge wads of notes. The kwacha is theoretically divided into 100 *ngwees*, but as you can buy nothing for one kwacha, an ngwee exists in name only, and any bill including ngwees will simply be rounded off. At the time of writing, the conversion rate was about ZK4,600 to the US$1.

Kwacha and U.S. dollars are welcome everywhere. It's a good idea to travel with plenty of small U.S. bills for tips and small purchases. Make sure you have only "big head" dollars, as the older, "small head" ones are no longer accepted. ⚠ Small bills are not exchanged for the same rate as larger denominations at the *bureaux de change*. Official banks have standard exchange rates across the board for all notes. International banks, along Mosi-oa-Tunya Road, have ATMs and exchange services. Banking hours are generally weekdays 8–2 (although some do open the last Saturday of the month). Bank ATMs accept only Visa.

⚠ You may be invited to do a little informal foreign exchange by persuasive street financiers. Resist the temptation—it's not worth the risk of being ripped off or arrested. There are many reputable exchange

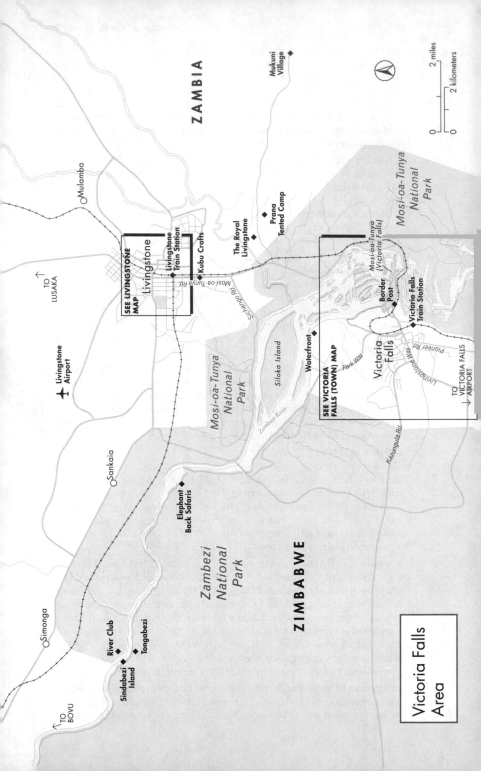

ZAMBIA

Mukuni
Village

TO
LUSAKA

Livingstone
Airport

Mulamba

SEE LIVINGSTONE
MAP

Livingstone
Train Station

Livingstone

Kubu Crafts

Prana
Tented Camp

The Royal
Livingstone

Mosi-oa-Tunya Rd.

Sichango Rd.

Mosi-oa-Tunya
National
Park

Siloka Island

Zambezi River

Waterfront

Mosi-oa-Tunya
(Victoria Falls)

Border
Post

Victoria Falls
Train Station

Victoria
Falls

Park Way

Pioneer Rd.

Livingstone Way

SEE VICTORIA
FALLS (TOWN) MAP

TO
VICTORIA FALLS
AIRPORT

Kazungula Rd.

Mosi-oa-Tunya
National
Park

Sankaia

Elephant
Back Safaris

Zambezi
National
Park

ZIMBABWE

Simonga

River Club

Sindabezi
Island

Tongabezi

TO
BOVU

2 miles

2 kilometers

Victoria Falls
Area

bureaus throughout town, though they are sometimes flooded with dollars and low on kwacha, generally toward the end of the month. MasterCard and Visa are preferred by business owners and banks to American Express or Diners Club. Business owners always prefer cash to credit cards, and some smaller hotels levy fees up to 10% to use a credit card.

Zambia has a 16% V.A.T. and a 10% service charge, which is included in the cost or itemized on your bill.

Tipping is less common in Zambia since service charges are included, but it's appreciated. Small notes or 10% is appropriate. Gas station attendants can be tipped, but tip a taxi driver only on the last day if you have used the same driver for a number of days.

> **DID YOU KNOW?**
>
> The uttering of the popular phrase "Dr. Livingstone, I Presume?" may never have happened. Although Livingstone did meet John Rowlands (the person reported to utter the phrase) in Tanzania in 1871, the famous quote is widely considered a figment of Rowlands's imagination. Mr. Rowlands was fond of a good story – he also told people that he was American (which he wasn't) and that his name was Henry Stanley (which it wasn't).

Electricity and voltage are the same in Zambia and South Africa. ⇨ *For more information, see Electricity in Travel Smart South Africa.*

SAFETY AND PRECAUTIONS

For minor injuries, a test for malaria, or the treatment of non–life-threatening ailments, you can go to the Rainbow or Southern medical centers or the Shafik clinic. For serious emergencies, contact SES (Specialty Emergency Services). Musamu Pharmacy is open weekdays 8–8, Saturday 8–6, and Sunday 8–1.

Homosexuality is technically illegal in Zambia, although it is widely accepted and presents no real problem.

TELEPHONES

Telephone rates in Zambia are much cheaper and more stable than those in Zimbabwe. Check numbers very carefully, as some are Zimbabwean mobile phones. Zambia and Zimbabwe now both have cell coverage, and there are certain areas where the networks overlap and mobile telephones work in both countries. If you have any trouble dialing a number, check with a hotel or restaurant owner, who should be able to advise you of the best and cheapest alternative. International roaming on your standard mobile phone is also an option, as coverage is quite extensive. Alternatively you could purchase a local SIM card with pay-as-you-go fill-ups. Pay phones are not a reliable option, and the costs of all telephone calls out of the country can be exorbitant.

The country code for Zambia is 260. When dialing from abroad, drop the initial 0 from local area codes. Note that all telephone numbers are listed as they are dialed from the country that they are in. Although the number for operator assistance is 100, you will be much better off asking your local lodge or restaurant manager for help.

EXPLORING

Sights below appear on the Livingstone map.

Batoka Gorge. Just below the falls, the gorge is split between Zambia and Zimbabwe and is more than 120 km (75 mi) long and 2,000 feet deep. It lies mostly within the Hwange Communal Land and is covered with mopane and riparian forests that are interspersed with grassland. On the Zambian side, the gorge is surrounded by the Mosi-oa-Tunya National Park, which contains a tropical rain forest that thrives on the eternal rainfall from the falls. Victoria Falls National Park in Zimbabwe surrounds the other side of the gorge.

Operators from both countries offer excursions to what is reputed to be the world's best one-day white-water rafting, with commercial rapids Class VI and down (amateurs can only do Class V and down) that have been given evocative nicknames like "The Ugly Sisters" and "Oblivion." If you're *"lucky"* enough to experience what locals call a "long swim" (falling out of the raft at the start of a rapid and body surfing through), your definition of the word *scary* will surely be redefined. The walk in and out of the gorge is quite strenuous on the Zimbabwe side, but as long as you are reasonably fit and looking for adventure, you need no experience. On the Zambian side though, operators use a cable car to transport you from the bottom of the gorge to your waiting transportation (and beverage) at the top.

☺ **Livingstone Museum.** The country's oldest and largest museum contains history, ethnography, natural history, and archaeology sections and includes materials ranging from newspaper clippings to photographs of Queen Elizabeth II dancing with Kenneth Kaunda (Zambia's first president) to historical information dating back to 1500. Among the priceless David Livingstone memorabilia is a model of the mangled arm bone used to identify his body and various journals and maps from the period when he explored the area and claimed the falls for his queen. ✉ *Mosi-*

oa-Tunya Rd., between civic center and post office ☎ *213/32–0495* 🖭 *US$5* ☉ *Daily 9–4:30.*

Fodor's Choice **Mosi-oa-Tunya (Victoria Falls).** Literally translated as "the Smoke that Thunders," the falls more than lives up to its reputation as one of the world's greatest natural wonders. No words can do these incredible falls justice, and it's a difficult place to appreciate in just a short visit, as it's always changing. Though the Zimbabwean side may offer more panoramic views, the Zambian side—especially the **Knife Edge** (a sharp headland with fantastic views)—allows you to stand virtually suspended over the Boiling Pot (the first bend of the river after the falls), with the deafening water crashing everywhere around you. From around May to August the falls are a multisensory experience, though you'll get absolutely drenched if you venture onto the Knife Edge, and there may be too much spray to see the bottom of the gorge. If you get the sun behind you, you'll see the magic play of multiple rainbows. A network of paths leads to the main viewing points; some are not well protected, so watch your step and wear good, safe shoes, especially at high water, when you are likely to get dripping wet. You will have dramatic views of the full 1½ km (1 mi) of the ironstone face of the falls, the Boiling Pot directly below, the railway bridge, and Batoka Gorge. During low water levels, it's possible to take a guided walk to Livingstone Island and swim in the **Devils Pool**, a natural pond right on the lip of the abyss. ⊠ *Entrance off Mosi-oa-Tunya Rd., just before border post* ☎ *No phone* 🖭 *US$10* ☉ *Daily 6–6, later at full moon.*

> **CHOBE: A GREAT DAY TRIP**
>
> If it is serious game-viewing you desire, join a one-day excursion to Chobe National Park in Botswana with **Bushtracks** (☎ *213/32–3232* ⊕ *www.gotothevictoriafalls. com*). The trip costs US$185 and includes transfers from Livingstone, a game drive, a boat cruise, and all meals. Bushtracks is also your best bet for a visit to the Mukuni Village (US$35). Reservations must be in writing and prepaid for both.

☉ **Mosi-oa-Tunya National Park.** This park is a quick and easy option for viewing plains game. In fact, you are almost guaranteed to spy white rhinos. You can also visit the Old Drift graveyard, as the park includes the location of the original settlement here. The park's guides are knowledgeable, but you can visit without one, though the roads get seriously muddy in the rainy season, and a guide who knows where to drive becomes a near-necessity. ⊠ *Sichanga Rd., off Mosi-oa-Tunya Rd., 3½ km (2 mi) from Livingstone* ☎ *No phone* 🖭 *US$10* ☉ *Daily 6–6.*

☉ **Mukuni Village.** Fascinated by the history, customs, and traditions of the area? Local guides can escort you on an intimate visit inside a house and explain the customs of the village. This is not a stage set but a very real village, so your tour will be different depending on the time of the day you go. For example, at mealtimes you can see how local delicacies are prepared. It is customary to sign in the visitor book and to pay a small fee to your guide. **Bushtracks** (☎ *213/32–3232* ⊕ *www.gotothevictoriafalls.com*) conducts organized visits. ☉ *Daily 6–6.*

8

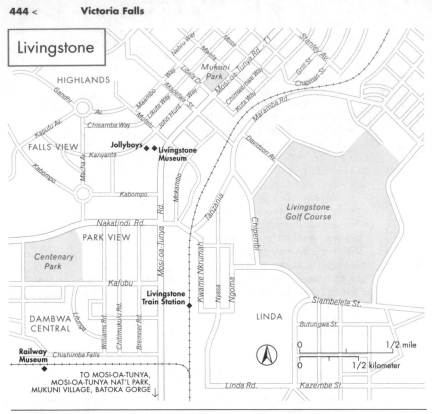

WHERE TO EAT

$ ✕ **Funky Munky.** Cheap and cheerful, this small pizzeria's reputation
PIZZA keeps spreading. On offer find thin-crust pizzas baked in a traditional
☺ wood-fired oven and named after primates. Try the popular bacon and
mushroom Baboon, the Chimpancheese four-cheese extravaganza, or
build your own. If you seek lighter fare, have a salad or head straight
for the classic gelato or Hawaiian shaved ice, which comes in flavors like
Tigerblood and Maitai. ⊠ *Mosi-oa-Tunya Rd.* ☎ *213/32–0120* ▭ *No
credit cards.*

$–$$ ✕ **Kamuza.** The Moghuls themselves might declare a meal here a feast.
INDIAN Spicy but not hot, the curries are lovingly prepared from ingredients
imported from India. The chicken Tikka Masala is a house specialty,
and the handmade saffron Kulfi is a great way to end a hot day in
Africa. ⊠ *Ngolide Lodge, Mosi-oa-Tunya Rd.* ☎ *213/32–1091* ▭ *MC,
V* ⊘ *No dinner Mon.*

$$$$ ✕ **Livingstone Island Picnic.** Available throughout the year except for a
CAFÉ couple of weeks when the water level is too high, this is a spectacular,
☺ romantic dining option. Livingstone Island is perched right on the edge
Fodor'sChoice of the abyss, where you'll sit around a linen-decked table while being
★ plied with a delicious buffet lunch (with salads) and drink by liveried
waiters. You get there by boat (two engines, just in case). Brunch and

afternoon tea are US$60 and US$90, respectively, and lunch is US$115, including transfers. The trips are run by Tongabezi Lodge, and there is a maximum of 16 guests. ⊠ *Livingstone Island* ☎ *213/32–7450* 🖃 *MC, V* ⊘ *Closed a couple of months around Feb.–June, depending on water levels. No dinner.*

$$$$ ✕ **Royal Livingstone Express Steam**
SOUTH AFRICAN **Train.** Walking the long stretch of red carpet alongside Locomotive 156 while it blows steam and rumbles in preparation for the journey is undeniably exciting and romantic. Ask to be seated in either the Wembley or Chesterfield dining carriage (both exquisitely restored) while the historic steam train pulls you through a shanty town, over the Sinde River bridge, and then back through Mosi-oa-Tunya National Park at sunset. The gourmet dinner is beautifully presented and perfectly prepared, offering guests no fewer than five set courses and a choice of main meal (special dietary requests can be catered to with advance notice). And yes, the train does give right-of-way for giraffes and elephants who decide to cross the tracks at sunset! ⊠ *Km 0 of the Mulebezi line on Mosi-oa-Tunya Rd.* ☎ *213/32–3232* ⊕ *www.royal-livingstone-express.com* ⚓ *Reservations essential* 🖃 *MC, V* ⊘ *Closed Mon. and Tues.*

A THREE-HOUR TOUR

Many park guides are knowledgeable, but the ultimate Mosi-oa-Tunya National Park experience is the three-hour guided walking safari offered by **Livingstone Safaris** (☎ *213/32–2267* ✒ *gecko@zamnet.zm*). Not only can you see the endangered white rhino and other plains game, but your professional guide and park scout will impart detailed information on birding, flora, and the modern use of plants by local people. Walks are conducted early in the morning and late in the afternoon and cost US$60, including transfers within Livingstone. Hopefully, your trip won't turn out like Gilligan's.

WHERE TO STAY

¢ 🖼 **Bovu.** The vibe of California and Marrakesh in the '60s and '70s is alive ☾ and well at this collection of thatched huts and campsites along the banks of the Zambezi, 52 km (32 mi) upstream of the falls. Take a good book or an excellent companion. Accommodations are basic but somehow quite perfect, each with gorgeous river views, and there are hot showers and flush toilets. The kitchen is the heart of the island, and the emphasis is on wholesome organic food. Vegetarian diners are always catered to, and the coffee is better than most of the upscale lodges serve. You can swim in a shallow section of small rapids naturally protected from crocodiles or hippos (or this is the theory). Warning: "island time" operates here and anything goes, so the staid or conservative are likely to find it unsuitable. The best way to reach Bovu is by guided *mokoro* trip run by BUNDU (⊕ *www.bunduadventures.com*). Don't forget to check out the hat collection behind the bar in the main camp and add your own to the mix. **Pros:** Bovu is *the* Zambian chill-out zone; a great way to combine an educational canoe trip with a basic overnight camp; the perfect balance between comfort and a real commune with nature. **Cons:** this might be too basic for travelers who like their little luxuries; meals are charged

8

separately. ⊠ *52 km (32 mi) upstream from Victoria Falls, on Zambezi River* ⌂ *Box 61122* ☎ *213/32–3708* ⊕ *www.junglejunction.info* ⤳ *8 huts* ⚭ *In-room: no phone, no TV. In-hotel: restaurant, bar, laundry facilities, laundry service, some pets allowed* ⊟ *No credit cards.*

¢ ⊞ **Jollyboys.** When the *New York Times* includes a backpacker lodge on
☺ the same list as two five-star resorts, your curiosity should be tweaked.
The entire design of this small establishment is user-friendly, inviting, and certainly aimed at both private relaxation and easy interaction with other travelers. Superbly maintained and professionally run, the lodge offers a variety of room types to suite every budget and need. There are eight unisex dorms varying from three to 16 beds, 10 private rooms with shared bathrooms, five private en suite rooms and one executive suite with a private kitchen. The suite, five en suite rooms, and two eight-bed dorms also have air-conditioning. The restaurant serves the usual hamburger but also has a number of surprises on the menu including a full roast on Sundays and exotic vegetarian soups made from local sweet potatoes and Indian spices. The swimming pool is large, and there is a public Jacuzzi as well. You can entertain yourself with board games or explore the extensive library that has information on absolutely everything you could ever need in Zambia and all neighboring countries. **Pros:** very central location; free daily transfers to the falls. **Cons:** it's a backpackers' lodge, so it's pretty basic; the location right in the middle of town might not exactly be where you like to spend your holiday. ⊠ *Kanyanta Rd.* ☎ *213/324–756* ⊕ *www.backpackzambia.com* ⤳ *24 rooms* ⚭ *In-room: safe (some), kitchen (some), refrigerator (some), Wi-Fi. In-hotel: restaurant, bar, pool, laundry service, Internet terminal, Wi-Fi, parking (free), some pets allowed* ⊟ *No credit cards.*

$$$ ⊞ **KaingU Safari Lodge.** KaingU Safari Lodge is a small camp comprised
☺ of a family house with two bedrooms and four classic en suite safari tents. The central *boma* and tents are raised on rosewood decks to provide ideal views over the river. It's also very remote—situated in the northern reaches of Kafue National Park. This combination of intimacy and seclusion lends an undeniable flavor of mystery and discovery to your stay. The thatched boma has a lounge, bar, and dining room where the hosted dinner conversations cover all topics. Big game is not an everyday occurrence, but the lodge's guiding team is particularly fine-tuned to the many different wildlife stories constantly unfolding in the bush. Two activities are included every day, and the selection ranges from chilled-out river safaris to serious birding excursions. The natural splendor of deepest Zambia takes precedent—at this camp even the swimming pool is a wholly natural Jacuzzi in the rapids of the Kafue! From of each nightly rate, $10 is paid into a registered Community and Conservation Trust. **Pros:** Africa untouched in all its glory; the owners have a true commitment to environmental and community development. **Cons:** difficult and expensive to reach; the area does not have an abundance of big game. ⊠ *North Kafue, 400 km north of Victoria Falls* ☎ *097/784–1653* ⊕ *www.kaingu-lodge.com* ⤳ *1 house, 4 tents* ⚭ *In-room: kitchen (some), refrigerator (some). In-hotel: restaurant, room service, bar, pool, children's programs (ages 2–11), laundry facilities, laundry service, Internet terminal, parking (free)* ⊟ *No credit cards* ⊙ *Closed Dec. 1–20* ⎸⎸*AI.*

$$$$ ⌘ **Old Mondoro Camp.** The legend of a great white-maned lion that used to call this area its home lives on in the name of this camp, which is Shona for the "king of cats."If you're looking for an African adventure of the original epic variety and love the opportunity to take lots of pictures, then you need to stay at Old Mondoro. The gin-and-tonics are cold, and the game-viewing sizzles with sightings of wild-dog dens and leopards in trees. Old Mondoro is decorated in old-school-safari style with canvas bucket showers and hand basins all lit by romantic lanterns. Tents are open (with canvas flaps at night) to maximize views of the surrounding floodplains, woodlands, and complex maze of waterways and hippo paths. The smell of fresh homemade bread introduces a back-to-basics bushveld kitchen repertoire that includes generous portions of hearty, flavorful meals. The entire experience manages to be marvelously satisfying without any fuss or complication. This is deliberately not a supercharged, over-the-top new safari palace where the design of the establishment completely usurps the natural environment and all local flavor is lost. **Pros:** great game drives led by top-notch wildlife guides; one of the few places to see wild dogs; best walking area in the Lower Zambezi. **Cons:** the open rooms have only canvas flaps to ward off the wild at night, and this might be too daring for some. ⊠ *Old Mondoro is a 1-hr motorboat ride or a 2-hr game drive from Chiawa Camp. Jeki Airstrip is only a 30-minute game drive away from Old Mondoro and can be reached in a 2-hr flight from Livingstone or a 40-minute flight from Lusaka.* ☎ *211/261–588* ⊕ *www.chiawa.com* ⟵ *4 tents* ♿ *In-room: no phone. In-hotel: restaurant, room service, bar, laundry service, Internet terminal, parking (free), no kids under 12* ▤ *MC, V* ☺ *Closed Nov.–May 1* ⍩ *AI.*

$$ ⌘ **Prana Tented Camp.** Taking its name from the Sanskrit for breathing, ☺ this exclusive camp offers the perfect opportunity for taking just that, a breather. Guests have the choice between staying in the main house or in one of the beautiful, well-appointed, en suite tents. Spread out along one of the highest points in the region, the camp overlooks the spray of Victoria Falls. Plenty of staff are on hand to look after you and take care of the cooking, cleaning, and you can book all of the area's adventure activities with reception. Prana also hosts yoga retreats, so you can book various treatments like shiatsu massage and individual yoga classes on the property. Because this property must be rented in full each night, the cost is about US$600 per night. However, the camp can sleep 12–14 adults, plus six children, so it works out to US$100 per couple—very affordable if you're traveling with a group. **Pros:** this is privately owned, managed, and takes only private bookings, so you are assured of personal attention and the luxury of having the entire camp exclusively; an affordable option for small groups traveling together; completely off the beaten track yet only 10 minutes from Livingstone and 10 minutes from the entry to the Mosi-oa-Tunya Park at the falls. **Cons:** self-catering is the only meal option; transfers must be booked for every activity. ⊠ *Off Mosi-oa-Tunya Rd.* ☎ *213/32–7120* ⊕ *www. pranazambia.com* ⟵ *4 tents, 2 rooms* ♿ *In-room: a/c (some), no phone, safe (some), kitchen (some), refrigerator (some). In-hotel: bar, pool, laundry service, parking (free)* ▤ *MC, V.*

8

$$$$ ▣ **River Club.** With split-level rooms that cling to the edge of the great
★   Zambezi, the River Club puts a modern spin on a Victorian house party.
The view from the infinity pool seems unbeatable, until you watch the
sun set from your claw-foot tub. Clever cooling mists of water draw
flocks of birds to the massage tent, and the library begs for a glass of
port and a serious book. History clings to the structure, built to the
plans of the original house, but decorations have been lovingly collected from past and present. You could spend an entire day reading
interesting anecdotes, old maps, *Punch* cartoons, and updates about
the River Club's support of the local village. A candlelight dinner is
followed by croquet on the floodlighted lawn before you retire to your
partially starlit room. You approach the lodge from the river—purely
for the spectacular effect—but it necessitates negotiating some steep
stairs. If you think you'll struggle, ask to be transferred by vehicle. **Pros:**
beautiful location with stunning views of the Zambezi; a/c and enclosed
rooms is a plus for those who don't want to give up too many modern
conveniences. **Cons:** colonial decor may not be Zambian enough for
some travelers; 20-minute drive from town for any activities that are not
in-house. ⊠ *About 18 km (11 mi) upstream from Victoria Falls town,
on Zambezi River* ✆ *Box 60469* ☏ *213/32–3672* ⊕ *www.wilderness-
safaris.com* ⇲ *10 rooms* ⚭ *In-room: safe. In-hotel: restaurant, room
service, bar, pool, laundry service, Internet terminal, parking (free), no
kids under 8* ▤ *MC, V* ⏃ *AI.*

$$$$ ▣ **The Royal Livingstone.** This high-volume, high-end hotel has an incredibly gorgeous sundowner deck, arguably on the best spot on the river,
just upstream from the falls. The attractive colonial safari-style buildings are set amid sweeping green lawns and big trees and have fantastic views, although passing guest traffic makes for a lack of real
privacy. The decor of the guest rooms and the public rooms is deliberately colonial and ostentatious. This resort is tremendously popular
and can be extremely busy, especially during peak times, but the staff
is always friendly and helpful. ▪**TIP➔** Vervet monkeys are an entertaining nuisance, so hang on to your expensive cocktail. **Pros:** the level of
service here is definitely that of a five-star international hotel; rooms
have air-conditioning, satellite TV, and fantastic snacks in the rooms.
Cons: volume of people can lead to problems, omissions, and errors,
with service standards struggling to match the high costs; if you're
traveling from other intimate safari properties, this big hotel might
feel very impersonal. ⊠ *Mosi-oa-Tunya Rd.* ☏ *213/32–1122* ⊕ *www.
suninternational.co.za* ⇲ *173 rooms* ⚭ *In-room: safe, refrigerator. In-
hotel: 3 restaurants, room service, bars, pool, spa, children's programs
(ages 2–12), laundry service, Internet terminal, Wi-Fi, parking (free)*
▤ *AE, DC, MC, V* ⏃ *BP.*

$$$$ ▣ **Sausage Tree Camp.** There is no formal dress code but this camp offers
the perfect backdrop for throwing practicality to the wind and dressing up for dinner. A genuine safari experience including beautiful bush
views, great creature sightings and dining alfresco by lamplight is perfectly balanced by a splendidly chic minimalist design that focuses on
space and pure white fabrics, which combine for a very satisfying and
perfectly decadent bush retreat. Sumptuous fabrics by night and lion

from canoe by day. Simply bliss! ⚠ **The closest airstrip is Jeki, and this is two hours from Livingstone and 40 minutes from Lusaka in a small aircraft. Sausage Tree Camp is a one-hour drive from Jeki.** Pros: gorgeous food and the services of a private *muchinda* (butler) to attend to every detail of your stay; the complimentary Mohini body-care products are infused with perfectly balanced Ayurvedic herbs. Cons: its remote location makes it very expensive and time-consuming to reach; if you don't like small aircraft transfers, avoid coming here. ⊠ *Lower Zambezi National Park* 🕾 *211/84–5204* 🖳 *www.sausagetreecamp.com* ↰ *5 tents, 3 suites* ⅀ *In-room: no phone, refrigerator (some). In-hotel: restaurant, room service, bar, pool, laundry service, Internet terminal, parking (free), no kids under 8* ▭ *MC, V* ☉ *Closed Nov. 15–Mar.* ⅃Ⓘ *AI.*

$$$
Fodor'sChoice
★

⌕ **Tongabezi and Sindabezi Island.** If you're looking for a truly African experience, Tongabezi and Sindabezi, its satellite island 4 km (2½ mi) downriver, won't disappoint. Never formal but flagrantly romantic, they are the frame around the picture, so to say, and do not upstage the Africa you have come to see. At Tongabezi, standard rooms are spacious cream-and-ocher rondavels featuring private verandas that can be enclosed in a billowing mosquito net. Three suites are built into a low cliff and incorporate the original riverine forest canopy, one suite hugs the water with a private deck extending over the river, and the Nuthouse breaks with Tongabezi tradition as it's entirely enclosed and also has an exclusive plunge pool. King beds set in tree trunks and covered by curtains of linen netting, oversize sofas in the sitting area, and giant bathtubs on the private decks are all unashamedly romantic. Every room has a local guide who acts as a personal valet and caters to your every whim. Room service is ordered via antique telephones, and the lodge has an in-house holistic therapist. **Sindabezi Island** is the most environmentally friendly property on the Zambezi. The island makes use of recycled wood chips and solar power for heating, all the gray water is recycled, and the chalets are constructed mainly from sustainable forests. The island has a strict 10-guest maximum and is separated only by a stretch of river from the Zambezi National Park. Each of the island's chalets is raised on a wooden deck built artistically around the existing trees, and they are all completely open to the river with spectacular private views (curtains drop down at night). Each guest can plan a completely private itinerary, and every need is anticipated. Two honeymoon chalets also have baths. There is absolutely no electricity on the island, and hot water is provided on demand only. If your party takes Sindabezi for itself, the guide, boat, and land vehicle are at your disposal. Dinner is served by lantern and candlelight on a sandbank or wooden deck under the stars. Pros: Tongabezi is the original open-fronted lodge; the property is owner-run, so lots of thought goes into every aspect of your stay; management is extremely environmentally and community aware. Cons: the use of local materials for building and decoration can make these properties seem shabby; individual itineraries are arranged for all guests, making it difficult to interact with other guests—but this might be a pro, too. ⊠ *About 20 km (12 mi) upstream from Victoria Falls town, on Zambezi River* ⌖ *Box 31* 🕾 *213/32–7450 or 213/32–7468* 🖳 *www.tongabezi.com* ↰ *5 suites,*

8

5 cottages ❧ In-room: safe, Wi-Fi. In-hotel: restaurant, room service, bar, laundry service, Internet terminal, Wi-Fi, parking (free), no kids under 14 at Sindabezi, no kids under 7 at Tongabezi ▤ MC, V ❑ AI.

$ ☷ **Waterfront.** There's a hive of happy activity here ranging from opportunistic monkeys relieving unsuspecting tourists of their lunch to serious late-night boozing to adventure enthusiasts (hangover optional) being whisked off to do their thing at all hours of the day. Curiously, the spacious rooms where families can stay are reached only via a steep exterior wooden staircase, but this is also a popular spot for camping. Restaurant service is notoriously slow and mediocre, and the choice of food is mostly limited to standard burger, chicken, and steak options. **Pros:** great location right on the river with beautiful sunsets; many of the adventure activities in the area are managed from the Waterfront. **Cons:** can be very noisy as it caters for campers; food is often disastrous. ✉ *Sichanga Rd., just off Mosi-oa-Tunya Rd.* ☎ *213/32–0606* ⊕ *www.safpar.com* ↻ *21 chalets, 24 adventure village tents, campsites accommodating 86 campers ❧ In-room: no phone, no TV. In-hotel: restaurant, room service, bar, laundry service, Internet terminal, Wi-Fi, parking (free)* ▤ *MC, V ❑ BP.*

SPORTS AND THE OUTDOORS

Livingstone can compete with the best as far as indulging the wildest fantasies of adrenaline junkies and outdoor enthusiasts goes. You can reserve activities directly with the operators, let your hotel or lodge handle it, or book through a central booking group. **Safari Par Excellence** (☎ *213/32–1629* ⊕ *www.safpar.net*) offers elephant-back safaris, game drives, river cruises, canoeing, kayaking, and rafting as well as trip combinations, which are a good option if your time is limited or you just want to go wild. Prices for combinations are available on request.

BOATING

Truly the monarch of the river, the **African Queen** (☎ *213/32–0058* ✉ *african.queen@thevictoriafalls.co.zm*)—no relation to the movie except in name—is an elegant colonial-style riverboat. Sunset cruises offer the maximum style and splendor. Costs start at US$55 for a 90-minute lunch cruise.

BUNGEE JUMPING

Bungee jumping off the 340-foot-high Victoria Falls Bridge with **African Extreme** (☎ *213/32–4231* ✉ *bungi@zamnet.zm*) is a major adrenaline rush, with 65 feet and three seconds of free fall and a pretty spectacular view. The jump costs from US$105, but it's also worth getting the photo and video (US$45), complete with *Top Gun* music track.

CANOEING

A gentle canoeing trip on the upper Zambezi is a great opportunity to see birds and a variety of game. Many of the lodges upriver have canoeing as an inclusive activity, but trips are also run by a number of companies, which are all reputable and provide similar value for your money. **Bundu Adventures** (☎ *213/32–4407* ⊕ *www.bunduadventures.com*) offers custom-made canoe trips that range from half-day outings to multiday excursions, with costs starting at US$80.

ELEPHANT-BACK RIDING

Elephant Back Safaris. Fancy the idea of meandering through the bush courtesy of your own ellie? Not only does this operation keep clients happy enough to forget their sore thighs the next day, it also has the elephants happy enough to keep having babies! Trips with **Safari Par Excellence** (☎ 213/32–1629 ⊕ www.safpar.net) cost US$160 for a ride.

FLYING

Batoka Sky (☎ 213/32–0058 ⊕ www.livingstonesadventure.com) offers weight-shift Aerotrike twin-axis microlighting (flying jargon for what resembles a motorized hang glider) and helicopter flights over the falls and through the gorges. There's a minimum of two passengers for helicopters. For microlighting you are issued a flight suit (padded in winter) and a helmet with a headset, but you may not bring a camera for safety reasons. Batoka Sky has been operating since 1992, and has a 100% microlighting safety record. Flights are booked for early morning and late afternoon and are dependent on the weather. Prices are US$115–US$240, depending on length of flight and aircraft. Your transfer and a day visa, if you are coming from Victoria Falls, are included. The Helicopter Gorge picnic (US$365) includes lunch and drinks for a minimum of six people.

HORSEBACK RIDING

You can take a placid horseback ride through the bush along the banks of the Zambezi with **Chundukwa Adventure Trails** (☎ 213/32–7452 ✎ chundukwa@zamnet.zm). If you are comfortable enough to keep your riding cool while a herd of elephants approaches, you may want to watch game from horseback or do a multiday trail ride. Costs are U$45 for 1½ hours; US$137.50 for a full day including lunch and drinks.

JETBOATING

If you want some thrills and speed but rafting seems a bit daunting, or you can't face the walk in and out, you'll probably enjoy jetboating with **Jet Extreme** (☎ 213/32–0058 ⊕ www.livingstonesadventure.com). A new cable-car ride, included in the cost of the jetboat ride (US$95 for 30 minutes), will mean no more strenuous walking out of the gorge. Jetboating can be combined with a rafting excursion, as the jetboat starts at the end of the rafting run, or with a helicopter trip out of the gorge. ■TIP→ **The rafting and heli must be booked separately, although big operators like Safari Par Excellence and Livingstone's Adventure offer combinations.** Children over seven can jetboat if they are accompanied by an adult.

RAPPELLING AND SWINGING

For something completely different, **Abseil Zambia** (☎ 213/32–1188 ✎ theswing@zamnet.zm) has taken some specially designed heavy-duty steel cables, combined them with various pulleys and rigs, one dry gorge, and a 100% safety record to entertain both the fainthearted and the daring. The full day (US$85) is a great value, as it includes lunch, refreshments, and as many repeats of the activities as you like. ⚠ **Keep in mind that you will have to climb out after the gorge swing and the rappel. A half day (US$95) is advised during the hot months of October–December.** Work up an appetite for more daring drops by starting on the zip line (or flying fox).

You run off a ramp while attached to the line, and the sensation is pure freedom and surprisingly unscary, as you are not moving up or down. Next rappel down into the 175-foot gorge, and, after you climb out, try it again facing forward. It's called a rap run. You're literally walking down the cliff face. End the day with the king of adrenaline activities, a whopping 175-foot, 3½-second vertical free-fall swing into the gorge (US$55 for one swing). Three-two-one-hoooo-ha!

RAFTING AND RIVER BOARDING

Safari Par Excellence (☎ *213/32–1629* ⊕ *www.safpar.net*) offers rafting excursions to Batoka Gorge that cost US$120 for a morning trip or US$145 for a full-day trip. The cable car transports rafters out of the gorge, so you only have to climb down. You can also do a combination helicopter-and-rafting trip. Bring secure shoes, dry clothes for the long drive home, a baseball cap to wear under your helmet, and plenty of sunscreen. You can also decide to try river boarding (from US$155), in which you hop off the raft onto a body board and surf suitable rapids.

SHOPPING

If you fall in love with the furniture in your lodge, visit **Kubu Crafts** (✉ *133 Mosi-oa-Tunya Rd.* ☎ *213/32–0320* ⊕ *www.kubucrafts.com*), a stylish home decor shop. Locally made furniture in hardwood and wrought iron is complemented by a selection of West African masks and weavings and the work of numerous local artists, including the fantastic oil paintings of Stephen Kapata. Prices can be ridiculously inflated. It's worth having a look through Mukuni Park before you buy the same article at a 500% markup. Kubu Crafts also sells tea, coffee, and cakes to enjoy in the garden.

Although the park at the entrance to the falls has stalls where you can find stone and wood carvings and simple bead and semiprecious-stone jewelry, the real gem of an African bazaar lies in the center of town, at **Mukuni Park Market** (✉ *Mosi-oa-Tunya Rd. and Libala Dr.* ☎ *No phone*). ■ TIP➜ This is the place to try your hand at bargaining. You'll be quoted top dollar initially, but shop around and watch the prices drop to roughly one-third of the original quote. Walk through the entire market before you commence buying. This will not only ensure that you get the best price but will give you the opportunity to gauge the level of craftsmanship that can be expected. Look out for individual and unusual pieces, as it is occasionally possible to find valuable antiques. The market is open daily approximately 7–6.

VICTORIA FALLS, ZIMBABWE

The town of Victoria Falls started with a little curio shop and slowly expanded until the 1970s, when it became the mecca around which the tourist phenomenon of Victoria Falls pivoted. The political problems following independence have been well documented in the world press and certainly continue to take their toll.

There has been significant poaching in the Zambezi National Park to the northwest. (If you really want to have the African game experience, take a day trip to Chobe National Park, only 70 km [44 mi] away in Botswana.) Regardless, the town enjoys the happy coincidence of being a curio shopper's paradise inside a national park. This means you can literally buy an elephant carving while watching the real McCoy march past the shop window. The town is extremely compact. Almost all the hotels are within walking distance, and the falls themselves are only 10 minutes away on foot. The main road that runs through town and goes to the falls in one direction and to the airport in the other is called Livingstone Way. Park Way is perpendicular. Most of the shops, banks, and booking agents can be found on these two streets, and this part of town is also where most of the hawkers operate. ■TIP➜ **Give these vendors a clear berth, as their wares are cheap for a reason (the boat cruise is substandard, it's illegal to change money, etc.).**

GETTING HERE AND AROUND
Very few tourists opt to fly into Vic Falls due to the political problems, high visa costs, and lack of reliable flights. It's actually more common for those visiting Zim to fly into Zambia and cross the border. However, if you do choose to fly into the Victoria Falls Airport, most hotels will send free shuttle buses to meet incoming flights and provide free transfers for departing guests; book in advance.

Hotels can summon reputable taxis quickly and advise you on the cost. Tipping is not mandatory, but change is always appreciated.

MONEY MATTERS
Zimbabwe's currency is the Zimbabwe dollar, but it's currently meaningless for tourists so avoid it. Instead, carry U.S. dollars in small denominations, because everyone accepts foreign currency. It's advisable to stick to U.S. dollars for all activity payments to both the Zimbabwean- and the Zambian-based operators. Credit card facilities are not readily available.

Electricity and voltage are the same in Zimbabwe and South Africa.

SAFETY AND PRECAUTIONS
The political situation in Zimbabwe is currently fairly stable but the damage from the lengthy dictatorship and internal strife is still very apparent. Prices have stabilized and the basic goods have reappeared on the shelves, but the tourist capital of Victoria Falls has by no means regained its status as a prime international destination. Most of the hotels are forced to import all their goods from South Africa or Zambia, making profit margins increasingly smaller while occupancy levels stay low. Unfortunately the tide has not yet turned convincingly, and the political climate remains unpredictable. All the activities, shopping, and dining options on offer on the Zimbabwean side can also be enjoyed across the border in Zambia—without any of the uncertainty and potential for sudden political and economical upheavals that could result in cancellations, substandard service, or threats to visitors' safety. ■TIP➜ **Until the rule in Zimbabwe has proven itself completely stable and the industry on the road to recovery, we recommend concentrat-**

ing on Zambia and only venturing into Zimbabwe with reputable Zambian tour operators.

MARS (Medical Air Rescue Services) is on standby for all emergencies. Dr. Nyoni is a trauma specialist and operates a hospital opposite the Shoestring lodge. Go to Victoria Falls Pharmacy for prescriptions.

Homosexuality is not illegal in Zimbabwe but can be a practical problem. Attitudes are improving, but it's advisable to be extremely circumspect.

Beware of street vendors. They'll try to rip you off in ways you'd never have believed possible.

TELEPHONE

The country code for Zimbabwe is 263. When dialing from abroad, drop the initial 0 from local area codes. Operator assistance is 962 for domestic and 965 for international inquiries, but it's better to ask a hotel or restaurant owner.

Zimbabwe has card-operated pay phones. Phone cards are available in several denominations, and a digital readout tells you how much credit remains. Telephone cards are available at newsstands and convenience stores.

PERUSING THE MARKETS

Original African art is hard to come by in curio markets, and unfortunately most of the pieces are crude replicas. Explore the markets with an open mind and simply buy a piece that tickles your fancy. Don't buy anything until you've walked the length of the market. This will give you a sense of what's on offer and the standard of workmanship. Look for objects carved from one solid piece of wood. Those made from more than one piece of wood are stuck together using very dodgy processes. Within a year you could find your beloved treasure in pieces.

ESSENTIALS

Airlines **Air Zimbabwe** (☎ 013/4–4316 ⊕ www.airzimbabwe.com). **Comair/ British Airways** (☎ 013/4–2053 or 013/4–2388 ⊕ www.british-airways.com). **South African Airways** (☎ 04/738–922 ⊕ www.flysaa.com).

Airport **Victoria Falls Airport** (✉ Livingstone Way ☎ 013/4–4250).

Embassies **U.S. Embassy** (✉ 172 Herbert Chitepo Ave., Box 4010, Harare ☎ 04/25–0593 ⊕ harare.usembassy.gov).

Emergency Services **Police** (☎ 013/4–4206 or 013/4–4681). **MARS** (✉ West Dr., opposite Shoestring ☎ 013/4–4646).

EXPLORING

Sights below appear on the Victoria Falls Town map.

☺ **Victoria Falls Bridge.** A veritable monument to Cecil Rhodes's dream of completing a Cape-to-Cairo rail line, this graceful structure spans the gorge formed by the Zambezi River. It would have been far easier and less expensive to build the bridge upstream from the falls, but Rhodes was captivated by the romance of a railway bridge passing over this natural wonder. A net was stretched across the gorge under

Continued on page 458

Victoria Falls

VICTORIA FALLS

by Kate Turkington

Expect to be humbled by the sheer power and majesty. Expect to be deafened by the thunderous noise, drenched by spray, and overwhelmed at the sight. Expect the mighty swath of roaring, foaming Victoria Falls—spanning the entire 1-mile width of the Zambezi River—to leave you speechless.

On a clear day the spray generated by the falls is visible from 31 mi (50 km) away—the swirling mist rising above the woodland savanna looks like smoke from a bush fire inspiring their local name, Mosi-Oa-Tunya, or the "Smoke that Thunders." The rim of the Falls is broken into separate smaller falls with names like the Devil's Cataract, Rainbow Falls, Horseshoe Falls, and Armchair Falls.

The Falls, which are more than 300 feet high, are one of the world's seven natural wonders and were named a UNESCO World Heritage Site in 1989. Upon seeing Victoria Falls for the first time Dr. David Livingstone proclaimed, "Scenes so lovely must have been gazed upon by angels in their flight." Truer words were never spoken.

FALLS FACTS

FORMATION OF THE FALLS

A basaltic plateau once stood where the falls are today. The whole area was once completely submerged, but fast-forward to the Jurassic Age and the water eventually dried up. Only the Zambezi River remained flowing down into the gaping 1-mile-long continuous gorge that was formed by the uneven cracking of the drying plateau.

WHEN TO GO

The Falls are spectacular at any time, but if you want to see them full, visit during the high water season (April–June) when more than 2 million gallons hurtle over the edge every second. The resulting spray is so dense that, at times, the view can be obscured. Don't worry though, the frequent gusts of wind will soon come to your aid and your view will be restored. If you're lucky to be there during a full moon, you might be able to catch a moonbow (a nighttime version of a rainbow) in the spray.

TO ZIM OR TO ZAM

Sorry Zambia, but the view from your side just doesn't stack up to the view from the Zimbabwean side. Only on the Zim side do you see infamous Devil's Cataract racing through the gorge; the entire width of the world's most spectacular waterfall; and the most rainbows dancing over the rapids—a bronze statue of Dr Livingstone's first sight of the falls is also here. You'll also get to walk through the glorious rain forest that borders the cliff edges, where wild flowers glow from greenery and monkeys chatter in ancient trees. This is also where accessible, flat-stone pathways—found immediately after you pass through the Zimbabwe entrance to the Falls—will take even the most unfit, tottery, or wheelchair-bound visitor right up to all the viewpoints. You don't need a map or a guide, as each path to the viewpoints is clearly marked.

CROSSING THE FALLS

Built in 1905, Victoria Falls Bridge is a monument to explorer, adventurer, empire-builder and former South African Prime Minister Cecil Rhodes's dream of creating a Cape-to-Cairo railway. Though the line was never completed, steam-powered trains still chug over the bridge, re-creating a sight seen here for over a century. From the bridge you get a knockout view of the falls, as well as the Zambezi River raging through Batoka Gorge. An added bonus: watching adrenaline junkies hurl themselves off the 364-foot-high Victoria Falls Bridge.

GREAT SCOT!

The first European to set eyes on the falls was the Scots explorer and missionary Dr. David Livingstone in the mid-1850s. Overcome by the experience he named them after his queen, Victoria.

EXTREME SPORTS

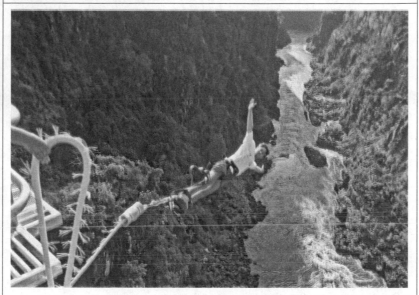

Bungee jumping off Victoria Falls Bridge above the Zambezi River

Victoria Falls is renowned for the plethora of adventure activities that can be organized on either side. It's best to arrange activities through your hotel, or a safari adventure shop, but if you want to go it alone, know that some operators only serve one side of the falls and operators have a tendency to come and go quickly.

▪ Bungee Jumping with **African Extreme** (☎ 213/32-4231 ✉ bungi@zamnet.zm) is a major adrenaline rush, with 65 feet and three seconds of free fall and a pretty spectacular view.

▪ If you fancy an elephant-back safari on your own elephant for a couple of hours in the morning or evening then **Safari Par Excellence** (☎ 213/1-4424 ⊕ www.safpar.com) will put you on board.

▪ **Livingstone Air Safaris** (☎ 213/32-3147) will take you over the falls in a fixed-wing aircraft while **Batoka Sky** (☎ 213/32-0058 ⊕ www.livingstones adventure.com) will put you in a helicopter or microlight plane.

▪ If you are comfortable enough to keep your cool while a herd of elephants approaches, go horseback riding along the banks of the Zambezi with **Chundukwa Adventure Trails** (☎ 213/32-7452 ✉ chundukwa@zamnet.zm).

▪ If you want some thrills and speed but rafting seems a bit daunting, go jetboating with **Jet Extreme** (☎ 213/32-1375 ✉ jetextremetony@microlink.zm). A cable-car ride, included in the cost of the jetboat ride, will save strenuous walking out of the gorge.

▪ Big operators like Safari Par Excellence and **Shearwater Adventures** (☎ 213/4-5806 ⊕ www.shearwatersadventures.com) can satisfy your every adventure whim with their combination packages that include jet-skiing, kayaking, rappelling, swinging, and of course, white-water rafting, reputed to be the best in the world with Class-6 rapids and down.

the construction site, which prompted the construction workers to go on strike for a couple of days. They resumed work only when it was explained that they would not have to leap into it at the end of every workday. Although the workers did not share the current adrenaline-fueled obsession with jumping into the abyss, the net probably had a lot to do with the miraculous fact that only two people were killed during construction. The bridge was completed in only 14 months, and the last two cross-girders were defiantly joined on April 1, 1905.

To get onto the bridge, you first have to pass through Zimbabwean immigration and customs controls, so bring your passport. Unless you decide to cross into Zambia, no visa is necessary. Depending on crowds, the simple procedure can take from five minutes to a half hour. The border posts are open daily from 6 AM to 10 PM, after which the bridge is closed to all traffic. From the bridge you get a knockout view of the river raging through Batoka Gorge as well as a section of the falls on the Zambian side. An added bonus is watching the bungee jumpers disappear over the edge. ⊠ *Livingstone Way.*

Victoria Falls National Park. Plan to spend at least two hours soaking in the splendors of this park. Bring snacks and water, and supervise children extremely well, as the barriers are by no means safe. Babies and toddlers can be pushed in a stroller. If you visit the falls during the high-water peak, between April and June, you'd do well to carry a raincoat or umbrella (you can rent them at the entrance) and to bring along a waterproof, disposable camera because you *will* be drenched in the spray from the falls, which creates a permanent downpour. Be prepared for limited photo opportunities due to the mist. ■TIP➔ **Leave expensive cameras, cell phones, and wristwatches in your hotel or lodge safe.**

The constant drizzle has created a small rain forest that extends in a narrow band along the edge of the falls. A trail running through this dripping green world is overgrown with African ebony, Cape fig, Natal mahogany, wild date palms, ferns, and deep red flame lilies. A fence has been erected to keep non-fee-paying visitors at bay. Clearly signposted side trails lead to viewpoints overlooking the falls. The most spectacular is **Danger Point,** a perilous rock outcropping that overlooks the narrow gorge through which the Zambezi River funnels out of the **Boiling Pot,** but be careful, as this viewpoint is hazardously wet and precarious. In low-water months (September–November) most of the water goes over the falls through the **Devil's Cataract,** a narrow and mesmerizingly powerful section of the falls visible from **Livingstone's statue.** Around the full moon the park stays open late so you can see the lunar rainbow formed by the spray—a hauntingly beautiful sight. Early morning and late afternoon are popular visiting times, as you can see the daylight rainbows then. A booklet explaining the formation and layout of the falls is available from the Victoria Falls Publicity Association for a small fee. ⊠ *Off Livingstone Way* ☎ *No phone* 🖃 *US$20* ⊙ *Daily 6–6; open later around full moon.*

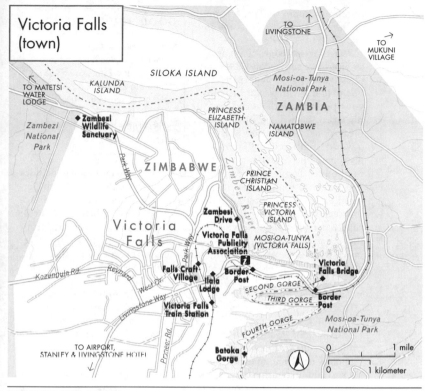

Victoria Falls
(town)

TO
LIVINGSTONE

TO
MUKUNI
VILLAGE

SILOKA ISLAND

Mosi-oa-Tunya
National Park

TO MATETSI
WATER
LODGE

KALUNDA
ISLAND

PRINCESS
ELIZABETH
ISLAND

ZAMBIA

Zambezi
National
Park

◆ Zambezi
Wildlife
Sanctuary

NAMATOBWE
ISLAND

ZIMBABWE

PRINCE
CHRISTIAN
ISLAND

Victoria
Falls

Zambesi
Drive ◆

Victoria Falls
Publicity
Association

PRINCESS
VICTORIA
ISLAND

MOSI-OA-TUNYA
(VICTORIA FALLS)

Kazungula Rd.

Reynard

Falls Craft
Village

Ilala
Lodge

Border
Post

Victoria
Falls Bridge

SECOND GORGE

THIRD GORGE

Border
Post

West Dr.

Livingstone Way

Victoria Falls
Train Station

FOURTH GORGE

Mosi-oa-Tunya
National Park

Pioneer Rd.

TO AIRPORT,
STANLEY & LIVINGSTONE HOTEL

Batoka
Gorge

0   1 mile

0   1 kilometer

8

WHERE TO STAY

It's important to know that inflation caused by the current political climate is causing prices to constantly rise. Getting an all-inclusive package tour is by far the best bet in this area.

$ **Ilala Lodge.** The lodge's elegant interior design is tempered with thatch roofs, giving it a graceful African look. Dining outside under the night sky at the Palm Restaurant ($$$), with the falls thundering 300 feet away, is a particularly enticing way to while away a Zimbabwean evening. The Palm also serves a great terrace lunch overlooking the bush. Guest rooms are hung with African paintings and tapestries and filled with delicately caned chairs and tables and with dressers made from old railroad sleepers. French doors open onto a narrow strip of lawn backed by thick bush. Unlike most hotels in town, Ilala Lodge has no fence around it, so at night it's not uncommon to find elephants browsing outside your window or buffalo grazing on the lawn. **Pros:** great central location; family-friendly; only 10 minutes from the falls by foot. **Cons:** the location in the center of town can ruin expectations if you are keen on the peace of the African bush; the noise from the helicopters and microlights can be disturbing. ⊠ *411 Livingstone Way, Box 18* ☎ *013/4–4737* ⊕ *www.ilalalodge.com* ⤻ *32 rooms, 2 suites* ♿ *In-room: safe, no TV (some), Internet (some), Wi-Fi (some). In-hotel:*

restaurant, room service, bar, pool, laundry service, Wi-Fi, some pets allowed ▭ *V* ❄ *BP.*

$$$ 🖾 **Matetsi Water Lodge.** "I am at your service from this second 24/7 until the second of your departure" may be the first words you'll hear from your personal butler. And true to his word, he will be informative, professional, and friendly and make a world of difference. River guides give comprehensive impromptu lec-

> **GOOD SOUVENIRS**
>
> Shona stone carvings from Zimbabwe, woven baskets from Botswana and Zambia, and soap-stone from Zambia and Zimbabwe make great souvenirs. Make sure you pack these things carefully, especially the soapstone, as it's all extremely fragile.

tures on the Zambezi River, the chef will make sure every meal includes your favorite food, and room attendants pepper the room with per-sonal touches and draw an end-of-the-day bath for you. With service this seamless and generous, you can only have a delightful time. **Pros:** superb personal butler service; 15 km of exclusive Zambezi waterfront that's bordered on both sides by unfenced national parks; interpre-tative wildlife experience with extensive information on fauna, flora, and history available for the telling by all the guides. **Cons:** 30 min-utes from town. ✉ *On southern banks of Zambezi River, 40 km (25 mi) upstream from Victoria Falls* 🕿 *Box X27, Benmore, Johannesburg 2010* ☏ *118/09–4300* ⊕ *www.andbeyond.com* ➧ *18 suites* ⚬ *In-room: safe (some), refrigerator (some), no TV. In-hotel: restaurant, room ser-vice, bar, pool, spa, children's programs (ages 2–14), laundry service* ▭ *No credit cards* ❄ *AI.*

$$ 🖾 **Stanley and Livingstone at Victoria Falls.** It's almost surreal to step from the surrounding bushveld into the meticulously composed rooms of this small hotel, which is set on a 6,000-acre private game reserve. Public rooms are luxuriously furnished in colonial style with some spectacular antiques and have verandas overlooking a water hole where elephants and other animals come to drink. The suites are large with Victorian flourishes, dark wood furnishings, wall-to-wall carpeting, heavy drapes, and an expensive chocolate on your pillow at night. The bathrooms are a calming study in white tile, green marble, and gold trim. Service is personal but slightly more casual than the decor would lead you to expect. The rate includes game drives and all on-site activities except elephant rides and transfers to the airport or to town. **Pros:** rooms have air-conditioning; 10 minutes outside town; unbelievably over-the-top and decadently indulgent decor. **Cons:** the design of this lodge owes very little to Africa, and once you close your door you could very well be almost anywhere in Europe; you might find yourself wanting to use words like "mahvelous" a lot! ✉ *Off Ursula Rd., 13 km (8 mi) south of Victoria Falls town* 🕿 *Box 160* ☏ *013/4–1003* ⊕ *www.stanleyan-dlivingstone.com* ➧ *16 suites* ⚬ *In-room: no phone (some), safe (some), refrigerator (some), DVD (some). In-hotel: restaurant, room service, bar, pool, laundry service, no kids under 12* ▭ *MC, V* ❄ *AI.*

Safaris in South Africa

WORD OF MOUTH

"To be in the bush and see the different animals up close, in their habitat, living their lives as they have forever (albeit without land rovers looking at them), was an absolutely amazing experience . . . Can't wait to return."

—cw

"Kruger (National Park) is a great experience, but I would not do it as my only safari experience. You are too limited in viewing capability (no off road) and the density of 'big 5' sightings is much lower than in a private camp. [If] you are going on safari for only 6–8 days, you need the 'concentrated safari experience.'"

—Cary999

By Kate
Turkington

Since 1994, when Nelson Mandela spearheaded its peaceful transition to democracy, South Africa has become one of the fastest-growing tourist destinations in the world. And it's not difficult to see why. The country is stable and affordable, with an excellent infrastructure; friendly, interesting, amazingly diverse people; and enough stunning sights, sounds, scenery, and attractions to make even the most jaded traveler sit up and take notice. And nearly everybody speaks English—a huge bonus for international visitors.

South Africa has always teemed with game. That's what drew the early European explorers, who aimed to bring something exotic home with them. After all, as Pliny the Elder, one of Africa's earliest explorers, wrote almost 2,000 years ago, *ex Africa semper aliquid novi*—out of Africa always comes something new. Sometimes it was a giraffe, a rhinoceros, a strange bird, or an unheard-of plant.

In the latter half of the 19th century, Dr. Livingstone, Scotland's most famous Christian missionary, opened up much of the interior on his evangelizing expeditions, as did the piratical Englishman Cecil John Rhodes, who famously made his fortune on the Kimberley diamond mines and planned an unsuccessful Cape-to-Cairo railway line. About the same time, lured by the rumors of gold and instant fortunes, hundreds of hunters came to the lowveld to lay their hands on much-sought-after skins, horns, and ivory. Trophy hunters followed, vying with one another to see how many animals they could shoot in one day—often more than 100 each.

Paul Kruger, president of the Transvaal Republic (a 19th-century Boer country that occupied a portion of present-day South Africa), took the unprecedented visionary step of establishing a protected area for the wildlife in the lowveld region; in 1898 Kruger National Park was born.

South Africa has 22 national parks covering deserts, wetland and marine areas, forests, mountains, scrub, and savanna. Hunting safaris are still popular but are strictly controlled by the government, and licenses are compulsory. Although hunting is a controversial issue, the revenue is substantial and can be ploughed into sustainable conservation, and the impact on the environment is minimal. Increasingly, wildlife conservation is linked with community development; many conservation areas have integrated local communities, the wildlife, and the environment, with benefits for all. Londolozi, MalaMala, Phinda, and Pafuri Camp are internationally acclaimed role models for linking tourism with community-development projects.

Although the "**Big Five**" was originally a hunting term for those animals that posed the greatest risk to hunters on foot—buffalo, elephants,

TOP REASONS TO GO

Big Game. You're guaranteed to see big game—including the Big Five—both in national parks and at many private lodges.

Escape the Crowds. South Africa's game parks are rarely crowded. You'll see more game with fewer other visitors than almost anywhere else in Africa.

Luxury Escapes. Few other sub-Saharan countries can offer South Africa's high standards of accommodation, service, and food amid gorgeous surroundings of bush, beach, mountains, and desert.

Take the Family. All the national parks accept children (choose a malaria-free one if your kids are small), and many private lodges have fantastic children's programs.

Bountiful Birds. Even if you're not a birder you'll be dazzled by hundreds of fascinating birds of all colors, shapes, and sizes.

---

leopards, lions, and rhinos—it is used today as the most important criterion for evaluating a lodge or reserve. But let the lure of the Big Five turn your safari into a treasure hunt and you'll miss the overall wilderness experience. Don't overlook the bush's other treasures, from desert meerkats and forest bush babies to antelopes, the handsome caracal, and spotted genets. Add to these hundreds of birds, innumerable insects, trees, flowers, shrubs, and grasses. Don't forget to search for the "Little Five": the buffalo weaver, elephant shrew, leopard tortoise, lion ant, and rhinoceros beetle. A guided bush walk may let you see these little critters and more.

Unfortunately, you probably won't be able to see all of the safaris that South Africa has to offer in one trip. We suggest that you *read* about all of them and then choose for yourself.

ORIENTATION AND PLANNING

GETTING ORIENTED

South Africa is a great place for first-time safari-goers to get their feet wet. There are plenty of options, from small private reserves like Shamwari Game Reserve in the Eastern Cape to large national parks like Kruger National Park, just a few hours from Johannesburg.

Kruger National Park. A visit to Kruger, one of the world's great game parks, may rank among the best experiences of your life. With its amazing diversity of scenery, trees, amphibians, reptiles, birds, and mammals, Kruger is a place to safari at your own pace, choosing from among upscale private camps or simple campsites.

Sabi Sands Game Reserve. The most famous and exclusive of South Africa's private reserves, this 153,000-acre park is home to dozens of private lodges, including the world-famous MalaMala and Londolozi. With perhaps the highest game density of any private reserve in southern Africa, the Sabi Sands fully deserves its exalted reputation.

KwaZulu-Natal Parks. Zululand's Hluhluwe-Imfolozi is tiny—less than 6% of Kruger's size—but delivers the Big Five plus all the plains game. It has one of the most biologically diverse habitats on earth, a unique mix of forest, woodland, savanna, and grassland that includes about 1,250 species of plants and trees—more than you'll find in some entire countries. Mkuze and Ithala are even smaller but well worth a visit, and if you're looking for the ultimate in luxury, then stay at Phinda or Thanda private reserves.

Kgalagadi Transfrontier Park. National parks in two countries—Botswana's Gemsbok National Park and South Africa's Kalahari Gemsbok National Park—together are known as Kgalagadi Transfrontier Park, one of the world's largest conservation areas, spanning more than 38,000 square km (14,670 square mi). Its stark, desolate beauty shelters huge black-maned Kalahari lions among other predators and provides brilliant birding, especially birds of prey.

PLANNING

GETTING HERE AND AROUND
AIR TRAVEL
Arriving by plane is the best and most viable means of transportation to most safari destinations. If you are visiting a game lodge deep in the bush, you will be arriving by light plane—and you really will be restricted in what you can bring. Excess luggage can usually be stored with the operator until your return. Don't just gloss over this: charter operators take weight very seriously, and some will charge you for an extra ticket if you insist on bringing excess baggage. ⇨ *For airline contact information, see Air Travel, in the Travel Smart South Africa chapter.*

HEALTH AND SAFETY
The most serious health problem you'll face while on Safari is malaria. It occurs in the prime game-viewing areas of Mpumalanga and Limpopo provinces (home to Kruger and Sabi Sands) and northern KwaZulu-Natal (site of Hluhluwe-Imfolozi, Mkuze, and Ithala game reserves, and Phinda and Thanda private reserves). Travelers heading to malaria-endemic regions should consult a health-care professional at least one month before departure for advice on antimalarial drugs. As the sun goes down, wear light-color long-sleeve shirts, long pants, and shoes and socks, and apply mosquito repellent generously. Always sleep in a mosquito-proof room or tent and keep a fan going. If you're pregnant or trying to conceive, avoid malaria areas if at all possible.

⚠ **All malaria medications are not equal.** Chloroquine is *not* an effective antimalarial drug in South Africa. And halofantrine (marketed as Halfan), which is widely used overseas to treat malaria, has serious heart-related side effects, including death. The CDC recommends that you do *not* use halofantrine.

You must be up-to-date with all of your routine shots such as measles/mumps/rubella (MMR) vaccine, diphtheria/pertussis/tetanus (DPT) vaccine, etc. If you're not up-to-date, usually a simple booster shot will bring you up to par.

CHOOSING A FIELD GUIDE

Arm yourself with specialized field guides on mammals and birds rather than a more general one that tries to cover too much. Airports, lodges, and camp shops stock a good range, but try to get hold of one in advance and do a bit of homework.

DEHYDRATION AND OVERHEATING

The African sun is hot and the air is dry, and sweat evaporates quickly in these conditions. You might not realize how much bodily fluid you are losing as a result. Wear a hat, lightweight clothing, and sunscreen—all of which will help your body cope with high temperatures.

Drink at least two to three quarts of water a day; in extreme heat conditions drink as much as three to four quarts of water or juice, and drink more if you're exerting yourself physically. If you overdo it at dinner with wine or spirits, or even caffeine, you need to drink still more water to recover the fluid lost as your body processes the alcohol. Antimalarial medications are also very dehydrating, so it's important to increase your water intake while you're taking this medicine.

Don't rely on thirst to tell you when to drink; people often don't feel thirsty until they're a little dehydrated. At the first sign of dry mouth, exhaustion, or headache, drink water, because dehydration is the likely culprit.

■ TIP→ **To test for dehydration, pinch the skin on the back of your hand and see if it stays in a peak; if it does, you're dehydrated.** Drink a solution of ½ teaspoon salt and 4 tablespoons sugar dissolved in a quart of water to replace electrolytes.

Heat cramps stem from a low salt level due to excessive sweating. These muscle pains usually occur in the abdomen, arms, or legs. When a child says he can't take another step, investigate whether he has cramps. When cramps occur, stop all activity and sit quietly in a cool spot and drink. Don't do anything strenuous for a few hours after the cramps subside. If heat cramps persist for more than an hour, seek medical assistance.

MOTION SICKNESS

If you're prone to motion sickness, be sure to examine your safari itinerary closely. Though most landing strips for chartered planes are not paved but rather grass, earth, or gravel, landings are smooth most of the time. If you're going on safari to northern Botswana (the Okavango Delta, specifically), know that small planes are the main means of transportation between camps; these trips can be very bumpy, hot, and a little dizzying even if you're not prone to motion sickness. If you're not sure how you'll react, take motion-sickness pills just in case. Most of the air transfers take an average of only 30 minutes, and the rewards will be infinitely greater than the pains.

9

DOCUMENT CHECKLIST

- Passport
- Visas, if necessary
- Airline tickets
- Proof of yellow-fever inoculation
- Accommodation and transfer vouchers
- Car-rental reservation forms
- International driver's license
- Copy of information page of your passport
- Copy of airline tickets

- Copy of medical prescriptions
- Copy of traveler's check numbers
- List of credit card numbers and international contact information for each card issuer
- Copy of travel insurance and medical-emergency evacuation policy
- Travel agent's contact numbers
- Notarized letter of consent from one parent if the other parent is traveling alone with their children

■TIP→ **When you fly in small planes, take a sun hat and a pair of sunglasses.** If you sit in the front seat next to the pilot, or on the side of the sun, you will experience harsh glare that could give you a severe headache and exacerbate motion sickness.

INTESTINAL UPSET

Microfauna and -flora differ in every region of Africa, so if you drink unfiltered water, add ice to your soda, or eat fruit from a roadside stand, you might get traveler's diarrhea. All reputable hotels and lodges have filtered, clean tap water or provide sterilized drinking water, and nearly all camps and lodges have supplies of bottled water. If you're traveling outside organized safari camps in rural Africa or are unsure of local water, carry plenty of bottled water and follow the CDC's advice for fruits and vegetables: boil it, cook it, peel it, or forget it. If you're going on a mobile safari, ask about drinking water.

TRAVEL INSURANCE

Get a comprehensive travel-insurance policy in addition to any primary insurance you already have. Travel insurance covers trip cancellation; trip interruption or travel delay; loss or theft of, or damage to, baggage; baggage delay; medical expenses; emergency medical transportation; and collision damage waiver if renting a car. These policies are offered by most travel-insurance companies in one comprehensive policy and vary in price based on both your total trip cost and your age.

It's important to note that travel insurance does not include coverage for threats of a terrorist incident or for any war-related activity. It's important that you speak with your operator before you book to find out how it would handle such occurrences. For example, would you be fully refunded if your trip was canceled because of war or a threat of a terrorist incident? Would your trip be postponed at no additional cost to you?

■ **TIP→ Purchase travel insurance within seven days of paying your initial trip deposit.** For most policies this will not only ensure your trip deposit but also cover you for any preexisting medical conditions and default by most airlines and safari companies. The latter two are not covered if your policy is purchased after seven days.

Many travel agents and tour operators stipulate that travel insurance is mandatory if you book your trip through them. This coverage is not only for your financial protection in the event of a cancellation but also for coverage of medical emergencies and medical evacuations due to injury or illness, which often involve use of jet aircraft with hospital equipment and doctors on board and can amount to many thousands of dollars.

If you need emergency medical evacuation, most travel-insurance companies stipulate that you must obtain authorization by the company prior to the evacuation. Unfortunately, a few safari camps and lodges are so remote that they don't have access to a telephone, so getting prior authorization is extremely difficult if not impossible. You should check with your insurance company before you leave to see whether it has this clause and, if so, what can be done to get around it. Good travel agents and tour operators are aware of the issue and will address it.

ABOUT THE CAMPS AND LODGES

Accommodations range from fairly basic huts to the ultimate in luxury at most of the private camps. The advantage of a private lodge (apart from superb game-viewing) is that often everything is included: lodging, meals, beverages including excellent house wines, game drives, and other activities. You'll also be treated like royalty. (Indeed, you may well brush shoulders with royals and celebs of all kinds.) Note that there are no elevators in any safari lodging facility in Kruger.

At most establishments, prices include a three- to five-course dinner plus a full breakfast. Most places now have at least one vegetarian course on the menu. Many lodges and hotels offer special midweek or winter low-season rates. If you're opting for a private game lodge, find out whether it accepts children (many specify kids only over 12), and plan to stay a minimum of two nights, three if you can.

Most national parks have self-catering accommodations (you buy and prepare your own food): budget huts from R250 per couple per night and much more expensive (but worth it) cottages in the more remote and exclusive bush camps that range from R600 to R1,100. Visit the South African National Parks Web site (⊕ *www.sanparks.org*) to get information and book accommodations. ■ **TIP→ Bookings open every September 1 for the following year. Make sure you book well in advance and, if possible, avoid July, August, and December, which are South African school vacations.** If you can, book by phone. It's quicker and your booking will be confirmed (and paid for if you wish) on the spot.

WHAT IT COSTS IN SOUTH AFRICAN RAND				
¢	$	$$	$$$	$$$$
Full-service Safari Lodging	under R2,000	R2,000– R5,000	R5,001– R8,000	R8,001– R12,000	over R12,000

Lodging prices are for a standard double room in high season, including 14% tax.

MONEY MATTERS

Most safaris are paid for in advance, so you need money only to cover personal purchases and gratuities. (The cash you take should include small denominations, like US$1, US$5, and US$10, for tips.) If you're not on a package tour and are self-driving, you need to carry more money. Credit cards—MasterCard, Visa, and, to a much lesser extent, American Express and Diners Club—are accepted throughout South Africa and at most group-owned lodges and hotels but often not elsewhere. Always check in advance whether your preferred card is accepted at the lodge. If you're self-driving, note that many places prefer to be paid in the local currency, so make sure you change money where you can.

TIPS FOR TIPPING

Plan to give the local equivalents (U.S. dollars are also fine) of about US$10 per person per day to the ranger and not much less to the tracker; an additional tip of US$25 for the general staff would be sufficient for a couple staying two days. Mark Harris, managing director of Tanzania Odyssey, a London-based tour operator, suggests that tipping roughly $15 a day (per couple) into the general tip box and approximately $15 a day to your specific driver is generous.

Guides should be tipped at least US$5 per person per day.

It's also a good idea to bring some thank-you cards with you from home to include with the tip as a personal touch. Fodor's Forum member atravelynn adds, "Put bills in an envelope for your guide and in a separate envelope with your name on it for the camp staff. Sometimes the camps have envelopes, but bringing some from home is also a good idea."

DISCOUNTS AND DEALS

If you're keen to explore South Africa's many wilderness areas, buying a Wild Card from South African National Parks might be worth your while, but be sure to read all the fine print. There are several types of passes covering different clusters of parks for individuals, couples, and families; at this writing the price of an individual pass ranges from about R200 to R1,000 (for an all-parks pass).

Contact **South African National Parks** (☎ *012/343–1991* ⊕ *www.sanparks.org*).

BATHROOM BREAKS ON SAFARI

On safari, particularly when you stop for sundowners, you'll be pointed to a nearby bush (which the ranger checks out before you use it). Carry tissues and toilet paper with you, although these are usually available on the vehicle. Bury any paper you may use. If you have an emergency, ask your ranger to stop the vehicle and check out a suitable spot.

WHAT TO PACK

You'll be allowed one duffel-type bag, approximately 36 inches by 18 inches and a maximum of 26 kilos (57 pounds)—less on some airlines— so that it can be easily packed into the baggage pods of a small plane. One small camera and personal-effects bag can go on your lap. Keep all your documents and money in this personal bag.

You only need three changes of clothing for an entire trip; almost all safaris include laundry as part of the package. If you're self-driving you can carry more, but washing is easy and three changes of clothes should be ample if you use drip-dry fabrics that need no ironing. On mobile safaris you can wear tops and bottoms more than once. Either bring enough underwear to last a week between lodges or wash them in the bathroom sink. Unless there's continual rain (unlikely), clothes dry overnight in the hot, dry African air.

For game walks, pack sturdy but light walking shoes or boots—in most cases durable sneakers suffice for this option. For a walking-based safari, you need sturdy, lightweight boots. Buy them well in advance of your trip so you can break them in. If possible, isolate the clothes used on your walk from the remainder of the clean garments in your bag. Bring a couple of large white plastic garbage bags for dirty laundry. ⇨ *For information on plug adapters, see Electricity in Travel Smart South Africa.*

TOILETRIES AND SUNDRIES

Most hotels and game lodges provide soap, shampoo, and insect repellent, so you don't need to overpack these items. In the larger lodges in South Africa's national parks and private game reserves, stores and gift shops are fairly well stocked with clothing, film, and guidebooks; in self-drive and self-catering areas, shops also carry food and drink. △ **The African sun is harsh, and if you're even remotely susceptible to burning, especially coming from a northern winter, don't skimp on sunscreens and moisturizers.** Also bring conditioner for your hair, which can dry out and start breaking off.

BINOCULARS

Binoculars are essential and come in many types and sizes. You get what you pay for, so avoid buying a cheap pair—the optics will be poor, and the lenses usually don't stay aligned for long, especially if they get bumped, and they will on safari. Whatever strength you choose, pick the most lightweight pair; otherwise you'll be in for neck and shoulder strain. Take them with you on a night drive; you'll get great visuals of nocturnal animals and birds by the light of the tracker's spotlight. Many people find that when they start using binoculars and stop documenting each trip detail in photos, they have a much better safari experience.

CAMERA SMARTS

All the safaris included in this chapter are photographic (game-viewing) safaris. That said, if you spend your entire safari peering through a camera viewfinder, you may miss all the other sensual elements that contribute to the great show that is the African bush. And more than likely, your pictures won't look like the photos you see in books about African safaris. A professional photographer can spend a full year in

PACKING CHECKLIST

Light, khaki, or neutral-color clothes are universally worn on safari and were first used in Africa as camouflage by the South African Boers and then by the British army that fought them during the South African War. Light colors also help to deflect the harsh sun and, unlike dark colors, are less likely to attract mosquitoes. Do not wear camouflage gear. Do wear layers of clothing that you can strip off as the sun gets hotter and put back on as the sun goes down.

- Three cotton T-shirts

- Two long-sleeve cotton shirts

- Two pairs shorts or two skirts in summer

- Two pairs long pants (three pairs in winter)

- Optional: sweatshirt and pants, which can double as sleepwear

- Optional: a smart/casual dinner outfit

- Underwear and socks

- Walking shoes or sneakers

- Sandals

- Bathing suit

- Warm, thigh-length, padded jacket and sweater in winter

- Lightweight jacket in summer

- Windbreaker or rain poncho

- Camera equipment, plenty of film, and extra batteries

- Contact lenses, including extras

- Eyeglasses

- Binoculars

- Small flashlight

- Personal toiletries

- Malaria tablets

- Sunscreen and lip balm with SPF 30 or higher, moisturizer, and hair conditioner

- Antihistamine cream

- Insect repellent

- Basic first-aid kit (aspirin, bandages, antidiarrheal, antiseptic cream, indigestion remedy, etc.)

- Tissues and/or premoistened wipes

- Warm hat, scarf, and gloves in winter

- Sun hat and sunglasses (Polaroid and UV-protected)

- Documents and money (cash, traveler's checks, credit cards), etc.

- A notebook and pens

- Travel and field guides

- A couple of large white plastic garbage bags

- U.S. dollars in small denominations ($1, $5, $10) for tipping the field to produce a book, so you are often better off just taking snaps of your trip and buying a book to take home.

■ TIP→ **Be sure to keep your camera tightly sealed in plastic bags while you're traveling to protect it from dust.** Tuck your equipment away when the wind kicks up. You should have one or more cloth covers while you're working, and clean your equipment every day if you can.

Learning some basics about the wildlife that you expect to see on your safari will help you capture some terrific shots of the animals. If you know something about their behavior patterns ahead of time, you'll be primed to capture action, like when the hippos start to roar. Learning from your guide and carefully observing the wildlife once you're there will also help you gauge just when to click your shutter.

WHAT'S YOUR BUDGET?

When setting a budget, consider how much you want to spend and keep in mind three things: your flight, the actual safari costs, and extras. You can have a low-budget self-catering trip in one of South Africa's national parks or spend a great deal of money in one of the small, pampering, exclusive camps in Botswana. Almost every market has high-priced options as well as some economical ones.

LUXURY SAFARIS

The most popular option is to book with a tour operator and stay in private lodges, which are owned and run by an individual or company rather than a government or country. Prices at these lodges include all meals and, in many cases, alcoholic beverages, as well as two three- to five-hour-long game-viewing expeditions a day. Occasionally high-end lodges offer extra services such as spa treatments, boat trips, or special-occasion meals served alfresco in the bush. Prices range from US$350 to US$1,600 per person per night sharing a double room. If you travel alone, expect to pay a single supplement because all safari-lodge rooms are doubles.

SAFARIS ON A SHOESTRING

Don't let a tight budget deter you. There are many opportunities for big-game experiences outside the luxury lodges. Your least expensive option is to choose one of the public game parks—Kruger National Park, for example—where you drive yourself and shop for and prepare all meals yourself. The price of this type of trip is approximately one-tenth of that for private, fully inclusive lodges.

Mobile safaris are another option. Travel is by 4x4 (often something that looks like a bus) and you sleep in tents at public or private camp-sites. You need to be self-sufficient and bush-savvy to travel this way.

Rates for national park camps, called rest camps, start at about $34 a day for a two-bed *rondavel* (a round hut modeled after traditional African dwellings) and go up to $85 for a four-bed bungalow. Budget about $6 for breakfast, $8 for lunch, and $12 for dinner per person for each day on the trip. You also need to factor in park entry fees (usually a onetime fee of approximately $20 per person).

9

Booking a private lodge in the off-season also saves a bundle of money. Many lodges—South Africa's Sabi Sands area, for example—cost about US$800 per person per night during the high season but can drop to about US$500 a night during the slower months of July and August.

THE EXTRAS

Besides airfare and safari costs, make sure you budget for tips, medications, film, and other sundries. Plan to stay at a city hotel on your first and last nights in Africa—it'll help you adjust to jet lag and make things altogether easier. Expect to pay from US$50 for basic accommodations to a maximum US$750 a night in the most luxurious hotels.

Not digital yet? Stock up on film before you head out into the bush; a roll costs about US$20 in a safari camp. And don't forget to save some money for souvenirs.

WHO'S WHO

There's no substitute for a knowledgeable tour operator or travel agent who specializes in Africa. These specialists look out for your best interests, are aware of trends and developments, and function as indispensable backups in the rare instance when something goes wrong.

African safari operator. Also referred to as a ground operator, this type of outfitter is a company in Africa that provides logistical support to a U.S.–based tour operator by seeing to the details of your safari. An operator might charter flights, pick you up at the airport, and take you on game-viewing trips, for example. Some operators own or manage safari lodges. In addition, an operator communicates changing trends and developments in the region to tour operators and serves as your on-site contact in cases of illness, injury, or other unexpected situations.

Africa tour operator. Based in the United States, this type of company specializes in tours and safaris to Africa and works with a safari operator that provides support on the ground. Start dates and itineraries are set for some trips offered by the operator, but customized vacations can be arranged. Travelers usually find out about these trips through retail travel agents.

Air consolidator. A consolidator aggressively promotes and sells plane tickets to Africa, usually concentrating on only one or a few airlines to ensure a large volume of sales with those particular carriers. The airlines provide greatly reduced airfares to the consolidator, who in turn adds a markup and resells them directly to you.

Retail travel agent. In general, a travel agent sells trip packages directly to consumers. In most cases an agent doesn't have a geographical specialty. When called on to arrange a trip to Africa, the travel agent turns to an Africa tour operator for details.

Before you entrust your trip to an agent, do your best to determine the extent of his or her knowledge as well as the level of enthusiasm he or she has for the destination. There are as many travel companies claiming to specialize in Africa as there are hippos in the Zambezi, so

SAFARI PLANNING TIME LINE

SIX MONTHS AHEAD
- Research destinations and options. Make a list of sights you want to see.
- Start a safari file to keep track of information.
- Set a budget.
- Contact a travel agent to start firming up details.
- Choose your destination and make your reservations.
- Buy travel insurance.

THREE TO SIX MONTHS AHEAD
- Find out which travel documents you need.
- Apply for a passport or renew yours if it's due to expire within six months of travel time.
- Confirm whether your destination requires visas and certified health documents.
- Arrange vaccinations or medical clearances.
- Research malaria precautions.
- Book tours, side trips, etc.

ONE TO THREE MONTHS AHEAD
- Create a packing checklist.
- Fill prescriptions for antimalarial and regular medications. Buy mosquito repellent.
- Shop for safari clothing and equipment.
- Arrange for a house and pet sitter.

ONE MONTH AHEAD
- Get copies of prescriptions. Make sure you have enough medicine to last you a few days longer than your trip.

- Confirm international flights, transfers, and lodging reservations directly with your travel agent.

THREE WEEKS AHEAD
- Using your packing list, start buying articles you don't have. Update the list as you go.

TWO WEEKS AHEAD
- Collect small denominations of U.S. currency ($1 and $5) for tips.
- Prepare to pack; remember bag size and weight restrictions.

ONE WEEK AHEAD
- Suspend newspaper and mail delivery.
- List contact numbers and other details for your house sitter.
- Check antimalarial prescriptions to see whether you need to start taking medication now.
- Arrange airport transportation.
- Make two copies of your passport data. Leave one copy, and a copy of your itinerary, with someone at home; pack the other separately from your passport. Make a PDF of these pages that can be accessed via e-mail.

A FEW DAYS AHEAD
- Get pets situated.
- Pack.
- Reconfirm flights.

ONE DAY AHEAD
- Check destination weather reports.
- Make a last check of your house and go through your travel checklist one final time.

9

it's especially important to determine which operators and agents are up to the challenge.

After choosing a tour operator or travel agent, it's a good idea to discuss with him or her the logistics and details of the itinerary so you know what to expect each day. Ask questions about lodging, even if you're traveling on a group tour. A lodge that is completely open to the elements may be a highlight for some travelers and terrifying for others, particularly at night when a lion roars nearby. Also ask about the amount of time you'll spend with other travelers. If you're planning a safari honeymoon, find out if you can dine alone when you want to, and ask about honeymoon packages.

TOUR OPERATORS

Our list of tour operators hardly exhausts the number of reputable companies, but those listed were chosen because they are established firms that offer a good selection of itineraries ranging from overland safaris, walking and fly-in safaris, under-canvas safaris or safari lodges. Although various price options are offered, we suggest that where possible you go for all-inclusive packages, which will cover every aspect of your safari from flights and road transfers to game drives, guided game walks, food, drinks, and accommodation.

Abercrombie & Kent (⊠ *U.S.* ☎ *800/554–7016* ⊕ *www.abercrombiekent. com*). In business since 1962, this company is considered one of the best in the safari business and is consistently given high marks by former clients. From your first decision to go on safari to its successful conclusion, A&K offers seamless service. It has a professional network of local A&K offices in all its destination countries, staffed by full-time A&K experts. It is also renowned for its top tour directors and guides. The head office in the States is located in Oak Brook, Illinois.

Africa Adventure Company (⊠ *U.S.* ☎ *954/491–8877* ⊕ *www.africa-adventure.com*). For more than 20 years this Florida-based company has planned safaris of all kinds. It also specializes in all sorts of tours that you can add on to your safari, from exploring cities, gorilla trekking, and fishing, to diving, beaching, and lots more.

Africa Travel Resource (⊠ *U.K.* ☎ *44/1306/880–770, 888/487–5418 in the U.S. and Canada* ⊕ *www.africatravelresource.com*). This is a Web-based resource site that provides you with numerous trip possibilities. After you've browsed to your heart's content and made all the relevant decisions, the operator will do the easy part and book the trip for you. So, if you're looking to plan a trip to Mt. Kilimanjaro, you can search through the huge resource base and choose your perfect trip.

&Beyond (⊠ *South Africa* ☎ *27/11/809–4300 in South Africa, 888/882–3742 in U.S.* ⊕ *www.andbeyond.com*). Formerly CC Africa, this highly experienced tour operator has 16 years of service to the safari-going public. It offers ready-made trips and tours to all parts of southern or East Africa or can tailor one to your needs, from the budget variety to the lavish. It offers some of the best destinations and accommodations in Africa (read: it owns and manages all its properties), from the

Okavango to remote Indian Ocean islands. It specializes in honeymoon packages.

Big Five (✉ *U.S.* ☎ *800/244–3483* ⊕ *www.bigfive.com*). Offering more than 100 tours to Africa, this Florida-based operator promises its clients a trip of a lifetime—if you're not happy with the tour choices, Big Five will custom-create one for you. You can be assured that whatever trip you do choose, your knowledgeable agent will be able to draw on personal experience to assist you. Founded in 1973, Big Five focuses on low-impact, sustainable tourism and patronizes environmentally responsible lodgings.

Fazendin Portfolio (✉ *U.S.* ☎ *303/993–7906* ⊕ *www.fazendinportfolio. com*). This Denver-based company is not a traditional operator but rather a portfolio representing operators, lodges, and safari experiences. It was developed specifically with the needs and desires of North American travelers in mind. From luxury tented camping safari experiences to unique cultural adventures, you'll find exactly what you're looking for and expecting out of this once-in-a-lifetime trip.

Ker & Downey (✉ *U.S.* ☎ *800/423–4236* ⊕ *www.kerdowney.com*). One of the oldest and most respected safari companies in Africa, Ker & Downey also has an office in Texas. The company utilizes its exclusive camps to provide traditional safari experiences. Accommodation options range from rustic to deluxe.

Micato Safaris (✉ *U.S.* ☎ *800/642–2861* ⊕ *www.micatosafaris.com*). Family-owned and -operated, this New York–based operator offers deliberately luxurious trips. Safari lodges enchant with such unadulterated luxuries as private plunge pools and personal butlers. Cultured safari guides educate, instruct, and amuse, while itineraries offer an irresistible array of experiences from the sophisticated pleasures of Cape Town to the celebrated savannas of the Serengeti and the near-spiritual beauty of the Kalahari.

Orient-Express Safaris (✉ *South Africa* ☎ *27/21/483–1600* ⊕ *www.orient-express-safaris.com*). A member of the Small Luxury Hotels of the World organization, this operator owns three strategically located camps in some of Botswana's most diverse ecosystems and most desirable destinations: Chobe National Park, Moremi Wildlife Reserve, and the Okavango Delta. All the camps have identical thatch tented lodging and furnishings plus plenty of bells and whistles.

Premier Tours (✉ *U.S.* ☎ *800/545–1910* ⊕ *www.premiertours.com*). Based in Philadelphia but owned and operated by people from Africa, Premier specializes in adventure tours for anyone from 18 to 55. It is a founding member of the United Nations Environment Program's initiative on sustainable tourism development and offers consolidated airfares to Africa.

Roar Africa (✉ *U.S.* ☎ *877/762–7237* ⊕ *www.roarafrica.com*). New York– and South Africa–based ROAR Africa offers a one-of-a-kind travel service for personalized, custom tours of southern Africa. The founders' family dates back to 1688 ensuring trips are designed by specialists whose wealth of information and well-established network can only come from years of actually living there.

9

QUESTIONS TO ASK A SAFARI SPECIALIST

Don't forward a deposit to a safari specialist (a general term for a safari operator or Africa tour operator) until you have considered his or her answers to these questions. Once you have paid a deposit, you're liable for a penalty if you decide to cancel the arrangements for any reason.

■ Do you handle Africa exclusively?

■ How many years have you been selling tours in Africa?

■ Are you or any of the staff native to the continent?

■ To which professional organizations do you belong? For example, the American Society of Travel Agents (ASTA) or the United States Tour Operators Association (USTOA)?

■ Has your company received any accolades or awards relating to Africa?

■ Can you provide a reference list of past clients?

■ How often do you and your staff visit Africa?

■ Have you ever visited Africa yourself?

■ What sort of support do you have in Africa?

■ Do you charge a fee? (Agents and operators usually make their money through commissions.)

■ What is your cancellation policy?

■ Can you handle arrangements from start to finish, including flights?

■ What is your contingency plan in case of war or terrorism?

Thompsons Africa (⊠ *South Africa* ☎ *27/11/770–7700* ⊕ *www.thompsonssa.com*). Thompsons, which has been given awards for excellence by the South Africa Travel Industry and South African Airways, works with every budget to plan all types of tours including day trips and safaris. Agents are available 24 hours a day to answer your questions.

Wilderness Safaris (⊠ *South Africa* ☎ *27/11/257–5000* ⊕ *www.wilderness-safaris.com*). One of Africa's most respected and innovative tour operators, Wilderness assures you of impeccable service, gorgeous destinations and accommodations, and game galore. It operates a seven-day fly-in safari from Windhoek, which covers most of the main tourist destinations in Namibia. It also owns the majority of lodges in Botswana and offers all kinds of packages, and a choice of "premier," "classic," "vintage," or "camping wild" camps in a great variety of locations and ecosystems, from the delta to the Kalahari Desert. It has mobile safaris and custom tours for all Botswana destinations and specializes in honeymoon packages.

SPECIAL CONSIDERATIONS

CHILDREN ON SAFARI
Most safari operators and private game reserves don't accept children under a certain age, usually under eight, but sometimes the age limit is as high as 12. This age limit is largely for safety reasons. Animals

often respond, not in a positive manner, to something that is younger, slower, or smaller than they are. And even though you might think your six- or seven-year-old adores all sorts of animals and bugs, you'd be surprised how overwhelmed kids can become, out of the comfort of their home and backyard, by the size and multitude of African insects and wildlife.

Take into account, also, that when you're following a strange schedule and getting in and out of small planes, safari vehicles, boats, and the like with other people whom you probably won't know, there often is no time to deal with recalcitrant children—and fussing will, you can be guaranteed, annoy the other people in your plane or lodge, who have spent a great deal of money for what may be a once-in-a-lifetime safari trip.

One option, if you can afford it, is to book a private safari where no other people are involved and you dictate the schedule. Many private lodges will rent you the entire property for the length of your stay; this is often the only way these camps allow children under age eight on safari. At the very least, a camp will require that you pay for a private safari vehicle and guide if you have children under 12. Be advised that, even if you're renting the whole camp, babies and toddlers still aren't allowed out on game-viewing trips.

One great family option is to stay with &Beyond, formerly CC Africa, a safari operator with children's programs at several of its upscale camps throughout southern and East Africa. While you follow your own program, your kids pursue their own wilderness activities; you all meet up later for meals and other activities.

A much cheaper alternative is also one of the most enjoyable for a safari as a family: a self-driving trip where you stay at national parks. No destination is better in this regard than Kruger National Park, where there are comfortable accommodations and lots of other families around. You'll be able to set your own schedule, rent a cottage large enough for the entire family, and buy and prepare food you know your children will eat.

It's best not to visit malarial areas with children under age 10. Young kidneys are especially vulnerable to both the effects of malaria and the side effects of malaria prophylactics. You might opt to practice stringent nonchemical preventive measures, but know the risks: malaria's effects on young children are much worse than they are on older people.

Going on safari with babies also isn't recommended. Some lodges, such as those at MalaMala, provide babysitting service for infants, but babies aren't allowed out in safari vehicles. The sound of an infant crying puts most predators on alert, and that can be dangerous to other passengers as well as the child. Keep in mind also that the bush is often a hot and dusty place with little in the way of baby-friendly amenities. You'd have to bring all your own supplies, and if something were to go wrong there would be no way to get immediate help until a flight could be arranged.

9

SHOULD YOU TAKE THE KIDS?

Consider the following if you're thinking about bringing children to a private safari lodge:

■ **Are they afraid of the dark?** A safari camp that runs on generator-powered batteries will have minimal lights at night.

■ **Are they startled easily?** Large animals may come quite close to rooms or tents or near safari vehicles.

■ **Are they comfortable with strangers?** Most meals at safari lodges are at communal tables and shared six-seat planes are the basic form of transportation between remote safari camps.

■ **Are they troubled by bugs?** The African bush can be filled with moths as big as small birds as well as a host of other flying and crawling insects.

■ **Are they picky eaters?** Meals are usually buffet style, and food for camps is often ordered at least a month in advance, so your child's favorite food may not be available.

PEOPLE WITH DISABILITIES

Having a disability doesn't mean you cannot go on safari. It's important, however, to plan carefully to ensure that your needs can be adequately met. South African lodges, especially the high-end private ones, are the easiest to navigate and have the fewest steps. Keep in mind that all-terrain 4x4 vehicles don't have seat belts, so you need enough muscle control to keep yourself upright while the vehicle bumps along the unpaved roads. Getting in and out of these elevated vehicles can also be challenging. MalaMala Game Reserve is completely accessible and even has specially equipped four-wheel-drive safari vehicles with harness seat belts. Many of Kruger's camps have special accommodations.

OLDER TRAVELERS

Safaris everywhere welcome older travelers. However, before you book a safari, find out as many details as possible about how taxing a trip might be both physically and mentally. Consider the types of accommodations (for example, find out whether a lodge is built on an incline or has many stairs, and whether bathrooms have grab bars) as well as how much time will be spent in the elements, such as in the hot sun where it's easy to dehydrate, and whether there are daily activities such as canoeing that are physically challenging. For travelers older than 55, Elderhostel arranges a number of annual educational trips to South Africa that consider special needs.

TYPES OF SAFARIS

Do you picture yourself zipping from camp to camp in a tiny Cessna, getting a bird's-eye view of a water hole? Or inspecting an animal track up close while on a multiday walk through the bush? Since there are many kinds of safaris, you should think hard about what approach suits you best. There are high- and low-end versions of each option, and you can always mix and match options to create your ideal itinerary.

LUXURY LODGE–BASED SAFARIS

The majority of safari-goers base their trips at luxury lodges, which pack the double punch of outstanding game-viewing and stylish, atmospheric accommodations. A lodge may be made up of stone chalets, thatch-roof huts, rondavels, or large suitelike tents. Mosquito nets, leather furnishings, and mounted trophies add to the ambience. Dinners are served in an open-air *boma* (traditional thatch dining enclosure). All have hot-and-cold running water, flush toilets, toiletries, laundry service, electricity, and, in most cases, swimming pools. Some lodges also have air-conditioning, telephones, hair dryers, and minibars. The most lavish places also have private plunge pools.

Make no mistake—you pay for all this pampering. Expect to spend anywhere from US$400 to US$1,300 per person per night, depending on the season. All meals, beverages, house wines, game drives, and walks are included. A three-night stay is ideal, but two nights is usually sufficient to see the big game.

A VOYAGE OF DISCOVERY

As you embark on your safari, consider how lucky you are to be witnessing these rare species in their natural habitat. To this day, researchers in Africa continue to unearth new species. In the summer of 2007, for example, a group of scientists on a two-month expedition in the eastern Democratic Republic of the Congo discovered six new species (a bat, a rodent, two shrews, and two frogs) in a remote forest that had been off-limits to scientists for almost 50 years. At that rate—almost one new species each week—one can't help but wonder what else is out there or who will find it and when.

The time you spend at a private lodge is tightly structured. With some exceptions, the lodges offer almost identical programs of events. There are usually two three- to four-hour game drives a day, one in the early morning and another in the evening. You spend a lot of time sitting and eating, and in the afternoon you can nap and relax. You can always opt for an after-breakfast bush walk, and many lodges now have spas and gyms. If you're tired after your night drive, ask for something to be sent to your room, but don't miss the bush *braai* (barbecue) and at least one night in the boma.

On game drives at bigger camps, rangers stay in contact with one another via radio. If one finds a rhino, for example, he relays its location to the others so they can bring their guests to have a look. It's a double-edged sword. The more vehicles you have in the field, the more wildlife everyone is likely to see. But don't worry, most lodges are very well disciplined with their vehicles and there are rarely more than three or four at a sighting. As your vehicle arrives, one already there will drive away. In choosing a game lodge, remember to check how much land a lodge can traverse and how many vehicles it uses. Try to go on a bush walk with an armed ranger—an unforgettable experience, as the ranger can point out fascinating details along the way.

9

All lodges arrange transfers from nearby airports, train stations, or drop-off points, as the case may be. In more remote areas most have their own private airstrips carved out of the bush and fly guests in on chartered aircraft at extra cost. If you're driving yourself, the lodge will send you detailed instructions because many of the roads don't appear on maps and lack names.

> **STAR STRUCK**
>
> You'll be awed by the brilliance of the night skies on safari, especially if you live in a city where lights obscure the stars. To add romance and interest to your stargazing, study up on the southern skies and bring a star guide. Also, most guides are knowledgeable about the stars, so ask questions.

FLY-IN SAFARIS

The mode of transportation for fly-in safaris is as central to the experience as the accommodations. In places such as northern Botswana, where few roads are paved, or northern Namibia, where distances make road transfers impractical, small bush planes take you from lodge to lodge. These planes are usually six-seat Cessna 206 craft flown by bush pilots. The planes have no air-conditioning and in summer can be very hot indeed, especially in the afternoon. But most flights are short—approximately 30 minutes or so—so bite the bullet or you'll miss out on some of the really fabulous destinations.

Flying from destination to destination is a special experience. The planes stay at low altitudes, allowing you to spot game along the way: you might see elephant and buffalo herds lined up drinking along the edges of remote water holes or large numbers of zebras walking across the plains. Fly-in safaris also allow you to cover more territory than other types of safaris. In Botswana, for example, the trip between the diverse game destinations of the Moremi Wildlife Reserve in the Okavango Delta and northern Chobe National Park is 40 minutes by plane; it would take six hours by vehicle, if a road between these locations existed.

Hopping from place to place by plane is so easy and fast that many travelers make the mistake of cramming their itineraries with too many lodges. Plan your trip this way and you'll spend more time at airstrips, in planes, and shuttling to and from the airfields than tracking animals or enjoying the bush. You will glimpse animals as you travel back and forth—sometimes you'll even see them on the airstrips—but you won't have time to stop and really take in the sights. If possible, spend at least two nights at any one lodge; three nights is even better.

The best way to set up a fly-in safari is to book an all-inclusive package that includes airfare. (It's impractical to try to do it yourself.) A tour operator makes all the arrangements, and many offer standard trips that visit several of its lodges. For example, in Botswana, Orient-Express Safaris has a package that includes three camps in three very different locations.

LIGHTEN UP

The key to fly-in safaris is to pack light. In southern Africa the maximum weight allowed for luggage is 26 kilos (even less with some airlines). Your bag should be a soft-sided duffel or something similar, so the pilot can easily fit it into the small cargo area. At most private lodges, laundry is included.

■**TIP**➔ If your bag is over the weight limit, or if you weigh more than 220 pounds, you will be required to purchase an additional plane seat (usually about US$100).

WALKING SAFARIS

Many lodges offer walks as an optional way to view game. On a walking safari, however, you spend most, if not all, of your time in the bush on foot, accompanied by an armed guide. Because you're trekking through big-game country, there's an element of danger. But it's the proximity to wilderness that makes this type of trip so enchanting—and exciting. Of course, you can't stop every step of the way or you'd never get very far, but you will stop frequently to be shown something—from a native flower to spoor to animals—or to discuss some aspect of animal behavior or of tracking.

Walking treks take place on what are known as wilderness trails, which are natural tracks made by animals and are traversed only on foot, never by vehicle, to maintain their pristine condition. These trails usually lead into remote areas that you would never see on a typical safari. In most cases porters or donkeys carry the supplies and bags. Accommodation is usually in remote camps or occasionally in tents.

■**TIP**➔ If you consider a walking safari, you must factor in your physical condition. You should be in good health and be able to walk between 4 and 10 mi a day, depending on the scope of the trip. Some trips don't allow hikers under age 12 or over age 60. Also, you shouldn't scare easily. No guide has time for people who freeze up at the sight of a beetle, spider, or something more menacing up close; guides need to keep their attention on the wilds around them and on the group as a whole. The guides are armed, and they take great caution to keep you away from trouble. Your best insurance against getting in harm's way is always to listen to your guide and follow instructions.

MOBILE AND OVERLAND SAFARIS

Most mobile-safari operations are expertly run but are aimed at budget-conscious travelers. They are mostly self-sufficient camping affairs with overnights at either public or private campgrounds, depending on the safari's itinerary and price. Sometimes you stay at basic lodges along the way. Travel is often by something that looks like a 4x4 bus.

For young people, or the young at heart, mobile safaris are a great way to see the land from ground level. You taste the dust, smell the bacon cooking, stop where and when you want (within reason), and get to see some of the best places in the region. Trips usually run 14 to 21 days, although you can find shorter ones that cover fewer destinations. Prices start at US$750 and climb to US$2,500 for all-inclusive trips. Not sure whether all-inclusive is right for you? Consider combining a mobile safari with a lodge-based one, which gives you the best of both worlds.

9

A minimum of 10 nights is recommended for such an itinerary.

SELF-DRIVE SAFARIS

A self-drive safari, where you drive yourself in your own rental vehicle, is a great option for budget travelers and for those who feel comfortable seeing the bush without a ranger at hand to search out game or explain what you're seeing. Popular and easy-to-navigate options for this kind of trip are Kruger National Park, Hluhluwe-Imfolozi Game Reserve, and Kgalagadi Transfrontier Park. These parks have accessible, well-marked roads and a wide range of accommodations that include family-size chalets, small huts, tents, and camping sites. You may buy your own groceries and cook for yourself at all of these areas; all national parks have restaurants and stores on-site.

> **KNOWLEDGE IS POWER**
>
> Arm yourself with specialized books on mammals and birds rather than a more general one that tries to cover too much. Airports, lodges, and camp shops stock a good range, but try to bring one with you and do a bit of boning up in advance. Any bird guide by Ken Newman (Struik Publishers) and the *Sasol Guide to Birds* are recommended.

If possible, rent a van or a 4x4, since the higher off the ground you are the better your chances of spotting game (although a two-wheel-drive car is fine), and you can stop and start at your leisure; remember that you have to stick to marked roads. In addition to patience, you'll need drinks, snacks, and a ready camera. Keep your eyes and ears open and you may come across game at any time, in any place.

■ TIP→ Purchase a good park map that shows roads, water holes, different ecozones, and the types of animals you can expect to find in each. It's no good driving around open grassland searching for black rhinos when the lumbering browsers are miles away in a woodland region. You can buy these maps when you enter a park or at rest-camp shops, and it would be foolish to pass them up.

When planning your day's game drive, plot your route around as many water holes and rivers as possible. Except during the height of the summer rains, most game must come to permanent water sources to drink. In winter, when the land is at its most parched, a tour of water holes is bound to reap great rewards. Even better, take a picnic lunch along and park at the same watering hole for an hour or two, especially in winter, when the car interior doesn't become too hot. Not only will you see plenty of animals, but you'll find yourself slipping into the drama of the bush. Has that kudu seen the huge crocodile? What's making the impala nervous? What's that sitting on my car?

KRUGER NATIONAL PARK

There's no getting away from it, and it's worth repeating: visiting Kruger is likely to be one of the great experiences of your life. Founded in 1898 by Paul Kruger, president of what was then the Transvaal Republic, the park is a place to safari at your own pace, choosing from upscale private camps or simple campsites.

Kruger lies in the hot lowveld, a subtropical section of Mpumalanga and Limpopo provinces that abuts Mozambique. The park cuts a swath 80 km (50 mi) wide and 320 km (200 mi) long from Zimbabwe and the Limpopo River in the north to the Crocodile River in the south. It is divided into 16 macro ecozones, each supporting a great variety of plants, birds, and animals, including 145 mammal species and almost 500 species of birds, some of which are found nowhere elsewhere in South Africa.

Maps of Kruger are available at all the park gates and in the camp stores, and gas stations are at the park gates and at the major camps. Once in the park, observe the speed-limit signs carefully (there are speed traps): 50 kph (31 mph) on paved roads, 40 kph (25 mph) on dirt roads. Leave your vehicle only at designated picnic and viewing sites, and if you do come across animals on the road, allow them to pass before moving on. Sometimes you have to be very patient, especially if a breeding herd of elephants is blocking your way. ■TIP→ **Animals always have the right-of-way.** Always be cautious. Kruger is not a zoo; you are entering the territory of wild animals, even though many may be habituated to the sights and sounds of vehicles.

GETTING HERE AND AROUND
AIR TRAVEL
Kruger Mpumalanga International Airport (KMIA), at Nelspruit, and Hoedspruit airport, close to Kruger's Orpen Gate, serve Kruger National Park. KMIA has a restaurant, curio shops, banking facilities, car-rental agencies, VIP lounges, information desks, and shaded parking; Hoedspruit has a restaurant and curio shop.

Three airlines—SA Airlink, SA Express, and Pelican Air—link Johannesburg to Kruger Mpumalanga International Airport. SA Airlink has daily flights, SA Express flies on weekends, and Pelican Air has flights on Tuesday and Friday.

Airport Information Hoedspruit (HDS) (⊕ hoedspruit-hds-airport.web-port.com). **Kruger Mpumalanga International Airport (KMIA)** (MQP) (☎ 27/13/753–7502 ⊕ www.kmiairport.co.za).

Airlines Pelican Air (⊕ www.pelicanair.co.za). **South African Airways/SA Airlink/South African Express** (☎ 011/978–1111 ⊕ www.flysaa.com).

9

WILDLIFE WATCHING DO'S AND DON'TS

WILDLIFE SAFETY AND RESPECT

Observe animals silently. Talking loudly can frighten animals away and disturb their natural activities. Likewise, never attempt to attract an animal's attention. Don't imitate animal sounds, clap your hands, pound the vehicle, or throw objects.

Never feed wild creatures. This is especially important to remember near lodges and in campgrounds where animals—especially baboons and monkeys—may have become accustomed to humans. In some places they sneak into huts, tents, and even occupied vehicles to snatch food. If you see primates around, keep all food out of sight, and keep your windows closed. (If a baboon gets into your vehicle, he will trash the interior as he searches for food and will use it as a toilet.)

Never try to pose with an animal. This is probably the biggest cause of death and injury on safaris, when visitors don't listen to or believe the warnings from their rangers or posted notices in the public parks. Regardless of how cute or harmless they look, these animals are not tame. An herbivore impala, giraffe, or ostrich can kill you just as easily as a lion, elephant, or buffalo can.

Show respect for your driver and guide's judgment. They have more knowledge and experience than you. If they say no, there's a good reason.

Doing a self-drive? Always stay in the vehicle and drive slowly and carefully, keeping ample distance between you and the wildlife.

On walking safaris. Stay downwind from the animals, keep noise to a bare minimum, and walk at an even stride. Don't make quick or excited movements. Obey your guide.

Never litter. Aside from the obvious disrespect for the environment, tossed items can choke or poison animals.

No smoking. The dry African bush ignites easily.

Dress in neutral-tone clothes. If everyone is wearing earth tones, the animal sees one large vegetation-colored mass.

No body fragrances. This is for the benefit of both the animals and your fellow travelers.

Never sleep out in the open. If you're sleeping in a tent, make sure it's fully zipped or snapped shut; if it's a small tent, place something between you and the side of the wall to prevent an opportunistic bite from the outside. Generally if you're in your tent and not exposed, you should be quite safe from animals. Malaria is a much more potent danger, so keep your tent zipped up tight at night to keep out mosquitoes. (Note: If you are menstruating, be sure to dispose of tampons and pads somewhere other than in or near your tent.)

Never walk alone. Nearly all camps and lodges insist that an armed ranger accompany you both during the day and at night, and rightly so.

BEST VIEWING TIMES

The best time to find game is in the early morning and early evening, when the animals are most active, although old Africa hands will tell you that you can come across good game at any time of day. Stick to the philosophy "you never know what's around the next corner," and keep your eyes and ears wide open all the time. If your rest camp offers guided night drives on open vehicles with spotlights—go for it. You'll rarely be disappointed, seeing not only big game but also a lot of fascinating little critters that surface only at night. Book your night drive in advance or as soon as you get to camp.

DRIVING DIRECTIONS

Approach animals cautiously and quietly and "feel" their response. As soon as an effect is noted slow down or stop, depending on the circumstances. Human presence among wild animals never goes unnoticed. Not all game guides and rangers are sensitive to this, their focus being on giving you the best sighting. But if you feel uncomfortable, say so.

MAKING A LIST, CHECKING IT TWICE

Many national parks have reception areas with charts that show the most recent sightings of wildlife in the area. To be sure you see everything you want, get yourself a spotting chart, or just chat with the other drivers, rangers, and tourists, who can tell you what they've seen and where.

KEEP IN MIND

Nature is neither kind nor sentimental. Don't interfere with the natural processes. Animals are going about the business of survival in a harsh environment, and you can unwittingly make this business more difficult. Don't get too close to the animals and don't try to help them. If you're intrusive, you could drive animals away from feeding and, even worse, from drinking at water holes, which may be their only opportunity to drink that day.

Immersion in safari lands is a privilege. In order to preserve this privilege for later generations, it's important that you view wildlife with minimal disturbance and avoid upsetting the delicate balance of nature at all costs. You're the visitor, so act as you would in someone else's home: respect their space. Caution is your most trusted safety measure. Keep your distance, keep quiet, and keep your hands to yourself.

9

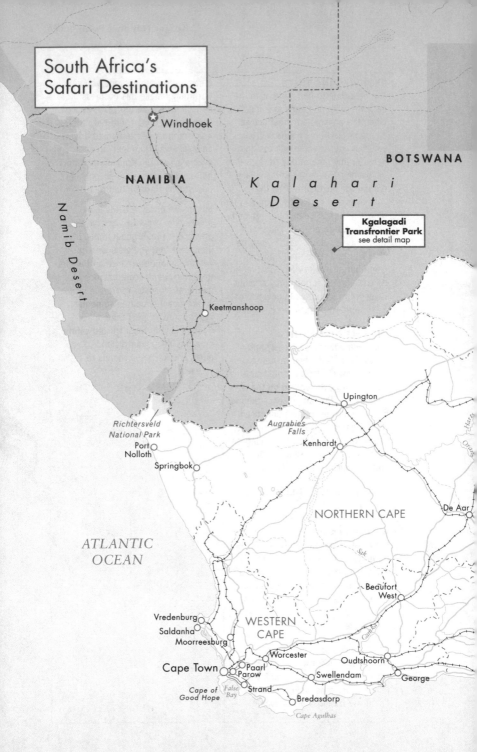

South Africa's Safari Destinations

Windhoek

NAMIBIA

BOTSWANA

*K a l a h a r i
D e s e r t*

Namib Desert

**Kgalagadi
Transfrontier Park**
see detail map

Keetmanshoop

Upington

*Augrabies
Falls*

*Richtersveld
National Park*

Kenhardt

Port
Nolloth

Springbok

NORTHERN CAPE

De Aar

*ATLANTIC
OCEAN*

Beaufort
West

Vredenburg

Saldanha

Moorreesburg

**WESTERN
CAPE**

Worcester

Oudtshoorn

Cape Town

Paarl
Parow

Swellendam

George

*Cape of
Good Hope*

*False
Bay*

Strand

Bredasdorp

Cape Agulhas

BUS TRAVEL

Only tour-company buses actually go through Kruger, but they're not recommended. Being in a big tour bus in the park is like being in an air-conditioned bubble, totally divorced from the bush. Also, the big tour buses aren't allowed on many of Kruger's dirt roads and have to stick to the main paved roads.

> ### PARK ESSENTIALS
>
> It's worth renting an eight-seater *combi* (van) or SUV. Though more expensive than a car, they provide more legroom, and you'll probably have better luck spotting and observing game from your lofty perch. Always reserve well in advance.

CAR TRAVEL

If you're driving to Kruger National Park there's generally no need to rent a 4x4 vehicle as all roads are paved. This accessibility means first-timers shouldn't worry about driving.

You can pick up rental cars at the KMIA and Hoedspruit airports. Avis, Budget, and Imperial all have desks at KMIA, whereas Hoedspruit offers Avis and Budget.

Rental Companies Avis (☎ 013/750–1015 at KMIA, 015/793–2014 at Hoedspruit ⊕ www.avis.co.za). **Budget** (☎ 013/751–1774 at KMIA, 011/398–0123 at Hoedspruit ⊕ www.budget.co.za). **Imperial** (☎ 013/751–1855 at KMIA ⊕ www.europcar.co.za).

BOOKING AND VISITOR INFORMATION

There are information centers at the Letaba, Skukuza, and Berg-en-Dal rest camps. There is a daily conservation fee, but Wild Cards, available at the gates or online, are more economical for stays of more than a few days. Reservations for all accommodations, bush drives, wilderness trails, and other park activities must be made through South African National Parks.

Contacts South African National Parks (☎ 012/343–1991 ⊕ www.sanparks.org ⊠ R120 daily conservation fee ⊙ Gates Apr.–Sept., daily 6–5:30; Oct.–Mar., daily 5:30 AM–6:30 PM, but sometimes vary).

TIMING

How and where you tackle Kruger will depend on your time frame. With excellent roads and accommodations, it's a great place to drive yourself. If you don't feel up to driving or self-catering, you can choose a lodge just outside the park and take the guided drives—but it's not quite the same as lying in bed and hearing the hyenas prowling round the camp fence or a lion roaring under the stars.

If you can spend a week here, start in the north at the very top of the park at the Punda Maria Camp, then make your way leisurely south to the very bottom at Crocodile Bridge Gate or Malelane Gate. With only three days or fewer, reserve one of the southern camps such as Berg-en-Dal or Lower Sabie and just plan to explore these areas. No matter where you go in Kruger, be sure to plan your route and accommodations in advance (advance booking is essential). Game spotting is not an exact science: you might see all the Big Five plus hundreds of other animals, but you could see much less. Try to plan your route to include water holes and rivers, which afford your best opportunity to see game. Old Africa hands claim that the very early morning, when the camp gates open, is the best time for game-viewing, but it's all quite random—you could see a leopard drinking at noon, a breeding herd of elephants midmorning, a lion pride dozing under a tree in the middle of the afternoon. You could also head out at dawn and find no wildlife at all. Be sure to take at least one guided night drive; you won't likely forget the thrill of catching a nocturnal animal in the spotlight.

WHEN TO GO

Kruger National Park is hellishly hot in midsummer (November–March), with afternoon rain a good possibility, though mostly in the form of heavy short showers that don't interfere with game-viewing for long. If you plan your drives in the early morning (when the gates first open) or in the late afternoon, you will manage even if you are extremely heat sensitive. ■ TIP→ **Don't drive with the windows up and the air conditioner on—you'll cocoon yourself from the reason you're there.** In summer the bush is green, the animals are sleek and glossy, and the birdlife is prolific, but high grasses and dense foliage make spotting animals more difficult. Also, because there's plenty of surface water about, animals don't need to drink at water holes and rivers, where it's easy to see them. There are also more mosquitoes around then, but you'll need to take malaria prophylactics whatever time of year you visit.

In winter (May through September), the bush is at its dullest, driest, and most colorless, but the game is much easier to spot, as many trees are bare, grasses are low, and animals congregate around the few available permanent water sources. Besides, watching a lion or leopard pad across an arid but starkly beautiful landscape could be the highlight of your trip. It gets very cold in winter (temperatures can drop to almost freezing at night and in the very early morning), so wear layers of warm clothes you can shed as the day gets hotter. Lodges sometimes drop their rates during winter (except July), because many foreign tourists prefer to visit in the South African summer months, which coincide with the northern hemisphere winter.

Spring (September and October) and autumn (March to early May) are a happy compromise. The weather is very pleasant—warm and sunny but not too hot—and there are fewer people around. In October migratory birds will have arrived, and in November many animals give birth. In April some migrating birds are still around, and the annual rutting season will have begun, when males compete for females and are often more visible and active.

MONEY MATTERS

Kruger accepts credit cards, which are also useful for big purchases, but you should always have some small change for staff tips (tip your cleaning person R20 per hut per day) and for drinks and snacks at the camp shops.

RESTAURANTS

Food is cheap and cheerful in Kruger's cafeterias and restaurants, and usually excellent in the private game lodges. Dinner is eaten 7:30-ish, and it's unlikely you'll get a meal in a restaurant after 9. At private

WALKING KRUGER

Kruger's seven wilderness trails accommodate eight hikers each. On three-day, two-night hikes, led by an armed ranger and local tracker, you walk in the mornings and evenings, with an afternoon siesta. You can generally get closer to animals in a vehicle, but many hikers can recount face-to-face encounters with everything from rhinos to lions.

Be prepared to walk up to 19 km (12 mi) a day. No one under 12 is allowed; those over 60 must have a doctor's certificate. Hikers sleep in rustic two-bed huts and share a reed-wall bathroom (flush toilets, bucket showers). Meals are simple (stews and barbecues); you bring your own drinks. In summer walking is uncomfortably hot (and trails are cheaper); in winter, nights can be freezing—bring warm clothes and an extra blanket. Reserve 13 months ahead, when bookings open. The cost is about R2,350 per person per trail.

Bushman Trail. In the southwestern corner of the park, this trail takes its name from the San rock paintings and sites found in the area. The trail camp lies in a secluded valley dominated by granite hills and cliffs. Watch for white rhinos, elephants, and buffalo. Check in at Berg-en-Dal.

Metsi Metsi Trail. The permanent water of the nearby N'waswitsontso River makes this one of the best trails for winter game-viewing. Midway between Skukuza and Satara, the trail camp is in the lee of a mountain in an area of gorges, cliffs, and rolling savanna. Check in at Skukuza.

Napi Trail. White rhino sightings are common on this trail, which runs through mixed bushveld between Pretoriuskop and Skukuza. Other possibilities are black rhinos, cheetahs, leopards, elephants, and, if you're lucky, nomadic wild dogs. The camp is tucked into dense riverine forest at the confluence of the Napi and Biyamiti rivers. Check in at Pretoriuskop.

Nyalaland Trail. In the far north of the park, this trail camp sits among ancient baobab trees near the Luvuvhu River. Walk at the foot of huge rocky gorges and in dense forest. Look for highly sought-after birds: Böhm's spinetail, crowned eagle, and Pel's fishing-owl. Hippos, crocs, elephants, buffalo, and the nyala antelope are almost a sure thing. Check in at Punda Maria.

Olifants Trail. This spectacularly sited camp sits on a high bluff overlooking the Olifants River and affords regular sightings of elephants, lions, buffalo, and hippos. The landscape varies from riverine forest to the rocky foothills of the Lebombo Mountains. Check in at Letaba.

Sweni Trail. East of Satara, this trail camp overlooks the Sweni Spruit and savanna. The area attracts large herds of zebras, wildebeests, and buffalo with their attendant predators: lions, spotted hyenas, and wild dogs. Check in at Satara.

Wolhuter Trail. You'll come face-to-face with a white rhino on this trail through undulating bushveld, interspersed with rocky kopjes, midway between Berg-en-Dal and Pretoriuskop. Elephants, buffalo, and lions are also likely. Check in at Berg-en-Dal.

9

lodges, dinner is served after the evening game drive, usually around 8:30. "Smart casual" is the norm. In Kruger you might put on clean clothes for an evening meal in a restaurant, but that's as formal as it gets. After an exciting nighttime game drive in a private reserve, you'll want to change or at least freshen up, but keep the clothes very casual. Wear long sleeves and long pants because of mosquitoes. Many higher-end restaurants close on Monday, and it's always advisable to make reservations at these in advance.

LODGES

Accommodations range from fairly basic in the Kruger Park huts to the ultimate in luxury at most of the private camps. You may forget that you are in the bush until an elephant strolls past. The advantage of a private lodge (apart from superb game-viewing) is that often everything is included—lodging, meals, beverages including excellent house wines, game drives, and other activities. The price categories used for lodging in this chapter treat all-inclusive lodges differently from other lodgings; see the price chart above for details.

Prices at most guest establishments on the escarpment include a three- to five-course dinner plus a full English breakfast. Most places have at least one vegetarian course on the menu. Many lodges and hotels offer special midweek or winter low-season rates. If you're opting for a private game lodge, find out whether it accepts children (many specify kids only over 12) and stay a minimum of two nights, three if you can.

WHERE TO STAY

It's impossible to recommend just one camp in Kruger. One person might prefer the intimacy of Kruger's oldest camp, Punda Maria, with its whitewashed thatch cottages; another might favor big, bustling Skukuza. A great way to experience the park is to stay in as many of the camps as possible. The SANParks Web site (⊕ *www.sanparks.org*) has a comprehensive overview of the different camps. The bushveld camps are more expensive than the regular camps, but offer much more privacy and exclusivity—but no shops, restaurants, or pools. If you seek the ultimate in luxury, stay at one of the private luxury lodges in the concession areas, some of which also have walking trails.

LUXURY LODGES

The lodges that follow are in private concession areas within Kruger.

$$ 🏨 **Singita Lebombo Lodge.** Taking its name from the Lebombo mountain ★ range, Singita Lebombo, winner of numerous international accolades and ecodriven in concept, has been built "to touch the ground lightly." It hangs seemingly suspended on the edge of a cliff, like a huge glass box

in space. Wooden walkways connect the aptly named "lofts" (suites), all of which have an uncluttered style and spectacular views of the river and bushveld below. Outdoor and indoor areas fuse seamlessly. Organic materials—wood, cane, cotton, and linen—are daringly juxtaposed with steel and glass. This is Bauhaus in the bush, with a uniquely African feel. Public areas are light, bright, and airy, furnished with cane furniture, crisp white cushions, comfy armchairs, and recliners. Service is superb, as is the food, and nothing is left to chance. You can buy African art and artifacts at the classy Trading Post or enjoy a beauty treatment at the spa. **Pros:** stunning avant-garde architecture; superb food and service. **Cons:** a bit over the top; avoid if you want the traditional safari lodge experience; very, very pricey. *Box 650881, Benmore 2010 021/683–3424 www.singita.co.za 15 suites In-room: a/c, safe, refrigerator. In-hotel: bar, pool, gym, spa, Internet AE, DC, MC, V FAP.*

$$ **Sweni Lodge.** Built on wooden stilts, Sweni is cradled on a low riverbank amid thick virgin bush and ancient trees. More intimate than its sister camp, Lebombo, it has six huge river-facing suites glassed on three sides, wooden on the other. At night khaki floor-to-ceiling drapes lined with silk divide the living area from the bedroom, which has a king-size bed with weighted, coffee-color mosquito netting and a cascade of ceramic beads. Hanging lamp shades of brown netting fashioned like traditional African fish traps, cream mohair throws, and brown leather furniture enhance the natural feel and contrast boldly with the gleam of stainless steel in the living room and bathroom. You can relax in a wooden rocking chair on your large reed-shaded deck while watching an elephant herd drink or spend the night under the stars on a comfy, mosquito-net-draped mattress. **Pros:** tiny, intimate; great location. **Cons:** game not overabundant; dim lighting; all those earth colors could become a bit depressing. *Box 650881, Benmore 2010 021/683–3424 www.singita.co.za 6 suites In-room: a/c, safe, refrigerator. In-hotel: bar, pool, gym, spa, Internet AE, DC, MC, V FAP.*

PERMANENT TENTED CAMPS

The camps of Rhino Post Plains Camp and Rhino Post Safari Lodge are situated in about 30,000 acres of pristine bushveld in the Mutlumuvi area of Kruger, 10 km (6 mi) northeast of Skukuza, the heart of Kruger Park; the area can be easily accessed by road or air. The concession shares a 15-km (9-mi) boundary with MalaMala, in the Sabi Sands Game Reserve, and there's plenty of game movement between the two.

$ **Pafuri Camp.** This gorgeous lodge stretches for more than a kilometer along the banks of the Luvuvhu River in Kruger's far north. The 240-square-km (93-square-mi) area embraces an amazing variety of landscapes and is one of the few places on earth where fever-tree and baobab forests intermingle. At Crooks Corner, where baddies-on-the-run of days-gone-by once lurked, a wide swath of sand stretching as far as the eye can see links Mozambique, South Africa, and Zimbabwe. There's great game plus ancient history—more than 1.5 million years ago, early humans lived here, and the area holds stone-age tools, rock engravings, and rock paintings. Pafuri also has the best birding in Kruger: this is the place to spot the rare and elusive Pel's fishing-owl. There's a superb children's program, and special family accommodations provide privacy for parents and kids. The tented rooms face the river. Pros: one of best locations in Kruger; terrific biodiversity; family friendly; adventurous three-night walking trail. Cons: accessible by road, but it's a long drive to get there. ⌂ *Safari Adventure Co., Box 5219, Rivonia 2120* ☎ *011/257–5111* ⊕ *www.safariadventurecompany. com* ⇨ *20 tents* ⚭ *In-room: safe. In-hotel: restaurant, bar, pool* ☰ *AE, DC, MC, V* ⎮◎⎮ *MAP.*

$ 🚹 **Rhino Post Plains Camp.** Overlooking a water hole amid an acacia knobthorn thicket deep in the heart of the Timbitene Plain, Plains Camp has comfortably furnished tents with wooden decks and great views of the plains. A deck with a bar and plunge pool is great for postwalk get-togethers, and there's a small tented dining area. The camp is simple, unpretentious, very friendly, and has great food. Pros: bang in the middle of Kruger and easily accessible by road or air; great game; fabulous night drives when everyone else in the Kruger camps is confined to barracks. Cons: surroundings a bit bleak, especially in winter; not much privacy between tents. ⌂ *Box 1593, Eshowe 3815* ☎ *011/467–1886* ⊕ *www.zulunet.co.za* ⇨ *4 tents* ⚭ *In-hotel: bar, pool* ☰ *AE, DC, MC, V* ⎮◎⎮ *FAP.*

$ 🚹 **Rhino Post Safari Lodge.** This lodge comprises eight spacious suites on stilts overlooking the Mutlumuvi riverbed. Each open-plan suite built of canvas, thatch, wood, and stone has a bedroom, private wooden deck, bathroom with a deep freestanding bath, twin sinks, a separate toilet, and an outdoor shower protected by thick reed poles. Pros: eco-friendly; great game; busy water hole. Cons: canvas makes the suites very hot in summer and very cold in winter. ⌂ *Box 1593, Eshowe 3815* ☎ *035/474–1473* ⊕ *www.zulunet.co.za* ⇨ *8 suites* ⚭ *In-room: safe. In-hotel: bar, pool, Internet terminal* ☰ *AE, DC, MC, V* ⎮◎⎮ *FAP.*

NATIONAL PARK ACCOMMODATIONS

Reservations for the following accommodations should be made through **South African National Parks** (☎ *012/428–9111* ⊕ *www.sanparks. org* ☰ *AE, DC, MC, V*). At this writing, some of the national park accommodations in Kruger are undergoing refurbishment, including installation of air-conditioning; if this is an important amenity for you, call or check the Web site to confirm its availability in the accommodation of your choice.

¢ 🚹 **Balule.** On the banks of the Olifants River, Satara's rustic satellite camp differs radically from the others because it really is simple, appealing to those who don't mind roughing it a bit and want to experience the true feel of the bush. There are no shops or restaurants—so bring your own food—and there's no electricity either (only lanterns). Accommodations are in basic three-bed huts with no windows (vents only); the shared bathroom facilities have running water. You must check in at Olifants, 11 km (7 mi) away. Pros: intimate; evocative hurricane lamps; captures history and atmosphere of the original Kruger Park. Cons: very rustic; no windows or electricity; shared refrigerator; no on-site shop (closest camp is Olifants, 15 minutes away on dirt road). ✍ *15 campsites, 6 huts.*

¢ 🏠 **Berg-en-Dal.** This rest camp lies at the southern tip of the park, in
☾ a basin surrounded by rocky hills. Berg-en-Dal is known for its white
★ rhinos, leopards, and wild dogs, but there's plenty of other game too.
A dam (often nearly dry in winter) by one side of the perimeter fence
offers good game-viewing, including a close look at cruising croco-
diles and munching elephants. One of the more attractive camps, it
has thoughtful landscaping, which has left much of the indigenous
vegetation intact, making for more privacy. It has an attractive pool
and well-stocked grocery–curio shop, and kids can run around safely
here. **Pros:** you can sit on benches at the perimeter fence and watch
game—particularly elephants—come and go all day; evening wildlife
videos under the stars; great food options for those on the go. **Cons:**
always crowded (although chalets are well spaced out); very slow ser-
vice when checking in at reception. ✍ *69 chalets, 23 family cottages,
2 guesthouses, 70 campsites ✍ In-room: kitchen (some). In-hotel: res-
taurant, pool, laundry facilities.*

¢ 🏠 **Crocodile Bridge.** In the southeastern corner of the park, this superb
small rest camp (it has won several awards for good service) doubles
as an entrance gate, which makes it a convenient stopover if you arrive
near the park's closing time and thus too late to make it to another
camp. Although the Crocodile River provides a scenic backdrop, any
sense of being in the wild is quickly shattered by views of power lines
and farms on the south side. The road leading from the camp to Lower
Sabie is famous for sightings of general game as well as buffalo, rhinos,
cheetahs, and lions, but it's often crowded on weekends and holidays
and during school vacations. A hippo pool lies just 5 km (3 mi) away.
Two of the bungalows are geared toward travelers with disabilities.
Pros: adjacent to one of best game roads in park; very well run. **Cons:**
close proximity to the outside world of roads and farms makes it very
noisy. ✍ *20 bungalows, 8 safari tents, 12 campsites ✍ In-room: kitchen
(some). In-hotel: laundry facilities.*

¢ 🏠 **Letaba.** Overlooking the frequently dry Letaba River, this lovely
☾ camp sits in the middle of elephant country in the central section of
the park. There's excellent game-viewing on the roads to and all around
the Englehardt and Mingerhout dams; be careful in the early morning
and as the sun goes down that you don't bump a hippo. The camp itself
has a real bush feel: all the huts are thatch (ask for one overlooking the
river), and the grounds are overgrown with apple-leaf trees, acacias,
mopane, and lala palms. The restaurant and snack bar, with attrac-
tive outdoor seating, look out over the broad, sandy riverbed. Even if
you're not staying at Letaba, stop at the superb elephant exhibit at the
Environmental Education Centre and marvel at just how big elephants'
tusks can get. Campsites, on the camp's perimeter, offer lots of shade
for your tent or trailer. **Pros:** lovely old camp full of trees, flowers, and
birds; restaurant deck overlooks Letaba riverbed, where there's always
game; interesting environmental center. **Cons:** a long way from the
southern entrance gates, so you'll need more traveling time; always
busy. ✍ *86 bungalows, 5 huts, 10 guest cottages, 2 guesthouses, 20*

9

safari tents, 60 campsites �& *In-room: kitchen (some). In-hotel: restaurant, laundry facilities.*

¢ ⊞ **Lower Sabie.** This is one of the most popular camps in Kruger for
☾ good reason: it has tremendous views over a broad sweep of the Sabie
★ River and sits in one of the best game-viewing areas of the park (along
with Skukuza and Satara). White rhinos, lions, cheetahs, elephants,
and buffalo frequently come down to the river to drink, especially in
the dry winter months when there is little surface water elsewhere.
Long wooden walkways that curve around the restaurant and shop
are particularly attractive; you can sit here and look out over the river.
Half the safari tents have river views. The vegetation around the camp
is mainly grassland savanna interspersed with marula and knobthorn
trees. There are lots of animal drinking holes within a few minutes'
drive. Don't miss the H10 road from Lower Sabie to Tshokwane, where
you'll almost certainly see elephants. **Pros:** great location right on the
river; superb game in vicinity; good atmosphere at the camp. **Cons:**
always crowded; surly restaurant staff. ⇗ *30 huts, 62 bungalows, 24
safari tents, 1 guesthouse, 33 campsites* �& *In-room: kitchen (some).
In-hotel: restaurant, pool, laundry facilities.*

¢ ⊞ **Malelane.** Small and intimate, this camp offering privacy and that
close-to-the-bush feeling is ideal for backpackers and do-it-yourselfers.
If you need supplies, a swim, or a bit more sophistication, you can head
over to Berg-en-Dal, just a few kilometers away. A bonus is that you're
within easy driving distance of good game areas around and toward
Lower Sabie. Guided bush drives are also on offer. You check in at
Malelane Gate, from which the camp is managed. **Pros:** private and intimate; great for campers and caravans. **Cons:** right on perimeter fence;
unattractive surroundings; lots of backpackers and happy campers; no
pool. ⇗ *5 bungalows, 15 campsites* �& *In-room: kitchen (some).*

¢ ⊞ **Maroela.** Orpen's small, cozy satellite campsite is just 3 km (2 mi)
away from the Orpen Gate. It can be hot, dry, and dusty at any time
of the year, but you'll feel close to the bush among thorn and maroela
(marula) trees. A small hide (blind) overlooks a water hole, and there's
lots of excellent game in the vicinity, including cheetahs, lions, and rhinos. **Pros:** hide (blind) overlooking water hole; good game. **Cons:** only
campers and caravans allowed; unattractive surroundings; no pool.
⇗ *20 campsites with power hookups.*

¢ ⊞ **Mopani.** Built in the lee of a rocky kopje overlooking a lake, this
camp in the northern section is one of Kruger's biggest. The camp is a
landscaped oasis for birds, people, and a few impalas and other grazing
animals amid not very attractive surrounding mopane woodlands. If it's
hippos you're after, from your veranda feast your eyes on a cavalcade of
these giants frolicking in the lake. Constructed of rough stone, wood,
and thatch, the camp blends well into the thick vegetation. Shaded
wooden walkways connect the public areas, all of which overlook the
lake, and the view from the open-air bar is awesome. The à la carte restaurant (reserve before 6 PM) serves better food than most of the other
camps, and the cottages are better equipped and larger than their counterparts elsewhere in Kruger. Ask for accommodations overlooking the
lake when you book. Mopani lacks the intimate charm of some of the

smaller camps, and the surrounding mopane woodland doesn't attract much game, but it's a really comfortable camp to relax in for a night or two if you're driving the length of the park. **Pros:** lovely accommodation; right on big lake; good restaurant and bar; easy to get bookings. **Cons:** so very little game in immediate vicinity. *45 bungalows, 12 cottages, 45 guest cottages, 1 guesthouse ☼ In-room: kitchen. In-hotel: restaurant, bar, pool, laundry facilities.*

¢ 🖫 **Olifants.** In the center of Kruger, Olifants has the best setting of all the camps: high atop cliffs on a rocky ridge with panoramic views of the distant hills and the Olifants River below. A lovely thatch-sheltered terrace allows you to sit for hours with binoculars and pick out the animals below. Lions often make kills in the river valley, and elephants, buffalo, giraffes, kudu, and other game come to drink and bathe. Try to book one of the thatch rondavels overlooking the river for at least two nights (you'll need to book a year in advance) so you can hang out on your veranda and watch Africa's passing show below. It's a charming old camp, graced with wonderful indigenous trees like sycamore figs, mopane, and sausage—so called because of the huge, brown, sausage-shape fruits that weigh down the branches. The only drawback, particularly in the hot summer months, however, is that it has no pool. **Pros:** hilltop location gives great views of the river below; elephants, elephants, and more elephants; lovely old-world feel; try for riverside accommodation. **Cons:** huts in the middle of the camp have no privacy; high malaria area; no pool. *107 rondavels, 2 guesthouses ☼ In-room: kitchen. In-hotel: restaurant, laundry facilities.*

¢ 🖫 **Orpen.** Don't dismiss this tiny, underappreciated rest camp in the center of the park because of its proximity to the Orpen Gate. It may not be a particularly attractive camp—the rooms, arranged in a rough semicircle around a large lawn, look out toward the perimeter fence, about 150 feet away—but there's a permanent water hole where animals come to drink and plenty of game is in the vicinity, including cheetahs, lions, and rhinos. The two-bedroom huts are a bit sparse, without bathrooms or cooking facilities (although there are good communal ones), but there are three comfortable family cottages with bathrooms and kitchenettes. And it's a blissfully quiet camp, as there are so few accommodations. **Pros:** permanent water hole; cheetahs and lions usually in vicinity; quiet and relaxing environment. **Cons:** very unattractive camp; close to main gate. *6 huts, 3 cottages ☼ In-room: kitchen (some).*

¢ 🖫 **Pretoriuskop.** This large, bare, nostalgically old-fashioned camp, conveniently close to the Numbi Gate in the southwestern corner of the park, makes a good overnight stop for new arrivals. The rocky kopjes and steep ridges that characterize the surrounding landscape provide an ideal habitat for mountain reedbuck and klipspringers—antelope not always easily seen elsewhere in the park. The area's *sourveld*—so named because its vegetation is less sweet and attractive to herbivores than other kinds of vegetation—also attracts browsers like giraffes and kudu, as well as white rhinos, lions, and wild dogs. There's not a lot of privacy in the camp—accommodations tend to overlook each other—but there is some shade, plus a great swimming pool. **Pros:** great landscaped pool; good restaurant; old-fashioned nostalgic feel; good cheetah country.

9

Cons: bleak and bare in winter, barracks-style feel. ◄🖉 *82 rondavels, 52 bungalows, 6 cottages, 45 campsites* ⚭ *In-room: kitchen. In-hotel: restaurant, pool, laundry facilities.*

¢ 🖼 **Punda Maria.** It's a pity that few foreign visitors make it to this lovely little camp in the far north end of the park near Zimbabwe, because in some ways it offers the best bush experience of any of the major rest camps. It's a small enclave, with tiny whitewashed thatch cottages arranged in terraces on a hill. The camp lies in *sandveld*, a botanically rich area notable for its plants and birdlife. This is Kruger's best birding camp: at a tiny, saucer-shape, stone birdbath just over the wall from the barbecue site, dozens of unique birds come and go all day. A nature trail winds through and behind the camp—also great for birding, as is the Punda/Pafuri road, where you can spot lots of raptors. A guided walking tour from here takes you to one of South Africa's most interesting archaeological sites—the stone Thulamela Ruins, dating from 1250 to 1700. Lodging includes two-bed bungalows with bathrooms and, in some cases, kitchenettes, plus fully equipped safari tents. There are also two very private six-bed family bungalows up on a hill above the camp; they're visited by an amazing variety of not-often-seen birds and some friendly genets. Reservations are advised for the restaurant (don't expect too much from the food), and only some of the campsites have power. **Pros:** possibly the most attractive of all the camps; delightful short walking trail in camp; best birding area in Kruger with some endemic species. **Cons:** very far north; game less abundant than the south; cottages very close together. ◄🖉 *22 bungalows, 2 family bungalows, 7 safari tents, 50 campsites* ⚭ *In-room: kitchen (some). In-hotel: restaurant, pool.*

¢ 🖼 **Satara.** Second in size only to Skukuza, this camp sits in the middle of the hot plains between Olifants and Lower Sabie, in the central section of Kruger. The knobthorn veld surrounding the camp provides the best grazing in the park and attracts large concentrations of game. That in turn brings the predators—lions, cheetahs, hyenas, and wild dogs—which makes this one of the best areas in the park for viewing game (especially on the N'wanetsi River Road, also known as S100). If you stand or stroll around the perimeter fence, you may see giraffes, zebras, and waterbucks and other antelope. Despite its size, Satara has far more appeal than Skukuza, possibly because of the privacy it offers (the huts aren't all piled on top of one another) and because of the tremendous birdlife. The restaurant and cafeteria are very pleasant, with shady seating overlooking the lawns and the bush beyond. Accommodations are in large cottages and two- or three-bed thatch rondavels, some with kitchenettes (no cooking utensils). The rondavels, arranged in large circles, face inward onto a central, open, grassy area. Campsites are secluded, with an excellent view of the bush, although they don't have much shade. **Pros:** superb location in middle of park; game galore; good on-site shop and restaurant. **Cons:** ugly buildings; unattractive surroundings inside and outside the camp; always crowded. ◄🖉 *152 rondavels, 10 guest cottages, 3 guesthouses, 100 campsites* ⚭ *In-room: kitchen (some). In-hotel: restaurant, pool, laundry facilities.*

¢ ⊞ **Shingwedzi.** Although this camp lies in the northern section of the
◔ park, amid monotonous long stretches of mopane woodland, it benefits
enormously from the riverine growth associated with the Shingwedzi
River and Kanniedood (Never Die) Dam. As a result, you'll probably
find more game around this camp than anywhere else in the region—
especially when you drive the Shingwedzi River Road early in the morning or just before the camp closes at night (but don't be late—you'll
face a hefty fine). The roof supports of thatch and rough tree trunks
give the camp a rugged, pioneer feel. Both the à la carte restaurant and
the outdoor cafeteria have views over the Shingwedzi River. Accommodations are of two types: A and B. Try for one of the A units, whose
steeply pitched thatch roofs afford an additional two-bed loft; some
also have fully equipped kitchenettes. The huts face one another across
a fairly barren expanse of dry earth, except in early spring, when the
gorgeous bright pink impala lilies are in bloom. Pros: lovely atmosphere
and recently refurbished accommodation; game-busy river road; pink
impala lilies in season; good restaurants. Cons: many of the accommodations are grouped in a circle around a big open space that is pretty
bleak and bare most of the year and affords little individual privacy;
roads south full of mopane trees so not much game. ⇥ *12 huts, 66
bungalows, 1 cottage, 1 guesthouse, 50 campsites ⚒ In-room: kitchen
(some). In-hotel: restaurant, pool, laundry facilities.*

¢ ⊞ **Skukuza.** It's worth popping in to have a look at this huge camp. More
like a small town than a rest camp, it has a gas station, police station,
airport, post office, car rental agency, grocery store, and library. It's
nearly always crowded, not only with regular visitors but with busloads
of noisy day-trippers, and consequently has lost any bush feel at all.
Still, Skukuza is popular for good reason. It's easily accessible by both
air and road, and it lies in a region of thorn thicket teeming with game,
including lions, cheetahs, and hyenas. The camp itself sits on a bank of
the crocodile-infested Sabie River, with good views of thick reeds, dozing hippos, and grazing waterbuck. Visit the worthwhile museum and
education center to learn something about the history and ecology of
the park. However, if you're allergic to noise and crowds, limit yourself
to a stroll along the banks of the Sabie River before heading for one of
the smaller camps. Pros: plumb in the middle of best game areas in the
park; easily accessible; beautifully located right on river; good museum.
Cons: you don't want to be here when the seemingly never-ending tour
and school buses arrive. making it horribly crowded and noisy. ⇥ *198
bungalows, 1 family cottage, 15 guest cottages, 4 guesthouses, 20 safari
tents, 80 campsites ⚒ In-hotel: restaurant, pool.*

¢ ⊞ **Tamboti.** Kruger's first tented camp, a satellite of Orpen and very close
to the Orpen Gate, is superbly sited on the banks of the frequently dry
Tamboti River, among sycamore fig and jackalberry trees. Communal
facilities make it a bit like an upscale campsite; nevertheless it's one of
Kruger's most popular camps, so book well ahead. From your tent you
may well see elephants digging in the riverbed for water just beyond the
barely visible electrified fence. Each of the walk-in, permanent tents has
its own deck overlooking the river, but when you book, ask for one in
the deep shade of large riverine trees—worth it in the midsummer heat.

9

All kitchen, washing, and toilet facilities are in two shared central blocks. Just bring your own food and cooking and eating utensils. Luxury tents have a shower, refrigerator, cooking and braai facilities. **Pros:** lovely location on banks of tree-lined riverbed; tents provide that real "in the bush" feel. **Cons:** food, drink, and cooking supplies not included; always fully occupied; shared bathrooms. ⤵ *30 safari tents, 10 luxury tents.*

> **WORD OF MOUTH**
>
> "My personal favorite is Tamboti camp, which is just outside Orpen. The safari tents are neat, there are resident animals like honey badgers within the camp, and it's small for a Kruger camp." —Gritty

¢ ⊞ **Tsendze Rustic Camp Site.** As its name suggests, this new camp is very rustic with no electricity (personal generators are not allowed) and solar-heated warm, not hot, water. It's 7 km (4 mi) south of Mopani Rest Camp. Although the camp itself has some lovely ancient trees, basically it's in the middle of a swathe of mopane woodland that doesn't offer much in the way of a variety of game, and what game there is, is difficult to see. However, you should see elephants (often on the tarred road between Tsendze and Mopani), and large herds of buffalo. The area is reputed to be the home turf for some of Kruger's big tuskers. If you're an ardent camper you'll enjoy the intimate bush experience, and if you're a birder you'll be in seventh heaven because what the area lacks in game it makes up for in birds—look out for the endangered ground hornbill. **Pros:** small and intimate; exclusive to campers and caravans; lovely ancient trees; good birding. **Cons:** situated in middle of unproductive mopane woodland so not much game other than elephants and buffalo; noisy when camp is full; no electricity; warm (not hot) water. ⤵ *30 campsites.*

BUSHVELD CAMPS

Smaller, more intimate, more luxurious, and consequently more expensive than regular rest camps, Kruger's bushveld camps are in remote wilderness areas of the park that are often off-limits to regular visitors. Access is limited to guests only. As a result you get far more bush and fewer fellow travelers. Night drives and day excursions are available in most of the camps. There are no restaurants, gas pumps, or grocery stores, so bring your provisions with you (though you can buy wood for your barbecue). All accommodations have fully equipped kitchens, bathrooms, ceiling fans, and large verandas, but only Bateleur has air-conditioning and TV, the latter installed especially for a visit by South Africa's president. Cottages have tile floors, cheerful furnishings, and cane patio furniture and are sited in stands of trees or clumps of indigenous bush for maximum privacy. Many face directly onto a river or water hole. There are only a handful of one-bedroom cottages (at Biyamiti, Shimuwini, Sirheni, and Talamati), but it's worth booking a four-bed cottage and paying the extra, even for only two people. The average cottage price for a couple is R850, with extra people (up to five or six) paying R180 each. If you have a large group or are planning a special celebration, you might consider reserving one of the two bush lodges, which must be booked as a whole: **Roodewal Bush Lodge** sleeps 19, and **Boulders Bush Lodge** sleeps 12. Reservations should be made with **South African National Parks** ✆ *Box 787, Pretoria 0001* ☎ *012/428–9111* ⊕ *www.sanparks.org* ⊟ *AE, DC, MC, V.*

$ ▦ **Bateleur.** Hidden in the northern reaches of the park, this tiny camp, the oldest of the bushveld camps, is one of Kruger's most remote destinations. Shaded by tall trees, it overlooks the dry watercourse of the Mashokwe Spruit. A raised platform provides an excellent game-viewing vantage point (don't forget to apply mosquito repellent if you sit here at dawn or dusk), and it's only a short drive to two nearby dams, which draw a huge variety of animals, from lions and elephants to zebras and hippos. The main bedroom in each fully equipped cottage has air-conditioning; elsewhere in each cottage there are ceiling fans, a microwave, and a TV. **Pros:** private and intimate; guests see a lot at the camp's hide; no traffic jams. **Cons:** long distance to travel; there's a TV, which can be a pro or a con depending on your point of view. ⇗ *7 cottages* ☩ *In-room: a/c, kitchen.*

$ ▦ **Biyamiti.** Close to the park gate at Crocodile Bridge, this larger-than-average, beautiful, sought-after bush camp overlooks the normally dry sands of the Biyamiti River. It's very popular because it's close to the southern gates, and the game is usually prolific. A private sand road over a dry riverbed takes you to the well-sited camp, where big shade trees attract a myriad of birds and make you feel almost completely cocooned in the wilderness. The vegetation is mixed combretum woodland, which attracts healthy populations of kudu, impalas, elephants, lions, and black and white rhinos. After the stars come out you're likely to hear lions roar, nightjars call, and jackals yipping outside the fence. **Pros:** easily accessible; lots of game; variety of drives in area. **Cons:** difficult to book because of its popularity; may be a bit too close to civilization for some—you can see adjacent sugarcane fields and farms. ⇗ *15 cottages* ☩ *In-room: kitchen.*

¢ ▦ **Shimuwini.** Birders descend in droves on this isolated, peaceful camp set on a lovely dam on the Letaba River. Towering jackalberry and sycamore fig trees provide welcome shade, as well as refuge to a host of resident and migratory birds. Away from the river, the riverine forest quickly gives way to mopane woodland; although this is not a particularly good landscape for game, the outstandingly beautiful roan antelope and handsome, rare black-and-white sable antelope move through the area. Resident leopards patrol the territory, and elephants frequently browse in the mopane. Be sure to visit the huge, ancient baobab tree on the nearest loop road to the camp—*shimuwini* is the Shangaan word for "place of the baobab," and there are lots of these striking, unusual trees in the surrounding area. Cottages have one, two, or three bedrooms. One disadvantage is that the camp is accessed by a single road, which gets a bit tedious when you have to drive it every time you leave or return to the camp. **Pros:** lovely situation on banks of permanent lake; isolated and tranquil; good chance to spot sable and roan. **Cons:** only one access road so coming and going gets monotonous; game can be sparse. ⇗ *15 cottages* ☩ *In-room: kitchen.*

¢ ▦ **Sirheni.** The most remote of all the bushveld camps and one of the
★ loveliest, Sirheni is a major bird-watching camp that sits on the edge

9

of the Sirheni Dam in an isolated wilderness area in the far north of the park. It's a long drive to get here but well worth the effort. Because there is permanent water, game—including lions and white rhinos—can often be seen at the dam, particularly in the dry winter months. Keep your eyes open for the resident leopard, who often drinks at the dam in the evening. A rewarding drive for birders and game spotters alike runs along the Mphongolo River. You can watch the sun set over the magnificent bush from one of two secluded viewing platforms at either end of the camp, but be sure to smother yourself with mosquito repellent. **Pros:** permanent water hole attracts lots of animals, especially in winter; really remote. **Cons:** high malaria area; difficult to access; no electrical plug points in accommodation; no cell phone reception, which can be a pro or con. ⊸ *15 cottages* ⅍ *In-room: kitchen.*

¢ ⊞ **Talamati.** On the banks of the normally dry N'waswitsontso River in Kruger's central section, this peaceful camp in the middle of a wide, open valley has excellent game-viewing. Grassy plains and mixed woodlands provide an ideal habitat for herds of impalas, zebras, and wildebeests, as well as lions, cheetahs, and elephants. You can take a break from your vehicle and watch birds and game from a couple of raised viewing platforms inside the perimeter fence. The accommodations are well-equipped and comfortable, with cane furniture and airy verandas. **Pros:** peaceful; good plains game; couple of good picnic spots in vicinity; bigger camps near enough to stock up on supplies. **Cons:** a bit bland and boring. ⊸ *15 cottages* ⅍ *In-room: kitchen.*

BUDGET LODGING

¢ ⊞ **Protea Hotel Kruger Gate.** Set in its own small reserve 110 yards from
↻ the Paul Kruger Gate, this comfortable hotel gives you a luxury alternative to the sometimes bare-bones accommodations of Kruger's rest camps. The hotel has two major advantages: fast access to the south-central portion of the park, where game-viewing is best, plus the impression that you are in the wilds of Africa. Dinner, heralded by beating drums, is served in a *boma,* a traditional open-air reed enclosure around a blazing campfire. Rangers lead guided walks through the surrounding bush, and you can even sleep overnight in a tree house, or you can book a guided game drive (note that all these activities cost extra). Rooms, connected by a raised wooden walkway that passes through thick indigenous forest, have Spanish-tile floors and standard hotel furniture. Self-catering chalets sleep six. Relax on the pool deck overlooking the Sabie River, have a cocktail in the cool bar, or puff on a cheroot in the sophisticated cigar bar while the kids take part in a fun-filled Prokidz program (during school vacations only). **Pros:** good for families; lots of activities from bush walks to game drives (although these cost extra); easily accessible; tree-house sleep-outs. **Cons:** you can't get away from the fact that this is a hotel with a hotel atmosphere. ⊠ *Kruger Gate, Skukuza* ☎ *013/735–5671* ⊕ *www.proteahotels.co.za* ⊸ *96 rooms, 7 chalets* ⅍ *In-room: refrigerator, kitchen (some), safe. In-hotel: 2 restaurants, bar, pool, tennis courts, parking, Internet terminal* ▤ *AE, DC, MC, V* ⊮⊙�⎮ *MAP.*

ADJACENT TO KRUGER PARK

MANYELETI GAME RESERVE

This public park, covering more than 54,000 acres, is owned by the Msini tribe with private concessions to the various lodges in the reserve. *Manyeleti* means "place of the stars" in Shangaan. You'll certainly see dazzlingly bright stars and also lots of game because there are no fences between this and its neighboring reserves. It's something of a Cinderella reserve compared with its more famous neighbors. Away from the major tourist areas, it's amazingly underused; you'll probably see very few vehicles while you're here. The park's grassy plains and mixed woodland attract good-size herds of general game and their attendant predators. You have a strong chance of seeing the Big Five, but the Manyeleti lodges focus more on providing an overall bush experience than simply rushing after big game. You'll learn about trees, birds, and bushveld ecosystems as you go on guided bush walks.

GETTING HERE AND AROUND

This relatively unknown part of Greater Kruger borders Kruger National Park, Sabi Sands, and the Timbavati game reserves. It's a five-hour drive from Johannesburg, or you can fly to Kruger Mpumalanga International Airport (KMIA) at Nelspruit where the lodges will pick you up or you can rent a car.

WHERE TO STAY

★ **Honeyguide Tented Safari Camps.** These platform tents are some of the best value in Mpumalanga, achieving the delicate balance of providing professional service with a casual atmosphere, a welcome relief if the over-attentiveness of some of the more upscale lodges isn't to your taste. Because the camps are small, an added bonus is that there are only six people per game vehicle. ✍ *Box 786064, Sandton 2146* ☎ *011/341– 0282* ⊕ *www.honeyguidecamp.com* ⊟ *AE, DC, MC, V* ❍⎮ *FAP.*

$ ⛺ **Khoka Moya.** This delightful, value-priced camp is situated on both
☾ sides of a riverbed. Simply designed and built of corrugated iron, the large lounge and dining areas overlook green lawns leading to the pool and outside bar. There's a private space in front of each tent, where you can chill out and take in the sights and sounds of the surrounding bush. Nice touches in your tent include a couch, cotton sheets, and damask linen bedspreads. As part of the Children's Safari activities, kids can make clay footprints, learn about the little bugs and critters they see on their guided walks, play soccer, swim, relax in the playroom, and then dig into a special kids' menu. **Pros:** excellent value for money; only six guests per game vehicle; situated away from major tourist areas; great kids' programs. **Cons:** no a/c, and it can get very hot in summer; usually lots of kids around so if you aren't childproof, stay away. ⟿ *12 tents* ☖ *In-hotel: bar, pool, children's programs (ages 4–14), Internet terminal.*

$ ⛺ **Mantonbeni.** This tented camp, minimalist but with surprising luxury touches, gives you the total bush experience without some of the bells and whistles of more upscale camps and at half the price. Designed

9

to reflect Hemingway's Africa, it sits in a tamboti grove overlooking a dry riverbed. You'll feel very close to the bush (but quite safe and secure) in your large, comfortable tent with its leather couch and open-air bathroom with concrete bath, double shower, and separate toilet. Spot game as you lounge on the swimming pool deck, or browse in the temperature-controlled wine cellar. Tea or coffee is served in your tent at dawn, and meals are served in a big safari tent around a long wooden table, where you can swap animal war stories with your fellow guests in an intimate, relaxed atmosphere. Children under 12 are not allowed. **Pros:** superb value for money; friendly, informal atmosphere; complimentary bar and well-stocked wine cellar; watch ellies from the pool deck. **Cons:** comfortable but far from five star; everything is under canvas so if you need more solid structures this is not for you. ↩*12 tents △ In-hotel: bar, pool, Internet terminal.*

TINTSWALO

$$$ ☶ **Tintswalo Safari Lodge.** This gorgeous ultraluxurious lodge, which aims
☾ to recapture the mid-19th century, is sited under huge jackalberry and fig trees overlooking a seasonal river, where game come down to drink and bathe. Each suite is themed for one of the great African explorers, including Burton, Speke, Livingstone, and Stanley, who would undoubtedly be amazed by such modern conveniences as air-conditioning, hair dryers, en suite bathrooms, and personal plunge pools. The suites are warmed by Persian rugs and honey-colored velvet chairs and ottomans. Dining is under the stars or in an elegant thatch dining room with open fireplace and sparkling chandelier. Although it's great to have a personal butler, sometimes it's rather disconcerting to be offered something every time you move a muscle. Stargaze by telescope, enjoy a complimentary spa treatment, visit a local Shangaan village, or, if you're both adventurous and romantic, opt for a moonlight sleep-out in the bush. There's a good children's program, but children are allowed only in the Presidential Suite. **Pros:** drop-dead luxury; all suites overlook a busy water hole; attractive architecture; exclusivity; moonlight sleep-outs. **Cons:** potentially over-attentive staff. ⌂ *Box 70378, Bryanston 2021* ☎ *011/300–8888* ⊕ *www.tintswalo.com* ↩*7 suites △ In-room: safe, refrigerator. In-hotel: bar, pool, spa, Internet terminal* ▭ *AE, DC, MC, V* ▮◎▮ *FAP.*

THORNYBUSH GAME RESERVE

This small game reserve, 35 acres of pristine Limpopo bushveld, is known for its fine lodges and good game sightings. It abuts the western boundary of Timbavati and Kruger.

GETTING HERE AND AROUND
South African Express Airways provides daily flights from Cape Town and Johannesburg to Hoedspruit. Road transfers can be arranged to most lodges.

If you want to drive, it's easy to do from Johannesburg and Hoedspruit.

WHERE TO STAY

$ ⊡ **Jackalberry Lodge.** This lodge offers understated luxury, excellent
☾ food, superb guiding, and the Big Five at half the price of some of the
better-known lodges. The air-conditioned thatch-and-stone chalets face
the purple Drakensberg Mountains and lie in pristine bushveld that
nudges the public areas and pool. It's commonplace to watch a warthog munching while you do the same, or a giraffe wander past as you
sun yourself. Chalets have stone floors, braided straw rugs with leather
bindings, deep armchairs, and beaded cushions in soft earth tones, all
echoing a simple but elegant African theme. Spacious bathrooms have
his-and-hers sinks, a tub with a bushveld view, and indoor and outdoor
showers. The rangers are terrific, the staff friendly and efficient, and a
particular bonus is that kids of all ages are welcome. Trained babysitters keep them occupied while you are off on game drives. For a little
extra you can book the two-bedroom family chalet or one of the two
large rooms where the bush comes right up to your doorstep. Don't
be surprised if a herd of curious zebras eyeballs you as you sit on your
large, private stoop. **Pros:** excellent value for money; very friendly staff
and super-knowledgeable rangers; great mountain views; perfect for
families; superb bird-watching. **Cons:** no children under six on game
drives (babysitters available, however); game not as prolific as Sabi
Sands and Timbavati. ⌖ *Box 798, Northlands 2116* ☎ *021/424-1037*
⊕ *www.jackalberrylodge.co.za* ↘ *7 rooms, 1 suite* ⅙ *In-hotel: bar, pool,
Internet terminal* ⊟ *AE, DC, MC, V* ⅙⎮ *FAP.*

TIMBAVATI GAME RESERVE

The 185,000-acre Timbavati, the northernmost of the private reserves,
has been collectively owned and managed since 1962 by the Timbavati Association, a nonprofit organization that strives to conserve the
biodiversity of the area. Timbavati is home to more than 40 mammal
species, including the Big Five, and more than 360 species of birds. It's
famed for its rare white lions; if you miss them here, you can see more
at the National Zoological Gardens in Tshwane. Timbavati also has a
large population of "regular" lions, and there's a good chance of finding leopards, elephants, buffalo, and spotted hyenas. Rhinos are now
more frequently seen, although they keep crossing back into Kruger.
You might get lucky and see wild dogs, as they migrate regularly to this
region from Kruger.

GETTING HERE AND AROUND

Timbavati borders Kruger National Park, Sabi Sands, and Manyeleti.
It's a five-hour drive from Johannesburg, or you can fly to KMIA at
Nelspruit, where the lodges will pick you up or you can rent a car.

WHERE TO STAY

NGALA

Ngala means "the place of the lion" and certainly lives up to its name.
There's wall-to-wall game, and you'll almost certainly see the King of
Beasts as well as leopards, rhinos, elephants, and buffalo, among others. Ngala lies in Timbavati's mopane shrubveld, and its main advantage over Sabi Sands is its proximity to four major ecozones—mopane

shrubveld, marula combretum, acacia shrub, and riverine forest—which provide habitats for a wide range of animals. As this camp is unfenced, always be sure to walk with a guide after dark. Ngala welcomes kids and puts on a range of activities for them. Ngala rangers, trackers, and general staff are specially trained to look after children and their needs, and, what's more, they seem to delight in their company. After the morning game drive, the kids are whisked away to go on a bug hunt, visit a local village, or bake cookies. ✒ *Private Bag X27, Benmore 2010* ☎ *011/809–4447* ⊕ *www.ngala.co.za* ▭ *AE, DC, MC, V* ⍣◎⍣ *MAP.*

$ ☷ **Main Camp.** This camp has Mediterranean style and a sophistication
☊ that is refreshing after the hunting-lodge decor of some other lodges. Track lighting and dark-slate flooring and tables provide an elegant counterpoint to high thatch ceilings and African art. A massive, double-sided fireplace dominates the lodge, opening onto a lounge filled with comfy sofas and chairs on one side and a dining room on the other. Dinner at Ngala is quite formal (kids on their best behavior, please!); it's served in a reed-enclosed boma or a tree-filled courtyard lighted by lanterns with crystal and silver. Air-conditioned guest cottages, in mopane shrubveld with no views, comprise two rooms, each with its own thatch veranda. Rooms make extensive use of hemp matting, thatch, and dark beams to create an appealing, warm feel. **Pros:** superb game and a bird-watcher's paradise; very child-friendly; open fires on cold nights; white rhino sightings increase during the dry season. **Cons:** expect lots of guests; kids dine with adults. ⇝ *20 rooms, 1 suite* ⚘ *In-hotel: bar, pool, Internet terminal.*

$ ☷ **Ngala Tented Safari Camp.** It seems that the marula seeds softly fall-
★ ing on the tents are applauding this gorgeous little camp shaded by a canopy of giant trees. You'll feel like a sultan as you lie beneath your billowing, honey-colored canvas roof, which acts as a ceiling for your basket-weave handmade bed and headboard. Polished wooden floors, gauze-screened floor-to-ceiling windows, and a dressing area with two stone washbasins and gleaming old-fashioned bath create a feeling of such roominess and elegance that it's hard to believe you're in a tent. The camp's dining area and lounge have an almost nautical feel. Huge wooden decks are tethered by ropes and poles on the very edge of the Timbavati River. It seems as if at any moment you could be gently blown into the sky over the surrounding bushveld. **Pros:** exclusivity; knowing you are right in the heart of the bush; palpable natural energy from the huge ancient trees. **Cons:** if you don't like to be too close to nature, this is not for you, as hippos (and other game) wander freely around the tents; no a/c. ⇝ *6 tents* ⚘ *In-hotel: pool, no kids under 12, Internet terminal.*

$ ☷ **Tanda Tula Safari Camp.** With a well-deserved reputation as one of
★ the best bush camps in Mpumalanga, Tanda Tula is very professional, yet makes you feel at home. When lions roar nearby, the noise sounds like it's coming from under the bed. The reason is simple: you sleep in a large safari tent with huge window flaps that roll up, leaving you gazing at the bush only through mosquito netting. Tanda Tula is decorated with colorful Africa-themed furnishings. Each thatch tent has electricity, a freestanding fan, a private bathroom with a Victorian-

style tub and outdoor shower, and a private wooden deck overlooking the Nhlaralumi River. You'll eat breakfast and lunch in a large, open, thatch lounge, but for dinner enjoy one of Tanda Tula's famous bush braais in the dry riverbed, with the moon reflecting off the dry sand. Although the lodge can sleep 24, it usually keeps numbers down to 16, which makes for added intimacy. First-class rangers give you a very thorough understanding of the environment, local history, and animals without concentrating solely on the Big Five. The Elephant Research Program's camp is housed here and accepts visitors. If you want real privacy, book the luxurious two-person lodge next to the tented camp; it comes with its own butler, vehicle, plunge pool, and in-house catering. **Pros:** ultra-knowledgeable rangers; emphasis on the whole bush experience, not just the Big Five; moonlit bush barbeques. **Cons:** if you don't like being under canvas, stay away; no a/c. ⌂ *Box 32, Constantia, Cape Town 7848* ☎ *021/794–6500* ∰ *www.tandatula.co.za* ⇨ *12 tents, 1 lodge* ⚭ *In-hotel: bar, pool, Wi-Fi, no kids under 12* ⊟ *AE, DC, MC, V* ⦿ *FAP.*

SABI SANDS GAME RESERVE

This is the most famous and exclusive of South Africa's private reserves. Collectively owned and managed, the 153,000-acre reserve near Kruger is home to dozens of private lodges, including the world-famous MalaMala and Londolozi. The Sabi Sands fully deserves its exalted reputation, boasting perhaps the highest game density of any private reserve in southern Africa.

Although not all lodges own vast tracts of land, the majority have traversing rights over most of the reserve. With an average of 20 vehicles (from different camps) watching for game and communicating by radio, you're bound to see an enormous amount of game and almost certainly the Big Five, and since only three vehicles are allowed at a sighting at a time, you can be assured of a grandstand seat. The Sabi Sands is the best area for leopard sightings. It's a memorable experience to see this beautiful, powerful, and often elusive cat—the most successful of all feline predators—padding purposefully through the bush at night, illuminated in your ranger's spotlight. There are many lion prides, and occasionally the increasingly rare wild dogs will migrate from Kruger to den in the Sabi Sands. You'll also see white rhinos, zebras, giraffes, wildebeests, most of the antelope species, plus birds galore.

If you can afford it, a splurge on a Kruger SKI ("spend the kids' inheritance") vacation could be the experience of a lifetime. Staying for two or three nights (try for three) at a private game lodge combines superb accommodations, service, and food with equally excellent game-viewing. Exclusivity on game drives (most lodges put only six people in a vehicle, along with a dedicated ranger and tracker) almost guarantees sightings of the Big Five. Words like "elegance," "luxury," and "privacy" are overused when describing the accommodations, but each lodge is unique. One place might have chalets done in modern chic, another lodges with a colonial feel, and a third open-air safari tents whose proximity to the bush makes up for what they lack in plushness. At all of them you'll be treated like royalty, with whom you may well rub shoulders.

Many accommodations have air-conditioning, minibars, room safes, ceiling fans, and luxurious en suite bathrooms. If mainline phone reception is available, there are room telephones. Cell-phone reception is patchy (depending on the area), but never take your cell phone on a game drive (or at least keep it turned off) to avoid disturbing the animals and annoying fellow passengers. All camps have radio telephones in case you need to make contact with the outside world. Chartered flights to and from the camps on shared private airstrips are available, or lodges will collect you from Hoedspruit airport or KMIA.

The daily program at each lodge rarely deviates from a pattern, starting with tea, coffee, and muffins or rusks (Boer biscuits) before an early-morning game drive (usually starting at dawn, later in winter). You return to the lodge around 10 AM, at which point you dine on a full English breakfast or brunch. You can then choose to go on a bush walk with an armed ranger, where you learn about some of the minutiae of the bush (including the Little Five), although you could also happen on giraffes, antelopes, or any one of the Big Five. But don't worry—you'll be well briefed in advance on what you should do if you come face-to-face with, say, a lion. The rest of the day, until the late-afternoon game drive, is spent at leisure—reading up on the bush in the camp library, snoozing, or swimming. A sumptuous afternoon tea is served at 3:30 or 4 before you head back into the bush for your night drive. During the drive, your ranger will find a peaceful spot for sundowners (cocktails), and you can sip the drink of your choice and nibble snacks as you watch one of Africa's spectacular sunsets. As darkness falls, your ranger will switch on the spotlight so you can spy nocturnal animals: lions, leopards, jackals, porcupines, servals (wildcats), civets, and the enchanting little bush babies. You'll return to the lodge around 7:30, in time to freshen up before a three- or five-course dinner in an open-air boma around a blazing fire. Often the camp staff entertains after dinner with local songs and dances—an unforgettable experience. Children under 12 are not allowed at some of the camps; others have great kids' programs (though children under five or six are not allowed to take part in any activities involving wild animals).

GETTING HERE AND AROUND
AIR TRAVEL
Kruger Mpumalanga International Airport (KMIA), at Nelspruit, and Hoedspruit airport, close to Kruger's Orpen Gate, serve Sabi Sands Reserve.

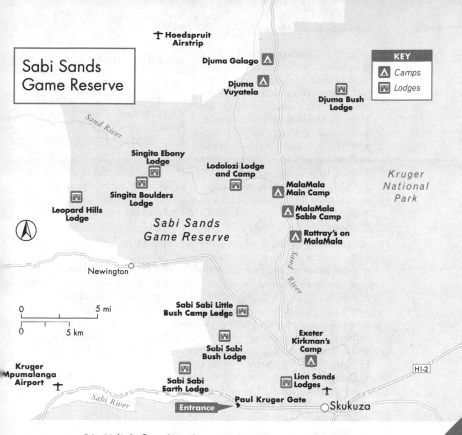

Sabi Sands Game Reserve

Hoedspruit Airstrip

Djuma Galago ▲

Djuma Vuyatela ▲

Djuma Bush Lodge 🏠

KEY
▲ Camps
🏠 Lodges

Sand River

Singita Ebony Lodge 🏠

Lodolozi Lodge and Camp 🏠

MalaMala Main Camp ▲

Kruger National Park

Singita Boulders Lodge 🏠

MalaMala Sable Camp ▲

Leopard Hills Lodge 🏠

Sabi Sands Game Reserve

Rattray's on MalaMala ▲

Sand River

Newington

0 ————— 5 mi
0 ————— 5 km

Sabi Sabi Little Bush Camp Lodge 🏠

Exeter Kirkman's Camp ▲

Sabi Sabi Bush Lodge 🏠

Kruger Mpumalanga Airport ✈

Sabi Sabi Earth Lodge 🏠

Lion Sands Lodges 🏠 ✈

H1-2

Sabi River

Entrance

Paul Kruger Gate

Skukuza

SA Airlink flies directly to MalaMala airstrip, which serves the Sabi Sands lodges.

9

Airport Information Hoedspruit *(HDS)* (⊕ *hoedspruit-hds-airport.webport.com*). **Kruger Mpumalanga International Airport (KMIA)** *(MQP)* (☎ *27/13/753–7502* ⊕ *www.kmiairport.co.za*).

Airlines South African Airways/SA Airlink/South African Express (☎ *011/978–1111* ⊕ *www.flysaa.com*).

CAR TRAVEL
You can drive yourself to the reserve and park at your lodge.

WHERE TO STAY

LUXURY LODGES

DJUMA
Djuma, Shangaan for "roar of the lion," is in the northeast corner of the Sabi Sands Game Reserve. Your hosts are husband-and-wife team Jurie and Pippa Moolman, who are passionate about their work (Jurie has a bachelor's degree in ecology). Although there's a good chance of seeing the Big Five during the bush walk after breakfast and the twice-daily game drives, Djuma also caters to those with special bushveld interests, such as bird-watching or tree identification. Djuma's

rangers and trackers are also adept at finding seldom-seen animals such as wild dogs, spotted hyenas, and genets. You'll find none of the formality that sometimes prevails at the larger lodges. For example, members of the staff eat all meals with you and join you around the nighttime fire. In fact, Djuma prides

itself on its personal service and sense of intimacy. Your dinner menu is chalked up on a blackboard (try ostrich pâté with cranberry sauce for a starter), as is the evening cocktail menu (how about a Screaming Hyena or African Sunrise?). ⬠ *Box 338, Hluvukani 1363* ☎ *021/424–1037* ⊕ *www.djuma.com* ▤ *AE, DC, MC, V* ⦾ *FAP.*

$$ ▦ **Bush Lodge.** Sitting in a lush grove of tamboti trees and overlooking a water hole, this homey safari camp contains thatch chalets with rugged wooden furniture and faux-animal-skin fabrics. Don't miss out on a trip to the local villages (the real thing—not tourist traps) of Dixie and Utah, where you'll be introduced to the families of the people looking after you at camp. **Pros:** family-owned and -run for years so boasts a genuine personal feel; floor-to-ceiling windows with great bushveld views; children always welcome; trips to local villages can be arranged. **Cons:** smallish bathrooms; no outdoor showers. ⬐ *8 chalets* ⬩ *In-room: a/c. In-hotel: bar, pool, Internet terminal.*

¢ ▦ **Galago.** A delightful and affordable alternative to the upscale lodges, Galago, which means "lesser bush baby" in Shangaan, is a converted U-shape farmhouse whose five rooms form an arc around a central fireplace. There's a big, shady veranda where you can sit and gaze out over the open plain before cooling off in the plunge pool. You can bring your own food and do your own cooking for less than half the all-inclusive price, or you can bring your own supplies and hire the camp's chef (R300 per day) to cook it for you. Game drives and walks are led by your own ranger. This is a perfect camp for a family safari or friends' reunion. **Pros:** real value for money; perfect for family or friends; do-it-yourself in style. **Cons:** hire a cook or you'll spend your time cooking and entertaining. ⬐ *5 rooms* ⬩ *In-room: a/c. In-hotel: pool.*

$ ▦ **Vuyatela.** Djuma's vibey, most upscale camp mixes contemporary African township culture with modern Shangaan culture, making it very different from most of the other private camps. Bright colors, trendy designs, hand-painted napkins, and candy-wrapper place mats combine with traditional leather chairs, thatch, and hand-painted mud walls. Look out for some great contemporary African township art, both classic and "naïf" artifacts, and especially for the chandelier made with old Coca-Cola bottles above the dining table. The camp is unfenced, and it's quite usual to see kudu nibbling the lawns or giraffes towering above the rooftops. Accommodations are in beautifully decorated chalets with private plunge pools. For something different in between drives, why not have your hair braided in funky African style at the Comfort Zone, the in-camp spa? **Pros:** amazing African art; the only genuinely innovative and funky lodge in Sabi Sands; legendary hosts;

trips to authentic villages. **Cons:** corrugated iron, recycled metals, and in-your-face glitzy township feel not everyone's taste. ⌐▷ *8 suites* ⚹ *In-room: a/c. In-hotel: bar, spa, gym, Internet terminal.*

LEOPARD HILLS

Owned by the Kruger family, whose distant family member Paul Kruger, president of the former Transvaal Republic, founded Kruger National Park in 1898, this hilltop lodge was built 100 years after the park's founding. Managed and run by the ultra-experienced Duncan and Louise Rodgers, the lodge has grown from its original five suites to the current complex of eight suites, private heated plunge pools, gym and *sala* (outdoor covered deck), library, and traditional Shangaan boma. As with many lodges in the area, Leopard Hills gives back to the community, and its on-site junior school provides an excellent education for the children of lodge staff throughout the Sabi Sands area. Expect to see the Big Five, take a guided bush walk, fly over the awesome Blyde River canyon in a helicopter, or visit the local village to meet the people and see how they live. ⌂ *Box 612, Hazyview 1242* ☎ *013/737–6626 or 013/737–6627* ⊕ *www.leopardhills.com* ⊟ *AE, DC, MC, V* ⏐⊙⏐ *FAP.*

$$ ⌸ **Leopard Hills Lodge.** Renowned for its relaxed and informal atmosphere, Leopard Hills is one of the premier game lodges in the Sabi Sands area. Set on a rocky outcrop with panoramic views of the surrounding bushveld, this small lodge offers privacy and luxury. Its main draw is its spectacular game-viewing; during a two-night stay you're almost guaranteed to see the Big Five at close quarters. Rangers are eager to share their knowledge and quick to rush guests off to see big game. The decor has an authentic bush theme, which gels well with the surroundings. Each double room has its own private heated pool (in addition to the main pool) and deck overlooking the bushveld. Bathrooms have his-and-her showers both indoors and out. Attention to detail is apparent in the leopard tracks and similar African motifs that appear in walkways, bedrooms, and bathrooms; check out the ceramic chameleon around the dressing table. **Pros:** very experienced and knowledgeable owners/managers; many rangers are expert photographers and offer great shooting tips; spacious suites. **Cons:** bit of a steep climb to the top of the hill and the main areas. ⌐▷ *8 rooms* ⚹ *In-room: a/c, safe, refrigerator. In-hotel: bar, pool, gym, spa, Internet terminal, Wi-Fi, no kids under 10.*

LION SANDS PRIVATE GAME RESERVE

Separated from Kruger National Park by the Sabie River, the Lion Sands Reserve has been owned and operated by the More family for four generations. Purchased in 1933 as a family retreat, the reserve was opened to the public in 1978 with two lodges and 10,000 acres of undisturbed wildlife that's available only to its guests. Today, under the watchful eyes of current owners and brothers, Nick and Rob More, the reserve offers guests four different lodging options: the ultraluxe Ivory Lodge, the more economical River Lodge, the once-in-a-lifetime Chalkley Treehouse (yes, it really is a bed on a platform in a tree, but nothing like the tree house in your backyard), and for larger groups the More family vacation home, the 1933 Lodge, complete with personal chef, guide, pool, gym, and wine cellar. The brothers are so committed to keeping the reserve as close to its original state that they employ a full-time ecologist, the only reserve in the Sabi Sands group to do so.

Guests of the Lion Sands Private Game Reserve can take direct scheduled flights to the MalaMala Airfield through SA Airlink (⇨ *Air Travel, in the Travel Smart South Africa chapter*). ⌂ *Box 30, White River 1240* ☎ *013/735–5330* ⊕ *www.lionsands.com* ▤ *AE, DC, MC, V* � *FAP.*

$$ ⌸ **Ivory Lodge.** If you seek the ultimate in luxury, privacy, and relaxation,
★ look no further than this gorgeous, exclusive lodge. Suites are really more like villas as each has its own private entrance and a separate sitting room and bedroom that are joined by a breezeway. Superb views overlooking the Sabi River and Kruger beyond are had from every point, especially on the decks, which come equipped with telescopes— you actually never have to leave your suite to catch views of incredible wildlife. The simple, uncluttered, elegant suites are decorated in contemporary African-European style with wood-burning fireplaces, a butler's passage-way where your morning tea is delivered, an indoor and outdoor shower, as well as a freestanding tub to relax in at the end of the day. You'll also have a personal butler and a plunge pool. Relax with intimate dinners and on-the-spot spa treatments, sample some of South Africa's finest wines in the on-site cellar, or head out on a game drive in a private vehicle with your own personal ranger. You won't even know if Brangelina or Ewan is in the next villa. ■**TIP**➡ **If you're looking for something even more special and over-the-top, inquire about spending the night at the Chalkley Treehouse.** Pros: exclusivity; great views from everywhere; attentive staff. Cons: suites are so comfortable you might not want to leave them; frequency of meals and abundance of good food may have you crying uncle. ⟿ *6 suites* ⚿ *In-room: a/c, safe, refrigerator, no TV. In-hotel: room service, bar, pool, spa, laundry service, Internet terminal, no kids under 12.*

$ ⌸ **River Lodge.** This friendly lodge is set on one of the longest and best stretches of river frontage in Sabi Sands. You can watch the passing animal and bird show from your deck or from the huge, tree-shaded, wooden viewing area that juts out over the riverbank facing Kruger National Park. The guest rooms are comfortable and attractively Africa themed, with honey-color stone floors with pebble inlays, cream wooden furniture, embroidered white bed linens, and lamps and tables of dark indigenous wood. The food is imaginative and tasty (try kudu stuffed with peanut butter with a mushroom-and-Amarula sauce), the young staff cheerful and enthusiastic, and the rangers highly qualified. After an exhilarating game drive, take a leisurely bush walk, go fishing, sleep out under the stars, or relax with a beauty treatment at Lalamuka Spa (*Lalamuka* means "unwind" in Shangaan). Public spaces are large and comfortable and lack the African designer clutter that mars some other lodges. There's a resident senior ecologist, plus a classy and interesting curio shop. Pros: fabulous river frontage; very friendly atmosphere. Cons: chalets built quite close together so not much privacy. ⟿ *20 rooms* ⚿ *In-room: a/c, safe, refrigerator. In-hotel: bar, pool, spa, gym, laundry service, Internet terminal, no kids under 10.*

LONDOLOZI

Formerly a family farm and retreat since 1926, Londolozi today is synonymous with South Africa's finest game lodges and game experiences. (*Londolozi* is the Zulu word for "protector of all living things.") Dave and John Varty, the charismatic and media-friendly grandsons of the original owner, Charles Varty, put the lodge on the map with glamorous marketing, superb wildlife videos, pet leopards and lions, visiting celebrities, and a vision of style and comfort that grandfather Charles could never have imagined. Now the younger generation, brother-and-sister team Bronwyn and Boyd Varty, are bringing their own creative stamp to the magic of Londolozi with a mission to reconnect the human spirit with the wilderness and to carry on their family's quest to honor the animal kingdom. Game abounds; the Big Five are all here, and the leopards of Londolozi are world famous. (You are guaranteed to see at least one.) There are five camps, each representing a different element in nature: Pioneer Camp (water), Tree Camp (wood), Granite Suites (rock), Varty Camp (fire), and Founders Camp (earth). Each is totally private, hidden in dense riverine forest on the banks of the Sand River. The Varty family lives on the property, and their friendliness and personal attention, along with the many staff who have been here for decades, will make you feel part of the family immediately. The central reception and curio shop are at Varty camp. ✉ *Londolozi, Box 41864, Hyde Park* ☎ *011/280–6655* ⊕ *www.londolozi.com* ▤ *AE, DC, MC, V* ❘◎❘ *FAP.*

$$$ ▥ **Founders Camp.** This camp takes you back to the early days of Lon-
♻ dolozi before ecotourism was invented—when it was more important to shoot a lion than to take the perfect shot of it. The stone-and-thatch chalets sit amid thick riverine bush and are linked to the other chalets by meandering pathways. Each has its own wooden viewing deck and is decorated in classic black-and-cream ticking fabric, with compass safari lamps, military chests, and faded family documents. Relax on the thatch split-level dining and viewing decks that jut out over a quiet backwater of the Sand River, and watch the mammals and birds go by. After your game drive or walk, cool off in the tree-shaded swimming pool, which also overlooks the river. **Pros:** has the first zero-emissions safari vehicles; children welcome. **Cons:** all the lodges are in very close proximity to one another, so it can be noisy. ⇛ *7 chalets* ♿ *In-room: a/c, safe, refrigerator. In-hotel: bar, pool, Internet.*

$$$ ▥ **Granite Suites.** Book all three private suites or just hide yourself away from the rest of the world like the celebrities and royals who favor this gorgeous getaway. Here, it's all about location, location, location. Huge, flat granite rocks in the riverbed, where elephants chill out and bathe, stretch almost to the horizon in front of your floor-to-ceiling picture windows, and the elephant prints and furnishings done in velvets and silvers, grays, and browns echo the shifting colors and textures of the mighty pachyderms. Bathe in your own rock pool. At night, when your suite is lit by scores of flickering candles, you may truly feel that you're in wonderland. **Pros:** among the best-situated accommodation in Sabi Sands with truly stunning views; the candlelit dinners. **Cons:** pricey. ⇛ *3 suites* ♿ *In-room: a/c, safe, refrigerator. In-hotel: bar, pool, Internet.*

9

$$ ⬛ **Pioneer Camp.** Pioneer Camp and its cottage suites are a loving tribute to the early days and legendary characters of Sparta, the original name of the Londolozi property. Channel into a past world through faded sepia photographs, old hunting prints, horse-drawn carts, gleaming silverware, and scuffed safari treasures, taking you back to a time when it took five days by ox wagon to get to Londolozi. In winter, sink deeply into your comfortable armchair in front of your own blazing fireplace; in summer sit outside in your outdoor dining room and listen to Africa's night noises. Keep your ears and eyes open for the resident female leopard as she hunts at night. The public rooms comprise a small, intimate boma, inside and outside dining areas, viewing decks, and a gorgeous S-shape pool nestling in the surrounding bush, where after your dip you can laze on padded lie-out chairs and be lulled to sleep by the birdsong. **Pros:** genuine and uncontrived romantic-safari atmosphere; only three suites; intimate. **Cons:** with only three suites it can be hard to book. ↪ *3 suites ☼ In-room: a/c, safe, refrigerator. In-hotel: bar, pool, Internet terminal, no kids under 12.*

$$$ ⬛ **Tree Camp.** The first Relais & Chateaux game lodge in the world, this
★ gorgeous camp, now completely rebuilt and redesigned (think leopards, lanterns, leadwoods, and leopard orchids), is shaded by thick riverine bush and tucked into the riverbank overlooking indigenous forest. Dave Varty has built more than 20 lodges around Africa, and he feels that this is his triumph. The lodge is themed in chocolate and white, with exquisite leopard photos on the walls, airy and stylish interiors, and elegant yet simple furnishings. Huge bedrooms, en suite bathrooms, and plunge pools continue the elegance, simplicity, and sophistication. From your spacious deck you look out onto a world of cool green forest dominated by ancient African ebony and marula trees. Treat yourself to a bottle of bubbly from the Champagne Library and then dine with others while swapping bush stories or alone in your private sala. **Pros:** the viewing deck; the ancient forest; state-of-the-art designer interiors. **Cons:** stylishness nudges out coziness. ↪ *6 suites ☼ In-room: a/c, safe, refrigerator. In-hotel: bar, pool, Internet.*

$$ ⬛ **Varty Camp.** This camp's fire has been burning for more than 80 years,
☾ making this location the very soul and center of Londolozi. It's also the largest of Londolozi's camps, centered on a thatch A-frame lodge that houses a dining room, sitting areas, and lounge. Meals are served on a broad wooden deck that juts over the riverbed and under an ancient jackalberry tree. The thatch rondavels, which were the Varty family's original hunting camp, now do duty as a library, a wine cellar, and an interpretive center, where you can listen to history and ecotourism talks—don't miss the Londolozi Leopard presentation. If you're looking for romance, have a private dinner on your veranda and go for a moonlight dip in your own plunge pool. In suites, the pool leads right to the riverbed. All rooms are decorated in African ethnic chic—in creams and browns and with the ubiquitous historic family photographs and documents—and have great bushveld views. Families are welcome, and the fascinating kids' programs should turn any couch potato into an instant wannabe ranger. **Pros:** superb children's programs; meals taken on lovely viewing deck. **Cons:** you need to be childproof; lacks the

intimacy of the smaller Londolozi lodges. ⌁2 *suites, 8 chalets* ⌂ *In-room: a/c, safe, refrigerator. In-hotel: bar, pool, Internet.*

MALAMALA

Fodor's Choice
★

This legendary game reserve (designated as such in 1929), which along with Londolozi put South African safaris on the international map, is tops in its field. It delights visitors with incomparable personal service, superb food, and discreetly elegant, comfortable accommodations where you'll rub shoulders with aristocrats, celebrities, and returning visitors alike. Mike Rattray, a legend in his own time in South Africa's game-lodge industry, describes MalaMala as "a camp in the bush," but it's certainly more than that, although it still retains that genuine bushveld feel of bygone days. Both the outstanding hospitality and the game-viewing experience keep guests coming back. MalaMala constitutes the largest privately owned Big Five game area in South Africa and includes an unfenced 30-km (19-mi) boundary with Kruger National Park, across which game crosses continuously. The variety of habitats ranges from riverine bush, favorite hiding place of the leopard, to open grasslands, where cheetahs hunt. MalaMala's animal-viewing statistics are probably unbeatable: the Big Five are spotted almost every day. At one moment your well-educated, friendly, articulate ranger might fascinate you by describing the sex life of a dung beetle, as you watch the sturdy male battling his way along the road, pushing his perfectly round ball of dung with wife-to-be perched perilously on top; at another, your adrenaline will flow as you follow a leopard stalking impala in the gathering gloom. Along with the local Shangaan trackers, whose eyesight rivals that of the animals they are tracking, the top class rangers ensure that your game experience is unforgettable. ⌂ *Box 55514, Northlands 2116* ☎ *011/442–2267* ⊕ *www.malamala.com* ⊟ *AE, DC, MC, V* ⎮◎⎮ *FAP.*

$$
☾

⌹ **Main Camp.** Ginger-brown stone and thatch air-conditioned rondavels with separate his-and-her bathrooms are decorated in creams and browns and furnished with cane armchairs, colorful handwoven tapestries and rugs, terra-cotta floors, and original artwork. Public areas have a genuine safari feel, with plush couches, animal skins, and African artifacts. Shaded by ancient jackalberry trees, a huge deck overlooks the Sand River and its passing show of animals. Browse in the air-conditioned Monkey Room for books and wildlife videos, sample the magnificent wine cellar, sun yourself by the pool, or stay fit in the well-appointed gym. The food—among the best in the bush—is delicious, wholesome, and varied, with a full buffet at both lunch and dinner. Children are welcomed with special programs, activities, and goody-filled backpacks; kids under 12 are not allowed on game drives unless they're with their own family group, and children under five are not allowed on game drives at all. One guest room is geared toward travelers with disabilities. **Pros:** you'll feel really in the heart of the bush when you look out over the sweeping wilderness views; not as fancy as some of the other camps but you can't beat the authenticity and history; delicious, hearty, home-style cooking; great kids' program; unparalleled game-viewing. **Cons:** rondavels are a bit old-fashioned, but that goes with

9

the ambience. ⌐518 rooms ⌂ In-room: a/c, safe, refrigerator. In-hotel: bar, pool, gym, children's programs, Internet terminal.

$$ ⊡ **Rattray's on MalaMala.** The breathtakingly beautiful Rattray's merges original bushveld style with daring ideas that run the risk of seeming out of place but instead work wonderfully well. Eight opulent *khayas* (think Tuscan villas) with spacious his-and-her bathrooms, dressing rooms, and private heated plunge pools blend well with the surrounding bush. Each villa's entrance hall, with art by distinguished African wildlife artists such as Keith Joubert, leads to a huge bedroom with a wooden four-poster bed, and beyond is a lounge liberally scattered with deep sofas, comfy armchairs, padded ottomans, writing desks (for those crucial nightly journal entries), antique Persian rugs, and a dining nook. Bird and botanical prints grace the walls. Floor-to-ceiling windows with insect-proof sliding doors face the Sand River and lead to massive wooden decks where you can view the passing wildlife. The main lodge includes viewing and dining decks, an infinity pool, lounge areas, and tantalizing views over the river. In the paneled library, with plush sofas, inviting leather chairs, old prints and photographs, and battered leather suitcases, the complete works of Kipling, Dickens, and Thackeray rub leather shoulders with contemporary classics and 100-year-old bound copies of England's classic humorous magazine *Punch*. After browsing the cellar's impressive fine wines, have a drink in the bar with its huge fireplace, antique card table, and polished cherrywood bar. **Pros:** accommodation so spacious it could house a herd of almost anything; heated pool; excellent lighting; fascinating library; unparalleled game-viewing. **Cons:** Tuscan villas in the bush may not be your idea of Africa. ⌐58 *villas* ⌂ In-room: a/c, safe, refrigerator, DVD, Internet. In-hotel: bar, pool, gym, no kids under 16.

$$ ⊡ **Sable Camp.** This fully air-conditioned, exclusive camp at the southern end of Main Camp overlooks the Sand River and surrounding bushveld. With its own pool, library, and boma, it's smaller and more intimate than Main Camp, but it shares the same magnificent all-around bush and hospitality experience. **Pros:** small and intimate; privacy guaranteed; unparalleled game-viewing. **Cons:** you might like it so much you never want to leave. ⌐57 *suites* ⌂ In-room: a/c, safe, refrigerator. In-hotel: bar, pool, gym, Internet terminal, no kids under 12.

SABI SABI

Founded in 1978 at the southern end of Sabi Sands, Sabi Sabi was one of the first lodges, along with Londolozi, to offer photo safaris and to link ecotourism, conservation, and community. Superb accommodations and the sheer density of game supported by its highly varied habitats draw guests back to Sabi Sabi in large numbers. There's a strong emphasis on ecology: guests are encouraged to look beyond the Big Five and to become aware of the birds and smaller mammals of the bush. ⌐D *Box 52665, Saxonwold 2132* ☎ *011/447–7172* ⊕ *www.sabisabi.com* ▤ *AE, DC, MC, V* ⦿¶ *FAP.*

$$ ⊡ **Bush Lodge.** Bush Lodge overlooks a busy water hole (lions are frequent visitors) and the dry course of the Msuthlu River. The thatch, open-sided dining area, observation deck, and pool all have magnificent views of game at the water hole. Thatch suites are connected by

walkways that weave between manicured lawns and beneath enormous shade trees where owls and fruit bats call at night. All have a deck overlooking the dry river course (where you may well see an elephant padding along) and outdoor and indoor showers. Chalets at this large lodge are older and smaller—although more intimate in a way—but still roomy; they are creatively decorated with African designs and have a personal wooden deck. Pros: always prolific game around the lodge; busy water hole in front of lodge; roomy chalets. Cons: big and busy might not be your idea of relaxing getaway. ⇌ *25 suites & In-room: a/c, safe, refrigerator. In-hotel: bar, pool, spa, Internet terminal, Wi-Fi.*

$$ ⊡ **Earth Lodge.** This avant-garde, eco-friendly lodge was the first to break away from the traditional safari style and strive for a contemporary theme. It's a cross between a Hopi cave dwelling and a medieval keep, but with modern luxury. On arrival, all you'll see is bush and grass covered hummocks until you descend a hidden stone pathway that opens onto a spectacular landscape of boulders and streams. The lodge has rough-textured, dark brown walls encrusted with orange seeds and wisps of indigenous grasses. The mud-domed suites are hidden from view until you're practically at the front door. Surfaces are sculpted from ancient fallen trees, whereas chairs and tables are ultramodern or '50s style. Your suite has huge living spaces with a sitting area, mega bathroom, private veranda, and plunge pool. A personal butler takes care of your every need, and there's a meditation garden. Dine in a subterranean cellar or in the boma, fashioned from roots and branches and lit at night by dozens of lanterns. Pros: out-of-the-ordinary avant-garde, eco-friendly architecture and interior design; warm earth colors. Cons: don't let your butler become too intrusive; although practical for guests who don't want to walk to their suites, golf carts seem alien in the bush. ⇌ *13 suites & In-room: a/c, safe, refrigerator. In-hotel: bar, pool, spa, Internet terminal.*

$ ⊡ **Little Bush Camp.** This delightful family camp combines airiness and
☺ spaciousness with a sense of intimacy. At night glowing oil lanterns lead you along a wooden walkway to your comfortable thatch-roof suite decorated in earthy tones of brown, cream, and white. After your action-packed morning game drive—during which you'll see game galore—and your delicious brunch, relax on the wooden deck overlooking the bush, have a snooze in your air-conditioned bedroom, or laze away the time between activities at the pool area. In the evening you can sip a glass of complimentary sherry as you watch the stars if you're a city slicker, you may never have seen such bright ones. Pros: perfect for families. Cons: it's popular with families. ⇌ *6 suites & In-room: a/c, safe, refrigerator. In-hotel: bar, pool, spa, Internet terminal.*

$ ⊡ **Selati Lodge.** For an *Out of Africa* experience, you can't beat Selati,
★ an intimate, stylish, colonial-style camp that was formerly the private hunting lodge of a famous South African opera singer. The early-1900s atmosphere is created by the use of genuine train memorabilia—old leather suitcases, antique wooden chairs, nameplates, and signals—that recall the old Selati branch train line, which once crossed the reserve, transporting gold from the interior to the coast of Mozambique in the 1870s. At night the grounds of this small, secluded lodge flicker with

9

the lights of the original shunters' oil lamps. Dinner is held in the boma, whereas brunch is served in the friendly farmhouse kitchen. Members of the glitterati and European royalty have stayed at the spacious Ivory Presidential Suite, with its Persian rugs and antique furniture. Pros: unique atmosphere because of its old railroad theme; secluded and intimate; Ivory Presidential Suite is superb value for money. Cons: some old-timers preferred the camp when it was just lantern-lit with no electricity. ➪ *8 suites ♿ In-room: a/c, safe, refrigerator. In-hotel: bar, pool, no kids under 10.*

SINGITA

Although Singita (Shangaan for "the miracle") offers much the same bush and game experience as the other lodges, nothing is too much trouble here. Its muted, low-key opulence, comforting organic atmosphere, truly spacious accommodations, superb food and wine, variety of public spaces—quiet little private dining nooks to a huge viewing deck built round an ancient jackalberry tree, comfortable library with TV and Internet, and attractive poolside bar—really do put this gorgeous lodge head and shoulders above the rest of the herd. Whether you fancy a starlit private supper, a riverside breakfast, or just chilling alone in your megasuite, you've only to ask. Forget the usual lodge curio shop and take a ride to the Trading Post where objets d'art, unique handmade jewelry, classy bush gear and artifacts from all over Africa are clustered together in a series of adjoining rooms and courtyards that seem more like someone's home than a shop. Pop into the wine cellars and learn about the finest South African wines from the resident sommelier, and then choose some to be shipped directly home. If you're feeling energetic, the bush bike rides are great. ➪ *Box 650881, Benmore 2010* ☎ *021/683–3424* ⊕ *www.singita.co.za* ➘ *AE, DC, MC, V* ⦿ *FAP.*

$$$
Fodor's Choice
★

⊡ **Boulders Lodge.** As you walk over the wooden bridge spanning a reed- and papyrus-fringed pond, you'll find yourself in the midst of traditional Africa at its most luxurious. The terra-cotta colors of the polished stone floors blend with the browns, ochers, creams, and russets of the cow-skin rugs, the hide-covered armchairs, the hand-carved tables, the stone benches, and the carefully chosen artifacts that grace the surfaces. Tall pillars of woven reeds, old tree trunks and stone walls reminiscent of Great Zimbabwe support the huge thatch roof, and from every side there are stunning bushveld views. You're guaranteed to gasp when you walk into your sumptuous suite. An entrance hall with a fully stocked bar leads into your glass-sided lounge dominated by a freestanding fireplace. Earth-colored fabrics and textures complement leather and wicker armchairs, a zebra-skin ottoman, desks and tables fashioned from organic wood shapes, with writing, reading, and watercolor materials. A herd of impalas could easily fit into the bathroom, which has dark stone floors, a claw-foot tub, his-and-hers basins, and an indoor and outdoor shower. Every door leads out onto a big wooden deck with a bubbling horizon pool, inviting sun loungers and bushveld views. ■TIP➔ **Request rooms 11 or 12, which overlook a water hole.** Pros: spacious accommodation; lovely organic, unpretentious bushveld feel; best food in Sabi Sands. Cons: it's quite a walk from some of the rooms to the main lodge (although transport is available); refuse the crackling log fire if you're at all congested. ↪ *9 suites ⟳ In-room: a/c, safe, refrigerator. In-hotel: bar, pool, spa.*

$$$ ⊞ **Ebony Lodge.** If Ernest Hemingway had built his ideal home in the African bush, this would be it. From the moment you walk into the main lounge with its genuine antique furniture, leather chairs gleaming with the polish of years of use, old photographs and paintings, mounted game trophies and hand-carved doors and windows, you'll be transported to a past where trendy urban designers had never heard of the bush, brimming glasses toasted the day's game activities, and deep laughter punctuated the fireside tales. This is really Old Africa at its best. Yellow, red, orange fabrics bring flashes of bright color to the old club atmosphere and are carried through to the viewing decks over the river below and into the comfortable dining room. Your room gives exactly the same feel—beautiful antiques, a claw-foot bathtub, photographs of royalty and original bush camps, lovely lamps and carvings, splashes of vivid color, a dressing room big enough to swing a leopard by the tail, and a carved four-poster bed that looks out over the bush below. Catch the sun or catch up on your journal at the antique desk or on the big inviting deck with pool and stunning views. **Pros:** this is the mother lodge of all the Singita properties, and it shows: maturity, warmth, hospitality, and furniture and fittings antique dealers would kill for; check out the cozy library with its amazing old books and magazines. **Cons:** the beds are very high off the ground—if you've short legs or creak a bit, ask for a stool; mosquito netting in rooms needs a bit of attention. ↪ *9 suites ⟳ In-room: a/c, safe, refrigerator. In-hotel: bar, pool, spa.*

EXETER PRIVATE GAME RESERVE

$ ⊞ **Kirkman's Kamp.** You feel as if you've stepped back in time at this camp. The cottages are strategically clustered around the original 1920s homestead, which, with its colonial furniture, historic memorabilia, and wrap-around veranda, makes you feel like a family guest the moment you arrive. That intimate family feeling continues when you sleep beneath a cluster of old photographs above your bed, slip into a leather armchair in front of a blazing log fire, or soak in your claw-foot bathtub in the nostalgia-laden bathroom. Cocoon yourself in your cottage with its private veranda looking out onto green sweeping lawns, or mingle with the other guests in the homestead where you'll find it hard to believe that you're in the 21st century. You'll see game galore in Sabi Sands (the size of New Jersey), which has the highest density of leopards in the world. Kirkman's is ideal for families and family reunions. **Pros:** more affordable than many other Sabi Sands lodges; one of Sabi Sands' best-loved camps for its old-time nostalgic atmosphere; superb game-viewing; easy road access from Johannesburg. **Cons:** malaria area; very busy when full; avoid school holidays if you can. ✆ *Private Bag X27, Benmore 2010* ☎ *011/809–4300* ⊕ *www.andbeyond.com* ↪ *18 cottages ⟳ In-room: no phone, safe. In-hotel: bar, pool, Internet terminal* ⊟ *AE, DC, V* ⊙ *FAP.*

$$ ⊞ **River Lodge.** Although this is one of Sabi Sands' oldest lodges, it has
★ somehow managed to keep itself something of a secret. Less glamorous than many of its more glitzy neighbors, it scores 10 out of 10 for

its quite gorgeous location—one of the best in the whole reserve—with lush green lawns sweeping right down to the Sabi River. The main sitting and dining areas have panoramic river views; if you want a quiet game-watching experience you can sink into one of the big comfy sofas on the deck, have your binoculars handy, and animals and birds of one kind or another are sure to happen along. If you go out on a game drive you'll see great game—almost certainly the Big Five—and the experienced rangers and staff, some of whom have been at the lodge for years, will guide, advise and look after you in a friendly, unfussy way. Your roomy air-conditioned suite (try to sleep with the windows open so you don't miss that lion roaring or hyena whooping) is decorated in soft earth colors and has its own plunge pool. Guests say that there's something about this lodge that melts effortlessly into its surroundings. It's a genuine African bush ambience. **Pros:** much more affordable than many of its neighbors; unpretentious feel; amazing river views; easy access by road from Johannesburg. **Cons:** malaria area; no triple rooms for guests with children. ⌖ *& Beyond, Private Bag X27, Benmore 2010* ☎ *011/809–4300* ⊕ *www.andbeyond.com* ⇲ *8 suites* ⌂ *In-room: no phone, safe. In-hotel: bar, pool, Internet terminal* ▤ *AE, DC, V* ⦿ *FAP.*

KWAZULU-NATAL PARKS

The province of KwaZulu-Natal is a premier vacation destination for South Africans, with some of the finest game reserves in the country, including the Hluhluwe-Imfolozi Game Reserve. The reserve is small compared to Kruger, but here you'll see the Big Five and plenty of plains game, plus an incredibly biologically diverse mix of plants and trees. The nearby Mkuze and Ithala game reserves are even smaller but are still worth a visit for their numerous bird species and game.

KwaZulu-Natal's best private lodges, including Phinda and Thanda private reserves, lie in northern Zululand and Maputaland, a remote region close to Mozambique. These lodges are sufficiently close to one another and Hluhluwe-Imfolozi Game Reserve to allow you to put together a bush experience that delivers the Big Five and a great deal more, including superb bird-watching opportunities and an unrivaled beach paradise.

GETTING HERE AND AROUND

AIR TRAVEL

The Richards Bay airport is the closest to the Hluhluwe-Imfolozi area—about 100 km (60 mi) south of Hluhluwe-Imfolozi and about 224 km (140 mi) south of Ithala.

There are daily flights from Johannesburg to Richards Bay; flight time is about an hour. Private lodges will arrange your transfers for you.

CAR TRAVEL

If you're traveling to Hluhluwe-Imfolozi from Durban, drive north on the N2 to Mtubatuba, then cut west on the R618 to Mambeni Gate. Otherwise, continue up the N2 to the Hluhluwe exit and follow the signs to the park and Memorial Gate. The whole trip takes about three hours, but watch out for potholes.

If you're headed to Ithala from Durban, drive north on the N2 to Empangeni, and then head west on the R34 to Vryheid. From here cut east on the R69 to Louwsburg. The reserve is immediately northwest of the village, from which there are clear signs. The journey from Durban takes around five hours and from Hluhluwe-Imfolozi about 2½ hours. Roads are good, and there are plenty of gas stations along the way.

HEALTH AND SAFETY

Malaria does pose a problem, however, and antimalarial drugs are essential.

WHEN TO GO

Summers are hot, hot, hot. If you can't take heat and humidity, then autumn, winter, and early summer are probably the best times to visit.

TOURS

By far the largest tour operator in Zululand, umHluhluwe Safaris offers a full range of half- and full-day game drives in Hluhluwe-Imfolozi, as well as night drives and bush walks. The company also leads game drives into the Mkuze Game Reserve and guided tours to the bird-rich wetlands and beaches of St. Lucia.

BOOKING AND VISITOR INFORMATION

Ezemvelo KZN Wildlife can provide information about the Hluhluwe-Imfolozi and Ithala **game reserves** and can help you book hikes on wilderness trails.

The Elephant Coast's Web site has information about dining and lodging, as well as attractions, towns you'll pass through, sports facilities, and much more. If you're visiting the Hluhluwe-Imfolozi Game Reserve, all activities can be booked through the Web site of the province's official conservation organization, Ezemvelo KZN Wildlife.

ESSENTIALS

Car Rentals Avis (☎ 035/789–6555). **Imperial** (☎ 035/786–0309).

Tour Operator umHluhluwe Safaris (☎ 035/562–0519 ⊕ www.hluhluwe-safaris.co.za).

Visitor Information Elephant Coast (☎ 035/562–0353 ⊕ www.elephantcoast.kzn.org.za). **Ezemvelo KZN Wildlife** (☎ 033/845–1000 ⊕ www.kznwildlife.com).

9

HLUHLUWE-IMFOLOZI GAME RESERVE

Reputedly King Shaka's favorite hunting ground, Zululand's Hluhluwe-Imfolozi (pronounced shloo-*shloo*-ee im-fuh-*low*-zee) incorporates two of Africa's oldest reserves: Hluhluwe and Imfolozi, both founded in 1895. In an area of just 906 square km (350 square mi), Hluhluwe-Imfolozi delivers the Big Five plus all the plains game and species like nyala and red duiker that are rare in other parts of the country. Equally important, it boasts one of the most biologically diverse habitats on the planet, a unique mix of forest, woodland, savanna, and grassland. You'll find about 1,250 species of plants and trees here—more than in some entire countries.

The park is administered by Ezemvelo KZN Wildlife, the province's official conservation organization, which looks after all the large game reserves and parks as well as many nature reserves. Thanks to its conservation efforts and those of its predecessor, the highly regarded Natal Parks Board, the park can take credit for saving the white rhino from extinction. So successful was the park at increasing white rhino numbers that in 1960 it established its now famous Rhino Capture Unit to relocate rhinos to other reserves in Africa. The park is currently trying to do for the black rhino what it did for its white cousins. Poaching in the past nearly decimated Africa's black rhino population, but as a result of the park's remarkable conservation efforts, 20% of Africa's remaining black rhinos now live in this reserve—and you won't get a better chance of seeing them in the wild than here.

Until 1989 the reserve consisted of two separate parks, Hluhluwe in the north and Imfolozi in the south, separated by a fenced corridor. Although a road (R618) still runs through this corridor, the fences have been removed, and the parks now operate as a single entity. Hluhluwe and the corridor are the most scenic areas of the park, notable for their bush-covered hills and knockout views, whereas Imfolozi is better known for its broad plains.

Compared with Kruger, Hluhluwe-Imfolozi is tiny—less than 6% of Kruger's size—but such comparisons can be misleading. You can spend days driving around this park and still not see everything, or feel like you're going in circles. Probably the biggest advantage Hluhluwe has over Kruger is that game-viewing is good year-round, whereas Kruger has seasonal peaks and valleys. Another bonus is its proximity to Mkuze Game Reserve and the spectacular coastal reserves of iSimangaliso Greater St. Lucia Wetland Park. The park is also close enough to Durban to make it a worthwhile one- or two-day excursion.

BUSH WALKS

Armed rangers lead groups of eight on two- to three-hour bush walks departing from Hilltop or Mpila Camp. You rarely spot much game on these walks, but you do see plenty of birds and you learn a great deal about the area's ecology and tips on how to recognize the signs of the bush, including animal spoor. Walks depart daily at 5:30 AM and 3:30 PM (6 and 3 in winter) and cost R200. Reserve a few days in advance at **Hilltop Camp** reception (☎ *035/562–0848*).

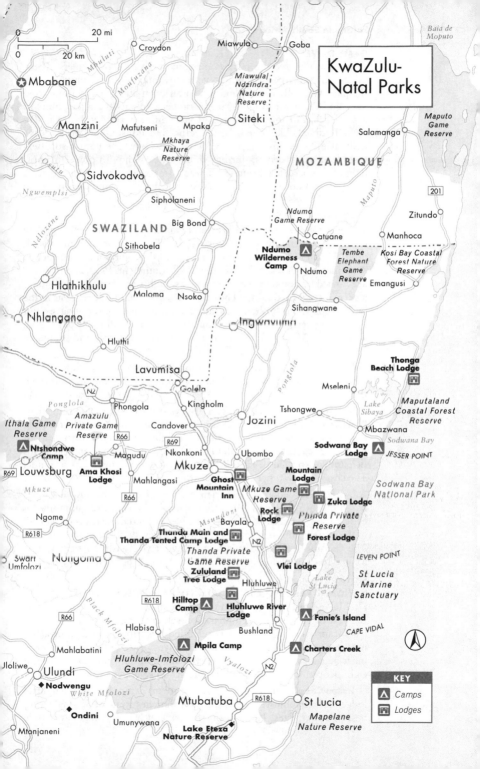

GAME DRIVES

A great way to see the park is on game drives led by rangers. These drives (R200 per person) hold several advantages over driving through the park yourself: you sit high up in an open-air vehicle with a good view and the wind in your face, a ranger explains the finer points of animal behavior and ecology, and your guide has a good idea where to find animals like leopards, cheetahs, and lions. Game drives leave daily at 5:30 AM in summer, 6:30 AM in winter. The park also offers three-hour night drives, during which you search with powerful spotlights for nocturnal animals. These three-hour drives depart at 7, and you should make advance reservations at **Hilltop Camp reception** (☎ *035/562–0848*).

WILDERNESS TRAILS

The park's **Wilderness Trails** are every bit as popular as Kruger's, but they tend to be tougher and more rustic. You should be fit enough to walk up to 16 km (10 mi) a day for a period of three days and four nights. An armed ranger leads the hikes, and all equipment, food, and baggage are carried by donkeys. The first and last nights are spent at Mndindini, a permanent tented camp. The other two are spent under canvas in the bush. While in the bush, hikers bathe in the Imfolozi River or have a hot bucket shower; toilet facilities consist of a spade and toilet-paper roll. Trails, open March–October, are limited to eight people and should be reserved a year in advance (R3,800 per person per trail).

Fully catered two- or three-night **Short Trails** involve stays at a satellite camp in the wilderness area. You'll sleep in a dome tent, and although there's hot water from a bucket shower, your toilet is a spade.

If that sounds too easy, you can always opt for one of the four-night **Primitive Trails.** On these treks hikers carry their own packs and sleep out under the stars, although there are lightweight tents for inclement weather. A campfire burns all night to scare off animals, and each participant is expected to sit a 90-minute watch. A ranger acts as guide. The cost is R1,870 per person per trail.

A less rugged wilderness experience can be had on the **Bushveld Trails,** based out of the tented Mndindini camp, where you're guaranteed a bed and some creature comforts. The idea behind these trails is to instill in the participants an appreciation for the beauty of the untamed bush. You can also join the Mpila night drive if you wish. Participation is limited to eight people and costs about R1,870 per person per trail.

WHERE TO STAY

NATIONAL PARK ACCOMMODATIONS IN HLUHLUWE-IMFOLOZI

Hluhluwe-Imfolozi offers a range of accommodations in government-run rest camps, with an emphasis on self-catering (only Hilltop has a restaurant). The park also has secluded bush lodges and camps, but most foreign visitors can't avail themselves of these lodgings, as each must be reserved in a block, and the smallest accommodates at least eight people. Conservation levies are R80 per person.

¢ 🏨 **Hilltop Camp.** It may be a government-run camp, but this delightful lodge in the Hluhluwe half of the park matches some of South Africa's best private lodges. Perched on the crest of a hill, it has panoramic views over the park, the Hlaza and Nkwakwa hills, and Zululand. Thatch and ocher-color walls give it an African feel. Scattered across the crown of the hill, self-contained chalets have high thatch ceilings, rattan furniture, and small verandas.

WORD OF MOUTH

"[Hluhluwe-Umfolozi] is a great park for elephant and rhino—we saw so many."   —Treepol

If you plan to eat all your meals in the restaurant or sample the evening *braai* (barbecue), forgo the more expensive chalets with fully equipped kitchens. If you're on a tight budget, opt for a basic rondavel with two beds, a basin, and a refrigerator; toilet facilities are communal. An à la carte restaurant, an attractive pub, a convenience store, and a gas station are on-site. Go for a stroll along a forest trail rich with birdsong, or take a bottle of wine to Hlaza Hide and join the animals as they come for their sundowners. **Pros:** floodlit water hole; great views; lovely little forest trail great for a stroll. **Cons:** surly, unhelpful staff; cottage needs a face-lift; cleaning of rooms not up to scratch. ⌖ *KZN Wildlife, Box 13069, Cascades, Pietermaritzburg 3202* ☎ *033/845–1000* ⊕ *www.kznwildlife.com* ⇨ *20 rondavels, 47 chalets* ♿ *In-room: kitchen (some). In-hotel: restaurant, bar, Internet terminal* ⊟ *AE, DC, MC, V.*

¢ 🏕 **Mpila Camp.** In the central Imfolozi section of the park, Mpila is humbler than the classy Hilltop Camp and more reminiscent of some of Kruger's older camps. Choose among one-room huts sharing communal facilities, two- and three-bedroom cottages, chalets, an en suite safari tent, or three secluded lodges. Gas is available, but you can only buy curios and sodas at the camp shop, so stock up with groceries before you arrive. Be sure to book your bush walks and game drives on arrival, as they work on a first-come, first-served basis. **Pros:** game comes right to your door (watch out for hyenas stealing your braai meat); lovely location. **Cons:** churlish staff; poor lighting; no mosquito mesh on windows; no electricity from 10 PM–8 AM. ⌖ *KZN Wildlife, Box 13069, Cascades, Pietermaritzburg 3202* ☎ *033/845–1000* ⊕ *www.kznwildlife. com* ⇨ *12 huts, 2 cottages, 6 chalets, 9 safari tents, 3 lodges* ♿ *In-room: kitchen (some)* ⊟ *AE, DC, MC, V.*

NATIONAL PARK ACCOMMODATIONS NEAR HLUHLUWE-IMFOLOZI

$ 🏕 **Hluhluwe River Lodge.** Overlooking False Bay Lake and the Hluhluwe
⛲ River flood plain, this luxurious, good-value, spacious, family-owned lodge set in indigenous gardens is the ideal base for visiting the game reserves and the iSimangaliso Greater St. Lucia Wetland Park. After a day spent game-viewing, canoeing, bird-watching, boating, fishing, or walking in the pristine sand forest, you can relax in a terra-cotta-color A-frame chalet with cool stone floors, wood and wicker furniture, and cream-and-brown decor and furnishings. Alternatively, sit out on your wooden deck overlooking the bush, the floodplain, and the lake. This lodge is the only one with direct access to the lake, and as you chug along through bird-filled papyrus channels decorated with water lilies en route to the broad expanses of the main body of water, you might easily feel as though you're in Botswana's Okavango Delta. Water activities are dependent on the seasonal rains, so check with the lodge

9

in advance. The food is excellent—wholesome country cooking with lots of fresh vegetables and good roasts. **Pros:** only 25 minutes from Hluhluwe-Imfolozi; boat trips (seasonal) reminiscent of Botswana's Okavango Delta; great for families; fun mountain- and quad bike trails. **Cons:** lots of kids in holiday times; activities cost extra. ⊠ *Follow signs from Hluhluwe village* ⌐Ɗ *Box 105, Hluhluwe 3960* ☎ *035/562–0246* ⊕ *www.hluhluwe.co.za* ↪ *12 chalets* ⚘ *In-room: a/c. In-hotel: restaurant, bar, pool, Internet terminal* ⊟ *AE, DC, MC, V* |◯| *MAP.*

¢ 🖫 **Zululand Tree Lodge.** About 16 km (10 mi) from the park, this lodge lies in a forest of fever trees on the 3,700-acre Ubizane Game Reserve, a small park stocked with white rhinos and plains game. It makes a great base from which to explore Hluhluwe, Mkuze, and St. Lucia. Built of thatch and wood, the open-sided lodge sits on stilts overlooking the Mzinene River. Rooms are in separate cottages, also on stilts, along the riverbank. The rooms themselves are small but tastefully decorated with mosquito nets covering old-fashioned iron bedsteads made up with fluffy white duvets, African-print cushions, wicker, and reed matting. If you want the experience of sleeping alfresco, fold back the huge wooden shutters dividing the bedroom from the open deck. A qualified ranger will take you for a bush walk or a game drive (which is included in your stay) through the small reserve or a little farther afield for a game drive in nearby Hluhluwe-Imfolozi. At the nearby Illala Weavers you can buy superb handwoven Zulu baskets. **Pros:** bird's-eye views over lovely game-filled surroundings; very friendly and attentive staff; authentic Zulu baskets available at nearby Illala Weavers. **Cons:** food not much to write home about. ⊠ *Hluhluwe Rd.* ⌐Ɗ *Box 116, Hluhluwe 3960* ☎ *035/562–1020* ⊕ *www.zululandtreelodge.co.za* ↪ *24 rooms* ⚘ *In-hotel: restaurant, bar, pool* ⊟ *AE, DC, MC, V* |◯| *MAP.*

MKUZE GAME RESERVE

This 88,900-acre reserve in the shadow of the Ubombo Mountains, between the Mkhuze and Msunduzi rivers, makes up the northwestern spur of the iSimangaliso Greater St. Lucia Wetland Park, now a World Heritage site. (The park itself is one of the most important coastal and wetland areas in the world with five interlinked ecosystems: a marine system, a coastal dune system, lake systems, swamps, and inland savanna woodlands. It is this often-pristine diversity that makes it both important and amazingly beautiful.) Mkuze is famous for its birds: more than 400 bird species have been spotted here, including myriad waterfowl drawn to the park's shallow pans in summer. Several blinds, particularly those overlooking Nsumo Pan, offer superb views. Don't miss out on the amazing 3-km (2-mi) walk through a spectacular rare forest of towering, ancient fig trees, some as big as 82 feet tall and 39 feet around the base. Although only a fraction of Kruger's size, this is the place to find rhinos; there's a healthy population of both black and white rhinos. You won't find lions, buffalo, or elephants, but the low-lying thornveld supports lots of other game, including zebras, giraffes, kudus, and nyalas. The reserve is 48 km (30 mi) north of Hluhluwe-Imfolozi. ■ TIP→ There are variant spellings of Mkuze in the area; you may

also see Mkuzi or Mkhuzi. ✉ *Off N2* ☎ *035/573–9004* *R35 per vehicle, R35 per person* ⏲ *Daily 6–6.*

WHERE TO STAY

¢ **Ghost Mountain Inn.** Swaths of scarlet bougainvillea run riot in the lush gardens of this family-owned country inn near Mkuze. It was here that Rider Haggard wrote some of his adventure stories, inspired perhaps by the mysterious lights and elusive flickering flames that give the mountain its spooky name. Rooms, each with a small veranda, are tastefully furnished in understated creams and browns with interesting historical prints. Large, invitingly restful public areas have terra-cotta tiles and comfortable cane furniture, and the cozy African lounge makes you feel like you've slipped back to the past. Don't miss the enthusiastic Zulu dancing before a succulent barbecue under the stars. At first light, wander down to the lake and watch the waterbirds wake up, or, later in the day, sit in the blind and watch them come home to roost. There's an excellent curio shop. The friendly staff can arrange tours to the neighboring game reserves and cultural sights or will fix you up to go bird-watching or fishing. **Pros:** good value for money; friendly staff. **Cons:** hotel-like atmosphere; tour buses overnight here. ✉ *Fish Eagle Rd., Mkuze* *Box 18, Mkuze 3965* ☎ *035/573–1025* *www.ghostmountaininn.co.za* *50 rooms* *In-room: a/c. In-hotel: restaurant, bar, pool, tennis courts, Internet terminal* *AE, DC, MC, V* *BP.*

> **SELF-GUIDED TRAILS**
>
> An unusual feature of Ithala is its self-guided walking trails, in the mountainside above Ntshondwe Camp. The trails give you a chance to stretch your limbs if you've just spent hours cooped up in a car. They also let you get really close to the euphorbias, acacias, and other fascinating indigenous vegetation that festoon the hills. Ask at the camp reception for further information.

9

ITHALA GAME RESERVE

In northern KwaZulu-Natal Province, close to the Swaziland border, Ithala (sometimes spelled "Itala"), at 296 square km (114 square mi), is small even compared with the relatively compact Hluhluwe-Imfolozi. Its size and its dearth of lions are probably why this delightful park 221 km (137 mi) northwest of Hluhluwe-Imfolozi is usually bypassed, even by South Africans—although they clearly don't know what they're missing. The other four of the Big Five are here—it's excellent for black and white rhinos—and the park is stocked with cheetahs, hyenas, giraffes, and an array of antelopes among its 80 mammal species. It's also an excellent spot for birders. The stunning landscapes and the relaxed game-viewing make this area a breath of fresh air after the Big Five melee of Kruger.

The reserve, founded in 1972 and run by KZN Wildlife, is a rugged region that drops 3,290 feet in just 15 km (9 mi) through sandstone cliffs, multicolor rocks, granite hills, ironstone outcrops, and quartz formations. Watered by nine small rivers rising in its vicinity and covered with rich soils, Ithala supports a varied cross section of vegetation, encompassing riverine thicket, wetland, open savanna, and acacia woodland. Arriving at its Ntshondwe Camp is nothing short of dramatic. The meandering road climbs from open plains to the top of a plateau dotted with granite formations, which at the last minute magically yield the rest camp at the foot of pink and russet cliffs.

WHERE TO STAY
NATIONAL PARK ACCOMMODATIONS

Although Ithala has several exclusive bush camps, these are booked up months in advance by South Africans, making the chalets at its main camp the only practical accommodations for foreign visitors. Two people sharing a two-bed unit at Ntshondwe will pay about R350 per person per night.

¢ 🔲 **Ntshondwe Camp.** In architecture, landscaping, and style, this beau-
★ tiful government-run rest camp, 69 km (43 mi) from Vryheid, comes closer than any other in the country to matching the expensive private lodges. Built around granite boulders and vegetation lush with acacias, wild figs, and giant cactuslike euphorbias, airy chalets with steep thatch roofs blend perfectly with the surroundings. Its two-, four-, and six-bed units can accommodate a total of 200 guests. Each self-catering chalet has a spacious lounge simply furnished with cane chairs, a fully equipped kitchen, and a large veranda surrounded by indigenous bush. Keep an eye open for eagles soaring above the pink and russet sandstone cliffs. A magnificent game-viewing deck juts out over a steep slope to provide views of a water hole and extensive panoramas of the surrounding valleys. Take a guided game drive (R150) or guided walk (R140), hike a self-guided trail, or follow one of the well-laid-out drives with markers at points of interest. Picnic at one of the many scenic picnic spots, all of which have barbecue facilities and toilets. A gas station, a store (with great curios), and a good restaurant are all on the premises. **Pros:** tarred road access; guided game drives or self-drive; spectacular surroundings. **Cons:** it's a busy conference and wedding venue. ⌂ *KZN Wildlife, Box 13069, Cascades, Pietermaritzburg 3202* ☎ *033/845–1000 or 034/983–2540* ⊕ *www.kznwildlife.com* ➟ *39 chalets* ⌂ *In-room: kitchen. In-hotel: restaurant, bar, pool* ▤ *AE, DC, MC, V.*

PHINDA PRIVATE GAME RESERVE

Established in 1991, this eco–award-winning flagship &Beyond (formerly CCAfrica) reserve is a heartening example of tourism serving the environment with panache. *Phinda (pin-duh)* is Zulu for "return," referring to the restoration of 54,360 acres of overgrazed ranchland in northern Zululand to bushveld. It's a triumph. You may find it impossible to believe the area wasn't always the thick bush you see all around you. The Big Five have established themselves firmly, and Phinda can claim a stunning variety of five different ecosystems: sand forest (which grows on the fossil dunes of an earlier coastline), savanna, bushveld, open woodland, and verdant wetlands.

Phinda can deliver the Big Five, although not as consistently or in such numbers as most lodges in Mpumalanga. Buffalo, leopards, lions, cheetahs, spotted hyenas, elephants, white rhinos, hippos, giraffes, impalas, and the rare, elusive, tiny Suni antelope are all here, and rangers provide exciting interpretive game drives for guests. Birdlife is prolific and extraordinary, with some special Zululand finds: the pink-throated twin spot, the crested guinea fowl, the African broadbill, and the crowned eagle. Where Phinda also excels is in the superb quality of its rangers, who can provide fascinating commentary on everything from local birds to frogs. It's amazing just how enthralling the love life of a dung beetle can be! There are also Phinda adventures (optional extras) down the Mzinene River for a close-up look at crocodiles, hippos, and birds; big-game fishing or scuba diving off the deserted, wildly beautiful Maputaland coast; and sightseeing flights over Phinda and the highest vegetated dunes in the world.

> **WORD OF MOUTH**
>
> "Phinda is a private and fenced game reserve so they have more control over seeing animals. [It] isn't exactly life in the "wild" but for a first-time person you see almost every animal you can imagine. So after three days in Phinda, we relaxed knowing we had seen all the important animals and were now ready to see them in a more wild or wide open setting... The guides, trackers, and lodge personnel are wonderful."
>
> —KSC2003

WHERE TO STAY

For all reservations, contact **&Beyond** ☎ *Private Bag X27, Benmore 2010* ☏ *011/809–4300* ⊕ *www.phinda.com* ▭ *AE, DC, MC, V* ⍰ *FAP*.

LUXURY LODGING

$ **Forest Lodge.** Hidden in a rare sand forest, this fabulous lodge over-
★ looks a small water hole where nyalas, warthogs, and baboons frequently come to drink. The lodge is a real departure from the traditional thatch structures so common in South Africa. It's very modern, with a vaguely Japanese Zen feel, thanks to glass-paneled walls, light woods, and a deliberately spare, clean look. The effect is stylish and very elegant, softened by modern African art and sculpture. Suites use the same architectural concepts as the lodge, where walls have become windows, and rely on the dense forest (or curtains) for privacy. As a result, you'll likely feel very close to your surroundings, and it's possible to lie in bed or take a shower while watching delicate nyalas grazing just feet away. Pros: magical feeling of oneness with the surrounding bush; light and airy, Zulu-Zen decor. Cons: being in a glass box could make some visitors nervous; not for traditional types. ⤙ *16 suites* ⚅ *In-room: a/c. In-hotel: pool, Internet terminal.*

$ **Mountain Lodge.** This attractive thatch lodge sits on a rocky hill over-
☾ looking miles of bushveld plains and the Ubombo Mountains. Wide verandas lead into the lounge and bar, graced with high ceilings, dark beams, and cool tile floors. In winter guests can snuggle into cushioned wicker chairs next to a blazing log fire. Brick pathways wind down the hillside from the lodge to elegant split-level suites with mosquito nets, thatch roofs, and large decks overlooking the reserve. African baskets, beadwork, and grass matting beautifully complement the bush atmosphere. Children are welcome, although those under five are not allowed on game drives and six- to 11-year-olds are permitted only

9

at the manager's discretion. **Pros:** great mountain views; very family-friendly. **Cons:** rather bland decor; pricey if you take the kids (pricey even if you don't take the kids). 🗷 *25 suites ⚐ In-room: a/c. In-hotel: bar, pool, Internet terminal.*

$ ⛆ **Rock Lodge.** If you get tired of the eagle's-eye view of the deep valley below from your private veranda, you can write in your journal in your luxurious sitting room or take a late-night dip in your own plunge pool. All of Phinda's activities are included—twice-daily game drives, nature walks, riverboat cruises, and canoe trips along the Mzinene River. Scuba diving, deep-sea fishing, and spectacular small-plane flights are extras. Don't miss out on one of Phinda's legendary bush dinners: hundreds of lanterns light up the surrounding forest and bush, and the food is unforgettable. **Pros:** Olé! If you fancy Mexico in the bush, then this hits the spot; your own plunge pool; great views. **Cons:** could be seen as inappropriately funky by Old Africa hands; stay away if you suffer from vertigo. 🗷 *6 suites ⚐ In-room: a/c. In-hotel: bar, pool.*

$ ⛆ **Vlei Lodge.** Accommodations at this small and intimate lodge are nestled in the shade of the sand forest and are so private it's hard to believe there are other guests. Suites—made of thatch, teak, and glass—have a distinct Asian feel and overlook a marshland on the edge of an inviting woodland. The bedrooms and bathrooms are huge, and each suite has a private plunge pool (one visitor found a lion drinking from his) and outdoor deck. The lounge–living area of the lodge has two fireplaces on opposite glass walls, a dining area, and a large terrace under a canopy of trees, where breakfast is served. The bush braai, with its splendid food and fairy-tale setting, is a memorable occasion after an evening game drive. **Pros:** superb views over the floodplains—you can lie on your bed and watch the ever-changing show of game; lovely warm romantic feel. **Cons:** you're so cosseted and comfortable you'll be hard put to make all those game drives; lots of mosquitoes and flying insects. 🗷 *6 suites ⚐ In-room: a/c. In-hotel: bar, pool.*

$$$$ ⛆ **Zuka Lodge.** An exclusive, single-use lodge for a family or small group
☾   of friends, Zuka (*zuka* means "sixpence" in Zulu) is a couple of miles from the bigger lodges. Thatch cottages overlook a busy water hole, and you'll be looked after by the camp's personal ranger, host, butler, and chef. Children are welcome. **Pros:** exclusivity; it's like having your own private holiday retreat; gives you the feeling of immediate celebrity status. **Cons:** this exclusivity comes at a high price; choose your fellow guests carefully—you're on your own here. 🗷 *4 cottages (which must be rented as one unit) ⚐ In-hotel: a/c, bar, pool.*

WALKING SAFARI

¢   ⛆ **Phinda Walking Safari.** This unusual experience is a delightful way to get close to the bush. Your home for three nights is a spacious safari tent (with bathroom) in the middle of a rare sand forest. Here crowned eagles may survey you as you take a postprandial nap in a hammock under giant fig trees, or a fishing owl may call as you swap safari stories under the stars. Each morning (depending on the consensus of the group) you amble through the forest or over the plains for four or five hours; then it's back to camp for a rest, then a presunset walk and night game drive. An armed security guard ranger makes sure you get home safely, and the camp chef keeps the calories coming. The walking safari is not offered in summer because of the heat. **Pros:** sleeping out in one of the world's rare sand forests is a privilege; walking every day really brings you in very close with the wilderness. **Cons:** food is fairly basic; stay away if you're not a natural survivor and you need strong walls and hate bugs. ↻4 *luxury tents* ⌂ *In-hotel: bar, no kids under 16* ☺ *Closed Dec.–Feb.*

THANDA PRIVATE GAME RESERVE

23 km (14 mi) north of Hluhluwe, 400 km (248 mi) north of Durban.

Located in a wildly beautiful part of northern Zululand, multi-award-winning Thanda is one of KwaZulu-Natal's newer game reserves. Like its neighbor Phinda did in the '90s, the 37,000-acre reserve is restoring former farmlands and hunting grounds to their previous pristine state, thanks to a joint venture with local communities and the king of the Zulus, Goodwill Zweletini, who donated some of his royal hunting grounds to the project. Game that used to roam this wilderness centuries ago has been reestablished, including the Big Five. *Thanda* (tan-duh) is Zulu for "love," and its philosophy echoes just that: "for the love of nature, wildlife, and dear ones." Rangers often have to work hard to find game, but the rewards of seriously tracking lions or rhinos with your enthusiastic and very experienced ranger and tracker are great. Because its owner is passionately committed not only to the land but also to the local people, there are many opportunities to interact with them. Don't miss out on Vula Zulu, one of the most magical and powerful Zulu experiences offered in South Africa. After exploring the village, including the chief's *kraal* (compound) and the hut of the *sangoma* (shaman), where you might have bones thrown and read, you'll be treated to the Vula Zulu show, a memorable blend of narration, high-energy dance, song, and mime that recounts Zulu history. The lodge can also arrange golf, scuba diving, snorkeling, whale-watching, and fishing expeditions.

GETTING HERE AND AROUND
Road transfers from Richards Bay and Durban airports can be arranged with the reserve.

WHERE TO STAY
For all reservations, contact **Thanda.** Both the tented camp and the main lodge have kids' programs and a customized Junior Ranger's course. ⌂ *Box 441, Hluhluwe 3960* ☎ *011/469–5082* ⊕ *www.thanda.com* ▤ *AE, DC, MC, V* ❂ *FAP.*

$$ ▦ **Thanda Main Lodge.** There's a palpable feeling of earth energy in this
☺ magical and exquisite lodge that blends elements of royal Zulu with
★ an eclectic pan-African feel. Beautiful domed, beehive-shaped dwellings perch on the side of rolling hills and overlook mountains and bushveld. Inside, contemporary Scandinavian touches meet African chic—from the "eyelashes" of slatted poles that peep out from under the thatch roofs to the embedded mosaics in royal Zulu red and blue that decorate the polished, honey-color stone floors. Creative light fixtures include

chandeliers made of handcrafted Zulu beads and lamps of straw or filmy cotton mesh. A huge stone fireplace divides the bedroom area from the comfortable and roomy lounge. Each chalet has a different color scheme and is decorated with beaded, hand-embroidered cushions and throws. Dip in your personal plunge pool after an exciting game drive, sunbathe on your private deck, or commune with the surrounding bush-veld in your cool, cushioned *sala* (outdoor covered deck). Later, after a meal that many a fine restaurant would be proud to serve, come back to your chalet to find a bedtime story on your pillow, marshmallows waiting to be toasted over flickering candles, and a glass of Amarula cream. Or dine alone in your private boma by the light of the stars and the leaping flames of a fragrant wood fire. The spacious, uncluttered public areas—dining decks, bomas, library, and lounge—are decorated in restful earth tones accented by royal Zulu colors, beads from Malawi, Ghanaian ceremonial masks, and Indonesian chairs. **Pros:** luxury unlim-ited; superb food and service; kids will love the Junior Ranger program; late-night snacks and drinks await you in your room. **Cons:** a bit over the top—some might say it's Hollywood in the bush; very near to the main road. ➴9 *chalets* ⟨ *In-room: a/c. In-hotel: bar, pool, spa, chil-dren's programs (ages 5–15), Internet terminal.*

$ 🏕 **Thanda Tented Camp.** Perfect for a family or friends' reunion, this
☺   intimate camp deep in the bush brings you into close contact with your surroundings. You might wake up in your spacious safari tent with en suite bathroom and private veranda to find a warthog or nyala grazing outside. The camp has its own vehicle, ranger, and tracker, and a huge sala with pool and sundeck. **Pros:** opportunities to learn stargazing; perfect for small (adults only) reunions or celebrations. **Cons:** not for the nervous type; only four tents so hope for pleasant fellow guests. ➴4 *tents* ⟨ *In-hotel: bar, pool, spa, no kids under 16.*

AMAZULU PRIVATE GAME RESERVE AND AMAKHOSI LODGE

GETTING HERE AND AROUND
The reserve is 155 km from Hluhluwe town; 245 km from Richards Bay; 426 km from Durban. Roads are good so you can self-drive. The nearest airport is Richards Bay, which has scheduled flights from all major cities. If necessary, AmaKhosi Lodge does road transfers from Richards Bay.

EXPLORING
Forty kilometers (21 mi) south of Phongola lies AmaKhosi Lodge, in the **Amazulu Private Game Reserve,** which covers some 25,000 acres of pristine wilderness on the perennial Mkhuze River. Different habitats range from rocky hillsides to thick bushveld, tamboti forests to broad wetlands. AmaKhosi has all of the Big Five, in addition to wildebeests, zebras, giraffes, and a variety of antelopes, including the shy nyala. Most animals have been reintroduced, with the exception of leopards, which remain secretive and very difficult to spot. In addition, a wide variety of bird species will delight birders.

WHERE TO STAY

$ ☆ **AmaKhosi Lodge.** In the heart of northern KwaZulu-Natal, amid countryside that South African author Alan Paton would have described as beautiful beyond any singing of it, this spectacular lodge overlooks the Mkhuze River, which carves its way through mountains, rolling hills, open plains, thick thornveld, and riverine bush. Birdlife is abundant, the Big Five are all here, and rangers work hard to find game, instead of relying on animals habituated to vehicles, as at some of the older camps. Superb air-conditioned suites (big enough to swing a pride of lions) have huge decks from which you can survey the river below. The staff excels, from management right down to the friendly gardeners, and the food would put many a posh restaurant to shame. Dine under the stars on a sprawling deck overlooking the river, in a gracious dining room if the weather is inclement, or in the staff-built branch-enclosed boma, entertained by local schoolchildren who practice their singing and dancing hard to help pay their school fees. For something very different, try a frog or insect safari: after a bush braai, you'll be supplied with gum boots and miners' lamps, and led on a hunt for more than 30 species of these fascinating and little-known creatures with the resident frog or insect expert. **Pros:** great river views; exciting, unique nighttime frogging expeditions. **Cons:** off the beaten track. ⊠ *Off the N2, south of Phongola* ✆ *Box 354, Phongola 3170* ☎ *034/414–1157* ⊕ *www.amakhosi.com* ↩ *6 suites* ⌕ *In-room: safe. In-hotel: bar, pool, Internet terminal* ⊟ *AE, DC, MC, V* ⊙⟨ *FAP.*

MAPUTALAND COASTAL FOREST RESERVE

300 km (186 mi) from Richards Bay.

GETTING HERE AND AROUND

Visitors fly into Richards Bay from Johannesburg and are picked up by the lodge, which will make all the flight and pickup arrangements. If you'd like to drive instead of fly, the lodge can arrange a car service to get you to and from Johannesburg. You could drive yourself, but it's really an unnecessary waste of time as you won't be able to use the vehicle once you're on the property. Plus, you'd need to rent a 4x4 as the last part of the road is very bumpy and muddy.

WHEN TO GO

The loggerhead and leatherback turtle egg-laying season goes from November through early March. During these months rangers lead after-dinner drives and walks down the beach to look for turtles, and you can expect to cover as much as 16 km (10 mi) in a night. From a weather standpoint, the best times to visit the lodge are probably spring (September–October) and autumn (March–May). In summer the temperature regularly soars past 38°C (100°F), and swimming during winter is a brisk proposition. August is the windiest month, and it's in summer that the turtles come ashore to dig their nests and lay their eggs—an awesome spectacle.

9

EXPLORING

Expect great swaths of pale, creamy sand stretching to far-off rocky headlands; a shimmering, undulating horizon where whales blow. Watch out for pods of dolphins leaping and dancing in the morning sun. If you're here in season (November to early March), one of nature's greatest and most spiritually uplifting experiences is waiting for you—turtle tracking. Nothing, not photographs, not wildlife documentaries, prepares you for the size of these creatures. On any given night, you might see a huge, humbling leatherback, 2 meters long and weighing up to 1,100 pounds, drag her great body up through the surf to the high-water mark at the back of the beach. There she will dig a deep hole and lay up to a 120 gleaming white eggs, bigger than a golf ball but smaller than a tennis ball. It will have taken her many, many years to achieve this moment of fruition, a voyage through time and across the great oceans of the world—a long, solitary journey in the cold black depths of the sea, meeting and mating only once every seven years, and always coming back to within 100m of the spot on the beach where she herself had been born. And if your luck holds, you might even observe the miracle of the hatchlings, when perfect bonsai leatherback turtles dig themselves out of their deep, sandy nest and rush pell-mell toward the sea under a star-studded sky.

WHERE TO STAY

$

Fodor's Choice

★

🖼 **Thonga Beach Lodge.** Dramatically sited, this lovely beach lodge makes the best of its unique situation. Twelve air-conditioned, thatch suites decorated in chic Robinson Crusoe style look out over indigenous coastal and forest bush a stone's throw from the sea. Chill out on your personal deck, lounge on the viewing deck or by the pool, or walk barefoot down the boardwalks leading to the beach, where you can recline on a lounge chair shaded by white cotton "sails." The food is delicious, creative, and you'll be amazed at just how hungry the sea air makes you. Dan, the resident snorkeling expert (half-man, half-fish), will walk along the beach with you to Island Rock, where at low tide, you can float among the rocks and pools. If you've never snorkeled, then now is your chance. Go for sundowners to Lake Sibaya, South Africa's largest, freshwater lake, with its spectacular birdlife, and watch out for lumbering hippos as they come out to graze. Take a guided walk through the forest, grassland, or wetlands around the lodge, or go diving to the pristine reefs offshore (one is as big as two football fields) or just stay on board and watch for whales and dolphins. Then relax with a treatment at the in-house Sea-Spa. **Pros:** Robinson Crusoe deluxe; privacy and tranquility; discover different (all magical) ecosystems. **Cons:** difficult to get to, so pricey. ⌂ *Box 1593, Eshowe 3185* 📠 *035/474–1473* ⊕ *www.isibindi.co.za* ⇝ *12 chalets* ♿ *In-hotel: bar, pool, Internet terminal* ⊟ *MC, V* ⭤ *FAP.*

KGALAGADI TRANSFRONTIER PARK

If you're looking for true wilderness, remoteness, and stark, almost surreal landscapes and you're not averse to forgoing the ultimate in luxury and getting sand in your hair, then this amazing, uniquely beautiful park within the Kalahari Desert is for you.

In an odd little finger of the country jutting north between Botswana in the east and Namibia in the west lies South Africa's second-largest park after Kruger. Kgalagadi was officially launched in 2000 as the first transfrontier, or "Peace Park," in southern Africa by merging South Africa's vast Kalahari Gemsbok National Park with the even larger Gemsbok National Park in Botswana. The name Kgalagadi (pronounced kalahardy) is derived from the San language and means "place of thirst." It is now one of the largest protected wilderness areas in the world—an area of more than 38,000 square km (14,670 square mi). Of this awesome area, 9,600 square km (3,700 square mi) fall in South Africa, and the rest in Botswana. Passing through the Twee Rivieren Gate, you will encounter a vast desert under enormous, usually cloudless skies and a sense of space and openness that few other places can offer.

The Kgalagadi Transfrontier is less commercialized and developed than Kruger. The roads aren't paved, and you will come across far fewer people and cars. There is less game on the whole than in Kruger, but because there is also less vegetation, the animals are much more visible. Also, because the game and large carnivores are concentrated in two riverbeds (the route that two roads follow), the park offers unsurpassed viewing and photographic opportunities. Perhaps the key to really appreciating this barren place is in understanding how its creatures have adapted to their harsh surroundings to survive—like the gemsbok, which has a sophisticated cooling system allowing it to tolerate extreme changes in body temperature. There are also insects in the park that inhale only every half hour or so to preserve the moisture that breathing expends.

The landscape—endless dunes punctuated with blond grass and the odd thorn tree—is dominated by two dry riverbeds: the Nossob (which forms the border between South Africa and Botswana) and its tributary, the Auob. The Nossob flows only a few times a century, and the Auob flows only once every couple of decades or so. A single road runs beside each riverbed, along which windmills pump water into man-made water holes, which help the animals to survive and provide good viewing stations for visitors. There are 82 water holes, 49 of which are along tourist roads. Park management struggles to keep up their maintenance; it's a constant battle against the elements, with the elements often winning. Similarly, the park constantly maintains and improves tourist roads, but again it's a never-ending struggle. A third road traverses the park's interior to join the other two. The scenery and vegetation on this road change dramatically from the two river valleys, which are dominated by

9

sandy banks, to a grassier escarpment. Two more dune roads have been added, and several 4x4 routes have been developed. From Nossob camp a road leads to Union's End, the country's northernmost tip, where South Africa, Namibia, and Botswana meet. Allow a full day for the long and dusty drive, which is 124 km (77 mi) one way. It is possible to enter Botswana from the South African side, but you'll need a 4x4. The park infrastructure in Botswana is very basic, with just three campsites and mostly 4x4 terrain.

The park is famous for its gemsbok and its legendary, huge, blackmaned Kalahari lions. It also has leopard, cheetah, eland, blue wildebeest, and giraffe, as well as meerkats and mongooses. Rarer desert species, such as the desert-adapted springbok, the elusive aardvark, and the pretty Cape fox, also make their home here. Among birders, the park is known as one of Africa's raptor meccas; it's filled with bateleurs, lappet-faced vultures, pygmy falcons, and the cooperatively hunting red-necked falcons and gabar goshawks.

> ## FOOD AND DRINK
>
> You can buy Styrofoam coolers at Pick 'n' Pay in Upington (or at any large town en route to the park) and then leave them behind for the camp staff when you exit the park. Pack ice and frozen juice boxes to keep your perishables chilled between camps. Ziplock bags are indispensable for keeping dust out of food (and for storing damp washcloths and swimsuits). You're not allowed out of your vehicle between camps, so keep your snacks and drinks handy inside the passenger area and not in the trunk.

The park's legendary night drives (R110) depart most evenings about 5:30 in summer, earlier in winter (check when you get to your camp), from Twee Rivieren Camp, Mata Mata, and Nossob. The drives set out just as the park gate closes to everyone else. You'll have a chance to see rare nocturnal animals like the brown hyena and the bat-eared fox by spotlight. The guided morning walks—during which you see the sun rise over the Kalahari and could bump into a lion—are also a must. Reservations are essential and can be made when you book your accommodations.

GETTING HERE AND AROUND

AIR TRAVEL

Upington International Airport is 260 km (162 mi) south of Kgalagadi Transfrontier Park; many lodgings provide shuttle service from the airport, or you can rent a car here.

CAR TRAVEL

Kgalagadi Transfontier National Park is approximately 250 km (155 mi) north of Upington in the far northern Cape and 904 km (562 mi) west of Johannesburg. If you drive from Johannesburg you have a choice of two routes: either via Upington (with the last stretch a 60-km [37-mi] gravel road) or via Kuruman, Hotazel, and Vanzylrus (with about 340 km [211 mi] of gravel road). The gravel sections on both routes are badly corrugated, so don't speed.

You can rent cars at the airport, or reserve a rental car through an agency in Upington and then pick up the car from the Twee Rivieren Camp. Under normal circumstances (no excessive rain, for example), a passenger car will be fine in Kgalagadi (except on the 4x4 routes). However, a 4x4 will give you greater access in the park and as you sit higher up, better game-viewing.

Airport Information Upington International Airport (📠 054/332 2161).

Airlines South African Airways/ SA Airlink/South African Express (📠 011/978–1111 ⊕ www.flysaa.com).

> **WHAT TO BRING**
>
> Winter or summer, bring a range of suitable clothing: shorts, T-shirts, and sun hats for the day, warm clothes for night. If you're going on a night drive (which is a must), wrap up with hats, scarves, coats, and blankets. You can boil and use park water for all cooking, but as it tastes very brackish (it has a high salt and mineral content), it's best to bring your own drinking water. You can fill up at the gateway town of Upington, or buy water from the camp shops.

BOOKING AND VISITOR INFORMATION

There is a daily conservation fee, but Wild Cards, available at the gates or online, are more economical for stays of more than a few days. Reservations for all accommodations, bush drives, wilderness trails, and other park activities must be made through South African National Parks.

Contacts Kgalagadi Transfrontier Park (✉ Park reception at Twee Rivieren Camp 📠 054/561–2000. **South African National Parks** (📠 012/426–5000 Pretoria, 021/552–0008 Cape Town ⊕ www.sanparks.org).

SAFETY AND PRECAUTIONS

Don't forget to take antimalarial drugs and use a mosquito repellent, especially during the summer.

WHEN TO GO

The park can be superhot in summer and freezing at night in winter (literally below zero, with frost on the ground). Autumn—from late February to mid-April—is perhaps the best time to visit. It's cool after the rains, and many of the migratory birds are still around. The winter months of June and July are also a good time. It's best to make reservations as far in advance as possible, even up to a year or more if you want to visit at Easter or in June or July, when there are school vacations.

WHERE TO STAY

LUXURY LODGING

$ 🛏 **!Xaus Lodge.** If you want to experience one of South Africa's most
Fodor's Choice beautiful and isolated parks without hassle, then this luxury lodge
★ owned by the Khomani San and Mier communities and jointly managed with SANParks is the place for you. You'll be picked up in a 4x4 from Twee Rivieren, fed, watered, taken on game drives and desert walks, and introduced to the local San. Located deep in the desert 32 km (20

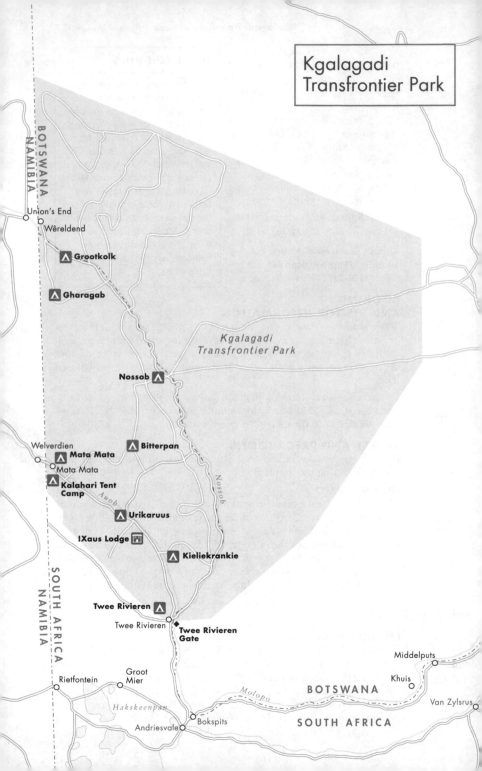

Kgalagadi
Transfrontier Park

BOTSWANA
NAMIBIA

Union's End
Wêreldend

△ **Grootkolk**

△ **Gharagab**

*Kgalagadi
Transfrontier Park*

Nossob △

Welverdien
△ **Mata Mata**
Mata Mata

△ **Bitterpan**

△ **Kalahari Tent
Camp**

Auob

Nossob

△ **Urikaruus**

!Xaus Lodge 🖼

△ **Kieliekrankie**

Twee Rivieren △
Twee Rivieren
◆ **Twee Rivieren
Gate**

SOUTH AFRICA
NAMIBIA

Middelputs

Khuis

Rietfontein

Groot
Mier

Molopo

BOTSWANA

Van Zylsrus

Hakskeenpan

Bokspits

SOUTH AFRICA

Andriesvale

San Culture and Language

Also called the /Xam, the hunter-gatherer San (Bushmen) have a culture that dates back more than 20,000 years, and their genetic origins are more than 1 million years old, contemporary humans' oldest. Fast-forward a few years—about 2,000 years ago, to be inexact—when Korana or Khoi (Khoe) herders migrated south, bringing their livestock and settling along the Orange (Gariep/Garieb), Vaal, and Riet rivers. During the 18th and 19th centuries, the Griquas—thought to be part Khoi and part slave—moved into the Northern Cape with their cattle and sheep.

At one time 20 to 30 languages pertaining to various clans flourished, but colonialism brought with it devastating results for the San's native tongue.

It lost out to Tswana and Afrikaans. In the nick of time in the 1870s, British doctor Wilhelm Bleek, who spoke /Xam, and Lucy Lloyd recorded the last activities of /Xam culture and tradition. (Some of these records can be found at the McGregor Museum in Kimberley.)

Still, thousands of Northern Cape residents today acknowledge an ancestral connection to the largest San or /Xam group of the 18th and 19th centuries. The two biggest remaining groups are the !Xu and Khwe, who live at Schmidtsdrift, 80 km (50 mi) from Kimberley. Among the best-known groups in South Africa today are the Khomani San, some of whom still speak the ancient Nu.

mi) from the Auob River road along a track that crosses the red dunes of the Kalahari, this enchanting lodge overlooks an amazingly scenic pan. The twin-bed, en suite chalets perch on sand dunes overlooking a water hole; each chalet has a private deck. A fan will keep you cool in summer, and a gas heater, hot-water bottle, and warm sheets will help you stay warm on winter nights. A welcome swimming pool is set in a deck overlooking the pan. The attractive rustic furniture and eye-catching artwork throughout this delightful, unique lodge are all made by local craftspeople and artists. Activities include game drives in an open safari vehicle, walks with San trackers, and a chance to watch San artists at work. At night the stars and planets are bright and clear; a telescope brings ancient tradition and modern technology together as the San interpret for you their legends of the night sky. But !Xaus (pronounced kaus) comprises so much more than its activities: it is solitude, peace, and silence as you "listen" to day turn into night, plus interaction with the cheerful and willing staff, the majority of whom come from the surrounding local communities. Negotiations are ongoing to establish a private airstrip nearby. **Pros:** unique wilderness setting; only private lodge in area; opportunities to interact with the local people. **Cons:** very long (almost an hour) roller-coaster approach road through dunes; game not abundant around lodge. ⌂ *Box 30919, Tokai, Cape Town 7966* ☎ *021/701-7860* ⊕ *www.xauslodge.co.za* ⟿ *12 chalets* ⚘ *In-room: no a/c. In-hotel: restaurant, bar, pool, Internet terminal* ▭ *AE, DC, MC, V* ⏻ *FAP.*

NATIONAL PARK ACCOMMODATIONS

Accommodations within the park are in three traditional rest camps and several highly sought-after wilderness camps (try to reserve these if possible), which are spread around the park. All of the traditional rest camps have shops selling food, curios, and some basic equipment, but Twee Rivieren has the best variety of fresh fruit, vegetables, milk, and meat, and is the only camp with a restaurant. Twee Rivieren is also the only camp with telephone and cell-phone reception (although cell-phone reception quickly disappears as you head into the dunes) and 24-hour electricity; the other camps have gas and electricity, but the electricity runs only part of the day, at different times in each camp.

For all national park accommodations, contact **South African National Parks,** or you can reserve directly through the park (☎ 054/561–2000) if you happen to be there and would like to stay a night or add another night onto your stay. ✉ Box 787, Pretoria 0001 ☎ 012/426–5000 Pretoria, 021/552–0008 Cape Town ⊕ www.sanparks.org ⊟ MC, V.

REST CAMPS

¢ 🏨 **Mata Mata.** This camp, 120 km (74 mi) from Twee Rivieren on the Namibian border, has good game-viewing due to the proximity of the water holes. The camp's facilities are not as modern as those at Twee Rivieren, although there is a small shop stocking basics and a swimming pool. **Pros:** you're allowed to drive into Namibia without visas for a certain distance; great water holes; giraffes galore. **Cons:** dry and dusty year-round; unattractive barracks-like buildings. ⟿ 2 6-person cottages, 3 2-person cottages ₺ In-room: kitchen. In-hotel: pool.

¢ 🏨 **Nossob.** In the central section of the park, this camp is on the Botswana border, 166 km (103 mi) from Twee Rivieren. Basic brick chalets come with an outside braai and real bush atmosphere and sleep from three to six people. Guesthouses have showers but no tubs. Most of the chalets are less than 50 yards from the fence, and there's also a stunning blind overlooking the water hole. You can see game without even leaving camp, but watch out for marauding jackals here; although they're not dangerous or aggressive, they're always on the lookout for unattended food. A small shop sells the basics. There's no electricity in the camp, and the generators are turned off at 11. **Pros:** this is the place to see predators, particularly lions; predator information center. **Cons:** barren, unattractive camp; no phone reception. ⟿ 15 chalets, 1 cottage, 2 guesthouses ₺ In-room: kitchen. In-hotel: pool.

¢ 🏨 **Twee Rivieren.** On the Kgalagadi's southern boundary, this camp is home to the park's headquarters. It's the biggest of the camps and has the most modern facilities; all units have fully equipped kitchens, and the camp shop here is the best. You can choose from a couple of types of accommodations, from a two-bedroom, six-bed family cottage to a bungalow with two single beds and a sleeper couch. Try for units 1–16, which look out over the dunes. Take a guided morning walk *and* a night drive—worth every penny. There are educational exhibits on the Kalahari's animal and plant life. From Upington to Twee Rivieren is 260 km (161 mi) on a relatively good road; only the last 52 km (32 mi) is gravel. **Pros:** modern, well-equipped chalets; on-site grocery store; not-to-be-missed guided morning and night drives; 24-hour electricity.

Cons: the biggest and noisiest camp in the area. *9 cottages, 21 bungalows, 1 family chalet In-room: kitchen, no TV. In-hotel: restaurant, bar, pool.*

CAMPING

There are a limited number of campsites (R130) at Mata Mata (20), Nossob (20), and Twee Rivieren (24). All campsites have a braai and access to electricity and water, and there are communal bathroom facilities and a basic communal kitchen. Before you arrive, be sure to arm yourself with the "blue camping plug"—available from any camping–caravanning shop—and a long extension cord. Try to find a shady spot.

WILDERNESS CAMPS

Kgalagadi is the first national park to provide accommodation deep in the wilderness, where several unfenced wilderness camps with their own water holes for game-viewing put you deep in the heart of the Kalahari. These enchanting camps are very popular, so make your reservations well in advance—a year ahead, if possible. Each camp is slightly different, but all have the same facilities and are similarly priced. All have an equipped kitchen with a gas-powered refrigerator, solar-powered lights, gas for hot water, and a deck with braai facilities. You do need to supply your own water and firewood.

As all of these camps are unfenced (which is part of their desirability and charm), you should *never* walk outside your accommodation at night—you don't want to come face-to-face with a hungry lion or scavenging hyena!

¢ **Bitterpan.** This camp overlooks an enormous expanse of sand and a water hole, where you can watch game come and go from your deck or from the communal areas. Four double cabins with their own bathrooms border a narrow walkway that leads to a large communal kitchen, dining room, and braai area. Bitterpan is accessible only by 4x4, and only guests here may use the road from Nossob to Urikaruus. **Pros:** spectacular game-viewing from your accommodation; spectacular desert scenery; only four cabins. **Cons:** 4x4s only; no children under 12; communal kitchen and eating area (cross fingers you share the camp with amenable visitors); it's a long drive to get here from any starting point; guests have to bring their own drinking water and firewood. *4 cabins In-hotel: no kids under 12.*

¢ **Gharagab.** Although you'll need a 4x4 to negotiate the two-track road to Gharagab, it's worth every dusty mile for the chance to feel like you're the only person on earth. Situated in the far northern region of the park close to the Namibian border, this camp provides stunning elevated views of Kalahari dunes and the thornveld savanna. Although the game isn't as abundant as in the Grootkolk area, you're likely to have unusual or even rare sightings, such as a honey badger, eland, or an aardvark, and the feeling of splendid isolation is unforgettable. You may never again feel this alone. Each long tent built on wooden stilts has a kitchen, bedroom, and bathroom, plus a wooden deck (with a braai) overlooking a water hole. **Pros:** you've probably never experienced solitary wilderness such as this. **Cons:** 4x4s only; no children under 12; not much in the way of big game; guests must bring their own drinking water and firewood. ⟲ *4 cabins* ⚭ *In-room: kitchen. In-hotel: no kids under 12.*

¢ ⊞ **Grootkolk.** Surrounded by camelthorn trees and close to the Nossob River bed, this lovely camp has good game-viewing, with lions, cheetahs, hyenas, and lots of antelope, including oryx and springbok. All four well-sited rustic desert cabins have a good view of the water hole, which is spotlighted for a couple of hours every night. Although the road to Grootkolk is heavily corrugated, you can negotiate it with a two-wheel-drive vehicle.

Pros: spotlit water hole; sublime wilderness; ceiling fans in the cabins. **Cons:** 4x4s or 2x4s only; no children under 12; chalets are made from canvas and sandbags so if you prefer something more substantial stay away. ⟲ *4 cabins* ⚭ *In-room: kitchen. In-hotel: no kids under 12.*

¢ ⊞ **Kalahari Tent Camp.** Many visitors say that this good game-viewing camp overlooking the Auob River bed and water hole is one of the most beautiful places in the park, so try to stay for more than one night. Your accommodation consists of a large walk-in tent with a spacious and attractive bedroom, shower, and toilet. There's a separate, fully equipped kitchen tent, also suitable as a dining room, and the terrace between these two tents has excellent views over the riverbed and its wildlife. At night, look out for jackals, lions, a resident family of meerkats, and spare-wheel-cover-eating hyenas around the tents—just be sure to stay in your tent at night and avoid walking around. The secluded honeymoon unit has a king-size bed and a bath and shower. The camp is near the Mata Mata shop and gas station. **Pros:** near Mata Mata, which has a shop and gas; excellent game; family-friendly; lovely honeymoon tent; ceiling fans in the tents. **Cons:** guests must bring their own drinking water and firewood. ⟲ *10 tents, 4 family tents, 1 honeymoon tent* ⚭ *In-room: kitchen. In-hotel: pool.*

¢ ⊞ **Kieliekrankie.** Perched high on a big sand dune only 8 km (5 mi) from the game-rich Auob River road, this small camp overlooks seemingly infinite red Kalahari sands, creating an amazing sense of space and isolation. To be among the red dunes at full moon is an unforgettable experience. The four cabins have stunning views over the desert and come with a kitchen tent, bedroom, bathroom, and deck and braai. Situated in the Twee Rivieren region, the camp can be easily reached with a two-wheel-drive vehicle. **Pros:** easily accessible with a sedan; you can start your game drives before residents of the other camps reach the area so you have the game to yourself for a while; the red Kalahari sands are unforgettable. **Cons:** no children under 12; guests must bring their own drinking water and firewood. ⟲ *4 cabins* ⚭ *In-room: kitchen. In-hotel: no kids under 12.*

¢ ⛛ **Urikaruus.** Four cabins with kitchens, bedrooms, and bathrooms are built on stilts among camelthorn trees overlooking the Auob River. You'll easily spot game as it comes to drink at the water hole close to the cabins. On-site wardens will help you interpret the spoor you find around your cabin. Set in the Mata Mata region, Urikaruus is accessible by two-wheel-drive vehicles. **Pros:** accessible with a sedan; stunning location; game to yourself on early-morning and late-afternoon drives; cabins have their own kitchen. **Cons:** no children under 12; guests must bring their own drinking water and firewood. ↪ *4 cabins* ∆ *In-room: kitchen. In-hotel: no kids under 12.*

BETWEEN KGALAGADI AND KRUGER

TSWALU KALAHARI RESERVE

300 km (186 mi) northwest of Kimberley, 270 km (168 mi) northeast of Upington.

GETTING HERE AND AROUND

It's easiest to fly to Kimberley or Upington and be picked up from there by the lodge. Daily flights are available from Johannesburg, Durban, and Cape Town with Airlink and Federal Air. Road transfers from Kimberley or Upington can be arranged, or you can book a charter flight from Johannesburg.

ESSENTIALS

Airlines **Federal Air** (⊕ www.fedair.com). **SA Airlink** (⊕ www.flyairlink.com).

EXPLORING

Near the Kgalagadi Transfrontier Park is the malaria-free **Tswalu Kalahari Reserve,** which at 900 square km (347 square mi) is the biggest privately owned game reserve in Africa; it's the perfect place to photograph a gemsbok against a red dune and an azure sky. Initially founded as a conservation project by the late millionaire Stephen Boler primarily to protect and breed the endangered desert rhino, it's now owned by the Oppenheimer family. Today it spreads over endless Kalahari dunes covered with tufts of golden veld and over much of the Northern Cape's Korannaberg mountain range. Its initial population of 7,000 animals has grown to more than 12,000, and it's now home to lions, cheetahs, buffalo, giraffes, and many species of antelope. It's the best place in Africa to see rhino—the reserve has more than 50 white and 20 black rhinos, which have amazingly adapted to living in the desert. Other rare species include roan and sable antelope, black wildebeest, and mountain zebra. There's not so much game as in some of Mpumalanga's private reserves because the land has a lower carrying capacity (the annual rainfall is only about 9¾ inches). But when you do see the animals, the lack of vegetation makes sightings spectacular. And the fact that only about three open-sided game vehicles traverse an area two-thirds the size of the entire Sabi Sands makes your escape all the more complete.

9

This is one of the most child-friendly game reserves in southern Africa. Children are welcomed and well catered for, with lots of freedom and special activities.

WHERE TO STAY

The emphasis at **Tswalu** is on exclusivity, which is why the entire reserve can accommodate no more than 30 people at a time. Nothing is left wanting at this exclusive Relais & Châteaux property. Children 12 and under stay free with adults, and there are discounted rates for older kids. ⌂ *Box 1081, Kuruman 8460* ☎ *011/274–2299* ⊕ *www.tswalu. com* ☰ *AE, DC, MC, V* ⏏ *FAP.*

LUXURY LODGES

$$ 🔲 **The Motse.** Tswalu's main lodge is made up of freestanding thatch-
☺ and-stone suites clustered around a large main building with a heated natural-color pool and a floodlit water hole. The decor—in keeping with the unusual and unique Tswalu experience—is minimalist and modern, echoing the landscape in colors and textures. **Pros:** a special children's room, and babysitting services and nannies available; unique desert landscape; same great wildlife as Tarkuni; wonderful library with rare books. **Cons:** no elephants. ⊠ *8 suites* ⚭ *In-hotel: a/c, bar, restaurant, pool, spa, gym, Wi-Fi.*

$$$$ 🔲 **Tarkuni.** In a private section of Tswalu, Tarkuni is an exclusive, self-
☺ contained house decorated similarly to Motswe and offering a comparable level of luxury. Perfect for small groups and families, Tarkuni sleeps 10 and comes with its own chef, game vehicle, and tracker. The food is almost as memorable as the scenery, and every meal is served in a different location: on a lantern-lighted dune or alongside a crackling fire in the lodge's boma. Apart from guided walks and drives, horseback trails (not included in the rate) that you traverse with a qualified guide offer close encounters with wildlife. Two sets of bunk beds, plus an adjoining nanny's quarters, are geared toward children. **Pros:** this is excellent value for money, and if there are 10 of you, it works out to be far more affordable than most other luxury lodges; a children's paradise; black-maned Kalahari lions, wild dogs, cheetah, and one-third of South Africa's endangered desert black rhino population; if you're a fan of TV's *Meerkat Manor,* you'll be in a seventh heaven. **Cons:** no elephants. ⊠ *1 house* ⚭ *In-hotel: a/c, bar, restaurant, pool, Internet terminal.*

PILANESBERG NATIONAL PARK

150 km (93 mi) northwest of Johannesburg.

GETTING HERE AND AROUND

To get to the national park from Johannesburg, get on the N4 highway to Krugersdorp and take the R556 off-ramp and follow the signs. The drive is about 2½ hours. There is a shuttle from Johannesburg to Sun City *(⇨ Chapter 7),* just outside the park, but public transport in and around the park is limited, so hiring a rental car or using a private transfer or tour company is your best bet.

TOURS

Pre-booking these tours is essential.

Continued on page 556

There's nothing quite like the feeling of first setting eyes on one of the Big Five—buffalo, elephant, leopard, lion, and rhino—in the African bush. Being just a few feet from these majestic creatures is both terrifying and exhilarating, even for the most seasoned safari-goer.

THE BIG 5

by Kristan Schiller

The Big Five was originally a hunting term referring to those animals that posed the greatest risk to hunters on foot—buffalo, elephant, leopard, lion, and rhino. Today it has become one of the most important criteria used in evaluating a lodge or reserve, though it should never be your only criterion.

THE AFRICAN BUFFALO

Often referred to as the Cape buffalo, this is considered by many to be the most dangerous of the Big Five because of its unpredictability and speed. Do not confuse them for the larger Asian water buffalo or, for that matter, with North American bison as this is an altogether heftier and more powerful beast. They have very few predators other than human hunters. Lion do prey on them, but it generally takes an entire pride or a large male lion to bring down an adult buffalo.

They can reach up to 1,800 pounds, and their lifespan is about 30 years, though they rarely make it to half that. Diets consist mainly of grass and water—they will not stay in a place where there is less than ten inches of rain per year.

Safari goers can expect to see Cape Buffalo in savannahs throughout sub-Saharan Africa, especially in Kenya, Tanzania, Botswana, Zambia, Zimbabwe, and South Africa. Herds generally number around a few hundred, however, buffalo have been known to gather in the Serengeti in the thousands during the rains. Herds mainly consist of females and their offspring. Males reside in bachelor groups, and the two come together only during the mating season. You shouldn't fear a herd, but do be on the look out for lone old males. Called dagha boys—dagha is the clay mixture used for building huts—they spend much of their days in mud wallows and are usually thickly coated in the stuff. While seemingly lethargic, these old guys can turn on a dime and run like lightening. If a buffalo charges you, run for the nearest cover. If it is upon you, your best bet is to lie flat on the ground; you can minimize the damage by playing dead.

IN FOCUS THE BIG 5

9

THE ELEPHANT

The largest of the land animals, it once roamed the continent by the millions. Today, according to the World Wildlife Fund (WWF), the population, mainly found in Southern and Eastern Africa, is about 600,000. The continent's forest elephants (of central and West Africa) are still under severe threat.

African elephants are divided into two species. Savannah elephants are the largest, at 13 feet and 7 tons, and can be found by lakes, marshes, or grass-lands. Forest elephants have an average height of 10 feet and weight of 10,000 pounds. They're usually found in cen-tral and West African rainforests.

An elephant's gestation period is 22 months—the longest of any land animal. The aver-

age calf is 265 pounds. When calves are born, they are raised and protected by the entire herd—a group of about 10 females led by the oldest and largest. Males leave the herd after 15 years, often living with other males or alone.

When an elephant trumpets in a showy manner, head up and ears spread, it's a mock charge—frightening but not phys-ically dangerous. If an elephant stomps the ground, holds its ears back and head forward, and issues a loud, high-pitched screech, this means real trouble. A charging elephant is extremely fast and surprisingly agile. If you're on foot make for the nearest big tree or embank-ment; elephants seldom negotiate these obstacles. If you're in a vehicle, hit the gas.

> 549

IN FOCUS THE BIG 5   9

THE RHINO

There are two species of these massive, primeval-looking animals in Africa: the black, or hooklipped, rhino and the white, or square-lipped, rhino. Both species have poor eyesight and erratic tempers and will sometimes charge without apparent reason; the rhino is surprisingly agile for its size. Both the black and white rhino are about 60 inches tall at their shoulders, but their weight differs. A black rhino can weigh up to one and a half tons, while a white rhino can grow to over 2 tons. Though they do share habitats and feeding grounds (both are vegetarians and feed on everything from grass and bushes to trees), the black rhino, the more aggressive of the two, is found in areas of dense vegetation, while the larger white rhino (pictured here) resides mainly in savannahs with water holes or mud wallows.

More often than not, rhinos live in sanctuaries, or protected areas, where they are safe from poachers. You'll spot them in Kenya, Tanzania, Botswana, Zambia, Zimbabwe, and South Africa. The black rhino tends to be solitary while the white rhino is more likely to travel in a herd, or "crash." Calves are born after 16 months in the womb; this may explain why the relationship between a female rhino and her calf is extremely close—it can last up to four years. As the calves get older, they may leave their mother's side to join a crash, but will eventually wander off to live on their own.

Sadly, the survival of this incredible mammal is under serious threat from poaching. Their numbers are down 85% since 1970 alone—black rhino horns are traded on the black market as symbols of wealth, mainly in the Middle East—but serious efforts by conservationists are underway to help save them.

⚠ When a rhino is about to attack, it lowers its head, snorts, and launches into a swift gallop of up to 30 miles an hour.

THE LION

Known as the king of beasts—the Swahili word for lion, "simba," also means "king," "strong," and "aggressive"—this proud animal was once found throughout the world. Today, the majority of the estimated 23,000 lions are found in sub-Saharan Africa—a small population are also found in India—in grasslands, savannah, and dense bush.

Watching a lion stalk its prey can be one of the most exciting safari encounters. Females do most of the hunting, typically setting up a plan of attack, which is then carried out by the pride. Lionesses take turns hunting and this collective labor allows them to conserve their energy and survive longer in the bush. They are most active from dusk to dawn. A pride consists of about 15, mostly female, lions. The males, identified by their gorgeous golden-red manes, are often brothers who behave territorially; their main task is to pro-tect the females and the cubs. Typically, the females in the pride will give birth at approximately the same time, and the cubs will be raised together. Litters usually consist of two to three cubs that weigh about three pounds each. Sometimes, males that take over a pride will kill existing cubs so that they can sire their own with the lioness.

Lions can sleep for up to 18 hours a day. Lounging about in the grass, lions will often lick each other, rub heads, and purr contentedly. But don't be fooled by their charms. When a lion moves, it can do so with awesome speed and power—a charging lion can cover 330 feet in four seconds. If you come face to face with a lion, never, ever turn your back and try to run—that is your death warrant. Your best bet is to "play dead" and to protect your neck with an arm or stick to prevent a paralyzing bite.

THE LEOPARD

Secretive and shrewd, leopard can live for about 10–15 years in the wild. They are extremely difficult to spot on safari, primarily because they are nocturnal and spend the daylight hours resting in tall trees or dense bush. Plus, they rarely stay in one area for more than a few days.

Leopard can vary in appearance, their coat ranging from a light tawny hue in dry areas to darker shades in the forest. Their spots, called rosettes, are round in East Africa, but square in Southern Africa. Leopard can also be found in India, China, Siberia, and Korea. The female leopard, whose litter usually ranges from about two to four cubs, will keep her young hidden for about two months after birth, then feed and nurse them for an additional three months or so until her cubs are strong enough to roam with her. What about dad? Male leopards play no part in rearing the cubs. In fact, the male is usually long gone by the time the female gives birth. He leaves her after they mate, although he has been known to return to kill the cubs, hence the reasoning behind keeping them hidden for the first few months of their lives.

Leopard use a combination of teeth and razor-sharp claws to kill their prey; it's not uncommon for a leopard's lunch to be taken away by lion or hyena. In order to avoid this, the leopard will often drag their larger kills into a tree where they can dine amongst the leaves in relative peace and quiet.

THE LITTLE 5

We've all heard of the Big Five, but keep a look out for the Little Five, a term given to the animals with names that include the Big Five: antlion, buffalo weaver, elephant shrew, leopard tortoise, and rhinoceros beetle.

RHINOCEROS BEETLE

The rhinoceros beetle grows up to two inches long. It has large spikes—similar in appearance to a rhino's tusks—that are used in battle with other rhino beetles, or for digging, climbing, and mating.

LEOPARD TORTOISE

The largest turtle in Africa, the leopard tortoise can grow up to two feet long and weigh up to 100 pounds. It lives in the grasslands of East and Southern Africa and doesn't mate until it's at least 12 years old. Its name stems from its black and yellow-spotted shell, which resembles a leopard's coat.

ELEPHANT SHREW

These ground-dwelling mammals range in size from that of a mouse to a large rabbit. They live in lowland forests, woodlands, rocky outcrops, and deserts and eat small fruits and plants. They get their name from their long nose, which resembles a miniature elephant's trunk.

ANTLION

Also known as a "doodlebug" because of the winding patterns it leaves in the sand when building traps, the antlion makes its home on dry, sandy slopes sheltered from the wind. Essentially larva, it eventually grows into an insect akin to a dragonfly.

BUFFALO WEAVERS

Similar in appearance to sparrows, buffalo weavers are found in East Africa. Their name comes from the way they weave their nests—found in the branches of tall trees—with grass, creating a complex maze of tunnels. Boasting a yellow plumage (sometimes with black), it lives in small groups where the bush is dry.

Game Trackers Outdoor Adventures (☎ 014/552–5020 ⊕ www.gametrac.co.za ☞ Elephant safaris, balloon safaris). **Pilanesberg Mankwe Safaris** (☎ 014/555–7056 ⊕ www.mankwesafaris.co.za). **Springbok Atlas** (☎ 011/396–1053 ⊕ www.springbokatlas.com). **Wilro Tours** (☎ 011/789–9688 ⊕ www.wilrotours.co.za).

EXPLORING

The 150,000-acre **Pilanesberg National Park** is centered on the caldera of an extinct volcano dating back 1.3 billion years that may well have once been Africa's highest peak. Concentric rings of mountains surround a lake filled with crocodiles and hippos. Open grassland, rocky crags, and densely forested gorges provide ideal habitats for a wide range of plains and woodland game, including rare brown hyenas, sables, and gemsbok. Since the introduction of lions in 1993, Pilanesberg (pronounced pee-*luns*-berg) can boast the Big Five. One of the best places in the country to see rhinos, it's also a bird-watcher's paradise, with a vast range of grassland species, waterbirds, and birds of prey. You can drive around the park in your own vehicle or join guided safaris with Pilanesberg Mankwe Safaris. The entertainment and resort complex of Sun City is nearby. ⊠ R556 ☏ Box 1201, Mogwase 0314 ☎ 014/555–1600 ⊕ www.pilanesberg-game-reserve.co.za ☒ R20 per vehicle, R45 per person ☼ Mar., Apr., Sept., and Oct., daily 6 AM–6:30 PM; May–Aug., daily 6:30–6; Nov.–Feb., daily 5:30 AM–7 PM. Check Web site for changes.

WHERE TO STAY
LUXURY LODGES

¢–$ ⊞ **Bakubung.** Abutting the national park, this lodge sits at the head of a long valley with terrific views of a hippo pool that forms the lodge's central attraction—it's not unusual to have hippos grazing 100 feet from the terrace restaurant. Despite this, the lodge never really succeeds in creating a bush feel, perhaps because it's such a big convention and family destination. Its brick buildings feel vaguely institutional. Nevertheless, the guest rooms, particularly the executive studios, are very pleasant, thanks to light pine furniture, colorful African bedspreads, and super views of the valley. The lodge conducts game drives in open-air vehicles, as well as ranger-guided walks. A shuttle bus (R40 round-trip) runs to Sun City, 10 km (6 mi) away. **Pros:** malaria-free; resident hippos; cheerful atmosphere. **Cons:** close to a main gate; always crowded. ⊠ Bakubung Gate, Pilanesberg National Park ☏ Box 294, Sun City 0316 ☎ 014/552–6000 lodge, 011/806–6800 reservations ⊕ www.legacyhotels.co.za ⇋ 76 rooms, 66 time-share chalets ☖ In-room: a/c.

FLORA SAFARIS

There are some fascinating plant-viewing safaris in national parks you could try if you have the time. On a plant safari in Ai-Ais/Richtersveld Transfrontier Park, you'll encounter some of the world's rarest and strangest plants. In August and September Namaqua National Park hosts one of the largest natural displays of wildflowers in full bloom anywhere in the world—a good time for a plant-viewing safari. Contact **South African National Parks** (☏ Box 787, Pretoria 0001 ☎ 012/343–1991 ⊕ www.sanparks.org) for more details on these three- to five-day specialty safaris.

In-hotel: restaurant, bar, tennis court, pool, Internet terminal ▭ AE, DC, MC, V 🍴 *MAP.*

$ 🏨 **Kwa Maritane.** The greatest asset of this hotel, primarily a time-share
🄫 resort, is its location: in a bowl of rocky hills on the edge of the national
★ park. The resort has a terrific blind overlooking a water hole and connected to the lodge via a tunnel; from your hotel room you can watch
a TV channel dedicated to filming what's there round-the-clock. Guest
rooms have high thatch ceilings and large glass doors that open onto a
veranda. It's best to secure a unit far from the noise of the reception, dining, and pool areas. You can pay to go on day or night game drives in
open-air vehicles or to go on guided walks with an armed ranger—both
worthwhile. The breakfasts at the restaurant are legendary. **Pros:** malaria-
free; you've got the best of both worlds: bushveld on your doorstep and
Sun City only 20 minutes away by free shuttle bus; children's playground
and pool. **Cons:** you can't get away from the hotel feel; packed during
school holidays; it gets noisy around reception, pool, and dining areas.
⊠ *Pilanesberg National Park* 📪 *Box 39, Sun City 0316* ☎ *014/552–5100
hotel, 011/806–6888 reservations* ⊕ *www.legacyhotels.co.za* 🛏 *90 rooms*
🛏 *In-room: a/c, kitchen. In-hotel: restaurant, bar, pools, tennis courts,
Internet terminal, Wi-Fi ▭ AE, DC, MC, V* 🍴 *MAP.*

$$ 🏨 **Tshukudu Game Lodge.** The most stylish option in the area, Tshukudu
★ is built into the side of a steep, rocky hill and overlooks open grassland
and a large water hole where elephants bathe. If you watch long enough,
you might see most of the Big Five from your veranda. Winding stone
stairways lead up the hill to thatch cottages with private balconies,
wicker furniture, African materials, and black-slate floors. Fireplaces
and mosquito nets are standard, and sunken bathtubs have spectacular
views of the water hole. At night you can use a spotlight to illuminate
game at the water hole below. **Pros:** malaria-free; most luxurious and
secluded accommodation in park; high on a hill with great views. **Cons:**
it's a 132-step climb to the main lodge from the parking area so avoid it
if you're not sound of wind and limb; game good, but not as abundant
as Kruger. ⊠ *Pilanesberg National Park* 📪 *Box 6805, Rustenburg 0300*
☎ *014/552–6255 lodge, 011/806–6888 reservations* ⊕ *www.legacyho-
tels.co.za* 🛏 *6 cottages* 🛏 *In-hotel: restaurant, pool, no kids under 12
▭ AE, DC, MC, V.*

BUDGET LODGING

¢ 🏨 **Manyane.** This resort is in a thinly wooded savanna east of Pilanes-
berg's volcanic ridges. Offering affordable accommodations in the Sun
City area, Manyane is simple but well located, efficiently run, and
clean. Thatch roofing helps soften the harsh lines of bare tile floors and
brick. You can choose from a two- or four-bed chalet with a small, fully
equipped kitchen and bathroom; the camping facilities are also very
popular. Self-guided nature trails lead from the chalets, providing inter-
esting background on the geology and flora of the park. You can also
take advantage of the outdoor chess and trampoline. **Pros:** good value
but quite downmarket. **Cons:** usually full of noisy campers and late-night
revelers. ⊠ *Pilanesberg National Park, Rustenburg* ☎ *014/555–1000*
⊕ *www.goldenleopard.co.za* 🛏 *20 4-bed chalets, 15 2-bed chalets* 🛏 *In-
room: a/c, kitchen. In-hotel: restaurant, bar, pools ▭ AE, DC, MC, V.*

9

EASTERN CAPE

ADDO ELEPHANT NATIONAL PARK

72 km (45 mi) north of Port Elizabeth.

GETTING HERE AND AROUND

The closest airport to Addo Elephant Park is Port Elizabeth (PLZ) airport. Flights arrive daily from all of South Africa's main cities via South African Airways, SA Airlink, and the budget airlines Kulula and 1time. Flights from Cape Town take one hour and from Johannesburg 1½ hours.

Traveling by car is the easiest and best way to tour this area as there's no public transport. Some roads are unpaved but are in decent condition. Most lodges will organize airport transfers for their guests.

ESSENTIALS

Airlines 1time (☎ *0861/345–345* ⊕ *www.1time.aero*). **Kulula** (☎ *0861/585–852* ⊕ *www.kulula-air.com*). **South African Airways/SA Airlink** (☎ *011/978–1111* ⊕ *www.flysaa.com*).

Airport Information Port Elizabeth Airport (☎ *041/507–7319* ⊕ *www.acsa.co.za*).

Car Rentals Avis (☎ *041/363–3014* ⊕ *www.avis.co.za*). **Budget** (☎ *041/581–4242* ⊕ *www.budget.co.za*). **Europcar** (☎ *0861/131–000* ⊕ *www.europcar.co.za*). **Hertz** (☎ *041/508–6600* ⊕ *www.hertz.co.za*).

EXPLORING

Smack in the middle of a citrus-growing and horse-breeding area, **Addo Elephant National Park** is home to more than 500 elephants, more than 400 buffalo, 48 black rhino, hundreds of kudu and other antelopes, and 21 lions. At present the park has about 420,000 acres, but it's expanding all the time and is intended to reach a total of about 600,000 acres. But Addo is a work in progress: not all of the land is contiguous, and parts of the land are not properly fenced in yet. The most accessible parts of the park are the original, main section and the Colchester, Kabouga, Woody Cape, and Zuurberg sections. The original section of Addo still holds most of the game and is served by Addo Main Camp. The Colchester section, in the south, which has one SANParks camp, is contiguous with the main area but is not properly fenced yet so there's not much game there. The scenic Nyati section is separated from the main section by a road and railway line; there are two luxury lodges in the Nyati section, and the game-viewing is excellent (but exclusive to guests staying in the lodges). Just north of Nyati is the mountainous Zuurberg section, which doesn't have a large variety of game but is particularly scenic, with fabulous hiking trails and horse trails. It is also the closest section of the park to Addo Elephant Back Safaris.

You can explore the park in your own vehicle, in which case you need to heed the road signs that claim DUNG BEETLES HAVE RIGHT OF WAY ... seriously. Addo is home to the almost-endemic and extremely rare flightless dung beetle, which can often be seen rolling its unusual incubator across the roads. Watch out for them (they're only about 2 inches long, but they have the right-of-way—as well as sharp spines that can puncture tires), and watch them: they're fascinating.

Instead of driving you could take a night or day game drive with a park ranger in an open vehicle from the main camp. A more adventurous option is to ride a horse among the elephants. Warning: no citrus fruit may be brought into the park, as elephants find it irresistible and can smell it for miles. ☎ 042/233–8600 ⊕ www.addoelephantpark.com ⊠ R130 ⊙ Daily 7–7 (may vary with seasons).

WORD OF MOUTH
"We went to Gorah for three nights and absolutely loved it! If you're going on safari in the Eastern Cape I highly recommend looking into Gorah." —finnaroo

☾ ★ **Addo Elephant Back Safaris** lets you get up close and personal with a small group of trained African elephants. You get to do a short elephant ride and then go for a scenic walk through the bush with them. You can touch them, feed them, and watch them as they bathe themselves with sand, water, or both (i.e., mud). The whole experience lasts about two to three hours and includes a meal either before or after the safari. You can also arrange for a fly-in day trip from Port Elizabeth. ☎ 042/235–1400 or 083/283–2359 ⊕ www.addoelephantbacksafaris.co.za ⊠ R675 ⊙ Daily 8 AM, 11 AM, and 3 PM.

Schotia Safaris. If you're short on time or budget, Schotia offers a good value, family run, no frills safari experience taking place in a privately owned wildlife reserve bordering the eastern side of Addo. Due to its small size (4,200 acres) and the fact that it's very densely stocked (more than 2,000 animals and 40 species) you're almost guaranteed to see a wide variety of wildlife—lion, giraffes, hippos, white rhinos, crocodiles, zebras, and all kinds of buck. The popular Tooth and Claw safari (R660) starts at 2:30 PM and includes a game drive and a tasty, generous buffet dinner served in an attractive open-air area with roaring fires. After dinner you're taken on a short night drive back to the reception area—keep your eyes peeled for some unusual nocturnal animals. There's also the option of going on a morning game drive into Addo, with lunch, and then the Tooth and Claw safari for R1,220. Other packages include one or two nights' accommodation on the reserve. Although you may see other vehicles during your drive, tours are very good value and well run, and the guides are excellent. The Tooth and Claw half-day safari can be easily done as a day trip from Port Elizabeth, as it's only a 45-minute drive away. A transfer from PE is R200. ☎ 042/235–1436 ⊕ www.schotia.com.

WHERE TO STAY
LUXURY LODGES

$$ ★ ⊞ **Gorah Elephant Camp.** A private concession within the main section of Addo, this lodge has accommodations in spacious, luxurious tents with thick thatch canopies that are furnished in colonial-era antiques. Each tent has an en suite bathroom with shower and a private deck with views. The lodge itself, a gracious old farmhouse dating from 1856,

9

overlooks a watering hole, so it's possible to watch elephants, buffalo, and other animals from your lunch table or the veranda. Everything is understated yet seriously stylish, including the swimming pool area, and the cuisine and service are outstanding. There's no electricity (although solar lamps are more than adequate), and dinner is served by romantic candlelight, either on the veranda or in the splendid dining room. The lodge operates two game drives a day, and the Web site has interesting updates on the animals viewed on recent game drives. **Pros:** the food and service are top-notch; guests are not required to sit together at meals. **Cons:** the wind can make the tents noisy at night; rooms do not have bathtubs. ⊠ *Addo Elephant National Park* ☚ *Box 454, Plettenberg Bay 6600* ☎ *044/501–1111* ⊕ *www.gorah.com* ⌕ *11 tents* ⚬ *In-room: safe, no TV. In-hotel: restaurant, room service, pool, laundry service, Internet terminal, Wi-Fi, no kids under 10* ⊟ *AE, DC, MC, V* ⓘⓄⓘ *AI.*

$ ⊡ **Nguni River Lodge.** Within the scenic Nyati section of Addo and close
★ to the main game area is this stylish lodge notable for its unusual decor. Each room takes its name and theme from a particular color pattern of the indigenous Nguni cattle. Stone, thatch, rough metal sculptures, and, of course, the skins of Nguni cattle work together to produce a funky contemporary interpretation of African architectural styles and legends. Indoor and outdoor showers and private plunge pools increase the living space of the already quite large rooms, and the enormous bathrooms have huge circular tubs. You'll see animals from your room and the open-air reception areas, which look out onto a natural watering hole. The food is cooked mostly on open fires and could best be described as fusion cuisine with an African twist. Two game drives per day are included. You leave your car at the reception just off the tarred road and are taken to the lodge in a 4x4, which means you don't need to drive on bumpy gravel roads. **Pros:** it's tranquil and secluded; you don't have to do your own driving on dirt roads. **Cons:** Internet reception is only available at the reception; the fireplaces in the rooms aren't operational. ⊠ *R342, about 7 km (4 mi) on the Paterson side of Addo Main Gate* ☚ *Box 2513, North End 6056* ☎ *042/235–1022 reservations* ⊕ *www.ngunilodges.co.za* ⌕ *8 rooms* ⚬ *In-room: safe, no TV. In-hotel: restaurant, bar, laundry service, Internet terminal, no kids under 8* ⊟ *AE, DC, MC, V* ⓘⓄⓘ *AI.*

$ ⊡ **River Bend Country Lodge.** Situated on a 34,594 acres private conces-
★ sion within the Nyati section of Addo, River Bend perfectly balances the idea of a sophisticated, comfortable country house with all the facilities of a game lodge. The spacious public rooms, filled with antiques and comfy couches, are in a beautifully renovated farmhouse and outbuildings. The guest rooms are in individual cottages with private verandas dotted around the lovely gardens; some have outdoor showers and each is uniquely decorated with a different color scheme. In addition to the usual game drives, you can tour the adjacent citrus farm and a small game sanctuary, where you may see animals not found in Addo— giraffes, white rhinos, blue wildebeest, nyala, and impala. There's also a safari villa that sleeps six. **Pros:** kids are welcome, and there's an enclosed playground; the food is excellent, especially the seven-course dinner menu. **Cons:** decor is more English colonial than African; only

the honeymoon suite has a plunge pool. ✉ *On R335, about 70 km (43 mi) north of Port Elizabeth* ☎ *Box 249, 6105* 🖹 *042/233–8000* 🌐 *www.riverbendlodge.co.za* 🖙 *8 suites* ⌂ *In-room: a/c, safe, refrigerator, DVD. In-hotel: restaurant, room service, bar, pool, spa, laundry service, Internet terminal, Wi-Fi* ▭ *AE, DC, MC, V* ⍩ *AI.*

BUDGET LODGING

¢ 🖳 **Hitgeheim Country Lodge.** This lovely lodge is set on a steep cliff over-
Fodor's Choice looking the Sundays River and the town of Addo. Classically decorated
★ rooms graced with lovely antiques are in separate thatch buildings, all with verandas overlooking the river. The bathrooms are spacious and luxuriously appointed with large tubs and enormous shower stalls. Some rooms have indoor and outdoor showers. Birds frolic in the natural vegetation that has been allowed to grow up to the edge of the verandas, and tame buck often wander around the garden. Hitgeheim (pronounced *hitch-ee-*hime) is situated on an eco-reserve and you can go for walks to observe birdlife and perhaps view some of the 11 indigenous antelope species found here. The food is fabulous, and most guests opt to stay for the six-course dinners (R325, guests only), although simpler dinner options can be tailor-made to your preferences. The lodge has its own game-viewing vehicle and guide, which can be booked at an extra cost, and can also organize elephant-back riding and day trips to the nearby Big Five game reserves. **Pros:** personal touches, such as a turndown service and luxury bath products by the South Africa Charlotte Rhys; friendly and helpful owners. **Cons:** not for independent travelers, as the owners like to arrange your activities for you; the restaurant is not open to nonguests. ✉ *18 km (11 mi) from Addo Main Gate on R335, then follow R336 to Kirkwood* ☎ *Box 95, Sunland 6115* 🖹 *042/234–0778* 🌐 *www.hitgeheim.co.za* 🖙 *8 rooms* ⌂ *In-room: safe, a/c, no phone, refrigerator, no TV. In-hotel: restaurant, bar, pool, laundry service, Internet terminal, no kids under 12* ▭ *AE, DC, MC, V* ⍩ *BP.*

NATIONAL PARK ACCOMMODATIONS

¢ 🖳 **Addo Elephant National Park Main Camp.** One of the best SANParks rest camps, this location has a range of self-catering accommodations, such as safari tents, forest cabins, rondavels, cottages, and chalets, and a shop that sells basic supplies as well as souvenirs. An à la carte restaurant with reasonable prices is open for all meals, and a floodlit water hole is nearby. Prices are calculated according to a complicated SANParks formula, which works by unit price, not per person, and is anything from R375 for up to two people sharing to R2,315 for four people sharing (luxury chalets). Camping rates are R150 for up to two people. Note that these are the minimum rates even if there's only one person booking the accommodation. There's also a conservation levy, which is paid per person per day in the park. **Pros:** great value; you get to enter the game area before the main gates open and go on night drives. **Cons:** the shop has only basic supplies; the rondavels have shared cooking facilities. ☎ *Box 52, Addo 6105* 🖹 *012/428–9111* 🌐 *www.addoelephantpark. com* 🖙 *46 chalets, 10 tents, 13 cottages, 2 guesthouses, 20 campsites* ⌂ *In-room: a/c (some), kitchen, TV (some)* ▭ *AE, DC, MC, V.*

9

SHAMWARI GAME RESERVE

45 km (72 mi) from Port Elizabeth.

GETTING HERE AND AROUND

The closest airport to Shamwari Game Reserve is Port Elizabeth (PLZ) airport, about 72 mi (45 km) away. Small and easy to navigate, the airport is served daily by South African Airways, SA Airlink, Kulula, and 1time. Flights arrive from Cape Town (1 hour) and Johannesburg (1½ hours). From here it's best to rent your own car, as there isn't any reliable public transport. If you are flying into Port Elizabeth and only visiting Shamwari, it may be easier to arrange an airport transfer with the reserve. As with all of the luxury game reserves, it's advised that you arrive by midday so you can check in and have lunch before the afternoon game drive.

Airlines 1Time (☎ *0861/345–345* ⊕ *www.1time.aero*). **Kulula** (☎ *0861/585–852* ⊕ *www.kulula-air.com*). **South African Airways/SA Airlink** (☎ *011/978–1111* ⊕ *www.flysaa.com*).

Airport Information Port Elizabeth Airport (☎ *041/507-7319* ⊕ *www.acsa.co.za*).

EXPLORING

In the Eastern Cape, **Shamwari Game Reserve** is, in every sense of the word, a conservation triumph. Unprofitable farmland has been turned into a successful tourist attraction, wild animals have been reintroduced, and alien vegetation has been, and is still being, eradicated. The reserve is constantly being expanded and now stands at about 62,000 acres. Its mandate is to conserve not only the big impressive animals, but also small things: the plants, buildings, history, and culture of the area. Shamwari has been named the World's Leading Conservation Company and Safari Lodge at the World Travel Awards for the past 12 years, and wildlife manager Dr. Johan Joubert, now the wildlife director for the Mantis Group, was voted one of South Africa's top 10 conservationists by the Endangered Wildlife Trust in 1999. ☎ *041/407–1000* ⊕ *www.shamwari.com*.

🅒
Fodor'sChoice
★

Part of the reserve has been set aside as the **Born Free Centres** (there's one in the northern part and one in the southern part of the reserve). Here African animals rescued from around the world are allowed to roam in reasonably large enclosures for the rest of their lives, as they cannot safely be returned to the wild. Although these are interesting tourist attractions, the main purpose is educational, and about 500 local schoolchildren tour the centers every month.

WHERE TO STAY

LUXURY LODGES

$$ 🏨 **Bayethe Tented Lodge.** Huge air-conditioned safari tents under thatch create characterful, comfortable accommodations, and private decks with plunge pools overlook the Buffalo River. One tent is wheelchair accessible. Suites, which are separated from the other rooms by the reception area and a walk of a hundred yards or so, are huge and impressive. Gleaming light-wood floors, fireplaces, and an enormous deck with the most beautiful loungers all contribute to a sense of restrained style

and opulence. As at all the lodges at Shamwari, you sit with your game ranger and other guests for breakfast and dinner. **Pros:** each tent has an amazing outside shower and hammock for napping; tents have fabulous bathrooms; the king-size beds have 400-thread-count sheets that immediately make you feel relaxed and pampered. **Cons:** dinner includes a barbecue every second night; there's no Wi-Fi. ⌂ *Box 113, Swartkops, Port Elizabeth 6210* ☎ *041/407–1000* ⊕ *www. shamwari.com* ⟳ *12 tents* ⚹ *In-room: safe, refrigerator, no TV (some). In-hotel: bar, pool, laundry service, Internet terminal, no kids under 12* ▤ *AE, DC, MC, V* ⧖ *AI.*

WORD OF MOUTH

"Our best elephant experience was at Shamwari. We saw several large family groups with some tiny babies—some of which got uncomfortably close at times. Not that we really minded!" —annhig

$$ ▦ **Eagles Cragg.** Very different from the other Shamwari options, this
Fodor'sChoice sleek, modern lodge makes use of light wood, pale sandstone, and
★ stainless-steel finishes. It's light and airy and spacious. All rooms have indoor and outdoor showers and private decks with plunge pools. Glass walls fold away to bring the feel of the bush into the room. You may also spot a movie star along with the wildlife; a number of celebrities have stayed here. As with all the lodges at Shamwari, breakfast and dinner are taken communally with your guide and other guests. Dinner alternates between a traditional South African braai cooked on open fires and an à la carte menu. **Pros:** a carefully selected choice of top local wines and spirits is included; the rooms are enormous. **Cons:** the reception areas are very large and can feel impersonal; rooms can be chilly in winter. ⌂ *Box 113, Swartkops, Port Elizabeth 6210* ☎ *041/407–1000* ⊕ *www.shamwari.com* ⟳ *9 suites* ⚹ *In-room: a/c, safe, refrigerator, no TV. In-hotel: bar, spa, laundry service, Internet terminal, no kids under 16* ▤ *AE, DC, MC, V* ⧖ *AI.*

$$ ▦ **Lobengula Lodge.** Rooms are set around a central lawn and pool area
★ but face outward for privacy. Thatch roofs and earth tones are part of the African decor. All rooms have outdoor and indoor showers and open onto a private veranda. Two rooms and the suite have private plunge pools. Meals are served around a fireplace, and you may choose wines from the extensive cellar. **Pros:** there are only six rooms, so it feels very exclusive; service is top-notch. **Cons:** only three rooms have private pools; meals are taken communally with other guests and your ranger. ⌂ *Box 113, Swartkops, Port Elizabeth 6210* ☎ *041/407–1000* ⊕ *www. shamwari.com* ⟳ *6 suites* ⚹ *In-room: safe, refrigerator. In-hotel: bar, pool, gym, spa, laundry service, Internet terminal, no kids under 16* ▤ *AE, DC, MC, V* ⧖ *AI.*

KWANDWE PRIVATE GAME RESERVE

Fodor'sChoice
★ *38 km (24 mi) northeast of Grahamstown.*

GETTING HERE AND AROUND

Kwandwe is a 20-minute drive from Grahamstown, and air and road shuttles are available from Port Elizabeth, which is a two-hour drive.

EXPLORING

Kwandwe Private Game Reserve is tucked away in the Eastern Cape, near the quaint, historic cathedral city of Grahamstown. Over a decade ago, the area was ravaged farmland and goat-ridden semi-desert. Today it is a conservation triumph—more than 55,000 acres of various vegetation types and scenic diversity including rocky outcrops, great plains, thorn thickets, forests, desert scrub, and the Great Fish River—that's home to more than 7,000 mammals including the Big Five. Your chances of seeing the elusive black rhino are very good, and it's likely you'll see game you don't always see elsewhere, such as the black wildebeest, the black-footed cat, caracal, Cape grysbok, and many rare and endangered birds. Kwandwe is also known for its nocturnal animals, so it's worth opting for a night drive, during which you stand a pretty good chance of unusual sightings like aardwolf, aardvark, porcupine, genet, and other creatures of the night.

Kwandwe means "Place of the Blue Crane" in Xhosa and you may well see South Africa's national bird on any of your thrilling game drives. If you come in winter, you'll see one of nature's finest floral displays, when thousands of scarlet, orange, and fiery-red aloes are in bloom, attended by colorful sunbirds.

WHERE TO STAY

There are four great places to stay within the reserve; guests can choose between classic colonial or modern chic. You'll be cosseted, pampered, well-fed, and taken on some memorable wildlife adventures. Kwandwe is a member of the prestigious Relais & Châteaux group. All the lodges listed here have cable TV in a communal area as well as a safari shop, and massages are available upon request. The child-friendly lodges have movies and games. In the single-use lodges, these are hidden away in a cupboard, so you can keep their existence a secret from your brood unless a rainy day makes them essential.

$$$ ⊞ **Ecca Lodge.** This classy lodge combines understated modern elegance with a touch of Scandinavian chic. High, white, open-raftered, wooden ceilings top warm, brown, paneled walls, and the burnt orange, green, charcoal, and rust colors of the interior furnishings complement and enhance the views outside the huge windows and viewing decks. Orange cushions echo the flowering aloes, soft greens repeat the surrounding wilderness, and the pillars of piled rough-hewn rock with russet-colored rugs at their base recall the kopjes and wildflowers that strew the reserve. Your bedroom may possibly qualify as one of the biggest you will ever sleep in. Keep the green, orange, and brown floor-to-ceiling curtains facing your king-size bed open at night so that you're woken by a dazzling dawn. Tiny pots of desert plants dot the lodge, but there's no designer clutter—simplicity is the key and space and light dominate. Chill by the rim-flow lodge pool, or just hang out at your own private plunge pool with only the birds and the sounds of the wilderness to keep you company. You'll dine in a big airy dining room with an interactive kitchen. Watch the chef whip up bobotie (spicy minced meat with savory custard topping)—the house special—toss a pancake or three, or stir some succulent sauce. If you find time, watch videos or read in the library or games room, or just sit on your massive wraparound deck and listen to the silence. **Pros:** superb guides; attentive well-trained local staff; a must-see community center and village. **Cons:** temperamental showers that ricochet between scalding hot and freezing cold; no tea and coffee in the rooms. ⌖ *&Beyond, Box X27, Benmore 2010* ☏ *011/809–4300* ⊕ *www.kwandwereserve.co.za* ⌖ *6 rooms* ⌂ *In-room: safe, refrigerator, no TV. In-hotel: pool, laundry service, Internet terminal, Wi-Fi, children's programs* ☰ *AE, DC, MC, V* ⊕ *FAP.*

$$$
Fodor's Choice
★
⌨ **Great Fish River Lodge.** If you've an artistic eye you'll immediately notice how the curving thatch roof of the main buildings echoes the mountain skyline opposite. Wooden steps lead down to the public areas—dining room, comfortable lounges, and library—that sprawl along the banks of the Great Fish River. Floor-to-ceiling windows bathe the stone walls, polished cement floors, Persian rugs, fireplaces with massive chimneys, deep armchairs, bookcases, handmade furniture and old prints and photographs in clear pristine light. At night the stars provide a dazzling display as lions call over the noise of the rushing river. All the spacious en suite bedrooms overlook the river, and you'll be hard put to tear yourself away from your personal plunge-pool-with-a-view to go chasing game. The generous-sized suites are decorated in greens, grays, browns, and creams that make you feel part of the natural world outside your picture windows. The whole lodge is permeated with a warm comfortable colonial ambience—the 21st century has never seemed so far away. **Pros:** spectacular river views; unusual habitats (it's not often you find lions clambering up and down rocky outcrops); ultra-friendly staff. **Cons:** avoid if you're a bit unsteady as there are lots of tricky steps. ⌖ *CC Africa, Box X27, Benmore 2010* ☏ *011/809–4300* ⊕ *www.kwandwereserve.co.za* ⌖ *9 suites* ⌂ *In-room: safe, refrigerator, no TV. In-hotel: room service, bar, laundry service, Internet terminal, Wi-Fi, no kids under 12* ☰ *AE, DC, MC, V* ⊕ *FAP.*

$$$
⌨ **Melton Manor.** Slightly bigger than Uplands, the Manor accommodates up to eight guests and offers the same superb service and exclusivity. It's a farmhouse in contemporary style with handmade clay chandeliers, cowhide rugs, vintage ball-and-claw armoires, and huge bathrooms with claw-foot tubs that look out over pristine wilderness. Built around a small central lawn with a swimming pool, the four spacious, light, and airy rooms look outward into the bush for privacy. You have your own chef and game ranger, and you call the shots. This is a great option for families, as you can take the little ones on game drives or leave them behind with babysitters. It's also a good deal for three couples traveling together (and a great deal for four). **Pros:** exclusivity deluxe; great food. **Cons:** as you're in your own group you miss out on the opportunity to meet other lodge guests. ⌖ *CC Africa, Box X27, Benmore 2010* ☏ *011/809–4300* ⊕ *www.kwandwereserve.co.za* ⌖ *4 rooms* ⌂ *In-room: no TV. In-hotel: bar, pool, laundry service, Internet terminal, Wi-Fi* ☰ *AE, DC, MC, V* ⊕ *FAP.*

$$$
⌨ **Uplands Homestead.** If you're a small family or a bunch of friends and want to have a genuine, very exclusive, *Out of Africa* experience, then stay at this restored 1905 colonial farmhouse. There are three spacious en suite bedrooms with separate balconies furnished in early Settlers style, and you'll have your own tracking and guiding team, plus a

9

dedicated chef. The game experience is excellent, and you'll have memorable moments sitting round a blazing log fire as you swap fireside tales in the evening. Try one of Kwandwe's specialist safaris that range from learning about the carnivore research and walking trails to excursions revealing the rich colorful past of this area, which is steeped in cultural, military, and archaeological history. **Pros:** perfect for that special family occasion or friends' reunion. **Cons:** you're in very close proximity with other guests, so it can be a bummer if you don't mesh well. ⌂ *CC Africa, Box X27, Benmore 2010* ☎ *011/809–4300* ⊕ *www.kwandwereserve.co.za* ⮌ *3 rooms* ⚭ *In-room: no TV. In-hotel: bar, pool, laundry service, Internet terminal* ☰ *AE, DC, MC, V* ⧖ *FAP.*

SAMARA PRIVATE GAME RESERVE

55 km (34 mi) southeast of Graaff-Reinet, 258 km (160 mi) north of Port Elizabeth.

GETTING HERE AND AROUND

There are daily flights from Johannesburg, Durban, and Cape Town to Port Elizabeth. Air charters from Port Elizabeth to Samara (gravel airstrip) can be arranged on request; it's a 45-minute drive from the airstrip to the reserve. Transfers to and from the airport or airstrip can be arranged through the reserve.

The drive from Port Elizabeth should take about three hours. Take the R75 toward Graaff-Reinet for 258 km (160 mi). Turn right onto the R63 toward Pearston/Somerset East for 7 km (4 mi). Turn left onto the Petersburg gravel road and drive 23 km (14 mi) to reach Karoo Lodge.

EXPLORING

Nestled among 70,000 acres of achingly beautiful wilderness, **Samara Private Game Reserve** is located in a hidden valley deep in the Karoo Mountains of South Africa's Eastern Cape. Owners Sarah and Mark Tompkins opened the reserve in 2005 with a promise to return former farmland to its natural state. The malaria-free reserve now encompasses 11 former farms and is home to a variety of protected species that have been reintroduced, including cheetah, Cape mountain zebra, white rhino, giraffe, black wildebeest, and a variety of antelope; there are even meerkats and aardvarks. Because there aren't predators to pose a threat, rangers stop the trucks often and guests get a completely different safari experience on foot. The lack of predators also makes this a great place for families with children.

WHERE TO STAY

$$ ⊞ **Karoo Lodge.** From the moment you reach this lovingly restored, 19th-century, green-roofed farmhouse set among purple mountains, 800-year-old trees, and rolling plains where cheetahs, rhinos, and giraffes roam, you'll forget another more stressful world even existed. The understated yet elegant colonial farmhouse and three lovely cottages await you after a day of game-watching, hiking, or picnicking in the desert. Super-attentive but unobtrusive staff and imaginative five-star cuisine add to the elegance of this exclusive resort. There's a history room with fossils and information about the area if your interest

is piqued and a curio shop if you want to bring a little something home. **Pros:** unique beauty; exclusivity; great for families. **Cons:** lack of accessibility. ✉ *Aapies Kloof, Petersburg Rd., Box 649, The Eastern Cape, Graaff-Reinet* ☎ *49/891–0880* ⊕ *www.samara.co.za* ➪ *3 rooms, 3 suites* ⚘ *In-room: safe, refrigerator, no TV. In-hotel: restaurant, room service, bar, tennis court, pool, laundry service, Internet terminal, children's programs* ⊟ *AE, DC, MC, V* ⦿ *AI.*

$$$ ▦ **The Manor House.** If you're looking for the perfect place to share a safari with a group of people, then look no further. One of the area's original homesteads, the Restoration Hardware meets African Pottery Barn–decorated house has four suites, each with its own veranda that overlooks the surrounding mountains. Bathrooms are huge, with double sinks, stone shower, toilet stall, and delicious Charlotte Rhys products—just try to resist getting into the claw-foot tub in which a bath has been drawn for you after the evening drive. The living space is made up of numerous cozy seating areas where you can while away hours reading, chatting, playing board games, or sipping drinks. The pool is lovely and refreshing after your morning drive and overlooks the property's natural water hole—you never know who you might see taking a drink. The house has a dedicated staff, including a ranger, who look after your every, and we mean every, need. **Pros:** complete run of the house for your group; attentive personal staff; lunch in the bush is an experience you'll not soon forget. **Cons:** not close to major airports; temperatures can get very hot. ✉ *Aapies Kloof, Petersburg Rd., Box 649, The Eastern Cape, Graaff-Reinet* ☎ *49/891–0880* ⊕ *www.samara.co.za* ➪ *4 suites* ⚘ *In-room: safe, no TV. In-hotel: bar, pool, laundry service, Internet terminal, children's programs* ⊟ *AE, DC, MC, V* ⦿ *AI.*

9

UNDERSTANDING SOUTH AFRICA

Chronology

Vocabulary

CHRONOLOGY

PREHISTORIC SOUTH AFRICA

South Africa's Great Karoo was once home to ferocious predators that became extinct more than 250 million years ago. Other fossils and artifacts suggest that the first humans in South Africa, and perhaps the world, lived more than 3 million years ago.

THE FIRST KNOWN INHABITANTS

AD 100 The San, descendants of the prehistoric Africans, were the only inhabitants of South Africa for thousands of years.

AD 200–400 People speaking various Bantu languages move into the area that is now South Africa's Eastern Cape and KwaZulu-Natal, bringing with them Iron Age culture.

AD 500–1300s The Khoikhoi, indigenous nomadic herders, settle in what is now western South Africa. Some Bantu speakers begin to group together and form large and powerful chiefdoms, especially the Sotho-Tswana people in the Highveld and the Nguni farther east.

EUROPEAN EXPLORATION AND COLONIZATION

1487 Portuguese explorer Bartolomeu Dias sets sail to explore the African coast in search of gold and a sea route to India. A storm sets the expedition back almost two weeks, depleting the food supply, and forcing the men to return to Portugal. Later that year Vasco de Gama is sent to expand upon Dias's discoveries. He reaches India, and the Portuguese establish informal trade for meat with the Khoikhoi people. The first detailed information on the indigenous inhabitants of South Africa is transmitted to Europe the following year.

1580 Sir Francis Drake sails around the world, passing the Cape of Good Hope.

1600s The first Europeans settle in South Africa as envoys of the Dutch East India Company, setting up a supply base in Cape Town in 1652 for ships traveling to and from the East Indies. In 1657 the company allows some employees to start their own farms east of Table Mountain and calls them free burghers (citizens) or Boers (farmers). The growing free burgher population wages war on the Khoikhoi, ending in their defeat in 1677. The Dutch East India Company offers free passage and land to new settlers from Europe in 1679. In 1688 French Huguenots escaping religious persecution also settle at the Cape.

Early 1700s Europeans occupy most of the fertile farmland around Cape Town. The Khoikhoi and San populations begin to decline. Khoikhoi living near areas of European settlement are forced into service for the colonists. Afrikaans, a new language that incorporates Dutch as well as words and sounds from the languages of other European settlers, Southeast Asian slaves, and San and Khoikhoi servants, develops, and those who speak it are called Afrikaners.

1770s White settlers spread into the area occupied by the Xhosa, a Bantu-speaking people, in what is now the Eastern Cape. In 1778 Dutch Governor Joachim van Plettenberg redefines the colony's boundaries, triggering frontier wars between the Xhosa and Trekboers (white cattle and sheep herders) who occupy the disputed area. The white population spreads about 480 km (300 mi) north and more than 800 km (500 mi) east of Cape Town. This area becomes known as Cape Colony. Out of a total population of about 60,000, nearly 20,000 are whites; the rest are Khoikhoi, San, and slaves.

1795 France conquers the Netherlands, and British troops occupy the Cape Colony to keep it out of French control.

1803–1815 The British return the Cape Colony to the Dutch, only to reoccupy it three years later. The Congress of Vienna (1815) formally recognizes the Cape as a permanent British colony.

THE MFECANE AND THE GREAT TREK

1818–1828 The Bantu-speaking Zulu clan, ruled by Shaka, evolves into the most powerful black African kingdom in southern Africa and occupies most of what is now KwaZulu-Natal. Less powerful chiefdoms flee to other parts of southeastern Africa. This period of forced migration and battles becomes known as the Mfecane (or Difaqane). The British government declares English the Cape Colony's only official language in 1828.

1834 The British free all slaves in the empire. Several thousand Boers leave the Cape Colony to escape British rule in a historic journey called the Great Trek. They become known as the Voortrekkers (pioneers) and travel into lands occupied by Bantu-speaking peoples, including the Zulu kingdom, hoping to establish an independent republic.

1837–1838 Afrikaner farmer and businessman Piet Retief leads a party of Voortrekkers and their servants into Zulu-dominated Natal and attempts to negotiate a land agreement with the Zulu king, Dingane. The following year the Zulus kill Retief and more than 500 Voortrekkers. In December 1838 a Boer raiding party led by the Afrikaner pioneer Andries Pretorius defeats the Zulu at the Battle of Blood River. The Voortrekkers then settle in Natal and set up the independent Republic of Natalia, now roughly the state of KwaZulu-Natal.

1843 The British annex Natalia and rename it Natal.

Early 1850s The British recognize the independence of two other Boer republics: the Transvaal (1852) and the Orange Free State (1854). In Natal and the Boer republics whites claim the best land and extend their control over black Africans and coloureds. Meanwhile, in 1853 the British government grants the Cape Colony a constitution. Colonists of all races who pass certain wage or property qualifications can vote for members of the legislature. That same year prospectors discover the first vein of gold at Pilgrim's Rest in Mpumalanga.

1856   The British government grants a constitution similar to that of the Cape Colony, effective for whites only, to Natal.

1858–1859   The Boers in the Transvaal name their government the South African Republic (SAR). Both the Transvaal and the Orange Free State then set up their own exclusively white governments.

1860–1864   The British import Indians to work as indentured laborers on sugarcane plantations in Natal. Under this system, the Indians work in exchange for payment of their voyage, food, clothing, shelter, and a small wage from the British.

DIAMONDS, GOLD, AND WAR

1867–1877   The discovery of diamonds in Kimberley marks an economic shift from agriculture to mining. After ousting several rival claimants, the British annex the diamond fields. The Cape Colony is granted self-government in 1872. Bantu-speaking farmers are required to remain in homelands, or Bantustans, outside Cape Colony borders. The British take advantage of a financial crisis in the SAR, annex the republic, and rename it the Transvaal in 1877.

1879   The British see the Zulu kingdom, now the region's only major African state, as a threat to their plan for a confederation of South Africa's colonies. They successfully invade the territory in what becomes known as the Zulu War, and the Zulu state falls under imperial control.

1880–1881   The Transvaal Boers rise in revolt in the First South African War (also called the Boer War, Anglo-Boer War, and Anglo-Transvaal War). They defeat the British, who agree to withdraw from the Transvaal under the Pretoria Convention. The Boers regain independence in the Transvaal and again name it the South African Republic.

1886   George Harrison discovers the Main Reef (large gold deposit) on the Witwatersrand and gold fever creates present-day Johannesburg. Investment and profits flow in, along with thousands of European immigrants hoping to make their fortunes, and new money makes possible the development of a modern transportation and communication network.

1888   The consolidation of diamond claims leads to the creation of De Beers Consolidated Mines, headed by Cecil Rhodes, who becomes prime minister of the Cape Colony (1890–1896) and pushes for the Glen Grey Act, one of a series of legislative maneuvers that systematically pushed minority farm dwellers off their lands to make way for industrial development.

1897   Zululand is incorporated into Natal.

1899–1902   The SAR and the Orange Free State declare war on the United Kingdom and fight what is now called the Second South African War (also referred to as the Anglo-Boer or Boer War). In 1902 the Boers surrender to Great Britain, the two Boer republics become British colonies, and the SAR is once again declared the Transvaal.

1907 The United Kingdom grants self-government to the Transvaal and to the Orange River Colony (the colonial name of the Orange Free State). Representatives from both colonies and from the Cape Colony and Natal meet at a national convention to protest the exclusion of blacks from government in the proposed union constitution—without success.

1909–1910 At a national convention held in Durban, white delegates pass the South Africa Act, which unites the British colonies of Cape Colony, Natal, Transvaal, and Orange River, thereby establishing the nation of South Africa. In 1909 a new constitution for a united South Africa is promulgated with British acceptance. The constitution agreed upon is largely the work of Jan Smuts, colonial secretary of the Transvaal, and his English secretary, R. H. Brand. Louis Botha, a former Transvaal premier, becomes the new Union of South Africa's first prime minister and founds the South African Party in 1910.

THE RISE OF AFRIKANER NATIONALISM

1912–1913 In response to the discriminatory nature of the South Africa Act, black political leaders set up the South African Native National Congress (SANNC). In keeping with the segregationist principles of the South African Native Affairs Commission, the first Union government establishes the Natives Land Act, which defines the borders of ancestral lands and declares illegal all land purchases and rent tenancy outside these reserves by blacks.

1914 In a breakaway from the ruling South African Party, James Barry Munnik Hertzog, a Boer general who had fought the British, founds the National Party to reflect Afrikaner nationalism.

1914–1918 During World War I, South Africa, as part of the British Empire, is de facto at war with Germany, and invades German South West Africa. White Afrikaners rebel and are suppressed, and South Africa occupies South West Africa from mid-1915.

1920 The League of Nations, a forerunner of the United Nations, gives South Africa control of South West Africa (now Namibia).

1923 The SANNC shortens its name to the African National Congress (ANC) and becomes the main political voice for blacks. That same year the Natives (Urban Areas) Act establishes the tenets of urban segregation and controls African mobility by means of pass laws.

1924–1925 Hertzog makes a pact with Labour Party leader Frederick H. P. Creswell for the upcoming general election. The two win and form the Pact government, of which Hertzog becomes prime minister in 1924. The Pact government makes Afrikaans, instead of Dutch, an official language along with English in 1925.

1931 South Africa gains full independence as a member of the Commonwealth of Nations, an association of the United Kingdom.

1933 Hertzog, who has lost some prestige due to the Great Depression, accepts a proposal from Jan Smuts to form a government of national unity with Hertzog as prime minister and Smuts as deputy.

1934 The National Party and the South African Party merge to form the United Party. In revolt, Afrikaner nationalist Daniel Malan forms a new National Party, and eventually becomes the first prime minister to promote apartheid.

1939–1945 During World War II Afrikaners again strongly oppose decisions to fight against Germany, which they support. Allied troops take shore leave in South African ports, boosting the economy. Africans pour into towns looking for work.

1945 South Africa becomes a founding member of the United Nations.

1948 The National Party wins the general election, and apartheid is adopted.

APARTHEID AND THE STATE OF EMERGENCY

1950 The National Party, under the leadership of Malan, begins to implement an apartheid program, coordinated by the white-male Afrikaner group the Broederbond. The cornerstone of apartheid is the Population Registration Act, under which all South Africans are classified according to race. The government establishes separate schools, universities, residential areas, and public facilities for each racial group.

1955 Opposition to apartheid grows swiftly under the leadership of ANC presidents James Moroka and later Albert Luthuli. The ANC, the Congress of South African Trade Unions, and other groups representing coloureds, Indians, and whites join to form the Congress Alliance, which meets at the Congress of the People in Kliptown (now part of Johannesburg). The alliance sets out a statement of goals called the Freedom Charter, which emphasizes equality of races, liberty, and human rights.

1956 On August 9, celebrated as South African Women's Day, more than 20,000 women march to the Union Buildings in Pretoria to protest the extension of pass laws to women.

1959 Members of the ANC leave to form the Pan-Africanist Congress (PAC) in opposition to the ANC's participation in the multiracial Congress Alliance. The PAC first targets the pass laws, which require all people classified as black to carry identity papers. PAC leaders encourage blacks to appear at police stations without their passes in protest.

1960 South Africa leaves the Commonwealth and becomes a republic. Prime Minister H. F. Verwoerd introduces the homeland policy, which delineates separate areas for each racial group. The policy uproots black Africans and denies them South African citizenship; the ANC and PAC begin waging armed struggle against the state. On March 21, in what comes to be known as the Sharpeville Massacre, police open fire on a peaceful demonstration that had gathered to oppose the pass laws; 69

people are killed. One week later the government declares a state of emergency, and detention without trial is introduced, forcing the ANC to go underground.

1964 The Rivonia Trial emerges as the most famous trial in the history of South African political resistance. Nelson Mandela and other prominent ANC leaders are sentenced to life imprisonment for sabotage and conspiracy against the South African government. While in prison, Mandela becomes a symbol of the struggle for racial justice.

1966 Prime Minister Hendrik Verwoerd, one of the architects of "modern" apartheid, is assassinated at his desk in the House of Assembly.

1970s The Black Consciousness Movement, led by Steve Biko, reawakens a sense of pride in black Africans. Opposition to white rule increases both inside and outside the country. In 1976 several thousand black African schoolchildren march through the township of Soweto to protest the use of Afrikaans in schools. During what becomes known as the Soweto Uprising, police kill more than 500 people, almost all of them black. In 1977 Steve Biko is killed in detention, and in 1978 P. W. Botha becomes prime minister.

GROWING OPPOSITION TO APARTHEID, AT HOME AND ABROAD

1980s International awareness of, and reaction to, apartheid grows. Government opponents, from journalists to student leaders, are arrested under security laws that permit detention without trial. Prominent apartheid opponents are killed in Zambia, Zimbabwe, Lesotho, Swaziland, and Mozambique. Sports teams traveling outside the country are heckled; countries launch travel boycotts to South Africa. South West Africa demands independence as the nation of Namibia, while South African forces chase rebel leaders into neighboring Angola and wage attacks there to quell the uprisings. More than 100 Dutch Anglicans in Pretoria denounce apartheid. South African Airways hires its first black flight attendants, integrating formerly all-white crews. Black golfers are admitted onto South Africa's tour. A new constitution voted on only by white South Africans restructures parliament to include three chambers: one each for whites, coloureds, and Indians; no provisions are made for black representation. Thousands boycott elections. A series of violent protests carried out by the military branches of the ANC and PAC end in guerilla attacks on government targets (1983–84). The European Community (the forerunner of the European Union), the Commonwealth of Nations, and the United States enact bans on certain kinds of trade with South Africa. The South African government begins to repeal apartheid laws, including the pass law, and more than 1 million black Africans move to cities. From 1984–89 the country is in a state of emergency, with thousands killed and beaten in racial violence, and media coverage severely curtailed.

1989–1990 F. W. de Klerk succeeds Botha as state president and abolishes most apartheid restrictions. He orders the release, in 1990, of Nelson

Mandela, after 27 years of imprisonment. De Klerk also lifts the ban on the ANC and ends South Africa's state of emergency.

1991 The South African government repeals the remaining laws that had formed the legal basis of apartheid. The government, the ANC, and other groups begin holding talks on a new constitution.

1992 Constitutional struggles persist between the majority black ANC and the minority white government, while violence continues to plague the country. South Africa sends its first racially integrated team to the Olympics, the country's first invitation to the games in 32 years.

1993 The government adopts an interim constitution that allows South Africa's blacks full voting rights. Nelson Mandela and F. W. de Klerk win the Nobel peace prize for negotiating the end of apartheid.

A DECADE OF DEMOCRACY

1994 The country holds its first elections open to all races. The ANC wins nearly two-thirds of the seats in parliament, which then elects Nelson Mandela president. South Africa resumes full participation in the UN and rejoins the Commonwealth, and remaining international sanctions are lifted. An interim constitution divides South Africa into nine provinces in place of the previous four provinces and 10 homelands.

1996 The government-appointed panel called the Truth and Reconciliation Commission (TRC), headed by Desmond Tutu, a former Anglican archbishop and winner of the 1984 Nobel peace prize, begins public hearings across the country to probe human-rights violations during the apartheid years.

1996 South Africa adopts a new constitution, guaranteeing freedom of religion; freedom of expression, including freedom of the press; and freedom of political activity. It also establishes the right to adequate housing, food, water, education, and health care.

1997 Mandela resigns as head of the ANC and is replaced by South Africa's deputy president, Thabo Mbeki.

1998 The TRC issues a report accusing the apartheid-era government of committing "gross violations of human rights," including kidnapping and murder. The report also criticizes anti-apartheid groups, including the ANC, which is found responsible for human-rights abuses.

1999 Mandela retires as president of South Africa. The ANC wins a majority in parliament, which elects Mbeki president in the second democratic national election.

2002 In his annual address to parliament, President Thabo Mbeki defines as national goals black economic empowerment, poverty eradication, and nation building driven by volunteerism. The organization of implementation is called the African Union.

2003 Parliament accepts the government's response to the TRC's final report. Out of the 22,000 people who appeared before the commission, 19,000 receive interim reparations.

2004 On the 10th anniversary of democracy in South Africa the ANC wins a landslide victory, assuring a second five-year term for Mbeki. Mandela retires from public life and praises Mbeki while advising him to address the crisis of the country's rising AIDS epidemic. South Africa wins a bid to host the 2010 World Cup. It's the first time the tournament has gone to an African nation.

2005 Bodies are exhumed in the TRC investigation into fates of hundreds who disappeared during apartheid. The Geographical Names Council recommends a name change from the capital, Pretoria, to Tshwane; hundreds of other places may be renamed to redress past injustices, with new names reflecting historic or oral traditions.

2006 South Africa becomes the first African country to permit same-sex unions.

2007 For the first time, apartheid appears in the South African high school curriculum. Jacob Zuma replaces Thabo Mbeki as president of the ANC. Zuma is indicted for fraud, corruption, and money laundering, but the charges are later dropped.

2008 President Thabo Mbeki resigns. Kgalema Motlanthe is named interim president. Congress of the People, a new political party, is formed by former ANC members.

VOCABULARY

South Africa has 11 official languages, including nine indigenous African languages. English is the lingua franca; in its everyday use it includes a rich assortment of terms from the other languages. Afrikaans, originally a Dutch dialect, has a shadowed history because of its role in apartheid politics, but it's still a very common language. Zulu is the most widely spoken indigenous African language; it doesn't hurt to know a few polite phrases if you're traveling to a Zulu-speaking area like KwaZulu-Natal. Below we've listed common terms, followed by some essential terms in Zulu and a menu guide.

BASICS

ablution blocks: public bathrooms
abseil: rappel
backpackers: hostel
bakkie: pickup truck (pronounced "bucky")
banda: bungalow or hut
berg: mountain
boma: enclosure; dining area in lodges
boot: trunk (of a car)
bottle store: liquor store
bra/bru/my bra: brother (term of affection or familiarity)
buck: antelope
burg: city
bushveld: generic term for the wild indigenous vegetation of the lowveld
Cape Malay/Malay: referring to descendants of Asian, largely Muslim, slaves, brought to the Cape starting in the 1600s and erroneously lumped together under the term
chommie: mate, chum
coloured: a term for people of Malay, Khoi-San, other black African, and/or European descent (⇨ See "A Note on the Term 'Coloured'" box in Chapter 3, The Winelands and Beaches)
dagga: marijuana, sometimes called *zol*
djembes: drums
dorp: village
Fanagalo: a mix of Zulu, English, Afrikaans, Sotho, and Xhosa
fynbos: the collective name for a variety of bush plants, which can be divided into four basic types (proteas, ericas or heather, restios or reeds, and ground flowers)
Highveld: the country's high interior plateau, including Johannesburg
howzit?: literally, "how are you?" but used as a general greeting
indaba: literally, a meeting but also a problem, as in "that's your indaba."
jol: a party or night on the town
kloof: river gorge
kokerbooms: quiver trees
koppies: hills (also *kopjes*)
kraal: traditional rural settlement of huts and houses, village
lekker: nice
lowveld: land at lower elevation, including Kruger National Park
marula: tree from which amarula (the liquor) gets its name
mokoro: dugout canoe, pluralized as *mekoro*
mopane: nutrient-poor land
moppies: vaudeville-style songs

more-ish: so good you will want more, mouthwatering
muthi: traditional (non-Western) medicine
plaas: farm
petrol: gasoline
robot: traffic light
rondawel/rondavel: a traditional round dwelling with a conical roof
sala: outdoor covered deck
sangoma: traditional healer or mystic
self-catering: with cooking facilities
shebeen: a place to drink, often used in townships
sis: gross, disgusting
sisi or usisi: sister (term of affection or respect)
South African War: the more inclusive name for the Boer War or Anglo-Boer War and
actually referring to either of two South African Wars (1880–81 and 1899–1902)
Spar: name of grocery market chain in Africa
spaza shop: an informal shop, usually from a truck or container
stoep: veranda
sundowner: cocktails at sunset
swenka: a local term for a hard-working man characterized by his natty style of dress.
Today weekly fashion contests (usually held Saturday night) for the best-dressed man
in town pay homage to the fashion trend which began in the 1950s.
takkie: (pronounced tacky) sneaker
veld: open countryside

ZULU ESSENTIALS

yes or hello: yebo
no: cha
please: uxolo
thank you: ngiyabonga
you're welcome: nami ngiyabonga
good morning/hello: sawubona
excuse me: uxolo
goodbye: sala kahle
Do you speak English?: uya khuluma isingisi?

MENU GUIDE

biltong: spiced air-dried (not smoked) meat, made of everything from beef to kudu
bobotie: spiced minced beef or lamb topped with savory custard, a Cape Malay dish
boerewors: Afrikaaner term for a spicy farmer's sausage, often used for a braai (pronounced "*boo*-rah-vorse")
braai: roughly, a barbecue or grill, with sausages, fish etc.
bredie: a casserole or stew, usually lamb with tomatoes
bunny chow: a half loaf of bread hollowed out and filled with meat or vegetable
curry
chakalaka: a spicy relish
gatsby: a loaf of bread cut lengthwise and filled with fish or meat, salad, and fries
kabeljou: one of the varieties of line fish
kingklip: a native fish
koeksister: a deep-fried braided, sugared dough

malva: apricot sponge cake pudding
melktert: a sweet custard tart
mogodu: beef or ox tripe
moroho: mopane worms
pap: also called *mielie pap,* a maize-based porridge
peppadews: a patented vegetable, so you may see it under different names, usually with the word *dew* in them; it's a sort of a cross between a sweet pepper and a chili and is usually pickled.
peri-peri: a spicy chili marinade, Portuguese in origin, based on the searing hot *piri-piri* chili; some recipes are tomato-based, while others use garlic, olive oil, and brandy
potjie: pronounced "*poy*-key" and also called *potjiekos,* a traditional stew cooked in a three-legged pot
rocket: arugula
rooibos: an indigenous, earthy-tasting red-leaf tea
samp: corn porridge
snoek: a barracuda-like fish, often smoked, sometimes used for *smoorsnoek* (braised)
sosaties: local version of a kebab, with spiced, grilled chunks of meat
waterblommetjie: water lilies, sometimes used in stews
witblitz: moonshine

Travel Smart

GETTING HERE AND AROUND

WORD OF MOUTH

"It's been my experience that flights from the US to SA do fill up fast. Going through Europe takes a day longer, but you're less jet-lagged when you arrive. September-October is a great time for weather—not too cold any more and not too hot yet."

—Celia

"On the subject of safety: Always be alert—alert and more alert. Do not look like a tourist—with camera and guidebook in hand."

—Judith18

GETTING HERE AND AROUND

You may have a few problems trying to find your way around South Africa, but it shouldn't be insurmountable. The newest wrinkle is the renaming of place names. Countless cities, towns, streets, parks, etc. have gotten or will get new monikers, both to rid the country of names that recall the apartheid era and to honor the previously unsung.

The names in this book were accurate at time of writing, but even if names are different by the time of your trip, don't worry; all of South Africa will be coping with these large-scale changes and will undoubtedly use both names for a while.

Another problem you may encounter is that geographical features, such as street and town names, are sometimes alternately signposted in English and Afrikaans. So, for example, Wale Street and Waalst are the same road. You can be driving the N2 toward Cape Town, but find that the major road signs point to Kaapstad, the city's Afrikaans name.

▌ AIR TRAVEL

When booking flights, check the routing carefully, as South Africa–bound flights from United States cities have refueling stops en route, and sometimes those stops can be delayed. Don't plan anything on the ground too rigidly after arriving; leave yourself a cushion for a connecting flight to a game lodge. Currently only South African Airways and Delta provide direct service from the United States to South Africa, but flights routed through Europe may be more pleasant. First, they allow you to stretch your legs and change planes, or even stop over on the way there or back. Second, most European flights bound for Africa are overnights, so you will arrive in South Africa in the morning, with plenty of time to make connections.

In peak season (midsummer and South African school vacations), give yourself at least a half hour extra at the airport for domestic flights, as the check-in lines can be endless—particularly on flights to the coast at the start of vacations and back to Johannesburg at the end.

If you are returning home with souvenirs, leave time for a V.A.T. inspection before you join the line for your international flight check-in. In Johannesburg, the O.R. Tambo international check-in area is in the process of being modernized, so it can be a jumble of people going to various destinations squeezed into a tight area at peak departure times, which can add to preflight stress.

O.R. Tambo's domestic terminal is far superior to the international terminal, with a large hall and plenty of room for you and your baggage trolley; baggage carts are widely available at South African airports at no charge. ▌TIP→ There are vast distances between gates and terminals at O.R. Tambo, particularly between the international and domestic terminals, so clear security before stopping for a snack or shopping, as you don't want to scramble for your flight.

All domestic flights within South Africa are no-smoking—the longest is only two hours—and all airports are smoke-free except for designated smoking areas.

If you are visiting a game lodge deep in the bush, you will be arriving by light plane—and you will be restricted in what you can bring. Excess luggage can usually be stored with the operator until your return. Don't just gloss over this: charter operators take weight very seriously, and some will charge you for an extra ticket if you insist on bringing excess baggage (⇨ *Charter Flights, below*).

Airlines and Airports **Airline and Airport Links.com** (⊕ *www.airlineandairportlinks.com*).

Airline Security Issues **Transportation Security Administration** (⊕ *www.tsa.gov*).

Air Travel Resources in South Africa **Airports Company South Africa** (⊕ *www.acsa. co.za*).

General Information Flight information (☎ *086/727-7888*).

AIRPORTS

South Africa's major airports are in Johannesburg, Cape Town, and, to a lesser extent, Durban. Most international flights arrive at and depart from Johannesburg's O.R. Tambo International Airport, 19 km (12 mi) from the city. The airport has a tourist information desk, a V.A.T. refund office, and a computerized accommodations service. Several international flights departing from Cape Town are also routed via Johannesburg. If you're leaving O.R. Tambo's international terminal, the domestic terminal is to your left and is connected by a busy and fairly long walkway. ■**TIP**➔ **Allow 10–15 minutes' walking time between international and domestic.** The Cape Town and Durban airports are much smaller and more straightforward. Cape Town International is 20 km (12½ mi) southeast of the city, and Durban International is 16 km (10 mi) south of the city. If you are traveling to or from either Johannesburg or Cape Town airport (and, to a lesser extent, Durban) be aware of the time of day. Traffic can be horrendous between 7 and 9 in the morning and between about 3:30 and 6 in the evening.

Just 40 km (25 mi) outside Johannesburg, Lanseria International Airport is closer to Sandton than O.R. Tambo and handles executive jets, company jets, domestic scheduled flights to and from Cape Town, and some charter flights to safari camps. It has a 24-hour customs and immigration counter, a café, and a high-end flight store. It's a popular alternative for visiting dignitaries and other VIPs.

The other major cities are served by small airports that are really easy to navigate. Most airports are managed by the Airports Company of South Africa.

Airport Information Airports Company of South Africa (☎ *021/937-1200, 086/727-7888 flight information* ⊕ *www.asca.co.za*).

International Airports Cape Town International Airport (*CPT* ☎ *021/937-1200*). Durban International Airport (*DUR* ☎ *031/451-6666*). Lanseria International Airport (*HLA* ☎ *011/659-2750*). O.R. Tambo International Airport (*JNB ORTIA* ☎ *011/921-6262*).

Domestic Airports Bloemfontein Airport (*BFN* ☎ *051/433-1772*). East London Airport (*ELS* ☎ *043/706-0304*). George Airport (*GRJ* ☎ *044/876-9310*). Kimberley Airport (*KIM* ☎ *053/851-1241*). Pilanesberg Airport (*NTY, next to Sun City* ☎ *014/552-1261*). Port Elizabeth Airport (*PLZ* ☎ *041/507-7348*). Upington Airport (*UTN* ☎ *054/337-7900*).

⇨ *For more information about airports, including ground transportation, see Getting Here and Around, in each chapter.*

TRANSFERS BETWEEN AIRPORTS
There are dozens of flights every day between O.R. Tambo and Cape Town airports. Although some of the discount airlines offer better fares for this flight, if your international flight is delayed, you may be left hanging until the next day. Even if it costs a bit more, it can be worth booking through SAA, as they run the bulk of the flights, and so if you miss one, it's usually easy to get on another.

FLIGHTS
South Africa's international airline is South African Airways (SAA). Several major United States carriers also fly to South Africa. Flight times from the U.S. East Coast range from 15 hours (from Atlanta to Johannesburg on Delta) to almost 20 hours (on Northwest, via Amsterdam). About 18 hours is the norm. When booking flights, check the routing carefully; some involve stopovers of an hour or two, which may change from day to day. You can usually spend a few days in your stopover location—charges for this vary but can be surprisingly low.

Three major domestic airlines have flights connecting South Africa's principal airports. SA Airlink and SA Express are subsidiaries of SAA, and Comair is a subsidiary of British Airways.

Recent years have seen an explosion of low-cost carriers serving popular domestic routes in South Africa with regularly scheduled flights. Kulula.com, Mango, and 1time provide reasonably priced domestic air tickets if you book a few weeks in advance. If you know your schedule, be sure to check their fares online. The only downside is they have fewer flights per day and aren't always cheaper than SAA.

Airlines Delta (📠 800/241-4141 ⊕ www. delta.com). **Northwest Airlines** (📠 800/225-2525). **South African Airways** (📠 800/ 521-4845 ⊕ www.flysaa.com). **United** (📠 800/538-2929).

Domestic Airlines British Airways/Comair (📠 011/921-0222 or 086/043-5922 ⊕ www. comair.co.za). **Kulula** (📠 086/158-5852 ⊕ www.kulula.com). **Mango** (📠 011/359-1222, 021/936-2848, or 086/116-2646 ⊕ ww5. flymango.com). **1time** (⊕ www.1time.aero). **South African Airways/SA Airlink/South African Express** (📠 011/978-1111 or 011/978-5577 ⊕ www.flysaa.com).

CHARTER FLIGHTS

Charter companies are a common mode of transportation when getting to safari lodges and remote destinations throughout southern Africa. These aircraft are well-maintained and are almost always booked by your lodge or travel agent. The major charter companies run daily shuttles from O. R. Tambo to popular tourism destinations, such as Kruger Park. On-demand flights, those made at times other than those scheduled, are very expensive for independent travelers, as they require minimum passenger loads. If it's just two passengers, you will be charged for the vacant seats. Keep in mind that you probably won't get to choose the charter company you fly with. The aircraft you get depends on the number of passengers flying and can vary from very small (you will

sit in the co-pilot's seat) to a much more comfortable commuter plane.

Due to the limited space and size of the aircraft, charter carriers observe strict luggage regulations: luggage must be soft-sided and weigh no more than 57 pounds (and sometimes less).

African Ramble flies out of Plettenberg Bay and Port Elizabeth and will take direct bookings. **Federal Air** is the largest charter air company in South Africa. It's based at Johannesburg Airport and has its own efficient terminal with a gift shop, refreshments, and a unique, thatched-roof outdoor lounge. It also has branches in Cape Town, Durban, and Nelspruit (near Kruger). **Sefofane** is a Botswana-based fly-in charter company that will take you anywhere there's a landing strip from its base in Jo'burg's Lanseria Airport.

Charter Companies African Ramble (📠 044/533-9006 or 083/375-6514 ⊕ www. aframble.co.za). **Federal Air** (📠 011/395-9000 or 031/563-8020 ⊕ www.fedair.com). **Sefofane** (📠 011/701-3700 ⊕ www.sefofane.com).

TICKETS

The least expensive airfares to South Africa are priced for round-trip travel and must usually be purchased in advance. Airlines generally allow you to change your return date for a fee; most low-fare tickets, however, are nonrefundable.

AIR PASS

The Star Alliance African Airpass can only be purchased by international passengers arriving to Africa on a Star Alliance carrier (United, Air Canada, South African Airways, etc.) and is good for 3 to 10 flights. The flights are sold in segments, priced by the distance between cities. These are only economy-class seats and can be expensive when compared to the discount airline pricing within South Africa, but they are a bargain for the longer routes, such as from Nairobi to Johannesburg for under $300. If your itinerary includes more than two of the 26 cities served in Africa, this may be a good choice.

The Oneworld Alliance's Visit Africa Pass uses a zone system between cities in South Africa, Namibia, Zambia, and Zimbabwe that British Airways services. The minimum purchase is two segments and the maximum is 20. It's a great value when compared to regular fares.

Air Pass Info Oneworld Alliance (⊕ *www.oneworld.com*). Star Alliance (⊕ *www.staralliance.com*).

▌ BUS TRAVEL

Greyhound, Intercape Mainliner, and Translux operate extensive bus networks that serve all major cities. The buses are comfortable, sometimes there are videos, and tea and coffee are served on board. Distances are long; for example, Cape Town to Johannesburg takes 19 hours. Johannesburg to Durban, at about seven hours, is less stressful. The Garden Route is less intense if you take it in stages, but the whole trip from Cape Town to Port Elizabeth takes 12 hours. Buses are usually pretty punctual. Greyhound and Intercape buses can be booked directly or through Computicket.

For travelers with a sense of adventure, a bit of time, and not too much money, the Baz Bus runs a daily hop-on/hop-off door-to-door service between backpackers' hostels around South Africa and other countries in the region. The rates are a bit higher than for the same distance on a standard bus, but you can break the journey up into a number of different legs, days or weeks apart, and the bus drops you off at the hostels so you don't need to find taxis, shuttles, or lifts. For example, you can do a loop between Johannesburg and Durban, via the Drakensberg one way and Swaziland the other, for R1,450.

▌**TIP→** It is illegal to smoke on buses in South Africa.

The Baz Bus offers a seven-day package for R1,300 and a 14-day package for R2,300. Each allows unrestricted travel; you can change direction as many times as you want and travel as far as you want. It's especially useful if you're planning a long leg followed by a few short ones before returning to your starting point.

Approximate one-way prices for all three major bus lines are R450–R550 Cape Town to Tshwane (Pretoria), R250–R320 Cape Town to Springbok, R160–R250 Cape Town to George, R250–R350 Cape Town to Port Elizabeth, R150–R230 Johannesburg to Durban, and R500–R520 Cape Town to Durban. Baz Bus also runs direct routes between cities, with comparable prices to major bus lines.

Contacts Baz Bus (☎ *021/439-2323* ⊕ *www.bazbus.com*). **Computicket** (☎ *083/909-0909* ⊕ *www.computicket.co.za*). **Greyhound** (☎ *083/915-9000* ⊕ *www.greyhound.co.za*). **Intercape Mainliner** (☎ *021/380-4400* or *0861/287-287* ⊕ *www.intercape.co.za*). **Translux** (☎ *0861/589-282* ⊕ *www.translux.co.za*).

▌ CAR TRAVEL

South Africa has a superb network of multilane roads and highways, so driving can be a pleasure. Remember, though, that distances are vast, so guard against fatigue, which is an even bigger killer than alcohol. Toll roads, scattered among the main routes, charge anything from R10 to R60.

⚠ **Carjackings can and do occur with such frequency that certain high-risk areas are marked by permanent carjacking signs** (⇨ *Safety*).

You can drive in South Africa for up to six months on any English-language license.

South Africa's Automobile Association publishes a range of maps, atlases, and travel guides, available for purchase on its Web site. Maps and map books are also available at all major bookstores.

The commercial Web site Drive South Africa has everything you need to know about driving in the country, including road safety and driving distances in its "Travel South Africa" section.

Maps and Information AA of South Africa's store (⊕ *www.aashop.co.za*). **Drive South Africa** (⊕ *www.drivesouthafrica.co.za*).

GASOLINE

■ TIP→ Credit cards are not accepted anywhere for fueling your tank, but nearly all gas stations are equipped with ATMs. Huge 24-hour service stations are positioned at regular intervals along all major highways in South Africa. There are no self-service stations; attendants pump the gas, check the oil and water, and wash the windows. In return, tip the attendant R2–R3. South Africa has a choice of unleaded or leaded gasoline, and many vehicles operate on diesel—be sure you get the right fuel. Older vehicles run on leaded fuel. Check when booking a rental car as to what fuel to use. Gasoline is measured in liters, and the cost works out to about R27 a gallon. When driving long distances, check your routes carefully, as the distances between towns—and hence gas stations—can be more than 100 mi. It's better to fill a half-full tank than to try to squeeze the last drop out of an unfamiliar rental car.

PARKING

In the countryside parking is mostly free, but you will almost certainly need to pay for parking in cities, which will probably run you about R7 per hour. Many towns have "human parking meters" that work for the municipality. An official attendant (should be wearing a vest of some sort) logs the number of the spot you park in; you're asked to pay up front for the amount of time you expect to park. When you return, if you've overstayed, you pay the balance. You won't receive money back if you leave early. At Pay and Display parking lots you pay in advance. Some parking garages expect payment at the exit. Many others (e.g., at shopping malls, airports) require that you pay for your parking before you return to your car (at kiosks located near the exits to the parking areas). Your receipt ticket allows you to exit. Don't forget to take the ticket with you and don't lose it before paying, as you will be fined for the lost ticket, as

well as the time parked. Just read the signs carefully.

You'll find informal parking guards in most cities; they also wear brightly colored vests or T-shirts. They don't get paid much (in fact some pay for the privilege of working a spot), so they depend on tips. You'll get the most out of these guys if you acknowledge them when you park, ask them politely to look after your car, and then pay them a couple of rand when you return and find it's safe.

DRIVING FROM	TO	RTE./DISTANCE
Cape Town	Port Elizabeth	769 km (478 mi)
Cape Town	Johannesburg	1,402 km (871 mi)
Johannesburg	Durban	583 km (361 mi)
Johannesburg	Kruger National Park	355 km (220 mi)
Kruger National Park	Victoria Falls, Zimbabwe	You cannot take rental cars into Zimbabwe from South Africa
Johannesburg	Pretoria	58 km (36 mi)

ROAD CONDITIONS

South African roads are mostly excellent, but it's dangerous to drive at night in some rural areas, as roads are not always fenced and animals often stray onto the road. In very remote areas only the main road might be paved, whereas many secondary roads are of high-quality gravel. Traffic is often light in these areas, so be sure to bring extra water and carry a spare, a jack, and a tire iron (your rental car should come with these).

RULES OF THE ROAD

South Africans drive on the left-hand side of the road. That may be confusing at first, but having the steering wheel on the right helps to remind you that the driver should be closer to the middle of the road.

Throughout the country, the speed limit is 100 kph (60 mph) or 120 kph (about 75 mph) on the open road and usually 60 kph (35 mph) or 80 kph (about 50 mph) in towns. Of course, many people drive far faster than that. Wearing seat belts is required by law, and the legal blood-alcohol limit is 0.08 mg/100 ml, which means about one glass of wine puts you at the limit. It is illegal to talk on a handheld mobile phone while driving.

South African drivers tend to be aggressive and reckless, thinking nothing of tail-gating at high speeds and passing on blind rises. During national holidays the body count from highway collisions is staggering. The problem is compounded by widespread drunk driving.

If it's safe to do so, it's courteous for slow vehicles to move over onto the shoulder, which is separated from the road by a solid yellow line. (In built-up areas, however, road shoulders are occasionally marked by red lines. This is a strict "no-stopping" zone.) The more aggressive drivers expect this and will flash their lights at you if you don't. Where there are two lanes in each direction, remember that the right-hand lane is for passing.

In towns, minibus taxis can be quite unnerving, swerving in and out of traffic without warning to pick up customers. Stay alert at all times. Many cities use mini-traffic circles in lieu of four-way stops. These can be dangerous, particularly if you're not used to them. In theory, the first vehicle to the circle has the right-of-way; otherwise yield to the right. In practice, keep your wits about you at all times. In most cities traffic lights are on poles at the side of the street. In Johannesburg the lights are only on the far side of each intersection, so don't stop in front of the light or you'll be in the middle of the intersection.

In South African parlance, traffic lights are known as "robots," and what people refer to as the "pavement" is actually the sidewalk. Paved roads are just called roads. Gas is referred to as petrol, and gas stations are petrol stations.

RENTAL CARS

The infrastructure of South Africa is so similar to that of the United States that many visitors decide to rent cars for some, if not all, of their trip. Renting a car gives you the freedom to visit what you'd like and set your own timetable. Most of Cape Town's most popular destinations are an easy drive from the City Bowl. Many people enjoy the slow pace of exploring South Africa's Garden Route by car, or a few days meandering through the Winelands on their own.

Rates in South Africa are similar to those in most U.S. destinations and can vary depending on the bells and whistles and where you intend to drive. Some companies charge more on the weekend, so it's best to get a range of quotes before booking your car. Request car seats and extras such as GPS when you book, and ask for details on what to do if you have a mechanical problem or other emergency.

At this writing, for a car with automatic transmission and air-conditioning, you'll pay around R450 per day for unlimited kilometers and slightly less for 200 km (125 mi) per day plus about R4 per extra kilometer. When comparing prices, make sure you're getting the same thing. Some companies quote prices without insurance, some include 80% or 90% coverage, and some quote with 100% protection.

The major international companies all have offices in tourist cities and at international airports, and their vehicle types are the same range you'd find at home. There's no need to rent a 4x4 vehicle, as all roads are paved, including those in Kruger National Park.

Maui Motorhome Rentals offers fully equipped motor homes, camper vans, and four-wheel-drive vehicles, many of which come totally equipped for a bush sojourn. Prices start at around R1,200 per day, not including insurance, and require a five-day minimum. Standard insurance coverage may be included or can be added for R160 to R285 per day.

You can often save some money by booking a car through a broker, who will access the car from one of the main agencies. Smaller, local agencies often give a much better price, but the car must be returned in the same city. This is pretty popular in Cape Town but not so much in other centers.

In order to rent a car you need to be 23 years or older and have held a driver's license for three years. Younger international drivers can rent from some companies but will pay a penalty. You need to get special permission to take rental cars into neighboring countries (including Lesotho and Swaziland). You cannot take rental cars into Zimbabwe. Most companies allow additional drivers, yet some charge. Get the terms in writing before you leave on your trip.

Leave ample time to return your car when your trip is over. You shouldn't feel rushed when settling your bill. Be sure to get copies of your receipt.

CAR-RENTAL INSURANCE

In South Africa it's necessary to buy special insurance if you plan on crossing borders into neighboring countries, but CDW and TDW (theft-damage waiver) are optional on domestic rentals. Any time you are considering crossing a border with your rental vehicle, you must inform the rental company ahead of time to fulfill any paperwork requirements and pay additional fees.

Local Agencies Car Mania (☎ 021/447–3001 ⊕ www.carmania.co.za). **Imperial Car Rental** (☎ 086/113–1000 ⊕ www.imperialcarrental. co.za). **Maui Motorhome Rental** (☎ 011/396–1445 or 021/982–5107 ⊕ www.maui.co.za). **Value Car Hire** (☎ 021/386–7699 ⊕ www. valuerentalcar.co.za).

Major Agencies Alamo (☎ 800/522–9696 ⊕ www.alamo.com). **Avis** (☎ 800/331–1084 ⊕ www.avis.com). **Budget** (☎ 800/472–3325 ⊕ www.budget.com). **Europcar** (☎ 0860/011–344 or 011/574–1000 ⊕ www.europcar.

co.za). **Hertz** (☎ 800/654–3001 ⊕ www.hertz. com). **National Car Rental** (☎ 877/222–9058 ⊕ www.nationalcar.com).

The Automobile Association (AA) of South Africa extends privileges to members of the American Automobile Association in the United States. Contact a local office in your home country for more information.

Auto Club Automobile Association of South Africa (☎ 011/799–1000 or 011/799–1001 in Johannesburg, 083/84322 24-hr toll-free emergency ⊕ www.aa.co.za).

Emergency Services General emergency number (☎ 112 from mobile phone, 10111 from landline).

▌ TRAIN TRAVEL

Shosholoza Meyl operates an extensive system of passenger trains along eight routes that connect all major cities and many small towns in South Africa. Departures are usually limited to one per day, although trains covering minor routes leave less frequently. Distances are vast, so many journeys require overnight travel. The service is good and the trains are safe and well maintained, but this is far from a luxury option, except in Premier Classe, the luxury service that runs between Cape Town and Johannesburg or Port Elizabeth and between Jo'burg and Durban and Hoedspruit (near Kruger). In Premier Classe, sleeping compartments accommodate two to four travelers, and single compartments are also available. Compartments include a/c, bedding, and limited room service (drinks only). The Jo'burg–Cape Town route has a compartment for vehicles (including 4x4s).

Tourist Class (the old first class) has four-sleeper (bunks) and two-sleeper compartments. Don't expect a/c, heat, or a shower in either class. Bathrooms are shared, compartments have a sink and bedding can be rented. The dining car serves pretty ordinary food, but it's inexpensive. Third class or Economy Class is referred to as "sitter class," because that's what you do—up to 25 hours on a hard seat with up to 71 other people in the car, sharing two toilets and no shower. You must reserve tickets Premier Classe and Tourist Class, whereas sitter-class tickets require no advance booking. You can book up to three months in advance with travel agents, reservations offices in major cities, and at railway stations.

A fun way to see the country is on the Shongololo Express. Though the train is as basic as the Shosholoza Meyl trains, while you sleep at night, it heads to a new destination. After breakfast, tour buses are loaded, and you explore the surroundings. In the evening, you reboard the train, have supper, and sleep while the train moves to the next stop. Trips include the Dune Adventure (the dunes of Namibia), the Good Hope Adventure (Cape attractions), and the Southern Cross Adventure (six African countries). Rates start at about R1,100 per person per night. By the way, a *shongololo* is a millipede.

Contacts Premier Classe (✆ 086/000-8888 ⊕ www.premierclasse.co.za). **Shongololo Express** (✆ 011/483-0657, 011/483-0658, or 011/483-0659 ⊕ www.shongololo.com). **Shosholoza Meyl** (✆ 086/000-8888 ⊕ www.shosholozameyl.co.za).

LUXURY TRAIN TRIPS

South Africa's leisurely and divine luxury trains come complete with gold-and brass-plated fixtures, oak paneling, and full silver service for every meal. The elegant Blue Train travels several routes, but the main one is between Cape Town and Tshwane (Pretoria). It departs once a week in each direction, takes 28 hours, and costs around R12,485 per person one way (peak season). The fare includes all meals (extravagant three-course affairs), drinks (a full bar and great selection of South African wines), and excursions (usually a two-hour stop in Kimberley). Only caviar and French champagne are excluded.

The Blue Train also goes to Durban from Tshwane and can arrange chartered trips that include stays in luxury lodges. All-inclusive tickets start at R9,680 per person for a four-day package that includes two nights on the Blue Train and two nights at Zimbali Lodge and golf course.

Rovos Rail's Pride of Africa runs from Cape Town to Tshwane every Monday (and sometimes other days). Fares are R9,860 for the 72-hour trip in Pullman Class; fancier suites cost up to R20,000. Rovos also includes all excursions, sumptuous meals, all drinks (except French champagne), and excellent butler service, but whereas the Blue Train excels in modern luxury, the Rovos creates an atmosphere of Victorian colonial charm (no cell phones or laptops in public spaces), and is the only luxury train in the world in which you can open the windows. Rovos also has four Cape Town–George trips a year; a seven-day trip Cape Town–Swakopmund round-trip in May; and a 14-day epic Cape Town–Dar es Salaam loop in July. Prices per person can reach R41,000 for the Royal Suite on the four-night, five-day trip from Cape Town to Victoria Falls.

All prices are for double occupancy; the single-occupancy supplement is 50%.

Contacts Blue Train (✆ 012/334-8459 or 021/449-2672 ⊕ www.bluetrain.co.za). **Rovos Rail** (✆ 012/315-8242, 631/858-1270 U.S. ⊕ www.rovos.co.za).

ESSENTIALS

■ ACCOMMODATIONS

The Tourism Grading Council of South Africa is the official accreditation and grading body for accommodation in South Africa. However, you may still find some establishments clinging to other grading systems. Hotels, bed-and-breakfasts, guesthouses, and game lodges are graded on a star rating from one to five. Grading is not compulsory, and there are many excellent establishments that are not graded. Those that are given a grade are revisited annually. Unlike North American ratings standards, AAA or Mobil, which are based on the presence of a constellation of facilities and services, these marks are purely subjective and reflect the comfort level and quality of the surroundings.

Most hotel rooms come with private bathrooms that are usually en suite, but they may, very occasionally, be across the corridor. You can usually choose between rooms with twin or double beds. A full English breakfast is often included in the rate, particularly in more traditional hotels. In most luxury lodges the rate usually covers the cost of dinner, bed, and breakfast, whereas in game lodges the rate includes everything but alcohol—and some include that. A self-catering room is one with kitchen facilities.

Be warned that in southern Africa words do not necessarily mean what you think they do. The term *lodge* is a particularly tricky one. A guest lodge or a game lodge is almost always an upmarket, full-service facility with loads of extra attractions. But the term *lodge* when applied to city hotels often indicates a minimum-service hotel, like the City and Town Lodges and Holiday Inn Garden Courts. A backpacker lodge, however, is essentially a hostel.

A *rondavel* can be a small cabin, often in a rounded shape, while its cousin, the *banda*, can be anything from a basic stand-alone structure to a Quonset hut. Think very rustic.

Price charts specific to each area are found in each chapter. We always list the facilities that are available—but we don't specify whether they cost extra: when pricing accommodations, always ask what's included. Price categories are based on a property's least expensive standard double room at high season (excluding holidays). Those indicated by a ⚹ are campgrounds with rustic camping accommodations (as opposed to the fairly luxurious safari tents at many private game lodges). Mailing addresses follow the street address or location, where appropriate.

Be sure you understand the hotel's cancellation policy. Some places allow you to cancel without any kind of penalty— even if you prepaid to secure a discounted rate—if you cancel at least 24 hours in advance. Others require you to cancel a week in advance or penalize you the cost of one night. Small inns and B&Bs are most likely to require you to cancel far in advance. Always have written confirmation of your booking when you check in.

■ TIP➜ Most hotels allow children under a certain age to stay in their parents' room at no extra charge, but others charge for them as extra adults, and some don't allow children under 12 at all. Ask about the policy on children before checking in and make sure you find out the cutoff age for discounts.

■ TIP➜ Assume that hotels operate on the European Plan (EP, no meals) unless we specify that they use the Breakfast Plan (BP, with full breakfast), Continental Plan (CP, Continental breakfast), Full American Plan (FAP, all meals), Modified American Plan (MAP, breakfast and dinner) or are all-inclusive (AI, all meals and most activities). In South Africa, most accommodations from hotels to guesthouses do include breakfast in the rate. Most game lodges have FAP. All hotels listed have private bath unless otherwise noted.

Contacts **Grading Council of South Africa** (⊕ www.tourismgrading.co.za). **Portfolio Collection** (☎ 021/689–4020, 072/371–2472 after hours ⊕ www.portfoliocollection.com).

HOTELS

Your hotel in South Africa will be similar to one at home; the more you pay, the better the quality and amenities. Some online booking sites have specials for more expensive properties that include a couple of extra nights at less popular locales. It's worth poking around to see if these can fit into your itinerary as they may save you some money if you're planning to visit several locations.

As at home, peak seasons mean peak prices. There are a few international chains represented in South Africa, so check with your frequent-stay program to see if you can get a better room or better rate. It might be more fun, though, to experience a local, or African establishment.

Almost every hotel stay will include breakfast in the hotel's dining room, and in South Africa that means a full array of meats, cheeses, and eggs cooked to order—a little bonus that makes it easier to ease into your touring day.

BED-AND-BREAKFASTS

B&Bs are ubiquitous in South Africa. Many are very small and personalized. For more information, contact the Bed and Breakfast Association of South Africa (BABASA) or the Portfolio Collection, which represents more than 700 lodging options in South Africa and publishes a respected list of South Africa's best B&Bs that may also be useful; it also offers a similar guide to small hotels and lodges.

Contacts **BABASA** (☎ 082/239–2111 ⊕ www.babasa.co.za). **Portfolio Collection** (☎ 021/689–4020, 072/371–2472 after hours ⊕ www.portfoliocollection.com). **SA-Venues** (⊕ www.sa-venues.com).

GUESTHOUSES

The term *guesthouse* may conjure up the image of a flophouse, but in South Africa guesthouses are a cross between an inn

and a B&B. Usually located in residential neighborhoods, they offer an intimate experience that benefits from the proprietor's tastes and interests, often at a vast savings over hotels. A guesthouse manager might make special arrangements to drive you to an attraction, whereas a hotel might charge extra transportation fees. Long-term visitors tend to choose guesthouses, where they can meet other like-minded travelers who are interested in experiencing the country, not just ticking off sites.

Contacts **Guest House Accommodation of South Africa** (☎ 021/762–0880 ⊕ www.ghasa.co.za). **Sleeping Out** (☎ 021/762–1543 ⊕ www.sleeping-out.co.za).

HOSTELS

Hostels can be found almost everywhere and they range from fabulous to downright scruffy. Most hostels are affiliated with BTSA (Backpacker Tourism South Africa). You can get a good overview of the hostel scene from "Coast to Coast" or "the Alternative Route," both of which are small free booklets that are regularly updated and found in hostels and tourist offices. The Baz Bus (⇨ *Bus Travel, above*) offers a handy door-to-door service to backpacker lodgings all around the country.

Contacts **Backpacking South Africa** (⊕ www.backpackingsouthafrica.co.za). **Coast to Coast** (⊕ www.coastingafrica.com). **Hostelling International South Africa** (☎ 021/788–2301 ⊕ www.hisa.org.za).

GAME LODGES

Game lodges in South Africa are often designed to fulfill your wildest wildlife fantasy. Top designers have created magical worlds in styles from African chic to throwback bush romance. At the highest end, you can enjoy dinner under starlight on your own deck, or swap stories around the boma at night. For some people the first glimpse of their accommodations is a thrill to rival the best game viewing. ⇨ *For park, lodge, and booking information see Chapter 9, Safaris in South Africa.*

FARM STAYS

Jacana Marketing and Reservations offers a range of farms, coastal and country cottages, and privately operated hiking, biking, and horse trails in country areas.

Contact Jacana Marketing and Reservations (☎ *012/734–2978* ⊕ *www.jacanacollection.co.za*).

HOME EXCHANGES

It is really unusual for a short-term vacationer to do a home exchange, but for visiting academics or business travelers who come for a long stay and bring their families, it might be a solution. Certainly a home gives you more space and a feel for the community.

HomeLink International is the largest home-exchange network in South Africa. Sabbatical Homes is a fee-based service for academics who need temporary housing in Cape Town and Johannesburg.

Contacts Home Base Holidays in South Africa (☎ *012/993–4310* ⊕ *www.homebase-hols.com/southafrica.shtml*). **Home Exchange.com** (☎ *800/877–8723* ⊕ *www.homeexchange.com*). **HomeLink International** (☎ *800/638–3841* ⊕ *www.homelink.org*). **Intervac U.S.** (☎ *800/756–4663* ⊕ *www.intervacus.com*). **Sabbatical Homes** (⊕ *www.sabbaticalhomes.com*).

∎ COMMUNICATIONS

INTERNET

Unless you have business in South Africa, leave the laptop at home and take memory cards for your vacation photos. You can check e-mail for a few rand either in the comfort of your hotel or at a public Internet café.

If you do bring your computer, you'll have no problem getting service in the cities. In the smaller towns you'll usually find a computer store, but it's unlikely you'll find anyone to service a Mac outside of Cape Town and Jo'burg. It's worth bringing a long phone cord, as some hotels have only one phone jack—right next to the bed. Many Internet cafés allow you to just plug into their phone line or, in some cases, their network. Back up all your data before leaving home.

Contacts Cybercafes (⊕ *www.cybercafes.com*).

PHONES

There are toll-free numbers in South Africa. There's also something called a share-call line, for which the cost of the call is split between both parties.

The country code for South Africa is 27. When dialing from abroad, drop the initial 0 from local area codes.

CALLING WITHIN SOUTH AFRICA

Local calls (from landline to landline) are very cheap, although all calls from hotels attract a hefty premium. Calls from a mobile phone or from a landline to a mobile are relatively expensive (up to R3 per minute). South Africa has two types of pay phones: coin-operated phones, which accept a variety of coins, and card-operated phones. Coin-operated phones are being phased out, and there aren't too many left in tourist destinations. Phone cards are the better option; they free you from the hassle of juggling handfuls of coins, and they're available in several denominations. In addition, a digital readout tells you how much credit remains while you're talking. Cards are available at newsstands, convenience stores, and telephone company offices. When making a phone call in South Africa, always use the full 10-digit number, including the area code, even if you're in the same area.

For directory assistance in South Africa, call 1023. For operator-assisted national long-distance calls, call 1025. For international operator assistance, dial 10903#. These numbers are free if dialed from a Telkom (landline) phone but are charged at normal cell-phone rates from a mobile—and they're busy call centers. Directory inquiries numbers are different for each cell-phone network. Vodacom is 111, MTN is 200, and Cell C is 146. These calls are charged at normal rates, but the call is timed only from when it is actually answered. You can, for an extra fee, get the call connected by the operator.

CALLING OUTSIDE SOUTH AFRICA

When dialing out from South Africa, dial 00 before the international code. So, for example, you would dial 001 for the United States.

The country code for the United States is 1.

■ TIP→ If you really want to save on international phone calls, the best advice is to provide a detailed itinerary back home and agree upon a schedule for calls. Internet calling like Skype also works well from the United States, but it's not always functional in South Africa, unless you're on a reliable high-speed Internet connection, which isn't available everywhere. However, if you have a South African "free" cell phone (meaning you can receive calls for free; all phones using an SA SIM card do this), someone in the United States can call you from their Skype account, for reasonable per-minute charges—you won't be charged.

Access Codes AT&T Direct (☏ 0800/990-123 from South Africa). MCI Worldwide Access (☏ 0800/990-011 from South Africa). Sprint International Access (☏ 0800/990-001 from South Africa).

MOBILE PHONES

Cell phones are ubiquitous and have quite extensive coverage. There are four cell-phone service providers in South Africa—Cell C, MTN, Virgin Mobile, and Vodacom—and you can buy these SIM cards, as well as airtime, in supermarkets for as little as R10 for the SIM card (if you purchase SIM cards at the airport, you will be charged much more). Bear in mind that your U.S. cell phone may not work with the local GSM system and/or that your phone may be blocked from using SIM cards outside of your plan. Basic but functional GSM cell phones start at R400, and are available at the mobile carrier shops as well as major department stores like Woolworths.

Cell phones also can be rented by the day, week, or longer from the airport on your arrival, but this is an expensive option. If you plan on bringing a U.S. cell phone while you're traveling, know that plans change frequently, so try to gather as many details before leaving to figure out which plan is right for you. Some allow free calls to your number, but charge rates close to landline calls if you call the United States. If you don't text message at home, you'll learn to in Africa, where a simple text message costs a fraction of the cost of making an actual call. This is a handy option for meeting up with friends, but for calling a hotel reservations line, it's best to make the call.

Cellular Abroad rents and sells GMS phones and sells SIM cards that work in many countries, but cost a lot more than local solutions. Mobal rents mobiles and sells GSM phones (starting at $49) that will operate in 150 countries. Per-call rates vary throughout the world. Vodacom is the country's leading cellular network.

The least complicated way to make and receive phone calls is to obtain international roaming service from your cell-phone service provider before you leave home, but this can be expensive. ■ TIP→ Verizon and Sprint customers cannot use their phones in Africa. Any phone that you take abroad must be unlocked by your company in order for you to be able to use it.

Contacts Cell C (☎ *084–140* ⊕ *www.cellc. co.za*). **Cellular Abroad** (☎ *800/287–5072 from U.S., 310/862–7100* ⊕ *www.cellulara-broad.com*). **Mobal** (☎ *888/888–9162 from U.S., 212/785–5800* ⊕ *www.mobal.com*). **MTN** (☎ *083/173* ⊕ *www.mtn.co.za*).**Virgin Mobile** (☎ *0860/000–181* ⊕ *www.virginmobile.co.za*). **Vodacom** (☎ *082–111 from landline, 111 from mobile phone* ⊕ *www.vodacom.co.za*).

▌ CUSTOMS AND DUTIES

Visitors may bring in new or used gifts and souvenirs up to a total value of R3,000 duty-free. For additional goods (new or used) up to a value of R12,000, a fee of 20% is levied. In addition, each person may bring up to 200 cigarettes, 20 cigars, 250 grams of tobacco, two liters of wine, one liter of other alcoholic beverages, 50 ml of perfume, and 250 ml of toilet water into South Africa or other Southern Africa Common Customs Union (SACU) countries (Botswana, Lesotho, Namibia, and Swaziland). The tobacco and alcohol allowance applies only to people 18 and over. If you enter a SACU country from or through another in the union, you are not liable for any duties. You will, how-ever, need to complete a form listing items imported.

The United States is a signatory to CITES, a wildlife protection treaty, and therefore does not allow the importation of living or dead endangered animals, or their body parts, such as rhino horns or ivory. If you purchase an antique that is made partly or wholly of ivory, you must obtain a CITES pre-convention certificate that clearly states the item is at least 100 years old. The import of zebra skin or other tourist products also requires a CITES permit.

South Africa Information Southern Africa Customs Union (⊕ *www.dfa.gov.za/foreign/ Multilateral/africa/sacu.htm*).

U.S. Information U.S. Customs and Border Protection (⊕ *www.cbp.gov*). **U.S. Fish and Wildlife Service** (⊕ *www.fws.gov*).

▌ EATING OUT

South Africa's cities and towns are full of dining options, from chain restaurants like the popular Nando's to chic cafés. Indian food and Cape Malay dishes are regional favorites in Cape Town, while traditional smoked meats and sausages are available countrywide. Children are allowed in all restaurants, but don't expect toys and games as in American restaurants.

The restaurants we list are the cream of the crop in each price category. Price cat-egories are charted in each chapter and are based on the costs of main courses or a prix-fixe meal (where that is the only option). If you love seafood, you should make a point of visiting one of the casual West Coast beach restaurants (⇨ *Chapter 3*), where you sit on the beach in a make-shift structure and eat course after course of seafood cooked on an open fire.

⇨ *For food-related health issues, see Health, below.*

MEALS AND MEALTIMES

In South Africa dinner is eaten at night and lunch at noon. Breakfast generally consists of something eggy and hot, but many people are moving over to muesli and fruit. South Africans may eat muf-fins for breakfast but draw the line at doughnuts. Restaurants serve breakfast until about 11:30; a few serve breakfast all day.

If you're staying at a game lodge, your mealtimes will revolve around the game drives—usually coffee and rusks (similar to biscotti) early in the morning, more cof-fee and probably muffins on the first game drive, a huge brunch in the late morning, no lunch, tea and something sweet in the late afternoon before the evening game drive, cocktails and snacks on the drive, and a substantial supper, or dinner, about 8 or 8:30.

LOCAL DO'S AND TABOOS

GREETINGS

The first words you should say to anyone in South Africa, no matter the situation, is "Hello, how are you?" It doesn't matter if you are in a hurry, African conversations begin with a greeting. To skip this and jump to the question, as we do in the United States, is considered rude. Slow down and converse, then ask for what it is you need. After a few weeks you'll get used to it and miss it when you return home to instant demands.

SIGHTSEEING

South Africa, unlike the rest of the continent, is relatively casual. Aside from top-end restaurants and houses of worship, you can dress fairly casually (shorts and sandals). In national parks and by the beach, rules are even more flexible, and many people stroll into cafés right off the beach, wearing only cover-ups.

If you're visiting a house of worship, dress modestly. This is especially true at mosques, where women should bring scarves to cover their heads, wear skirts below the knees, and cover their shoulders. Some mosques prefer non-Muslims to remain outside.

OUT ON THE TOWN

When out at a restaurant or a club, behave as you would at home. Be polite to waitstaff and don't call out.

HOUSE CALLS

If you are invited to someone's home, it's a good idea to bring a small gift. If you know your hosts' habits, you can bring a bottle of wine, chocolates, or flowers. If you've been invited to a very humble home—as can happen in rural areas—and your hosts are struggling to feed their children, they may prefer something a bit more pragmatic than a bunch of flowers. This is delicate territory so, when in doubt, ask a trustworthy, knowledgeable third party. Dress nicely and modestly when visiting homes, especially in the townships or Muslim areas.

DOING BUSINESS

Arrive on time for appointments, and hand over a business card during introductions. Handshakes are the proper form of greeting in a business setting. Gifts are not part of the business culture. Address colleagues by their titles and surnames.

It's not uncommon for business to be conducted over a meal. You may be inclined to rush proceedings along and force decisions, but this is not the African way. Slow down and relax.

Men generally wear a jacket and tie to meetings, but a suit isn't necessary, unless it's a really high-powered meeting. Women can get away with anything from a pretty floral dress to a suit, but take your cue from the general purpose of the meeting and other participants. Trousers are perfectly acceptable for women.

LANGUAGE

⚠ **While many Americans consider the term "coloured" offensive, it's widely used in South Africa to describe South Africans who are descended from imported slaves, the San, the Khoekhoen, and European settlers. Over the years the term has lost any pejorative connotations.**

South Africa has 11 official languages: Afrikaans, English, Ndebele, North Sotho, South Sotho, Swati, Tsonga, Tswana (same as Setswana in Botswana), Venda, Xhosa, and Zulu. English is widely spoken, although road signs and other important markers often alternate between English and Afrikaans.

If you're particularly interested in food, stay at a guesthouse selected by Good Cooks and Their Country Houses, which are noted for superior cuisine. In order for a guesthouse to qualify for inclusion, the chef must be the owner (or one of them).

Unless otherwise noted, the restaurants listed in this guide are open daily for lunch and dinner.

Contacts Good Cooks and Their Country Houses (⊕ *www.goodcooks.co.za*).

PAYING

Many restaurants accustomed to serving tourists accept credit cards, usually Visa and American Express, with MasterCard increasingly accepted.

⇨ *For guidelines on tipping, see Tipping, below.*

⇨ *For restaurant price charts specific to each area, see Planning, at the beginning of each chapter.*

RESERVATIONS AND DRESS

Most restaurants welcome casual dress, including jeans and sneakers, but draw the line at shorts and a halter top at dinner, except for restaurants on the beach. Very expensive restaurants and old-fashioned hotel restaurants (where colonial traditions die hard) may welcome nicer dress, but other than the Blue Train, few require a jacket and tie.

WINES, BEER, AND SPIRITS

You can buy wine in supermarkets and many convenience stores. Beer is available only in "bottle shops," which are licensed to sell spirits. Most restaurants are licensed to sell wine and beer, and many also sell spirits. From Saturday at 8 PM through Sunday, you can buy alcohol only in restaurants and bars. You may not take alcohol onto beaches, and it's illegal to walk down the street with an open container. You can, however, drink with a picnic or enjoy sundowners (cocktails at sunset) in almost any public place, such as Table Mountain or Kirstenbosch. The beach rule is also somewhat relaxed at sundowner time, but be careful.

⇨ *For more information on food and drink, see "Flavors of South Africa," in Chapter 1.*

▌ ELECTRICITY

The electrical current is 220 volts, 50 cycles alternating current (AC); wall outlets in most of the region take 15-amp plugs with three round prongs (the old British system), some take the European two narrow prongs, and a few take the straight-edged three-prong plugs, also 15 amps.

If your appliances are dual voltage, you'll need only an adapter. In remote areas (and even in some lodges) power may be solar or from a generator; this means that delivery is erratic both in voltage and supply. In even the remotest places, however, lodge staff will find a way to charge video and camera batteries, but you will receive little sympathy if you insist on using a hair dryer or electric razor.

Consider making a small investment in a universal adapter, which has several types of plugs in one lightweight, compact unit. Most laptops and mobile phone chargers are dual voltage (i.e., they operate equally well on 110 and 220 volts), so require only an adapter. These days the same is true of small appliances such as hair dryers. Always check labels and manufacturer instructions to be sure. Don't use 110-volt outlets marked FOR SHAVERS ONLY for high-wattage appliances such as hair dryers.

Contacts **Steve Kropla's Help for World Travelers** (🌐 *www.kropla.com*). **Walkabout Travel Gear** (🌐 *www.walkabouttravelgear.com*).

■ EMERGENCIES

If you specifically need an ambulance, you can get one by calling the special ambulance number or through the general emergency number. Europ Assistance offers professional evacuation in the event of emergency. If you intend to dive in South Africa, make sure you have DAN membership, which will be honored by Divers Alert Network South Africa (DANSA).

Embassies U.S. Embassy (✉ *1 River St., Killarney, Tshwane* ☎ *011/644-8000*). **U.S. Consulate, Cape Town** (✉ *2 Reddam Ave., Westlake, Cape Town* ☎ *021/702-7300* 🌐 *southafrica.usembassy.gov*).

General Emergency Contacts Ambulance (☎ *101 / /*). **DANSA** (☎ *0800/020-111 or 010/209-8112 Emergency hotline* 🌐 *www. dansa.org*) **Europ Assistance** (☎ *0860/635-635* 🌐 *www.europassistance.co.za*). **General emergency** (☎ *10111 from landline, 112 from mobile phone*). **Police** (☎ *10111*).

■ GEAR

Goods in South Africa's pharmacies and grocery stores are very similar to those in the States. If you have a favorite brand of toiletry, bring it; otherwise expect to pay average prices for items you may have left at home. Minimarts at gas stations also stock the same range of candies and sodas you would expect of a roadside shop.

Take care to bring enough prescription medicines and a copy of your prescription if you anticipate needing a refill. Ask your doctor to write down the ingredients so that a pharmacist will find a suitable substitute if necessary. Obtain your antimalarials at home.

Incidents of theft from checked baggage in Cape Town and Johannesburg airports make luggage wrapping a popular option. For a few rand, the process of wrapping a bag in impenetrable cellophane is a great deterrent against crime. Bags can be rewrapped. ⚠ **Fragile items in softsided bags can be crushed in the process, so remove breakable items or place them in the center of the bag to prevent their getting squeezed.** The wrapping can be removed by hand or with a knife. Security accepts wrapped bags.

In southern Africa it's possible to experience muggy heat, bone-chilling cold, torrential thunderstorms, and scorching African sun all within a couple of days. The secret is to pack lightweight clothes that you can wear in layers, and at least one lightweight fleece pullover or sweater. Take along a warm jacket, too, especially if you're going to a private game lodge. It can get mighty cold sitting in an open Land Rover at night or on an early morning game drive. It really and truly does get very cold in almost every part of southern Africa, so don't fall into the it's-Africa-so-it-must-always-be-hot trap.

South Africans tend to dress casually. Businessmen still wear suits, but dress standards have become less rigid and more interesting since ex-president Nelson Mandela redefined the concept of sartorial elegance with his Madiba shirts. You can go almost anywhere in neat, clean, casual clothes, but you can still get dolled up to go to the theater or opera.

It's easy to get fried in the strong African sun, especially in mile-high Johannesburg or windy Cape Town, where the air can feel deceptively cool. Pack plenty of sunscreen (SPF 30 or higher), sunglasses, and a hat. An umbrella comes in handy during those late-afternoon thunderstorms but is almost useless in Cape Town in the winter, as it will get blown inside out. But do take a raincoat.

If you're heading into the bush, bring binoculars, a strong insect repellent (with a good amount of DEET), and sturdy pants (preferably cotton) that can stand up to the wicked thorns that protect much of the foliage. Avoid black, dark blue, white, and garish clothing, which will make you more visible to animals and insects; medium tones will make you blend in most. Leave behind perfumes, which attract insects. Bring lightweight hiking boots if you plan to hit the trails; otherwise, a sturdy pair of walking shoes should suffice. For the coast, "water shoes" are a great option. ⇨ *For more details on what to pack for a safari, see Chapter 9, Safaris in South Africa.*

Some hotels do supply washcloths; some don't. It's always a good idea to have at least a couple of tissues in your bag, and moist towelettes as there may not be a restroom (or toilet paper) just when you need it. Even an hour in a safari vehicle on a dry day can cover you with dust.

Make copies of all your important documents. Leave one set in one bag, another at home, and try to save them online in a PDF file, which may be the fastest way to access data if you need to replace anything. Consider carrying a small card with emergency contact numbers on it, such as the local U.S. embassy, in case things go terribly wrong.

If your luggage does get lost, your best bet for replacing staple items will be Woolworths (a quality brand in South Africa, with both department and food stores). Edgars and Truworth are also fine. You can find all three in most big shopping malls. Mr. Price is South Africa's Target equivalent, but with less-reliable quality. Cape Union Mart is great for safari stuff. You'll find a wide supply of toiletries in Clicks.

▌HEALTH

The most serious health problem facing travelers is malaria, which occurs in the prime South African game-viewing areas of Mpumalanga, Limpopo Province, and northern KwaZulu-Natal and in the countries farther north. The risk is medium at the height of the summer and very low in winter. All travelers heading into malaria-endemic regions should consult a health-care professional at least one month before departure for advice. Unfortunately, the malarial agent *Plasmodium sp.* seems to be able to develop a hardy resistance to new prophylactic drugs pretty quickly, so even if you are taking the newest miracle drug, the best prevention is to avoid being bitten by mosquitoes in the first place. After sunset wear light-colored, loose, long-sleeve shirts, long pants, and shoes and socks, and apply mosquito repellent generously. Always sleep in a mosquito-proof room or tent, and if possible, keep a fan going in your room. If you are pregnant or trying to conceive, avoid malaria areas entirely.

Generally speaking, the risk is much lower in the dry season (May–October) and peaks immediately after the first rains, which should be in November, but El Niño has made that a lot less predictable.

Many lakes and streams, particularly east of the watershed divide (i.e., in rivers flowing toward the Indian Ocean), are infected with *bilharzia* (schistosomiasis), a parasite carried by a small freshwater snail. The microscopic fluke enters through the skin of swimmers or waders, attaches itself to the intestines or bladder, and lays eggs. Avoid wading in still waters or in areas close to reeds. If you have been wading or swimming in doubtful water, dry yourself off vigorously with a towel immediately upon exiting the water, as this may help to dislodge any flukes before they can burrow into your skin. Fast-moving water is considered safe. If you have been exposed, pop into a pharmacy and purchase a course of treatment and take it to be safe. If your trip is ending shortly after your exposure, take the medicine home and have a checkup once you get home. Bilharzia is easily diagnosed, and it's also easily treated in the early stages.

On hot days and days when you are on the move, especially after long flights, try to drink a few liters of water. If you're prone to low-blood sugar or have a sensitive stomach, consider bringing along rehydration salts, available at camping stores, to balance your body's fluids and keep you going when you feel listless. Alcohol is dehydrating, so try to limit consumption on hot or long travel days.

These days everyone is sun sensitive, so pack plenty of your favorite SPF product from home, and use it generously.

Be aware of the dangers of becoming infected with HIV (which is a big problem in Africa) or hepatitis. Make sure you use a condom during a sexual encounter; they're sold in supermarkets, pharmacies, and most convenience stores. If you feel there's a possibility you've exposed yourself to the virus, you can get antiretroviral treatment (post-exposure prophylaxis or PEP) from private hospitals, but you must do so within 48 hours of exposure.

Rabies is extremely rare in domesticated animals in South Africa but is more common in wild animals—one more reason you should not feed or tease wild animals. If you are bitten by a monkey or other wild animal, seek medical attention immediately. The chance of contracting rabies is extremely small, but the consequences are so horrible that you really don't want to gamble on this one.

As a foreigner, you'll be expected to pay in full for any medical services, so check your existing health plan to see whether you're covered while abroad, and supplement it if necessary. South African doctors are generally excellent. The equipment and training in private clinics rivals the best in the world, but public hospitals tend to suffer from overcrowding and underfunding.

On returning home, if you experience any unusual symptoms, including fever, painful eyes, backache, diarrhea, severe headache, general lassitude, or blood in urine or stool, be sure to tell your doctor where you have been. These symptoms may indicate malaria, tick-bite fever, bilharzia, or—if you've been traveling north of South Africa's borders—some other tropical malady.

The drinking water in South Africa is treated and, except in rural areas, is absolutely safe to drink. Many people filter it, though, to get rid of the chlorine, as that aseptic status does not come free. You can eat fresh fruits and salads and have ice in your drinks.

■TIP➜ If on safari or camping, check your boots and shake your clothes out for spiders and other crawlies before getting dressed.

In summer ticks may be a problem, even in open areas close to cities. If you intend to walk or hike anywhere, use a suitable insect repellent. After your walk, examine your body and clothes for ticks, looking carefully for pepper ticks, which are tiny but may cause tick-bite fever. If you find a tick has bitten you, do not pull it off. If you do, you may pull the body off, and the head will remain embedded in your skin, causing an infection. Rather, smother the area with petroleum jelly, and the tick will eventually let go, as it will be unable to breathe; you can then scrape it off with a fingernail. If you are bitten, keep an eye on the bite. If the tick was infected, the bite will swell, itch, and develop a black necrotic center. This is a sure sign that you will develop tick-bite fever, which usually hits after about 8 to 12 days. Symptoms may be mild or severe, depending on the patient. This disease is not usually life-threatening in healthy adults, but it's horribly unpleasant. Most people who are bitten by ticks suffer no more than an itchy bump, so don't panic.

Also, obviously, keep a lookout for mosquitoes. Even in nonmalarial areas they are extremely irritating. When walking anywhere in the bush, keep a lookout for snakes. Most will slither away when they feel you coming, but just keep your eyes peeled. If you see one, give it a wide berth and you should be fine. Snakes really bite only when they are taken by surprise, so you don't want to step on a napping adder.

OVER-THE-COUNTER REMEDIES

You can buy over-the-counter medication in pharmacies and supermarkets, and you will find the more general remedies in Clicks, a chain store selling beauty products, some OTC medication, and housewares. Your body may not react the same way to the South African version of a product, even something as simple as a headache tablet, so bring your own supply for your trip and rely on pharmacies just for emergency medication.

SHOTS AND MEDICATIONS

South Africa does not require any inoculations for entry. Travelers entering South Africa within six days of leaving a country infected with yellow fever require a yellow-fever vaccination certificate. The South African travel clinics and the U.S. National Centers for Disease Control and Prevention (CDC) recommend that you be vaccinated against hepatitis A and B if you intend to travel to more isolated areas. Cholera injections are widely regarded as useless, so don't let anyone talk you into having one, but the newer oral vaccine seems to be more effective.

If you are coming to South Africa for a safari, chances are you are heading to a malarial game reserve. Only a handful of game reserves are nonmalarial. Millions of travelers take oral prophylactic drugs before, during, and after their safaris. It's up to you to weigh the risks and benefits of the type of antimalarial drug you choose to take. If you're pregnant or traveling with small children, consider a nonmalarial region for your safari.

The CDC provides up-to-date information on health risks and recommended vaccinations and medications for travelers to southern Africa. In most of South Africa you need not worry about any of the above, but if you plan to visit remote regions, check with the CDC's traveler's health line. For up-to-date, local expertise, contact SAA Netcare Travel Clinics.

Health Warnings **National Centers for Disease Control and Prevention (CDC**

877/394–8747 international travelers' health line ⊕ www.cdc.gov/travel). **South African Airways Netcare Travel Clinics** (☎ 0860/638–2273 toll-free in South Africa ⊕ www.travelclinic.co.za). **Travel Health Online** (⊕ www.tripprep.com). **World Health Organization** (WHO ⊕ www.who.int).

Medical-Only Insurers **International Medical Group, South Africa** (☎ 800/628–4664 ⊕ www.imglobal.com). **International SOS Assistance, South Africa** (☎ 011/541–1000, 011/541–1300 24-hr emergency ⊕ www. internationalsos.co.za). **Wallach & Company** (☎ 800/237–6615 ⊕ www.wallach.com).

▎HOURS OF OPERATION

The most surprising aspect of South Africa's business hours, especially for tourists who come to shop, is that shopping centers, including enclosed secure indoor malls, almost always close by 6 PM. This is starting to change in Cape Town's malls, with summer hours increased until 7 or 8, but don't expect it. It's rare for a store to remain open after dinner.

Business hours in major South African cities are weekdays from about 9 to 5. Most banks close in midafternoon, usually about 3:30, but dedicated currency exchange offices usually stay open longer. In addition, post offices and banks are open briefly on Saturday mornings from about 9, so get there early. In rural areas and small towns things are less rigid. Post offices often close for lunch, and, in very small towns and villages banks may have very abbreviated hours.

Most museums are open during usual business hours, including Saturday mornings, but some stay open longer.

Most pharmacies close about 6, but there's generally an all-night pharmacy in towns of a reasonable size. If not, look for an emergency number posted on a pharmacy.

Many gas stations are open 24 hours, and urban gas stations have 24-hour convenience stores, some of which have an impressive range of goods.

HOLIDAYS

National holidays in South Africa are New Year's Day (January 1), Human Rights Day (March 21), Good Friday, Easter, Family Day (sometime in March or April), Freedom Day (April 27), Workers Day (May 1), Youth Day (June 16), National Women's Day (August 9), Heritage Day (September 24), Day of Reconciliation (December 16), Christmas Day (December 25), and Day of Goodwill (December 26). If a public holiday falls on a Sunday, the following Monday is also a public holiday. Election days are also public holidays, so check calendars closer to your time of travel for those, which are not on fixed dates.

In Cape Town, January 2 is also a holiday, known as *tweede nuwe jaar* (second new year). School vacations vary with the provinces, but usually comprise about 10 days over Easter, about three weeks around June or July, and then the big summer vacation from about December 10 to January 10.

▋ MAIL

The mail service in South Africa is reasonably reliable, but mail can take weeks to arrive, and money and other valuables may be stolen from letters and packages. You can buy stamps at post offices, open weekdays 8:30 to 4:30 and Saturday 8 to noon. Stamps for local use only, marked STANDARDISED POST, may be purchased from newsstands in booklets of 10 stamps. PostNet franchises—a combined post office, courier service, business services center, and Internet café—are in convenient places like shopping malls and are open longer hours than post offices.

All overseas mail costs the same. At the post office a postcard is about R4.20, and a letter ranges from R4.15 to about R19, depending on size and weight.

ADDRESSES

Note that the first floor of a building is the one between the ground floor and the second floor. Mailing addresses are pretty straightforward. If they're not a street address, they're either a P.O. Box or a Private Bag—essentially the same, just differing in size. The only vaguely tricky variation is a postnet suite, which consists of a number, followed by a private bag and then a post office (e.g., Postnet Suite 25, Private Bag X25, name of town, postal code). Even the smallest town has its own postal code, and suburbs may have different postal codes—one for a street address and one for P.O. boxes.

SHIPPING PACKAGES

If you make a purchase, try your best to take it home on the plane with you, even if it means packing your travel clothes and items into a box and shipping those to your home, or buying a cheap piece of luggage and paying the excess weight fees. If you buy something from a store accustomed to foreign visitors, it will likely already have a system for getting your items to you, often in a surprising few weeks' time.

Federal Express and DHL offer more reliable service than regular mail, as do the new Fast Mail and Speed Courier services, yet even these "overnight" services are subject to delays. PostNet, South Africa's version of Kinko's, also offers courier services. A parcel of up to about a pound (half a kilogram) will cost between R285 and R860 to send to the United States, and a one-kilogram parcel (2.2 pounds) will cost anywhere from R420 to R1,200.

Express Services DHL (☎ *0860/345–000* ⊕ *www.dhl.co.za*). **FedEx** (☎ *011/923–8000, 080/953–9599 toll-free in South Africa* ⊕ *www.fedex.com*). **PostNet** (☎ *0860/767– 8638* ⊕ *www.postnet.co.za*).

▋ MONEY

Because of inflation and currency fluctuations, it's difficult to give exact exchange rates. It's safe to say, though, that the region is a good value, with high-quality accommodations and food at about two-thirds or half the cost they would be at home.

A bottle of good South African wine costs about the equivalent of $6 (double or triple in a restaurant), and a meal at a prestigious restaurant won't set you back more than $40 per person; an average restaurant, with wine, might be about $30 for two. Double rooms in the country's finest hotels may cost $300 a night, but $130 is more than enough to secure high-quality lodging in most cities, and charming, spotless B&Bs or guesthouses with full breakfasts can be under $60 in many areas.

Not everything in South Africa is cheap. Expect to pay international rates and more to stay in one of the exclusive private game lodges in Mpumalanga, Limpopo Province, or KwaZulu-Natal—with a fly-in charter figured into the price, expect to pay between $1,500 and $2,000 per couple per night. Flights to South Africa are expensive, but the rash of new low-cost carriers makes popular domestic routes less expensive, with most trips under $100 one way. Taxis are uncharacteristically expensive, compared to other vacation needs.

ITEM	AVERAGE COST
Cup of coffee	$1
Glass of beer	$1.50–$2
Quarter of roasted chicken with salad and drink at a fast-food restaurant	$5–$7
Room-service sandwich in a hotel	$5–$7
2-km (1-mi) taxi ride	$6–$8

Prices throughout this guide are given for adults. Substantially reduced fees are almost always available for children, students, and senior citizens.

■ TIP→ Banks never have every foreign currency on hand, and it may take as long as a week to order. If you're planning to exchange

funds before leaving home, don't wait till the last minute.

ATMS AND BANKS

South Africa has a modern banking system, with branches throughout the country and ubiquitous ATMs, especially at tourist attractions, in gas stations, and in shopping malls. Banks open at 9 in the morning weekdays and close at 3:30 in the afternoon; on Saturday they close at 11 in the morning, and they are closed Sunday. Many banks can perform foreign-exchange services or international electronic transfers. The major South African banks are ABSA, First National Bank, Nedbank, and Standard.

If your card gets swallowed, *stay at the ATM* and call the help line number displayed. If possible, withdraw money during the day and choose ATMs with security guards present or those inside stores.

CREDIT CARDS

MasterCard, Visa, and American Express are accepted almost everywhere, but Diners Club is not. Discover is not recognized. Throughout this guide, the following abbreviations are used: **AE**, American Express; **DC**, Diners Club; **MC**, MasterCard; and **V**, Visa.

It's a good idea to inform your credit-card company before you travel, especially if you're going abroad and don't travel internationally very often. Otherwise, the credit-card company might put a hold on your card owing to unusual activity—not a good thing halfway through your trip. Record all your credit-card numbers—as well as the phone numbers to call if your cards are lost or stolen—in a safe place, so you're prepared should something go wrong. MasterCard, Visa, and American Express all have general numbers you can call collect if you're abroad.

If you plan to use your credit card for cash advances, you'll need to apply for a PIN at least two weeks before your trip. Although it's usually cheaper (and safer) to use a credit card abroad for large purchases (so you can cancel payments or be reimbursed if there's a problem), note that some credit-card companies *and* the banks that issue them add substantial percentages to all foreign transactions, whether they're in a foreign currency or not. Check on these fees before leaving home, so there won't be any surprises when you get the bill.

■ TIP→ Before you charge something, ask the merchant whether or not he or she plans to do a dynamic currency conversion (DCC). In such a transaction the credit-card processor (the shop, restaurant, or hotel, not Visa or MasterCard) converts the currency and charges you in dollars. In most cases you'll pay the merchant a 3% fee for this service in addition to any credit-card company and issuing-bank foreign-transaction surcharges.

Dynamic currency conversion programs are becoming increasingly widespread. Merchants who participate in them are supposed to ask whether you want to be charged in dollars or the local currency, but they don't always do so. And even if they do offer you a choice, they may well avoid mentioning the additional surcharges. The good news is that you *do* have a choice. And if this practice really gets your goat, you can avoid it entirely thanks to American Express; with its cards, DCC simply isn't an option.

Reporting Lost Cards **American Express** (📞 *800/528-4800 in the U.S., 336/393-1111 collect from abroad* ⊕ *www.americanexpress.com).* **Diners Club** (📞 *800/234-6377 in the U.S., 303/799 1504 collect from abroad* ⊕ *www.dinersclub.com).* **MasterCard** (📞 *800/627-8372 in the U.S., 636/722-7111 collect from abroad* ⊕ *www.mastercard.com).* **Visa** (📞 *800/847-2911 in the U.S., 0800/990-475 toll-free in South Africa, 410/581-9994 collect from abroad* ⊕ *www.visa.com).*

CURRENCY AND EXCHANGE

The unit of currency in South Africa is the rand (R), with 100 cents (¢) equaling R1. Bills come in R10, R20, R50, R100, and R200 denominations, which are differentiated by color (beware of the similar color of the R50 and R200 notes). Coins are minted in 5¢, 10¢, 20¢, 50¢, R1, R2, and R5 denominations.

At this writing, the rand is trading at about R7.50 to $1. It's a good bargain given the quality of lodgings, which cost probably two-thirds the price of comparable facilities in the United States.

To avoid administrative hassles, keep all foreign-exchange receipts until you leave the region, as you may need them as proof when changing any unspent local currency back into your own currency. You may not take more than R5,000 in cash out of South Africa. For more information you can contact the South African Reserve Bank.

■ TIP→ Even if a currency-exchange booth has a sign promising no commission, rest assured that there's some kind of huge, hidden fee. And as for rates, you're almost always better off getting foreign currency at an ATM or exchanging money at a bank.

Currency Information **South African Reserve Bank** (📞 *012/313-3911* ⊕ *www.reservebank.co.za).*

Currency Conversion **Oanda.com** (⊕ *www.oanda.com).* **XE.com** (⊕ *www.xe.com).*

■ PASSPORTS

American citizens only need a valid passport to enter South Africa for visits of up to 90 days; this includes infants. Check the expiration date. If your passport will expire within six months of your return date, you need to renew your passport in advance, as South Africa won't let you enter with a soon-to-expire passport. ⚠ **You will be denied entry to the country if you do not have two blank, facing pages in your passport.**

Before your trip, make two copies of your passport's data page (one for someone at home and another for you to carry separately). Or scan the page and e-mail it to someone at home and/or yourself.

U.S. Passport Information U.S. Department of State (☎ 877/487–2778 ⊕ travel.state.gov/ passport).

U.S. Passport and Visa Expediters A. Briggs Passport & Visa Expediters (☎ 800/806–0581 or 202/338–0111 ⊕ www.abriggs.com). **American Passport Express** (☎ 800/455–5166 ⊕ www.americanpassport.com). **Passport Express** (☎ 800/362–8196 ⊕ www. passportexpress.com). **Travel Document Systems** (☎ 800/874–5100 or 202/638–3800 ⊕ www.traveldocs.com). **Travel the World Visas** (☎ 866/886–8472 or 202/223–8822 ⊕ www.world-visa.com).

▌ RESTROOMS

All fuel complexes on the major roads have large, clean, well-maintained restrooms. In cities you can find restrooms in shopping malls, at some gas stations, and in restaurants—most of which are quite happy to allow you to use them.

Find a Loo The Bathroom Diaries (⊕ www. thebathroomdiaries.com) is flush with unsanitized info on restrooms the world over—each one located, reviewed, and rated.

▌ SAFETY

South Africa is a country in transition, and as a result experiences growing pains that reveal themselves in economic inequities, which result in high crime rates. While the majority of visitors experience a crime-free trip to South Africa, it's essential to practice vigilance and extreme care.

Crime is a major problem in the whole region, particularly in large cities, and all visitors should take precautions to protect themselves. Do not walk alone at night, and exercise caution even during the day. Avoid wearing jewelry (even costume jewelry), don't invite attention by wearing an expensive camera around your neck, and don't flash a large wad of cash. If you are toting a handbag, wear the strap across your body; even better, wear a money belt, preferably hidden from view under your clothing. When sitting at airports or at restaurants, especially outdoor cafés, make sure to keep your bag on your lap or between your legs—otherwise it may just quietly "walk off" when you're not looking. Even better, loop the strap around your leg, or clip the strap around the table or chair.

Carjacking is another problem, with armed bandits often forcing drivers out of their vehicles at traffic lights, in driveways, or during a fake accident. Always drive with your windows closed and doors locked, don't stop for hitchhikers, and park in well-lighted places. At traffic lights, leave enough space between you and the vehicle in front so you can pull into another lane if necessary. In the unlikely event you are carjacked, don't argue, and don't look at the carjacker's face. Just get out of the car, or ask to be let out of the car. Do not try to keep any of your belongings—they are all replaceable, even that laptop with all that data on it. If you aren't given the opportunity to leave the car, try to stay calm, ostentatiously look away from the hijackers so they can be sure you can't identify them, and follow all instructions. Ask again, calmly, to be let out of the car.

Many places that are unsafe in South Africa will not bear obvious signs of danger. Make sure you know exactly where you're going. Purchase a good map and obtain comprehensive directions from your hotel, rental-car agent, or a trusted local. Taking the wrong exit off a highway into a township could lead you straight to disaster. Many cities are ringed by "no-go" areas. Learn from your hotel or the locals which areas to avoid. If you sense you have taken a wrong turn, drive toward a public area, such as a gas station, or building with an armed guard, before attempting to correct your mistake, which could just compound the problem. When parking, don't leave anything visible in the car; stow it all in the trunk—this includes clothing or shoes. As an added measure, leave the glove box open, to show there's nothing of value inside (take the rental agreement with you).

Before setting out on foot, ask a local, such as your hotel concierge or a shopkeeper, which route to take and how far you can safely go. Walk with a purposeful stride so you look like you know where you're going, and duck into a shop or café if you need to check a map, speak on your mobile phone, or recheck the directions you've been given. ⚠ **Don't walk while speaking on a cell phone.**

Lone women travelers need to be particularly vigilant about walking alone and locking their rooms. South Africa has one of the world's highest rates of rape. If you do attract someone who won't take a firm but polite *no* for an answer, appeal immediately to the hotel manager, bartender, or someone else who seems to be in charge. If you have to walk a short distance alone at night, such as from the hotel reception to your room in a dark motel compound or back from a café along a main street, have a plan, carry a whistle, and know what you'll do if you are grabbed.

⇨ *For destination-specific information, see Safety in each chapter.*

Contact Transportation Security Administration (*TSA* ⊕ *www.tsa.gov*). **South Africa Police Service** (*SAPS* ☎ *10111 Emergency Number* ⊕ *www.saps.gov.za*).

▌TAXES

All South African hotels pay a bed tax, which is included in quoted prices. In South Africa the value-added tax (V.A.T.), currently 14%, is included in the price of most goods and services, including hotel accommodations and food. To get a V.A.T. refund, foreign visitors must present their receipts (minimum of R250) at the airport and be carrying any purchased items with them or in their luggage. You must fill out Form V.A.T. 255, available at the airport V.A.T. refund office. Whatever you buy, make sure that your receipt is an original tax invoice, containing the vendor's name

and address, V.A.T. registration number, and the words TAX INVOICE. Refunds are paid by check, which can be cashed immediately at an airport bank, or refunded directly onto your credit card, with a small transaction fee. Be sure you visit the V.A.T. refund desk in the departures hall before you go through check-in procedures, and try to organize your receipts as you go, to make for easy viewing. Officials will go through your receipts and randomly ask to view your purchases.

Contacts V.A.T. Refund Office (☎ *011/394–1117* ⊕ *www.taxrefunds.co.za*).

▌TIME

South Africa operates on SAST (South African Standard Time), which is two hours ahead of Universal Time (UT). That makes it seven hours ahead of North American eastern standard time (six hours ahead during eastern daylight saving time). South Africa doesn't follow any daylight saving time.

▌TIPPING

Tipping is an integral part of South African life, and it's expected that you'll tip for services that you might take for granted at home. Most notable among these is getting gas, as there are no self-service stations. If the attendant simply fills your tank, tip R2–R3; if he or she offers to clean your windshield, checks your tires, oil, or water, and is generally helpful, tip R4–R5. In restaurants the size of the tip should depend on the quality of service, but 10% is standard, unless, of course, a service charge has already been added to the bill. Give the same percentage to bartenders, taxi drivers, and tour guides.

TIPPING GUIDELINES FOR SOUTH AFRICA	
Bartender	10% of your bill is common
Bellhop	R5 per item
Hotel concierge	Hotel managers say it's not necessary to tip a concierge. If one goes out of his way for you, getting tickets to a sold-out event, say, then anything from R70–R175 would be appropriate.
Hotel doorman	R5, but it's not expected
Hotel maid	Tips are not expected for maids in South Africa, as hotels add service charges to the bill that are distributed to staff
Hotel room-service waiter	R5 per delivery is nice but not expected
Porter at airport or train station	R5 per bag
Skycap at airport	R5 per bag checked
Taxi driver	10%, but round up the fare to the next dollar amount
Tour guide	10% of the cost of the tour
Valet parking attendant	R5 when you get your car
Waiter	10%; nothing additional if a service charge is added to your bill
Car guards	R2–R5

At the end of your stay at a game lodge, you're expected to tip both the ranger and the tracker and the general staff. Different lodgings handle it differently and checking with the management is one way to make sure you tip properly. However, a good model to follow is to factor 10% of your total room bill. Fifty percent of this figure should go to your ranger/tracker, and 50% should go to the general staff. If you have a personal butler, factor an additional 10% (of your total tip figure). If you have your laundry done, leave R5–R10 for the laundress in a special envelope. Envelopes are usually provided in safari rooms and tents for tipping, but it's a nice touch to bring your own note cards to write a personal message.

Informal parking attendants operate in the major cities in South Africa and even in some tourist areas. Although they often look a bit seedy, they do provide a good service, so tip them R2–R5 if your car is still in one piece when you return to it.

▌TOURS

It's wise to go with a guide and only a guide to experience the townships on a day tour, for example.

Whenever you book a guided tour, find out what's included and what isn't. A "land-only" tour includes all your travel (by bus, in most cases) in the destination, but not necessarily your flights to and from or even within it. Also, in most cases prices in tour brochures don't include fees and taxes. Remember to tip your guide (in cash) at the end of the tour.

PHILANTHROPIC TRAVEL

Volunteering in South Africa has grown in popularity, and several international volunteer vacation organizations offer some combination of touring and service. A true volunteer experience usually requires more than providing your travel dates and sending a check, therefore it is advisable to research a range of types of commitment before picking one. Professionals can often consult their own organizations for opportunities to transfer skills in South Africa, while students can find suitable student-oriented programs through their universities.

Fees for volunteer programs are comparable to costs for a vacation, but standards are almost always lower than those of a typical pleasure trip. Rooms are shared, meals are self-catering, and toilet facilities will not be five-star-hotel caliber. Those that look more fun than work-oriented, with smiling bikini-clad teens on their Web pages, are generally most expensive.

Aviva, a vacation-oriented volunteer agency, offers leisure-friendly activities like teaching surfing or helping conserve penguins. It's good for students with spare time, and plenty of spare cash. Cross Cultural Solutions organizes teams of volunteers for projects worldwide. Global Volunteer Network is a New Zealand–based volunteer placement agency with environmental projects in South Africa. Transitions Abroad lists dozens of South African volunteer opportunities with a range of requirements and destinations.

Contacts Aviva (☎ 021/557-4312 ⊕ www.aviva-sa.com). **Cross Cultural Solutions** (☎ 800/380-4777 ⊕ www.crossculturalsolutions.com). **Global Volunteer Network** (☎ 800/963-1198 ⊕ www.volunteer.org.nz). **Transitions Abroad** (⊕ www.transitionsabroad.com).

∎ TRIP INSURANCE

Comprehensive trip insurance is valuable if you're booking a very expensive or complicated trip (particularly to an isolated region) or if you're booking far in advance. Comprehensive policies typically cover trip cancellation and interruption, letting you cancel or cut your trip short because of illness, or, in some cases, acts of terrorism in your destination. Such policies might also cover evacuation and medical care. For trips abroad you should have at least medical-only coverage (⇨ *Health, above*). Some also cover you for trip delays because of bad weather or mechanical problems as well as for lost or delayed luggage.

Another type of coverage to consider is financial default—that is, when your trip is disrupted because a tour operator, airline, or cruise line goes out of business. Generally you must buy this when you book your trip or shortly thereafter, and it's available to you only if your operator isn't on a list of excluded companies.

Always read the fine print of your policy to make sure that you're covered for the risks that most concern you. Compare several polices to be sure you're getting the best price and range of coverage available.

Insurance Comparison Info Insure My Trip (☎ 800/487-4722 ⊕ www.insuremytrip.com). **Square Mouth** (☎ 800/240-0369 or 727/564-9203 ⊕ www.squaremouth.com).

Comprehensive Insurers Access America (☎ 800/284-8300 ⊕ www.accessamerica.com). **Travel Guard** (☎ 800/826-4919 ⊕ www.travelguard.com). **CSA Travel Protection** (☎ 800/711-1197 ⊕ www.csatravelprotection.com). **HTH Worldwide** (☎ 610/254-8700 ⊕ www.hthworldwide.com). **Travelex Insurance** (☎ 800/228-9792 ⊕ www.travelexinsurance.com). **Travel Insured International** (☎ 800/243-3174 ⊕ www.travelinsured.com).

∎ VISITOR INFORMATION

See the individual chapter Essentials sections for details on local visitor bureaus.

ONLINE TRAVEL TOOLS

The official South Africa Tourism Web site is reasonable for general tourism information and pretty good on events, but you'll really struggle to find a decent hotel or other tourism product with its search engine. Another government-sponsored Web site, SouthAfrica.info, is full of useful but general country information and is a far better bet than the SA Tourism site. If most of your independent travel will be in and around Cape Town, visit the Tourism Cape Town Web site for everything from comprehensive event listings by date to accommodation links, and an e-mail newsletter that will come to your in box.

INSPIRATIONS

To learn about the issues of apartheid, pick up Nelson Mandela's *Long Walk to Freedom* (1995). The book examines Mandela's life and the political road ahead. History buffs will also enjoy *A History of South Africa, Third Edition* (2001). It's a comprehensive and interesting examination of South Africa's history.

If you're interested in learning a bit about a safari from your armchair, pick up *The Wildlife of South Africa: A Field Guide to the Animals and Plants of the Region*. If birds are more your thing, *Birds of Southern Africa* is the most comprehensive and authoritative guide.

There are also a few great movies you might want to watch before your trip. The 2006 Oscar winner for foreign film, *Tsotsi* (2005), offers insight into the harsh life of South Africa's townships. It's based on the novel by Athol Fugard. *Red Dust* (2004), based on the novel by Gillian Slovo, follows an attorney through the harrowing weeks of a Truth and Reconciliation Commission hearing in the Eastern Cape. *Catch a Fire* (2006), starring Tim Robbins, is set in the 1980s and highlights the anti-government sabotage common to that era. *Yesterday* (2004) follows one woman's struggles against HIV, and its impact on her life and on that of her young daughter.

The Iziko South African Museum Web site lists details for more than a dozen of Cape Town's museums. For the latest information on arts performances and exhibits, as well as a nationwide calendar of creative events, there is no better place to start than Artslink.co.za. The South Africa National Parks Web site outlines where the parks are, provides detailed maps, and includes information on accommodations, animals, park activities, and booking.

To stay abreast of news and events in South Africa, check out the online version of Independent Newspapers, which is the biggest newspaper group in South Africa. The *Mail & Guardian* provides a useful selection of South African and international news and insightful comments. *All Africa* culls English-language news articles from regional papers.

All About South Africa South Africa National Parks (⊕ *www.sanparks.org*). **South-Africa.info** (⊕ *www.southafrica.info*).

All About Africa Africa Adventure (⊕ *www.africa-adventure.org*). **Getaway** (⊕ *www.getawaytoafrica.com*). **The All Africa Internet Guide** (⊕ *www.goafrica.co.za*).

Culture Artslink.co.za (⊕ *www.artslink.co.za*). **Iziko South African Museum** (⊕ *www.iziko.org.za*). **Mail & Guardian** (⊕ *www.mg.co.za*).

Media All Africa (⊕ *www.allafrica.com*). **Independent Newspapers** (⊕ *www.iol.co.za*).

Visitor Info South African Tourism (☎ *800/593–1318 in U.S., 011/895–3000 in South Africa* ⊕ *www.southafrica.net*). **Cape Town** (⊕ *www.tourismcapetown.co.za*).

Weather African Weather Forecasts (⊕ *www.africanweather.net*). **South Africa Weather Service** (⊕ *www.weathersa.co.za*).

INDEX

NOTES

NOTES

NOTES

NOTES

NOTES

NOTES

ABOUT OUR WRITERS

Jade Archer works as a journalist for Flow Communications, a Johannesburg-based communications company. She has traveled through the countries of the East African coast, in Eastern and Western Europe, and in Southeast Asia. Since returning to Johannesburg she has immersed herself in the culture and cuisine to be found right on her doorstep and enjoys exploring "Jozi's" little-known gems.

Claire Melissa Baranowski is a freelance travel editor and writer. After 10 years in Zimbabwe, 10 years in South Africa, and 10 years in London, she has washed ashore in Cape Town and waits to see what adventure greets her next. Some of her favorite travel destinations are the beaches of Tobago, the city of Barcelona, and backpacking in Laos.

Brian Berkman is regularly called a legend in his own lunchtime. Although his girth is the subject of gossip columns, it is proof of an unquenchable appetite that rolls from gluttony to gastronomy. When not eating and traveling for a living, Brian runs a PR consultancy. He writes dining-out and luxury-travel columns and features for newspapers and magazines.

Sanja Cloete-Jones started life in the Kalahari Desert and has slept under the stars in most countries of southern, eastern, and northern Africa. Travel writing her way around Australasia, she completed guides to eight countries. She has now returned to the continent that remains her first love and lives in Zambia.

Tracy Gielink, a born and bred Durbanite, loves the individuality and creativity that distinguish her coastal city. A freelance journalist specializing in entertainment and food features, Tracy follows her taste buds—which means she's extremely well fed—and has a diploma in wine.

Debra A. Klein caught the Africa travel bug while on assignment for *Condé Nast Traveller*. A year later, she returned for a long-term assignment: as a volunteer in a Ugandan HIV/AIDS NGO. She's contributed travel news and features to many publications, among them, *Newsweek* and *The New York Times*.

Lee Middleton, originally from Hawaii, has traveled, worked, and studied in over 35 countries. Having previously found employment fishing in Alaska and researching tigers in Thailand, she has been working as an environmental journalist and travel writer in central and southern Africa since 2005. Lee is based in Cape Town.

Karena du Plessis is the author of travel books *The Overberg: Inland from the Tip of Africa* and *The West Coast: Cederberg to Sea*. She freelances for various publications and is passionate about the Western Cape and gathering stories from the area. Together with her husband, she can't wait for her kids to be a bit older before she can take them exploring.

Kate Turkington is one of South Africa's best-known journalists. Her live Sunday-night radio show, *Believe It or Not,* is the longest-running radio show in South Africa. She started traveling in World War II, when she was evacuated from London to East Anglia, in eastern England, and has not stopped traveling since. Her travel beat covers the world, but her heart and home are in Africa where she lives in Johannesburg. She's been held up by Ethiopian tribesmen armed with Kalashnikovs in the Rift Valley, broken bread with Buddhist monks in Tibet, rafted down the Ganges, and sipped coffee surrounded by a million and a half migrating wildebeest in the Serengeti.

Tara Turkington has lived all over South Africa, from the small diamond-mining town of Kimberley to Johannesburg. She has written and photographed for more than 20 publications and has taught journalism at university level. She is now the CEO of Flow Communications, which specializes in journalism, graphic design, and Web development. Tara has been writing for Fodor's for more than 10 years.